Teaching
Today's
Mathematics
in the Middle Grades

D1621583

Teaching
Today's
Mathematics
in the Middle Grades

Art Johnson
Boston University

Kit Norris
Educational Consultant

Boston   New York   San Francisco
Mexico City   Montreal   Toronto   London   Madrid   Munich   Paris
Hong Kong   Singapore   Tokyo   Cape Town   Sydney

Series Editor: *Traci Mueller*
Editorial Assistant: *James Neal*
Senior Marketing Manager: *Krista Clark*
Editorial Production Service: *Omegatype Typography, Inc.*
Composition and Manufacturing Buyer: *Andrew Turso*
Electronic Composition: *Omegatype Typography, Inc.*
Cover Administrator: *Kristina Mose-Libon*

For related titles and support materials, visit our online catalog at www.ablongman.com.

Copyright © 2006 Pearson Education, Inc.

All rights reserved. No part of the material protected by this copyright notice may be reproduced or utilized in any form or by any means, electronic or mechanical, including photocopying, recording, or by any information storage and retrieval system, without written permission from the copyright owner.

To obtain permission(s) to use material from this work, please submit a written request to Allyn and Bacon, Permissions Department, 75 Arlington Street, Boston, MA 02116 or fax your request to 617-848-7320.

Between the time website information is gathered and then published, it is not unusual for some sites to have closed. Also, the transcription of URLs can result in typographical errors. The publisher would appreciate notification where these errors occur so that they may be corrected in subsequent editions.

Library of Congress Cataloging-in-Publication Data

Johnson, Art
    Teaching today's mathematics in the middle grades / Art Johnson, Kit Norris.—1st ed.
      p. cm.
    Includes bibliographical references and index.
    ISBN 0-205-43359-6 (pbk.)
    1. Mathematics—Study and teaching (Elementary)—United States.   2.
  Mathematics—Study and teaching (Secondary)—United States.   I. Norris, Kit.   II. Title.

QA135.6.J64 2006
510'.71'2—dc22

                    2005049173

Printed in the United States of America

10 9 8 7 6 5 4 3 2 1   10 09 08 07 06 05

For my wife, Juanita,
whose loving support and
encouragement make
so many things possible

       —AJ

For my grandchildren,
Carolyn and Judson,
the great motivators

       —KN

Contents

section **one**

Teaching Mathematics in the Middle Grades

chapter **1**

Mathematics for the Twenty-First Century   1

chapter **2**

The Challenge of Middle School Learners   16

Effective Instruction in the Mathematics Classroom

chapter **3**

The Practice of Effective Instruction   34

chapter **4**

Assessment: Balanced and Varied   65

chapter **5**

Problem Solving: An Approach to Teaching and Learning Mathematics   94

section **three**

Mathematics Topics

chapter **6**

Making Sense of Number and Operations   127

chapter **7**

Algebra: The Gateway   173

chapter **8**

Geometry: Moving beyond Formulas   212

chapter **9**

Measurement: Behind the Units   259

chapter **10**

Data Analysis: The Process   296

chapter **11**

Probability: Measures of Uncertainty   327

chapter **12**

Teaching as a Career: The Journey Begins   360

Preface

Teaching Today's Mathematics in the Middle Grades focuses on the critical grades in mathematics education. The middle grades are the bridge between the introductory and intuitive mathematics of the primary grades and the content-specific courses at the high school level. The foundations laid in the primary grades must be nurtured and developed in the middle grades or students will not advance beyond the minimum levels of mathematics in their secondary schooling. The number of middle school mathematics initiatives funded by the National Science Foundation (NSF) testifies to the importance of the middle grades in fostering competence in mathematics.

Adolescents in the middle grades are growing into adulthood. They are developing personalities and habits of life that will remain with them long after they graduate. They also begin to develop likes and dislikes about everything, including mathematics. In surveys of children in primary grades, mathematics is nearly always a favorite subject. By the end of the middle grades, students rarely select mathematics as their favorite.

There are a number of factors that account for this. Many students' earlier experiences with mathematics have been simply computations with memorized methods. They rarely had the opportunity to create their own understanding of mathematics. When students enter middle school, the focus changes from whole numbers to rational numbers, along with a new set of relationships and algorithms. Rote practice is not an effective means for many students to succeed in mathematics and certainly will not engender a love of numbers. A curriculum that stresses rules and procedures promotes memorization. Creativity, the joy of discovery, and student engagement are lost. Consequently, it is incumbent upon middle school teachers to provide an engaging curriculum that maintains this early interest in mathematics. The goal of *Teaching Today's Mathematics in the Middle Grades* is to help teachers capture and maintain students' interest while developing their understandings and capabilities in mathematics.

Teaching Today's Mathematics in the Middle Grades focuses exclusively on the middle school learner and the middle school mathematics curriculum. Although each chapter discusses foundational mathematics concepts from earlier grades and previews topics that will follow the middle grades, the emphasis is on the middle school. This narrow focus allows for proper development of critical topics in the middle school, such as proportionality and algebraic thinking. The integral role of manipulatives is addressed in detail that is impossible in a text that includes mathematics topics from elementary or secondary grade levels. Assessment and problem solving are also considered from the viewpoint of effective practices for middle grades students.

Teaching Today's Mathematics in the Middle Grades contains a number of engaging activities and interesting problems for middle school mathematics students. These activities and problems support our chapter discussions of the important mathematics in each content chapter rather than become the focus of the text. Our objective is to illuminate the critical mathematics concepts for the middle grades, not to produce a collection of problems and activities. We believe that the appealing activities and problems that we have chosen to include in *Teaching Today's Mathematics in the Middle Grades* will further assist teachers to understand and teach the important mathematics topics to their middle school students.

Much of *Teaching Today's Mathematics in the Middle Grades* concentrates on mathematics topics that have been identified as critical by the National Council of Teachers of Mathematics (NCTM): number and operations, algebra, geometry, measurement, data, and probability. According to NCTM, an effective classroom must also emphasize key mathematics processes: problem solving, reasoning and proof, communication, connections, and representation. Because these processes are an integral part of teaching and learning, we have included specific comments about these processes in each content chapter. Although we discuss problem solving in each content chapter, we have devoted a full

Point Well Taken

"Elementary students who experience a narrow mathematics curriculum that consists only of rules, facts and procedures and who 'learn' mathematics by memorizing and mimicking are unlikely to understand the power of mathematics or be interested in it in middle and high school."

—*B. Reys & F. Fennel (2003, January). Who should lead mathematics instruction?* Teaching Children Mathematics, *280.*

Conceptual Icon of the Process and Content Standards

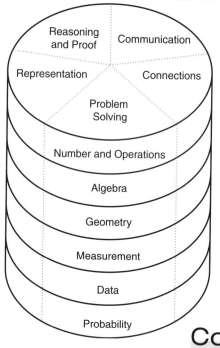

chapter to analyzing problem solving from a middle grades perspective. The image here represents our view of how the content topics and mathematical processes must combine to enable students to build their mathematics understanding. These process standards penetrate each layer of the content standards to engage students as they construct their understanding of mathematics. The order of the content standards in the image does not reflect any hierarchy or sequence of study. Rather these are the same content standards, in the same order, as described by NCTM in *Principles and Standards for School Mathematics*.

Along with problem solving, assessment plays a critical role in teaching and learning mathematics. Assessments are the means by which a teacher can determine if students have achieved the objectives for an activity, a project, or a chapter. We have devoted a full chapter to effective and meaningful assessments in the mathematics classroom.

As well as addressing mathematical content and processes, we also consider the art of teaching. We delineate the specific nature of middle school students and the impact this has on teaching mathematics. We also discuss how to teach special needs students and English-language learners and organizing the classroom into cooperative groups. Of course, any mathematics class has to have a mathematics focus, and so we have reviewed various *Standards*-based middle school series and other sources of mathematics content for the middle school classroom, including high-stakes tests. Finally, we offer suggestions, methods, and activities for teachers to bring excitement to their students' study of mathematics.

Contents of *Teaching Today's Mathematics in the Middle Grades*

Chapter 1, Mathematics for the Twenty-First Century, reviews the recent mathematics reforms starting with the "new math" of about 50 years ago. We also discuss the role of the National Council of Teachers of Mathematics in the developments in mathematics education and various NSF initiatives. The chapter concludes with a consideration of the implications of new and emerging technologies on mathematics teaching and learning.

In Chapter 2, The Challenge of Middle School Learners, we take into account the specific audience of middle grades learners and how to effectively teach those students who are on the brink of adolescence. Part of our discussion also includes English-language learners, special needs students, and gifted learners. We also examine different learning styles and intelligences.

Chapter 3, The Practice of Effective Instruction, focuses on the components of effective instruction. We include lesson plans, collaborative learning, and curriculum resources in our discussion. We also take into account *Standards*-based programs when reviewing mathematics curriculum resources.

Effective assessments offer information to the learner and teacher. Chapter 4, Assessment: Balanced and Varied, explores both formative and summative assessments and offers specific examples of each type. The chapter also discusses high-stakes testing at the national and international levels.

As one of the process standards described in NCTM's *Principles and Standards for School Mathematics*, problem solving offers opportunities for students to challenge and build their understanding. Chapter 5, Problem Solving: An Approach to Teaching and Learning Mathematics, examines the role of problem solving in today's classrooms and the components involved in its implementation. The chapter also includes examples of how the problem-solving strategies are used outside of the classroom.

Chapter 6, Making Sense of Number and Operations, explores a variety of methods that allow students to develop meaningful understandings of proportional reasoning and operations with whole and rational numbers. We stress the importance of developing conceptual understanding before formally introducing an algorithm. This chapter offers several concrete models to help students solidify their understanding of number relationships and describes ways to link fractions, decimals, and percents.

Algebra, seen by many as a barrier to continuing study in mathematics, is presented here as a gateway. Chapter 7, Algebra: The Gateway, looks at foundational concepts, such as the meaning of a variable and the equal sign, and then proceeds to stress the importance of multiple representations, referred to as the Rule of 5, as middle school students work with a variety of problems.

In Chapter 8, Geometry: Moving Beyond Formulas, we review the implication of the van Heile levels of geometry understanding for the classroom. Among several geometry topics, we stress the importance of spatial sense for middle school and include several effective activities to help middle school students to develop their spatial sense.

The emphasis in Chapter 9, Measurement: Behind the Units, is on helping students gain a foundational understanding of the relationships of linear, area, and cubic measures by classroom activities. The chapter also clarifies the relationships of various common area formulas via class explorations.

As suggested by the title of Chapter 10, Data Analysis: The Process, data analysis is a cyclical process. This chapter presents that process, offers graphical representations, defines and presents measures of central tendency and measures of dispersion, and discusses misleading graphs.

A solid understanding of probability requires students to perform many explorations and experiments. In Chapter 11, Probability: Measures of Uncertainty, we have included some model activities along with discussions that will assist students to build a solid understanding of probability and its applications.

Chapter 12, Teaching as a Career: The Journey Begins, offers some suggestions as one gets started on a teaching career. Questions to anticipate in the interview process and suggestions about getting started during the first few weeks are discussed. This chapter also includes ways to participate in continuing professional development.

We have included a number of innovative features in each of the content chapters. We have listed these features here with a brief description.

Marginal Notes

- *React/Reflect.* This marginal note appears several times in each chapter. React/Reflect contains a question for you to think about and then offers an opinion or recollection.
- *Point Well Taken.* This marginal note is a brief quotation that captures a key thought in the chapter. These thoughts are taken from a wide range of educators and researchers.
- *Author's Recall.* We include in each chapter one or more remembrances from our many years as classroom teachers. These recalls highlight an aspect of the chapter with a personal anecdote.
- *Did You Know?* These margin notes are brief, interesting factoids about mathematics, mathematicians, or mathematics in our world. Did you know that the cofounder of the probability theory also invented the game of roulette?

Boxes

- *Math in the Media.* Mathematics is a frequent topic for media coverage. We reference media topics in mathematics in each content chapter. Topics include the role of geometry in determining facial beauty and the discovery of a new largest prime number.
- *Research.* In each chapter we highlight recent research and the implications of the research on classroom practice. For example, recent research findings suggest that virtual electronic manipulatives may be as effective as the real manipulatives in helping students understand mathematics.

- *Misconception.* This feature highlights common mistakes or misconceptions that confound many middle schoolers. Knowledge about these misconceptions is a valuable component of any effective lesson plan, and we suggest activities to help remedy these misconceptions.
- *Process Standards.* This feature discusses the four process standards from NCTM: Connections, Communication, Reasoning and Proof, and Representation.
- *Assessment Tip.* In this feature we suggest classroom-tested ideas to improve assessment in middle grades mathematics.
- *Reaching Diverse Learners.* In many chapters we have incorporated an example of how to reach diverse learners. Diverse learners might be English language learners, students from different backgrounds, students with physical disabilities, or students with learning disabilities. Although space limitations do not allow for the many ways to reach diverse learners, the suggestions we have made in each chapter will help teachers generate additional ideas to reach these students.
- *Try This.* These activities appear throughout the chapters. They focus on the mathematics at hand and ask the reader to apply the math skills being discussed.

On the Lighter Side

We believe that humor is an essential part of any middle grades classroom. The cartoons we have selected for each chapter humorously highlight some aspect of mathematics.

Student Performance on International and National Assessments

At the ends of most chapters, we have incorporated problems from the National Assessment of Educational Progress (NAEP) and the Trends in International Mathematics and Science Study (TIMSS). These problems illuminate the achievement of American students on the concepts in that chapter.

Chapter Exercises

- *From the Reading*
- *On Your Own*
- *Portfolio Question.* We have placed a portfolio question in each chapter. We encourage you to respond to each of these questions—as well as to the other chapter exercises, the React/Reflect questions, and the Try This questions. Doing so will supply you with material to create your own portfolio at the end of the course. (See Chapter 12.)
- *Scenes from a Classroom.* For analysis and discussion we have developed a vignette for a typical middle school mathematics classroom for each chapter. The vignette will highlight a common scenario and a problem that you need to find a solution for.
- *Preparing for Praxis.* We have included a test question from released items of the Middle School Mathematics Test in each chapter. These questions exemplify the mathematical knowledge in the chapter's content area that is expected for middle school teachers who take the Praxis Middle School Mathematics Test.

Chapter Resources

- *Math–Literature Connections.* This section is a list of reading books that have mathematics themes. These are not activity books or collections of brainteasers. Rather, they are books with story lines that have strong mathematics components. The books range from serious literature such as *Gulliver's Travels* to the whimsical adventures of *Sir Cumference.*

- *Teacher's Bookcase.* In this section we list those texts that should be on the wish list of any teacher who teaches the content in that particular chapter.
- *For Further Reading.* We suggest texts and journal articles that comment further on the topics in the chapter. These articles are from the pages of *The Mathematics Teacher*, *Teaching Mathematics in the Middle School*, and other educational journals.
- *Links.* Here we have listed Internet sites that support interactive web pages where students can do activities, or informational sites that can help students develop mathematical understanding.

Blackline Masters

Several Blackline Masters (BLM) are included at the ends of select chapters. Each BLM outlines an activity and is easily reproducible for immediate classroom use.

By addressing both content and processes, *Teaching Today's Mathematics in the Middle Grades* will prepare preservice teachers to be effective mathematics educators, both by virtue of their improved understanding of the mathematics they will teach and by their knowledge of the best ways to instruct middle school students. *Teaching Today's Mathematics in the Middle Grades* also serves as an excellent resource for middle school teachers by providing activities and problems to use with their middle school students.

We believe that mathematics is the gateway to success in many different fields and occupations. Middle school is the critical stage for maintaining an interest and confidence in mathematics for most students. We are confident that the principles and concepts presented in *Teaching Today's Mathematics in the Middle Grades* will help you to maintain and engender the love of mathematics that middle school students bring to mathematics from their elementary school experiences.

Acknowledgments

We would like to thank the following reviewers for their comments on this manuscript: Rick Billstein, The University of Montana; Rainy M. Cotti, Rhode Island College; Virginia Horak, The University of Arizona; Dr. Gerold H. Jarmon, Central Michigan University; Henry S. Kepner, Jr., University of Wisconsin–Milwaukee; Dr. Marina Krause, California State University Long Beach; Edna O. Schack, Morehead State University; Eugenia Tsankova, Roger Williams University; Jeffrey X. Watt, Indiana University–Purdue University; and Janet A. White, Millersville University.

About the Authors

Art Johnson is a professor of mathematics education at Boston University. Before teaching at the college level, he taught middle and high school mathematics for over two decades. During that time, Art won a number of awards, including the Presidential Award for Excellence in Mathematics Teaching, New Hampshire Teacher of the Year, and the Christa McAuliffe Sabbatical. Art is a frequent speaker at regional and national mathematics conferences. His books include *Guiding Children's Learning of Mathematics* (Wadsworth), *Math Matters* (Math Solutions Publications), and *Famous Problems and Their Mathematicians* (Teachers Ideas Press).

Kit Norris is currently an educational consultant working with area districts, charter schools, and private schools supporting the teaching and learning of mathematics. She is also an adjunct professor at Simmons College. Her honors include the Presidential Award for Excellence in Mathematics Teaching and the Klingenstein Fellowship. She has served on the board of the Association of Teachers of Mathematics in Massachusetts and the Association of Teachers of Mathematics in New England, and she is a frequent speaker at national and regional conferences.

chapter one

Mathematics for the Twenty-First Century

Teaching has always been a highly honored profession. In every culture from the earliest societies those who have educated young people have been well esteemed. Socrates, Aristotle, Buddha, Jesus, Confucius, and Thomas Aquinas are a few of the great teachers from the past. In today's society teaching is a critically important profession. Our government looks to the schools to educate students for the twenty-first century, to equip students with the skills and motivation necessary to succeed in a rapidly changing society. By one estimate "60% of all new jobs in the 21st Century will require skills that are possessed by only 20% of the current work force" (National Commission on Mathematics and Science Teaching, 2002, p. 29). In addition to educating our youth, the schools now provide meals, health care, social functions, and even moral training via character-building activities. Today's teachers rise to the challenge and look to meet the increasing demands put upon them to serve the students in their classrooms. It is no exaggeration to say that teaching is the fullest possible engagement with our times.

Mathematics teaching is at an especially critical point in the United States. Many of the new jobs for the twenty-first century require better mathematics knowledge and skills than did many jobs in industry during the last century, and so outstanding mathematics teaching is a must. Rising student enrollments combined with an aging faculty mean there will need to be many mathematics teachers hired during the next decade to meet larger numbers of students and to replace the thousands of retiring mathematics teachers. Over the next few years, nearly 20,000 teachers will be needed to teach mathematics and science in our schools (National Commission on Mathematics and Science Teaching, 2002, p. 29). The responsibility for teaching mathematics to our youth in the next decade falls on the shoulders of new and preservice teachers.

Each level of school, from prekindergarten to senior high school, presents its own set of special circumstances. Certainly middle school students can be a challenge to the most dedicated, energetic teacher. Middle school is a transition from elementary school to secondary school, and it is also a transition from childhood to preadolescence. As middle school students struggle with physical and emotional changes that are a part of the maturation process, they also begin to develop their personal identity with an energy level that is difficult to predict from day to day, all while they are expected to develop their mathematics knowledge and abilities. We discuss the challenge of teaching middle school students more fully in the next chapter. We next discuss the challenge of teaching mathematics in a culture that values it yet disparages it.

Society's View of Mathematics

One objective of every mathematics teacher is to mitigate the widely held negative perceptions of mathematics. In our society a deficiency in mathematics is not considered a

Point Well Taken

"In a completely rational society, the best of us would be teachers and the rest of us would have to settle for something less."
—*Lee Iaccoca, former CEO of Chrysler Corporation*

Point Well Taken

"In the Industrial Age we burned fossil fuels to drive the engines of society. In the Information Age, the fuel we burn is mathematics."
—*Keith Devlin, mathematics educator and author*

fault that needs remedying. It is permissible, even expected, to reveal one's mathematical shortcomings and perhaps even brag about them. It is not unusual to hear someone boast about his or her inability to keep a balanced checkbook. Few people would admit they have trouble reading a newspaper because of all the big, confusing words or confess that they are confused by the portraits of the people on our coins and currency. Yet the same individuals will freely admit they carry a tip chart in their wallet to help them determine a restaurant tip because the mathematics involved is too confusing.

The average person's perception of mathematics extends beyond his or her own perceived inabilities. Most think of mathematics as a difficult discipline in which "you get it, or you don't." Too often parents consider mathematics ability a result of the right genes, that you are born with math ability or you aren't, and no amount of effort will change things much. Part of the problem is that few people really understand what it means to do mathematics. Their background in mathematics involved memorizing relationships and procedures and applying them by rote to skill and drill problems rather than employing them to solve engaging problems with real-world applications.

With much of their time spent on mind-numbing drills in the classroom, few students have had as much as a glimpse of the real people behind the discipline. Few adults can name any mathematician, much less a living one, or relate any recent advances in mathematics. Not so in science or English or social studies. Advancements in these fields are always in the media as are their practitioners, but not mathematics. Part of the problem is that new mathematics is highly abstract, and so advancements and discoveries in mathematics are by their very nature difficult to comprehend or apply to real-world settings. Nevertheless, there are continual applications of mathematics being made to new and emerging technologies and related industries. In each mathematics content chapter we have included some mention of mathematics in the media.

Another factor determining society's view of mathematics is how mathematics was taught several decades ago, at the time when many parents were still in public school. Many mathematics classrooms consisted of drill activities that focused on memorized algorithms and procedures. Most textbooks emphasized this rote aspect of mathematics as well. The material in mathematics textbooks was rarely updated to reflect new applications of mathematics. As a consequence, entire generations of parents left public school with the notion that mathematics is a discipline that only a gifted few can master. The prevailing view of mathematics today is a dance of symbols that are rearranged according to memorized procedures.

A recent international survey of upper elementary school children assessed their opinions about mathematics (Bruxelles, 2003). Their responses were similar to what might be expected of older children and adults. For one thing, they all agreed that mathematics was extremely important but thought it was tedious and uninteresting. Their image of a mathematician was stereotypical: an older white male with glasses and a pocket full of pens and pencils, who always had a bad hair day and little, if any, social life. Not the most flattering image! At times commercial products add to the poor image of mathematics. A popular doll was marketed one holiday season with a string to pull for a short message. Some of the dolls responded to the pulled string with "Gosh, math is tough!" A popular snack food delivered the following advertisement catch phrase: "Math is hard enough. Make math go down easier with Pop-Tarts." Both of these products and many others exploited the popular perception of mathematics as a difficult subject that few can master.

Given how society looks at mathematics, one of the key objectives in the middle school classroom is to help students see its beauty and elegance in addition to its acclaimed utility. Elementary school students think of mathematics as one of their favorite subjects. By the end of middle school few list it as a favorite. It is obvious that much needs to be done to maintain students' interest in mathematics. An underlying theme of this text is that students should appreciate not only the utility of mathematics but also its logic and beauty. An interesting way to examine students' views of mathematics is to ask them to complete a mathematics metaphor such as: "If mathematics were a breakfast cereal (or vegetable,

Point Well Taken

"Only in the United States do people believe that learning mathematics depends on special ability."

—*National Research Council, 1989*

REACT | REFLECT

Rank-order the subjects you will teach (reading, math, science, history, art) from favorite to least favorite. Why did you rank math where you did?

AUTHOR'S **Recall**

I can recall memorizing postulates in geometry that were a word-for-word translation from the original Greek of Euclid's geometry of 300 B.C.E.

Point Well Taken

"Although students in the early grades like mathematics, middle school students begin to perceive mathematics as a special subject in which only students with special ability succeed; the rest merely get by or fail."

—*Middleton, 1999*

Point Well Taken

"Inability in mathematics is not considered a particularly critical handicap in our society."

—*Dan Rosenberger, mathematics educator*

On the Lighter Side

Calvin reveals his view of math.

Calvin and Hobbes © 1991 Watterson. Distributed by Universal Press Syndicate. Reprinted with permission. All rights reserved.

or sound, or . . .), what would it be?" Students should complete the sentence and then explain their reasons for their answer. Most students will select a cereal that is healthy, such as oatmeal, but will admit to finding oatmeal dull or uninteresting, just as they see a value to mathematics but also find it to be dull and uninteresting.

TRY THIS

Complete one of these math metaphors and then ask several people to complete the same metaphor. Compare their metaphors to the one you completed.

It is our hope that you will join us in helping students maintain an interest in mathematics. We are convinced that middle school students can be helped to appreciate the beauty of mathematics, value its applications in so many real-world settings, and enjoy explorations in mathematics using concrete manipulatives, data collections, and experimentations. The world has changed in the last 25 years and so must mathematics education. We invite you to be an agent of this change and an advocate of interesting, engaging mathematics for middle school students.

In order to fully understand the landscape of mathematics education in the United States, it is helpful to consider three factors: pertinent issues in the recent history of mathematics education that still affect mathematics teaching and learning, the role of the National Council of Teachers of Mathematics, and the effects and consequences of high-stakes tests and educational technology.

Point Well Taken

"Kids who like math get better and better at it, and those who don't, don't."

—*Robert Plomin,*
mathematics educator

Recent History of Mathematics Learning in the United States

Mathematics education in the United States during the mid-1950s was pretty much what it had been for decades. It was focused on basic skills and computation. However, more schools were offering advanced mathematics (Algebra II and beyond), but it was studied by only about 10% of high school students, few of them young women. Still, there was reason to be proud of a national school system that was graduating a higher percentage of students and sending more of them to college. The sense of satisfaction with mathematics education vanished in the twinkling of an eye in 1957. The evidence of the failure of mathematics and science education was visible to all in the form of a flashing light moving across the night sky.

The New Math

The Soviet Union had launched the *Sputnik* satellite, thus demonstrating its superiority in mathematics and science and causing educators, politicians, and the military to look to improve mathematics and science education, and fast. As early as 1959 the College Board Commission of Mathematics met to examine the state of mathematics education and made recommendations about the need to move beyond computations and algorithms to more conceptual applications. One of the results of this commission was the School Mathematics Project and the School Mathematics Study Group, both of which produced materials for school mathematics during the next decade that were used by a wide audience of school districts. Content was expanded and deepened. The mathematics curriculum was adjusted to include such topics as set theory, vectors, and number bases. This new curriculum was termed the *new math* by supporters and critics alike. It was doomed to failure from the start because it was a top-down approach to curriculum reform. That is, the programs were conceived and developed at the college level with little input from public school educators. Teachers who had taught traditional mathematics for years were expected to institute this dramatically new curriculum within a single year, and students were expected to assimilate the new concepts as they were presented, regardless of their lack of any foundational experiences with the concepts.

> **AUTHOR'S Recall**
>
> In the same year I taught traditional computational mathematics to two middle school classes, and set theory, number systems from past civilizations, and modular arithmetic to three others. (They had the new books.)

Back to Basics

By the end of the 1960s Americans had put a man on the moon and so the Russian challenge had been met. Educators could relax and maintain the status quo in schools. The results of the first National Assessment of Educational Progress (NAEP) shook the education community. Students were not learning as much with the new math as was thought, and in some cases students seemed to be regressing to levels below what the 1950s showed. The outcome during the late 1970s was a swing back to a focus on basic mathematics and calculation excellence. The resulting mathematics program had a strong computational component and was termed *back to basics* by its advocates. One framework for this return to less conceptual and abstract mathematics had begun in the 1960s. The Comprehensive School Project focused on mastery of critical portions of mathematics and sought to begin various mathematics topics earlier in school so that students could advance farther in mathematics during their school years. By the end of the 1970s the back to basics movement that resulted in reaction to the perceived failure of the new math was itself exposed as flawed by the mathematics scores of American students on the second NAEP and on the Second International Mathematics and Science Study.

National Initiatives

The decade of the 1980s proved to be a seminal decade for mathematics education. In 1980 the National Council of Supervisors of Mathematics published a Position Statement about Basic Skills. The accepted list of basic skills was to be expanded to include problem solving, reasoning, computer literacy, and a wider and deeper curriculum. This report was followed by a paper from National Council of Teachers of Mathematics (NCTM) entitled *Agenda for Action*. In this report NCTM listed a number of recommendations for improving mathematics education, including expanded problem solving, increased use of calculators and computers, increases in the number of years spent studying mathematics, and increased public support for mathematics teachers and mathematics education. School mathematics was to focus on problem solving and conceptual understanding rather than on rote memorization and computation. Both of these reports were written for professional audiences, and both were circulated within the small groups of mathematics educators.

In 1983 the National Commission on Excellence in Education published *A Nation at Risk: The Imperative for Educational Reform*. This report was addressed to general audiences and was essentially an indictment of the entire educational system, mathematics education included. It offered evidence that the nation's schools were not producing a wide range of excellence in mathematics or other areas. "America's position in the world may once have been reasonably secure with only a few exceptionally well-trained men and women. It is no longer" (p. 6). Comparisons of American students' achievements to those of other nations found the United States in poor positions. "Secondary school curricula have been homogenized, diluted, and diffused to the point that they no longer have a central purpose" (p. 18). This call to arms recommended a longer school day and a longer school year. Colleges and textbook publishers were challenged to do more. Local school boards were cited as needing to more closely evaluate the education of their children. In mathematics education the recommendation was three years of high school mathematics for all, with some specific content recommendations for those courses, and appropriate preparation in mathematics before high school. *A Nation at Risk* succeeded in getting the attention of policy makers and more consideration was given to improving our schools on a national basis and not simply on a local stage.

The end of the decade marked two significant events in the development of mathematics education in the United States. The first was the publication *Everybody Counts: A Report to the Nation on the Future of Mathematics Education* by the Mathematical Sciences and Education Board, under the auspices of the National Research Council. This report was designed for general audiences, not mathematics educators, and spoke the language of the general population. "The national spotlight is on mathematics as we appreciate its central role in the economic growth of this country. . . . It must become a pump instead of a filter in the pipeline" (p. 7). In essence, the report envisioned a time when mathematics would be a gateway to further education and economic advancement rather than the barrier to advancement that they perceived. The report also itemized adjustments needed in the areas of human resources, mathematics topics, curricula, and teaching. The report suggested national reforms to improve mathematics education, including a national curriculum, revisions of teacher preparation, improved teaching methods, and further development of effective mathematics materials. The report mobilized school communities across the country to examine their mathematics education program and to take steps to begin to improve it.

> **REACT | REFLECT**
>
> In your school experience did you find math was a gateway or a barrier for you? Why?

Curriculum and Evaluation Standards for School Mathematics

Hard on the heels of *Everybody Counts* came another milestone in mathematics education, NCTM's *Curriculum and Evaluation Standards for School Mathematics.* This document was a landmark event in mathematics education in America. It was the first time any national group attempted to specify topics, concepts, and critical processes in a specific discipline. According to NCTM, "These standards are one facet of the mathematics education community's response to the call for reform in the teaching and learning of mathematics. . . .They reflect, and are an extension of, the community's responses to those demands for change. . . . Inherent in this document is a consensus that all students need to learn more, and often different, mathematics and that instruction in mathematics must be significantly revised" (NCTM, 1989, p. 2). The council saw a twofold objective in releasing the *Standards:*

1. Create a coherent vision of what it means to be mathematically literate both in a world that relies on calculators and computers to carry out mathematical procedures and in a world where mathematics is rapidly growing and is extensively being applied in diverse fields.
2. Create a set of standards to guide the revision of the school mathematics curriculum and its associated evaluation toward this vision.

For the first time a teacher in San Diego and a teacher in Boston could have a common curriculum. They could compare their own classroom activities and topics to national standards suggested by NCTM. The *Standards* document quickly became the basis for a national curriculum. Textbook publishers and authors consulted the *Standards* as they wrote new texts, ancillary materials, and other curriculum resources. Writers of state frameworks used the *Standards* as a guide as they detailed the expectations of the mathematics programs in their states. Local districts looked to the *Standards* to help them develop curriculum materials and course sequences. The *Standards* addressed mathematics topics at three levels, K–4, 5–8, and 9–12. At each level, standards for mathematics processes were discussed: problem solving, reasoning, communication, and connections. In addition, there were content topics appropriate to each grade level, such as algebra, synthetic geometry, and decimals and fractions. It was a text written for the practitioner in the classroom and was an immediate catalyst for needed changes in mathematics programs across the country.

The *Standards* were also revolutionary in calling for changes across the entire mathematics curriculum, specifying those concepts and processes that needed increased attention and those that needed decreased attention. For example, in Number and Operations these are the specific concepts that are cited for increased or decreased attention (NCTM, 1989):

Increased Attention	**Decreased Attention**
Developing number sense	Memorizing rules and algorithms
Developing operation sense	Practicing tedious paper-and-pencil
Creating algorithms and procedures	computations
Using estimation both in problem solving and in checking the reasonableness of results	Finding exact forms of answers
	Memorizing procedures such as cross-multiplication without understanding
Exploring relationships among representations of, and operations on, whole numbers, fractions, decimals, integers, and rational numbers	Practicing rounding numbers out of context
Developing an understanding of ratio, proportion, and percent	

This brief snapshot of the *Standards* captures NCTM's overarching vision of mathematics as a conceptual study rooted in real-world applications in contrast to the traditional view of mathematics as a rote, computational discipline that revolves around practice.

In the years since the publication of the *Standards* and *Everybody Counts*, there have been a number of additional reports that call for specific improvements in mathematics education, mathematics teacher preparation, and mathematics curricula. NCTM published companion standards to the *Curriculum and Evaluation Standards for School Mathematics*. In 1991 NCTM published *Professional Standards for Teaching Mathematics*, a set of standards for teachers and the teaching profession that paralleled the curriculum standards of 1989.

In *Professional Standards for Teaching Mathematics* (NCTM, 1991), NCTM suggested several seismic shifts in the environment of mathematics classrooms:

• Toward classrooms as mathematical communities	• Away from classrooms as simply a collection of individuals
• Toward logic and mathematical evidence as verification	• Away from the teacher as the sole authority for right answers
• Toward mathematical reasoning	• Away from merely memorizing procedures
• Toward conjecturing, inventing, and problem solving	• Away from an emphasis on mechanistic answer-finding
• Toward connecting mathematics, its ideas, and is applications	• Away from treating mathematics as a body of isolated concepts and procedures

In 1995 NCTM published *Assessment Standards for School Mathematics* (NCTM, 1995) that focused on the wide range of assessment practices appropriate for school mathematics.

In *Assessment Standards for School Mathematics*, NCTM suggested that assessment should focus on concepts and relationships between concepts instead of isolated concepts and procedures, and posited several shifts in thinking about assessment in mathematics:

- Toward a rich variety of mathematical topics and problem situations, and away from just arithmetic
- Toward investigating problems, and away from memorizing and repeating
- Toward questioning and listening, and away from telling
- Toward evidence from several sources judged by teachers, and away from a single test judged externally
- Toward using concepts and procedures to solve problems, and away from just mastering isolated concepts and problems

Principles and Standards of School Mathematics

Most noteworthy of NCTM's recent publications is *Principles and Standards of School Mathematics* (NCTM, 2000). It is a revision and expansion to the original *Standards* document. *Principles and Standards* is based on six major principles.

1. *The equity principle.* Excellence in mathematics education requires equity—high expectations and strong support for all students.
2. *The curriculum principle.* A curriculum is more than a collection of activities: It must be coherent, focused on important mathematics, and well articulated across the grades.
3. *The teaching principle.* Effective mathematics teaching requires understanding what students know and need to learn and then challenging and supporting them to learn it well.
4. *The learning principle.* Students must learn mathematics with understanding, actively building new knowledge from experience and prior knowledge.
5. *The assessment principle.* Assessment should support the learning of important mathematics and furnish useful information to both teachers and students.
6. *The technology principle.* Technology is essential in teaching and learning mathematics; it influences the mathematics that is taught and enhances students' learning (NCTM, 2000).

In *Principles and Standards*, school grades are now divided into four levels: pre-K–2, 3–5, 6–8, and 9–12. Each grade band contains ten strands, five content stands, and five process strands. (More detailed strands for middle grades are in each of the mathematics content chapters: Chapters 6–11.) The general themes for the content strands are as follows:

1. *Number and operations.* Instructional programs from prekindergarten through grade 12 should enable all students to
   - Understand numbers, ways of representing numbers, relationships among numbers, and number systems
   - Understand meanings of operations and how they relate to one another
   - Compute fluently and make reasonable estimates
2. *Algebra.* Instructional programs from prekindergarten through grade 12 should enable all students to
   - Understand patterns, relations, and functions
   - Represent and analyze mathematical situations and structures using algebraic symbols
   - Use mathematical models to represent and understand quantitative relationships
   - Analyze change in various contexts
3. *Geometry.* Instructional programs from prekindergarten through grade 12 should enable all students to
   - Analyze characteristics and properties of two- and three-dimensional geometric shapes and develop mathematical arguments about geometric relationships
   - Specify locations and describe spatial relationships using coordinate geometry and other representational systems

- Apply transformations and use symmetry to analyze mathematical situations
- Use visualization, spatial reasoning, and geometric modeling to solve problems

4. *Measurement.* Instructional programs from prekindergarten through grade 12 should enable all students to
  - Understand measurable attributes of objects and the units, systems, and processes of measurement
  - Apply appropriate techniques, tools, and formulas to determine measurements

5. *Data analysis and probability.* Instructional programs from prekindergarten through grade 12 should enable all students to
  - Formulate questions that can be addressed with data and collect, organize, and display relevant data to answer them
  - Select and use appropriate statistical methods to analyze data
  - Develop and evaluate inferences and predictions that are based on data
  - Understand and apply basic concepts of probability

Each grade band also contains five process strands: problem solving, reasoning and proof, connections, communication, and representation. The general themes for the process strands are as follows:

1. *Problem solving.* Instructional programs from prekindergarten through grade 12 should enable all students to
  - Build new mathematical knowledge through problem solving
  - Solve problems that arise in mathematics and in other contexts
  - Apply and adapt a variety of appropriate strategies to solve problems
  - Monitor and reflect on the process of mathematical problem solving

2. *Reasoning and proof.* Instructional programs from prekindergarten through grade 12 should enable all students to
  - Recognize reasoning and proof as fundamental aspects of mathematics
  - Make and investigate mathematical conjectures
  - Develop and evaluate mathematical arguments and proofs
  - Select and use various types of reasoning and methods of proof

3. *Communication.* Instructional programs from prekindergarten through grade 12 should enable all students to
  - Organize and consolidate their mathematical thinking through communication
  - Communicate their mathematical thinking coherently and clearly to peers, teachers, and others
  - Analyze and evaluate the mathematical thinking and strategies of others
  - Use the language of mathematics to express mathematical ideas precisely

4. *Connections.* Instructional programs from prekindergarten through grade 12 should enable all students to
  - Recognize and use connections among mathematical ideas
  - Understand how mathematical ideas interconnect and build on one another to produce a coherent whole
  - Recognize and apply mathematics in contexts outside of mathematics

5. *Representation.* Instructional programs from prekindergarten through grade 12 should enable all students to
  - Create and use representations to organize, record, and communicate mathematical ideas
  - Select, apply, and translate among mathematical representations to solve problems
  - Use representations to model and interpret physical, social, and mathematical phenomena

In this text we refer to the *Principles and Standards* quite often. We have chosen to devote entire chapters (Chapters 6–11) to the same content chapters that the *Principles and Standards* itemize: Number and Operations, Algebra, Geometry, Measurement, Data

Analysis, and Probability. We have also focused on problem solving in an individual chapter because we view problem solving as a foundational approach to all the middle school mathematics topics. It is also a focus of many high-stakes tests. We discuss the four other processes in Chapters 6–11 as they relate to the mathematics content topics in each of these chapters. Some general comments on each of these processes are appropriate here.

Reasoning and Proof

Reasoning and proof is "a habit of mind, and like all habits it must be developed through consistent use in many contexts" (NCTM, 2000, p. 56). Middle school students must have ample opportunities to explore relationships and form conjectures based on the data they gather. The reasoning process continues as they examine their conjectures and look for a case to refute their conjectures or work to offer evidence that their conjecture is always true. Part of the process involves working with classmates to explore and formulate these inductive conjectures and to examine the conjectures that classmates propose. Although middle school is not the place to expect students to design formal proofs, they are capable of deductive reasoning and so can gather evidence and present arguments to support their conjectures. We have included proofs in several of the content chapters. We suggest that these proofs can be presented to students as further verification of the relationships they have already discovered during their investigations. At this level the focus is not so much on writing formal proofs as it is on gathering evidence, making conjectures, and constructing supporting arguments that outline formal proofs.

Communication

This is an essential part of mathematics learning. When middle grade students communicate their findings or understandings, they clarify their thinking. Students can explain their conjectures, their problem-solving strategies, or their data findings to the class as part of the typical mathematics classroom. When students listen to others, they develop their own understandings by enlarging their knowledge base, adding to their repertoire of problem-solving strategies, or expanding their understanding of mathematical relationships.

Connections

The connections here focus on connections within mathematics. To be sure, mathematics should be connected to real-world situations and applications. Middle school students should also see the connections within mathematics. Fractions, decimals, and percents should be studied in concert, not as independent, discrete topics. Students should be able to relate various problems to problems they have seen in a different content or in a previous study.

Representation

In the middle grades students should use various representations to solve problems and to portray, clarify, or extend mathematical ideas (NCTM, 2000, p. 68). Students should have opportunities to not only employ conventional forms of representation but also to explore formats that resonate with them. Students should create models to represent and then solve mathematical problems.

The ultimate goal of the *Principles and Standards* is to

- Set forth a comprehensive and coherent set of goals for mathematics for all students from prekindergarten through grade 12 that will orient curricular, teaching, and assessment efforts during the next decades
- Serve as a resource for teachers, education leaders, and policymakers to use in examining and improving the quality of mathematics instructional programs
- Guide the development of curriculum frameworks, assessments, and instructional materials
- Stimulate ideas and ongoing conversations at the national, provincial or state, and local levels about how best to help students gain a deep understanding of important mathematics (NCTM, 2000, p. 2)

As these goals reveal, there is much more to do to improve mathematics education in the United States, and NCTM and other organizations continue to provide guidance and materials to help teachers, administrators, and teacher training institutions to do so.

A recent development across all education disciplines is the focus on the results of standardized tests. Although it is true that some tests such as the SAT (Scholastic Aptitude Test) and California Achievement Tests have been administered to large numbers of students for decades, this new wave of standardized tests involves state departments of education and even the federal government.

High-Stakes Testing

As attention has become more focused on education and student competency, there is an increasing number of what some educators term *high-stakes testing programs* that are being instituted across the country. The term *high-stakes tests* refers to standardized tests that carry with them some evaluation of students and school programs. In some states, students' scores are used to evaluate the educational program of a school. Many states require students to pass a test to graduate from high school. Here we discuss two well-known assessment programs and a new one that is still being developed.

NAEP

In the last part of the 1950s the Soviet Union launched the first man-made satellite. Scientists, politicians, and educators were shocked, especially in view of the implications in the existing cold war atmosphere. Many different initiatives were instituted to close the "space gap" and to improve mathematics and science education. One of the more far-reaching initiatives was proposed by the commissioner of education, who formulated an ambitious plan to determine U.S. students' achievement across many subjects. The result, in 1969, was the National Assessment of Educational Progress (NAEP), referred to by many as "the nation's report card." In the 1970s states voluntarily tested their students in mathematics, reading, science, and other subjects such as history, geography, and art. In 1988 the Hawkins-Stafford Elementary and Secondary Improvements Amendments further expanded the NAEP program and authorized statewide participation in the NAEP testing program. In 1990 a majority of states tested their fourth-, eighth-, and twelfth-grade students in mathematics, reading, and various other subjects. NAEP tests were also administered in 1992, 1996, 2000, and most recently in 2003/2004. Although a majority of states had participated in each test year, it was not until 2003 that all 50 states and the District of Columbia tested their students. That test was given to a national sample of 686,000 students in 13,600 school districts. The current NAEP program calls for tests in mathematics and reading every four years, along with other subjects on a rotating basis.

Student scores on the NAEP test have helped to shape the framework of mathematics education in the United States. Test scores have focused attention on deficiencies in mathematics and have also showed the effectiveness of recent reforms in mathematics education advocated by NCTM and others. For information about the NAEP tests and recent student performances, see Chapter 4, Assessment: Balanced and Varied.

TRY THIS

Go to http://nces.ed.gov/nationsreportcard/naepdata and compare your state results on the grade 8 NAEP mathematics to the nation as a whole.

TIMSS

TIMSS is the acronym for Trends in International Mathematics and Science Study, an international testing program administered in a four-year cycle. At one point TIMSS was the acronym for Third International Mathematics and Science Study, administered in 1995. It was preceded by the First International Mathematics and Science Study (FIMSS) in 1964 and the Second International Mathematics and Science Study (SIMSS) in 1980–1982. The current TIMSS program is organized by the International Association for the Evaluation of Educational Achievement (IEA). The first test in this program was conducted in 1995 at five grade levels in more than 40 countries. In 1999 TIMSS measured the mathematics achievement of eighth-grade students in 38 countries, including 13 states and 14 districts or consortia of districts across the United States. In 2003 students in grade 4 (27 countries) and grade 8 (49 countries) were tested. The purpose of TIMSS is to "provide important information for policy development, to foster public accountability, to allow areas of progress or decline to be identified and monitored, and to address concerns of equity" (http://timss.bc.edu/timss2003.html).

When national scores are released, comparisons between programs in different countries are cause for adjustment in national curricula, teaching practices, and mathematics frameworks. In addition, TIMSS scores can be the source of national pride and/or anxiety. For more on TIMSS see Chapter 4, Assessment: Balanced and Varied.

In each of the mathematics content chapters (Chapters 6–11) we have included one middle grades test item from NAEP and one from TIMSS. With each test item we have indicated the percentage of students who correctly answered the question. We invite you to try to answer these questions and then reflect on how difficult a middle school student might find them.

TRY THIS

Go to http://timss.bc.edu/timss2003.html and compare the United States grade 8 students' scores on the most recent TIMMS to scores of students from other nations.

No Child Left Behind

As of 2005 the U.S. government has stipulated that every child in grades 3–8 will be tested in mathematics and reading and in various other subjects. The details of the testing program in the No Child Left Behind legislation (NCLB) are still unclear. As this is being written, each individual state is responsible for testing its students, so there may be a wide variety of tests and a broad range of test difficulty. Many states are prepared to extend their own testing programs to all grades, whereas others seem ready to offer simple multiple-choice tests to meet the letter of the law as stipulated in the NCLB regulations. The results of the NCLB tests will be important to educators across the country. Sanctions are possible for those schools whose students display failing grades over a period of time. Poor scores may jeopardize federal funding, teacher positions, and ultimately, the viability of a school itself. The ramifications of NCLB are unclear, and the details of the program will likely be developed on an ongoing basis influenced by funding and political factors.

Whatever tests each state administers, the topics covered by these tests will likely be aligned with existing state mathematics frameworks. It may be beneficial to examine the state frameworks and the testing program in your own state. As previously mentioned, many states link students' scores on a high-stakes test to their graduation from high school. As of the publication date of his text, 27 states tied high school graduation to a student's score on some type of qualifying test. A developing consequence of focusing on high-stakes tests is that the classroom focus is shifting from engaging mathematics that students experience in explorations to an emphasis on those skills and topics found on the end-of-year tests. Many of the questions on these tests are multiple choice and open response, requiring a single answer. Few of these tests include open-ended questions because of the time and expense needed to evaluate these types of questions. Consequently, it is not only the mathematics curriculum that may be adversely impacted by such testing programs but also the classroom activities, as more time is spent on the problems, topics, and types of questions that students will find on their high-stakes test at the end of the year.

Point Well Taken

"Teachers focus 100 percent on educating and teaching children rather than preparing them for tests." Pasi Sahlberg, former official in the Finnish Education Ministry, when explaining Finland's top ranking in international mathematics testing for 15-year-olds.

—From U.S. Department of Education at www.ed.gov/news/pressreleases/2004/12/12062004a.html.

TRY THIS

Is there a high-stakes type of test for middle schoolers in your state? If so, what kinds of questions does it include?

The impact of technology on the middle grades classroom cannot be overstated. The calculator, computer, and the Internet can be effective tools for the middle grades teacher. We briefly discuss the development of technology here and refer to specific uses of technology in the mathematics content chapters.

Technology

One of the greatest factors to affect the ecosystem of mathematics education is the advancement in new and emerging technologies. Even the best visionaries of 25 years ago were not able to predict the full impact that technology has had and will have on mathematics teaching and learning. The changes in mathematics education due to advances in technology in the last two decades surpass any changes to mathematics education in the previous 2,500 years.

Handheld calculators are not new to education. Affordable calculators have been available since the early 1970s. As useful as these early calculators were, they were essentially computation devices and were limited to explorations involving computations and number relationships. Calculators now available to middle school students have capabilities that were impossible a generation earlier. Calculators designed for the middle school, such as the TI-15 and the TI-73, enable students to graph functions, develop spreadsheets, solve algebraic equations, explore geometric relationships, perform statistical analyses, and conduct classroom experiments using sensory accessories. Calculators are now permitted on state tests, college entrance examinations, and other high-stakes test programs.

Despite the utility of calculators in the classroom, students still need to master basic facts and relationships in mathematics, but this is no longer the sole focus of their study. Calculators in the classroom enable students to put aside tedious calculations and focus on the mathematics in a situation, mathematics that is revealed when students can look beyond the computations necessary to reveal it. For example, students might use a calculator when they explore a relationship first found by Greek mathematician Diophantus. He found an interesting result when he multiplied a triangular number (1, 3, 6, 10, 15, 21, 28 . . .) by 8 and then increased the product by 1. A triangular number is one that may be represented by dots in the form of an equilateral triangle, as shown in Figure 1.1 for the first four triangular numbers.

Students who are relieved from performing pencil-and-paper computations will be more likely to explore this relationship. In the mathematics content chapters we suggest how calculators may be beneficially used in the classroom.

Computers have, of course, become part of our daily life, for better or for worse. One way computers have affected education is by the scores of computer programs available to teachers, parents, and students. These programs

Texas Instruments TI-15 Calculator

Courtesy Texas Instruments.

Did You **Know**?

Tim Berners-Lee invented and named the World Wide Web in 1989.

Did You **Know**?

Jim Clark and Marc Andreessen founded Netscape and launched the first commercial Internet browser in 1994.

Did You **Know**?

The symbol @ was first used by Ray Thomlinson in 1969. He reasoned that whomever he sent messages to would be "at" the computer he designated.

Point Well Taken

"Appropriately using calculators during instruction improves paper-and-pencil skills for low-, average-, and high-ability students."

—*Lee Stiff, president of NCTM.* NCTM News Bulletin, *2003, March, p. 2*

figure **1.1**

Triangular Numbers

1   3   6   10

run the gamut from drill and practice and tutorials to simulations and interactive explorations. New and improved programs are developed every year to reflect new research findings and improved computer capabilities. Although we do not endorse any specific computer software, we do refer to generic programs that may be beneficial to students such as those dynamic geometry software programs that students can use to explore various geometry relationships.

Another factor that will impact computer use in the classroom is that now textbook publishers are providing electronic textbooks. School districts can obtain the rights from publishers to allow their students to access their textbook on the Internet or to use a CD version of the textbook at home. The paper and electronic textbooks are identical but the CD version may contain interactive explorations, animated examples, and updated references. It is unclear how this new use of technology will impact mathematics teaching, but you may be in a classroom where students do not have an assigned text, but rather access the textbook at home via their laptop computer, and use a classroom copy of the text when in school. Time will tell how light students' backpacks will become.

The last technology aspect to consider is scarcely 10 years old. The Internet was a curiosity in the early 1990s but is now an essential tool for every business and industry and even in our personal lives. The Internet is also a growing factor in mathematics education. There are literally hundreds of sites that contain mathematics problems, lesson plans, interactive lessons, explorations, and references. New sites emerge weekly, while some older sites become defunct. It is impossible to compile a list of all the useful websites. However, in each of the mathematics content chapters we refer to Internet sites that provide interactive activities to help students build mathematical relationships, explore mathematical concepts, and engage in problem solving. Some research suggests that experiences with virtual-reality manipulatives can be as effective as working with the concrete materials (Keller, Wasburn-Moses, & Hart, 2002). We encourage you to visit the sites we list and engage in the activities yourself to build appreciation for the potential the Internet will have on your classroom practice.

One final factor in mathematics education is the National Council of Teachers of Mathematics (NCTM). For over 100 years this organization of mathematics educators has been the preeminent mathematics teaching organization for public school teachers. Its membership is over 125,000 mathematics educators across the United States and Canada. NCTM provides a wide range of conferences, workshops, and professional development opportunities every year. In addition to the texts cited earlier, NCTM publishes scores of books designed to improve mathematics teaching in grades pre-K to 12 across a wide range of mathematics education topics from assessment and problem solving to content topics and language minority students. NCTM also publishes four monthly journals: *Teaching Children Mathematics*, designed for pre-K–6 teachers; *Mathematics Teaching in Middle School* for middle school teachers; *The Mathematics Teacher*, for secondary mathematics teachers; and *The Journal for Research in Mathematics Education*, a journal of current research findings for all levels. We suggest you learn more about NCTM at www.nctm.org.

In closing this first chapter, we reiterate and expand our goal for this text. It is critical that we prepare our middle school students to do more than memorize algorithms and perform rote procedures. They must become mathematically astute students who can solve skill, open-ended, and nonroutine problems, alone or in a group, by applying their mathematical knowledge across a wide range of concepts. In order to prepare such mathematically confident students, middle grades teachers must have a deep understanding of the important mathematics concepts middle schoolers should study and the knowledge to present these concepts in the forms of problems and challenges that engage students and stimulate their thinking. Today's middle school mathematics teacher draws support from recent research about how students learn mathematics, new and emerging technologies, and innovative and effective mathematics programs. Our goal, then, is to present to you the critical mathematics concepts middle school students should study, suggest ways to develop conceptual mathematics understanding in middle schoolers, and assist you to employ the many tools that are available to help you become an outstanding middle grades mathematics teacher.

Did You **Know**?

Douglas C. Engelhart invented the computer mouse in 1969.

SUMMARY

In the past 50 years mathematics education has moved from a computation-based study to the "new math" and then "back to basics." Mathematics education is now poised to continue the best of both movements in the twenty-first century. Mathematics education in the United States is entering an era of great changes. Lessons from research about how mathematics is learned, new and emerging technologies, and the effects of high-stakes tests will all shape mathematics education in the next decade. In addition, mathematics educators must prepare students to do more than mimic mathematical procedures; they must be able to apply mathematics to real-world situations that might not yet exist.

The following are highlights of this chapter:

- The popular view of mathematics is that you are born to do math.
- The NCTM is an important factor in mathematics education in the United States and Canada.
- "Back-to-basics" and "new math" are two opposing views of mathematics education.
- NAEP, TIMSS, and NCLB are three prominent high-stakes testing programs.
- *Principles and Standards for School Mathematics* is a document that serves as a source for mathematics frameworks across the United States.

EXERCISES

From the Reading

1. What do the following acronyms represent: NCTM, TIMSS, NAEP, NCLB?

2. List the six principles for *Principles and Standards of School Mathematics* (PSSM).

3. What are the five content strands of PSSM? The five process strands?

4. Do you think there should be a national curriculum (a curriculum that all mathematics teachers must follow) in mathematics in the United States as there is in other countries? Explain your answer.

5. How has the Internet impacted your precollege formal education?

6. How will electronic textbooks impact mathematics education? Give two potential benefits and two potential difficulties.

On Your Own

1. Interview a local middle school mathematics teacher. Ask what effect, if any, high-stakes tests have had on his or her teaching practice.

2. Visit a local middle school to determine the effect of having textbooks on CDs.

3. Compare your state's frameworks for middle school mathematics to the NCTM *Standards* for grades 6–8.

4. Go to www.phschool.com and follow the links to samples of its middle school series on line. How do the features you access compare to what you remember about middle school mathematics textbooks?

5. Subscribe to the NCTM journal *Mathematics Teaching in the Middle School*. (See www.nctm.org.)

Portfolio Question

What intrigues you about teaching as a career?

Preparing for Praxis

The Praxis tests are aligned with the NCTM *Standards* (see Chapter 4). Becoming familiar with these *Standards* and the resulting implications for the middle school mathematics curriculum will help prepare you for the Praxis Middle School Mathematics Tests.

RESOURCES

Teacher's Bookcase

National Council of Teachers of Mathematics. (2004). *Empowering the beginning teacher of mathematics in middle school.* Reston, VA: NCTM.

This is a compilation of many articles written by classroom teachers ranging from professional growth and equity issues to classroom organization and assessment.

National Council of Teachers of Mathematics. (2000). *Professional standards for school mathematics.* Reston, VA: NCTM.

This text is an updated version of the 1989 Standards. *It is more comprehensive and delineates standards across four grade bands compared to three in the 1989* Standards.

National Council of Teachers of Mathematics. (1995). *Assessment standards for school mathematics.* Reston, VA: NCTM.

> This is the third volume in the Standards *trilogy and focuses on assessment in mathematics programs.*

National Council of Teachers of Mathematics. (1991). *Professional standards for teaching mathematics.* Reston, VA: NCTM.

> This text is a companion to the 1989 Standards *with the focus on the process of teaching mathematics rather than on the content.*

National Council of Teachers of Mathematics. (1989). *Curriculum and evaluation standards for school mathematics.* Reston, VA: NCTM.

> This is the seminal text for teaching mathematics. It was the first set of standards for teaching in any discipline and set the stage for other disciplines to follow.

National Council of Teachers of Mathematics. (1982). *1982 yearbook: Mathematics for the middle grades (5–9).* Reston, VA: NCTM.

> This yearbook contains short articles about content, process, and preparation for teaching middle grades mathematics.

National Research Council. (2000). *Mathematics education in the middle grades: Teaching to meet the needs of middle grades learners and to maintain high expectations.* Washington, DC: National Academy Press.

> This report describes effective middle school mathematics programs and classrooms and suggests strategies to effect mathematics learning.

For Further Reading

Middelton, J., & Spanias, P. (1999). Motivation achievement in mathematics: Findings, generalizations, and criticisms of the research. *Journal for Research in Mathematics Education, 30,* 65–88.

> These research findings detail how motivation affects mathematics learning in middle school students.

National Commission on Excellence in Education. (1983). *A nation at risk: The imperative for educational reform.* Washington, DC: U.S. Department of Education.

> This report was the first to call attention to the shortcomings of education in the United States. It was the first of many reports dedicated to a general public audience.

National Commission on Mathematics and Science Teaching. (2002). *Before it's too late: A report to the nation from the National Commission on Mathematics and Science Teaching for the 21st Century.* Washington, DC: U.S. Department of Education.

> This report examines the current state of mathematics and science in the United States and makes recommendations for improvements.

National Research Council. (1989). *Everybody counts: A report to the nation about the future of mathematics education.* Washington, DC: National Academy Press.

> This report is another milestone in a series of reports that examined mathematics education in the United States and made recommendations for its improvement.

Links

Information about the high-stakes tests in each state may be found at
www.rowan.edu/mars/depts/math/milou/STATES/Page1

State mathematics and science frameworks for each state may be found at
www.ccsso.org/mathsci.html

NCTM Principles and Standards for School Mathematics may be found at
www.nctm.org/standards

REFERENCES

Bruxelles, S. (2003, January 3). Pupils sum up math teachers as fat nerds. *The Times* (London).

Devlin, K. (1998). Devlin's angle: Math + rigor = college. www.maa.org/devlin_1_98.html.

Keller, B., Wasburn-Moses, J., & Hart, E. (2002). *Improving students' spatial visualization skills and teachers' pedagogical content knowledge by using on-line curriculum-embedded applets.* Ongoing research and development project sponsored by NCTM.

Middelton, J., & Spanias, P. (1999). Motivation achievement in mathematics: Findings, generalizations, and criticisms of the research. *Journal for Research in Mathematics Education, 30,* 65–88.

National Commission on Mathematics and Science Teaching. (2002). *Before it's too late: A report to the nation from the National Commission on Mathematics and Science Teaching for the 21st Century.* Washington, DC: U.S. Department of Education.

National Council of Teachers of Mathematics. (2000). *Principles and standards for school mathematics.* Reston, VA: NCTM.

National Council of Teachers of Mathematics. (1995). *Assessment standards for school mathematics.* Reston, VA: NCTM.

National Council of Teachers of Mathematics. (1991). *Professional standards for teaching mathematics.* Reston, VA: NCTM.

National Council of Teachers of Mathematics. (1989). *Curriculum and evaluation standards for school mathematics.* Reston, VA: NCTM.

National Research Council. (1989). *Everybody counts: A report to the nation about the future of mathematics education.* Washington, DC: National Academy Press.

2

The Challenge of Middle School Learners

Middle school is the bridge between elementary school and high school, the time when students begin the many changes in personality, physique, attitudes, and likes and dislikes that will mark who they are as adults. It is the time when students start to clarify their thinking about a great many topics and when they determine the academic subjects they like and dislike. Middle school is the place where students begin to seek their life's path. Yet, in spite of the critical role middle school plays in the academic and developmental life of students, the concept of middle school is a fairly recent one in education.

Today's middle school had its beginning at the turn of the twentieth century. Up to that point all public school education was divided into elementary school (K–6) and secondary school (7–12). Some educators thought the transition from elementary school to secondary school was too abrupt and that teachers needed to take into consideration the many changes students were experiencing when they left elementary school in grade 6 for high school in grade 7. Their solution was the junior high school, which consisted of grades 7 and 8. Through the years the junior high school has taken different forms from grades 7–8 and 7–9 to 6–8 and 6–9.

Today junior high school has, to all intents and purposes, been replaced by the middle school, typically a 6–8 or 5–8 grade span. The decision about which grades will be assigned to a middle school is less an educational decision than an economic one. Will the school building designated as a middle school accommodate grades 5–8 or only 6–8? Do our elementary schools have enough room to keep the grade 5 students (and maybe even the grade 6 students) in their school? Some smaller school districts have maintained the traditional K–8, 9–12 program of studies for their schools. Most school districts, however, recognize the need for a middle school and have some format that allows young adolescents to be grouped together in their own school with their own curriculum. Interestingly, some urban districts are returning to the original K–8, 9–12 format. The rationale is that students who remain in the same school for their first nine years of schooling will be well known to all the faculty, who thus will be able to help them through their difficult adolescent years. Time will tell if this will become a widespread trend across the country.

Middle School: A Time of Change

Middle school students are a unique challenge in the public school setting, students who need support and understanding as they make the transition from elementary to middle school. In middle school new students have left the womb of elementary school for the confusing and chaotic world of the middle grades. In elementary school students stayed with their teacher all day and rarely left their own classroom except for recess and lunch. They bonded with their teachers, who essentially became surrogate parents to their stu-

On the Lighter Side

Junior high school teachers are fearless.

Copyright Grimmy Inc. Reprinted with permission of King Features Syndicate.

dents while they were in school. In middle school, students regularly see four to six teachers per day and can rotate through classrooms across the entire school building. This routine, so natural to high school students, can be harrowing to middle schoolers who are not used to crowded corridors and rotating schedules. In addition, the typical middle school is composed of students from several elementary feeder schools, and so there are new faces to recognize, new personalities to assimilate, new friendships to make, and so much more to become accustomed to. The fact that middle school teachers no longer treat their students as children but as young adults can further complicate the difficult transition these students are making in middle school.

Of course, things are changing with middle school students themselves. They are growing, some awkwardly, some too fast, and some reluctantly. The physical changes are troubling for some and painful for others. As voices change and signs of maturation reveal themselves, middle school students become overly self-conscious. Their self-esteem is at stake over the smallest skin blemish or a single stubborn hair. The need to be popular becomes ever more important at this age, as students begin to form friendships based on something other than family or their neighborhood. It is a time when friends begin to assume a greater importance than parents, and peer approval can (and in many cases does) become more important than parental approval (or teacher approval). All of this social and personal turmoil can take its toll on even the most well-adjusted middle grades student.

During middle school, students make decisions about many likes and dislikes that they will maintain all their lives, from music, colors, and sports teams to recreation and school subjects. The favorite subjects of elementary school are pared down to a favorite one or two, or perhaps to none at all in a not uncommon reaction to school in general. It is in middle school that students set their self-perceived role as a student: the effort they are satisfied with expending, the grades they are satisfied with attaining, the relationship with their teacher, and their view of school as useful either now or in the future.

Mathematics in the middle school presents its own particular challenges to students. Middle grades students change their focus from whole numbers to rational numbers, from concrete concepts to more abstract topics, and from the absolute to the hypothetical. Middle grades mathematics is no longer within the grasp of most parents. Parents may view mathematics as important, but they do not feel confident enough in the discipline themselves to help their children, and so students can no longer rely on their parents for assistance. Many middle schoolers think mathematics is valuable but only in a generic sort of way. Few see any prospect of mathematics being important to them personally once they finish school. Finally, mathematics begins to become a more complex study for middle school students at a time when their universe is expanding beyond their small world

Point Well Taken

"Students at this level [middle school] can aptly be called children in transition."
—*NCTM, 1989, p. 68*

Point Well Taken

"For many students middle school represents the last chance to develop a sense of academic purpose and personal commitment to academic goals."
—*Sowder, 2001, p. 3*

Point Well Taken

"At no other point in human development is an individual likely to encounter so much diversity in relation to oneself and others."
—*Sims & Sims, 2002, p. 6*

Point Well Taken

"Middle school is the place where kids have the most problems, the place where parents reach the level where they're not able or willing to help the kids with math anymore."

—*Johnny Lott,
NCTM president, 2004*

Did You **Know**?

A recent research study found lack of sufficient sleep in middle grades students showed a high correlation to lower self-esteem, lower grades, and higher levels of depression.

—*Science Daily, February 4, 2004*

Point Well Taken

"Confidence in learning mathematics was the best affective predictor of later mathematics achievement."

—*Hart & Walker, 1993, p. 26*

Point Well Taken

"A recognition of individual differences must be basic to an educator's philosophy."

—*Guild & Garger, 1998, p. 48*

and their attention is divided among peers, new ideas, new foods, and new customs. These collide for the first time in middle school.

Teaching middle school is never dull. Adolescents are open with their thoughts and feelings, engage their teachers at many different levels, and can still carry the enthusiasm of elementary school to their study of mathematics. The energy level of middle school students is at times astronomical. A high energy level combined with accompanying mood swings for which adolescents are notorious means that every day can be a leap into the unknown for a teacher. The quiet, reserved student of Monday is a loud, boisterous student on Wednesday and then quiet again on Friday. Effective middle grades teachers are aware of all these factors that help to shape their students, support their students as they face them, regularly make allowances for them, and find appropriate ways to harness their energy.

The affective side of middle school students is an important consideration for middle school mathematics teachers. As noted earlier, elementary school students like mathematics, whereas middle schoolers show a declining interest in it. A key to helping middle school students maintain an interest in mathematics is to boost their confidence in their own mathematics ability. Confidence is a dominant feature of a successful mathematics student in middle school. Student confidence shapes their perception of mathematics and their future studies in it. Nearly as important as confidence for middle grades students is their view of the usefulness of mathematics. When middle schoolers understand the value of a concept, process, or information, they are eager to master the discipline. This aspect of middle grades students' attitude is an important one for middle school teachers to recognize. Teaching the material is not enough—middle school teachers must also engage students in its discovery.

Learning Styles

Today educators recognize that the one-size-fits-all practices of the last century no longer work with today's students. Research has clearly found that not all students learn the same way, few students find the same approaches in mathematics persuasive, and few students benefit from a single approach to mathematical concepts or processes. Rather, different students best learn mathematical concepts in a variety of different ways that they find appealing and compelling. Clearly, this diversity in ways of learning has an important role to play in the day-to-day teaching practices of a middle school teacher. We discuss classroom practice in Chapter 3, The Practice of Effective Instruction, but feel it is appropriate here to expand on the need to recognize that in a typical middle school classroom there are many different learning styles.

Gardner's Multiple Intelligences

There are a number of paradigms that portray students' different learning styles or thinking methodologies. In this scheme of things educators recognize that students have strengths and weaknesses in their comfort level and ability to learn in various settings, by various means, and in various contexts. One format is the Multiple Intelligences of Howard Gardner. Gardner postulates that there are eight distinct types of intelligences or intellectual strengths that students bring to the classroom. A student's specific intelligence type indicates that student's particular cognitive strengths and what context or activity he or she may find engaging.

Gardner suggests that teachers can better help their students when they are able to identify which of these eight intelligences are predominant in the students. Once this is done, the teacher can select activities, aspects of concepts, and appropriate tasks that play to the strength of the particular student. In mathematics this can be a critical part of classroom lesson planning. Although Gardner's scheme of Eight Intelligences applies to students at any level, it is especially pertinent at the middle grades. As previously discussed, middle school students begin to feel threatened by the increasingly complex mathematics they study and by the many changes they are experiencing. Thus, they will benefit from having a means of learning and expressing themselves that plays to their strengths. As a result, they can focus on the mathematics content and mathematics process and not worry about the activity or situation they are using to learn it. They will be comfortable in the settings and tasks assigned to them and so can devote their energies to mastering the mathematical relationships that are imbedded within their tasks or activities. They will feel less threatened and more capable of achieving the mathematics learning that is demanded of them when they are in a task setting that is secure for them. The following are brief descriptions of Gardner's Eight Intelligences (Smith, 2002):

- *Logical-mathematical.* This student is quite capable in mathematics and problem solving. Sequential thinking is his or her strength. Appealing activities are sorting or classifying, mathematics problems, riddles, and explorations.
- *Spatial.* This student's strong imagination is reflected in drawing, puzzles, and mazes. Appealing activities are sketching, sculpture, creating posters, and visualization activities.
- *Interpersonal.* This student communicates well, works well with peers, and is an organizer. Appealing activities are cooperative and partner work, discussions, and collaboration.
- *Bodily-kinesthetic.* This student is constantly fidgeting or moving around. Appealing activities are manipulatives, role-play, and active experimentation.
- *Verbal-linguistic.* This student is a talker who talks to himself or herself and others, tells jokes, and listens well to others. Appealing activities are reports, oral presentations, and research in books.
- *Intrapersonal.* This student prefers to work alone, likes personal reading, and can work well to attain personal goals. Appealing activities are journal writing and thinking exercises.
- *Musical-rhythmic.* This student has an easily recognizable love of music, evidenced by humming, tapping, and singing. Appealing activities include background music, oral presentations, and music-related activities.
- *Naturalist.* This student is knowledgeable and concerned about a variety of natural and societal flora and fauna from birds and trees to sneakers and cars. Appealing activities include problems and tasks in the context of naturalist settings such as weather, animal care, and forestry.

The preceding list displays the wide range of learning styles covered by the Eight Intelligences and the resulting task settings that appeal to each intelligence. Again, middle school students are especially vulnerable to the stresses of new or uncomfortable situations. A student who is strong in intrapersonal intelligence might find it difficult to learn mathematics in the same group activity compared to a student who is strong in verbal-linguistic intelligence. Consequently, it is beneficial to students when their teacher provides task settings that allow them to work in their learning style. It is worth noting here that teachers have their own learning styles, and the tendency is for teachers to feature their own learning styles and identify with students who demonstrate the same styles.

> **REACT | REFLECT**
>
> Which of the intelligences seem to be predominant in you? Explain your answer.

McCarthy's 4MAT Inventory of Learning Styles

Bernice McCarthy is another educator with a system to categorize different learning styles. McCarthy views all student academic activity through the lens of their learning styles. In the case of McCarthy's 4MAT Inventory of Learning Styles, students are more comfortable in a particular activity that fits well with their particular learning style. McCarthy has thoughts similar to Gardner's regarding how classroom teachers should make use of their students' learning styles. According to McCarthy teachers should endeavor to identify each student's learning style and take this into account when developing activities for students. Giving students the opportunity to participate in activities within their learning style allows them to work within their strengths. They can then put effort into the specific concepts or relationships at hand rather than have to expend energy in a role that does not dovetail well with their learning style.

McCarthy's 4MAT system recognizes four learning styles (Silmer, 2003):

- *Type I: innovative learners.* Type I learners are interested in personal meaning. They need to have a personal connection with concepts either by personal experiences or usefulness in daily life or in the future. This type of learner performs well in groups and cooperative settings.
- *Type II: analytic learners.* Type II learners are focused on acquiring facts and knowledge to deepen their understanding of concepts and algorithms. They work well in lecture formats, readings, and research.
- *Type III: common-sense learners.* Type III learners are interested in practical aspects of concepts, how things work, and how they are useful. They learn best in concrete experiential settings such as using manipulatives.
- *Type IV: dynamic learners.* Type IV learners are focused on a journey of the self. They rely on intuition and look to make personal discoveries. They learn best in independent study and exploration.

As suggested with Gardner's Eight Intelligences, middle grades students have begun to concentrate on one of these learning styles. Providing opportunities for students to learn mathematics in a way that aligns with their learning style will promote better mathematics learning.

It is not possible to develop different activity settings and tasks for every student for every period of mathematics. Rather, the point is that during a unit of study there would be the opportunity for the Type III learner to explore concepts and relationships with manipulatives and for the Type I learner to work in small groups to examine mathematics relationships by questioning and discussing. The Type II learner should have the chance to collect, collate, and analyze the information generated by group explorations and discussions. Finally, the Type IV learner needs the occasion to make meaningful and personal connections to the mathematics concepts in the unit.

There is one factor about the concept of learning styles that is good to keep in mind. Middle grades students should be challenged with tasks, activities, and topics that require them to stretch their learning style repertoire and step out of their comfort zone. That is, a student who is comfortable in the role of a bodily-kinesthetic, for example, should be given the opportunity to work in a different intelligence style such as verbal-linguistic. A student who is a Type IV learner needs to develop the ability and comfort level to work well within a small group. It is not clear that students in middle grades are forever set within a single learning style, or that they are not still evolving to the intelligence they will best utilize for the rest of their lives. Whether they already have a well-defined intelligence and/or learning style or not, it is important that middle school students experience other modes and can function in a variety of settings. Middle grades students who are devoted to a single learning style and/or intelligence to the exclusion of all others will be severely handicapped as they continue their education in secondary school and beyond. It is a key role of the middle grades teacher to expand their students' learning styles and intelligences while at the same time recognizing the value of playing to students' strengths when they do mathematics in the classroom.

REACT | REFLECT

What learning style is most descriptive of the way you learn? Explain your answer.

Equity in Mathematics

A key aspect to teaching mathematics is ensuring all students have the same opportunities to succeed. The first of six overarching principles in *Principles and Standards for School Mathematics* is the Equity Principle: Excellence in mathematics education requires equity— high expectation and strong support for all students.

In the United States there is a diverse population in the public schools, including groups that have traditionally been denied the opportunity to achieve in mathematics. Fe-

Point Well Taken

"Addressing gender equity in the mathematics classroom is a complex issue."
—*Ambrose et al., 1997, p. 241*

males, English-language learners, and special needs students should all have a level playing field when it comes to learning mathematics. That does not mean treating every student the same or seeing that every student receives identical instruction. Rather, as NCTM suggests, ". . . reasonable and appropriate accommodations should be made as needed to promote access and attainment for all students" (2000, p. 112). We discuss here how to begin to employ the Equity Principle to meet the needs of these three subgroups.

Gender Equity

As recently as three decades ago a given truism was "mathematics is for boys and English is for girls." It was the rare female who ventured into advanced mathematics classes in high school, and rarer still the one who majored in mathematics at the university level.

Studies and test results seemed to bear out that boys could do math and girls could not. As recently as the mid-1970s the maleness of mathematics was a forgone conclusion (Fennema, 1982, p. 12).

Fortunately, society's attitudes have shifted. Recent studies support high-level potential in mathematics for both genders. No longer is mathematics presented as the male prerogative, the exclusive discipline for men. Today's middle grades classroom teachers support mathematics equity for both boys and girls. Yet some unrecognized residue of "math is for boys" can still reveal itself in subtle ways in the mathematics classroom. For example, some studies have shown that teachers are more attentive to boys when asking leading questions, frequently prompting boys to the correct mathematical answer. Girls are given less help and fewer prompts, as if they would not benefit from such because of limited ability and chance of success. Another not-uncommon practice is for a teacher to commend boys on their insight or knowledge in mathematics but commend girls on their hard work. Again, this implies that boys have an innate ability to succeed in mathematics but girls do not. When students have a difficult time with a mathematical concept, it is not unusual for a middle grades teacher to blame boys' failure on a lack of proper motivation and girls' failure on poor mathematical ability and talent. Even parents contribute to this *genderizing* of mathematics. Two longitudinal studies of school-age children and their parents found that parents are more likely to attribute a boy's success in mathematics to "natural talent," and a girl's success to "hard work" (Barnett & Rivers, 2004).

In all of the preceding situations, the gender stereotype of "math is for boys" persists, but it is not overt. In many studies, the teachers who exhibited such behaviors were unaware they were doing so and in interviews stated that they had no gender bias in mathematics. They believed that boys and girls could succeed equally well in mathematics. Still, as these experiences exhibit, the ill-conceived notions of gender superiority in mathematics can be stubbornly enduring. Recent test results in NAEP and TIMSS show that any gender differences in mathematics are focused on the upper grades and seems to be more a factor of the numbers of boys and girls who take advanced courses than any specific ability of boys over girls. The small differences between boys' and girls' scores (1–3 points) on the NAEP tests for both grade 4 and grade 8 students remain consistent, even as scores have risen since 1990. Thus, as a percentage of test scores, the difference between boys' and girls' scores shows a steady decrease. On the 2003/2004 NAEP the average mathematics scores were boys 277 and girls 275, a difference so small as to have no significance. In addition, a meta-analysis of SAT scores for 3 million students found that girls and boys had virtually identical scores in mathematics (Barnett & Rivers, 2004). Despite this equity in ability, girls do not study as much math in secondary school. According to the National Science Foundation, females account for only 35% of student enrollment in mathematics, science, and computer programming. The fact that more boys than girls pursue advanced mathematics shows that gender differences in mathematics is still an issue that must be confronted, and the place to do it is in the middle grades.

One area of mathematics where there appears to be a dramatic gender difference is spatial sense. Among early elementary school children, only 17% of girls score at the boys' average score on tests of spatial sense, especially mental rotation. Such differences may

Point Well Taken

"The vision of equity in mathematics education challenges a persuasive societal belief in North America that only some students are capable of learning mathematics."
—*NCTM, 2000, p. 12*

AUTHOR'S **Recall**

I can remember a guidance counselor asking about his daughter's work in my math class. After I gave him a brief summary of her fine successes, the counselor commented in hushed tones, "Well, that's good. But what will she ever use mathematics for anyway? She is a girl!"

Point Well Taken

"When gender differences [in mathematics achievement] are found, they are typically small."
—*Leder, 1992, p. 616*

AUTHOR'S **Recall**

When I was an undergraduate majoring in mathematics, there were only two female students in all of my mathematics classes. The popular thinking then was to wonder why they were taking mathematics and not history or English.

Point Well Taken

"Common notions about gender appropriate behavior are frequently internalized by individuals and lead to different beliefs and expectations in areas critical to the learning of mathematics."
—*Leder, 1992, p. 616*

AUTHOR'S **Recall**

I remember being told, "You don't really need to take math in college. After all, you're only going to get married after you graduate."

REACT | **REFLECT**

Have you seen gender differences in any of your mathematics classes? Have boys been treated differently than girls? In what ways?

REACT | **REFLECT**

Do you feel confident in your mathematics abilities? Why or why not?

be eliminated with a careful course of study that includes developing and expanding spatial sense. Without attention to spatial sense, the differences persist and even increase (Linn & Petersen, 1986). We discuss spatial sense in Chapter 8, Geometry: Moving beyond Formulas.

In elementary school, mathematics is universally popular for both boys and girls. In middle school it begins to lose some of its luster for both groups, but more so among girls, even though the achievement of boys and girls in the middle grades is essentially the same. Why might this be? Part of the reason may be due to how the boys and girls are treated in mathematics class, as outlined in the preceding paragraphs. Other factors to consider are how mathematics is presented in the classroom and assessment practices. Boys tend to be risk takers while girls in middle school stay within the bounds established by their teachers. Although this is beneficial for the smooth running of a classroom and school, staying within the bounds in mathematics can work to one's disadvantage. A mathematics student who follows only tried and true algorithms and problem-solving strategies and employs only those techniques that have been fully explored may not fare well when working on nonroutine problems or in nontraditional contexts. Girls (or boys) who succeed in middle grades mathematics by following the prescribed regimen of problem-solving techniques will have difficulty in new situations and falter in ways that students willing to take risks and try something new or unusual will not.

For all students, mathematics class is full of successes and mistakes. The mistakes should be simply part of the mathematics landscape and viewed as an opportunity to learn. Essentially, girls and boys in middle grades mathematics classes have to maintain confidence in their mathematics understanding and abilities. Girls and boys must have the opportunities to step into unfamiliar settings and take new and unexpected approaches to problems in a way that they do not perceive as threatening to them. The more they do so and the more they succeed, the stronger their confidence in their abilities becomes and the better they are able to succeed in the higher-level mathematics courses.

The structure of class assessments and activities can do much to build students' confidence and so help to ensure gender equity. Assessments in mathematics classes should provide opportunities for girls to work in collaborative, cooperative settings and not exclusively in competitive settings that tend to favor risk-taking boys. In point of fact both girls and boys can benefit from a variety of class settings and assessments (see Chapter 4, Assessment: Balanced and Varied). One way to bolster students' confidence in their mathematics ability is to provide many occasions for students to work in small, collaborative groups. Confidence in mathematics, or a lack of it, can be a critical factor in predicting success in middle grades mathematics and beyond. "There is some evidence that on average females are somewhat less confident about their ability to do mathematics" (Leder, 1992, p. 616). The manner in which middle grades boys and girls view their failures or successes in mathematics is instructive. Boys think ability is responsible for any successes or failures in mathematics, whereas for girls it is a matter of luck, good or bad. Thus, boys see mathematics as a discipline in which they can succeed if they develop their ability, but girls see no such connection and blame unseen forces for their fate in mathematics (Morris, 1995). Furthermore, those girls in middle school who lack confidence in mathematics will tend to self-select less demanding mathematics courses when given the chance, even if their mathematics ability is up to the task. By doing so they deny themselves the opportunity to take higher-level mathematics courses and so deny themselves entry to many professions that demand a strong mathematics background.

Another aspect that works against girls having a positive attitude about their ability in mathematics is the lack of role models. Most people can list two or three mathematicians, but their list is unlikely to include a woman. Middle grades teachers need to humanize mathematics for all their students by introducing the names behind the mathematics in the classroom. Included in the mathematicians of the past should be women mathematicians such as Hypatia, Mary Fairfax Somerville, Maria Agnesi, Emily du Chatelet, Ada Lovelace, Mary Everest Boole, and Sonya Kovalavsky.

TRY THIS

Read a biography of one of these women mathematicians at www.groups.dcs.st-and.ac.uk/~history/BiogIndex.html. What difficulties did she have to overcome to pursue mathematics?

Closely aligned to introducing women who used mathematics in the past is the need for mathematics to have a practical use for middle school girls. Girls who do well with mathematics in the middle grades but who see no use for it in their futures will be unlikely to pursue advanced mathematics courses in high school. The real-world applications that should be part of every mathematics class can focus on how mathematics is used in common activities of adult life and in real-world settings by professionals in interesting and unusual careers. Teachers can seek out women in the community who use mathematics every day in their careers and refer to them or have them address students in class. When designing open-ended problems and word problems, the setting should appeal to both boys and girls. For example, sports settings should employ sports that interest both genders such as soccer, basketball, swimming, and track and field rather than only football and baseball. Similarly, career-based settings should include men and women in the roles of professionals rather than the settings of a 1960s' textbook where men were the ones who had jobs and women were the ones who worked around the house. A physician in a real-world application problem can be measuring medicine dosages for *her* patients.

Clearly, it is important to be cognizant of the gender issue in the middle grades mathematics classroom. One study found that an instructive program changed the girls' attitudes toward mathematics and most of the middle grades girls studied mathematics all four years of high school. The control group in the study received no such program and "bought deeper over time into the myth that boys are smarter than girls in mathematics" (Koonz, 1997, p. 191). Thus, teachers who simply ignore the issue, reasoning they will conduct a class that is fair to all, may well penalize one gender over another because they do not take into consideration the needs of both boys and girls at this level. Each middle grades mathematics teacher must find the balance between changing a class to cater to girls' (or boys') needs or demanding that the girls (or boys) change to adapt to the given structure of the class. Neither extreme will benefit students in mathematics. In some school districts, middle school boys and girls learn mathematics and science in separate classes. It is still not clear that segregation by gender is beneficial for learning mathematics. Most teachers teach mixed-gender classes, so it is incumbent on a successful mathematics teacher to provide activities that meet the needs of both genders and nurture their confidence in their potential to do mathematics and in their ability to succeed in mathematics.

The most recent data indicate that girls take high school mathematics as often as boys do. Yet they still have less-than-positive attitudes about mathematics. By grade 12 fully 50% of girls declare their dislike for mathematics compared to only 9% in grade 4 (Chacon & Soto-Johnson, 2003). A study by the Organization for Economic Cooperation and Development found that compared to boys of the same age, 15-year-old girls consistently reported "much lower interest in and enjoyment of mathematics" (Norris, 2004, p. 23). Enrollments in college mathematics courses support this declaration. Although 60% of college students are women, only 44% of mathematics majors are women. The reason for the difference seems to be young women's attitudes toward mathematics (Chacon & Soto-Johnson, 2003). As discussed earlier, it is critical that teachers engender and maintain young women's interest in mathematics and build up their confidence in their ability to do mathematics.

English-Language Learners

There are now over 4 million English-language learners in the public schools, speaking some 460 different languages. The number of English-language learners is growing much faster than the general school population. Between 1990 and 2001, the general school

Point Well Taken

"In order for gender equity to be attained, teachers will have to attend to it directly in their classroom."

—Ambrose et al., 1997, p. 236

Point Well Taken

"Recommendations of how English Language Learners can best learn mathematics and how they should be taught do not differ significantly from what is best for other groups."

—*Flores, 1997, p. 90*

Point Well Taken

"Whenever possible, students' cultural backgrounds should be integrated into the learning experience."

—*NCTM, 1989, p. 5*

Point Well Taken

"For Americans, errors tend to be interpreted as an indication of failure in learning the lesson; for Chinese and Japanese, they are an index of what still needs to be learned."

—*Siger & Stevenson, 1991, p. 44*

population had grown 12% but the English-language learners population had grown over 105% (Kindler, 2002). In the past English-language learners were concentrated in distinct regions across the United States, but that is no longer true. As a result, the issue of equity for English-language learners must be considered by teachers in every school district. It is the rare district or school that has no English-language learners. In 2002, 43% of all K–12 teachers had at least one English-language learner in their classroom (Zehler et al., 2003). In addition, the trend in some states has been to eliminate bilingual education in favor of immersion, meaning that those students who speak no English whatsoever are placed in regular classes almost immediately after enrolling in their local school. For example, in 1997 the voters in California overwhelmingly approved Proposition 227, an initiative that essentially eliminated bilingual education in the California schools. The result has been even more students who do not speak adequate English in mathematics classrooms.

As noted in Chapter 1, Mathematics for the Twenty-First Century, middle school mathematics classes are dealing with many different pressures in addition to learning mathematics. Middle grades students who must navigate all these factors (and others we have not mentioned), and do it in what is for them a foreign language, need extraordinary persistence and motivation. They also need appropriate help from caring teachers. In many instances, English-language learners simply need good teaching by a teacher who is sensitive to the needs of all students. Such teachers take a personal interest in their students, try to meet their needs, and are respectful of who they are as individuals. Such affective qualities are indispensable for teachers with English-language learners in their classrooms.

Knowing something about an English-language learner's background can help the teacher in the classroom. Some English-language learners show respect for the position of a teacher by never making direct eye contact with their teacher, even when the teacher is talking to them. A teacher who is unaware of this cultural background could mistake the downcast eyes as disrespect and demand that the student "look at me when I'm talking to you." In the typical middle grade classroom the teacher expects, or at least hopes, that students will ask questions. In some cultures, asking questions is a sign of weakness. In others it is a sign of disrespect. A student asking the teacher a question is as much as telling the teacher that the teacher has failed to make things clear, and that is never done. Some cultures work well in competitive situations whereas others thrive in collaborative settings. Again, having some knowledge about these tendencies will help a teacher more effectively meet the needs of English-language learners.

An effective teacher speaks slowly enough to be easily understood by all students and avoids unfamiliar slang and vocabulary. All students benefit from a teacher who couches concepts and relationships in familiar real-world settings and who knows something about the community and the students' backgrounds. An effective mathematics classroom provides students with the opportunities to explore mathematics in a meaningful way and provides opportunities for students to explain their reasoning, present their findings, and reflect on their mathematics progress. All of the foregoing factors will benefit all students, but are especially important for English-language learners.

Although the preceding factors and others in the same line of thinking will help English-language learners, these students will benefit from additional considerations. Many of these will fall into the categories we have listed here.

The Teacher

It is critical to recognize some commonalities of all English-language learners. Their mathematics English will trail their social English by about three years. The student who can speak conversational English out in the corridor may not be able to follow the English mathematics in the classroom. The vocabulary and syntax of a typical middle grades mathematics class are not the same as social English, so teachers must be sensitive to students who seem to be at par in their comprehension of conversational English but are below par in their mathematics English.

Class Design

Another factor that can be critical to English-language learners is the class itself. We discuss the benefit of using groups in Chapter 3, The Practice of Effective Instruction, but some comments about grouping practices with English-language learners is appropriate here. When composing groups to include English-language learners, there are several possible configurations to consider, each of which can benefit them. An English-language learner might be placed in a group with all English-speaking students. In such a group English-language learners will learn appropriate behavior routines and will improve their English as they work with the other members in the group. Another group composition could be to place English-language learners in a group with bilingual students. In this group English-language learners will benefit from working with students who can help them with difficult terms or directions by explaining things in their native language. At the same time the bilingual students serve as role models who have improved their English to the point that they are able to learn effectively in English. However, they can still converse in their native language and this enables English-language learners to feel pride in their own language. Finally, English-language learners may be placed in a group with other English-language learners. In this case the students can communicate easily and work together without any language hurdles to cross. Such a group validates their native language and culture as one that can achieve in a mathematics class where English is spoken.

Assessment

Assessment is an aspect of a mathematics class that might be adjusted to benefit English-language learners. Naturally it is important to discern whether any low achievement in mathematics is due to difficulties with mathematical concepts or to problems with the English language. For example, in the case of English-language learners working together in a group, their product, an oral report or a written explanation, will be in their native language. This could then be translated by the teacher or by a bilingual student in the class or in another class. The same is true of individual work by English-language learners. By examining these work products and comparing them to what these students can manage in English, a perceptive teacher can determine if English-Language Learners are having difficulty and, thus, need remediation with the mathematics concepts the class is exploring.

It is important to be aware of what is termed the *Matthew Effect*. "This occurs when teachers, for example, only call on English-Language Learners to answer only low-level knowledge questions or when teachers do not provide limited English proficient students with opportunities to develop higher-order thinking skills" (Padron & Waxman, 2002, p. 514). Teachers who do assign low-level work to English-language learners are not doing so because they deem these students less able, but because they want them to succeed and so do not challenge them. Most English-language learners can perform mindless computations adequately, and so giving English-language learners only computation problems to solve is usually a misguided attempt to allow them to succeed. Rather than performing only rote computations, English-language learners can work at higher levels when given the opportunity to work in their own language or with those who can speak their language, as noted previously.

Multicultural Aspects

Teachers who expect their students to understand and speak mathematics English can serve as role models by learning some vocabulary and phrases in the student's language. Closely aligned with knowing something about a student's language is knowing something about the student's ethnic and cultural heritage. Teachers who have some knowledge about the ethnic and cultural backgrounds of their students can converse about these at times and get to know these students better. Many cultures observe different dates on the calendar. Teachers who acknowledge these dates and observances help English-language learners feel that their culture is validated in their mathematics class by both their peers and their teacher.

Point Well Taken

"By equipping language minority students with effective strategies for critical thinking and problem solving, some of the barriers to academic success faced by these students may be removed."
—*Padron, 1992, p. 515*

Problem contexts and real-world applications can reflect the diversity in the classroom. A problem setting that simply poses a consumer problem in a bodega and not a store or that describes a recipe for pad Thai instead of spaghetti can help students begin to understand the universality of mathematics. More meaningful settings and contexts as taken from a culture's literature or history for problems and explorations will help all students in the class appreciate the importance of mathematics to all cultures. The algorithms that are so familiar to middle school students in the United States may be quite new to English-language learners. For example, our method for finding the product of multi-digit numbers may not be used by English-language learners. Instead, many students have been taught the lattice method of multiplication. Allowing English-language learners to share their customary algorithm with the class can help both the English-language learners and the rest of the class to respect the many different approaches that various cultures have developed to solve mathematics problems, while expanding students' problem-solving repertoire.

It can be beneficial to teacher and student to know something about the basic mathematics in a different culture. For example, in some Asian cultures, fractions are read from bottom to top. The fraction $\frac{2}{3}$ is read "thirds, two of them." In some Latino countries decimals are placed where we place commas in whole numbers, and commas replace the decimal point in rational numbers. Does this sound confusing? Imagine trying to master this in a foreign language and you have some sense of how difficult it can be for English-language learners to succeed in their early mathematics classes.

One last aspect of the curriculum in the mathematics class that should be reviewed for multiculturalism is the history of mathematics. Just as studying famous women in mathematics can do much to promote gender equity, so including a review of the mathematical history of other cultures can help engage English-language learners in their study of mathematics. The number systems of the Maya, Japanese, and Egyptians are interesting topics for students, as is the calendar of the Aztecs. The accomplishments of Persian mathematicians such as Al-Kashi and Al-Khowarizimi, Hindu mathematicians such as Bramagupta and Bhaskara, and many mathematicians from other backgrounds can help all students understand that contributions are made to mathematics by all cultures.

Special Needs Students

It was only a few decades ago that students with special needs were sequestered in a single room of the school or shuttered in a "special school" separated from the rest of the school population. Fortunately, such practices are in the past and students attend local schools with neighborhood children. However, students with severe disabilities may be transported to a district or institution that can assist them better than the local school district, but the intent is still to provide these students with interpersonal contacts with students their own age.

While in elementary school, decreased expectations for special needs students meant they were easily accommodated in a self-contained classroom. In middle school there is increased attention to preparing students for the rigors of secondary school and for standardized tests. Too, by middle school special needs students become acutely aware they are different because of their special needs and so are even more burdened by adolescence than the rest of their peers. As a result, these students require even more attention, understanding, and accommodations for them to succeed in their study of mathematics.

The provisions for special needs students follow the Education for All Handicapped Children Act (1975). This act mandates that special needs children be placed in the least restrictive environment to learn, which for the most part is inclusion in a regular school classroom. The act has been extended by Public Law 105-17, the Individuals with Disabilities Act. A mandate of the federal law for students with special needs is the Individualized Education Program (IEP). The IEP is drafted by parents, teachers, and special needs educators, and in some cases the students themselves. This plan determines the most beneficial and comprehensive educational program appropriate for the student. Accord-

Point Well Taken

"The most important feature of multicultural mathematics is to let students' motivation to do mathematics grow out of their natural cultural environment."

—D'Ambrosio, 1997, p. 247

REACT | REFLECT

Can you recall any instances when your teachers included multiculturalism in any of your classes, particularly your mathematics classes?

Point Well Taken

"Culturally relevant teaching is a pedagogy that empowers students intellectually, socially, emotionally, and politically by using cultural referents to import knowledge, skills, and attitudes."

—Wagner, 2000, p. 114

AUTHOR'S **Recall**

I recall growing up in a neighborhood that had a "special school." Fortunately, such practices are no longer the norm. The special school across the street from my family home is now itself a private home, and special needs students are for the most part mainstreamed into regular classrooms.

Point Well Taken

"The overriding goal is to help students learn to compensate for their learning disabilities and to deal effectively with mathematics both in academic and everyday situations."

—Bley & Thornton, 2001, p. xii

ing to an extension of that federal law, the classroom teacher will have "appropriate" input into the structure of the plan. The IEP can be reviewed and adjusted during the school year, but generally the plan is updated only at the end of the school year. The IEP details what accommodations will be made for the student, such as extra time to complete an exam, a scribe to write out notes, or use of a calculator at all times. The IEP also cites the responsibilities of the special needs student in the class, such as taking notes and completing all homework. The plan may even determine where a student should sit in the class to gain the most benefit. Many times the plan will stipulate an aide to assist the special needs student in the classroom, and so the aide must also be well aware of the particulars of the plan. A well-conceived IEP will benefit both the special needs student and the teacher and should be implemented as well as possible. With a well-conceived IEP a teacher can plan lessons that are tailored to the special needs student's strengths as well as stretching the student in areas that need improvement. The IEP will also help the teacher formulate reasonable expectations for the special needs student and clarify reasonable assessment expectations.

It is not our intent to review the full ramifications of special needs education. Such a discussion is made in a number of effective texts and programs cited at the end of this chapter. We do want to recognize the needs of these children. The goal of education is to provide opportunities for children to reach their full potential as adults, no matter what that level may be. Some critics of special education are concerned that these students consume a larger and larger portion of the education funds of a community and wonder if it is worth putting so much into the education of so few students who will never return that investment to society. We suggest that such critics need only to imagine that the special needs student was their child. Any parent of a special needs child is grateful for the needed assistance provided by school districts and concerned educators. Another apprehension that a well-meaning citizen may present is that all students should be treated the same. They imply that it is unfair to make accommodations for special needs students and not make them for all students. In this case, they argue, it is unfair not to treat all students in the same way. Actually, fairness requires giving all students the same opportunity to succeed. The vast majority of special needs students have disabilities that will never change and that will be with them for the rest of their lives. Special needs students need the accommodations cited in their IEP so that they have the same opportunities to develop their talents and abilities as do students without disabilities.

Gifted and Talented Students

Programs for gifted and talented students are on the decline, especially as funds for schools are strained by difficult economic times. There is no provision in the No Child Left Behind (NCLB) program for gifted and talented education. In fact, one unintended consequence of the NCLB has been a sharp drop in gifted and talented programs. As of 2004, 22 states did not contribute any funds to gifted and talented programs, and five others earmarked only $250,000 to support gifted and talented education. At present, only $.02 of every $100.00 in federal funds for education is dedicated to gifted and talented learning (Bilger, 2004). An example of how gifted and talented funding is drying up can be found in Illinois. In 2002 Illinois provided $19,000,000 for gifted and talented programs. In 2004 all gifted and talented funding was eliminated (Shemo, 2004). The NCLB focuses attention on underachieving groups, seeking to raise their mathematics performance, but ignores the gifted and talented students. Special education for students with special needs is generally deemed more important than gifted education, the reasoning being that gifted students can achieve quite well without any extra attention and help. Therefore, funds should be devoted to those who will not succeed without any assistance. We advocate that above-average students are as deserving of attention as any other needful students in a school population. They are the high achievers, the potential leaders of tomorrow, and so deserve full support as they hone their abilities and talents. However, the consequences of current trends to curtail or eliminate funding for gifted and talented programs means

Point Well Taken

"It is a wise man who once said that there is no greater inequality than the equal treatment of unequals."

—*Felix Frankfurter, Supreme Court Justice*

REACT │ REFLECT

Do you think that nondisabled students benefit from having special needs students included in their classroom? Explain.

that middle school mathematics teachers may have a number of gifted and talented students in their classes with no program to meet their needs.

It is critical to enhance gifted and talented students' experiences in mathematics in the middle grades, particularly if their elementary school experiences have not fully engaged their mathematical abilities. Middle school is likely the last real opportunity to invest all gifted and talented students in mathematics (Karp, 2002). To be sure, some students will maintain their interest in mathematics and continue to develop their extraordinary mathematical talents, but others will fall prey to boredom and frustration. Learning mathematics at what they perceive as a snail's pace is not something gifted and talented students take to. If their boring experiences at the elementary level are repeated in middle school, it is no wonder that we lose the interest of many gifted and talented students in mathematics by the time they reach high school. In fact, many gifted and talented students do not make it through high school. A 2002 study by Joseph Renzulli and Sunghee Park found that of the 3,520 gifted students they tracked, 5% dropped out before graduating from high school, nearly matching the 5.2% dropout rate for the general student population (Thornburg, 2004).

Recognizing the gifted and talented student in mathematics is not as simple as looking for high-achievement test scores. Some gifted and talented students do not test well for a variety of reasons, and so it is helpful to have some description by which to identify gifted and talented students in mathematics. Russian psychologist V. Krutetskii (1976) developed the following characteristics of mathematically talented students:

Resourcefulness	Flexibility
Economy of thought	Use of visual thinking
Ability to reason	Ability to generalize
Mathematical memory	Ability to abstract
Enjoyment of mathematics	Mathematical persistence

Point Well Taken

"Few aspects of the U.S. Educational system have been met with more ambivalence than the question of how to provide for gifted and talented students."

—*House, 1999, p. 1*

Naturally, not every gifted and talented student will exhibit all of these characteristics, but they can serve as indicators of a talent in mathematics, even if the student appears to be bored and disinterested.

Gifted and talented students are mentally advanced, usually creative in a number of fields, and show high motivation in areas that interest them. On the other hand, gifted students can become easily disengaged when class material is not challenging, when classroom tasks are quickly completed, and when the curriculum is a repetition of skills they have already mastered. The task of the middle school mathematics teacher with gifted students in the room is to challenge them while maintaining an appropriate class curriculum for the rest of the students. A typical response to the student who has completed the class problem set is to give that student more problems to do. That is a recipe for shutting down the gifted students' diligent work ethic. Students whose teacher gives them extra work to occupy their time will quickly learn not to work very hard. As an alternative, the problem set could include one or two challenging problems at the end of the set that are designed to engage those students who quickly complete the problems. These challenging problems may not be completed by the majority of students in the class, but those who do so can share their findings with their classmates so all benefit from their efforts. However, such problems should be available to all students. Teachers are occasionally surprised by which students select a challenge task to work on, either in class or at home.

Another possibility is to collect thought-provoking problems, interesting explorations, and counterintuitive problems for students to work on when they have completed class work that most of the other students will need more time to complete. These should not be merely fun puzzles, but rather mathematics challenges with an application or preview to meaningful mathematics. Again, the gifted students can share their findings at times with the rest of the class. Certainly it is appropriate to expect some written explanation for their findings.

Another factor to consider with gifted students in the classroom is how to place them in small groups. We discuss grouping practices more fully in Chapter 3, The Practice of Effective Instruction, but it is appropriate to discuss small groups and the gifted student here. Gifted students can be grouped with their classmates in two ways: scattered into different groups or grouped together in the same group. We recommend both combinations during the course of the school year. Gifted students need to work effectively with others, and so they should be placed in groups with average classmates. The interpersonal skills and communication skills they will develop in their group will transcend their mathematics ability and benefit them in future classes. In addition, their classmates will benefit from the gifted students' work ethic, insights into mathematical relationships, and persistence in completing an engaging task. When gifted students are placed in the same group, they benefit from working with students who can build mathematics relationships and insights as quickly as they can. The group will move rapidly to concepts and relationships they all will find challenging and engaging. Naturally this group will be expected to produce or achieve a high quality of results.

Technology

One additional aspect of equity involves new and emerging technologies. Access to computers (and possibly calculators) can be an issue in some communities. In this text we will suggest ways to employ both computers and calculators in middle grades mathematics classes. There is also the new trend of textbook publishers to provide electronic textbooks on a CD to all students. Clearly, students in today's mathematics classes will need access to a computer or calculator. Access to a computer is more an issue than is access to a calculator. Many schools have classroom sets of calculators for students to use in school and at home. Not all students have access to a computer in the home, either because their family does not have one, or because it is used by one or both parents who work from home. In either case some students must use a computer in another setting. All schools and community libraries have computers with Internet access for students to use. The question of equity arises in what access is available to students and at what personal cost in added time and effort.

Not long ago students were given assignments to do research with an encyclopedia in the library. Using the computer for Internet access in the library can be viewed as a modern counterpart to a pencil-and-paper research assignment. However, the teacher should consider how difficult it is for a student to get to the library, whether in the school or the community. If transportation is difficult or impossible, such assignments should be carefully examined for fairness to students without a home computer. Another aspect is the frequency of assignments. Asking students to spend four afternoons a week using a school or public computer is probably unfair. Each class and community will have its own set of circumstances that will enable a perceptive teacher to incorporate technology in the classroom and make electronic assignments that are within equitable reach of all students.

SUMMARY

Middle grades students are in a state of transition socially, physically, emotionally, intellectually, and academically. A middle grades teacher must acknowledge the transitory stages of middle school students and channel their energy to learning authentic mathematics. A critical part of teaching in the middle grades classroom is taking steps to ensure all students have the opportunity to develop their mathematics knowledge and skills and to enhance their appreciation of mathematics. In assuring all students have the opportunity to achieve, the matter of equity is a primary consideration. English-language learners, special needs students, gifted and talented students, and both boys and girls should have the prospect of a mathematics class where they can meet their full potential. A discerning mathematics teacher will ensure that this is so.

The following are highlights of this chapter:

- Students have different leaning styles and intelligences that will affect their classroom performance.
- English-language learners will master social English several years before they master mathematics English.
- It is important to determine if an English-language learner is having difficulty with the mathematics or with English.
- Many special needs students must have appropriate accommodations in order to have a fair opportunity to achieve in mathematics.
- There is no gender difference in mathematics ability and potential. Gender differences in achievement in mathematics are due to societal views and affective factors.
- Gifted and talented students deserve challenging mathematics programs that help them fully develop their talents and abilities.
- Knowing a student's background and culture can help teachers work effectively with their students.
- All students should see pictures and references to adults from their cultures who have contributed to the field of mathematics.

EXERCISES

From the Reading

1. Describe Howard Gardner's Eight Intelligences.

2. How can knowing a student's leaning style benefit the classroom teacher?

3. Describe Bernice McCarthy's four learning styles.

4. Why was junior high school first developed?

5. What are the predominant groups of English-language learners in your community?

6. Describe your experiences with special needs students when you were in school.

7. Why does proficiency in mathematics English lag behind social English?

On Your Own

1. Sit in on a middle grades mathematics class. Do you see any accommodations being made to ensure equity?

2. What bilingual programs exist in your state?

3. Research the laptop computer program instituted in the state of Maine. How does equity play a role in this program?

4. Examine a student's IEP in a local school. Describe how detailed the plan is.

5. Research the contributions of an African American to mathematics from one of the following Internet sites.
   www.math.upenn.edu/History/bh/text99.html
   www.princeton.edu/~mcbrown/display/profession/
       m2.html#Medical
   www.h-net.msu.edu/~women/bibs/bibl-aframermath.
       html

6. Research the lattice method of multiplication. Compared to the traditional multiplication method used in the United States, what are its advantages and disadvantages?

7. Observe a classroom and keep a tally of how many times students ask questions or give answers. (Compare girls and boys.)

Portfolio Question

How do you feel about giving only some students in a class accommodations to help them to achieve?

Scenes from a Classroom

First-year teacher Marty Euler is trying to get his students (12 boys, 10 girls) to discover the pattern involved in the Fibonacci sequence (1, 1, 2, 3, 5, 8, 13, 21, 34 . . .). He has written the first three terms of the sequence on the overhead and is asking the class to determine the next few terms.

Euler: OK class, what do you think the next term is?

Harold: That's easy, it's 5!

Euler: Yes, that's right. Now what's next?

Juan: Next comes 8.

Euler: Yes, now what's next? How about you, Juanita?

Mark: I know. It's 12.

Jake: No, it's not. It's 13.

Mark: No, it's 12.

Jake: No, it's 13. You added wrong.

Mark: Oh, yeah. That's right. It is 13.

Euler: So then, what's next?

Jon: Now you get 21.

Euler: That's great. Now let's do one more and then we can try to describe the pattern. What do you think, Sonya?

Sonya: I think . . .

Deano: It's easy, the next one is 34.

Jaime: That's right. Piece of cake.

Before reading our comments, respond to these questions.

1. What is happening to the young women in the class?
2. Is Mr. Euler purposely favoring the boys in the class?
3. What might Mr. Euler do to remedy the situation?

The problem here is that Mr. Euler has not established appropriate classroom behaviors with his students. The students are eager to respond to the task at hand, but the boys are taking over all the answering. The girls are not blurting out the answers like the boys but are waiting to be called on by Mr. Euler. But even when he calls on the girls in his class, the boys still shout out answers. Unless the situation is corrected, the boys will be the ones who actively participate in the class and the girls will play a diminished role and perhaps accept the myth that mathematics is for boys.

To remedy the situation, Mr. Euler might insist that students take a few seconds for reflection and then write their answers on a piece of note paper. Then he can ask a volunteer to give the next term. This will help keep students from simply shouting out answers. He might also observe that students who wish to give an answer have to be called on to do so; otherwise only a few in the class will be able to participate. When a student does blurt out an answer, Mr. Euler should kindly remind the student of the need to be called on and then ask a different student to give the answer.

Preparing for Praxis

A teacher is trying to help nonfluent speakers of English understand an English text. During the class, the teacher asks the students to read aloud and focuses on correcting errors in pronunciation. Which of the following is a principle of second-language development that this approach fails to take into account?

A. For most nonfluent speakers of a language, the fastest way to learn the language is to imitate the way native speakers speak it.

B. Reading skills have to be well established before a student of a language can learn a language.

C. Nonfluent speakers of a language can understand what they are reading before they can accurately pronounce all the sounds in the language.

D. Students should not attempt to read aloud before they can read grade-level texts silently with understanding.

RESOURCES

Teacher's Bookcase

Alcoze, T., et al. (1993). *Multiculturalism in mathematics, science, and technology: Readings and activities.* Reading, MA: Addison-Wesley Publishing Company.
The authors set out a variety of ready-to-use classroom activities to promote multiculturalism in mathematics, ranging from Navajo weaving designs and Inca quipu patterns to the number systems of different cultures.

Bennet, C. (2003). *Comprehensive multicultural education: Theory and practice* (5th ed.). Boston: Allyn & Bacon.
This text presents an overview of effective multicultural education and describes several program approaches to serving the needs of minority students in mathematics. The author also considers assimilation and pluralism issues for minority students.

Bley, N., & Thornton, C. (2001). *Teaching mathematics to students with learning disabilities.* Austin, TX: Pro-Ed.
This is a comprehensive text for teaching mathematics to students with learning disabilities. A very helpful feature is error analysis from the viewpoint of students with learning disabilities.

Guild, P., & Garger, S. (1998). *Marching to different drummers* (2nd ed.). Alexandria, VA: Association for Supervision and Curriculum Development.
This text presents generic overviews for teaching students with learning disabilities.

Irons, C., & Burnett, J. (1993). *Mathematics from many cultures.* Denver, CO: Mimosa Publications.
This text presents mathematics from different cultures via the history of number systems, different approaches to algorithms, and notations.

Lumpkin, B. (1997). *Algebra activities from many cultures.* Portland, ME: J. Weston Walsh Publishers.
As the title suggests, this text is full of classroom-ready activities in algebra that stress multiculturalism approaches and sources.

Malloy, C. E. (Ed.). (1998). *Challenges in the mathematics education of African-American children.* Reston, VA: NCTM.
This NCTM text specifies difficulties and remedies for teaching mathematics to African American students.

National Council of Teachers of Mathematics. (1997). *Multiculturalism and gender equity.* Reston, VA: NCTM.
The focus of this NCTM text is gender equity. The text links multicultural activities with similar activities that promote gender equity in mathematics classes.

National Council of Teachers of Mathematics. (1999). *Developing mathematically promising students.* Reston, VA: NCTM.
This NCTM text suggests ways of helping promising and gifted students to reach their full potential in mathematics, both in the classroom and outside it.

National Council of Teachers of Mathematics. (1997). *Multicultural and gender equity in the mathematics classroom: The gift of diversity.* Reston, VA: NCTM.

This NCTM yearbook is a compilation of articles dealing with gender equity, including descriptions of programs and activities that have been effective in promoting gender equity in the mathematics classroom.

Padron, Y., & Waxman, H. (2001). *Teaching and learning risks associated with limited cognitive mastery in science and mathematics for limited English proficient students.* Proceedings of the Third National Research Symposium on Limited English Proficient Student Issues: Focus on Middle and High School Issues, vol. 2. Washington, DC: U.S. Department of Education.

This text contains keynote presentations of a conference that focused on the learning difficulties of language minority students in mathematics. Many articles describe programs in place to help these students learn mathematics.

Secada, W. G. (Ed.). (1999). *Changing the faces of mathematics: Perspectives on Latinos.* Reston, VA: NCTM.

One of a series of texts from NCTM that focuses on programs and practices for teaching mathematics to a specific minority group, in this case Latinos.

Secada, W. G. (Ed.). (1999). *Changing the faces of mathematics: Perspectives on Asian Americans and Pacific Islanders.* Reston, VA: NCTM.

One of a series of texts from NCTM that focuses on programs and practices for teaching mathematics to a specific minority group, in this case Asian Americans and Pacific Islanders.

Secada, W. G. (Ed.). (2000). *Changing the faces of mathematics: Perspectives on African Americans.* Reston, VA: NCTM.

One of a series of texts from NCTM that focuses on programs and practices for teaching mathematics to a specific minority group, in this case African Americans.

Siger, J., & Stevenson, H. (1991). How Asian teachers polish each lesson to perfection. *American Educator, 15*(11), 44–49.

In this article, the authors describe how Asian teachers carefully develop lesson plans by collaborating with colleagues and observing each other as they present the lesson. Further revisions are made after each observation until all are satified with the lesson plan.

Tiedt, P., & Tiedt. I. (2002). *Multicultural teaching: A handbook of activities, information and resources.* Boston: Allyn & Bacon.

As the title implies, this book is full of useful ideas, resources, suggestions, and diverse information to help the teacher with multicultural approaches to teaching across all subjects, not just mathematics.

Tucker, B., Singleton, A., & Weaver, A. (2002). *Teaching mathematics to all children: Designing and adapting instruction to meet the needs of diverse learners.* Upper Saddle River, NJ: Prentice Hall.

The focus of this book is how to adapt routine classroom instructional practices to meet the needs of diverse learners, including those with learning disabilities.

Winebrenner, S. (2001). *Teaching gifted kids in the regular classroom: Strategies and techniques every teacher can use to meet the academic needs of the gifted and talented.* Minneapolis, MN: Free Spirit Publishing.

The author delivers specific activities and strategies for the classroom teacher who has gifted students in the classroom.

Zaslavsky, C. (1993). *Multicultural mathematics: Interdisciplinary cooperative-learning activities.* Portland, ME: J. Weston Walsh Publishers.

The author is known for her contributions to multicultural learning. In this text she combines multicultural activities with cooperative learning for engaging activities for middle school students.

For Further Reading

Gilbert, M., & Gilbert, L. (2002). Challenges in implementing strategies for gender-aware teaching. *Mathematics Teaching in the Middle School,* 7(9), 522–527.

The article details a program for establishing a safe learning environment for a gender-neutral mathematics learning experience.

Hainer, V., Fagan, B., Bratt, T., Baker, L., & Arnold, N. (1990, Summer). Integrating learning styles and skills in the ESL classroom: An approach to lesson planning. *NCBE Information Guide Series,* pp. 1–28.

The authors explore the research findings on learning styles and develop a program to adapt their findings to language-minority students.

Koonz, T. (1997). Know thyself: The evolution of an intervention gender-equity program. In *Multicultural and gender equity in the mathematics classroom: The gift of diversity—1997 NCTM yearbook.* Reston, VA: NCTM.

The author describes a program that successfully built up appreciation and ability in mathematics in middle grades females while in a regular middle school mathematics class.

Perkins, I. (2002). Mathematical notations and procedures of recent immigrant students. *Mathematics Teaching in the Middle Grades,* 7(6), 346–352.

This article demonstrates the benefits of being aware of the differences in standard notation and algorithms of different cultures when planning lessons and activities.

Siger, J., & Stevenson, H. (1991). How Asian teachers polish each lesson to perfection. *American Educator,* 15(11), 44–49.

The authors show the difference in teaching and planning in Asian and American cultures. The resulting student expectations are helpful when working with Asian students in the classroom.

Short, D. (1993). Assessing integrated language and content instruction. *TESOL Quarterly,* 27(4), 45–58.

The author suggests various effective alternate assessments that can be used to benefit language-minority students.

Tannenbaum, J. (1996). Practical ideas on alternative assessment for ESL students. www.cal.org/ericcll/digest/tannen01.html.

In this article the author describes many classroom-tested ideas for assessing language minority students, including portfolios, oral and written products, and presentations.

Links

African American Mathematicians
www.math.upenn.edu/History/bh/text99.html

Hispanic Mathematicians
www.lansing.lib.il.us/Web/HomeworkHelp/Biography.htm

Minorities and Mathematics
www.mathforum.org/social/math.minorities.html
www.mcpasd.k12.wi.us/~kms/math/math.html

Non-English Language Mathematics Resources
www.mathforum.org/teachers/nonenglish.html
Mathematics Biographies

REFERENCES

Ambrose, R., Levi, L., & Fennema, E. (1997). The Complexity of teaching for gender. In *Multicultural and gender equity in the mathematics classroom: The gift of diversity. 1997 NCTM Yearbook*. Reston, VA: NCTM.

Barnett, R., & Rivers, C. (2004, October 13). The persistence of gender myths in math. *Education Week*, p. 39.

Bilger, B. (2004, July 26). Annals of childhood: Nerd camp. *The New Yorker*, p. 71.

Bley, N., & Thornton, C. (2001). *Teaching mathematics to students with learning disabilities*. Austin, TX: Pro-Ed.

Chacon, P., & Soto-Johnson, H. (2003). Encouraging young women to stay in the mathematics pipeline: Mathematics camp for young women. *School Science and Mathematics, 103*(16), 274–284.

D'Ambrosio, U. (1997). Diversity, equity, and peace: From dream to reality. In *Multicultural and gender equity in the mathematics classroom: The gift of diversity. 1997 NCTM Yearbook*. Reston, VA: NCTM.

Fennema, E., (1982). Gender and mathematics: The crucial middle grades. In *Mathematics for the middle grades: 1982 NCTM Yearbook*. Reston, VA: NCTM.

Flores, A. (1997). "*Si Se Puede*, It Can Be Done": Quality mathematics in more than one language. In *Multicultural and gender equity in the mathematics classroom: The gift of diversity. 1997 NCTM yearbook*. Reston: NCTM.

Guild, P., & Garger, S. (1998). *Marching to different drummers* (2nd ed.). Alexandria, VA: Association for Supervision and Curriculum Development.

Hart, L., & Walker, J. (1993). The role of affect in the teaching and learning of mathematics. In D. Owens (Ed.), *Research ideas for the classroom: Middle grades*. Reston, VA: NCTM.

House, P. (1999). Promises, promises, promises. In L. Sheffield (Ed.), *Developing mathematically promising students*. Reston, VA: NCTM.

Jacobs, J., & Becker, J. (1997). Creating a gender-equitable, multicultural classroom using feminist pedagogy. In *Multicultural and gender equity in the mathematics classroom: The gift of diversity. 1997 NCTM yearbook*. Reston, VA: NCTM.

Karp, A. (2002). Beautiful minds need able beholders: Preparing middle school teachers to identify and nurture mathematical talent. *NCSM Journal of Mathematics Education Leadership, 6*(1), 42.

Kindler, A. (2002). Survey of the states' limited English proficient students available educational programs and services, 2000–2001 summary report. National Clearinghouse for English Language Acquisition and Language Instruction Educational Programs.

Koonz, T. (1997). Know thyself: The evolution of an intervention gender-equity program. In *Multicultural and gender equity in the mathematics classroom: The gift of diversity. 1997 NCTM yearbook*. Reston, VA: NCTM.

Krutetskii, V. (1976). *The psychology of mathematical abilities in schoolchildren* (J. Kilpatrick & I. Wirszup, Eds.; J. Teller, Trans.). Chicago: University of Chicago Press.

Leder, G. (1992). Mathematics and gender: Changing perspective. In D. Grouws (Ed.), *Mathematics handbook of research on mathematics teaching and learning*. Reston, VA: NCTM.

Linn, M. C., & Petersen, A. (1986). A multi-analysis of gender differences in spatial ability: Implications for mathematics and science students. In J. S. Hyde & M. C. Linn (Eds.), *The psychology of sense: Advances through meta-analysis* (pp. 67–100). Baltimore: The Johns Hopkins Press.

Lott, J. (2004, January 18). Pop quiz; math in the middle. *New York Times*, p. 43.

Morris, C. (1995). *Female and male differences in attributional explanations for leisure success and failure*. The 1995 Leisure Research Symposium. www.indiana.edu/~lrs/lrs95/cmorris95.html.

National Council of Teachers of Mathematics. (2000). *Professional standards for school mathematics*. Reston, VA: NCTM.

National Council of Teachers of Mathematics. (1989). *Curriculum and evaluation standards for school mathematics*. Reston, VA: NCTM.

Norris, F. (2004, December 7). U.S. students fare badly in international survey of math skills. *New York Times*.

Padron, Y., & Waxman, H. (2002). Teaching and learning risks associated with limited cognitive mastery in science and mathematics for limited English proficient students. Proceedings of the Third National Research Symposium on Limited English Proficient Student Issues: Focus on Middle and High School Issues, vol. 2. Washington, DC: U.S. Department of Education.

Secada, W. G. (Ed.). (2000). *Changing the faces of mathematics: Perspectives on African Americans*. Reston, VA: NCTM.

Shemo, D. (2004, March 2). Schools facing tight budgets leave gifted programs behind. *New York Times*, p. 1.

Siger, J., & Stevenson, H. (1991). How Asian teachers polish each lesson to perfection. *American Educator, 15*(11), 44.

Silmser, Lisa: An Internet hotlist on learning styles. (2003). www.kn.pacbell.com/wired/fil/pages/listlearningli2.html.

Sims, R., & Sims, C. (2002). *Middle school mathematics: A survival guide to implementing instruction*. New York: The Regency Group.

Smith, M. K. (2002). Howard Gardner and multiple intelligences. *The Encyclopedia of Informal Education*. www.infed.org/thinkers/gardner.htm.

Sowder, J. (2001). Middle grades mathematics: Linking research and practice. Proceedings of a National Convocation and Action Conference in Middle Grades Mathematics. Washington, DC: National Academy Press.

Thornburg, J. (2004, September 27). Saving the smart kids. *Time Magazine*, pp. 56–57.

Zehler, A., Fleischman, H., Hopstock, P., Stephenson, T., Pendzick, M., & Sapru, S. (2003). Descriptive study of services to LEP students and LEP students with disabilities. Volume I: Research report. Submitted to the U.S. Department of Education, OELA. Arlington, VA: Development Associates.

chapter three

The Practice of Effective Instruction

Excellence in teaching can be difficult to define but is easy to identify by anyone who sees it in action. Good teaching has many common characteristics regardless of the setting, grade level, or subject. Indeed, every teacher has his or her own talents to adapt to the classroom. In this chapter we review some characteristics of good mathematics instruction for the middle grades, including class planning, teaching styles, and class organization, as a means to build a foundation for teaching excellence. The many teaching styles appropriate for middle grades mathematics might be divided into two groups: teacher-centered and student-centered styles. As each implies by its title, these two approaches focus on either the teacher or the student as class is conducted, activities planned, and assessments made. There are variations in between these two methods of teaching. We will highlight the variations as we discuss these approaches.

Teaching Styles

Teacher-Centered Learning

Traditional mathematics classes of years past were classic examples of teacher-centered classes. All the desks are neatly lined up, all attention is directed at the teacher, and all communication is to and from the teacher and not between students. The class is a series of lectures, demonstrations, or modeling sessions. A typical class might begin with a review of the homework, with the teacher either asking for questions and providing answers at the board or assigning a single student to show a solution at the board. The new lesson consists of the teacher explaining the new concept(s), perhaps demonstrating its relationship to earlier concepts, and possibly showing some derivation of the new concepts. The lesson continues with the teacher modeling how to solve typical problems involving the same concepts. The teacher might repeat the model solution demonstration with a different problem. The teacher then directs students to begin their homework, and students work alone on the assignment. The next day will be remarkably similar to this day and to most days. The topic changes, but not much else is different.

This is an extreme example of a teacher-centered classroom, but it is one that is still all too common in middle grade classrooms across the United States. The teacher is the "sage on the stage," the expert on mathematics, and the students are empty vessels that the teacher will fill with mathematical knowledge. A slight variation of teacher-centered instruction gives students more of a role in the class activities. Students still take lecture notes from the teacher and model their problem solutions after the solution strategy has been shown. However, students can work in pairs and groups to display and/or discover mathematics relationships. For example, if students were trying to develop a formula for the area of a trapezoid, each small group would perform identical explorations, in this case dissecting a trapezoid to produce a related parallelogram (see Chapter 8, Geometry: Moving Beyond Formulas). All students have the same experience, and all should reach the same conclusion. Even though students are working in small groups, the teacher directs all the steps for the exploration and the conclusions. The teacher might ask questions along the way, as students cut and paste the various dissected parts of the trapezoid to form a parallelogram. Students are then directed, step by step, to each develop the formula for the area of a trapezoid from the area formula for a parallelogram. In their small groups students can work together on the activity, discuss their findings, and help one another. This may appear to be a student-centered approach, but it is not. All the students are working at the same pace, and they all reach the same deductions after a scripted activity because they have been carefully led to the desired goal, a conclusion, strategy, or algorithm. Thus, although this is more interactive than the traditional teacher-centered model, it is still teacher-centered. Every student has the same experiences, the same expectations, the same discoveries, and the same conclusions. Still, the students are actively participating in their learning.

Student-Centered Learning

A truly student-centered classroom consists of teacher and students working together to achieve new learning. The foundation of a student-centered classroom is the belief that all students must build their own personal understanding of mathematics. The educational theory that supports this type of classroom is constructivism. The term *constructivism* is fairly new, emerging only within the last 30 years or so, but the concept of students building their understanding is centuries old. Plato recorded how Socrates taught a slave, Meno, to understand the relationship between the areas and perimeters of similar figures by leading the slave to construct his own understanding of the concepts involved. Centuries later Galileo wrote, "You cannot teach a man anything, you can only help him find it within himself." More recently Jean Piaget described the need of students to gain equilibrium in their understanding. This means that when there is a dissonance between what a student understands and a new fact or experience, the student will work to bring the new fact into harmony or equilibrium with what is already known. By doing this, students are constructing their own understanding, an understanding that harmonizes this new fact with what was previously understood. Russian psychologist Lev Vygotsky also viewed the learner from the vantage of learning in a personal way. He used the Zone of Proximal Development (ZPD) to refer to the distance or gap between the actual mathematical development of an individual student and the level of potential development possible when under adult guidance or in collaboration with more capable peers.

We maintain that students will not effectively construct personal understanding by listening to a lecture or trying to mimic solution strategies they watch their teacher model. Students need to perform experiments and explorations. They need to work with other students and ask questions, learn how their peers view a problem solution, and they need to hear how others in the class comprehend a particular concept. Some educators understand constructivism to mean that each student makes his or her own discoveries independently and creates a unique understanding of a concept. This is an extreme view of constructivism and is considered *radical constructivism* by some. In general, from the constructivist point of view, students need to work together to support one another as they discuss how to approach a problem, understand an algorithm, or comprehend a concept. Their personal understanding may be developed independently by listening to a student in their group or from hearing a student report group findings to the class. Their personal understanding may, in fact, mirror other students' understandings, but that does not make their understanding any less personal or any less valid to them because they constructed it in a way that made sense to them.

For example, consider the same activity that we discussed in the preceding section on teacher-centered teaching from a constructivist slant. The teacher passes out several congruent trapezoids to each group and challenges them to develop a method for determining the area of the trapezoid. The teacher may suggest that any single trapezoid might be cut into pieces to resemble a more familiar quadrilateral or simply challenge students to develop an area formula for a trapezoid. Students then work to develop a method for finding the area of their trapezoid. After each group has had sufficient time to explore different ways of cutting up their trapezoid and forming quadrilaterals, each group reports their results to the class via the group's reporter. After each report, students discuss the validity and value of their findings. After all the groups have reported to the class, the teacher asks the students to write their conclusion about how to determine the area of a trapezoid in their notebooks or in their journals, and then these are submitted to the teacher. The teacher may then ask one or two students to relate their conclusions to the entire class, and then the class briefly discusses the students' conclusions. This last report or discussion serves as a summary of the activity and provides an additional opportunity for students to clarify the concepts and relationships revealed during class. It is important to note here that effective group practices evolve over time, and the class described here reflects previous efforts and activities that developed the group processes portrayed. Simply putting students' desks together will not result in students working cooperatively. We describe groups and group process later in this chapter (see pages 48–53).

In a traditional lecture-demonstration classroom, there are always some students who will do well in mathematics. These students construct their understandings just as much as do students who work in small groups and experiment with concepts and manipulatives. In this case, these students are able to construct their own understanding via hearing a lecture, whereas most students in such a setting cannot. Most students need experience with manipulatives and the opportunity to explain their own thinking and hear how others perceive a concept or solve a problem in order to understand a relationship. In the words of one student, "Once I can get it into my gut, then I can bring it to my brain." Teachers need to provide experiences that enable all students to get the mathematics at hand in their gut. They will then be able to construct the personal understandings that can bring it to their brain.

Another critical part of the middle school classroom is what is taught. We next discuss the resources for teachers to use for the mathematics classroom.

REACT | REFLECT

Were your mathematics classes more teacher-centered or student-centered? Explain.

Determining the Mathematics Content for Your Class

An important decision for any middle grades mathematics teacher is what textbook to use. In about half the states across the country the local school district can select any textbook series on the market. In the remaining states, districts select textbook series from a list of qualifying texts that is drawn up by each state department of education. In either case, several commercial publishers have produced middle school mathematics series, including Prentice Hall, Glencoe, McDougal Littell, and McGraw-Hill. Although it is not our intent to recommend any one middle school program over another, it is appropriate here to describe the four series for middle school mathematics that were funded by the National Science Foundation.

Standards-Based Programs

These *Standards*-based programs were produced in response to a call for improved mathematics education in America's schools. Accordingly, the National Science Foundation funded a number of mathematics program developments at the elementary, middle, and secondary school levels. We will briefly discuss the four middle school programs. Each of these programs is a *Standards*-based program. That is, each one addresses the recommendations of the National Council of Teachers of Mathematics in *Curriculum and Evaluation Standards for School Mathematics* (1989), and they align with the NCTM *Standards and Principles for School Mathematics* (2000) in both content and approach to teaching mathematics. Thus, the NCTM *Standards* are the starting point for each program, and their respective goals focus on helping middle grades students meet the benchmarks that NCTM established.

Standards-based programs support the following premises:

- Reach *all* students
- Focus on challenging and motivating investigations
- Explore significant mathematics topics that extend to high school
- Engage students as active learners
- Require teachers and students to assume different roles, such as coach and coinvestigator
- Use alternate forms of evaluation
- Provide strong real-world contexts for problems and explorations

These programs are designed for either individual or group work, but they are especially beneficial when used with group settings. All of the programs have been field-tested and many teachers have found them to be effective in helping students learn meaningful mathematics. Although these four textbook series were originally funded by the National Science Foundation, each of them is now published by a commercial publishing house and each one is used in school districts across the United States.

Connected Mathematics

Connected Mathematics Program was developed at Michigan State University and stresses connections among the core ideas of mathematics. The 6–8 program materials are organized around problem-centered themes that are broken down into three phases: launch, explore, and summarize. Each grade level consists of eight units. The developers believe this instructional model encourages higher-level thinking and problem solving. The program covers the following strands: number and operation, geometry, measurement, algebra, and statistics and probability. The goal is to foster and examine connections among various mathematics concepts and between mathematics and other disciplines.

Mathematics in Context

The Mathematics in Context program was developed at the Wisconsin Center for Education and Research at the University of Wisconsin. The focus of the 40-unit program is mathematics in real-world settings. In this program real-world problems drive the mathematics curriculum in contrast to the typical textbook presentation, in which the mathematics is presented first, and then real-world settings are developed from the mathematics. The grade 5–8 program covers the following strands: number and operation, geometry, algebra, and data analysis.

MathScape: Seeing and Thinking Mathematically for Grades 6–8

MathScape was developed by the Educational Development Center in Newton, Massachusetts. The program presents mathematics as a "historical human endeavor" with a focus on learning mathematics in the "context of planning, predicting, designing, creating, explaining, comparing, and deciding." Topics are found throughout the world and in historical settings. The 21-unit program covers the following strands: number, geometry, algebra, and data analysis. Each unit of 12 lessons takes five to six weeks to complete.

MATH Thematics

The MATH Thematics program was developed by the Department of Mathematical Science at the University of Montana. Each of the modules of the program revolves around a theme that bases the mathematics of each module in a real-world context. There are eight modules per grade level, each requiring approximately four weeks to complete. Subsequent problems and explorations in each module are related to the original context. The strands of the grade 6–8 program are number concepts, measurement, probability, statistics, geometry, algebra, and discrete mathematics.

The Show-Me Center in Missouri has developed an Internet site that describes each of these programs in more detail and includes lesson plans from each of them. We have used one of these lesson plans later in this chapter. For more information about these *Standards*-based middle grades mathematics programs see http://showmecenter.missouri.edu.

An important consideration for curriculum planning is the content of district and state mathematics frameworks or curriculum standards. These frameworks generally delineate the topics and specific content for mathematics at various grade levels. These frameworks form the content of high-stakes tests that all states require from their students. It is vital that teachers are familiar with the mathematics frameworks for their grade and supplement any classroom text when necessary to ensure that all students are familiar with the concepts and relationships deemed important by state and district educators.

Planning for High-Stakes Tests

We have already discussed some of the requirements of the No Child Left Behind legislation. One aspect of the legislation is that, in addition to any existing state-level testing programs, all students in grades 3 to 8 will be tested in mathematics. These state and national test results can be used to evaluate schools, programs, and teachers. As a consequence of present state testing programs, many middle grades mathematics teachers already find themselves teaching to the test rather than teaching mathematics as they normally would. Although we would decry anyone teaching to the test, it is understandable that a teacher would want his or her students to do well on any high-stakes tests. Students feel the pressure of these high-stakes tests as much as teachers do. If the coming tests are constantly referenced, students can fall victim to test anxiety and simply fear the test in and of itself. We recommend approaching high-stakes tests in a more supportive manner, as another component of the mathematics curriculum, rather than teaching to the test. We discuss high-stakes tests in more detail in Chapter 4, Assessment: Balanced and Varied.

In addition to learning relationships, concepts, and mathematical processes, students should also develop a sense of mathematical proficiency, a holistic way to think about mathematics.

Mathematical Proficiency

Jeremy Kilpatrick, Jane Swafford, and Bradford Findell, editors of *Adding It Up—Helping Children Learn Mathematics*, worked with a team of leading mathematics educators to investigate the latest research on the teaching and learning of mathematics. As a result of this intensive study, the meaning of *mathematical proficiency* was developed to define the essential components critical to learning mathematics. These five components or strands are as follows:

1. *Conceptual understanding.* Comprehension of mathematical concepts, operations, and relations
2. *Procedural fluency.* Skill in carrying out procedures flexibly, accurately, efficiently, and appropriately
3. *Strategic competence.* Ability to formulate, represent, and solve mathematical problems
4. *Adaptive reasoning.* Capacity for logical thought, reflection, explanation, and justification
5. *Productive disposition.* Habitual inclination to see mathematics as sensible, useful, and worthwhile, coupled with a belief in diligence and one's own efficacy. (Kilpatrick et al., 2001, p. 116)

These strands intertwine and define the ultimate goals in teaching and learning mathematics. Before reading further, work on the problem in "Try This." It is designed to demonstrate and solicit the strands of mathematical proficiency.

TRY THIS

Find the sum of three consecutive integers. Look for a pattern. Is there another way to find the sum that does not involve addition? As you work through this task, note your strategies. What strands of mathematical proficiency did you demonstrate?

The sum of three consecutive integers can be approached in a variety of ways. Students may struggle to get beyond finding the sum without adding. Hints such as "What is the relationship between the consecutive numbers?" might stimulate their thinking. A series of sums such as the following may also help to guide students' thinking:

$$14 + 15 + 16 = \text{_____} \; (45)$$
$$29 + 30 + 31 = \text{_____} \; (90)$$
$$99 + 100 + 101 = \text{_____} \; (300)$$

As the pattern for the sum emerges, three times the middle number, students can investigate whether or not the pattern holds true for any three consecutive integers. They can also explore larger series of consecutive values. What happens if you have an odd number of integers? What happens if there is an even number of integers? Eventually, students should offer a convincing argument or proof as to why this pattern holds true. When asked how they might prove this pattern, students typically respond that they can continue to try different values. Such an endless endeavor does not prove the pattern, however. This leads to the use of a variable as a generalized statement for any value. (Refer to Chapter 7, Algebra: The Gateway, for more information on using variables.) By using a variable that represents any value, students begin to see the benefit in such a tool.

REACT | **REFLECT**

Did you attempt to solve the "Try This" problem or did you read ahead for the answer? How does your response characterize your interest in mathematics?

TRY THIS

Develop a proof verifying that the sum of five consecutive integers is five times the middle number.

Finding the sum of consecutive integers represents a task that leads to other insights and knowledge. Building generative knowledge is a key component in conceptual understanding, the first strand in mathematical proficiency (Kilpatrick et al., 2001, p. 119). Students demonstrate the second and third strands, procedural fluency and strategic competence, as they look for ways to represent the sum without adding. Strand four, adaptive reasoning, becomes apparent as students work through the task using logic and seeing the connection between the middle value and the sum of the series. The fifth strand, productive disposition, is also exhibited as students work on this task. Do the students try several approaches? Do they stick with the problem or do they try one ineffective avenue and then stop working? Finding the pattern and proving why the pattern holds true is not a procedure to be memorized. The value of the task comes from the experience of discovery and the extension to verify the pattern.

In *Adding It Up*, Kilpatrick and colleagues extend the definition of mathematical proficiency to the teaching of mathematics. According to Kilpatrick (2001, p. 380), proficiency requires

- *Conceptual understanding* of the core knowledge required in the practice of teaching
- *Fluency* in carrying out basic instructional routines
- *Strategic competence* in planning effective instruction and solving problems that arise in instruction
- *Adaptive reasoning* in justifying and explaining one's instructional practices and in reflecting on those practices to improve them
- *Productive disposition* toward mathematics, teaching, learning, and the improvement of practice

Working to help students develop mathematical proficiency as well as building that capacity in our own professional practice is a journey. Such capacities develop over time and through rich and meaningful tasks.

Daily Planning

An important aspect of classroom teaching is planning the content of a class lesson, which in turn focuses on lesson plans. Curriculum planning for a middle grades mathematics class will likely revolve around daily and weekly lesson plans. The middle grades curriculum for a whole year will usually be defined by the textbook series, high-stakes tests such as those mandated by No Child Left Behind, and state and local mathematics frameworks. We suggest that lesson plans be based on units, modules, or chapters in whatever text or series the district has determined for the particular grade level. For each unit, the teacher should determine the important mathematical concepts, the big ideas. After identifying the big ideas, teachers can then formulate what might be termed *essential questions*. Essential questions serve as guideposts for the big idea(s) in the unit and focus student attention on what students will be able to do (know) at the end of the unit. The essential questions help students reflect on the important mathematics in the unit. In a chapter on rational numbers, essential questions might include the following:

- What is the connection among fractions, decimals, and percents?
- How are all three representations useful?
- What are the advantages and disadvantages to each representation?

In some series, a single problem situation functions as the means to examine the essential question(s). The problem situation places the essential question in a real-world context. For example, in Growing, Growing, Growing: Exponential Relationships, a unit in the grade 8 Connected Mathematics series, the introductory problem asks students to cut a stack of cards in half, form a new stack with the resulting half-cards, and cut in half again. This is repeated several more times, and students are encouraged to look for a pattern to the number of cards produced after each cut. The pattern is exponential and serves to set the stage for studying exponential functions. The initial problem is then recalled throughout the unit as students explore the many relationships involving exponential functions. In particular, Connected Mathematics has reflective questions at the end of each chapter. These questions might be used at the beginning of the chapter to help students focus on the essential mathematics in the chapter.

Usually the textbook series used in a particular grade level will supply chapter goals and objectives to help a teacher plan out the entire chapter. Typical of what various textbook publishers provide for teachers is seen in the Lesson Planner, a teacher resource with the Connected Mathematics Program. In Connected Mathematics the Lesson Planner (Lappan, Fey, Fitzgerald, Friel, & Phillips, 2003) lists the following for each unit:

- Materials
- Mathematics in the Unit
- Essential Vocabulary
- Big Ideas
- Prior Work
- Future Work

Each lesson (investigation) in the unit lists mathematical and problem-solving goals, worksheets, resources for teachers, and problems in the investigation. Support materials from Prentice Hall mathematics texts include the following information for each lesson (Bass et al., 2004):

- Objectives
- New Vocabulary
- Introduce and Facilitate
- Needed Skills/Knowledge

As these examples show, information for single-lesson or class-period plans is not minutely delineated but focuses more on the topic and helpful teaching hints. The material in these ancillary resources might need to be fully fleshed out in order to plan for an effective class. In addition, there will be times when topics that are not part of the textbook curriculum will be the focus of a class, necessitating lesson plans that are developed by the classroom teacher. Thus, every teacher should be able to compose effective lesson plans. Again, middle school mathematics series provide information for each unit or chapter, so the long-range planning needed beyond what the ancillary materials of the text provide for an entire unit is minimal. It is the daily lesson plan that needs attention by a middle grades mathematics teacher.

Lesson Plans

Lesson plans can be very brief or quite detailed. The details of a lesson plan depend on the topic, the teacher's experience and teacher's style, and the type of class the lesson plans describe. Regardless of the specifics of the class, it is absolutely critical that each lesson is carefully crafted to ensure that the material is accessible to students. The skill of writing an effective lesson plan involves matching the needs of students with the curriculum content. Lesson plans may differ by discipline, grade level, and school district, to say nothing of how each individual teacher will write out a lesson plan. Nevertheless, there are some common elements that will benefit any lesson plan and we present them here.

Objective

This is the goal of any specific class, project, or unit. It is the reason for conducting the class. The objective may be as simple as reviewing for a test or as complex as introducing proportional reasoning. Many times the objective will include some indication of assessment level after the lesson or unit is completed as, for example, "students will score 80% or better on the chapter test." The objective really sets the stage for the entire lesson. Sharing the objective with students can specify the value of the lesson to the students. The objective might also note whether the class will be based on student exploration, guided discovery, or will be teacher-directed. This decision will affect many of the remaining details of the lesson plan.

Materials

Here is where the teacher lists all the materials that will be used in the lesson, from scrap paper and rulers to calculators and geoboards. By planning ahead for the lesson materials, the teacher can be sure there are sufficient manipulatives or supplies for each student or group and that the manipulatives are on hand in the classroom, not in a storage office, a closet, or another classroom. Listing all the needed manipulatives and supplies also reminds the teacher to make any special arrangements for the manipulatives in the lesson plans. In the case of a new manipulative, for example, the teacher would need to allow some free exploration time in the lesson and may need to have a student demonstrate proper use of the manipulative. Materials might also include prepared data sheets, worksheets, and activity sheets. Many times these are included in the unit plans from a textbook or with lesson plans in ancillary sources, including the Internet.

Prior Knowledge

Mathematics is a sequential discipline. By and large, mathematics knowledge builds on prior experiences and knowledge. (However, middle school students do not always learn and understand mathematics concepts and relationships in sequence. See Chapter 6,

Making Sense of Number and Operations, for more on this point). Thus, for any lesson topic, it is important to cite what previous knowledge is needed to fully benefit from the lesson. A lesson plan on circle areas would likely list circle circumference, square units, area measure, and π as previous knowledge, in addition to exponents, that would help students benefit from the lesson. If some part of the prior knowledge is missing from the students' backgrounds, then this might require the teacher to build in a review of this prior knowledge as part of the lesson in order to bring the students' knowledge up to the proper level.

New Terms and Knowledge

The objective of the lesson will specify the mathematics the lesson will introduce. It is important to identify new terms and knowledge in the lesson and then distinguish the terms students should retain as compared to those that are not part of the objectives. For example, in a lesson on irrational numbers, the teacher might introduce imaginary numbers as a means of further defining irrational numbers. Although the comparison to imaginary numbers may help students understand rational numbers, the teacher might not expect students to make imaginary numbers part of their vocabulary and mathematics knowledge. However, by introducing the term *imaginary numbers* and making it part of the discussion, the teacher has laid the groundwork for studying them at a later time.

Time

This lists the length of time the lesson will cover, ranging from part of a class period to several days. This can be the most difficult part of planning for a new teacher. The best-planned lessons can run beyond a class period, whereas others fall far short of the full period. In the case of a plan that takes up less time than expected, there are several ways to make good use of the remaining time. One way to use the remaining time (but not very beneficial) is to tell students to start their homework. Usually the intent here is to jump-start students who may be having some difficulty with the assignment. One unconstructive consequence of always providing homework time at the end of a class is that some students tend to "tune out" as instructions are given. They reason that there is no need to listen because, if they have any questions, they can always ask them during homework time. When the material has been presented by following an effective lesson plan, students will have few questions about the assignment. Rather, the unexpected free time can be spent on a challenging problem, a brainteaser, or an extension of the lesson. New teachers can begin to build a library of engaging problems and interesting applications for the material they teach for such times. Test items from high-stakes tests that deal with the same topics that students are studying might also be given as challenge problems to solve.

What if the lesson takes more time than planned? In this case it is important to keep an eye on the clock and set some time benchmarks. When a teacher can see well before the end of the class period that the activity will not conclude before the period ends, then there is ample time to consider alternative plans for carrying the activity over to the next class. For example, a teacher might plan to have students conclude their explorations with manipulatives with 20 minutes left in class, and use the remainder to develop conclusions and ask students to report their findings to the class. If students are still working with manipulatives and there is only 10 minutes left in the class, an alternative lesson plan is needed. It might be beneficial to plan for students to reflect on their findings at home and report their conclusions at the start of the next class. In the same fashion, a time benchmark can help a teacher plan additional activities for a lesson that is running short.

Class Organization

The class may be organized in a number of different ways ranging from individual students to pairs or small groups, as we will discuss further in this chapter. The mathematics and lesson objectives will likely determine the class organization.

Procedure

This is a brief description of what will happen during class. An interesting introductory problem, exploration, or challenge to engage students is usually cited here. This might be a time to consider a problem from a high-stakes test. Any activities are referenced here, as are any pages or problems in the textbook. The specificity here will generally decrease as a teacher gains experience. A brief reference to using folding paper to demonstrate how the area of a triangle compares to the area of a rectangle with the same height and base length will be sufficient for an experienced teacher. A newer teacher may detail the expected procedure students might employ to show the relationship of the two areas.

Evaluation

This section details how to tell if the lesson was successful. There is a variety of methods to assess the success of a lesson (see Chapter 4, Assessment: Balanced and Varied). Reports from each of the small groups can serve as an assessment, as might a spot quiz, homework, or whole-class discussion. The specific means of evaluation is not at issue. What is important is that there should be some means by which to determine how successful the lesson plan was. In many cases an "exit ticket" at the end of class will suffice. Such an exit ticket evaluation might be a problem all students solve before class ends that summarizes the lesson. At other times, students might respond to a journal prompt dealing with the class and its mathematics content, as suggested earlier in this chapter. These and similar exit tickets can provide an effective evaluation of that day's lesson. An ineffective lesson needs to be remedied the next day or students will not have the needed foundation for subsequent concepts and relationships.

Pacing

It is important to make full use of class time for mathematics, whether the length of each day is the same or not. Recently more and more time is being devoted to mathematics instruction, so it is critical that lesson plans make full use of this time. Longer blocks of time allow for more exploration activities and postactivity debriefing to be sure every student understands the mathematics underlying the activity. As suggested earlier, every mathematics class should begin with a warm-up problem or challenge. An engaging warm-up immediately sets students to thinking about mathematics. The warm-up may be a problem from an earlier chapter, a problem from a high-stakes test, or a challenge problem that establishes the activities for the rest of the class. In addition, every lesson plan should have an engaging problem, a wrap-up problem or question to fill in any time left at the end of the class to make effective use of all the class time.

It can be helpful to examine effective lesson plans, and so we present several at this point. Notice that the lesson plans differ in format, class organization, and emphasis, yet they all contain the same basic components.

Sample Lesson Plans

The first lesson plan is from the Educator's Reference Desk, part of the ERIC database. More lesson plans from the Educator's Reference Desk are at www.eduref.org/cgi-bin/printlessons.cgi/Virtual/Lessons/Mathematics.html.

Find a Pattern with *One Grain of Rice*

Created by: Patricia Engel

School/University/Affiliation: Middle River Middle School,
Baltimore, Maryland

Description: Students use the problem-solving strategy of "find a pattern" to predict the number of grains of rice Rani (from *One Grain of Rice*) will receive after thirty days. Students use a table to assist with making predictions.

Goals:
1. Apply guess and check, find a pattern, draw a diagram, and other problem-solving strategies to develop inductive and deductive thinking.
2. Students will algebraically represent, model, analyze, and solve mathematical and real-world problems involving patterns and functional relationships.

Objectives:
1. Students will apply find a pattern and make-a-table strategies in order to solve problems.
2. Students will be able to record data from an Indian folktale.
3. Students will explore, describe, and extend patterns.
4. Students will be able to make a generalization about a pattern.

Teacher Materials:
- *One Grain of Rice: A Mathematical Folktale* (Demi, Hitz. 1997, Scholastic, Inc.)
- overhead projector with markers
- transparency of table worksheet
- rice—a small handful

Student Materials:
- pencils
- calculators—one for each student or pair of students
- tables/worksheet
- New vocabulary: patterns, table
- Story vocabulary: *Rani*—girl's name in the story, *raja*—Indian king, *famine*—extreme lack of something

Procedure:
Explain the objectives of the lesson and then begin reading *One Grain of Rice*. [Brief summary of story: During a famine, Rani outsmarts the raja by asking him to give her one grain of rice to be doubled every day for 30 days.]

Discuss book vocabulary as it comes up in the reading. Show one grain of rice on the overhead, then two, four, and eight. Stop at the ninth day in the story. Revisit the objective by asking, "What are we doing today and how?" [I have a Problem-Solving Guidelines poster in my room.] Ask students, "What is a pattern?" (A list that occurs in some predictable way.) Pass out the table worksheets and have students fill in the table, stopping at the ninth day. Ask students to share any patterns that they notice. Most likely, students will say that the pattern doubles every day. Students will predict how many grains of rice Rani will receive in all after the thirtieth day. In pairs, students will complete the rest of the table. (Calculators will be needed, as numbers get into the millions.) As students are working, ask if anyone can find an easier way to calculate the next day's rice count without adding. (Usually someone notices that you can multiply by 2.) Tell students to complete the table using this new pattern. (Students should fill in the table faster now.) After the tables are completed, ask for students' predictions for the number of grains of rice on the thirtieth day. Finish reading the story to see if students' calculations were correct. As you read the story, students should check their answers with the story to make sure that they calculated correctly.

Assessment: Independently, students will answer the following questions:
1. Find out how many grains of rice Rani received in all. Explain how you got your answer. (1,073,741,823—more than 1 billion grains of rice)
2. What do you notice about the grains of rice received each day? Describe the pattern you see in the table (doubles or "times 2").

In this lesson plan it is important to note that students are expected to work productively in pairs. One additional point to consider about this lesson plan is that it is written for other teachers to use in their classroom. As a result, it has much more detail than would be necessary if the author were to use it for her own classroom—for example, the comments in parentheses.

This lesson plan has been used successfully at the middle school level by one of the authors.

Consecutive Sums

Objectives:
  Process: Experience work in cooperative groups
                    Play specific role within the group
  Mathematics: Find, analyze, and extend patterns
                    Make conjectures
                    Substantiate those conjectures

Materials: 1 activity sheet for each group
                    Recording sheets for each student
                    Transparency or newsprint for group summaries

Lesson:
1. As they enter the room, students write the number of the problems that they would like the class to discuss on homework board.
2. Warm-up problem reviewing yesterday's lesson   (5 minutes)

   Place parentheses to make this statement true:
   $8 + 4/2 + 3 = 2$

3. Review agenda for the day
   Warm-up
   Group work: Consecutive Sums
   Homework demos by students
   Wrap up

4. Consecutive sums   (40 minutes)
   Students sit in groups of four. Remind them to rotate their jobs clockwise.

   Highlight the math abilities that this task requires:
       Looking for patterns
       Extending patterns
       Finding efficient use of patterns
       Analyzing patterns
       Making conjectures
       Drawing conclusions
       Summarizing group's work

   Remind students that no one has *all* of these abilities yet, but each and every one of us has some of these abilities. That is why group work is so important. Remind students of the community guidelines and the importance of playing the assigned role for the group.

   Resource Manager gets task card as students in groups consider what abilities on the list that they have to share with the group.

Students work in their groups to determine the patterns of the sums and why powers of 2 cannot be stated as the sum of consecutive numbers. (See task card, Blackline Master 3.1)

Teacher observes students working and documents those who are clearly playing their appropriate role. Record positive actions by each group on transparency while students work. Give 10-minute warning to Resource Managers.

5. Presentations by students summarizing group's work.   (10–15 minutes)
   Teacher and students ask any questions for groups to clarify.
   Teacher summarizes those collaborative processes in which groups excelled.

6. Students volunteer to write homework problems on the board and explain their thinking. These problems were specified by students as they entered the class.

7. Wrap-up to lesson:
   Students write an exit card and give it to the teacher as they leave the classroom:
   Describe two or more patterns that your group used in today's activities.
   What mathematical abilities did you contribute to your group today?

The final lesson plan is from one of the *Standards*-based programs, Mathematics in Context. This lesson plan and many others are available at http://showmecenter.missouri.edu.

Student Page

Source: http://showme center.missouri.edu/ showme/Lesson/ mainMiC.shtml. Used by permission of Encyclopedia Britannica, Inc. Copyright © 2003 Encyclopedia Britannica, Inc. All rights reserved.

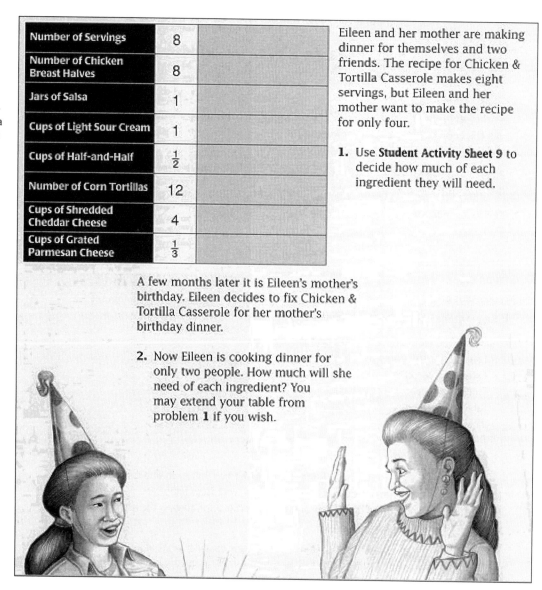

Number of Servings	8	
Number of Chicken Breast Halves	8	
Jars of Salsa	1	
Cups of Light Sour Cream	1	
Cups of Half-and-Half	$\frac{1}{2}$	
Number of Corn Tortillas	12	
Cups of Shredded Cheddar Cheese	4	
Cups of Grated Parmesan Cheese	$\frac{1}{3}$	

Eileen and her mother are making dinner for themselves and two friends. The recipe for Chicken & Tortilla Casserole makes eight servings, but Eileen and her mother want to make the recipe for only four.

1. Use **Student Activity Sheet 9** to decide how much of each ingredient they will need.

A few months later it is Eileen's mother's birthday. Eileen decides to fix Chicken & Tortilla Casserole for her mother's birthday dinner.

2. Now Eileen is cooking dinner for only two people. How much will she need of each ingredient? You may extend your table from problem **1** if you wish.

Solutions and Samples
of student work

Hints and Comments

1.

Number of Servings	8	4
Number of Chicken Breast Halves	8	4
Jars of Salsa	1	$\frac{1}{2}$
Cups of Light Sour Cream	1	$\frac{1}{2}$
Cups of Half-and-Half	$\frac{1}{2}$	$\frac{1}{4}$
Number of Corn Tortillas	12	6
Cups of Shredded Cheddar Cheese	4	2
Cups of Grated Parmesan Cheese	$\frac{1}{3}$	$\frac{1}{6}$

2.

Number of Servings	8	4	2
Number of Chicken Breast Halves	8	4	2
Jars of Salsa	1	$\frac{1}{2}$	$\frac{1}{4}$
Cups of Light Sour Cream	1	$\frac{1}{2}$	$\frac{1}{4}$
Cups of Half-and-Half	$\frac{1}{2}$	$\frac{1}{4}$	$\frac{1}{8}$
Number of Corn Tortillas	12	6	3
Cups of Shredded Cheddar Cheese	4	2	1
Cups of Grated Parmesan Cheese	$\frac{1}{3}$	$\frac{1}{6}$	$\frac{1}{12}$

Materials Student Activity Sheet 9 (one per student), fraction strips, optional (one set per student)

Overview Students complete a ratio table to determine the quantity of each ingredient needed for a recipe when the number of servings decreases.

About the Mathematics In this situation, students begin to informally divide fractions by two or to multiply fractions by one-half.

It is not important that students use formal notation such as $\frac{1}{2} \times \frac{1}{2} = \frac{1}{4}$. The primary goal is for students to find relationships between fractions, such as half of $\frac{1}{2}$ is $\frac{1}{4}$, half of $\frac{1}{3}$ is $\frac{1}{6}$, and half of $\frac{1}{4}$ is $\frac{1}{8}$. Students may use their fraction strips for visual support.

Planning Students can work individually or in pairs on problems **1** and **2**. Discuss these problems with the class.

Comments about the Problems

1. Some students may need to use their fraction strips. Have students explain what they did with the given numbers, so that the relationships between simple fractions can be emphasized. For example, students may explain that "half of $\frac{1}{2}$ cup is $\frac{1}{4}$ cup."

2. **Homework** This problem may be assigned as homework.

Extension You may ask students to write the relationships they discover between fractions. The same relationship may be expressed in different ways. For example: half of $\frac{1}{4}$ cup is $\frac{1}{8}$ cup;

Teacher Page

Source: http://showmecenter.missouri.edu/showme/Lesson/mainMiC.shtml. Used by permission of Encyclopedia Britannica, Inc. Copyright © 2003 Encyclopedia Britannica, Inc. All rights reserved.

Notice that each plan contains the essential elements of a lesson plan, but they are not identical. So too, will lesson plans differ from text to text, district to district, and teacher to teacher. The key point is that the lesson plans are an integral part of any mathematics class. Lesson plans help a teacher to effectively plan so that each class period provides the greatest benefit to students. Thus, teachers may find commercially prepared lesson plans for use with their classroom text are inadequate or inappropriate for their class. We encourage teachers to improve those plans so they fit the needs of their students. A classroom teacher knows best how his or her students learn, what activities they need, and what assessments will be effective. If your plans contain the major elements discussed earlier, you will be well on the way to producing an effective class lesson.

There are literally thousands of mathematics lesson plans available on the Internet. A search for "math lesson plans" on Google turns up nearly half a million sites! One way to cut down on so many choices is to focus attention on a grade level and on a specific topic. There are two general Internet sites for lesson plans in mathematics that allow a teacher to narrow a lesson plan search. These two sites will link to many other sites by grade level and/or topic.

www.thegateway.org
www.LessonPlanz.com

REACT | REFLECT

What type of lesson plan do you plan to use? Why?

REACT | REFLECT

What aspect of daily lesson plans seems to be the most challenging for you? How can you meet that challenge?

Point Well Taken

"There is clear and compelling evidence that small-group instructional models can facilitate student achievement (in mathematics)."

—*Good et al., 1992, p. 167*

Point Well Taken

"They [middle school students] can try out ideas in the relative privacy of small groups before opening themselves up to the entire class."

—*NCTM, 2000, p. 272*

Point Well Taken

"Because African American students (and also Native American students) excel in a cooperative learning environment, teachers should encourage students to learn collaboratively and expect them to take responsibility for each other."

—*Cousins, 2000, p. 18*

Point Well Taken

". . . math anxiety has an impact during the original learning of difficult arithmetic and mathematics."

—*Ashcraft, 2001, p. 226*

Point Well Taken

"Grouping students to maximize the effectiveness of instructional techniques can be a powerful tool for teaching and classroom management. Done without planning and careful thought, it can also lead to an inefficient use of teacher and student time."

—*Kizlik, 2004*

A word of caution is in order for anyone looking for lesson plans on the Internet. Some sites offer excellent plans whereas others present nothing more than worksheets and simple activities that in some cases can actually be damaging to students. One lesson plan on an Internet site stipulated offering candy to students who completed their assignments early! A suggestion for ensuring the quality of a lesson plan site is to determine whether the site posts lesson plans that have been screened for quality. Many sites ask teachers to submit their favorite plans. Although soliciting lesson plans is well-meaning, if the plans that are contributed are not screened, then any plan, no matter how poorly conceived, will appear on the site. Ultimately, a teacher's good judgment can be the best sifter of an effective lesson plan. At the worst, a poor plan can spark an idea that an astute teacher can develop into an effective lesson plan.

Organizing the Students for Effective Learning

Using Small Groups

It is clear from research that using small groups will facilitate middle school students' constructing their knowledge of mathematics (Johnson et. al., 1981; Slavin et al., 1984; Slavin et al., 1985). The effective use of small groups requires more than simply clustering students together. In this section we will discuss the principles for working with cooperative groups.

In small groups, students can take risks, make mistakes, and ask questions without any fear of revealing their inadequacies to the entire class. In small groups students are able to discuss, reason, investigate, adjust, and readjust their thinking without worry because they are working with only a small number of peers who themselves are making mistakes, taking risks, and forming erroneous conjectures (NCTM, 1989). When a small group reports its findings and conclusions to the entire class, there is safety in numbers. Such settings allow middle school students to be part of a group that reveals its results to the class as a unified whole rather than as individual students.

Students in small groups feel less threatened in mathematics class and are able to focus on mathematics rather than on the affective aspects of the class. Students who learn mathematics in small groups generally like mathematics better than those who do not. "Students are more apt to like and enjoy mathematics and want to take advanced mathematics courses when mathematics is taught cooperatively than when it is taught competitively or individualistically" (Johnson & Johnson, 1992, p. 109). Middle school students tend to be very social, and small groups allow them to be social and productive at the same time.

Small groups may be used effectively with a wide range of typical classroom activities. As seen in the following list, there are very few activities in a typical middle grades mathematics classroom that may not be adjusted to lend themselves to small group work.

Homework problems or class problems	Homework review
Exam preparation	Class explorations
Developmental lessons	Enrichment activities
Real-world applications of mathematics	Research projects
Class presentations	

Characteristics of Effective Groups

David and Richard Johnson are professors and educational researchers who have devoted many years to exploring cooperative learning across the curriculum. They specify a number of identifying characteristics or norms of cooperative learning that differentiate it from simply grouping students together for instruction (Johnson, Johnson, Holobec, & Roy, 1984).

1. Cooperative Groups Are Based on Positive Interdependence

Positive interdependence ensures that all group members work together to achieve the goal or complete the task. When students depend on one another, they are unlikely to work alone or make decisions without consulting others in the group. When students work in an atmosphere of positive interdependence, they are more at ease asking questions, giving help to others in the group, and revealing their own shortcomings about the mathematics at hand.

One way to begin to build positive interdependence is to give the group the information and materials needed to solve a problem and each member a specific role to perform. Thus, the team must read and interpret the task and then perform individual roles, such as recorder, checker, materials manager, facilitator, and so forth. Some educators suggest that no roles should be assigned, reasoning that all students in the group should play all the roles as needed. We disagree. Some roles, such as those listed previously, can be filled only by a single individual. By assigning specific roles for students to play teachers enable each student to contribute to the task. The roles should vary according to the specific situation. Regardless of the roles used in cooperative groups, those that are filled by a single student should be rotated frequently within the same group. That way all students gain the experience of fulfilling various group roles.

Skill builders are tasks used to help students acquire cooperative skills and to give students experiences of working in groups. These tasks often use an interdependency format in which each person is given a clue or piece of information. The group then needs to produce the desired outcome according to specific rules about sharing their clues. The main goal of these exercises is for students to realize that they need each group member's information in order to complete the task. For specific skill-building tasks, see Cohen, 1994; Davidson, 1990; and Shaw, 1992.

2. Each Member in a Cooperative Group Is Individually Accountable

This is a key component in cooperative groups that can be lost in the details of setting up small groups. Cooperative groups commonly receive a group evaluation for their final product whether it is a completed problem, research assignment, report to the class, or an artifact such as a poster, scale model, or a map. In addition, each student should be individually assessed. The individual assessment can take many forms. Each student may take a quiz or answer questions about the material covered by the group task. Students might submit their own reports on the group explorations or experiments. Finally, students may be assessed by how they worked cooperatively with the group members. Figure 3.1 is one way to observe and assess students as they work cooperatively. (See Chapter 4, Assessment: Balanced and Varied, for more on observing and assessing students' work.)

3. Cooperative Groups Tend to Be Heterogeneous

We will discuss group compositions in more detail later in this chapter, and the baseline of heterogeneous groups fits well into the cooperative groups model. Students should have

Point Well Taken

"The social setting in which materials are used may account in part for their effectiveness (or ineffectiveness) in helping students understand [build understanding]."
—*Hiebert & Carpenter, 1992, p. 87*

Point Well Taken

"The positive outcomes of cooperative learning strategies have been documented by studies conducted at all grade levels and in all subject areas."
—*Artzt, 1994, p. 4*

figure **3.1**

Chart for Evaluating Group Work

Name _____			
Skill	Frequently	Rarely	Not yet
Shares in group work			
Offers praise/suggestion			
Asks/answers questions			

the opportunity to work together in cooperative settings with every student in their class and not only with close friends.

4. All Group Members Share Responsibility

In a cooperative group no one student fills the role as leader. Such a role runs counter to the spirit of cooperative learning, where all students cooperate and collaborate to reach a common goal. A leader suggests that one student is ultimately in charge, responsible for the success or failure of the group, and is somehow able to decide the roles, duties, and responsibilities of others in the group. We have referred to a team captain in some of the lesson plans in the content chapters. The team captain ensures that all members of the group participate and fulfills the role of any missing member within the group. There are some tasks that might be assigned to individual members such as materials manager, teacher contact member, and others. The responsibilities for these roles might be clarified by a class discussion and then posted in the classroom. By specifying what each role entails, students can appreciate the value that each role brings to the group. The fact that a single member has responsibility for a specific role does not imply that the responsibility is solely his or hers. With positive interdependence other group members can assist if asked and make suggestions where needed, and all are responsible for the smooth completion of any assignment in their group.

5. Responsibility for Each Other's Learning in the Group Is Shared

In the spirit of the preceding points, it is not only the completion of the group task that is every group member's responsibility. Each group member is responsible for the progress and learning of fellow group members. In a truly cooperative group a key norm is that all members work together to ensure that they all individually, as well as the group, succeed. In short, every member supports the group and receives support from the group.

6. Focus Is on Both Learning and on Maintaining Working Relationships

In order for cooperative groups to function properly, it is important to place the emphasis on two aspects of the groups: the task and the process. In most classrooms that use groups, the process gets short shrift, and all the attention is placed on the task and its assessment. Although it is obvious that the goal of any group activity is the most important concern, just as important in a cooperative setting is the process by which students in their groups reach the goal. Both matter, and that should be clear to students. As stated earlier in point 2, individual student process development can be one source of individual accountability in a cooperative setting. Notice that in several lesson plans in the content chapters, the wrap-up consists of two questions, one dealing with content and one dealing with group process.

7. Social Skills Needed for Cooperative Groups Are Explicitly Identified

Many times middle school teachers mistakenly assume students have developed the tools to work successfully in small groups. Usually all that these students have learned is to vote on any differences and let the majority rule. There is much more to group process than that. Students must work for consensus rather than a majority vote. Voting can discourage those students whose opinions were rejected by the vote. Working toward consensus takes time and effort, but it is critical for effective and productive work by the group.

It is also important for the teacher to identify various skills to work cooperatively so that they become norms for working together in groups. For example, the role of a praiser, which every student should assume in every group, can be discussed so that all students know what is involved in that role and will feel comfortable giving and receiving praise. The helper role (another role all students assume) calls for students to help one another. Students should understand that giving help does not mean simply supplying the answer or the correct solution strategy. Rather, giving help means leading group members to solving the problem themselves. Every group member has the right to ask questions and receive help, and every group member has the responsibility to provide help when asked.

Point Well Taken

"It is a great mistake to assume that students (or adults) know how to work with each other in a constructive collegial fashion."

—*Cohen & Lotan, 1997, p. 28*

A key element of being an effective member of a cooperative group is to develop good listening and questioning skills. These skills are important lifelong assets. Spending the time to help students understand what good listening looks like and sounds like in the classroom pays dividends beyond the small group process. To help students develop this skill (or others), teachers can create a T-chart entitled "Good Listening." One side of the chart is labeled "Sounds Like" and the other side is labeled "Looks Like." As students discuss the characteristics of good listening, the teacher places students' statements on the appropriate side of the chart. Entries under "Looks Like" might include a group member asking clarifying questions such as "Did you mean . . . ?" or "Is that like . . . ?" Another entry might include statements such as "One person talking at a time." On the other side of the chart, entries might include body language characteristics such as one person leaning in toward the speaker or group members making eye contact. As students work within their small groups, they can add characteristics to their T-chart or develop additional T-charts. Students also need to be encouraged to use "I" statements to help clarify their own personal needs and boundaries when working in a small group. For example, "I" statements might be "I can't hear you both if you talk at once," or "I need you to speak more slowly so I can understand."

8. The Teacher Evaluates and Gives Feedback on the Group Process

One effective way to help students develop these skills and norms is to debrief every group activity, however briefly. In a debriefing session for a cooperative activity, both mathematical concepts and cooperative skills are discussed. Regarding cooperative skills, the teacher can identify positive skills in a particular group and draw the entire class's attention to how that skill was demonstrated. Skills or processes that need more attention or adjustment might be analyzed individually, with each group, or with the entire class. In either case, students need lots of feedback as they begin to work cooperatively. Collaborative classrooms take time to develop. Middle school students are quick learners and will develop strong cooperative skills quickly, so that the process of cooperative groups does not overwhelm the product, the mathematics concepts at hand.

TRY THIS

Describe what you might see and hear when four students are effectively collaborating.

Composition of Cooperative Groups

A critical part of making effective use of small groups is their size and composition. We suggest small groups with four students. With four students in a group, the group has enough members to divide up various tasks but not so many that it is difficult to get anything done. In a four-member group students can discuss mathematics and review fundamentals with others in the group but not fret that the group has so many people in it that they feel embarrassed or threatened to ask for an explanation. An additional advantage of a four-member group is that it frequently is advantageous to have students work with a partner at the computer or with an exploration or simulation. A four-member group can easily split up into two pairs for such activities and then recompose to compare results and report their findings to the class. When in pairs, students may employ what is called the think-pair-share technique. Students using this process *think* about a problem or task individually and then discuss it as a *pair* with their partner. Then they *share* their conclusions with the rest of their group for further refinement and extensions.

Group composition is another important consideration. One suggested composition for four-member groups is one high-ability student, one low-ability student, and two middle-ability students. Another combination is two high-ability students and two low-ability students, or all middle-ability students. In research studies each of these has been advantageous for the most part to the group members. Another factor to consider when forming groups is language-minority students and special needs students. We have already addressed considerations for grouping English-language learners (see Chapter 2, The Challenge of Middle School Learners). Special needs students should be included in groups along with other students. In this case, however, it might be beneficial to be sure there are tasks that are within the reach of special needs students as they work along with their peers, so the students will be an integral part of the group efforts. Gender is another factor to consider when grouping students. For example, a small group composed of three rowdy boys and one shy girl may not be beneficial for all in the group, nor might a group of three mature young women and an awkward, immature boy. For the most part, however, gender need not be a focus when composing small groups.

Another aspect of group composition is learning styles or intelligences (see Chapter 1, Mathematics for the Twenty-First Century). A teacher might try to ensure that each group has a combination of learner strengths in its members. If, for example, the end product of a project includes a poster or other artistic product, then it will be beneficial if each group has at least one member who is comfortable in that creative environment.

After students have had experience working in groups and have worked with many of their classmates, groups may be selected randomly. Students can count off and students with some combination of numbers or multiples can be placed in the same group. Or students can pick numbers or different-colored milk caps or number cards out of a bag. On some occasions, however, random selection may produce groups that will not benefit all students in the group, as mentioned earlier. When this happens the groups can work together for a short time on a small task, such as going over a class problem, and then the groups can be recomposed the next day. In any event, all students should understand that they will work in a group with every other student in class during the course of the year. Teachers should not allow students to select their own groups, however. Inevitably, some students are not selected and they feel left out. Teachers may ask students to write down the names of six students with whom they would like to work. Teachers can then use the list as a guide when creating the groups.

TRY THIS

What stereotype of group practices does the cartoon below suggest? How has your experience in groups supported or disproved this outlook?

One of the affective goals of having students work in small groups is for them to learn to work with different students and to expand their socialization skills. We suggest re-

On the Lighter Side

Jeremy explains his view of group work.

Copyright Zits Partnership. Reprinted with permission of King Features Syndicate.

grouping students quite frequently, perhaps at the end of a unit or even more frequently. It can be helpful to students to know how long they will work in a particular group. Students should have the opportunity to work with all their peers and with different combinations of peers. Changing groups fairly often can also help students who are not as comfortable working with some students as with others. Although it is true that working with all students can help socialization skills, the fact that the groups will only last a short time can also be encouraging to the students who may be uncomfortable in their group.

For more information on ability and instructional grouping, see www.adprima.com/grouping.htm.

Classroom Climate

A key component of successful teaching is to establish classroom norms that define and delineate what is expected of students in the classroom, regardless of the setting, the task at hand, or the class organization. Classroom norms benefit both the teacher who uses small groups extensively and the teacher who mostly lectures to the students. The time spent in the beginning of the year establishing norms for a productive and respectful classroom climate pays great dividends throughout the course of the year. We have focused on norms for cooperative groups in this chapter.

General Social Norms

Social norms are those understandings that students and their teacher construct about behavior and student interactions. For middle school students, these norms, often referred to as "community guidelines," set parameters for acceptable behavior. The norms are developed by the class and discussed at length and can evolve over the course of the year. Teachers can also present predetermined norms and then help students understand the rationale for each stated norm. Allowing middle school students a voice in the establishment of the norms gives them a sense of ownership. Students are more likely to uphold the norms if they contributed to the development of them. As discussed earlier, many norms for cooperative learning may be developed in debriefing sessions and by teacher feedback.

In addition to the norms for cooperative groups we have considered, there are specific sociomathematical norms that are designed to be used in mathematics classes.

Sociomathematical Norms

Sociomathematical norms support behaviors, beliefs, and dispositions about mathematics (Rasmussen et al., 2003). "Show steps leading to your solution," and "Explain your reasoning" are norms specific to mathematics. Another sociomathematical norm involves defining the components of an explanation or proof. Teachers can ask students about the evidence for their statements or encourage them to look for a counterexample. A sociomathematical norm includes a disposition such as keeping an open mind or reflecting on a particular task as part of the problem-solving process (Rasmussen et al., 2003). Both social and sociomathematical norms are part of the culture in any classroom. Unfortunately, not all norms are positive and productive. We have all been in classes in which students blurt out answers, pass notes, interrupt the teacher, or make negative statements about others in the class. The norms in such a classroom tolerate those disruptive behaviors. By giving students specific training in cooperative learning skills and norms, group work contributes to the positive learning environment.

In some cases groups can become dysfunctional. Many times groups experience difficulties dealing with status issues. Status is a critical factor that influences the success of small groups. Teachers need to be mindful of status issues and be ready to address them as they occur.

Status Issues

The issue of status plays into any working group. Status can be given, perceived, or withdrawn all without an individual's knowledge. Status functions in every group dynamic.

REACT | REFLECT

What group activities do you remember from middle school mathematics? How confident were you when working in your group(s)?

Point Well Taken

"Students do slightly better on basic skills achievement tests with direct or traditional (teacher-centered) teaching, but students do better on creativity and problem-solving tests with open classroom (small group) approaches to instruction."
—*Padron & Waxman, 1992, p. 6*

Point Well Taken

"There can be little doubt that cooperation promotes higher achievement in math class than do competitive and individualistic efforts."
—*Johnson & Johnson, 1992, p. 106*

Middle school students tend to give status to others based on popularity, athleticism, academic performance, and common interests. With status comes power to monopolize, make decisions, and control the group's interactions. When students do not feel they are heard or that they do not have a chance to contribute, they withdraw from participating. These students are the ones seen on the periphery of a small group. They become distracted and feel devalued. They may look as though they do not care about the task. These low-status students do not have access to the task. Low-status students can feel isolated and lonely.

In such instances intervention by the teacher is necessary and should be approached in a positive manner. By assigning specific roles that are detailed and important to the task, the teacher provides each student with a way to make a contribution. Teachers can make role tags that students wear like name tags. These tags help remind students to perform their role and the tags help teachers observe students functioning in their roles. Making certain that students have access to the task and a role to play within the group are critical features for successful group work.

TRY THIS

Try to remember a time in which you felt left out of a conversation. You may have tried to contribute, but you did not feel that others heard you. Explain the circumstance in which this occurred. How did you feel in the moment? What did you do? Did anyone in the group try to include you?

Another method for improving the status of students in a group involves the teacher calling one student from each group who all play the same particular role together and hold a conference with these students. Suppose the teacher observes status issues within several groups. The teacher can decide to call the facilitators from each group together to remind them to ensure that all members in their groups are contributing. The teacher can offer the facilitator specific questions to ask their groups such as, "Does anyone have anything else to add?" or "I'd like to check in with Isaac. Isaac, do you have a question or something to say?"

Teachers can raise the status of an individual student by stating to the group, "I don't think you heard what Juanita said. She can help this group." Naturally, this statement can only happen if the teacher has indeed heard Juanita speaking. If the teacher senses that a student has withdrawn or the group is ignoring someone, a reminder as to the importance of everyone contributing to the group can be made.

As the year progresses, students can learn to check in with each other about how they are feeling in terms of their participation in the group. Frequently, status is assigned to various students for arbitrary reasons. For example, students might perceive that Roberto is good in math because he answered a question in class or he did well on the last test. As a result, they look to Roberto to take control. Reminding students to perform their roles for the group can help balance the contributions of everyone in the group. There has been significant work done on the assignment of status within groups, notably the work of Cohen and Lotan (1997). (See resources at the end of this chapter.)

Teachers often have difficulty determining whether or not to intervene when a group is not working well. If students appear to be struggling with the task, teachers want to support the students by guiding them toward the solution. Teachers need to allow students the right to grapple with problems. Working through the difficulties, making errors, and then using the knowledge gained to try another path lead students to greater understanding and build confidence. However, if a teacher senses that the building frustration in a group is to the point that students are ready to abandon the task, then some guidance and direction may be in order. Teachers also need to intervene when students need clarification with directions. Teachers may also decide to redirect a group that is pursuing an approach that is off track. This is a delicate decision, and the allocation of time may be another determining factor to consider.

Point Well Taken

"Successful groups require careful planning, from the activities and group composition to the responsibilities of the students and appropriate assessments."

—*Johnson, 2004, p. 18*

In *Designing Groupwork*, Elizabeth Cohen suggests that with each intervention, the teacher may be interrupting the flow of the group's thinking. There are times when intervention is important. Cohen suggests that teachers intervene under the following circumstances:

- When the group is hopelessly off-task
- When the group does not seem to understand enough to get started or carry out the task
- When the group is experiencing sharp interpersonal conflict
- When the group is falling apart because it cannot organize itself to get the task done (Cohen, 1994, p. 108)

It is important that teachers evaluate the situation before they move to intervene. Understanding the cause of the difficulty determines how and what the teacher should do. For example, if the group needs help organizing, the teacher can suggest that students refer to the roles. The teacher might suggest that the facilitator guide a discussion to clarify the task and determine what needs to happen first. If group members had been working well and now seem stuck, the teacher can ask a few carefully chosen questions to help them refocus. Sometimes groups don't seem to get started because they may be having trouble with the directions. The wording of the text may be difficult, for example. It is important that teachers find out what students know specifically before offering any suggestions. A teacher might highlight important components of the task or explain some of the vocabulary involved. Here the teacher is working to get the group started rather than suggesting a method of solution. Suppose the group is engaged in an interpersonal conflict. In this case, it is important that the teacher keep the authority of the group within the group. The teacher can ask students to consider alternative strategies for resolving the conflict. If they have been provided with alternative strategies for conflict management, this task is a reasonable request. If not, the teacher can remind students of the norms established by the class. The teacher can ask students what they can do to move the group forward as a group (Cohen, 1994, p. 109).

If the group continues to be dysfunctional, a teacher may decide to disband the group and suggest that they work on the task independently. This is a last resort! A teacher should make a mental note to incorporate conflict resolution training in future work. For the moment, noting the individuals involved in the conflict can help the teacher avoid placing them together in a group in the near future. The teacher should also talk with the members of the group individually and then as a group to try to resolve the issue at some other point during the day or as soon as possible. It is important that students have the appropriate language in which to work through conflicts. Using "I" statements rather than statements that accuse or blame others is an important ingredient. For more on conflict resolution, refer to Cohen, 1994, and Crawford and Wood, 1998.

Other Instructional Formats

Although we strongly support using small groups in middle grades mathematics classes, there are other ways to organize a class for effective mathematics learning. In a traditional lecture or question-and-answer class, an instructor can impart explicit information in a short time. If the information is straightforward and does not require building a foundational understanding, this may be a reasonable approach. For example, a teacher may review mathematics concepts from a previous year's material to set the stage for an extension of these concepts. Another teacher may use a lecture format to introduce and discuss order of operations. Some educators suggest the lecture-in-front-of-the-classroom approach is best for the first few days or even weeks of the school year, when the teacher needs to quickly review previously studied concepts in order to get students up to par before beginning a study of new concepts. We suggest that early in the school year is the time for working on cooperative skills and engaging students in activities that build mathematics knowledge and group process skills.

Point Well Taken

"Over-reliance on one learning experience, such as independent work, at the expense of another, such as group work, is not conducive to the effective learning of children."

—*Vause, 2004, p. 83*

Point Well Taken

"Throughout this period (middle school) concrete experiences should continue to provide the means by which they construct knowledge."

—*NCTM, 1989, p. 68*

Point Well Taken

"Despite the dramatically increased role of mathematics in or society, mathematics classrooms in the United States today too often resemble their counterparts of a century ago. Many mathematics teachers still spend the bulk of their time demonstrating procedures and supervising students while they practice those procedures."

—*National Research Council, 2002, p. 3*

Point Well Taken

"Students' attitudes towards mathematics are improved through the long-term use of concrete instructional materials."

—*Sowell, 1989, p. 501*

Related to the lecture or question-answer format is the teacher demonstration. This can be effective when the teacher plans to model or demonstrate a particular concept or relationship employing a single manipulative or teaching aid as, for example, a balance scale to show the balance aspect of algebraic equations. With but a single balance scale in the classroom, it is impractical for each group to spend time exploring how the scale works and how it might represent algebraic concepts. Thus, the teacher may choose to demonstrate how to use the scale and perhaps show how it represents algebraic equations. It will be beneficial for students to take turns in small groups using the scale to work out algebraic concepts while other groups are engaged with a related task or activity.

Finally, all students need to have the opportunity to work at mathematics individually. We referenced the think-pair-share format, which includes some individual thinking or examining. Another opportunity for independent work can be incorporated into the small-groups classroom. Before having students move into small groups for a task or activity, teachers can provide individual processing time. Students find that having this processing time to think independently gives them ideas to offer to their group when they begin to work together. In addition, students need to have opportunities to work independently to solve problems, to review notes, and to be evaluated. High-stakes tests, job and college interviews, and other activities in life require individual efforts by students, and so it is important that students have the opportunity to develop the skills that will enable them to work independently or in individual settings. Thus, some combination of these approaches to teaching may be the most beneficial to students.

Another important aspect of a successful middle grades mathematics class is how manipulatives are used, either in small groups or by individual students.

Manipulatives

Using Manipulatives in the Classroom

Do manipulatives have a place in the middle grades mathematics classroom? Although most elementary school classrooms frequently use manipulatives when studying mathematics, few middle school classrooms do.

For many middle school mathematics teachers, middle school is the time for leaving behind concrete experiences in mathematics and studying mathematics through an abstract lens. We disagree.

Manipulatives should be an integral part of any mathematics classroom, from pre-K to high school. According to the National Council of Teachers of Mathematics, learning new concepts in the middle grades is just as complex a task as learning new concepts in the elementary grades (Lannin, 2003, p. 342). Numerous studies have found that students who have used manipulatives in their mathematics classroom have a higher achievement level in mathematics, are better problem solvers, and have higher-level thinking skills (Erickson & Niess, 1996; Garnett, 2004). However, the evidence is that manipulatives play only a small role, if any, in many middle school mathematics classrooms. One survey found that less than half the teachers in the middle grades used manipulatives more than three times a month (Martine & Stramel, 2003). In many of these cases, the manipulatives were used for "fun" activities without any strong connection to mathematics being studied in the classroom.

A case might be made that as mathematics topics become more complex and abstract, the effective use of manipulatives in the classroom becomes all the more critical. For example, students who are studying polyhedrons will benefit from using actual polyhedron models. Students can use these models to explore nets as a means to understand and compute surface area. The models can help students visualize the hidden edges that appear as dotted lines in a drawing. They can use the models to count edges, faces, and vertex points as they explore Euler's Formula. Students who are beginning their study of algebra can use two-color counters to represent the four operations with integers. Algebra tiles can help students understand binomial multiplication, combining like terms, and the difference between x^2 and $2x$. There are many other manipulatives that middle grades mathematics students can use to explore or clarify mathematics concepts from patty paper for paper folding to MIRAS and geoboards. We have cited various manipulatives in the content chapters as we discuss specific mathematics topics.

With clear evidence of the benefits of using manipulatives, it is worth considering some reasons why many middle grades teachers do not use them. Many teachers (and many students) consider manipulatives to be childish, suitable only for elementary-level mathematics. While it is true that manipulatives play a large role in elementary-level mathematics, they can help middle school students understand middle grades topics such as those cited earlier. Middle school students need to understand that the role of manipulatives in the middle grades is to help them master topics that are far too complex for elementary-level students to study. They must be helped to reason that although a specific manipulative, such as pattern blocks, might be used in a third-grade mathematics class to help students recognize and form various patterns, the same manipulative is now helping middle grades students learn a more difficult mathematics topic than third-grade students might study, such as symmetry across a line or the sum of interior angles of polygons. Many of the activities in the content chapters employ manipulatives to clarify concepts and relationships for students.

Another concern with manipulatives can be classroom management. Again, some forethought can help eliminate this concern before it becomes a reality. Students who work in small groups will best benefit from using manipulatives, and so the group can become the focus of managing the manipulatives. One student in the group can be assigned the responsibility of gathering and returning the manipulative of the day. This lessens time needed to distribute and collect manipulatives.

A related concern about manipulatives is that students may misuse them. Some middle school students tend to consider the rubber bands that accompany a geoboard as more a projectile than something useful for mathematics. Students should be given a rationale for using the manipulative, instructed in the proper use, and expected to use the manipulative responsibly. One helpful suggestion is to allow students a bit of free time to explore with a manipulative whenever a new manipulative is introduced. This enables students to examine, explore, and in general familiarize themselves with the specific learning aid before they engage in the activities for the day. With the geoboard, for example, many students have a deep-seated need to plunk a taut rubber band to produce some snappy music. If students have a minute to do so, then they will not try to play any music when they are performing mathematics explorations. Any attempt to sidestep this informal, introductory stage will result in students experimenting and exploring when they should be using the manipulative for mathematics. It is also important to establish with students the norms of reasonable behavior with manipulatives as, for example, a geoboard, by having students agree that the rubber bands are not meant for shooting at one another. It can also be beneficial to establish consequences for behavior that does not meet expectations and follow through if necessary.

A well-worn cliché about teaching is "You teach the way you were taught." In the case of manipulatives there may be some truth to this statement. A teacher who never used manipulatives as a student may be reluctant to use manipulatives at a teacher. We encourage any teacher to break away from the cliché and use manipulatives to illuminate mathematics for students.

Probably the greatest concern among teachers who are reluctant to use manipulatives is that they are not helpful. As noted earlier, research clearly demonstrates the benefits of effective use of manipulatives. The key point here is *effective use*. Manipulatives are a concrete representation of a mathematics relationship. Students first need to discover through explorations and experiments with manipulatives the specific relationships intended with the manipulative. It is then critical for students to take the relationship beyond the concrete level to a representational level. This connection may be made during the same class session or in a following session. Students need to draw or explain the relationship demonstrated by the manipulative. They will also benefit from representing

Point Well Taken

"Teachers must provide ample opportunities for students to use manipulatives to connect concrete and abstract reasoning."
—*Martine & Stramel, 2003, p. 333*

AUTHOR'S **Recall**

I remember the math chair of a middle school telling me that the grade 8 math students had no time for hands-on activities. They had to use all their class time "to get ready for high school."

Point Well Taken

"Active involvement is emphasized when students construct their own knowledge, using a variety of manipulatives and tools."
—*Martine & Stramel, 2003, p. 332*

AUTHOR'S **Recall**

The only manipulatives I can recollect using in middle school mathematics class was a protractor and compass, and these are really tools, not manipulatives, because they do not help model or represent mathematics concepts.

Point Well Taken

"Learning is enhanced when students are exposed to a concept in a variety of manipulative contexts."
—*Martine & Stramel, 2003, p. 332*

Point Well Taken

"Once a concept is learned using one material, students can explore the same concept using another manipulative and thereby generalize the concept."

—Owen, 1993, p. xiv

Point Well Taken

"You don't understand anything until you learn it more than one way."

—Marvin Minsky

the relationship with a different manipulative. That way they do not link the concept exclusively with a particular manipulative. The final stage is for students to move from the representational stage to the abstract, where they can explain the relationship without reference to any manipulative. If students do not move to the abstract from the concrete, the mathematical relationship remains linked to the manipulative and is never generalized or conceived apart from the manipulative.

Jerome Bruner termed these last two stages of mathematical conceptualization as *ikonic* and *symbolic*. In the ikonic stage students would represent the relationship in a different format. In the symbolic stage students would represent the mathematical relationship in abstract or symbolic form. For example, a teacher might use string or ribbon, rulers, and lids from various jars and plastic tubs to help students learn about the circumference of a circle. The students use the string to form the circumference of the disk and compare that length to the length of string needed to trace the diameter. They discover that the string around the circle is a little more than three times as long as the diameter length. The ikonic stage would perhaps involve students drawing their own circle, and, without making any measurements, indicating how the diameter is related to the circumference. The symbolic stage might require students to write a relationship such as $C = 3d$ or $C = \pi d$.

There are many vendors that produce mathematics manipulatives for the classroom. The list that follows contains both telephone and Internet contacts. These vendors will send out a catalogue of their manipulatives to anyone who requests one.

Classroom Products
P.O. Box 26
Bloomington, IL 60108
888-271-8305
www.classroomproducts.com

Master Innovations, Inc.
P.O. Box 906
Alpha, NJ 08865-0906
www.themasterruler.com
908-859-1788

Didax
395 Main St.
Rowley, MA 01969-1207
800-458-0024
www.didaxinc.com

Nasco Math
901 Jamesville Ave.
Fort Atkinson, WI 53538-0901
800-558-9595
www.enasco.com

ETA/Cuisenaire
500 Greenview Court
Vernon Hills, IL 60061-1862
800-445-5985
www.etacuisenaire.com

Scott Resources
401 Hickory Street
Fort Collins, CO 80522
800-289-9299
www.hubbardscientific.com

REACT | REFLECT

What manipulatives do you remember using in middle school? What were the mathematics concepts the manipulative was meant to clarify?

Virtual Manipulatives

One last aspect of manipulatives to consider is the number of virtual manipulatives found on the Internet. Today's middle schoolers are the first generation of students who have the opportunity to use electronic manipulatives in place of, or in addition to, the real thing. One obvious concern about virtual manipulatives is whether they are effective. Can they possibly be as good as the real thing? The research into the effectiveness of virtual manipulatives is still in the informal stages, but early results are promising, indicating that students who work with electronic manipulatives show the same benefits as those who work with concrete manipulatives (Keller et al., 2002). In the area of spatial visualization, virtual manipulatives may advance students' achievement more than concrete manipulatives (Olkun, 2003). Our position with regard to virtual manipulatives is that students benefit from observing concepts and relationships in multiple representations, and so concrete and electronic manipulatives should be used in tandem for the greatest benefit. As a result, students will generalize the concept or relationship to all appropriate settings.

In each of the content chapters we have listed Internet sites for exploring specific mathematics concepts. The list that follows contains general sites of interactive mathematics activities that employ virtual manipulatives.

National Library of Virtual Mathematics Manipulatives
http://nlvm.usu.edu/en/nav/vlibrary.html
This site is sponsored by Utah State University and catalogues applets by grade bands: pre-K–2, 3–5, and 6–8.

NCTM Illuminations
http://illuminations.nctm.org
This site is maintained by the National Council of Teachers of Mathematics. It includes "mathlets" at all grade bands and subject strands, listed by topic or grade band. Also included are electronic activities contained in *Principles and Standards for School Mathematics*.

Educational Java Programs
www.arcytech.org/java/
Archytech Research labs in Palo Alto, California, contains three interesting applets: Base 10, Pattern Blocks, and Fraction Bars.

Shodor Interactive Activities
www.shodor.org/interactivate/activities/index.html
The Shodor Educational Foundation is a nonprofit research organization for advancement of mathematics and science education. The site contains many applets grouped by topic: number, algebra, geometry, measurement, data, and probability.

International Education Software
www.ies.co.jp/math/indexeng.html
The International Educational Software Company is a Japanese company. The site consists of many applets, in particular ninety-one middle school applets in geometry.

BBC Interactive Math Games
www.bbc.co.uk/education/mathsfile
This site from British Broadcasting Corporation contains twelve interactive games with excellent mathematics content for elementary and middle school students.

Mathsnet Interactive Mathematics
www.mathsnet.net
This British site is maintained by the Anglia Multimedia Corporation and is housed at Hewett School in Norwich, England. It contains many different interactive sections including fractions, geometry, graphs, and algebra.

Eisenhower National Clearinghouse
www.enc.com
The Eisenhower National Clearinghouse for Education in Mathematics and Science links to many sites across geometry, number, data and probability, measurement, algebra, and applied mathematics.

RekenWebGames
www.fi.uu.nl/rekenweb/en/welcome.xml
This site is sponsored by the Freudenthal Institute in the Netherlands. It contains over twenty-five interactive challenges and games for ages 4–12 with very good mathematics content.

Annenberg & Corporation for Public Broadcasting Math and Science Project
www.learner.org/teacherslab/index.html
This site presents interesting applets in two areas: shape and space in geometry and patterns in mathematics.

Planning for effective instruction begins and ends with the classroom teacher. In between there are many decisions to be made about content, classroom organization, grouping practices, and class procedures. A well-conceived lesson plan can clarify all of these and lay a foundation for a class lesson in which students learn meaningful and engaging mathematics.

SUMMARY

Proper preparation is the key to effective teaching. Text selection, lesson plans, classroom organization, and teaching style are all part of planning to teach. They all relate to one another and affect one another. There are many resources to assist teachers in their plans, from Internet resources and textbook ancillary materials to state and district mathematics frameworks. Ultimately the careful preparation and execution of teaching plans is the most significant part of the teaching process. In brief, teachers do the bulk of their work *before* class; students do the bulk of their work *in* class.

Teaching styles can be at the extremes of teacher-centered or student-centered approaches or someplace in between. Research conclusively supports a student-centered approach that employs manipulatives and cooperative groups. In such groups middle grades students, especially, are more likely to construct their own personal understanding of mathematics concepts.

The following are highlights of this chapter:

- Teaching styles can lie at either of two extremes, teacher-centered and student-centered, or someplace in between.
- Constructivism is a theory of learning that suggests students learn mathematics best when they can build or construct their own personal understanding of concepts and relationships.
- Two key components of cooperative learning groups are individual accountability and positive interdependence.
- As students work within groups, teachers need to be mindful of status issues.
- Manipulatives are a key means of helping students move from concrete understandings to abstract understandings.
- Specific responsibilities for roles in small groups must be clearly understood by students.
- Two sources of classroom materials are commercial textbooks and *Standards*-based series.
- Teaching to high-stakes test can be destructive to an effective mathematics curriculum if that is the only focus of the class.
- Both teachers and students build an effective classroom climate.

EXERCISES

From the Reading

1. What are some characteristics of cooperative groups?

2. List some of the student norms for cooperative groups.

3. What are some ways to prepare students for high-stakes mathematics tests besides teaching to the test?

4. What are the standards that form the basis for *Standards*-based mathematics texts? How do such tests differ from traditional mathematics texts?

5. What are the three stages for using manipulatives to acquire mathematical understanding?

6. Explain how small groups can benefit a self-conscious middle grades student in mathematics.

7. What are the integral parts of an effective lesson plan?

8. What is positive interdependence in cooperative groups? Why is it important?

9. Is constructivism a theory of teaching or a theory of learning? Explain.

10. In terms of cooperative groups, what is status? How does it impact the group's productivity?

11. When students work in cooperative groups, what are some ways in which individual students can be held accountable?

On Your Own

1. Find examples of released items from a recent high-stakes test. Look at the items for a specific grade level. What types of questions on the test do you find surprising? Why?

2. Visit one of the interactive mathematics Internet sites and review two of the activities. What is the mathematics involved? Was the site engaging? Effective?

3. Critique a lesson plan from a textbook series. How would you adjust it? What is missing?

Portfolio Question

How comfortable are you with small groups in your classroom?

Scenes from a Classroom

Ms. Mary Somerville has been using small groups successfully now for several months with her seventh graders. Today she has decided to allow them to choose their own groups.

She has planned to have six students act as captains and choose the groups by standing in front of the classroom and picking their group members, like choosing sides in playground basketball.

Things go well at first, and each captain makes two selections. Each team now has one pick left. Things are about to change—and fast.

Shawna: Boy, now who do we pick? There's nobody left.

Curt: You said it. There's no one I want on my team.

Hector: Well, we've got to pick one more. At least we're not last. There's six kids left. How about Smitty?

Curt: Oh no, not him. He doesn't know anything about math. Maybe Effie.

Shawna: Her? No way! Just look at her.

Hector: It's hopeless, there is no one left to pick.

We stop here before total chaos breaks out for Ms. Somerville.

Before reading our comments, respond to these questions.

1. What was the flaw in Ms. Somerville's plan to allow students to pick their own groups?

2. How might students be allowed to select their own groups?

3. Do you think allowing students to select their own groups is a good idea? Why or why not?

One possibility for composing groups is to allow students to pick their own groups. This can have some troublesome aspects. When students pick their own groups, invariably they pick their own friends. The result can be that there is little gained by group efforts in terms of explorations or discussions because all the group members see, think, and reflect in the same way. A more worrisome aspect is the process by which students pick their groups. If six students stand in front of the class and take turns picking group members, as portrayed here, someone is always the last to be picked. It is cruel and unthinking to put any student in such a situation. One way for students to pick groups is to have students write the names of four to six other students they want in their group. Then the teacher can do his or her best to match names and groups but with no guarantee to students that the students on their lists will be in their respective groups.

There is one benefit to allowing students to select their group members by making out a short list, as described in the previous paragraph. They may quickly learn that they cannot work in a group with their friends unless they adopt a different persona, that of being serious mathematics students. That does not mean they cannot enjoy one another's company, but typically groups composed of friends initially will get very little done. That can be a learning experience. If that is the goal for a small-group activity, the duration should be very short, a single class period, and involve a short-term activity that will benefit all students at the end of the group session as successful groups report their findings to the entire class.

Preparing for Praxis

Mr. Rose wants to improve the quality of responses and the level of participation by students during class discussion. Which of the following techniques has the greatest potential for improving thoughtfulness of students' responses and stimulating wider participation?

A. Keeping a seating chart on which he keeps a record of each student's participation.
B. Using peer tutoring in which more-able students work with less-able students.
C. Waiting longer between posing a question and calling on students to respond.
D. Giving verbal and visual clues to the kind of response he is seeking.

RESOURCES

Teacher's Bookcase

Artz, A., & Newman, C. (2004). *How to use cooperative learning in the mathematics classroom* (2nd ed.). Reston, VA: NCTM.

This book is an excellent resource of ideas and strategies to implement cooperative learning in mathematics.

Cohen, E. (1994). *Designing groupwork: Strategies for the homogeneous classroom* (2nd ed.). New York: Teachers College Press.

The focus of the text is in its title: using small groups to mitigate the difficulties of a homogeneous classroom.

Erikson, T. (1989). *Get it together—Math problems for groups grades 4–12.* Berkeley, CA: Equals.

The problems presented are designed for group work. The author provides many topics ranging in difficulty along with instructional suggestions, such as questions to ask during the debriefing sessions.

Erikson, T. (1996). *United we solve.* Oakland, CA: Eeps Media.

This resource offers 101 problems employing the power of group work. The problems are designed so that each member of the group has one piece of the necessary information needed to solve the problem.

Johnson, D., Johnson, R., Holobec, E., & Roy, P. (1984). *Circles of learning: Cooperation in the classroom.* Alexandria, VA: Association for Supervision and Curriculum Development.

This book is a seminal text in the development of cooperative education by the leading educators in the field of cooperative learning.

Shaw, V. (1992). *Community Building in the Classroom.* San Clemente, CA: Kagan.

This resource offers a vast amount of team building, relationship skill building, and cooperative skill exercises from which to select.

For Further Reading

Artzt, A. (1994). Integrating writing and cooperative learning in the mathematics classroom. *The Mathematics Teacher, 87*(2), 80–85.

In this article the author presents classroom methods and the rationale for using writing activities to enhance communication with cooperative learning.

Goos, M. (2004). Learning mathematics in a classroom community of inquiry. *Journal for Research in Mathematics Education, 35*(4), 258–296.

The author describes the successful application of Vygotsky's theory of zone of proximal development in a middle school mathematics class. Students develop their mathematics via inquiry and class discussions.

Martine, S., & Stramel, J. (2003). Manipulatives in the middle school. *Mathematics Teaching in the Middle School, 9*(6), 330–334.

This article describes several manipulatives and the explorations and investigations in which they can be used in middle grades topics.

Sutton, C. (1992). Cooperative learning works in mathematics. *The Mathematics Teacher, 85*(1), 63–66.

This article sets out a number of suggestions for a teacher who is starting out with cooperative groups, emphasizing the affective and social aspects of students working together.

Links

Cooperative Learning Center (Johnson & Johnson)
www.co-operation.org

Cooperative Learning Techniques
www.jigsaw.org

U.S. Department of Education
www.ed.gov

REFERENCES

Ashcraft, M. (2001). *Cognition.* Upper Saddle River, NJ: Prentice Hall.

Bass, L., Charles, R., Johnson, A., & Kennedy, D. (2004). *Informal geometry planning guide.* Needham, MA: Prentice Hall.

Cohen, E., & Lotan, R. (Eds.). (1997). *Designing group work—Strategies for the heterogeneous classroom.* New York: Teachers College Press.

Cohen, E., & Lotan, R. (Eds.). (1997). *Working for equity in heterogeneous classrooms.* New York: Teacher's College Press.

Cousins, C. (2000). Teacher expectations and their effects on African American students' success in mathematics. In W. Sacada (Ed.), *Changing the face of mathematics: Perspectives on African Americans.* Reston, VA: NCTM.

Crawford, L., & Wood, C. (1998). *Guidelines for the responsive classroom.* Greenfield, MA: Northeast Foundation for Children.

Damian, C. (2004). Grouping that leads to real learning. www.adprima.com/grouping.htm.

Davidson, N. (Ed.). (1990). *Cooperative learning in mathematics: A handbook for teachers.* Reading, MA: Addison-Wesley.

Erickson, D., & Niess, M. (1996). Focusing on NCTM's *Standards*: Teachers' choices and decisions related to student achievement in middle school mathematics. *Research in Middle Level Education Quarterly, 19,* 23–42.

Fennema, E., & Peterson, R. (1987). Learning mathematics with understanding: Cognitively guided instruction. In J. Brophy (Ed.), *Handbook of Research on Teaching* (3rd ed.). New York: Macmillan.

Gabler, C., & Schroeder, M. (2003). *Constructivist achievement for the secondary classroom.* Boston: Allyn & Bacon.

Good, T., Mulryan, C., & McCaslin, M. (1992). Grouping for instruction in mathematics: A call for programmable research in small-group processes. In D. Grouws (Ed.), *A handbook for research in mathematics education.* Reston, VA: NCTM.

Hiebert, J., & Carpenter, T. (1992). Learning and teaching with understanding. In D. Grouws (Ed.), *A handbook for research in mathematics education.* Reston, VA: NCTM.

Johnson, A. (2004). Small groups in my classroom? In M. Chappell & T. Pateracki (Eds.), *Empowering the beginning teacher of mathematics in middle school.* Reston, VA: NCTM.

Johnson, D., & Johnson, R. (1990). Using cooperative learning in mathematics. In N. Davidson (Ed.), *Cooperative learning in mathematics: A handbook for teachers.* Reading, MA: Addison-Wesley.

Johnson, D., & Johnson, R. (1993). *Cooperation in the classroom.* Edina, MN: Interactive Books.

Johnson, D., Johnson, R., & Holubec, E. (1983). *Circle of learning.* Edina, MN: Interaction.

Johnson, D., Johnson, R., Holobec, E., & Roy, P. (1984). *Circles of learning: Cooperation in the classroom.* Alexandria, VA: Association for Supervision and Curriculum Development.

Johnson, D. W., Johnson, R., & Maruyama, G. (1981). Effects of cooperative, competitive, and individualistic goal structures on achievement: A meta-analysis. *Psychological Bulletin, 89,* 47–62.

Keller, B., Wasburn-Moses, J., & Hart, E. (2002). *Improving students' spatial visualization skills and teachers' pedagogical content knowledge by using on-line curriculum-embedded applets.* Ongoing Research and Development Project sponsored by NCTM.

Kilpatrick, J. et al. (2001). Adding it up: Helping children learn mathematics. Washington DC: National Academy Press.

Kizlik, R. (2004). Ability and instructional grouping. www.adprima.com/grouping.htm.

Lannin, J. K. (2003). Developing algebraic reasoning through generalization. *Mathematics Teaching in the Middle Grades, 8*(7), 342.

Lappan, G., Fey, T., Fitzgerald, W., Friel, S., & Phillips, E. (2003). *Connected mathematics: Lesson planner for grades 6, 7, and 8.* Needham, MA: Prentice Hall.

Martine, S., & Stramel, J. (2003). Manipulatives in the middle school. *Mathematics Teaching in the Middle School, 9*(6), 330–334.

National Council of Teachers of Mathematics. (1989). *Curriculum and evaluation standards for school mathematics.* Reston, VA: NCTM.

National Council of Teachers of Mathematics. (2000). *Principles and Standards of School Mathematics.* Reston, VA: NCTM.

National Research Council. (2002). *Helping children learn mathematics.* Mathematics Learning Study Committee. J. Kilpatrick and J. Swafford (Eds.). Center for Education, Division of Behavioral and Social Sciences and Education, Washington, DC: National Academy Press.

Olkun, S. (2003). Computer versus concrete manipulatives in learning 2-D geometry. *The Journal of Computers in Mathematics and Science Teaching, 22*(2), 43–56.

Owen, D. (1993). Introduction in *Research ideas for the classroom: Middle grades.* Reston, VA: NCTM.

Padron, Y., & Waxman, H. (1992). Teaching and learning risks associated with limited cognitive mastery in science and mathematics for limited english proficient students. In *Proceedings of the Third National Symposium on Limited English Proficient Students: Focus on Middle and High School Issues, 1992.* Washington, DC: U.S. Department of Education.

Rasmussen, C., Yackel, E., & King, K. (2003). Social and socio-mathematical norms in the mathematics classroom. In H. Schoern & C. Lester (Eds.), *Teaching mathematics through problem solving, grades 6–12.* Reston, VA: National Council of Teachers of Mathematics.

Slavin, R., & Karweit, N. (1985). Effects of whole-class, ability grouped, and individualized instruction on mathematics achievement. *American Educational Research Journal, 22,* 351–367.

Slavin, R., Leavy, M., & Madden, N. (1984). Combining cooperative learning and individualized instruction: Effects of students mathematics achievement, attitudes, and behaviors. *Elementary School Journal, 84,* 409–422.

Sowell, E. (1989, November). Effects of manipulative materials in mathematics instruction. *Journal for Research in Mathematics Education,* 501.

Vause, L. (2004). Ontario's early math strategy. In C. Greenes & J. Tsankova (Eds.), *Challenging young people mathematically.* Golden, CO: National Council of Supervisors of Mathematics.

Wagner, L., Roy, F. C., Ecatoin, E., & Rousseau, C. (2000). Culturally relevant mathematics teaching at the secondary school level: Problematic features and a model for implementation. In M. Strutchens, M. L. Johnson, and W. F. Tate (Eds.), *Changing the faces of mathematics: Perspectives on African Americans.* Reston, VA: NCTM.

Webb, R. (1985). Student interaction and learning in small groups. In R. Slavin et al. (Eds.), *Learning to cooperate, cooperating to learn.* New York: Putnam.

Consecutive Sums

OBJECTIVES

- Experience work in cooperative groups
- Play role as defined on task card
- Experience the multiple abilities as individuals and as a group

MATERIALS

- One task card
- Recording sheets
- Summary transparency

ROLES

Facilitator: Make sure that group reads this entire card all the way through before beginning the task. *Who wants to read? Does everyone understand what to do?* Make sure everyone's ideas are heard. *Did anyone see it a different way?*

Records/Reporter: Your group needs to summarize any patterns discovered on the transparency. Were any patterns helpful in finding certain values? If the group has remaining questions, please record these as well.

Resource Manager: Get materials for your team. You may call the teacher over to your group when your group has a question. Remember, the question must be one held by every member of the group before the teacher responds. Inform group as to the amount of time remaining.

Team Captain: Remind your team to use patterns to help find new patterns. Search for connections. If there is a conflict, facilitate the discussion so that the conflict is resolved. Resolution is found through consensus, not a vote. Take on role of any missing member in the group.

PROBLEM STATEMENT

Using the sum of consecutive whole numbers, represent the values from 1 to 40. You may use as many consecutive numbers as you want for any value. You may not repeat a number within any value's representation.

Your team needs to present their findings on a transparency. The findings include:

- Strategies used
- Patterns found
- Any remaining questions

From Johnson & Norris, *Teaching Today's Mathematics in the Middle Grades.* Copyright © 2006 Allyn and Bacon, Pearson Education, Inc.

chapter four

Assessment: Balanced and Varied

Assessments play integral roles in the learning and teaching of mathematics. Assessments measure the progress of individual students, particular student groups, and the effectiveness of the curriculum. Formative assessments, including observations, interviews, journal entries, homework, class exercises, and tests and quizzes, inform teachers about students' understandings in that moment. These assessments provide information to help teachers plan lessons and implement appropriate strategies. Summative assessments such as unit tests, gradewide examinations, projects and presentations, and high-stakes tests lead to comparisons between students' performances or district and statewide rankings or comparisons among nations. In the last twenty years, assessment has taken a higher place on the national agenda, and assessment has raised the level of accountability in the classroom.

In this chapter, we look at the six standards for assessment in mathematics as presented by NCTM. We also present an overview of the goals for assessment. We discuss both formative and summative assessment strategies and look at evaluating these assessments using rubrics. We also address grading issues in this chapter. We discuss the high-stakes assessments used in many states and current national tests and international tests, NAEP and TIMSS.

> ### Did You **Know**?
>
> Eduventures, Inc., reports that the K–12 assessment market, representing a $2 billion industry, will grow at a rate of 9% annually. This market includes test materials and services supporting preparation.

NCTM Standards

The *Assessment Standards for School Mathematics* (NCTM, 1995) presents six standards for mathematics assessment:

1. Reflect the mathematics that students need to know and be able to do
2. Enhance mathematics learning
3. Promote equity
4. Be an open process
5. Promote valid inference
6. Be a coherent process

These six standards provide guidelines for evaluating the effectiveness of mathematics assessments as well as assessment programs. Considering the wide range of assessments both formative and summative, all assessment tools should present the meaningful mathematics that students should know and be able to use. Assessments should also reflect the context and vision presented in the NCTM *Principles and Standards for School Mathematics*. Because students are actively involved in opportunities to explore, analyze, and reason mathematically, assessments should promote those activities as well. Procedural skills should be tested in context as they are used to solve problems. Some teachers feel that they can either teach procedural skills or work on conceptual understanding. In *Making*

Point Well Taken

"Although assessment is done for a variety of reasons, its main goal is to advance students' learning and inform teachers as they make instructional decisions."

—*NCTM, 1995, p. 13*

Point Well Taken

"Every student has the right to reflect on, and communicate about, mathematics. Understanding is not just the privilege of the high-achieving group."

—*Hiebert et al., 1997, p. 11*

Sense, Hiebert and colleagues state that conceptual understanding and procedural skills should not be taught as separate entities, but rather these develop concurrently (Hiebert, 1997, p. 6). We agree. It is important, therefore, that conceptual understanding and procedural skills are linked in assessment. The second item in the assessment standards calls for increased learning in the assessment process.

Learning takes place during the assessment as students apply their mathematical tools in new situations. The process of weaving their understandings together and applying the knowledge in new ways continues to build students' competencies. Students are learning what is valued through the assessment process. Teachers are also learning throughout the assessment process as they use the information in lesson planning.

RESEARCH

Researchers Burkhardt, Fraser, and Ridgeway (1990) discuss the "WYTIWYG phenomenon—what you test is what you get." They found that testing can have a positive or negative effect on instruction. Tests emphasizing problem solving and applications encourage teachers to use and value these activities. Tests with multiple-choice questions that focus only on basic skills influence instruction to remain at that same basic level.

The third assessment standard promotes equity. Every student has a right to a meaningful mathematics program. A meaningful program includes assessment that focuses on each student's learning. By doing so, expectations for all students are raised to a higher level. In order for the assessment to be equitable, the special needs of students must be addressed. "Assessment is equitable when students with special needs or talents have access to the same accommodations they receive in instruction" (NCTM, 1995, p. 15).

The fourth assessment standard calls for an open process. All students have the right to know what they are expected to know and demonstrate on a particular assessment. They also should know the consequences of the outcomes of the assessment. Students should understand the impact of a successful performance as well as the consequences of a poor performance. Openness also improves communication with the community including parents, policy makers, business partners, and other concerned individuals. High-stakes tests such as those used in most states as a high school graduation requirement have significant influence in the community. For example, school performance on such tests impacts real estate values significantly. Another aspect of the need for openness in the assessment process includes involving teachers in the construction and evaluation of the assessment tools.

The fifth standard states the case for the promotion of valid inferences about mathematics learning. A valid inference "is a conclusion about a student's cognitive processes that cannot be observed directly. The conclusion has to be based on a student's performance" (NCTM, 1995, p. 19). Valid inferences rely on more than one assessment tool. The better the quality of the evidence, the more reliable the inferences are likely to be. Using both formative and summative assessments addresses the needs of diverse learners and supports and broadens the teacher's understanding of students' current development of mathematical concepts. Teachers need to look for balance between formative and summative assessments as they select the assessment strategies in the course of a unit or grading period.

The sixth standard states the importance of a coherent process. This standard includes three areas: coherence as a whole process, coherence in terms of the purpose, and alignment with curriculum and instruction. All of the components of an assessment program must fit together to form a cohesive whole; all of the components must meet the purpose of the program; and the assessment instruments must be aligned with curriculum and instruction. An assessment program includes a variety of instrument tools, including summative assessments developed outside of the school or district such as the high-stakes tests.

Testing must reflect what is valued in terms of meaningful mathematics. As stated earlier, if multiple-choice tests are used exclusively, the accompanying instruction will encourage students to value short, one-correct-answer problems without having to document their thinking. Effective assessment programs meet the criteria stated earlier and are considered balanced.

Goals of Assessment

As illustrated in Figure 4.1, the purposes of assessment vary. NCTM summarizes these goals in four categories seen in the ellipse and the corresponding actions in the rectangles in the diagram.

Monitoring student progress is one of the goals of an assessment program and it is a continuous process that provides feedback to the student and teacher alike. Students can also take an active role in reflecting on their own progress. Teachers use information on student progress to plan future lessons. Thus, making instructional decisions is a second goal for assessment. As they evaluate student work and observe students as they share ideas in small groups, teachers gain insights about students' understandings and their misconceptions. This information then helps teachers tailor lesson plans and improve instruction for students. The third goal of assessment involves evaluating student achievement. This is accomplished by examining a variety of evidence illustrating whether or not a particular student has met the expectations. The reporting procedure varies from school to school. The more specific details that are included in the reports, the more beneficial they can be for the learners. Taking the time to value student achievement is an important piece of an assessment program. The fourth goal of assessment includes evaluating the instructional program. Whether or not the current program is delivering a quality mathematics curriculum for all students needs to be determined. The result of this assessment leads to modification in the program (NCTM, 1995, pp. 25–26). Formative and summative assessment strategies work toward delivering the goals of assessment and can be evaluated in terms of the six standards referred to earlier in the chapter.

figure **4.1**

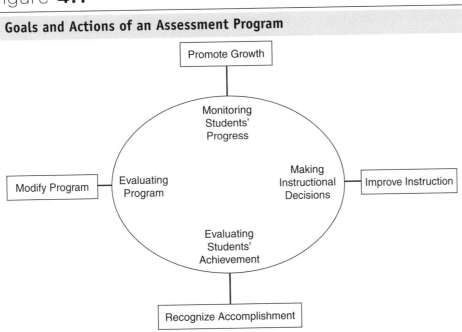

Goals and Actions of an Assessment Program

Source: Reprinted with permission from *Assessment Standards for School Mathematics,* copyright 1995, by the National Council of Teachers of Mathematics. All rights reserved.

Point Well Taken

"Formative assessment in the classroom, which depends on teachers' gathering evidence from multiple sources and then acting on that evidence, can be one of the most powerful forces for learning. Listening to students, asking them good questions, and giving them the opportunity to show what they know in a variety of ways are all affirmed by research to be important ways to increase student learning."

—*Wilson & Kenney, 2003, p. 64*

figure **4.2**

Formative Assessments

- Journal
- Challenge Problems
- Notebook
- Observations
- Interviews
- Homework and Classwork
- Do Nows

Formative Assessments

Formative assessments occur daily. These assessments can be informal in design, such as observing students as they collaborate, or they can be more formal such as a quiz or test. The formative assessments take on a diagnostic role in that they provide information about the current thinking of the students. These assessments can continue throughout the year and function as quick snapshots of students' understanding at that time. See Figure 4.2 for a list of formative assessments.

Journals

Students' journal responses can be extremely informative as well as influential in their learning process. Journal entries can serve as a tool to understand prior knowledge about a particular concept. Consider, "write down everything you know about $\frac{3}{5}$." Students may discuss vocabulary associated with fractions; they may relate the fraction to a concrete situation, or they may discuss the various meanings of fractions such as rates or parts of a whole. (See Chapter 6, Making Sense of Number and Operations, for more details on work with rational numbers.) Journal entries can be shared as a way to activate a discussion, or they can be collected and then returned to the student after the teacher writes a quick response. Students value and anticipate a teacher's response to their writing. The teacher models the importance of writing by responding to students' entries in writing. The information gained as a result of such a quick prompt can help the teacher understand individual needs as well as when the class should begin a particular unit and what topic should be first introduced. Journal entries can also be used to summarize a particular lesson or concept. Examples of prompts as summarizers are provided in Figure 4.3.

TRY THIS

Select either of the last two bullets in Figure 4.3 and write a response as if it were a journal entry.

Journals give students the opportunity to provide feedback about how the class is working for them. Prompts can address such issues as length of assignments, pacing of tests, and students' feelings regarding their own level of success in the class. Journals can provide a window into a student's thinking and feelings.

MISCONCEPTION

When students demonstrate a particular computational skill, teachers may think that the students actually understand the mathematics involved. This may not always be the case. In an article in the *1993 NCTM Yearbook* entitled "Just Because They Got

figure **4.3**

Writing Prompts as Summarizers

- Discuss what happened in today's lesson. Be as specific as you can.
- As a result of today's activity, what did you understand?
- What was the most difficult problem on last night's homework? Why was it more difficult than others?
- Explain the process used to make equivalent fractions. Be sure to include examples and explain why the fractions are equivalent.
- Explain the difference between an altitude and a median in a triangle.

It Right, Does It Mean They Know It?," Susan Gay and Margaret Thomas cite many examples in which students obtained correct answers. When questioned orally, students revealed their misconceptions and faulty logic. Teachers need to provide many opportunities for students to explain their thinking both orally and in writing.

Frequency of assignments involving journals requires pacing. A teacher can become overwhelmed by trying to respond to all the students' journals at once. Some teachers collect a representative sample of journals from a class making sure to record whose journals have been read. Some teachers use large note cards for students to use as their journals. Each card contains one entry. Students can write a second entry on a new note card even if the teacher has not returned the first entry at that point. Responding quickly to students' entries is important in terms of the communication established with students and the impact of the writing for student learning. These cards can be placed in a card file with each student having his or her own section. These entries can help to document each student's progress over time. Journals provide an ongoing opportunity for students to be reflective and work to develop their writing and communication skills.

Challenges of the Week

Challenges of the Week, another formative assessment tool, provide an opportunity for students to apply what they know to situations that they have not seen before. The time needed to solve these problems tends to be longer than any class period, and it is beneficial for students to work together at least in the initial stages of the problem-solving process. Problems selected by teachers usually reflect the current unit of study. (See Chapter 5 for more details on the problem-solving process.) Students benefit from participating in discussions about the problem. They can share their assumptions about the problem and they can suggest strategies that might be used to solve the problem. Students might even work together as they implement their strategy. Each student should submit his or her own solution including each step of the problem-solving process.

TRY THIS

What is the sum of the whole numbers from 1 to 100?

There are many ways that students can approach finding the sum of the numbers from 1 to 100. Some students might attempt to list the numbers and then begin adding. Hopefully, these same students will abandon that strategy and begin investigating more efficient methods. Students reveal their thinking through their choice of strategy and, therefore, provide the teacher with insights about their mathematical development. A student who makes a list and then adds demonstrates perseverance and is thinking at a very concrete level, for example. By having opportunities to explore the problem in small groups, students can share their thinking and try several approaches. Before teachers present the first Challenge of the Week, students need to understand the format required for the solution and how the solutions will be graded. Teachers find that rubrics serve as a tool to help communicate and clarify expectations for a given task. Rubrics tend to fall into two types, analytic and holistic.

Analytic Rubric

An analytic rubric assigns points to the phases involved in the task and provides descriptions of the points assigned. Analytic rubrics focus students' attention on the requirements of a successful completion with clear criteria on which to judge their own work. (See Figure 4.4.) Clarifying with students the expectations for the task before they actually engage in the task enables students to do their best work. Students can critique their performance in terms of the rubric and make modifications as necessary. Editing their

figure **4.4**

Analytic Rubric	
PROBLEM-SOLVING STEP	**POINTS**
Get Started	2: Read problem carefully, defined vocabulary, and restated the question in own words. Include an estimate. 1: Restatement of question missed some aspect or information or the statement did not match the question. May include estimate. 0: No restatement of the question or estimate.
Make a Plan	2: Plan clearly stated and could lead to correct answer if implemented. 1: Plan has slight design flaw. 0: Faulty plan that will not lead to correct answer.
Take Action	2: Implemented plan and correctly used the necessary tools to lead to an appropriate response. 1: Implemented plan but errors made in the process. 0: No action taken.
Reflect	2: Demonstrates the use of reflection by going back and checking to ensure that the question is answered. Compares answer to estimate for appropriateness. This might include a statement making a connection between this problem and others completed earlier. 1: Checks answer for accuracy but neglects one of the components stated above. 0: No reflection demonstrated.

work in terms of the rubric places the evaluative role in the students' hands and thereby increases the likelihood that the students become invested in the process. Another type of rubric is referred to as holistic.

Holistic Rubric

A holistic rubric presents one overall score for the task rather than scoring the component parts as seen in the analytic rubric. See Figure 4.5 for an example of a holistic rubric.

Holistic rubrics provide one score, are relatively quick to use, and provide a framework on which to base the evaluation of student work. Holistic rubrics can be used when there are a large number of papers or there are several scorers as in a gradewide assessment. Both analytic and holistic rubrics can be made more specific in terms of the task to be evaluated.

A site that assists teachers in creating rubrics is http://rubistar.4teachers.org.

AUTHOR'S **Recall**

I remember referring to Challenges of the Week as Problems of the Week. The students quickly began calling these longer problems POWs. After one faculty meeting, an administrator pulled me aside to say that he had received a complaint from a parent about referring to a math task as "POW."

ASSESSMENT TIP

Many teachers have invited their class to participate in the development of the rubric after the students have had plenty of opportunities to work with them. Students gain a clear understanding of the requirements as they work to develop the rubric.

Many of the problems detailed in Chapter 5, Problem Solving: An Approach to Teaching and Learning Mathematics, can be used as Challenges of the Week. Challenges of the Week provide information about the mathematical tools that students use in their solu-

figure **4.5**

Holistic Rubric

Excellent Response: *(6 points)*

The response is complete and includes a clear and accurate explanation of the techniques used to solve the problem. It includes accurate diagrams (as appropriate), identifies important information, and shows full understanding of the mathematical concepts and processes, often showing multiple representations of the solution. The response also includes possible connections to other topics or problems solved previously.

Competent Response: *(5 points)*

The response is fairly complete and includes reasonable explanation of ideas and processes used. Supportive evidence of conclusion is presented, but some aspect may not be clearly or completely explained.

Satisfactory with Some Errors: *(4 points)*

The problem is completed satisfactorily as the correct answer is stated. Explanation lacks detail or supporting evidence. Student appears to understand the concepts but diagram and/or description is not clear.

Nearly Satisfactory but Has Serious Errors: *(3 points)*

The response is not complete. The solution contains errors and the explanation may be flawed.

Begins Problem: *(2 points)*

Response is started but does not reach a conclusion. There is little evidence of understanding. Explanation is faulty or not clear.

Fails to Begin Problem: *(1 point)*

Parts of the problem may have been copied but steps toward a solution are not evident.

No Attempt: *(0 points)*

No paper submitted.

tion. These insights can help teachers select appropriate problems and plan lessons according to students' needs.

Notebooks

Notebooks serve to organize students' work. Notebooks usually include class work, notes taken as examples, vocabulary, and homework. Sections are created in the notebook identifying each of these categories. Middle school students should learn how to take appropriate notes and time should be dedicated to this important preparation for high school. Notes should include an example with explanations of the steps included. Using a T-chart design can help organize the note-taking process. (See Figure 4.6.)

In accordance with the adage that students value what is graded, teachers need to grade notebooks. Organization and comprehensiveness are critical factors to be considered. See Figure 4.7 for an analytic rubric that can be used for the evaluation of notebooks.

Observations

Observations are quick, noteworthy statements about a student's understanding on a particular concept. Observations may also include documenting class behavior or contributions in class. Teachers make these observations repeatedly throughout the day; the challenge lies in developing a system to record the observations.

Some teachers use large Post-it Notes. As an observation is made, they quickly jot a note on the pad including the student's name or initials and a brief note to help them

figure **4.6**

Taking Notes

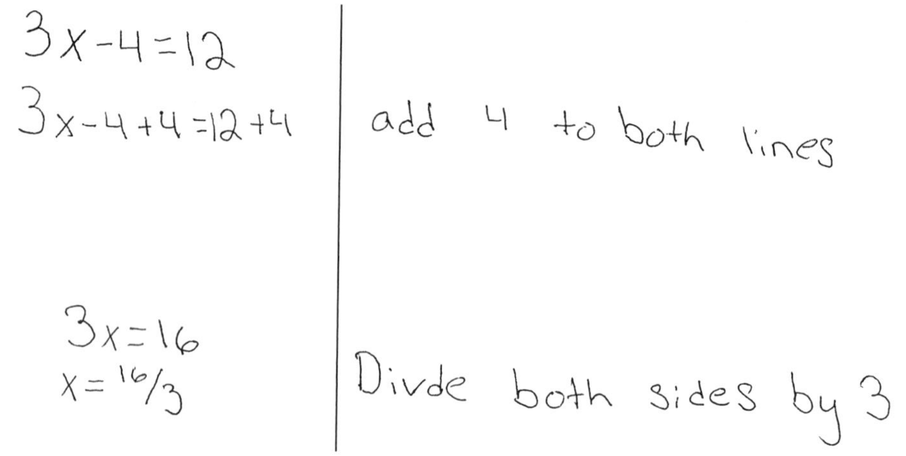

$$3x - 4 = 12$$
$$3x - 4 + 4 = 12 + 4 \qquad \text{add } 4 \text{ to both lines}$$

$$3x = 16$$
$$x = {}^{16}\!/_{3} \qquad \text{Divde both sides by 3}$$

figure **4.7**

Analytic Rubric for Notebooks	
Contents	2: Papers placed in proper sections; notes and Do Nows complete; all tests included.
	1: Some papers may be missing or in wrong section.
	0: Papers misplaced; entire section(s) missing.
Organization	2: All required sections clearly labeled.
	1: Some sections missing.
	0: No attempt made to have sections.

remember the observation. At the end of the day, all of these Post-it Notes are placed in a notebook containing one page for every student. Next to the note, the teacher writes several descriptive phrases about the observation. As the grading period progresses, teachers refer to the notebook to identify any students who have not been observed as frequently as others. Another system to record observations uses note cards on a clipboard. A series of cards with each student's name is taped onto a clipboard. As the teacher makes an observation, a note is taken on the appropriate card.

Teachers have also developed matrices with students' names across the top and mathematical concepts, skills, and/or cooperative processes along the side. Such a matrix helps teachers track students' demonstrated achievements in the moment that they occur. These checklists can also document students' growth over a period of time. (See Figure 4.8.) The matrix can also be changed to fit the particular task and skills to be featured. Teachers should inform students about the skills that will be noted in the chart before work begins. Such information helps students remain focused on the skills that the teacher values. Teachers can then summarize the activity by publicly acknowledging those students who demonstrated the skills.

These informal observations help teachers make decisions as to specific questions to include in the next lesson for an individual student as well as provide insights about future investigations and lesson plans. These continuing formative assessments impact the teacher's awareness of students' understandings and, therefore, improve student learning.

figure **4.8**

Checklist of Skills

Date: _____

Names:

	Juanita	Billy	Erna	Chelsea	Sheilah	Matthew	Carlo
Identified patterns							
Extended pattern							
Made connections to exponents							
Calculated accurately							
Asked clarifying questions							
Played role in group effectively							
Helped group stay on task							

RESEARCH

Research indicates that making assessment an integral part of classroom practice is associated with improved student learning. Black and William (1998) reviewed 250 research studies and concluded that the learning of students, including low achievers, is generally enhanced in classrooms where teachers include attention to formative assessment in making judgments about learning and teaching (NCTM, 2000, p. 22).

Interviews

Interviews offer opportunities to talk with students individually. Teachers can probe into the student's thinking to gain insights as to that student's current understanding. Interviews can be carefully planned and structured or they can be informal conversations with students to gain an understanding of the student's thinking on a particular task. Interviews are particularly beneficial for students who are struggling. Teachers can identify misconceptions and then work with the student to challenge his or her thinking. Misconceptions are usually ingrained so that a student may need many experiences confronting the misunderstanding before it is replaced with a correct concept. Interviews are also beneficial for students who may have difficulty with language. These students can show what they know by using concrete objects or drawings. With a teacher at their side, students can convey what they know through the interactions with the teacher and in response to carefully posed questions. Throughout the interview process, the teacher should avoid taking notes as this action can be distracting to the student. After the interview is completed, however, the teacher should document any insights. As with all assessments, students should understand prior to the interview what the purpose is and such details about how long it will last. Interviews are time consuming, but those teachers using interviews as a formative assessment testify to their value.

Teachers have found a variety of ways to implement interviews. One way is to plan to interview each student over the course of a term. The conversation can take place while the rest of the class is engaged in individual tasks or small-group work. Teachers frame the interview based on a recent problem and use similar questions designed to gain insights into the student's understanding of the mathematics involved in the problem. A second way to implement interviews is to speak with a team of students at once. Questions

Point Well Taken

"Advantages of using interviews include the opportunity to delve deeply into students' thinking and reasoning, to better determine their level of understanding, to diagnose misconceptions and missing connections, and to assess verbal ability to communicate mathematical knowledge."

—*Huinker, 1993, p. 80*

in this case can also include techniques that the students used in working as a group as well as their understanding of the mathematics involved in the task. Interviews can also be incorporated as a part of the portfolio process. As students select items to be included in the portfolio, teachers can ask them to explain their rationale for selecting each piece. (See Summative Assessments in this chapter for more details on portfolios.)

Homework and Classwork

Homework and classwork can also serve as formative assessments. Solutions shared by students frequently offer insights as to their thinking. As students demonstrate their solutions with the class, they explain their thinking. Students as well as the teacher can ask questions, often probing deeper in order to highlight the concepts involved. Time spent on homework problems can vary greatly depending on the objectives for the day's lesson and the questions that students raise.

There is a variety of ways to go over homework without spending the entire class period doing so. Some teachers demonstrate a particular problem on the board when more than one student had difficulty on that task. If only one student had trouble on the problem, then the teacher asks to talk with the student separately or asks for a volunteer to help that student. Unfortunately, this method highlights the fact that only one student did not know how to do the problem. The student may be embarrassed and decide not to ask questions about the homework in the future. Some teachers take advantage of small groups to go over the homework. (See Chapter 3 for a thorough discussion of cooperative groups.) When students understand group roles and guidelines for working in groups, they support each other in a positive atmosphere. Students understand that giving help does not mean doing the problem for another student, but rather help means guiding that student's thinking. Students also understand that they have a right to ask for and receive help as needed, and they have an obligation to give help when asked. As students go over homework problems in their groups, a teacher works with the group only when the *entire* group has a question. A third way to address questions on the homework requires that students write down the problems that they had difficulty with as they enter the class. Some teachers have a transparency ready with the problem numbers and students put their initials by the problem number. Others ask for students to write the problem number in a particular area on the board. Seeing the variety and number of questions as the class begins allows the teacher to make a decision as to how to proceed. If there are very few questions, the teacher can decide to address them at the end of class or go over those particular problems immediately. If there are many questions on a wide variety of the problems, the teacher may decide to change the lesson plan entirely for the day. Homework as a formative assessment quickly informs the teacher as to the success of the previous lessons.

Do Nows

Do Nows, sometimes called Fast Fives, serve as a set of short problems that students solve at the very beginning of the class. These problems are usually skill based involving a review of past concepts, a check on yesterday's lesson, or a preview of upcoming work. Do Nows also function as techniques to get students into their seats with pencil and paper ready to work. Students also need to understand the purpose of these problems.

All of these formative assessments are continuous and provide regular feedback to teachers about what the students understand, the impact of the lesson, and useful information to be used for future lessons. A second type of assessment, summative assessment, is used to put closure on a unit of study and document students' understanding.

Summative Assessments

Summative assessments, such as portfolios, unit tests, and performance assessments, document progress and growth.

Portfolios

Portfolios can serve as tools to help students reflect about their term's work and provide showcases for best work or improved work. Portfolios are especially effective in showing progress over time and can also serve as a vehicle promoting communication between home and school.

In order to prepare for the portfolio, a filing system needs to be created for the students' work. Ideally, the students' folders should be kept in a place that is easily accessible and visible within the classroom, serving as a constant reminder of the portfolio's importance. As students complete work such as a homework assignment, a group report, or a challenge problem, they can store the work in the folders. Toward the end of the term, students can review all of the work and select appropriate pieces for their portfolios. Teachers help students in the selection process ensuring balance in terms of the type of work selected. Teachers can restrict the number of tests to be included, for example. Most portfolios contain six to eight pieces of work representing the activities occurring in class. See Figure 4.9 for a list of entries in one teacher's class.

Some teachers ask students to select a theme for their portfolio. As they review the term's work, students look for characteristics in their work to address in their portfolio. For example, a sixth grader's theme was "When I study, I do better," and another student selected "Improvement" as her theme. Conducting individual interviews as the class is engaged in reviewing their folders can help students select the theme, the work supporting the theme, and ensure that the portfolios include the required types of work as seen in Figure 4.9. Such conversations can also provide insights as to the student's understanding of the recent concepts covered and attitude toward mathematics and present opportunities for the teacher to value the student's strengths. Teachers complimenting students in these individual conversations motivate students to continue building on that strength. Students are more likely to try to improve other areas that may have been discussed as well. After collecting the pieces, students write a paragraph about the selection including reasons why the work was selected for the portfolio and why it reflects the chosen theme. Most portfolios include a cover letter focusing the reader's attention on the theme and the pieces selected. This letter also presents specific goals for the coming term. A third component of the portfolio includes students presenting their completed portfolio to their parent or guardian. By presenting their portfolio, students have another opportunity to communicate their understanding of the concepts covered throughout the term. This presentation also gives the parent an opportunity to see the student's work and the range of activities experienced. Parents then may respond to a series of questions that can be answered in terms of "yes" or "no." (See Figure 4.10.) Parents also have a chance to communicate with the teacher about the portfolio at the end of the response form.

Portfolios may used in several ways. Some teachers have students work on their portfolios on a regular basis throughout the year; these teachers refer to the work as "process-folios." As students reflect on their entries, they remove ones that no longer illustrate their theme such as "My Best Work," for example. Process-folios are consistently reviewed and updated and, as a continuous task, are considered to be formative assessments. Portfolios may be assigned at the end of the term to summarize the work to date and establish goals for the coming term. Both informative and summative forms of the portfolio provide students with opportunities to reflect on their work and assess their own progress.

Unit Tests

Unit tests provide opportunities for students to demonstrate what they know. These tests can be designed by the teacher or be supplied by the publisher. Teacher-designed tests are beneficial as they are tailored to the instruction and should reflect the particular

figure **4.9**

Selections for the Portfolio

You may choose to include the following:

1 Test

2 Challenges of the Week

1 Group project

2 Journal entries

1 Teacher selection

figure **4.10**

Parents' Questionnaire for Portfolio

Parents: Thank you for your participation in your child's portfolio presentation. Please respond to the questions below in terms of "yes" or "no." Your child will earn 1 point for each "yes" response. There is room for any comments that you wish to make at the bottom of the page. Thanks again for your participation.

Did your child . . .

1. State the purpose of the portfolio?   _____

2. Describe each entry?   _____

3. Explain why each entry is included?   _____

4. State goals for the coming term?   _____

5. Answer any questions that you had?   _____

Comments: _____

_____

_____

emphasis placed during the lessons. Textbook publishers also provide electronic databases from which teachers can select problems to create their own tests.

Unit tests are intended as evaluative tools to answer the question: How well have the students mastered the material? Tests can also be diagnostic in terms of an individual student's weaknesses and strengths. Test results can play a significant role in planning future lessons. If many students in the class missed a particular question on the test, a teacher needs to investigate to find the reasons for their errors. Was the question poorly written? Did the teacher devote enough time to the particular topic? The answers to these questions help direct future lessons. Creating tests can be challenging, especially for new teachers.

On the Lighter Side

Feedback can sometimes be harsh.

Peanuts copyright © by Charles Schultz. Reprinted by permission of United Feature Syndicate, Inc.

Creating Tests

Writing appropriate test questions can be a daunting task. Teachers should take advantage of the resources around them beginning with their colleagues! Asking for feedback about a particular question or an entire test can help both parties involved—the teacher asking the question and the teacher providing support. Both individuals benefit from the exchange of ideas. It is important to build those supportive collegial relationships. In designing tests, teachers can also use questions provided by the textbook publisher. Most programs provide quizzes and unit tests; publishers also provide enrichment as well as review questions. These can also be used to build test questions.

When constructing a test, many teachers prefer to begin the test with a straightforward skill. For example, a unit test on fractions might begin with finding equivalent fractions. Beginning with a skill that the teacher is relatively confident that all students understand can help the students build confidence as they proceed. Some questions on every test should be open-ended. (See Figure 4.11.)

This first question in Figure 4.11 promotes students' thinking beyond a procedure. It requires that the student understands the vocabulary and draws conclusions based on the information. A problem is considered to be open-ended if it can be approached using a variety of strategies. A closed problem limits the solution method and usually requires that the student select the answer rather than generate one. Some educators make a distinction between open response questions and open-ended questions. An open response question calls on the student to find the solution. An open-ended question is more complicated than an open response question in that it involves several criteria that need to be met. Both open and closed questions have a place in a test, depending on the objective to be assessed and the anticipated information to be gained. Effective test questions place the concept in a context. Consider the following two questions:

1. Maurice wants to build a fence for his puppy. He has already purchased 36 yards of fencing, and he wants the biggest possible area for his puppy to run around in. What should the length and the width of the fencing be in order to have the largest area?
2. Find the area and perimeter of a square whose sides measure 9 yards.

TRY THIS

These two problems involving the area and perimeter can be characterized as either an open response question or an open-ended question. Which problem is an example of an open response question? Explain your answer.

Although these two questions focus on the same skills, the first one establishes a context. Even if the student did not remember the difference between area and perimeter, he or she might be able to determine what the problem is asking through the given context.

figure **4.11**

Example of Open and Closed Questions

Open-ended question:

A friend asks you to play "Guess my number." Your friend says that when his number is divided into 100, the quotient is between 1 and 2 and is a repeating decimal.

Write three statements that must be true about your friend's number. Explain your reasoning.

Closed question:

Divide 100 by 17. Round your answer to the nearest tenth.

a. 5.8   b. 6.0   c. 6.1   d. 5.9

The second problem, although straightforward, does not offer contextual support. The first question challenges the student to determine the rectangle that contains the largest area given a fixed perimeter of 36 feet. The second question is simply a matter of recalling formulas and computing an answer. This second question is an example of an open response question. Another guideline in creating tests involves the length of the test.

Length of Test

One way that teachers judge how long students will take on a particular test is to time themselves taking the test. Teachers need to write down the steps that they expect their students to show as they take the test. By multiplying their time by a factor of 4 or 5, teachers will have an estimate of how long their students might take to complete the test. By taking the test, teachers also gain an answer key and an understanding of exactly what each question requires. Teachers are also likely to find any typographical errors as they take the test. One last consideration for designing tests involves answer columns.

Recording Answers

Many publishers provide answer columns for students to write their answers in on tests. This practice adds an additional step for the student although it seemingly makes the job of correcting the tests easier. Using an answer key raises some serious issues. Students can easily make an error copying their answer into the column. The message sent to students by including the answer column is that the teacher values only an answer. Students think that the work leading to the answer is not important. For multiple-choice tests, an answer column or "fill in the bubble" style answer sheet makes sense as it provides practice for many of the standardized tests. For routine tests within classrooms, we strongly advise encouraging students to present their work leading to the answer rather than using an answer column that separates the work from the answer.

Grading

Some teachers view grading as a necessary evil in classrooms that cannot be avoided. In *The Skillful Teacher*, Jon Saphier and Robert Gower recommend a system of "A, B and not yet" (Saphier & Gower, 1997, p. 321). Such a system recognizes accomplishments in achieving certain standards and yet does not demoralize those who have yet to reach these standards. Inherent in such a grading system is the implied belief that all students will reach the standard. Teachers have little influence regarding the system used in their building, but having a clear philosophy about grading that is articulated to the students in the beginning of the year is important.

In order to make grading consistent and fair, teachers need to make some decisions about their grading policies. They should consider the following:

- Will you use partial credit?
- If a student makes a computational error somewhere along the line, will that work earn some credit?
- How will points be assigned?
- Typically, teachers assign more points to the more difficult problems. If partial credit is not given, do the hard problems influence the final grade too heavily?
- Will the lowest test performance be dropped at the end of the term?
- Will you provide makeup tests for those students who perform badly on the first test?

TRY THIS

Respond to each of the questions in the bullets. Provide reasons for your answers.

Every teacher needs to address these questions and decide what is correct for him or her and right for the students. We offer a few suggestions.

Partial credit values students' thinking and documentation of their work. Partial credit also balances out the impact of the more difficult questions. If students can begin a difficult problem, they can earn some credit. Whether or not a teacher decides to drop the lowest test performance depends on how many tests have been taken during that grading period and how many other grades are contributing to the term grade. Dropping a low test from the average tends to help every student's average but should not be stated as a policy in the beginning of the term because students will think that they have one "throw-away" test. Therefore, they do not prepare well for all of them. By delaying the decision whether or not to drop the lowest test, the teacher can factor in unforeseen circumstances. Providing makeup tests for those who did not find success the first time tends to encourage many students to make a minimal effort until after the first test. Teachers offering regular second chances end up doing most of the work! Students do not have to try until after they see how they did on the first test. Of course, there are always individual exceptions to any evaluation system. Having a philosophy in place supports the teacher in making decisions while remembering to remain flexible based on the individual circumstances. There are also different ways to structure quizzes or tests.

Team Quizzes

Teachers can consider having students take quizzes or tests in small groups. The process can vary, but initially each student completes the test independently. The teacher may collect these tests to get an overview of students' initial performance. Teachers can also create a chart identifying problems missed by each student to document changes later. At this point, the teacher does not write on the tests or give any indication of an error. During the next class period, students work with a partner quietly comparing answers and discussing problems. After a specified period of time, the students change partners and once again compare answers and their solutions. By the end of the third round, most of the students' original errors have been corrected. Students who performed well on the initial opportunity to take the quiz become increasingly more confident as they explain their solutions. Other students engage in the process of correcting, listening to procedures, and asking clarifying questions. After the three rounds, teachers collect the quizzes and grade them for each individual student. When passing back the quizzes, teachers can illustrate the class's improvement in a stem-and-leaf plot or a box-and-whisker plot comparing the initial work to the final quiz submitted by each student. (See Figure 4.12. For more on these graphical representations see Chapter 10, Data Analysis: The Process.) Using students' scores, even to demonstrate improvement, can be controversial. Some students do not want to see where they stand in comparison to their classmates. Showing the grades can make other students more competitive. The box plot stresses the trend of improvement and might be the better choice for some classes. Teachers need to decide what is best for their students.

figure **4.12**

Two Graphs Using the Data from the Before and After Team Quiz

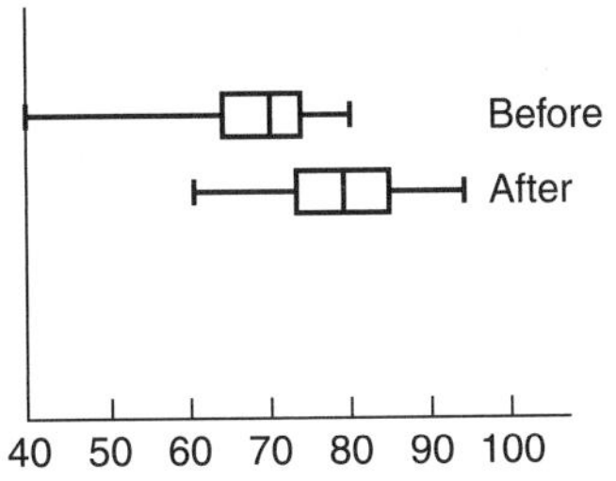

PROCESS STANDARDS

Connections

Using graphs in the context of students' achievement models the appropriate use of the graphs and many students enjoy seeing data about themselves. Students can discuss how the different representations tell the story of the class's progress. Students can also compare the different features of the two graphs.

This team quiz promotes student discussions and helps create a community working together for a common goal. Team quizzes also provide opportunities for students to evaluate their own work. The partners used in team quizzes can be established early. It is best for the students to have selected their potential partners prior to the day of the quiz. Many teachers use some variation of a "dance card." Figure 4.13 shows one tool for finding partners. Students make appointments with each other using the Prime Partners organizer. Students place their names on someone else's sheet and record that person's name on their own sheets. As the teacher states, "find your prime partner number 43," students refer to their sheets to find the name of partner 43. Using the Prime Partner organizer gives students a voice in determining with whom they want to work while providing teachers options to call for certain prime partners based on past experience of which teams work well together. Performance assessment is a third type of summative assessment.

figure **4.13**

Prime Partners

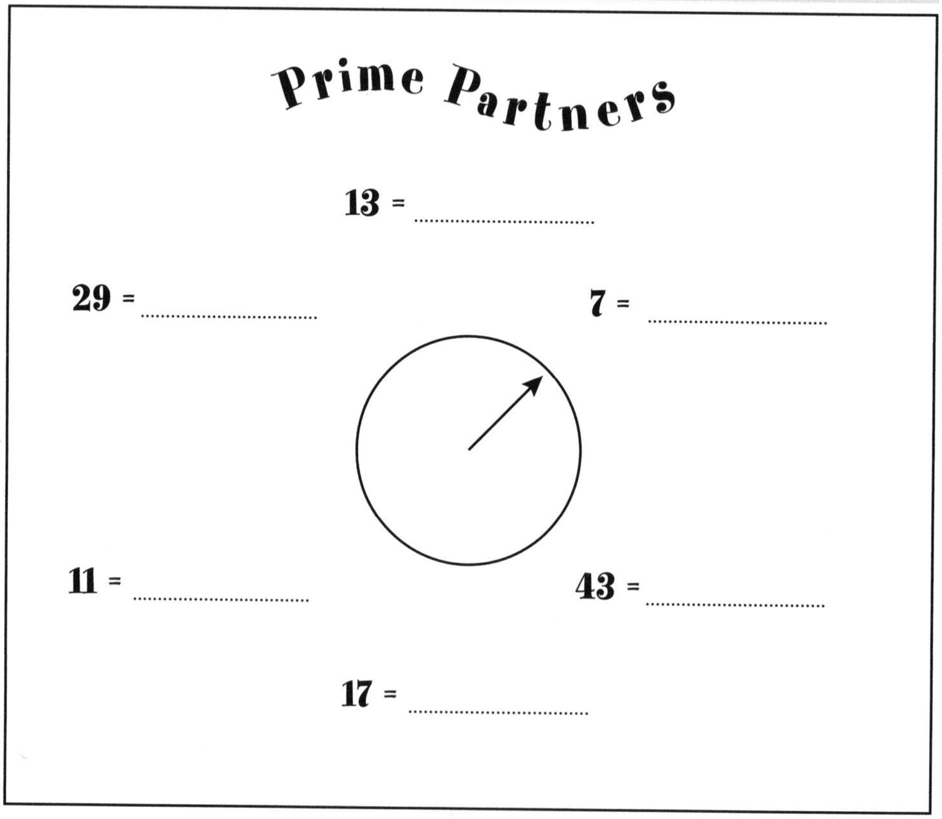

Prime Partners

13 = ...

29 = ...   7 = ...

11 = ...   43 = ...

17 = ...

Performance Assessments

Performance assessments provide students with opportunities to apply what they understand in a realistic setting. In athletics or drama, the performance assessment occurs on game days or opening nights. For an athlete or an actor, all of the work is done in the context of the upcoming performance. Students understand that the drills, conditioning training, rehearsals, voice training, and role modeling have a purpose of enhancing their performance as individuals and as a group. The same objectives should be apparent in mathematics classrooms as well.

Example from a Data Analysis Unit

For example, a teacher is planning a data analysis unit for seventh graders. He must identify those conceptual understandings and skills that he wants his students to know and be able to use as a result of the unit. By identifying these objectives up front, he can share them with his students and use them to monitor the class's progress throughout the unit. The teacher can also create or identify the performance assessment. Suppose that the teacher wants his students to be able to analyze data in terms of a five-point summary (i.e., range, median, mean, and first and third quartiles), use appropriate graphing techniques, and draw conclusions based on the findings. In the beginning of the unit, the performance assessment is described to the students. As the unit proceeds, students can focus on the upcoming assessment asking questions, further defining terms and techniques as necessary. Figure 4.14 shows an example of the performance assessment for this unit. The teacher can refer to this assessment as the unit proceeds. The Nielsen ratings for a particular week can be found in newspapers such as *USA Today*. The teacher needs to

figure **4.14**

Data Analysis: Performance Assessment

Imagine that you are working for a marketing firm. Your client wants to place an advertisement on television. It is your task to decide which network might stimulate the greatest return on your client's investment.

This is your opportunity to demonstrate what you know about data analysis. By using Nielsen Ratings,* apply your data analysis skills to present a case for your decision regarding the selection of a broadcasting company in which your client should invest advertising dollars.

An excellent presentation includes:

Name for your company.

A letter to your client describing the process you used to determine which network will bring the best results.

Statistical evidence demonstrating your conclusion.

Visual displays supporting your conclusion.

Remember, you are trying to convince your client that your decision is correct. Convincing evidence both in terms of the analysis and visual display is crucial to the success of your company's presentation. Neatness and clarity contribute as well.

Companies will be formed on Wednesday, March 10.

Date Due: Wednesday, March 24

*Nielsen Ratings is the system used to determine the number of viewers watching a particular show. Based on the sample of homes throughout the country, the Nielsen Company assigns a rank. The higher the rank, the more popular the show is regarded to be.

clarify further details in terms of a scoring rubric so that students understand the criteria on which they will be graded.

Performance assessments place students in a realistic situation in which they can apply their knowledge. These tasks enable students to integrate their understandings and, thus, they are learning in the process of completing the assessment. Some teachers refer to performance assessments as projects. Although similar, performance assessments are not chosen by the students. Performance assessments also tend to push students toward the integration of knowledge. This is not always the case in projects. With some projects, the mathematics gets lost somewhere along the production process. Teachers need to help students focus on the mathematics in their projects. (See Chapter 5, Problem Solving: An Approach to Teaching and Learning Mathematics, for more on performance assessments.) Another important aspect in performance assessment is that it tends to promote self-assessment.

Self-Assessment

Self-assessment refers to the "process of actively monitoring one's own progress in learning and understanding and of examining one's own mathematical knowledge, processes, and attitudes" (Kenney & Silver, 1993, p. 229). Getting students to evaluate their own work, to judge their own progress, and to use their conclusions to help them plan their next steps are goals that are not easily attained. We offer some strategies to give students guidance in building the important skill of self-assessment.

RESEARCH

There is strong evidence from research that indicates involving students in understanding the objectives and having them evaluate their own progress increases their performance. Given daily opportunities to self-assess significantly improves student achievement (Fernandes & Fontana, 1996).

Rubrics provide guidelines for students as they begin a performance assessment task. The expectations for the task can be clearly defined and specified in a rubric. For that reason, analytic rubrics can be tailored to the particular task. As students use rubrics, they are judging their current work in terms of the expectations as stated in the rubric. They are evaluating whether or not they have included all of the requirements. Students then make plans for the next steps. In some cases, students may be satisfied with their work. In other cases, students might decide to add more details. Self-assessment is reflective as well as a monitoring process.

Error Analysis

Using error analysis can help students begin to experience the benefit of self-assessment. See Figure 4.15 for an example of an error analysis worksheet. Teachers can create a worksheet to match the specific test. Getting students involved in the process of analyzing their mistakes promotes self-assessment and self-adjustment. Because students are required to find strategies to help avoid similar mistakes in the future, they are more likely to embrace those strategies. Self-assessment features self-awareness and self-evaluation. These metacognitive skills are critical life assets. Self-awareness and self-evaluation transcend the realm of mathematics as they are skills that students can employ throughout their lives.

Student-Led Parent Conferences

Another form of summative assessment engages students and parents. Student-led parent conferences are a relatively new idea and combine many features of summative and

figure **4.15**

Error Analysis

Look at each of the errors you made on the test. Decide whether the error involved one or more of these reasons:

   a. Calculation error
   b. Misread the problem
   c. Did not follow directions
   d. Copy error
   e. Did not understand the concept
   f. Did not answer question being asked

Next to the number of the problem, write down the type of error that you think you made.

1. _____
2. _____
3. _____
4. _____
5. _____

From this analysis, what patterns did you notice?

What strategies might help you avoid making these errors in the future?

performance assessments. Students gather evidence of their performance throughout the course of the year or term. They then organize their work according to specific guidelines. Similar to the process of creating a portfolio, students select pieces of their work and then write short paragraphs explaining why those items were selected. Students also establish goals for the coming term. Many teachers provide a checklist of items to be discussed by students as they lead the discussion in the conference. Parents also receive information in the mail regarding what to expect during the conference. Specifically, parents are informed that their child will lead the discussion while showing them pieces of their work. Parents should feel free to ask questions about the work presented, plans that the student has for improvement, and goals for the coming term. The teacher attends each conference solely as a facilitator. The teacher may begin the conference by thanking the parents and students for coming and then briefly present an agenda reflecting the letter that has already been sent to the parents. Many schools offer parents three opportunities throughout the course of the year for conferences. The first and the third conferences are more traditional, as parents speak individually with teachers. The second conference held in the middle of the year is the student-led conference.

As with any form of assessment, student led conferences have advantages and disadvantages. Student-led conferences tend to increase students' involvement in their learning. Students take an active role in the preparation for and participation in the conference. Students are essentially pushed to reflect about their strengths and weaknesses in the learning process. Students take greater ownership in the strategies for improvement as they are integral to the process of creating these plans. For teachers, student-led conferences provide more opportunities to listen to individual students. Teachers help prepare students for the role of leading the discussion with parents. If difficult news needs to be shared, such as missing work, teachers can model in a role-play how the information might be shared. Another advantage of student-led conferences is that schools are finding that they increase parent participation. Parents who participate in the conference can gain a sense of pride and an understanding of how they might help their child at home. Those parents who want individual time with the teacher can schedule another appointment at a different time. A disadvantage for this format occurs when a parent does not attend. Students are disappointed and sometimes embarrassed especially after working hard to prepare for the conference. There are several resources for further information on student-led conferences:

> www.middleweb.com/mw/resources/ParentConfs.html
> www.education-world.com/a_admin/admin112.shtml

Also see the resources in the Teacher Bookcase section at the end of the chapter.

The last category that we will address in terms of assessment involves those instruments that are externally designed and statewide, national, or international in scope. Standardized tests are playing an increased role in educational circles today. These tests not only include student tests but tests for teachers as well.

Standardized Tests

As mentioned earlier in Chapter 1, there is an increased emphasis on standardized testing. Many states now mandate passing a test as a high school graduation requirement. These tests, referred to as high-stakes tests, influence lesson plans at the local level. These high-stakes tests are criterion referenced as they set benchmark levels for students to achieve.

Criterion-Referenced and Norm-Referenced Tests

Criterion-referenced tests do not make comparisons among students. All students' results are compared with levels of proficiency such as "advanced," "proficient," or "needs improvement." Criterion-referenced tests differ from norm-referenced tests. Norm-referenced tests results are based on a population of students, and individual scores are compared to that population or norm group. Norm-referenced tests usually report findings in terms of percentiles. These percentiles can be misleading unless we understand the characteristics of the norm group. For example, if a student scores in the 92nd percentile on an achievement test, what does that say about the student's understanding of mathematics? Suppose the norm group was third graders and the student who scored in the 92nd percentile was in the eighth grade. On the other hand, suppose the norm group was composed of high school seniors. Knowing the composition of the norm group places greater meaning on an individual student's results on norm-referenced tests.

The Dilemma Regarding State Tests

Most of the high-stakes testing programs mandated by individual states are criterion referenced and teachers feel obligated to prepare students for this graduation requirement. Many classrooms focus on the skills of the test for months prior to the testing date. Rather than rely on quality lessons that deliver state guidelines, many teachers focus on multiple-choice tests and questions similar to those on the previous year's test. Many educators have mixed feelings about teaching to the test in this manner. On the positive side, teachers can feel that they have done everything possible to prepare students. On the negative side, the curriculum becomes narrowly focused, and students view mathematics just as a tool to pass the test. "Teach to the test" classrooms tend to focus on computational skills.

Higher-order thinking and problem solving receive minimal attention as a consequence. We recommend approaching high-stakes tests as an integrated component of the curricula rather than taking time to teach to the test as a separate unit.

MATH IN THE MEDIA

On the statewide test in Massachusetts, one student challenged the answer that the Department of Education had posted on its website. Jennifer Mueller persuaded state officials that there was a second interpretation to a problem involving a pattern. Her initiative allowed 449 other students to pass the test. By being able to explain her reasoning, this student challenged the system and won!

All states post released items from their past high-stakes tests. It is helpful to know the material that is on the coming tests and the types of questions the tests include. If a test asks questions about nets of a cube or pyramid, then similar questions can be included in material dealing with spatial sense when it comes up in the course of the normal mathematics curriculum. Similarly, other topics that are included in high-stakes tests can be reviewed as the topics are studied during the year by including actual released problems on tests, worksheets, and class problems. Teachers should identify these problems for students and point out that similar problems may appear on a future high-stakes test. As students successfully solve these problems, their confidence will build and their anxiety will decrease.

Another consideration for high-stakes tests is how students in a school score on portions of the test. If there are parts of the test where students scored poorly, then these topics could be compared to the grade-level curriculum to determine if the topics are included. If the students' test scores show gaps in their mathematical knowledge that are not part of the school curriculum, then teachers may decide to review and readjust the mathematics curriculum at each grade level.

Teachers themselves should solve each of the released problems. Doing so will not only familiarize teachers with the specific content on the test but will also help them to fully understand the mathematics needed to respond to the test questions. Many times the problems on high-stakes tests involve several steps, each employing a different concept of mathematics. By taking the time to solve each problem, teachers can become familiar with all the mathematics required for these tests.

The problem types that are on high-stakes tests should also be included in the normal scope and sequence of mathematics activities. If a high-stakes test asks students to solve open-ended problems, then open-ended problems could easily be included in regular class work (if not done so already). By the same token, students should have regular experience solving multiple-choice problems, so that they will not be at a disadvantage when they see multiple-choice problems on their state tests. When students have the opportunity to solve multiple-choice problems in class, they can also learn test-taking strategies such as eliminating incorrect answers before solving the problem itself. When these aspects of high-stakes tests are layered into the everyday mathematics that students study, there is no need for the teacher to teach to the test. Students will learn the mathematics appropriate for their grade as they progress through the course. Students will not need to worry about the coming high-stakes test because they will be learning all the mathematics they need throughout the year in their normal curriculum.

A site that links to all state testing programs is www.rowan.edu/mars/depts/math/milou/STATES/Researchstatehsexam.pdf.

TRY THIS

Find examples of released items from a recent high-stakes test. Look at the items for a specific grade level. What content on the test do you find surprising? Why?

A site that links to all state curriculum standards is www.enc.org/professional/standards/state.

TRY THIS

Look up your state mathematics frameworks for a specific grade and compare that to the frameworks for a local school district.

Along with state-level tests, the National Assessment of Educational Progress and the Trends in International Mathematics and Science Study play significant roles in assessment.

NAEP

In 2003, all 50 states participated in the National Assessment of Educational Progress (NAEP). The NAEP is commonly referred to as the nation's report card as it is the only national test covering a variety of disciplines and given regularly on a national level. In mathematics, the test has evolved to integrate conceptual understanding, procedural knowledge, and problem solving with the content strands similar to those listed in NCTM's *Principles and Standards of School Mathematics*. The content strands covered in the NAEP test are

- Number sense, properties, and operations
- Measurement
- Geometry and spatial sense
- Data analysis, statistics, and probability
- Algebra and functions

TRY THIS

Compare the list of content strands in NAEP to the content standards used by NCTM.

Figure 4.16 illustrates the overall structure of the NAEP. The NAEP framework is described as follows:

> Mathematical power is conceived as consisting of mathematical abilities (conceptual understanding, procedural knowledge, and problem solving) within a broader context of reasoning and with connections across the scope of mathematical content and thinking. Communication is viewed as both a unifying thread and a way for students to provide meaningful responses to tasks. (National Assessment Governing Board, 2003, pp. 11–12)

The NAEP stresses mathematical abilities, conceptual understanding, procedural knowledge, and problem solving throughout all of the content areas. The ability to reason, make connections, and communicate are the fundamental tools used as students develop their mathematical abilities.

The NAEP attempts to balance these strands throughout the test and uses families of tasks to evaluate the depth of a student's knowledge. The NAEP is scored according to three basic categories: basic, proficient, and advanced. The results from the NAEP 2003 are encouraging. In the fourth grade, Hispanic students reaching the basic level rose from 42% to 62% and African American students achieving at the basic level increased from 36% to 54%. As of 2004, three-fourths of the fourth graders have reached this basic level. This is up from two-thirds in 2000. Two-thirds of all eighth graders have achieved the basic rank growing from about half in 1990. Students reaching the proficient level have also increased since the 1990 test. Fourth graders currently at 32% rose from 13% and the eighth graders climbed from 15% to 29%. Unfortunately, many minority students fall behind their white counterparts at this level. Addressing and closing this racial gap

figure **4.16**

Framework for NAEP Used in 1996, 2000, 2003

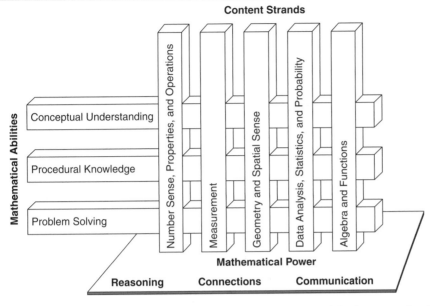

Source: National Assessment Governing Board. (2003). *Mathematics framework for the 2003 national assessment of educational progress.* Washington, DC: National Center for Education Statistics, p. 11.

needs national attention (Stevens, 2003). See http://nces.ed.gov/nationsreportcard/states for more information on the NAEP.

TIMSS

TIMSS, Trends in International Mathematics and Science Study, raised the bar of accountability for mathematics and science education in the United States. The International Association for Evaluation of Educational Achievement has conducted three international tests beginning in 1995, repeated in 1999, and most recently given in 2003. Regarding the results in grade 8 in 1995, the fact that the United States ranked only in the middle rather than in the top 10% compared with other countries using student test results and analysis of videotaped lessons sent shockwaves around the United States. The results of the TIMSS studies placed mathematics and science as a top priority for the national agenda and caused adjustments in the national curricula. TIMSS also brought increased comparisons between pedagogical practices used in the United States and those countries in the top 10%.

The 1999 TIMSS study ranked the following countries as the top ten achievers in mathematics:

1. Singapore
2. Korea, Republic of
3. Chinese Taipei
4. Hong Kong SAR
5. Japan
6. Belgium-Flemish
7. Netherlands
8. Slovak Republic
9. Hungary
10. Canada

These countries scored significantly higher than the United States, which was ranked nineteenth out of the 38 countries participating. Some of the conclusions based on the 1999 TIMSS study concerning the United States are as follows:

- U.S. boys and girls performed similarly in the eighth-grade test.
- U.S. students reported using computers and technology in their math classes 12% of the time as compared to their international peers who reported using technology 5% of the time.
- Between 1995 and 1999, there was no significant change in mathematics achievement overall. However, eighth-grade African American students showed improvement in mathematics.

In terms of the content strands, students in the United States scored higher than the international average on fractions and number sense, data representation, analysis, and probability, but these students performed below the international average in measurement and geometry (National Center for Education Statistics, 2001, p. 16).

In 2003, 46 countries participated in TIMSS at either the fourth-grade level or eighth-grade level, or both. Internationally, the United States improved its rank to the twelfth position. The TIMSS data also revealed interesting trends regarding mathematical achievement within the United States:

- Both eighth-grade boys and eighth-grade girls gained 12 points from 1995 to 2003. The boys are still scoring higher than the girls by 5 points.
- Both African American and Hispanic students continued to make improvements in their scores on the mathematics test. In 1995, U.S. African American eighth-grade students improved by 19 points. Hispanic eighth-grade students raised their average score by 22 points.
- The gap in achievement between European American and African American eighth-grade students narrowed between 1995 and 2003.

In the 1995 TIMSS Video Study, researchers videotaped math lessons in three countries, Japan, Germany, and the United States. The 1999 TIMSS Video Study extended this study to include seven countries, including more countries whose students had scored higher than the U.S. students in the TIMSS assessment. Evaluating lessons across cultures helps educators define those factors that contribute to student learning and provides opportunities for educators to broaden their perspectives and stimulate debate on effective practices. The videotapes provide opportunities to examine lessons in detail and then articulate the national and international trends in mathematics education. The results of the analysis revealed that all lessons shared some of the same characteristics. There were also distinct differences.

Differences between countries as articulated through TIMSS include the following (National Center for Education Statistics, 2003, p. 4):

- Introduction of new content
- Coherence across mathematical problems and within their presentation
- Topics covered
- Procedural complexity of the mathematical problems
- Classroom practices regarding individual student work and homework in class

In Japan, 60% of the lesson time was spent on introducing a new topic. The U.S. lessons spent 23% of the time presenting new material. Most of the other countries spent more time, varying from 56 to 76%, introducing and practicing new material. In the United States, there was no difference between the time spent reviewing previous content and studying new material. The topics covered in all seven countries included whole numbers, fractions, linear equations, and trigonometry. Most all of the lessons, 82%, focused on numbers, geometry, and algebra. One country, Hong Kong SAR, spent 14% of lessons on trigonometry. A wide variation among the countries is seen in terms of the complexity of the problems. Japan's lessons spent 45% of the time on moderately complex tasks and 39% on highly complex tasks. Australia's lessons spent 77% of the time on low complexity tasks, 16% on moderately complex tasks, and 8% on highly complex problems. The United States spent 67% of the time on low-level problems, 27% on moderately complex tasks, and 6% on highly complex tasks. In Japan, more time is spent on making connections (54%) rather than on stating concepts (5%) and using procedures (41%).

TRY THIS

Compare Japan's percentage of time on types of problems presented to the United States. In United States, time spent on making connections is 17%, stating concepts is 13%, and using procedures is 69%. What are the implications of these varying time allotments between the two countries?

In terms of class work, students in Australia, Switzerland, and the Netherlands spent more time working individually or in small groups as opposed to whole class instruction primarily used in Japan, Hong Kong, Czech Republic, and the United States. In terms of the format of the lesson, many lessons included a statement of the objective. The Czech Republic and Japan used objective statements 91% of the time as compared to the lowest-ranking country for this category, the Netherlands, at 21%. The TIMSS study also noted the number of lessons that incorporated a summary of the lesson objective at the end of the lesson. In Japan, the Czech Republic, and Hong Kong SAR, summary statements were used 21% of the time. Australian lessons included summary statements 10% of the time whereas other nations used such statements minimally, between 2% and 6%. The TIMSS study also notes that in all of the high-performing countries there is not one single approach to teaching mathematics. A variety of methods is used. Yet the common trend between two of the highest-performing countries, Japan and Hong Kong, is that both countries spent a vast amount of time making and highlighting connections. Teachers in these countries emphasized activities that challenged students to look for similarities, analyze differences, and critique efficiency of methods. Researchers concluded that such work enhances understanding and increases retention.

For more information on TIMSS go to http://nces.ed.gov/TIMSS. This site provides opportunities for students to answer questions from previous versions of the TIMSS assessment: http://nces.ed.gov.nceskids/eyk.

Standardized Tests for Teachers

Many states require prospective teachers to pass a test of their content knowledge and pedagogical skills. Of the states that require such tests, 44 use the Praxis Series of Professional Assessments for Beginning Educators. The various individual Praxis tests cover all subject and pedagogical areas at various grade levels. The tests are designed to assess teacher candidates when they enter a teacher-training program, when they apply for licensure, or when they are in their first year of teaching. There is a Middle School Mathematics Content Test and a Middle School Teaching Foundations: Mathematics Test. The Middle School Mathematics Content Test consists of 45 multiple-choice questions (75% of the total score) and three short constructed-response questions (25% of the total score). According to the Educational Testing Service, the test is designed to conform to the recommendations of the National Council of Teachers of Mathematics (Educational Testing Service, 2004). The Foundations Test consists of 50 multiple-choice items (34–36% total score) and two constructed-response items (64–66% of the total score). Among the topics covered by the Foundations Test are Human Development, Assessment, Classroom Practices, and Teaching Methods in Mathematics. For more on the Praxis tests see www.ets.org/praxis/#sasat. This site, www.testprepreview.com, offers practice tests.

Implementing an Assessment Program

As stated earlier, assessments play multiple roles in the learning and teaching of mathematics. Rather than an end result, assessment serves as a tool integral to the attainment of educational goals. Assessments provide information to the student and the teacher about the student's current mathematical understanding and areas of strength and weaknesses and indicate direction for future work. Providing feedback on students' work is an important component in teaching.

Feedback can function as a motivating force for students. Direct responses from a teacher regarding a contribution in class, an aside, supportive comment, or public compliment, contribute to a student's willingness to engage in the learning process. Grades, comments on homework assignments, or journal responses all provide information to the student. Students also need opportunities to self-assess their own progress. Providing students with exemplary models can help them evaluate their own performance. Students can also give themselves a score on a rubric and then compare their scores with the teacher's evaluation. This process opens lines of communication and helps the student and teacher clarify their understanding of the work.

PROCESS STANDARDS

Communication and Representation

Teachers who incorporate both formative and summative assessments into their teaching practices provide opportunities for students to communicate their understanding and demonstrate their reasoning. These two process standards stimulate students' thinking and are paths to solidify students' understandings. Representation, a third process standard, is also highlighted in many assessment tools. Students make connections as they work to represent their ideas in a variety of forms. (Refer to the Rule of 5 in Chapter 7, Algebra: The Gateway, for further discussion on multiple representations.)

Point Well Taken

"Because different students show what they know and can do in different ways, assessments should allow for multiple approaches, thus giving a well-rounded picture and allowing each student to show his or her best strengths."
—*NCTM, 2000, p. 23*

As we mentioned earlier, understanding how an assessment tool will be graded is an important factor contributing to the students' success. Students have a right to know how their work will be judged, and they have a right to know the consequences of their performance on a particular assessment. Will the results of the standardized tests be used to create class sections in the coming year? Will the results be used to identify areas of weakness in the curriculum? Will these results contribute to class comparisons within the district?

Incorporating formative and summative assessments into a teacher's repertoire can appear overwhelming. When planning an assessment program, there may be some assessments that are mandated by schools, districts, or state. Teachers need to understand the purpose and content of those tests. Knowing those components will help teachers balance the remaining pieces of the assessment program.

We encourage teachers to work collaboratively. Working with grade-level teams and other math teachers to share ideas, information, and the work can streamline the process. Teachers can begin by accessing the information that is provided by state standards. They can then identify approximately four critical mathematical concepts to focus on for a given time period. Teachers can then list two activities for each concept and create a rubric to identify the specific actions and understandings that students will know and be able to demonstrate. The next step involves selecting the type of assessment to be used. After all four mathematical concepts have been matched with an activity or lesson design and assessment strategy, teachers need to reflect on the balance of those assessments. If all of the assessments involve long-term projects, timing could interfere with the success of the program. Similarly, if all of the assessments are formative, then students miss the experience of a culminating project or performance assessment.

We encourage teachers to take the implementation process in small steps. Incorporate one or two strategies, evaluate these strategies, and then assess to make the appropriate changes. Expand the types of assessments over time. Teachers need to reflect on the assessment program to evaluate its strengths and weaknesses. The craft of teaching involves matching students' needs to curricula, curricula to assessments, and assessment results to students' needs.

SUMMARY

Assessments play an increasingly complex role in today's classrooms. Assessments provide information to the student and the teacher. An assessment may highlight a topic that needs to be reviewed, and students can gain an understanding of topics that they have mastered. Students can strengthen their communication skills by presenting their approaches to Challenges of the Week to their peers; they, in turn, can benefit from hearing other students' approaches to the same task. Students can clarify their thinking as they summarize an activity in their journals. Assessments also offer teachers information about individual students as well as the entire class. Assessments impact lesson planning and help teachers gauge the progress of their students.

Assessments at the state, national, and international levels stimulate broader thinking. Such assessments may cause changes in curricula and promote critical conversations among all invested parties: educators, parents, administrators, local and state interests, business partners, and national policy makers.

An assessment program must be varied so that students have opportunities in a variety of formats to demonstrate their understanding. The assessment program is, therefore, balanced by using both formative and summative tools that reflect the state and national standards.

Effective assessment programs are ones that

- Reflect the NCTM's *Assessment Standards*
- Provide a variety of instruments including formative and summative assessments
- Are balanced
- Align with state and national standards
- Inform students and teachers
- Evolve over time
- Increase communication for all constituencies

Teachers support student learning through assessments by

- Making expectations known at the beginning of the unit
- Providing grading rubrics
- Clarifying grading policies
- Highlighting students' accomplishments
- Involving students in the process of self-evaluation
- Using standardized test data to inform instruction

Point Well Taken

"When teachers use assessment techniques such as observations, conversations and interviews with students, or interactive journals, students are likely to learn through the process of articulating their ideas and answering the teacher's questions."

—*NCTM, 2000, p. 22*

EXERCISES

From the Reading

1. Explain the difference between formative and summative assessments.

2. Describe one formative assessment mentioned in this chapter. How might you use this assessment tool in your teaching?

3. Describe one summative assessment mentioned in this chapter other than unit tests. How might you use this assessment tool in your teaching?

4. What are performance assessments?

5. Develop a rubric for the performance assessment placing students in the role of working in a marketing firm using data analysis.

6. Create a closed question. Then rewrite your question so that it becomes an open response question.

7. What is the "WYTIWYG" phenomenon? What are its implications for the classroom?

8. Take a stand in the argument about teaching to the statewide tests. Are you in favor of directly teaching to these tests? Why or why not?

9. Describe in your own words the implications of the NAEP diagram in Figure 4.16 (p. 87).

On Your Own

1. What role should calculators play in the assessment of skills in mathematics?

2. Go to http://nces.ed.gov.nceskids/eyk and try some of the TIMSS questions.

3. Look at your state standards and identify five mathematical concepts in the number and operations strand.

4. Go to your state's department of education website and locate released test questions. Identify the mathematical concepts and/or skills that the test question is addressing.

5. Take a test question from a middle school textbook. Rewrite the question so that it becomes open-ended.

6. Go to www.ets.org/praxis/prxstate.html and determine what tests your state requires for licensure.

Portfolio Question

Using ideas and suggestions from this chapter and your own experiences as a student, define your grading philosophy. Be as specific as possible and be certain to address the following:

- Will you grade homework?
- How will you communicate expectations for tests, projects, or any graded material?
- Will you provide makeup tests?
- If the class does not perform as well as expected on a particular test, what action will you take?

Scenes from a Classroom

The grading period is about to close. Mr. Aljendro is sitting at his desk coincidentally looking at his grade book. One of his eighth-grade students tentatively knocks on the door. "Mr. Aljendro? Can I speak with you?" Mr. Aljendro looks over his glasses and invites Ingrid to come in and take a seat near his desk. Ingrid looks a little nervous;

Mr. Aljendro jokingly tells her that he "doesn't bite." Ingrid notices that he has his grade book, and she says, "I haven't been doing well this term. I'm wondering if there is any work that I can do for extra credit?" Mr. Aljendro turns the page in his grade book and sees that Ingrid has had at least six missing assignments and two low test scores in the last month. He knows her to be a reasonably consistent student so the last two tests were a little surprising.

Before reading further, respond to the following question:

> How would you respond to Ingrid? Be specific and provide reasons for your response to this student.

Providing some students with extra credit opportunities can raise issues of fairness with other students. If one or two students are being given chances to improve their grades, all students deserve to earn bonus points. Teachers need to consider the additional work that offering extra credit involves. First, teachers need to plan and develop the assignment. Teachers need to develop a grading rubric. How much will this extra credit affect a term grade? If the grade is raised five points as a result of extra credit, is it fair that the extra credit is weighted so heavily? There are other lessons involved here for Ingrid to learn. Working consistently on homework, for example, would help those test grades. Waiting until the end of the term to look for ways to improve a grade can result in disappointment. However, this student might have extenuating circumstances that need to be considered.

Mr. Aljendro has several options. He can suggest that she make up the missing assignments so that she doesn't have a low homework grade. He can also strategize with Ingrid how she might avoid this situation in the future. He could also suggest an extra credit project and then offer the opportunity to everyone in the class. No matter what action he selects, he should begin the conversation with Ingrid by asking her if there is something going on in her life currently that is perhaps interfering with her work.

Preparing for Praxis

Which of the following describes an informal assessment that a teacher might use to check individual students' understanding of a lesson or unit in progress?

A. The teacher has students work in groups of three to solve a problem they have not seen before and keep careful records of their reasoning.

B. The teacher has students work in groups of four to solve a problem and has a representative of each group come to the board to write out the group's solution.

C. The teacher asks each student to write two sentences that answer a question on a topic the teacher has put on the board midway though the class.

D. The teacher facilitates a brief whole class discussion, eliciting questions from students about a topic.

RESOURCES

Teacher's Bookcase

Kinney, P., Munroe, M., & Sessions, P. (2003). *A school-wide approach to student-led conferences: A practitioner's guide.* Westerville, OH: National Middle School Association.

Authors provide strategies to implement student-led conferences including organizing frameworks and guidelines.

Pokay, P., & Tayeh, C. (2000). *256 assessment tips for mathematics teachers.* Parsippany, NJ: Dale Seymour Publishing.

This book is a collection of tips from teachers for presecondary mathematics teachers. Topics range from journals and portfolios to observations and interviews.

Warloe, K. (1993). Assessment as a dialogue: A means of interacting with middle school students. In *Assessment in the middle school classroom.* Reston, VA: NCTM.

The author offers a range of projects and assessment strategies for middle school students.

For Further Reading

Gay, S., & Thomas, M. (1993). Just because they got it right, does it mean they know it? In N. L. Webb & A. Cox-ford (Eds.), *Assessment in the mathematics classroom: 1993 yearbook* (pp. 130–134). Reston, VA: NCTM.

Authors provide instances in which students held a misconception and yet were able to arrive at correct answers. By observing and questioning these students, the authors present ways to challenge students' thinking in order to replace a misconception with an appropriate understanding.

Parke, C., Lane, S., Silver, E., & Magone, M. (2003). *Using assessment to improve middle-grades mathematics teaching and learning.* Reston, VA: NCTM.

Developed through the QUASAR project, Quantitative Understanding: Amplifying Student Achievement and Reasoning, this resource presents assessment tasks along with student work and rubrics.

Stutzman, R., & Race, K. (2004). EMRF: Everyday rubric grading. In *Mathematics Teacher, 97*(1), 34–39.

The authors discuss using a four-level rubric that does not involve a number scale. They recommend using letters: E for excellent, M for meets expectations, R for revisions required, and F for fragmentary. The authors suggest that using letters rather than numbers focuses students' attention on the meaning of the letter and what needs to be done as a result of that letter. The authors moved away from numbers because students remained focused on the percent equivalent. For example, a student earning a 3 on a 4-point scale, considers the grade to be a 75%.

REFERENCES

Black, P., & William, D. (1998, October). Inside the black box: Raising standards through classroom assessment. *Phi Delta Kappan,* 139–148.

Burkhardt, H., Fraser, R., & Ridgeway, J. (1990). The dynamics of curriculum change. In I. Wirszup and R. Streit (Eds.), *Developments in school mathematics around the world: Proceedings of the Second UCSMP International Conference on Mathematics Education, 7–10 April, 1988* (pp. 2–30). Reston, VA: NCTM.

Educational Testing Service. (2004). *The Praxis series: Professional assessments for beginning teachers.* www.ets.org/praxis/prxtest.html#sasat.

Fernandes, M., & Fontana, D. (1996). Changes in control beliefs in Portuguese primary pupils as a consequence of the employment of self-assessment strategies. *British Journal of Educational Psychology, 19,* 95–107.

Hiebert, J. et al. (1997). *Making sense. Teaching and learning mathematics with understanding.* Portsmouth, NH: Heinemann.

Huinker, D. M. (1993). Interviews: A window to students' conceptual knowledge of operations. In N. L. Webb & A. Cox-ford (Eds.), *Assessment in the mathematics classroom: 1993 yearbook* (pp. 80–86). Reston, VA: NCTM.

Kenney, P., & Silver, E. (1993). Student self-assessment in mathematics. In N. Webb & A. Coxford (Eds.), *Assessment in the mathematics classroom: 1993 yearbook* (pp. 80–86). Reston, VA: NCTM.

National Assessment Governing Board. (2003). *Mathematics framework for the 2003 National Assessment of Educational Progress.* Washington, DC: National Center for Education Statistics.

National Center for Education Statistics. (2001). *Pursuing excellence: Comparisons of international eighth-grade mathematics and science achievement from a U.S. perspective, 1995 and 1999.* Washington, DC: U.S. Department of Education.

National Center for Education Statistics. (2003). *Highlights from TIMSS 1999 video study of eighth-grade mathematics teaching.* Washington, DC: U.S. Department of Education.

National Council of Teachers of Mathematics. (1995). *Assessment standards for school mathematics.* Reston, VA: NCTM.

National Council of Teachers of Mathematics. (2000). *Principles and standards for school mathematics.* Reston, VA: NCTM.

Saphier, J., & Gower, R. (1997). *The Skillful Teacher.* Carlisle, MA: Research for Better Teaching.

Stenmark, J. K., & Bush, W. (Eds.). (2001). *Mathematics assessment. A practical handbook.* Reston, VA: NCTM.

Stevens, J. (2003). *Statement on NAEP 2003 mathematics and reading results.* Released on November 13, 2003.

Wilson, L., & Kenney, P. (2003). Classroom and large-scale assessment in Kilpatrick, Martin, and Schifter (Eds.), *A research companion to principles and standards for school mathematics.* Reston, VA: NCTM.

chapter five

Problem Solving: An Approach to Teaching and Learning Mathematics

Today's emphasis on problem solving moves beyond an intriguing problem or challenging activity. Today's emphasis involves using problem solving as a tool for teaching and learning mathematics.

NCTM Standards

Problem solving is one of the five process standards articulated by the National Council of Teachers of Mathematics in *Principles and Standards for School Mathematics*. The Problem Solving Standard is defined as follows:

> Instructional programs from prekindergarten through grade 12 should enable all students to
> Build new mathematical knowledge through problem solving;
> Solve problems that arise in mathematics and in other contexts;
> Apply and adapt a variety of appropriate strategies to solve problems;
> Monitor and reflect on the process of mathematical problem solving. (NCTM, 2000, p. 256)

Problem solving engages students in the development of their conceptual understanding of mathematics. As stated in the standard, students generate knowledge through the process of problem solving. Problem solving as a process involves reasoning, persistence, learning from mistakes as one proceeds, looking for multiple representations, making connections with previous work, reflecting back on the process and communicating the results. Thus, all of the other four process standards, representation, reasoning and proof, communication and connections, are included in the problem-solving process. From the teaching and learning perspective, the problem-solving process—the analysis, the demonstrated understanding of the mathematics, and the connections made as a result of the work—constitutes the true value of problem solving. Because of its overarching impact on the teaching and learning of mathematics, we have devoted an entire chapter to problem solving.

This chapter further defines the meaning of problem solving and connects it with the meaning of understanding. We examine what problem solving looks like in classrooms and the components involved in the process of implementation. The chapter explains the teacher's role before, during, and after the lesson. This chapter identifies the habits of mind that are developed through problem solving and provides examples of many of the problem-solving strategies. We take the time to highlight these problem-solving strategies so that teachers can recognize them as they become intertwined in the broader open-ended problem-solving emphasis in today's curricula. The National Council of Teachers of Mathematics highlights the importance of placing problems in a meaningful context for students. As context can vary so greatly according to locale and environment, we have presented problems in a more general manner. We encourage teachers to adapt these problems according to their specific locations and students' interests. This chapter also presents changes in emphasis on problem solving and recent findings from research.

What Is Problem Solving?

Problem solving is essentially a process that is intrinsically linked to understanding. It is a process through which mathematics becomes meaningful and relevant. Students work in a variety of contexts applying the mathematics that they have mastered and build new understandings as they do so. As a result of the problem-solving process, an answer happens to occur, but the answer is secondary in terms of its importance. Problem solving is "the means by which individuals take skills and understandings that they have developed previously and apply them in unfamiliar situations" (Krulik et al., 2003, p. 92). Many textbooks include word problems in each chapter. For the most part, these problems practice only the skills previously demonstrated in the chapter or earlier chapters. Students view these tasks as procedural and the problems rarely require significant thought. These word problems tend to focus on one particular strategy and students work to get the correct answer by applying the intended strategy. In the May 2003 issue of *Mathematics Teaching in the Middle School*, Ferrucci, Ban-Har Yeap, and Carter quote a recent study by Verschaffel, De Corte, and Vierstraete (1999) stating that "extensive experiences with traditional arithmetic word problems induces in pupils a strong tendency to approach word problems in a mindless, superficial, routine-based way to identify the correct arithmetic operation needed to solve a word problem" (Verschaffel et al., 1999, p. 265). Many students never move beyond knowing the procedures by rote. Students frequently say that they can do the problems, but they will also admit that they do not understand the mathematics. Such rote learning is fragile; procedures become entangled and confused or even lost over time. Rote learning does not demonstrate understanding.

Understanding

Understanding is the ability to think and act flexibly with what is known (Perkins, 1992). For students in mathematics, this means, for example, that they can apply procedures, make connections, analyze and critique varying approaches, and pose new questions. As a result of their work, students build new knowledge.

TRY THIS

Note the active verbs used in the paragraph about understanding. What are the implications for instruction?

Understanding can also be thought of as a continually growing web of interrelated ideas. This web is similar to a hammock "in which knots are joined to other knots in intricate webbing. Even if one knot comes undone, the structure does not collapse but still bears weight—as opposed to what might happen if each individual rope was strung only from one point to another, with no interweaving" (Russell, 1999, p. 4). The interconnectedness of ideas strengthens over time. As a new idea comes forward and challenges prior knowledge, the struggle to resolve the conflict leads the student to construct new knowledge.

Finding those connections, linking ideas to one another, and extending those ideas to new areas represent the work involved in problem solving.

Problem solving is an integral part of the study of mathematics. Students who analyze, create conjectures and look for patterns, and make connections will view mathematics as more than a series of rote calculations. The study of mathematics is an active endeavor.

Point Well Taken

"Problem solving should be the central focus of the mathematics curriculum. As such, it is a primary goal of all mathematics instruction and an integral part of all mathematical study. Problem solving is not a distinct topic, but a process that should permeate the entire program and provide the context in which concepts and skills can be learned."
—*Leiva, 1991, p. 2*

Point Well Taken

"Learning with understanding—making sense of new ideas by connecting them with existing knowledge in coherent ways—is, admittedly, often harder to accomplish and takes more time than simply memorizing or mimicking; yet, the benefits of learning with understanding outweigh the challenges."
—*Lambdin, 2003, p. 7*

Point Well Taken

"Problem solving is not only a goal of learning mathematics but also a major means of doing so."
—*NCTM, 2000, p. 52*

Problem solving offers students the opportunity and the challenge to develop their abilities to reason effectively, increase their self-confidence in the process, and build their understanding.

What Problem Solving Looks Like in Classrooms

Because problem solving involves students who are actively engaged in the process, the classroom can appear less structured than a traditional class. The traditional classroom places the teacher in front with students interacting by responding to questions. The classroom appears orderly and the teacher is clearly in charge. In classrooms using a problem-solving approach, it is not always clear where the teacher is located. He or she might be kneeling by the desk of one student, standing behind a group of students and listening to their conversations, or meeting with a representative from each group of students to provide further directions. Problem-solving classrooms can be noisy as groups are talking and working together. A visitor to the class might see small groups of students working so deliberately that their heads are literally touching. Groups of students may have their materials spread out on the floor around the room as they work on a poster. Students may be moving around the classroom to get supplies, posting summaries of work on the bulletin board, or going to the front of room to make presentations. The problem-solving classroom is action oriented and student centered.

Teacher's Role: Before, during, and after the Lesson

Problem solving requires a classroom climate that provides students with specific strategies so that they can work respectfully with each other. It is a climate that allows all students to be heard and actively participate. It values thinking and reasoning and taking risks. Establishing such environments is not an easy task; it requires ongoing attention. (Refer to Chapter 3, The Practice of Effective Instruction, for more details on classroom climate.)

Before

The teacher's role in the implementation process of problem solving begins long before the students enter the classroom. As soon as possible, teachers identify the big mathematical ideas to be addressed within the course of the year and then within each unit of study. This work is usually presented to a new teacher in terms of a curriculum guide and a scope and sequence. The new teacher must study these resources. With the support and collaboration of colleagues, the teacher needs to identify worthwhile tasks for students to explore.

Worthwhile tasks are those that students do not know how to solve on first reading. A problem is simply not a problem if students already know how to solve it! When exploring worthwhile tasks, students apply their skills and understandings in new and interesting ways. In order for students to be willing to approach such challenges, the problems need to be established in a familiar context. Marilyn Burns (2000, p. 17) offers the following criteria for mathematical problems:

1. There is a perplexing situation that the student understands.
2. The student is interested in finding the solution.
3. The student is unable to proceed directly to the answer.
4. The solution requires use of mathematical ideas.

Good problems attract and maintain students' interest. They present the problem in an understandable context and avoid culturally exclusive information (Leinwand, 2000, p. 51). Worthwhile tasks are also accessible to diverse learners as such tasks offer students multi-

On the Lighter Side

A relevant context can make a difference for students.

FoxTrot © 1995 Bill Amend. Reprinted with permission of Universal Press Syndicate. All rights reserved.

ple solution paths and lead students to important mathematical ideas. When determining the value of a problem, teachers need to consider what the students gain from the experience. Are they left remembering a fun activity or are they connected with the mathematics involved in a more meaningful way? In *Making Sense*, James Hiebert refers to "residue" as "leftovers" from the experience. Two significant types of residue are "insights into the structure of mathematics" and "the strategies or methods for solving problems" (Hiebert et al., 1997, p. 23). In selecting the problem-solving task, the predicted residue of the task should be a determining factor. Worthwhile tasks also promote communication and reflection. When given opportunities to reflect and communicate their understandings, students demonstrate a greater rate of retention. Worthwhile tasks move students through a compelling activity to the engagement of their higher-order thinking skills.

Newspapers often provide stimulating contexts for problems. Stock quotes, sports statistics, graphs and charts, and even news headlines can offer problem-solving opportunities. Math in the Media provides an example of questions taken from a newspaper article. Students can often find articles that interest them and then pose problems to address. Other resources for worthwhile tasks include *Standards*-based curricula such as Connected Mathematics, Mathematics in Context, Middle Grades MATH Thematics, and MathScape. These curricula present entire units based on the problem-solving approach. (See Chapter 3, The Practice of Effective Instruction.) Professional journals such as *Teaching Mathematics in the Middle School* provide articles and regular features on problem solving. The National Council of Teachers of Mathematics' *Navigation Series* provides many rich and meaningful tasks. A traditional textbook approach can also be modified so that students explore a concept rather than being told a procedure. For example, instead of demonstrating how to change a mixed number to an improper fraction, teachers can ask student groups to explore ways to express the mixed number as a single fraction. By attending professional development conferences and workshops, teachers can build files of worthwhile tasks. Websites also offer a vast array of problem-solving opportunities. The following are some Web resources for problem-solving tasks:

www.c3.lanl.gov/mega-math

This site provides unusual and interesting problems for grades 4–12. Teacher support material and information are also available.

www.eduplace.com/math/brain

This site offers weekly opportunities to solve problems and submit them. The problems are ranked by grade-level range (3–4, 5–6, 7 and up).

Point Well Taken

". . . a mathematical task is a problem only if the problem solver reaches a point where he or she does not know how to proceed."
—*Knoll & Miller in Owens, 1993, p. 59*

Point Well Taken

"The teacher is responsible for shaping and directing students' activities so that they have opportunities to engage meaningfully in mathematics. Textbooks can be useful resources for teachers, but teachers must also be free to adapt or depart from texts if students' ideas and conjectures are to shape teachers' navigation of the content. The tasks in which students engage must encourage them to reason about mathematical ideas, to make connections, and to formulate, grapple with, and solve problems. Students also need skills. Good tasks nest skill development in the context of problem solving."

—NCTM, 1991, p. 32

http://pegasus.cc.ucf.edu/~mathed/problem.html

Weekly problem-solving contests offer prizes. Winners are selected randomly from all of those submitting correct answers.

www.mathchannel.com

This site was originally called Wonderful Ideas and presents activities and mathematical games for grades 3–8 as well as research and current topics.

(See resources at the end of the chapter for more problem-solving websites.)

The planning for a course of study must begin with the important mathematical ideas. Selecting tasks, teaching strategies, and planning each lesson follow from the identification of the critical ideas for students to understand. In the following content chapters, we present many of the important ideas for each of the NCTM standards with suggested teaching strategies. The "Before" work for teachers is vast and can appear overwhelming. It is important that new teachers establish a support network. Your class in the methods course is the beginning of such a network.

ASSESSMENT TIP

Teachers identify the important mathematical concepts to be addressed as they plan a unit. Teachers also need to decide what kind of evidence will indicate that students are mastering those ideas. Knowing what assessments will be used and sharing those with students at the beginning of the unit helps teachers and students alike. By identifying the assessment strategies, teachers clarify their expectations and know where each lesson is leading the class. Students understand the expectations from the beginning and they can work toward them. Many students find that knowing the goal of the unit as the work begins helps them remain focused and involved.

Another aspect of a teacher's "Before" work is the extension of establishing norms. (See Classroom Climate in Chapter 3, The Practice of Effective Instruction.) Before students work on a task, teachers need to reinforce the norms and highlight one or two that will be featured in the process of solving the task. It is also important for the teacher to state what abilities the group needs to use in order to be successful in completing the task. For example, the lesson plan in Chapter 3 entitled "Consecutive Sums" lists the multiple abilities to be used in the task:

- Looking for patterns
- Extending patterns
- Finding efficient use of patterns
- Analyzing patterns
- Making conjectures
- Drawing conclusions
- Summarizing group work

It is critical for students to realize that they do not possess all of these abilities, but as a group working together, they can be successful because each member of the group will contribute his or her individual skills. The multiple abilities help students realize that they can contribute to the work. By identifying with one or more abilities, students find an entry point into the work. Students may not feel as confident with the mathematical content, but they realize that they can participate by offering their abilities to the group. By identifying the abilities and highlighting the group processing norms, the teacher is featuring what is valued in terms of the social and sociomathematical norms. This is the "Before" work for teachers.

During

After the class has reviewed the norms and identified the multiple abilities that they can offer to their groups, the students are ready to engage in the task. During this time for group work, the teacher observes students exhibiting the desired strategies. The teacher listens carefully as students engage in the problem-solving process. The teacher also looks at various indicators to determine whether or not all students are participating equally, using cooperative strategies and working toward the important mathematical ideas. The teacher can note body language and listen to the verbal interchange between group members. The issues regarding when the teacher should intervene and how this intervention takes place are significant. See Chapter 3, The Practice of Effective Instruction, for the discussion on status issues.

Another critical role that the teacher plays during a problem-solving task is conducting and facilitating the discussion. Usually, the class comes together as a summarizing activity and the reporter from each group presents the work of the group. This full-class discussion has four main purposes:

1. Provides opportunities for students to share their thinking and strategies used
2. Gives the teacher a chance to ask questions and extend students' thinking
3. Allows the teacher to commend groups and individual students on demonstrating specific norms
4. Influences the lesson planning process for future lessons

This discussion, therefore, is more than a gathering of each group's findings. Students can see the different approaches used and this may stimulate their thinking to make a connection between approaches or deepen their understanding of a concept. Teachers can highlight the important mathematical thinking exhibited and ask students to explain further by asking, "What factors contributed to your strategy?" or "What conclusions can we make now based on this evidence?" Teachers might even offer another approach to be considered. Students then have opportunities to compare the various approaches.

Because groups of students have been working together, it is important that they have individual opportunities to process and clarify their thinking. Teachers can ask students to write in their journals. Providing a writing prompt that asks students to go beyond the summary of the process used in the task helps focus their thinking. Prompts should also ask about the student's evaluation of his or her contribution to the group's work. In Chapter 3, the lesson plan, "Consecutive Sums," presented two writing prompts as summarizers:

Describe two or more patterns that your group used in today's activities.

What mathematical abilities did you contribute to your group today?

Such writing opportunities help to hold individuals accountable for the work achieved by the group. Teachers have also found that a norm such as "No one is finished until every member of the group is finished" stimulates group ownership of the task and its solution. (See Chapter 4, Assessment: Balanced and Varied, for more details on journal writing.)

After

Just as students need opportunities to reflect on their thinking, teachers need time to evaluate the effectiveness of a lesson. Did the task help students gain an understanding of the intended concept? Did the students find a variety of approaches to the task? How might this lesson be extended? What changes need to be made to improve this lesson? As part of the reflection process, teachers also need to judge where the students are in their individual development of a particular concept. (See Chapter 4, Assessment: Balanced and Varied, for specific strategies documenting students' growth in their mathematical thinking.) This information helps plan the content and structure of future lessons.

Point Well Taken

"By modeling respect for students' thinking and conveying the assumption that students make sense, teachers can encourage students to participate within a norm that expects group members to justify their ideas."
—*NCTM, 1991, p. 36*

Point Well Taken

"Solving problems can be regarded as the most characteristic human endeavor."
—*George Polya*

From the Students' Perspective

When problem solving is first introduced in the classroom, some students may have to confront their belief that all math problems can be solved quickly. Faced with more challenging tasks, these students may demonstrate their impatience and become frustrated. Students may wait for the teacher to show them or simply give up trying to solve the problem. Students may also believe that there is only one right answer and one right way of solving a problem. Students may consider access to the answer is beyond them, so they will not begin to address the problem. Teachers can use the power of cooperative groups to alleviate some of the anxiety for these students. Teachers can also gain an understanding of students' attitudes by giving them a survey. Questions might include those similar to the questions in Black Line Master 5.1, Attitude Survey. Surveys such as this might be repeated later in the year to see how students' dispositions have changed. Such surveys function as another form of self-assessment as discussed in Chapter 4, Assessment: Balanced and Varied. As students find success working with challenging tasks, they gain confidence and become more willing to try.

Students' Disposition

Students' positive disposition toward problem solving contributes significantly to their success. Successful problem solvers are willing to try various approaches, are mindful of their progress, and are receptive to the possibility that their chosen approach is not working. Students begin a task by reading the question and clarifying any vocabulary. Students who patiently read the problem and then reread the problem gain insights into the problem. Some students use subvocalization in order to hear as well as see the information as they read. Subvocalization, or hearing the words in their head, taps into two learning modalities and helps students make greater meaning of the words in the context of the problem. Some teachers assign reading the problem as a job within the small groups. This helps students with less competent reading and comprehension skills.

As students begin to make a plan to solve the problem, they need to consider the desired outcome and what strategy might lead them toward that outcome. Students also realize that there may be several approaches. This forward thinking helps students remain focused on the desired outcome and, therefore, students remain connected to the problem. As students develop a plan, they need to be mindful of their thinking. This involves self-monitoring and evaluation. These metacognitive activities help students gain control of the problem (Posamentier & Stepelman, 1999, p. 104). Students may choose to break the problem into smaller parts or make a simpler problem by using smaller values. They may classify a problem as being similar to one solved previously. These strategies represent the students' attempt to gain control of the problem.

As students move through the problem-solving process, they need to continue to monitor their thinking. Students need to evaluate their progress as they work through a task. They also need to check their result in terms of the context of the problem and then reflect back on their process in terms of its efficiency and effectiveness.

Just as teachers pose problems to explore, students can ask their own questions. Being able to pursue a line of inquiry excites and motivates middle school students. Students also begin to see mathematics as a tool to help them explore, discover, and hypothesize. As young mathematicians, we want students to ask, "What if . . .", "Suppose . . .", "How come. . . ." Asking questions is one of the habits of mind that are reinforced through problem solving.

Habits of Mind

Monitoring progress and posing questions are habits of mind. Providing students with a coherent sequence of meaningful problems helps them build constructive habits of mind. "Students develop these habits of mind as a by-product of learning mathematics through

Point Well Taken

"The difference between a successful student and an unsuccessful student is that the successful student knows what to do when s/he doesn't know what to do."

—Sheila Tobias

Point Well Taken

"An awareness of the problem-solving process is the first step for attaining control. This control enables the learner to find a proper solution path."

—Posamentier & Stepelman, 1999, p. 104

Point Well Taken

"Good problem solvers realize what they know and don't know, what they are good at and not so good at; as a result they can use their time and energy wisely. They plan more carefully and more effectively and take time to check their progress periodically. These habits of mind are important not only in making students better problem solvers but also in helping students become better learners of mathematics."

—NCTM, 2000, p. 260

problem solving" (Levasseur & Cuoco, 2003, p. 27). Habits of mind such as looking for patterns, making conjectures, using several representations, justifying statements, and analyzing strategies are forms of thinking.

Habits of mind and problem-solving strategies are closely intertwined. Using certain strategies can lead to the development of the habits of mind. Similarly, using the habits of mind can provide insights as to the nature of problem-solving strategies. Habits of mind and strategies are not synonymous, however. One distinction is that habits become ingrained and called upon easily; strategies are processes that students try out and explore as they work on a particular problem.

Point Well Taken

"*Thinking*, we think, must be at the core of all school learning. This concept is perhaps so basic to use that it is like a postulate, something accepted without reasons. Mathematics is certainly a discipline whose principal component is thinking."

—*Goldenberg, Shteingold, & Feurzeig, 2003, p. 29*

Problem-Solving Strategies

In this section we present many problem-solving strategies with specific examples that can be used in the classrooms. By taking the time to detail these strategies, we feel that teachers will recognize these approaches when applied in more open-ended tasks. By knowing specific strategies, teachers can suggest a different approach if the need arises. NCTM places an increased emphasis on situating problem solving in realistic contexts. As contexts vary so greatly from region to region, we have chosen straightforward examples that can be adapted for students in terms of contexts as well as the level of difficulty. Selecting specific problems that are appropriate for their individual students and placing the problem in an appropriate context are essential tasks for today's teachers. We begin this section with the general four-step problem-solving guideline, heuristic.

Heuristic

The first component of the problem-solving process involves a heuristic or plan. In order to get started with problem solving, students need to be introduced to a general plan. In 1945, George Polya, considered the father of problem solving in mathematics, presented the following heuristic:

1. Understand the problem.
2. Devise a plan.
3. Carry out the plan.
4. Look back.

Many textbooks offer similar heuristics. The specific plan used by students is not as important as the thinking involved in the implementation of the plan. In this book, we will use the following problem solving heuristic:

1. *Get Started.* Read the problem. What is the problem asking? What is the action involved? Is there sufficient information? Make an estimate.
2. *Make a Plan.* Organize the information using a list, table, or chart. Select a strategy or choose an operation.
3. *Take Action.* Solve the problem by implementing the plan.
4. *Reflect.* Look back to see that problem's question has been answered. Does the result make sense? Can the result be verified by using another method to solve the problem?

Note that a heuristic is not the same as an algorithm. An algorithm is a procedure applied and used on a particular set of problems. Heuristics are general and applicable to many different types of problems (Krulik & Rudnick, 1987, p. 21). Simply stated, heuristics offer guidelines for solving all types of problems. Understanding each step in this heuristic is a critical component to success in the problem-solving process.

The first step, Get Started, involves careful reading of the problem. Students need to interpret the problem and restate the problem in their own words. Students should look for any missing information or any unnecessary information as they restate the problem. Students should also make an estimate or try to define the range of the possible answer.

figure **5.1**

Problem-Solving Strategies	
• Find a pattern	• Act it out
• Make a picture	• Use an equation or number sentence
• Make a chart/graph	• Solve a simpler problem
• Build a model (use manipulatives)	• Account for all possibilities
• Work backwards	• Adopt a different point of view
• Use intelligent guessing and checking	• Use unit analysis

Taking the time to carefully identify the meaning of the problem helps to clarify the next step in the heuristic, Make a Plan. By focusing on the action of the problem, students can select the appropriate operation or series of operations. They can organize the information into a chart and begin pulling information from what is known. At this point, students can select a strategy to begin working toward the answer. Strategies are numerous. (See Figure 5.1.) Each of these strategies will be discussed in detail in the context of a specific problem.

MISCONCEPTION

Key words have been used to help students select an appropriate operation. Placing a strong emphasis on key words can be misleading for many students. Many students are taught to use the word *of* to indicate multiplication as seen in "Find $\frac{1}{2}$ *of* $\frac{3}{4}$." These students are then challenged by "$\frac{1}{2}$ *of what number is* $\frac{3}{4}$?" where *of* indicates multiplication but division is used in the process of solution. Similarly, addition or subtraction, depending on the given context, might solve questions involving statements like "how many more?" If students simply focus on the key word *more*, they may misinterpret the problem entirely. Students need to focus on the action involved in the problem rather than performing a word search as their problem-solving strategy.

Point Well Taken

"If truth be known, as far as the teacher is concerned, the answer is probably the least important part of the process. It is the solution—the analysis, strategy selection, and method of attack—that is critical if the learner is to become a problem solver and reasoner."

—*Krulik et al., 2003, p. 93*

Take Action is the third step in the heuristic. Students implement the strategy selected and use a variety of computational, geometric, algebraic, and/or reasoning skills to arrive at an answer. It is important to note that the answer is not equivalent to the solution. The answer is an outcome from the entire problem-solving process. The problem-solving process is the solution.

The fourth step in the heuristic is Reflect. This critical final step engages students in the process of making certain that their solution is thorough in its development and that the answer makes sense. Students can compare the answer with the original estimate. Does the answer address the original question? Does the answer make sense? Is anything else needed? Are there connections between this problem and others that have already been explored?

TRY THIS

There are 330 students going on a field trip. Each bus holds 25 students. How many buses will be needed to transport all of the students?

Answers given by students: a) $13\frac{1}{5}$ b) 13   c) 14

What might a student be thinking if he or she selected one of the preceding answers? Write an explanation for each response.

The importance of the fourth step, Reflect, is seen in the bus problem. A student who states $13\frac{1}{5}$ as the answer has calculated correctly but ignores the fact that $\frac{1}{5}$ of a bus does not make sense. A student who presents 13 as the answer has performed the correct calculation and has chosen to ignore the remainder or has followed the rule for rounding and rounded $13\frac{1}{5}$ down to 13. Using 13 buses for the trip leaves 5 students behind. The correct answer is 14 buses.

This heuristic, or problem-solving plan, needs to be explicitly taught and modeled with students. The four-step approach, Get Started, Make a Plan, Take Action, Reflect, is easily remembered, but students need to use it frequently. Students require many successful experiences in order to build their confidence. As their confidence grows, their reasoning skills develop and they tend to remain receptive to the process.

Providing students with examples of problems whose solution can demonstrate a particular strategy also needs to be supported by direct discussion about the strategy after students have had a chance to explore the problem. In some cases, problems might require more than one strategy. Figure 5.1 lists the problem-solving strategies discussed in this section. Some students entering middle school have had vast experience in problem solving. If that is the case, working through each strategy is not necessary. We offer these problem-solving techniques to help teachers recognize the possibilities. Each strategy is presented in the context of a problem that is appropriate for middle school students, and we explore the relevance of each strategy as it is demonstrated outside of the mathematics classroom. We also discuss discrete mathematics in this section. Discrete mathematics is a relatively new field in mathematics, and it is not considered a separate strand for middle school curricula. However, discrete math offers a vast resource for middle school problems illustrating many of the problem-solving strategies identified in this section.

Find a Pattern

Find a Pattern is the first in a series of options that students can select as they make a plan according to step 2 in the heuristic.

TRY THIS

Find the sum of the first 20 odd numbers.

Students may want to take a "brute force" approach to finding the sum of the first 20 odd numbers. This approach can lead to a correct result, but it is time consuming and likely to have errors. By looking for a pattern, students can easily state the sum and make a connection with square number values. (See Figure 5.2.) Students should recognize the square values representing the sum for the number of values in the series. Consequently, the sum for the first 20 odd values is 20^2 or 400.

The problem-solving strategy, Find a Pattern, has many applications outside of mathematics. Doctors recognize patterns in the symptoms patients exhibit, musicians employ the power of patterns as they compose music, and police look for patterns as they search a crime scene for clues. Patterns exist in nature as seen in plant growth and ripples in the pond after a pebble breaks the water. Teachers notice patterns in students' behavior. Looking for patterns can lead to discovery and connections within the mathematics curriculum.

Make a Picture

Students often gain insights into a problem simply by creating a diagram or drawing. Consider the following:

> A log can be cut into 4 pieces in 12 seconds. How long will it take to cut the log into 8 pieces?

Point Well Taken

"Through guided reflection, students can focus on the mathematics involved in solving a problem, thus solidifying their understanding of the concepts involved."

—*NCTM, 2000, p. 260*

Point Well Taken

"An emphasis on problem solving closes the apparent gap between the mathematics learned in the classroom and the mathematics needed to be a problem solver in the real world."

—*Krulik et al., 2003, p. 91*

Did You **Know**?

Carl Friedrich Gauss (1777–1855) used a pattern to find the sum of the first 100 consecutive numbers when he was in elementary school. By recognizing that there are 50 pairs of numbers in the series each totaling 101, he quickly found the sum, 5050.

figure **5.2**

Finding the Sum of the First 20 Odd Integers	
ADDENDS	**SUM**
1	1
1 + 3	4
1 + 3 + 5	9
1 + 3 + 5 + 7	16
1 + 3 + 5 + 7 + 9	25

figure **5.3**

Cutting the Log

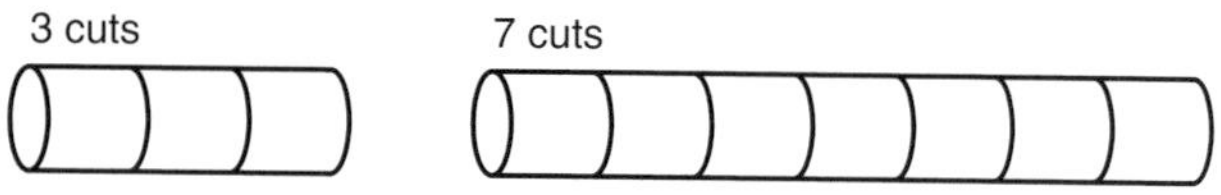

3 cuts

7 cuts

Many students fall into the trap of simply doubling the time needed to cut the log for four pieces. By making a drawing, students realize that only three cuts are needed to make the four pieces and, therefore, each cut takes 4 seconds to complete. As seen in Figure 5.3, seven cuts are needed to create the eight sections.

Students frequently discover that by making a drawing they gain a better understanding of the problem. They may decide to implement a different strategy simply as a result of making the drawing.

TRY THIS

Place this problem in a meaningful context for middle school students in your geographic area.

This problem-solving strategy is used in a wide variety of contexts. Diagrams are frequently used to help clarify a statement. Newspapers and professional journals provide many examples of diagrams. Maps, either quick drawings when giving directions or published maps, are ways to present information visually.

Make a Chart

This strategy is very similar to Find a Pattern. A chart can serve as a way to find out more about a problem. By looking for patterns that may emerge from the chart, students can gain insights that lead toward an answer.

TRY THIS

How many ways can you make change for $1.00 using only quarters, dimes, and nickels?

Students are often surprised to discover that there are twenty-seven ways to make change for a dollar using only quarters, dimes, and nickels. An organized chart, as in Figure 5.4, helps keep track of all possibilities, and students quickly recognize patterns in the chart, such as when using two quarters, the number of dimes can decrease by one as the nickels increase by multiples of two. On the other hand, if only one quarter is used, the number of nickels increases by two starting with one nickel, leading to an odd pattern for the number of nickels.

Tables and charts can be seen in a wide variety of contexts. Advertising, medicine, pharmaceuticals, farming, and city planning all use tables and charts to convey information. Another problem-solving strategy involves making a model.

Make a Physical Model

Students can gain a great deal from representing the problem in a physical form. Blocks, coins, chips, and cookies can all be used to represent the problem depending on the context presented. Look at the problem in Figure 5.5. In this case, students can build the towers as seen in the diagram to help them determine the emerging pattern. Many students find that building a model helps them begin the task and gain insights into the problem as they do so.

Make a Physical Model is a strategy used in many careers. For example, city planners, developers, engineers, architects, and fashion designers all use models in their creative process. Archeologists also build models to depict how an an-

figure **5.4**

Organized List

CHANGE FOR $1.00

Quarters	Dimes	Nickels
4	0	0
3	2	1
3	1	3
3	0	5
2	5	0
2	4	2
2	3	4
2	2	6
2	1	8
1	7	1
1	6	3
1	5	5
1	4	7
1	3	9
1	2	11
1	1	13
1	0	15
0	9	2
0	8	4
0	7	6
0	6	8
0	5	10
0	4	12
0	3	14
0	2	16
0	1	18
0	0	20

figure **5.5**

Building Block Dilemma

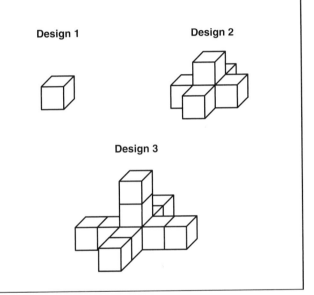

Building Block Dilemma

Your teacher watched her nephew building block towers. She noticed that the higher the center tower became, the more blocks her nephew placed on each side of the tower. If this pattern continues, how many blocks will be needed in a design 5 that has a tower 5 blocks high? How many blocks will be needed for a 10-block-high tower?

Design 1   Design 2

Design 3

cient civilization might have appeared, and scientists use prototypes to gain an understanding of different functions of their designs.

PROCESS STANDARDS

Representation

Graphs, diagrams, and tables are various ways to represent the information presented in the problem-solving task. Students should be encouraged to use several of these strategies in order to gain insights into the task. As students work to solve problems, they can think about the Rule of 5. The Rule of 5 refers to the five ways to represent problems:

1. Concrete representation
2. Tabular representation
3. Graphical representation
4. Symbolic representation
5. Verbal representation

For a more detailed description of the Rule of 5, see Chapter 7, Algebra: The Gateway.

MATH IN THE MEDIA

The adage, "Just sleep on it" as a problem-solving strategy turns out to have a foundation in research. Ulrich Wagner and Jan Born at the Universities of Lubeck and Cologne summarized their research showing that the brain remains active integrating recent knowledge with prior understandings while we sleep. As reported in January 2004 in the *Boston Globe* summarizing an article appearing in *Nature*, sixty-six subjects were trained on a mathematical task. After training, some of the subjects slept while others stayed awake. The subjects who slept were twice as likely to outperform their peers on a task involving the trained skill.

Work Backwards

This problem-solving strategy can appear to be counterintuitive. After all, if we knew the result, then there isn't really a problem to solve. However, in some cases, the end result is known and the task requires finding out how to arrive at the end result. The game of Poison involves logic, and using the strategy, Work Backwards, proves beneficial.

Students are given thirteen objects. These can be anything including cubes, coins, pencils, and so on. For purposes of this discussion, coins will be used. The game is played with two people and the objective of the game is to avoid removing the last coin as this coin represents the poison. Each player in turn removes one or two coins. Students should play the game several times and then be instructed to look for patterns or strategies that enable them to win most of the time. Knowing that they do not want to take the last coin, the fourth coin from the end becomes crucial.

TRY THIS

Why is it critical not to remove the fourth coin?

Students develop game-winning strategies based on key positions of the coins. Whether or not to go first is another decision to be made. Here is another problem in which the working backwards strategy proves beneficial.

> Samantha currently has an 80 average (arithmetic mean). Her teacher tells the class that they can drop their lowest test score out of the 11 tests. Samantha is thrilled to drop the 50 she earned two weeks ago. What is her new average?

Many students decide to guess and check to find Samantha's new average. Such guessing may take a very long time and may never lead to a correct solution. Working backwards from Samantha's mean of 80 indicates that the total of the 11 test scores must have been 880. Students can then subtract the low score of 50 and then divide by 10, the new number of test scores. Samantha's new mean is 83.

Working Backwards is a problem-solving strategy used by doctors as they proceed to diagnose patient's illnesses. Doctors begin with the symptoms and work backwards to their probable cause. Police investigate crime scenes working backwards from the clues as they establish what may have happened. When business executives plan trips, they often work backwards from the scheduled appointment in order to determine the appropriate flight to catch. Another problem-solving strategy for students to consider is Intelligent Guessing and Checking.

Use Intelligent Guessing and Checking

Random guessing allows students to engage in the problem, but random guessing alone is not a productive or efficient strategy. Using Intelligent Guessing and Checking is frequently coupled with a chart to track the guesses and then check the results.

Students are planning an after-school party. They have decided that 2 people will share a pizza, 3 students will share chips, and 5 students will share a salad. If there are a total of 62 options for food, how many students are attending the party? (Assume that there will not be any food left over.)

In this problem, students may recognize that they are working with multiples of 2, 3, and 5 and, therefore, a multiple of 30. Students may begin by selecting 30 students and then checking the results in terms of food. A chart as seen in Figure 5.6 will help students organize their work.

The strength of this problem-solving strategy rests on the intelligent guessing. Using some of the parameters in the task as in the previous problem allows the guesses to be more focused and targeted. This eliminates random guessing and streamlines the process. Gaining experiences in solving these problems provides a foundation as students learn to approach the task using variables and equations. Eventually, these algebraic tools focus their work so that guessing, even Intelligent Guessing and Checking, is no longer required.

Intelligent Guessing and Checking is seen outside of the classroom as contractors offer bids on projects. They calculate labor and material costs and estimate the time necessary to complete the project. These factors taken together compose the contractor's intelligent guess. Money managers use their expertise to make intelligent guesses in terms of investments. Another problem-solving strategy for students to consider is Act It Out.

figure **5.6**

Using Intelligent Guessing and Checking

Students	Pizza	Chips	Salad	Total
30	15	10	6	31
60	30	20	12	62

Act It Out

Using the problem-solving strategy, Act It Out, students dramatize the problem.

How many handshakes occur if 10 people meet for the first time?

In this problem, students might demonstrate the process of meeting each other. They quickly realize as they track the number of handshakes that there are a great number of them. In this case, students might consider trying a smaller number of people to see if they can determine a pattern. By physically shaking hands, students begin to notice that once one person has greeted everyone else in the group, that person is no longer involved. (See Chapter 7, Algebra: The Gateway, for more information on this handshake problem.) Another problem that encourages students to Act It Out involves traveling across a river.

Eight adults and 2 children are standing on shore trying to figure out how they can all get across the river. A small rowboat is available, and this boat can hold 1 adult or 1 child or both children. Thus, the possibilities for combinations of people in the boat are 1 adult alone, 1 child alone, or both children. Everyone can row the boat. How many one-way trips are needed to get everyone to the opposite shore?

TRY THIS

Solve the Crossing the River problem. Note your problem-solving strategy and your thinking process as you work toward the solution.

Students can act out this problem by creating two lines representing the banks of the river. Eight students represent the adults and 2 students play the role of the children. Everyone should wear some identifying badges as to their role in this problem. Post-it Notes labeled with an "A" for adult or "C" for child work well. By acting out the process of crossing the river, students begin to see an emerging pattern. Students discover that both children need to cross the river first and then 1 child returns to bring 1 adult over. This pattern continues until all of the adults are on the other side of the river and both children have

AUTHOR'S **Recall**

When I first started teaching, I presented problems in categories. I demonstrated each type of problem and then students practiced that type of problem. As a result, students successfully solved each type of problem, but they became confused if the wording varied slightly. I knew that I needed an alternative approach when I heard a student say, "But you haven't taught me that."

made their final trip. Students begin to realize that given 2 children who are doing most of the work, it takes 4 crossings for every 1 adult to cross. This can be expressed as $T = 4A + 1$ when T represents the number of trips and A represents the number of adults. This is the case when 2 children are involved. Interesting extensions can be explored by changing the number of children involved.

TRY THIS

Place the Crossing the River problem into a meaningful context for students in your area.

Act It Out is a popular strategy because students enjoy working together and having opportunities to move about the classroom. This is particularly true for those kinesthetic learners. (See Chapter 1, Teaching Mathematics for the Twenty-First Century.) Act It Out is similar to the Make a Physical Model strategy. In Act It Out, students are a part of the physical representation of the problem.

This problem-solving strategy can be seen outside of the classroom in the way many therapy groups use role modeling. Participants play a role so that they can act out what a person might be feeling in a particular situation. Lawyers use role playing to help prepare their clients or witnesses to take the stand in a trial. Using an Equation is another strategy that is available for students to select in the second stage of the heuristic, Make a Plan.

Use an Equation or Number Sentence

In some cases, identifying the variable and writing an equation to solve is the appropriate problem-solving strategy. We have included the term *number sentence* because some cases do not require the use of a variable in the solution process.

The sum of three consecutive integers is –39. Find the integers.

As students read the problem and verify the meaning of consecutive integers, they can use a variable, n, to establish the relationships. If n is the first integer, then $n + 1$ represents the second integer and $n + 2$ is the third. Some students may want to represent the integers by using subtraction. In this case, the three integers can be represented as n, $n - 1$, and $n - 2$. Interesting discussions occur as students compare their different approaches.

Use an Equation occurs in many different occupations. Investors work with equations as models for profit and loss statements; scientists use equations in terms of relationships and interactions of chemicals, and engineers solve problems using equations as they analyze stress loads on support beams. Another problem-solving strategy involves making a simpler problem.

Solve a Simpler Problem

The handshake problem mentioned earlier on page 107 can be solved by making a simpler problem and then searching for a pattern. Rather than beginning with ten handshakes, students might begin with three people meeting. The Solve a Simpler Problem strategy can also be used to approach the problem for finding the number of squares on an 8×8 grid. (See Figure 5.7.)

Students frequently try to outline the various-sized squares on the diagram. This soon becomes a confusing mess! An alternative approach involves working with a simpler problem. Students can first work with a smaller grid and then look for patterns that might be extended to the 8×8 square. Students might begin considering a 4×4 grid. Students quickly observe that one square measures 4×4. As they consider the number of 3×3 squares in the 4×4 grid, they need to think about the fact the 9 square units can be moved around the grid to four different locations. (See Figure 5.8.)

As students work to find the number of 2×2 squares that exist in the 4×4 grid, a paper model of a 2×2 grid can help students organize their thinking and keep track of

figure **5.7**

Solve a Simpler Problem

How Many Squares?

How many squares can you find on the checkerboard below?

Your task is to find out exactly how many squares are on the board. Show all of your work; explain your thinking and identify all strategies you use to solve the problem.

figure **5.8**

The Four Positions in a 3 × 3 Grid

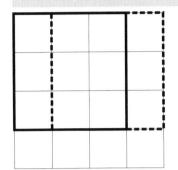

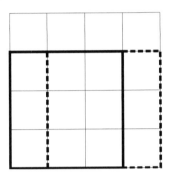

figure **5.9**

Finding the Number of Squares in a 4 × 4 Grid

SQUARE SIZE	NUMBER
4 × 4	1
3 × 3	4
2 × 2	9
1 × 1	16

figure **5.10**

Finding the Number of Squares in an 8 × 8 Grid

SQUARE SIZE	NUMBER
8 × 8	1
7 × 7	4
6 × 6	9
5 × 5	16
4 × 4	25
3 × 3	36
2 × 2	49
1 × 1	64

all of the locations. When students realize that there are 9 squares measuring 2 × 2 units, a pattern begins to emerge. (See Figure 5.9.)

Students readily see that there are 16 squares with a measure of 1 unit. By realizing that all of the numbers representing the quantities for the particular size squares in the chart are perfect squares, students can then make a conjecture that this pattern will continue when using the larger grid. By checking out a few larger sizes, students confidently conclude that the pattern indeed continues. (See Figure 5.10.)

By adding the total number for each size square, students find that there are 204 squares in the 8 × 8 grid.

This strategy, Solve a Simpler Problem, occurs frequently in our lives. Faced with a task such as learning how to use a new software tool, we tend to approach the learning the tool in small steps. Rather than sitting down to learn all that there is to know, we tend to take on smaller chunks at a time. When challenged to reorganize an office or a room, we tend to approach such a large task by breaking it down into smaller sections. Another problem-solving strategy looks to account for all possibilities.

Account for All Possibilities

This strategy uses organized lists in order to be certain that all the possibilities are included.

When 4 coins are tossed, what is the probability that there will be at least 2 heads?

figure **5.11**

Sample Space for Flipping 4 Coins				
HHHH	THHH	HHTT	HTTT	TTTT
	HTHH	HTHT	THTT	
	HHTH	HTTH	TTHT	
	HHHT	TTHH	TTTH	
	THHT			
	THTH			

figure **5.12**

Possible Areas Given 24-Ft Perimeter	
DIMENSIONS (ft.)	AREA (sq. ft.)
6 × 6	36
7 × 5	35
8 × 4	32
9 × 3	27
10 × 2	20
11 × 1	11

Middle school students can work with this problem by making a sample space of all of the possible outcomes. Organizing their list according to their identified approach assures them that they indeed have all of the possibilities. It is important that the students create their own organizing structure rather than being presented with a model to complete the task. There are several ways to set up the chart and having students compare their approaches leads to fruitful discussions and increased learning. (See Figure 5.11 for the sample space listing the results of flipping four coins.)

After the sample space has been created, students can simply count the number of outcomes that meet the conditions of the problem. The probability that the four coins will show at least two heads is $\frac{11}{16}$. Creating sample spaces when working with theoretical probabilities is discussed further in Chapter 11, Probability: Measures of Uncertainty. Another problem that can be solved using the strategy of Account for All Possibilities involves the comparison of two areas.

Two neighbors wanted to build sandboxes for their children. The sandboxes for both families have perimeters of 24 feet but the areas of the sandboxes differ by 8 square feet. What are the possible areas for the sandboxes? (Consider only integral measurements.)

Students can account for all the possibilities by setting up a chart. Knowing that the perimeters remain constant, students can determine the dimensions of the rectangular sandboxes. (See Figure 5.12.)

Now students simply need to select the areas that differ by 8 square feet. Students find that the sandboxes must measure 9 × 3 ft and 7 × 5 ft. A very similar strategy to accounting for all possibilities involves eliminating possibilities.

Ms. Jones researched her family tree to discover that several of her relatives had been born in Africa, specifically, Zimbabwe, Angola, and Botswana. Her ancestors' names were Shahid, Muhammad, and Elijah. Use the clues that follow to match the names with their places of birth:

1. Elijah is older than Muhammad.
2. Shahid's family moved to Botswana before he was born.
3. The youngest member of the Jones family was born in Angola.

Eliminating possibilities is one way to approach this logic puzzle. Students can eliminate options as they proceed through the clues. Creating a chart such as the one seen in Figure 5.13 helps organize the possibilities.

The second clue tells us that Shahid was born in Botswana and, therefore, we can eliminate Muhammad and Elijah in terms of being born in Botswana. Students use the first clue combined with the third to determine that Muhammad was born in Angola and Elijah was born in Zimbabwe.

Accounting for all possibilities and eliminating possibilities are similar strategies. We use these strategies frequently as we make choices. For example, we use these strategies as we select a movie. We might look in the newspaper for listings of movies in our area, eliminate ones we have seen or choose not to see, and then make our selection from the remaining options. Another problem-solving strategy students can select involves adopting a different point of view.

Adopt a Different Point of View

This is one of the hardest strategies to implement with students. If students see a way to approach a problem, even if it

figure **5.13**

Eliminating the Possibilities			
	Jones Family		
	Shahid	Muhammad	Elijah
Zimbabwe			
Angola			
Botswana	Yes	X	X

is not the most efficient method, they want to proceed with that approach. It is sometimes difficult to watch students solve a problem using "brute force" when a more elegant solution is available. Allowing students to solve the problem in their way and then discussing the various approaches taken provides stimulating learning opportunities. Some students will appreciate the more elegant approach found by their peers; other students will hold on to their own method. By hearing and seeing other solutions, these students may be more receptive during the next problem-solving opportunity. If students do not offer the solution that the teacher had hoped they would, the teacher may present the solution as another option. See Figure 5.14 for an example of using a different point of view in a geometric context.

Some students may attempt to find the area of the two shaded triangles. They may conclude that they need a different approach because they don't know the length of the base for either one of the shaded triangles. Another approach that students might select is to calculate the area of the unshaded triangle and then subtract that area from the area of the rectangle. Following this line of reasoning, students calculate the area of the triangle using the formula $\frac{1}{2}bh$ and arrive at the result of 36 cm^2. Subtracting the area of the triangle from the area of the rectangle yields the final result of 36 cm^2 (72 cm^2 – 36 cm^2). Still another point of view connects the area of the white triangle to the area of rectangle. Looking at this relationship, students may see that any triangle that shares the same base and the same height with the rectangle will always have one-half the area of that rectangle. Students may come to this same conclusion after subtracting the area of the white triangle from the rectangle.

We come to appreciate this problem-solving strategy as we are presented with a conflict to resolve. When we can see another individual's point of view, it can lead to a compromise or a better understanding of the issues involved in reaching a solution. In an athletic contest and many board games such as chess, understanding strategies that an opponent might use provides more useful information in establishing one's own options.

figure **5.14**

Using a Different Point of View

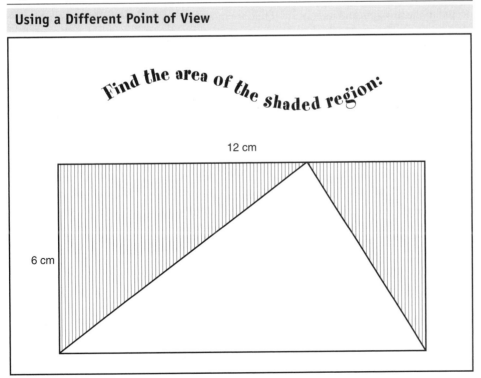

Find the area of the shaded region:

12 cm

6 cm

Use Unit Analysis

Middle school students can focus on the units as they approach such problems as finding the number of seconds in two years.

TRY THIS

Find the number of seconds in two years that are not leap years.

Students frequently make errors on such tasks as they can forget an important factor in the conversion from years to seconds. If they keep track of the units, they are not as likely to prone to such errors.

$$2 \; years \times \frac{365 \; days}{1 \; year} \times \frac{24 \; hours}{1 \; day} \times \frac{60 \; min}{1 \; hour} \times \frac{60 \; sec}{1 \; min}$$

Students need to recognize that days divided by day produces a value of 1 whole just as a number divided by itself is 1. As seen in Figure 5.15, the remaining units are seconds, which is the required unit stated in the problem.

Students simply need to perform the calculations to determine that there are 63,072,000 seconds in two years.

TRY THIS

Use unit analysis:

If you could count at the rate of one number per second, how long will it take you to count to a million?

If you could count at the rate of one number per second, how long will it take you to count to a billion?

Unit analysis puts the appropriate emphasis on the units. Many teachers require labeling an answer as a last step, but by keeping track of the units, students remain connected to the problem and its context. They are more likely to reflect on the reasonableness of an answer when they view the answer in terms of the appropriate number of units. See Chapter 6, Making Sense of Number and Operations, for more on unit analysis.

Unit analysis links many disciplines, particularly branches of science. Biology, physics, botany, and geology, for example, all use unit analysis to ensure that the calculations have been set up correctly. If the units simplify to meet the requirements of the problem, scientists are reassured that they have included the necessary components of the problem.

As seen in several of the problems presented thus far, there are several strategies that can be used effectively with any one task. Frequently more than one strategy can be used to solve typical tasks presented in middle school. When students are given the opportunity to explore problems and solve them using various strategies, they will frequently use a new or unprecedented solution process. It is important to recognize these new approaches and have students share their processes with the class. Giving students experiences in using the entire list of strategies helps them become more comfortable and increases their options as they look to Make a Plan. Finding problems to present to stu-

figure **5.15**

Unit Analysis

$$2 \; years \times \frac{365 \; days}{1 \; year} \times \frac{24 \; hours}{1 \; day} \times \frac{60 \; min}{1 \; hour} \times \frac{60 \; sec}{1 \; min}$$

dents can be challenging. The area in mathematics referred to as discrete mathematics offers a vast resource for problems that are appropriate for middle school students.

Discrete Mathematics

Although many of the ideas in discrete mathematics have been around since the days of Euclid (300 B.C.), discrete mathematics found new attention with advances in the field of mathematics, particularly those spawned by the technology eruption approximately 40 years ago.

Discrete mathematics, as defined by John Dossey, is characterized as "mathematics of finite situations that require the establishment of the existence of a solution, the number of possible alternatives, or the identification of the best solution for a specified problem" (Dossey, 1991, p. 3). The NCTM's 1989 *Curriculum and Evaluation Standard* defines discrete mathematics as "the study of mathematical properties of sets and systems that have only a finite number of elements" (NCTM, 1989, p. 176). These definitions offer a framework that suggests the vast range of topics included in discrete mathematics. For example, sets, counting techniques, iteration and recursion, networks and graphs, models, probability, and the study of algorithms all contribute to discrete mathematics. Discrete mathematics provides challenging experiences for middle school students to develop their problem-solving strategies. Discrete mathematics offers varied and interesting real-world contexts in which students apply the various problem-solving techniques. Furthermore, discrete mathematics provides opportunities for students to experience and develop skills in the other NCTM process standards: reasoning and proof, communication, connections, and representation. Discrete mathematics offers opportunities for students to develop an intuitive foundation on which to build as they proceed to more advanced and symbolic approaches in high school. In this section, we will explore four topics in discrete mathematics: counting techniques, sets, patterns, and networks and graphs.

Point Well Taken

"The interaction of discrete mathematics and computers has made possible powerful new applications, has focused attention on new kinds of problems, and has forced us to look at traditional mathematics in new ways."

—*Gardiner, 1991, p. 10*

TRY THIS

As you explore each of the discrete mathematics problems in this section, take note of the problem-solving strategies you use.

Counting Techniques

The fundamental counting principle can be applied in many relevant contexts for middle school students.

> The class is selecting pizza for their upcoming celebration. They can order either thin or thick crusts, and the toppings include extra cheese, green peppers, onions, sausage, and pepperoni. To make the ordering easier, the students decide that they only want one topping on each pizza. How many different types of pizza can the class order?

As students apply the problem-solving heuristic, Get Started, Make a Plan, Take Action, Reflect, to this pizza problem, the context is familiar to them. Getting the students to articulate what the problem is asking helps verify that they understand the task. Step 2 in the heuristic, Make a Plan, can involve several different strategies. Some students might select to account for all possibilities and use a chart; others might make a picture and others may act it out. Once students have had a chance to explore the problem independently or in small groups, they can share their findings with the class. After hearing students' suggestions, the teacher can explicitly demonstrate a tree diagram as a way of recording all of the possible pizzas. (See Figure 5.16.)

figure **5.16**

Tree Diagram Pizza Options

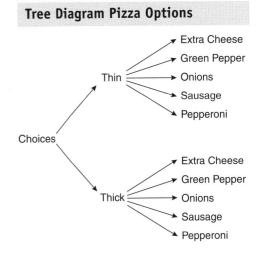

Point Well Taken

"Consideration of discrete scenarios provides a natural method for improving problem solving skills, practicing arithmetic, developing algebraic concepts, appreciation of algebra, and eliciting advanced mathematical ideas and formalism."

—Hersberger, Frederick, & Lipman, 1991, p. 51

By counting the last set of branches in the diagram, students determine that there are ten different pizzas they can order. After several experiences with such problems, teachers can probe whether or not students see similarities in the solution methods. As students reflect back on these problems, they realize that multiplying the number options led to the solution. At this point, teachers can direct the students' attention to the Fundamental Counting Principle: *If there are* m *ways to make one choice and* n *ways of making a second choice, then there are* (m)(n) *ways to make the first choice followed by the second.*

There are many contexts that are familiar to middle school students in which they can explore the Fundamental Counting Principle. Possible selections of outfits given six blouses and four pairs of slacks, designing a baseball uniform, selecting items from a menu, selecting one president for student council out of five candidates and then choosing a vice president out of a pool of six different candidates are just a few examples.

Another counting principle is referred to as the Pigeonhole Principle. Essentially, this principle states that if you have a certain number of pigeonholes with a greater number of pigeons than places for them, some pigeons need to occupy the same hole. Middle school students are always interested in problems relating to themselves. The Pigeonhole Principle is illustrated in the following problem involving students' birthdays.

> This morning I wrote all of your names and birthday months on separate slips of paper. I am going to reach into the bag without looking and pull out a name with the month in which that person was born. How many slips of paper must I select in order *to be certain* that I will have two people born in the same month?

For the sake of discussion, we will assume that there are twenty-eight students in the class. Using an overhead transparency of a 2 by 6 array with the months of the year labeled in each section provides a concrete representation of the task. Some teachers have labeled egg cartons to help students visualize the problem. Teachers can begin to draw a student's name and then place the paper or a chip on the corresponding square representing the month of birth. Teachers can guide students' thinking at this point by asking how likely is it that we will get a match on the next draw. Do you think that is more likely that we will not get a match? These questions can be repeated after each time a name is drawn. Students begin to see the pattern to realize that they would need thirteen selections to guarantee a match. Asking how many times we would have to draw names to guarantee that three students would have the same birth month can extend this idea. For three students having the same birth month, the worst-case scenario helps students realize that on the twenty-fifth selection, we are assured of getting three students having the same birth month. Students should be encouraged to reflect back on the solutions to articulate a pattern and then to state the pattern symbolically. The problem-solving strategy, Make a Chart, can help in this process. (See Figure 5.17.)

If students refer to n as the number of people, then $12(n - 1) + 1$ represents the number of draws required for that many people to have matching months. $12(n - 1)$ represents all of the draws without meeting the condition and the remaining $+1$ guarantees the result (Spangler, 1991, pp. 55–58). By encouraging students to reflect back and look for the pattern, teachers help students solidify their understanding and take it to a higher level, the symbolic representation.

figure **5.17**

Matching Birth Months	
NUMBER OF PEOPLE	**NUMBER OF DRAWS NEEDED**
2	13
3	25
4	37
5	49
6	61

Counting techniques, such as the Fundamental Counting Principle, also include the exploration of permutations and combinations. Before any formalized procedure is introduced, however, students need many experiences simply solving these types of problems.

> There are 4 runners competing in the 100-meter run. How many different ways might these runners be assigned to the lanes on the track?

Because this problem is in a context that middle school students understand, they may jump to step 2 in the heuristic. Before they do so, however, it is important that they state the problem in their own words so that they are certain that they understand the task. For this problem, some students might want to personalize the runners by giving them names as a first step. Students have several choices as they select a strategy. Act It Out might involve students standing in a line as if they were on a track. One student exchanges place with another and the new arrangement is recorded. Solve a Simpler Problem might entail using a smaller number of runners and then looking for a pattern. A third appropriate strategy, Account for All Possibilities, might use a chart and make an organized list. After the students have had a chance to explore, implement their strategy, and reflect back as to the reasonableness of their answers, students need time to exchange their ideas about the problem. After the students have had a chance to share their understandings, the teacher may introduce the concept of factorials. In the lane assignment problem, each runner is assigned to one lane. The officials of the race have four choices in terms of whom they can select for lane 1. Once that choice has been made, the officials have three remaining choices for runners to occupy lane 2. This process continues until all of the runners have been assigned. Students can make the connection with the reason for the operation, multiplication, as they compare their answers to the solution presented in Figure 5.18.

Teachers can present the term *factorial* and the notation at this point. 4! represents the solution to the runners' arrangement. This problem can be extended to ask, "What is the probability that Frederica is assigned to the first lane?" Students can analyze the complete sample space to realize that each individual is in the first lane for 6 out of 24 arrangements. Another way to think about the problem is to consider that there are only 4 lanes and, therefore, Frederica has a 25% chance of being in the first lane.

In this problem the arrangement of the runners was a significant factor. When order matters, as in this case, the possible arrangements are called permutations. Not all situations include order as a primary consideration.

> A class is designing a lottery to be used during a fund-raising event. The students who purchase a ticket select two numbers from 1 to 6. To win, they need to match two numbers that have been written on Ping-Pong balls. The balls are mixed up and then drawn from a bin. (The selected ball is not replaced in the bin before the next one is drawn.) How many combinations of two numbers can be selected from the six digits?

In this case, the students need to match the digits with no regard to order. Students can create a sample space of all of the ways that the two Ping-Pong balls might be selected from the bin. See Figure 5.19.

At this point, students will likely ponder whether 3,2 is the same as 2,3. As the contestants in the lottery were asked to simply match the numbers, order is not important. Students can then cross out all of the duplicates in the sample space to reveal that there are 15 ways that the numbers can be selected 2 at a time from a set of 6 numbers. Students might also approach the problem in terms of selections. For the first number, there are 6 options, and there are 5 options for the second number. Therefore, there are 30 ways to select the 2 numbers. Each option is repeated and, therefore, it is necessary to divide by 2. Dividing by 2 into the 30 ways gives the result of 15 ways to select the 2 numbers. Because order does not matter in this context, the problem involves combinations.

Students need many opportunities to work with permutations and combinations using numbers that are small enough so that students can determine the sample spaces. As students become comfortable with determining when order counts and when it does not count, they can be challenged to look for patterns in the solution process. Students can then understand the necessity of dividing to avoid repetitive combinations when order does not matter in the context of the problem.

figure **5.18**

Number of Ways Runners Can Be Assigned to Lanes

Lane 1	Lane 2	Lane 3	Lane 4
4 possibilities	3 possibilities	2 possibilities	1 possibility

$4 \times 3 \times 2 \times 1 = 24$ ways

Did You **Know**?

French mathematician Christian Kramp (1760–1826) first used ! as a symbol for factorials in 1808.

figure **5.19**

Sample Space for 6 Numbers Selected 2 at a Time

1,2	2,1	3,1	4,1	5,1	6,1
1,3	2,3	3,2	4,2	5,2	6,2
1,4	2,4	3,4	4,3	5,3	6,3
1,5	2,5	3,5	4,5	5,4	6,4
1,6	2,6	3,6	4,6	5,6	6,5

PROCESS STANDARDS

Reasoning and Proof

By placing problems in a context that is understood by students, teachers can help students reason effectively about the situation. By using strategies that empower them to make sense of the situation, students learn how to make conjectures and then test their thinking. Even pursuing inappropriate paths toward an answer can contribute to students' understanding.

figure **5.20**

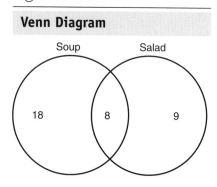

Venn Diagram

Sets

Throughout the primary and elementary curriculum, students have had many experiences working with sets. Sorting and classifying various shapes according to a variety of attributes are typical tasks students experience in the primary-grade levels. As students progress into the middle school, students can work with Venn diagrams to sort and classify. See Figure 5.20.

> At the local restaurant, 42 customers ordered lunch yesterday: 26 ordered soup with their meal, 17 ordered a salad with their lunch, and 8 people ordered both soup and a salad. How many people ordered just soup with their meal? How many did not order either soup or salad?

Using a Venn diagram can help students logically approach this problem.

The intersection of the two circles represents the number of customers that ordered both the soup and salad with their meal. Consequently, 18 people ordered just the soup with their meal and 9 ordered the salad. Adding up the number of customers in the diagram, students find that 35 people ordered soup and/or salad, indicating that 7 customers did not order either of those items.

Venn diagrams can also be used as a tool to gather information about the class. Students can be asked to select their favorite sports, academic subjects, and movie or rock bands given three options. Students then write their initials or use a sticky dot to indicate their preferences. They can use the intersection of the circles if they cannot decide between two options. Students can also place their sticker in the intersection of all three circles indicating that they have no preference given those choices. Data about the class preferences and characteristics can be gathered over a period of time and then used in a data analysis unit to find out about the "average" class member. Venn diagrams can serve as a data collection device, a vehicle to enhance logical reasoning and a problem-solving tool.

Patterns

As seen earlier in this chapter, looking for patterns, a habit of mind, is also a strategy used in discrete mathematics. In the elementary grades students extend numerical patterns by filling in blanks in a series.

Middle school students can explore recursive patterns as in the Fibonacci series. (See Chapter 7, Algebra: The Gateway, page 194, for the pattern's development and further explorations within the pattern.) In Figure 5.21 students investigate the number of ways that can be traveled to reach location 7.

An additional condition of this problem is that progress always proceeds to the right. One cannot backtrack to the left. As students work to explore the number of routes, they may decide to work with a simpler problem, such as the number of ways to get to location 1, then 2, and then 3. By building a chart, students may begin to see the Fibonacci series at work. There is only one way to get to location 1, but there are two ways to get to location 2. There are three ways to arrive at location 3. At this point, the students can be encouraged to predict how many ways they can proceed to get to location 7. After tracing the number of ways to arrive at location 4, students may make the connection with

figure **5.21**

Finding the Number of Ways to Reach a Location

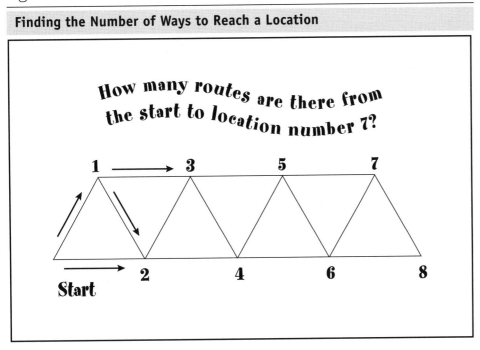

the Fibonacci series. These students can explore the application in terms of why it is an example of the application of the series. Students can now extend the chart to find that there are twenty-one ways to get to location 7. If students have not worked with this series, exploration of the Fibonacci series and its connections to art, architecture, music, and nature provide students with a new perspective on the relevancy of mathematics. The Fibonacci series is recursive in that the next value in the series depends on the two values preceding it. Middle school students can explore recursive patterns further in the Tower of Hanoi problem. (See Figure 5.22.)

In this problem, the students are asked to find the smallest number of moves to transfer all seven disks to another post if a larger disk cannot be placed on a smaller one and only one disk can be moved at one time. Students need time to explore this problem. They may decide to solve a simpler problem and build up to solving the task with all seven disks. Students can use a chart to keep track of each move that they make. See Figure 5.23 for a chart of the moves 1 through 5.

figure **5.22**

Tower of Hanoi

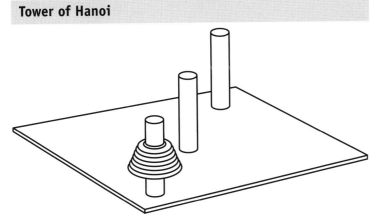

figure **5.23**

Tower of Hanoi Problem

NUMBER OF DISKS	MINIMUM MOVES NEEDED
1	1
2	3
3	7
4	15
5	31

Point Well Taken

"Each problem that I solved became a rule which served afterwards to solve other problems."
—*René Descartes*

At this point, students may recognize that the pattern involves powers of 2. The minimum number of moves is one less than a power of 2. If m = number of moves and n = the number of disks to be moved, students can write the equation, $m = 2^n - 1$. They can then use this equation to find the number of moves needed to move seven disks. Students might also consider the recursive nature of this problem: To move three disks, the moves required for moving two disks are used plus three additional moves; to move four disks, the moves required in moving all three previous disks are used plus an additional four moves. A characteristic of discrete mathematics is suggested in the Tower of Hanoi problem. The recursive nature seen in proceeding from moving one disk to the next indicates the possibility to find a rule governing this process. Finding and deriving rules or algorithms represents a significant aspect of discrete mathematics typically studied in high school and college.

Networks and Graphs

In the realm of discrete mathematics, a graph is a connection of vertex points and edges. A vertex is represented by a solid dot and an edge is a line segment connecting the vertices. A vertex is said to be odd if there is an odd number of edges connecting that vertex with other vertices. A vertex is even if there is an even number of edges connecting that vertex with others. The relationship of even and odd number of vertex points becomes apparent as students explore whether or not networks are traceable. In other words, can the network be traced without going back over an edge a second time? Blackline Master 5.2, Network Exploration, explores networks. By looking at the relationships between the odd and even number of vertices, students can make conjectures about whether or not a particular network is traceable. They can make up examples and then look for counterexamples to disprove their conjectures. In *Network Exploration* all networks except network 3 are traceable. Networks are traceable if they have only even vertices or they are traceable if they have exactly two odd vertices. In example 3 in Blackline Master 5.2, the network displays two even vertices but three odd vertices.

The Seven Bridges of Konigsberg intrigued Leonard Euler, and, as a result of his work, graph theory came into being in 1736. The question posed originally asked whether or not the citizens of Konigsberg could travel over all seven bridges without going back over any one of them a second time. Six of the bridges connected two islands to the shoreline and the seventh bridge connected the two islands. (See Figure 5.24.)

figure **5.24**

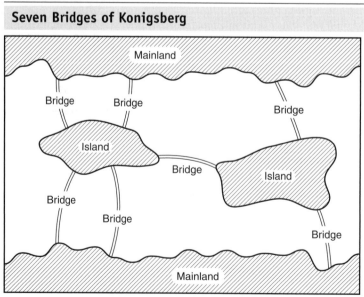

Seven Bridges of Konigsberg

After exploring networks, students can determine whether or not these seven bridges can be crossed once and only once as part of the same walk. Students will notice that all of the vertices are odd; the task cannot be accomplished.

Two professors at Princeton University, John Conway and Michael Paterson, developed an interesting game called Sprouts. Two players begin with any number of dots. In turn, players connect two of the dots and then place a new dot or sprout on the line just created. The object of the game is to be the last person to connect two dots. This game, based on networks, has two simple rules: The dots can have no more than three line segments coming from them and the line segments cannot cross over each other.

TRY THIS

Play Sprouts with a partner. Begin with three dots and look for a pattern for winning strategies. Is it better to start first? Why or why not? Does the pattern work if there is an even number of dots?

Discrete mathematics offers a rich resource for problems that are engaging for middle school students and lead to the development of important concepts in mathematics. Counting techniques, sets, patterns, and networks and graphs offer a variety of contexts in which students can explore their problem-solving strategies while building their knowledge base in mathematics and enhancing their abilities to reason, communicate, make connections, and use multiple representations.

Changed Emphasis on Problem Solving

The problem-solving strategies as illustrated in the many examples provided in the previous section became an emphasis of curriculum reform in the late 1980s. These strategies were directly taught by teachers and practiced by students. In middle school classes today, students are presented with worthwhile tasks, and it is through the students' explorations, discoveries, conjectures, and conclusions that important mathematical concepts, specific problem-solving strategies, and computational skills are developed. The emphasis places a priority on problem solving. In many classrooms, a problem is posed at the beginning of the lesson and the lesson itself entails what students do to make sense of the problem. Students present their strategies to the whole class and the teacher facilitates the discussion to highlight the mathematics and deepen students' understandings.

Problem solving can take on a variety of structures within a single classroom. Teachers can present a problem and then ask individuals to think about the problem by themselves before joining a group or just one other student. Providing individual processing time allows students an opportunity to think independently. Many students state that they need this time to think so that they have ideas to contribute to the group.

A strategy teachers have found successful in covering several topics at once is called a jigsaw. For example, a teacher wants to work on four different problem-solving strategies: Find a Pattern, Act It Out, Make a Physical Model, and Adopt a Different Point of View. Each team member is assigned one of those strategies. Each student moves to a station assigned to that problem-solving strategy and members from the different groups work together to develop ways that they will use to teach the strategy to their teammates when they return to their own groups.

A major change for many veteran teachers adopting a problem-solving approach involves the delegation of authority. As students become involved in group work, they take ownership of many of management concerns. Acquiring the supplies, tracking progress of their work, making certain that team members understand the work, asking clarifying questions, and challenging each other's thinking all fall on students' shoulders. The teacher's preparation before class in the careful planning and structuring of the tasks enables the

Did You **Know**?

A traceable network that begins and ends with the same vertex is called an Euler circuit; an Euler path is a traceable network that begins at one vertex and ends at a different vertex.

REACT | **REFLECT**

Which problem-solving strategies did you use in the solution process of those problems from discrete mathematics?

students to work hard during the class. As students take on more of the management issues throughout the course of the class period, teachers can observe students, listen attentively to their thinking, and ask them questions to deepen their understanding.

RESEARCH

Educational research on problem solving is vast with a great deal of emphasis on the process of problem solving itself. More recently, however, research has looked at the impact of problem solving on student learning. Stein, Boaler, and Silver summarize the current research that focused on the impact of reform curricula on student performance as determined by various standardized tests. In spite of the varying formats of the studies, Stein, Boaler, and Silver (2003, p. 248) draw the following conclusions:

> [S]tudents taught using the reform curricula, compared with those taught using more traditional curricula, generally exhibited greater conceptual understanding and performed at considerably higher levels with respect to problem solving (Boaler, 1997; Huntley et al., 2000; Thompson & Senk, 2001). Second, these gains did not come at the expense of those aspects of mathematics measured on more conventional standardized tests. Compared with students taught using conventional curricula, students who were taught using reform curricula performed at approximately the same level on standardized tests that assessed mathematical skills and procedures (Boaler et al., 2002; Riordan & Noyce, 2001; Schoenfeld, 2002; Thompson & Senk, 2001).

Stein, Boaler, and Silver also point out that the research indicates that students exhibited a positive attitude and saw greater applications and usefulness of mathematics using the reform curricula (2003, p. 248).

SUMMARY

Problem solving must not be relegated to the end of a set of exercises. Middle school students, by their very nature, need to explore, analyze, create, discover, prove, and disprove conjectures. They need to make connections between topics, and they need to build confidence in their problem-solving skills by taking control over their choices and monitoring their progress. Middle grade students need to discuss, explore, and participate in the construction of the rules. By placing the problem solving up front in their curricula, teachers are providing opportunities for students to engage in the discovery of mathematics and see mathematics as relevant, useful, and elegant.

Problem solving requires that teachers have a vast mathematical knowledge base; it demands that teachers incorporate ongoing assessments of students' understandings so that they can make informed decisions as to next steps. Administrators need to support the implementation of problem solving by providing time for teachers to collaborate and funding professional development opportunities. Problem solving serves to engage students as young mathematicians. Every student deserves the right and the privilege of such meaningful work.

The highlights from this chapter include the following points:

- Problem solving involves the four other process standards: connections, communication, representation, and reasoning and proof.
- Problem solving engages students and helps develop conceptual understandings.
- Problem solving makes mathematics relevant.
- Components of a problem-solving program include using a heuristic, finding worthwhile tasks, explicitly addressing problem-solving strategies, and providing appropriate problem-solving tools.
- The teacher's role in the problem-solving process includes finding worthwhile tasks, promoting classroom discourse, helping the class identify group norms, establishing collaborative groups, monitoring groups' progress, and providing rubrics for judging outcomes of the process.

- Students' role in the problem-solving process includes developing collaborative skills, providing appropriate support to members in the group, displaying an open disposition, and monitoring their own problem-solving process.
- There are many problem-solving strategies. Some tasks may be approached using several different strategies or a combination of strategies.
- Discrete mathematics offers a wide variety of problems for middle school students to explore.

Student Performance on International and National Assessments

TIMSS

In a sequence of starts and stops, an elevator travels from the first floor to the fifth floor and then to the second floor. From there, the elevator travels to the fourth floor and then to the third floor. If the floors are 3 m apart, how far has the elevator traveled? (53% correct)

- **A.** 18 m
- **B.** 27 m
- **C.** 30 m
- **D.** 45 m

NAEP

How many hours are equal to 150 minutes? (58% correct)

- **A.** $1\frac{1}{2}$
- **B.** $2\frac{1}{4}$
- **C.** $2\frac{1}{3}$
- **D.** $2\frac{1}{2}$
- **E.** $2\frac{5}{6}$

EXERCISES

From the Reading

1. What is "residue?" How does it impact lesson planning?

2. The cartoon illustrating Paige Fox and her attitude as she reads a math problem asks her to apply her knowledge of area and percents. Rewrite the problem and place the same topics in a more engaging context.

3. The title of this chapter is "Problem Solving: An Approach to Teaching and Learning Mathematics." Review the major points made in this chapter. What questions remain for you?

4. Solve this problem. Try to note your strategies as you proceed.

   If $\frac{x}{y} = 1$ *and* $x + y = 1$, find the value of *xy*.

5. Solve this problem. Try to note your strategies as you proceed.

   The high school football team scored a total of 21 points. Points can be earned in the following ways:

Touchdown (TD)	6 points
Point After (PAT)	1 point
Safety (S)	2 points
Field Goal (FD)	3 points

   How many ways could the team have scored 21 points? (Note: The PAT can only occur after a touchdown.)

6. If automobile plates display three letters followed by three digits, what is the total number of plates that can be made if no repetitions are allowed?

7. Mr. Williams gets dressed in the morning without turning on a light. He has some brown, blue, black, and grey unmatched socks. Since he cannot see in the dark, how many socks will Mr. Williams have to select before he is assured of having a matching set to put on?

8. There were 230 high school students who completed a survey about languages that they have studied:

   74 students studied German
   99 students studied Spanish
   90 students studied French
   56 students studied French and German
   65 students studied German and Spanish
   81 students studied both Spanish and French
   6 students studied all three languages

   How many students studied German but not French or Spanish? How many students did not study any foreign languages?

9. A box contains four slips of paper. Each piece has either a 3, 5, 6, or 7 written on it. Each piece is selected from the box and then placed on a table in the order that it was selected. How many four-digit numbers are possible to select? How many even numbers are possible? How many prime numbers are possible?

10. Betty tells Veronica a secret on June 1. Veronica tells two friends on June 2 and these two friends tell two friends on June 3. This process repeats until the end of the day on June 10. How many people know Betty's secret?

11. Select two problems from the previous questions. Compare your approaches with that of other classmates. What insights did you gain in this process?

12. Explain why it is beneficial for students to solve a problem in their own way. Are there any disadvantages?

13. Solve this problem using unit analysis:

> Find the approximate cost of traveling 5,600 miles if your car gets 18 miles for every gallon of gas and gas costs $1.68 per gallon on average throughout your trip.

On Your Own

Visit three websites listed in this chapter. Summarize the sites' offerings and try some of the problems presented. Be ready to share your findings with the class.

Portfolio Question

How confident are you as a problem solver? How might you develop your skills further?

Scenes from a Classroom

A seventh-grade teacher, Mr. Fermat, has just completed an explanation of how to solve linear equations in one and two steps. Students appeared attentive and he was pleased with their engagement. After concluding his explanation, Mr. Fermat asked the students if they had any questions. Mr. Fermat knew that if he waited patiently, someone might come up with a question. In this instance, the students remained quiet. Mr. Fermat then suggested that the students open their books and begin the assignment as there were 15 minutes remaining in the class. As students began working, Mr. Fermat walked around the room observing their work. As he approached Malia's desk, she stopped him and asked a question about a problem. Mr. Fermat repeated a point he had made in his explanation and reminded Malia that she needed to maintain the balance in the equation. Mr. Fermat then moved on to another student. This next student asked a similar question. Suddenly, Mr. Fermat found that he was repeating the exact same explanation to many students. As more students continued to ask similar questions, Mr. Fermat became more frustrated. He then called for all students' attention to the board. He waited for the class to quiet down and then he went over the steps for solving equations with the entire class. Students recognized that their teacher was frustrated because his voice was becoming louder, and he repeatedly banged his fist on the board as he pointed to each step. Fortunately, the class period ended and Mr. Fermat headed toward the teacher's lounge. "I can't believe that class. Right after I had finished the explanation, the students didn't have any questions. When they started to do some problems, then they had questions! It felt as though no one was listening the first time! What am I going to do?"

Write a response in your journal to Mr. Fermat's dilemma. What suggestions would you make in terms of his lesson plans for the coming days? Be as specific as possible.

RESOURCES

Teacher's Bookcase

Crawford, L., & Wood, C. (1998). *Guidelines for the responsive classroom.* **Greenfield, MA: Northeast Foundation for Children.**

The authors provide activities, suggestions, and strategies for building respectful and productive classroom communities.

Danielson, C. (1997). *A collection of performance tasks and rubrics: Middle school mathematics.* **Larchmont, NY: Eye On Education.**

As the title suggests, this resource offers performance assessment tasks and rubrics. The author includes standards that are addressed as well as some student work that has been evaluated according to the rubric.

Dunn, A. (Ed.). (1980). *Mathematical bafflers.* **New York: Dover Publications.**

This is a collection of problem-solving tasks that includes algebra, geometry, probability, and logic. The grade range is vast and the resource provides one method of solution.

Frohlichstein, J. (1967). *Mathematical fun, games and puzzles.* **New York: Dover Publications.**

This resource offers a great supply of number puzzles, games, and number tricks. The author provides solutions as well as rankings as to difficulty.

Gardner, M. (1987). *Mathematical puzzles and diversions.* **Chicago: University of Chicago Press.**

Martin Gardner is the master. This edition of his problems, complete with solutions and his engaging commentary, provides many areas to explore with middle school students.

Johnson, A. (1999). *Famous problems and their mathematicians.* **Englewood, CO: Libraries Unlimited.**

This resource presents over 100 problems from the history of mathematics and includes particularly engaging comments about the mathematicians who posed and/or solved them.

Pappas, T. (1989). *The joy of mathematics.* **San Carlos, CA: Wide World of Publishing.**

This resource includes problems to explore along with a little history and connections to everyday life. The author demonstrates connections with mathematics and architecture, art, and nature, for example.

Polya, G. (1957). *How to solve it.* **Garden City, NY: Doubleday.**

As the creator of the first heuristic and as one who is referred to as the father of problem solving, reading Polya's work provides insights into the process of problem solving.

For Further Reading

Baroody, A., & Wilkins, J. (2004, February). Triangular array: Involving students in mathematical inquiry. *Mathematics Teaching in the Middle School.*

Students are challenged to find the fewest number of moves to invert a triangle of thirty-six pennies. Students explore number patterns and many problem-solving strategies as they engage in a meaningful inquiry.

Buschman, L. (2004, February). Teaching problem solving in mathematics. *Teaching Children Mathematics,* **302.**

The author explores some of the pitfalls inherent in the implementation of a problem-solving program. From a teacher's insecurity about his or her own problem-solving abilities to finding appropriate tasks, suggestions are made as to how to plan and take the important steps toward effective learning strategies.

English, L. (1997, November). Promoting a problem-posing classroom. *Teaching Children Mathematics,* **172.**

Students take on the task of posing problems as a result of solving other problems.

Friedler, L. (1996, March). Problem solving with discrete mathematics. *Teaching Children Mathematics,* **426.**

The author explores problems involving discrete mathematics that are appropriate for fifth graders. Students work with scheduling conflicts to discover patterns in the networks.

National Council of Teachers of Mathematics. (1980). *Problem solving in school mathematics. 1980 yearbook.* **Reston, VA: NCTM.**

A collection of articles on problem solving covering all grade levels.

Tobias, S. (1993). *Overcoming math anxiety.* **London: W. W. Norton.**

The author presents realistic approaches for dealing with math anxiety.

Tratton, P., & Midgett, C. (2001, May). Learning through problems: A powerful approach to teaching mathematics. *Teaching Children Mathematics,* **7, 532.**

The authors present the case for using problem solving as a tool for learning. Using specific examples from the classroom, students' strategies are highlighted and factors contributing to the effectiveness of problem solving are explained.

Links

This site offers famous problems from the history of mathematics.
http://mathforum.org/isaac/mathhist.html

These sites offer problems of the week.
www.mathforum.com.
www.mathcounts.org
www.wits.ac.za/ssproule/pow.htm
www.mathsurf.com/teacher

These sites present brainteasers and puzzles.
www.cut-the-knot.com
www.mathpuzzle.com
www.greylabyrinth.com/puzzles.htm
www.dse.nl/puzzle/index_us.html
www.aimsedu.org/puzzle/index.html
http://barryispuzzled.com
www.logicville.com
www.puzzles.com/P

REFERENCES

Boaler, J. (1997). *Experiencing school mathematics: Teaching styles, sex and setting.* Buckingham, UK: Open University Press.

Boaler, J., Brodie, K., Chou, R., Gifford, H., Hand, V., Pilsner, K., Shahan, E., Somerfield, M., Staples, M., Strauss, J., Whalen, S., & White, T. (2002). Stanford University mathematics teaching and learning study: Initial report—A comparison of IMP1 and Algebra 1 at Greendale School. www.stanford.edu/~joboaler.

Burns, M. (2000). *About teaching mathematics—A K–8 resource.* Sausalito, CA: Math Solutions Publications.

Cohen, E. (1994). *Designing group work—Strategies for the heterogeneous classroom.* New York: Teachers College Press.

Cohen, E., & Lotan, R. (Eds.). (1997). *Working for equity in heterogeneous classrooms.* New York: Teachers College Press.

Davidson, N. (Ed.). (1990). *Cooperative learning in mathematics.* New York: Addison-Wesley Publishing Co.

Dossey, J. (1991). Discrete mathematics: The math for our time. In *Discrete mathematics across the curriculum.* Reston, VA: NCTM.

Gardiner, A. (1991). A cautionary note. In M. J. Kenney (Ed.), *Discrete mathematics across the curriculum.* Reston, VA: NCTM.

Goldenberg, E., Shteingold, N., & Feurzeig, N. (2003). Mathematical habits of mind for young children. In F. Lester & R. Charles (Eds.), *Teaching mathematics through problem solving, prekindergarten–grade 6* (pp. 3–13). Reston, VA: NCTM.

Herr, T., & Johnson, K. (1994). *Problem solving strategies—Crossing the river with dogs.* Berkeley, CA: Key Curriculum Press.

Hersberger, J. R., Frederick, W. G., Lipman, M. J. (1991). Discrete mathematics in the traditional middle school curriculum. In *Discrete mathematics across the curriculum.* Reston, VA: NCTM.

Hiebert, J., Carpenter, T., Fennema, E., Fuson, K., Wearne, D., Murray, H., Oliver, A., & Human, P. (1997). *Making sense.* Portsmouth, NH: Heinemann.

Huntley, M. A., Rasmussen, C. L., Villarubi, R. S., Sangtong, J., & Fey, J. T. (2000, May). Effects of standards-based mathematics education: A study of the core-plus mathematics project algebra and functions strand. *Journal for Research in Mathematics Education, 31,* 328–361.

Kroll, D., & Miller, T. (1993). Insights from research on mathematical problem solving in the middle grades. In D. Owens (Ed.), *Research ideas for the classroom—Middle grades mathematics.* New York: Simon and Schuster.

Krulik, S., & Rudnick, J. (1987). *Problem solving—A handbook for teachers.* Boston: Allyn & Bacon.

Krulik, S., Rudnick, J., & Milou, E. (2003). *Teaching mathematics in the middle school.* Boston: Pearson Education, Inc.

Lambdin, D. (2003). Benefits of teaching through problem solving. In F. Lester (Ed.), *Teaching mathematics through problem solving, prekindergarten–grade 6* (pp. 3–13). Reston, VA: NCTM.

Leinwand, S. (2000). *Sensible mathematics—A guide for school leaders.* Portsmouth, NH: Heinemann.

Leiva, M. A. (Ed.). (1991). *Curriculum and evaluation standards for school mathematics: Addenda series, grades K–6, kindergarten book.* Reston, VA: NCTM.

Levasseur, K., & Cuoco, A. (2003). Mathematical habits of mind. In H. Schoen & R. Charles (Eds.), *Teaching mathematics through problem solving, grades 6–12* (pp. 27–37). Reston, VA: NCTM.

National Council of Teachers of Mathematics. (1989). *Curriculum and Evaluation Standards.* Reston, VA: NCTM.

National Council of Teachers of Mathematics. (1991). *Professional standards for teaching mathematics.* Reston, VA: NCTM.

National Council of Teachers of Mathematics. (2000). *Principles and standards for school mathematics.* Reston, VA: NCTM.

Perkins, D. (1992). *Smart schools—Better thinking and learning for every child.* New York: The Free Press.

Posamentier, A., & Stepelman, J. (1999). *Teaching secondary mathematics—Techniques and enrichment units.* Upper Saddle River, NJ: Merrill/Prentice Hall.

Rasmussen, C., Yackel, E., & King, K. (2003). Social and sociomathematical norms in the mathematics classroom. In H. Schoen & C. Lester (Eds.), *Teaching mathematics through problem solving grades 6–12.* Reston, VA: NCTM.

Riordan, J., & Noyce, P. E. (2001). The impact of two standards-based mathematics curricula on student achievement in Massachusetts. *Journal for Research in Mathematics Education, 32,* 368–398.

Russell, S. J. (1999). Mathematical reasoning in the elementary grades. In L. Stiff (Ed.), *Developing mathematical reasoning in grades K–12* (pp. 1–12). Reston, VA: NCTM.

Schoen, H., & Lester, C. (Eds.). (2003). *Solving grades 6–12.* Reston, VA: NCTM.

Schoenfeld, A. (2002). Making mathematics work for all children: Issues of standards, testing and equity. *Educational Researcher, 31*(1), 13–25.

Spangler, D. (1991). The pigeon hole principle: A counting technique for the middle grades. In M. J. Kenney (Ed.), *Discrete mathematics across the curriculum.* Reston, VA: NCTM.

Stein, M., Boaler, J., & Silver, E. (2003). Teaching mathematics through problem solving: Research perspectives. In H. Schoen (Ed.), *Teaching mathematics through problem solving.* Reston, VA: NCTM.

Stein, M., Smith, M., Henningsen, M., & Silver, E. (2000). *Implementing Standards-based mathematics instruction.* New York: Teachers College Press.

Thompson, D. R., & Senk, S. L. (2001). The effects of curriculum on achievement in second-year algebra: The example of the University of Chicago school mathematics project. *Journal for Research in Mathematics Education, 32,* 58–84.

Verschaffel, L., De Corte, E., & Vierstraete, H. (1999). Upper elementary school pupils' difficulty in modeling and solving nonstandard additive word problems involving ordinal numbers. *Journal for Research in Mathematics Education, 30*(3), 265–286.

Attitude Survey

Read the question and then circle the most appropriate response.
T = True, F = False

1. I look forward to coming to math class.   T   F

2. Sometimes I do not know how to begin a problem.   T   F

3. I usually give up on hard problems.   T   F

4. I continue to work on challenging problems; I do not   T   F
   want to give up.

5. I would rather work in a small group than by myself.   T   F

6. I liked mathematics when I was younger, but now it   T   F
   is too hard.

7. I like to do a lot of problems of the same kind rather T   F
   than doing problems that need different strategies.

8. There is more to math than getting the right answer.   T   F

Place an X on the scale where you think that you belong:

|———|

I am NOT   **I am great**
good at math   **at math**

Network Exploration

For each network, state the number of even vertices and the number of odd vertices. Next determine whether or not the network is traceable.

1.

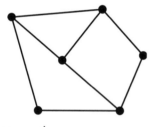

Even vertices: _____
Odd vertices: _____
Traceable: Yes   No

2.

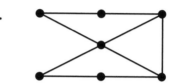

Even vertices: _____
Odd vertices: _____
Traceable: Yes   No

3.

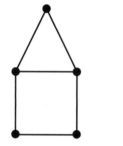

Even vertices: _____
Odd vertices: _____
Traceable: Yes   No

4.

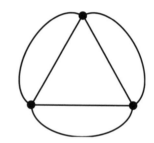

Even vertices: _____
Odd vertices: _____
Traceable: Yes   No

5.

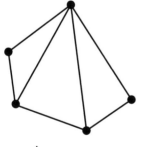

Even vertices: _____
Odd vertices: _____
Traceable: Yes   No

6.

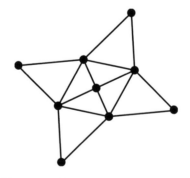

Even vertices: _____
Odd vertices: _____
Traceable: Yes   No

 From Johnson & Norris, *Teaching Today's Mathematics in the Middle Grades.* Copyright © 2006 Allyn and Bacon, Pearson Education, Inc.

chapter six

Making Sense of Number and Operations

Do any of these statements sound familiar?

- "Write the number and carry the other one to the next column."
- "Shift the decimal point over the number of places in the top, but sometimes the point just comes down."
- "Flip this one upside down and then multiply."

Students offer these rules as they discuss their solutions to various arithmetic problems. Asked why the rule works, students' responses range from "I don't know" to "my teacher said so" or "just because." These rules are memorized, practiced over and over, and yet many students, even the most capable ones, do not understand why the rules work. Worse yet, students retain only a piece of the rule. That piece combines with bits of other rules until the student feels confused and overwhelmed. Students claim that they are doing what is expected but the answers are not coming out right. Mathematics becomes a guessing game in which students fudge the numbers until the teacher's answer pops up.

In NCTM's *Principles and Standards of School Mathematics*, the Learning Principle stresses the importance of building understanding:

> Students who memorize facts or procedures without understanding often are not sure when or how to use what they know, and such learning is often quite fragile. (NCTM, 2000, p. 20)

As students work to memorize arithmetic procedures, teachers find that they need to reteach topics from the previous year. Many students do not retain their mathematical knowledge from one year to the next. No wonder the mathematics curriculum in the United States repeats itself in grades 4–8.

TRY THIS

Find a mathematics textbook series and compare the table of contents in several consecutive grades. What percent of new topics is presented from one year to the next?

Some middle school classrooms spend nearly 90% of the time practicing calculations in sixth grade, seventh grade, and perhaps again in the eighth grade. In many classrooms, students rarely employ computational skills in a practical context. Constant drilling of skills leads to student apathy and frustration. Students rightfully claim that they "did this last year." Educators reply, "This year, we will be doing more complicated work with multiplication of decimals." Teachers in this school of thought refer to the spiraling curriculum in which each year cycles back to refresh skills and then uses those skills to explore more complicated problems. Is this repetition necessary?

Point Well Taken

"When a pupil readily concludes without batting an eyelid, that 317 – 81 = 376, perhaps there is something rotten in the educational kingdom."

—*Dahaene, 1997, p. 135*

Did You **Know**?

The symbol for division is called an *obelus*.

In this chapter, we will investigate the role of algorithms, specifically the introduction and use of the traditional algorithms in comparison to students' invented strategies. We will also discuss the importance of estimation and mental math in the middle school curriculum. One of the major tasks for middle school students involves the development of proportional reasoning. This chapter will explore this critical process. We will investigate these important ideas as seen within the context of rational numbers, including integers.

NCTM Standards

In *Principals and Standards for School Mathematics*, the National Council of Teachers of Mathematics presents the Number and Operation Standard for all students in grades K–12. This standard states that students be able to

Understand numbers, ways of representing numbers, relationships among numbers, and number systems

Understand meanings of operations and how they relate to one another

Compute fluently and make reasonable estimates (NCTM, 2000, p. 148)

The importance of multiple representations of number, the meanings of operations and their relationships to one another, and the use of estimation as well as computation lay the foundation for mathematical proficiency. In grades 3–5, the focus is on whole number operations with an introduction to rational numbers, including integers. Students in this grade span work with operations as they appear in context. In the middle grades, the focus is on rational numbers. In grades 6–8, the NCTM standards state that students should:

- Work flexibly with fractions, decimals, and percents to solve problems
- Compare and order fractions, decimals, and percents efficiently and find their approximate locations on a number line
- Develop meaning for percents greater than 100 and less than 1
- Understand ratios and proportions to represent quantitative relationships
- Develop an understanding of large numbers and recognize and appropriately use exponential, scientific, and calculator notation
- Use factors, multiples, prime factorization, and relatively prime numbers to solve problems
- Develop meaning for integers and represent and compare quantities with them
- Understand the meaning and effects of arithmetic operations with fractions, decimals, and integers
- Use the associative and commutative properties of addition and multiplication and the distributive property of multiplication over addition to simplify computations with integers, fractions, and decimals
- Understand and use the inverse relationships of addition and subtraction, multiplication and division, and squaring and finding square roots to simplify computations and solve problems
- Select appropriate methods and tools for computing with fractions and decimals from among mental computation, estimation, calculations or computers, and paper and pencil, depending on the situation, and apply the selected methods
- Develop and analyze algorithms for computing with fractions, decimals, and integers and develop fluency in their use
- Develop and use strategies to estimate the results of rational number computations and judge reasonableness of the results
- Develop, analyze, and explain methods for solving problems involving proportions, such as scaling and finding equivalent ratios

In both elementary and middle grades, students solve problems in ways that are clear to them and then they share their solutions and procedures. A classroom climate that stimulates discussions encourages students as they compare their solution strategies. As students are actively engaged in sharing techniques, they build their understanding and retain that knowledge over time.

Role of Algorithms

Since the 1970s, researchers have studied the impact on student learning of direct teaching of the traditional algorithms. An algorithm can be defined as an established procedure used to solve a particular set of problems. The development of algorithms, generally speaking, took generations of mathematicians. The discovery and refinement of the procedure took years to become established as the method of choice. In many classrooms today, these discoveries are presented as facts to replicate.

Students attempt to model the process they have seen presented by their teachers. In the NCTM 1998 Yearbook, Zalman Usiskin comments that algorithms, designed to be efficient and accurate, are powerful and reliable. "When we know an algorithm, we can complete not just one task but all tasks of a particular kind and we are guaranteed an answer or answers. The power of the algorithm derives from the breadth of its applicability" (NCTM, 1998, p. 10). The mature mathematical mind comes to appreciate the beauty and power of these procedures. This is not true for the mind of adolescents. For elementary and middle school students, algorithms are rules to be memorized in order to get the correct answers. As students attempt to memorize the steps, most do not understand why the procedures work. Even when students can use the algorithm correctly, they may overuse it to the extent that they miss a fundamental understanding. For example, some students insist on multiplying 745 by 1000 using the algorithm:

$$
\begin{array}{r}
745 \\
\times\ 1000 \\
\hline
000 \\
000\ \\
000\ \ \\
745\ \ \ \\
\hline
745{,}000
\end{array}
$$

Students who hang on to every step do not understand that the product is 1000 times greater and, therefore, the digits shift over three place values. These students miss the fact that the zeros function as place holders and the digits 745 shift over so that the 7 moves from the hundreds place to the hundred thousands place. A student with deeper understanding of multiplication would reason that a product that is 1000 times greater than 745 has to be 745,000.

Research indicates that the direct teaching of one established procedure can be detrimental, especially if that procedure is presented before conceptual understanding occurs (Owens, 1993, p. 139). When students strive to mimic an established procedure, they lose sight of the meaning of the task. Students arrive at an answer feeling a sense of accomplishment that they got all of the steps, and they are satisfied, even if the answer makes no sense in the context of the problem. Referring to early elementary grade levels, Constance Kamii notes two reasons "that algorithms are harmful: (1) They encourage children to give up their own thinking, and (2) they 'unteach' place value, thereby preventing children from developing number sense" (NCTM Yearbook, 1998, p. 135). Requiring students to focus on procedures in isolation can be detrimental. We need to look at conceptual understanding and procedural fluency as intertwined.

Using Manipulatives

For middle school students who have not gained a sense of number, manipulatives such as base-ten blocks provide a vehicle for them to see the conceptual underpinnings of the algorithms at work. Using concrete representations of numbers helps middle school students confront their misconceptions about those procedures. Students compare their

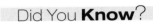
Did You **Know**?

The word *algorithm* is derived from the Latin translation of a book by Persian mathematician Al-Khwarizimi (c. 850).

action with the blocks to steps seen in the algorithms. They reflect on and critique both representations as a way to build their understanding. It is important to note that research indicates that students need time to interpret the connection between the physical model and the written mathematical procedures (McClain, Cobb, & Bowers, 1998). Manipulatives such as base-ten blocks are models that clearly demonstrate one of the big ideas in our number system—that 10 ones equal 1 ten. For many students manipulatives play an important role by representing mathematical concepts in concrete ways. Throughout this book, we refer to a variety of manipulatives and models to use with middle school students.

More Than One Algorithm
TRY THIS

Consider the following procedures. Write a brief explanation of the steps the student used to arrive at the correct solution.

a)
```
      32
   ×  46
      92
     138
    1472
```

b)
```
      32
   ×  46
      12
     180
      80
    1200
    1472
```

c)
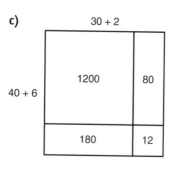

d)
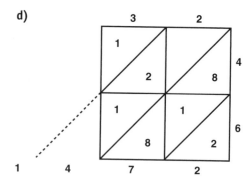

Which example was clear to you? How closely does the example follow the way that you were taught to find the product of two-digit factors?

REACHING DIVERSE LEARNERS

Number and operations provide the opportunity to invite students with different backgrounds to present the algorithms they have learned for various operations. These same students might also display and discuss the notation they used in a different country. Many students with learning disabilities can learn algorithms when the teacher uses "effective physical and pictorial models" (Tucker et al., 2002). Throughout this chapter, we have included these models to help students develop a conceptual understanding before proceeding to the formal algorithm.

PROCESS STANDARDS

NCTM

Communication

These algorithms for two-digit multiplication represent a sample of the varied procedures used in classrooms today. All four of these procedures can be used effectively. Students in the middle school can explore these various procedures and compare them to their own ways of multiplying two-digit quantities. Students will realize that the procedures vary in terms of the number of steps required. They also come to realize that in some of the algorithms the steps are not easily understood. These comparisons offer students rich opportunities to communicate orally and in writing as to their findings. Such an exercise leads to a greater appreciation of the various methods as well as a deeper understanding of the mathematics behind the process. Analyzing algorithms challenges students to raise their level of thinking. Such analysis forges connections, deepens understanding, and increases retention.

In mathematics classrooms, students need to engage in such activities as making charts and graphs, discovering and extending patterns, making and testing conjectures, and writing and reflecting on their understandings. All of these actions involve the process of "mathematizing." This term, credited to Hans Freudenthal, a highly regarded Dutch mathematics educator, highlights the critical importance of the student making mathematics. The role for the teacher focuses on establishing an appropriate environment and presenting the tasks, as well as asking those probing questions that help students develop their mathematical abilities.

Before moving on to rational numbers, the primary focus for middle school students, this chapter considers our base-ten number system, its development and expansion over time. We also look at orders of magnitude, scientific notation, different number bases, and estimation and mental mathematics as tools to enhance middle school students' number sense.

Base-Ten Number System

Our base-ten number system evolved according to the needs of society. In the beginning the counting numbers, also referred to as natural numbers {1, 2, 3, 4, 5 . . . }, served to count objects and compare quantities. The set of whole numbers is defined as the natural numbers with the addition of zero {0, 1, 2, 3, 4 . . . }. Over time, situations arose that could not be resolved using just the whole numbers. For example, merchants wanted to track financial matters. Thus, integers { . . . –3, –2, –1, 0, 1, 2, 3 . . . } were introduced. Integers, natural numbers, and their opposites including zero were used to record increases and decreases. People were able to now work with a problem involving such quantities as 8 – 14. When the need arose to create equal shares in units smaller than one whole, the set of rational numbers evolved.

Rational numbers are defined as values that can be stated as a ratio in which the numerator and denominator are integers, with the additional condition that the denominator cannot equal zero. Rational numbers provided smaller units and more precise measurements. (See Figure 6.2 for examples of rational numbers.) When a hypotenuse of a right triangle could not be measured precisely using rational numbers, however, our number system was extended yet again to irrational numbers. Irrational numbers such as $\sqrt{2}$, π, and $\sqrt{3}$ are numbers that cannot be expressed as a ratio of two integers. The decimal form of irrational numbers is nonterminating and nonrepeating. Rational and irrational numbers compose the set of real numbers.

Some middle school students may appreciate a proof that $\sqrt{2}$ (and by extension other numbers) is irrational. The following proof was written by Aristotle and extends to algebraic representations the earliest proof of irrational numbers that was written by Hippasus, a member of the Pythagorean Brotherhood (c. 400 B.C.E.). It was this proof by Hippasus that exposed the imperfect nature of numbers and so undermined the Pythagorean belief in the perfection of all numbers.

The proof is an indirect proof. Although most of the proofs students will study in high school will be direct, deductive proofs, we believe that it is important for middle school students to develop a sense of the logic involved with indirect proofs. An indirect proof begins with a statement of fact that is the opposite (*AC* is rational) of what is to be

Point Well Taken

"When students are engaged in trying to figure out the meaning of a suggested algorithm, they are becoming more aware of what it means to think mathematically. The kind of thinking that goes into inventing and evaluating procedures for solving problems can be intriguing, rewarding, and stimulating. It is part of the work of mathematicians."

—*Campbell et al. in Morrow & Kenney, NCTM, 1998, p. 54*

Did You **Know**?

Some mathematics historians claim that Hippasus was drowned at sea by fellow Pythagoreans for revealing the irrational nature of numbers to those outside the Pythagorean Brotherhood.

figure **6. 1**

√2 Is Irrational

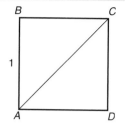

proved (*AC* is irrational). The indirect proof then draws a series of conclusions from that statement, using accepted definitions, properties, and relationships as reasons for these conclusions. Eventually the conclusions lead to an impossible statement. Thus, either the logical reasoning is faulty or the original statement of fact is untrue. In an indirect proof the reasoning is sound, so the original statement is untrue. If the original statement (*AC* is rational) is untrue, then its opposite (*AC* is not rational, or *AC* is irrational) must be true, and the proof is concluded.

This proof depends on the definition of rational numbers as numbers that may be expressed as a ratio between two integers. (See Figure 6.1.)

Given a square *ABCD*, with $AB = 1$, then $AC = \sqrt{2}$ by the Pythagorean Theorem ($1^2 + 1^2 = AC^2$, $AC = \sqrt{2}$). If *AC* is rational, then it may be expressed as a ratio with the side of the square. In other words, $AB/AC = n/m$, with n/m in lowest terms (*m* and *n* have no common factors). Let $AC^2/AB^2 = m^2/n^2$. According to the Pythagorean Theorem, $AB^2 + BC^2 = AC^2$, and in the square $AB = BC$, so

$$AB^2 + AB^2 = AC^2$$
$$2AB^2 = AC^2$$
$$\text{Thus, } 2n^2 = m^2$$

At this stage we can say that *m* must be an even number because m^2 is equal to an even number ($2n^2$). If *m* is even, *n* must be odd, because *m* and *n* have no common factors. Now let $m = 2k$, then $m^2 = 4k^2$, and so $4k^2 = 2n^2$ or $2k^2 = n^2$. Since n^2 is equal to an even number ($2k^2$), then *n* must be an even number.

We have concluded that *n* is both an odd number and an even number, which is impossible. The reasoning is correct through all of the proof, so the original statement, that there is a ratio, *m/n*, that represents *AC/AB*, must be false. The conclusion is that there is no such ratio and *AC* cannot be represented by a ratio of two integers. Thus, √2 is not rational because it cannot be represented by a ratio of two integers.

MATH IN THE MEDIA

The Last Stand of Fermat's Last Theorem

Mathematics, itself, reflects the process of refinement over time. Those early understandings and discoveries have been justified, refined, and enhanced. For some theorems, the justification has taken decades. Fermat's Last Theorem took over three centuries to prove.

Pierre Fermat, a lawyer by training and mathematical enthusiast, died in 1665. After his death, his son collected his writings and comments he had written in margins of books. In *Arithmetica*, by Diophantus, Fermat wrote $x^n + y^n = z^n$. Fermat stated for $n > 2$, the equation has no nonzero solutions for *x, y,* and *z*. Along with the equation, Fermat wrote, "I have discovered a truly remarkable proof which this margin is too small to contain." For centuries mathematicians wished that the margin had been wider as they struggled to develop the proof of this theorem. Euclid, Sophie Germaine, Krummer, and Faltings all worked toward the advancement and verification of this theorem. In 1993, Andrew Wiles, professor at Princeton University, presented his proof of Fermat's Last Theorem at a conference. Although other mathematicians found errors in his work, by 1994 Wiles had corrected his proof of Fermat's Last Theorem and it was verified by the mathematical community.

For more information on the development of the proof of Fermat's Last Theorem, see www-gap.dcs.st-and.ac.uk/~history/HistTopics/Fermat's_last_theorem.html.

Students can extend their understanding of the relationships within our number system by representing them as a series of nested shapes. (See Figure 6.2) The smaller shapes representing the subsets are contained in the larger shapes. Students can be given the set of shapes and the appropriate labels and then asked to place different numbers in the appropriate places. Teachers can also ask questions such as "Are all natural numbers integers?" and "Are all rational numbers also integers?" Such questions invite further discussion and help students understand the relationships among the sets of numbers.

Understanding our number system based on human needs helps to demystify mathematics as a discipline. The very fact that new branches of mathematics are continuing to evolve adds to the excitement and significance of the discipline. The universe of numbers does not stop with the real numbers, however. Mathematicians created the complex number system that includes real numbers and imaginary numbers. Imaginary numbers were created so that mathematicians could work with the square root of negative numbers. Consequently, the value of $i = \sqrt{-1}$ and $i^2 = -1$. Although intriguing to middle school students, the complex number system as a unit of study is best left to the high school curriculum. Middle school students deepen their understanding of the base-ten number system as they represent values using other base systems.

Did You **Know**?

German mathematician Cristoff Rudolff (c.1500–c.1547) invented the radical sign ($\sqrt{}$) but without the elongated horizontal line. That was added decades later by French mathematician René Descartes (1590–1650).

TRY THIS

Write 46 in base two.

As students work to translate 46 from base ten to base two, they need to understand place value based on powers of 2. Just as the base ten system works with ten digits, 0–9, the base-two system functions with two digits, 0 and 1. (See Figure 6.3.)

Therefore, the base-ten number 46 can be written as 101110_{two}. It is interesting to note that many mathematicians prefer to write out the words for bases other than base ten. This practice places an emphasis on the change to a different base as compared to our traditional system.

Another way to represent 46 in base two clearly demonstrates the use of powers of 2: $(1 \times 2^5) + (0 \times 2^4) + (1 \times 2^3) + (1 \times 2^2) + (1 \times 2^1)$. Just as students can explore base

figure **6.2**

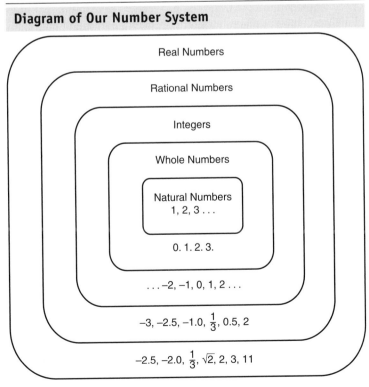

Diagram of Our Number System

Real Numbers

Rational Numbers

Integers

Whole Numbers

Natural Numbers
1, 2, 3 . . .

0. 1. 2. 3.

. . . –2, –1, 0, 1, 2 . . .

–3, –2.5, –1.0, $\frac{1}{3}$, 0.5, 2

–2.5, –2.0, $\frac{1}{3}$, $\sqrt{2}$, 2, 3, 11

figure **6.3**

Comparison of Base Ten and Base Two

Base Ten   46

$10^2 \rightarrow 0$	$100 \times 0 = 0$
$10^1 \rightarrow 4$	$10 \times 4 = 40$
$10^0 \rightarrow 6$	$1 \times 6 = \underline{6}$
	46

Base Two   46

$2^5 \rightarrow 1$	$32 \times 1 = 32$
$2^4 \rightarrow 0$	$16 \times 0 = 0$
$2^3 \rightarrow 1$	$8 \times 1 = 8$
$2^2 \rightarrow 1$	$4 \times 1 = 4$
$2^1 \rightarrow 1$	$2 \times 1 = 2$
$2^0 \rightarrow 0$	$1 \times 0 = \underline{0}$
	46

two as a way to deepen their understanding of the base-ten number system, students can work with scientific notation to help them understand orders of magnitude.

MISCONCEPTION

Middle school students typically think about putting zeros at the end of a number when multiplying by powers of 10. When asked to find the value of 28×10^2, students typically respond by stating that "you just add two zeros on the end." Of course, they mean using zero as a place holder to shift the 28 over two places, thereby creating a value 100 times greater. In order to place the emphasis on the fact that 28 is becoming 100 times greater, teachers can use a place value chart so that students understand what happens to the value of the number as it is multiplied. (See Figure 6.4.)

When students focus on the place value of the number, they readily see the connection between the power of 10 used as the multiplier and the number of places that the numbers shift. The purpose of zero as a place holder also becomes apparent. Students understand that as soon as the chart is removed the zeros are necessary to indicate the appropriate value. Teachers can readily use the place value chart to help students understand division by powers of 10 as well.

TRY THIS

1. Find the product: 2.3×10^4
2. Find the quotient: $23 \div 10^4$

When working with decimals, textbooks typically show little arrows that indicate that the decimal point jumps around according to the power of 10. This notation is a matter of convenience. Students need to understand that the decimal point indicates where the units place in the number is located. As the number is multiplied or divided by a power of 10, it is helpful for students to think about the shift occurring on the place value chart that is extended to include tenths, hundredths, and so on. Teachers have found that linking multiplication and division with the place value chart provides a strong visual representation that helps students understand and retain the material.

TRY THIS

1. Find the number of thousands in 1 billion.
2. How many hundreds are in a million?

figure **6.4**

Place Value Table Used to Demonstrate Multiplying 28 by 100

	Thousands	Hundreds	Tens	Ones
28 × 1			2	8
28 × 100	2	8	0	0

Thinking flexibly about the composition of numbers helps students understand the magnitude of number. To some students finding the number of thousands in 1,000,000,000 can seem daunting. Reading the place value to the thousands and then looking to the left indicates the number of thousands remaining in 1 billion, or 100,000 thousands. Teachers can ask students to explore the number of tens in 326 as a starting point. In most curricula, questions regarding place value focus on the digit in the tens place. Students also need to explore how many tens are in the number. If we were to build 326 using only tens and ones, how many tens would be needed? After building several examples, students begin to look for the pattern that would enable them to move beyond the concrete representation. They soon realize that there are 32 tens in 326. Ideally, this understanding of the composition of numbers is solidified before middle school. If that is not the case, it is critical for students to have the time to focus on this fundamental skill. Getting students to explain their thinking orally and in writing helps them develop and retain their understanding. Students are then ready to tackle large values and represent them in a variety of ways. Middle school students can use scientific notation to represent 860,000,000,000 as 8.6×10^{11} or 8.6 ten billions.

Understanding scientific notation helps students realize the value of the display on their calculators: 8.6 E 11 indicates 8.6×10^{11}, for example. As students work with scientific notation and all four arithmetic operations, they realize the efficiency and accuracy of the notation. Estimation and mental math also play important roles as students build a sense of number.

Did You **Know**?

In 1974, Marva Drew finished typing all the numbers from one to one million using a typewriter. The task took six years and 2,473 sheets of paper to complete.

MATH IN THE MEDIA

The largest prime number known to date was discovered on November 17, 2003. Michael Shafer had been participating in an eight-year-old-project, Great Internet Mersenne Prime Search, when his computer announced the discovery. This prime number is 6,320,430 digits long and would require between 1400 and 1500 pages to write it out. As this new prime is a Mersenne prime, it can be expressed as $2^{20996011} - 1$.

Source: Irwin, J. (2003, December 11). Student finds largest prime number. *Boston Globe.*

Note: On May 15, 2004, Josh Findley discovered the forty-first Mersenne prime, followed by the discovery of the forty-second Mersenne prime by Martin Nowak on February 18, 2005. The search continues! (Weinstein, 2005)

Mental Math and Estimation

The role of mental math and estimation contributes significantly to students' development of number sense. Mental math and estimation skills should be practiced routinely so that the skills become imbedded in a student's repertoire of calculation strategies. By using the commutative, associative, and distributive properties, students think flexibly to apply varying approaches to fit the situation. Teachers can present quick problems to be done mentally at the beginning of the class or at the end of class. (See Chapter 4, Assessment: Balanced and Varied, for greater detail on Do Nows.) Discussion about how the students found their answers is often varied and helps to deepen students' understanding of the options available to them.

TRY THIS

Solve using mental math strategies:

$$50 \times 24$$

There is a variety of approaches to this problem. Students might double 50 and then take half of the product, which is the same as dividing by 2: $100 \times 24 = 2400$ and then divide by 2 to arrive at 1200. During the discussion of this approach, teachers can ask students to verify why multiplying by 2 and then taking half is an effective strategy. Other students might view the problem in terms of the distributive property: $50(20 + 4) = 50 \times 20 + 50 \times 4$. Some students might break each number down into factors such as $5 \times 10 \times 8 \times 3$. They can then apply the commutative property to work with $5 \times 8 \times 10 \times 3$ or 40×30.

To introduce such strategies to students with little experience, teachers can present a series of simpler problems involving addition and subtraction. Asking students to find the missing part when the whole is 100 and one part is 63 is another example that can also be approached in a variety of ways. Students can subtract 60 from 100 to get 40 and then take away 3 more to obtain the result of 37. Students might also increase 100 to 103 and then subtract 63. They now need to subtract 3 more to compensate for the change made

figure **6.5**

Shifting the Numbers on the Number Line

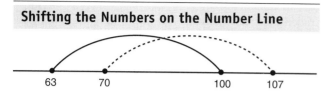

to 100. Some students might think of the number line to shift the numbers to more convenient numbers while maintaining the distance between them. (See Figure 6.5)

The resulting task of subtracting 70 from 107 is one that students can perform mentally.

Teachers can also present problems involving division such as $3\overline{)156}$. Students can consider 156 as 150 and 6 more. Therefore, there are 50 groups of 3 in 150 and 2 more groups of 3 in 6 resulting in 52 groups of 3.

AUTHOR'S **Recall**

As I watched my student use the number line for subtraction, I asked her to tell me what she was thinking. She replied that she thought of a handle on a suitcase. She was lifting the handle and moving it to place it down on a new spot.

Point Well Taken

"Estimation requires a flexibility of calculation that emphasizes adaptive reasoning and strategic competence, guided by children's conceptual understanding of both the problem situation and the mathematics underlying the calculation."

—*Kilpatrick, Swafford, & Findell, 2001, p. 216*

Front-End Estimation

Front-end estimation and rounding are two strategies to be explored with middle school students. Front-end estimation is particularly effective when working with values that are relatively close to one another.

> Shalemya has $50 in her bank account. She wants to purchase some gifts for her family. She wants to buy a book for $21.89, a toy for $14.95, and a pen for $6.78. Does she have enough money to make these purchases?

Using front-end estimation, students look at the digit in the largest place value or the digit that occurs first in the number as it is read from left to right. Regarding Shalemya's purchases, students use the tens digits: 2 + 1 + 0 or approximately 30 dollars. Students then look at the units digits to see if any adjusting needs to be done to their initial estimate. In this case, students add 1 + 4 + 6 for a total of 11 dollars. Students now adjust the estimate to be $41 and they can answer the original question that Shalemya does indeed have enough money. Front-end estimation can be applied to situations involving multiplication and division. The first digits are again used as with addition and then adjustments can be made.

> There are 46 seats in each row in the community theater and there are 72 rows. Approximately how many seats are in the theater?

Students can find the product using the tens digits to arrive at their initial estimate, 40 × 70, or 2800 seats. They can then look to the units digits to see if they want to make any adjustment. Students need to consider the fact that the units digits multiply with the tens digit of the other factor. Consequently, students need to consider (2 × 40) + (6 × 70) and increase the estimate by 500. The product of the units digit in each factor can be dropped as it does not significantly increase the total.

MISCONCEPTION

It is important that students keep track of the tens when making the estimate. Using the seats in the theater problem, students tend to say 4 × 7 to arrive at an estimate of 28 tens or 280. Being mindful of the place value by thinking about 4 tens × 7 tens or 40 × 70 helps avoid this error.

Suppose we were told that the theater had 3,312 seats and we knew that there were 72 rows, and we wanted to estimate how many seats were in one row. Using front-end estimation, students would divide 3000 by 70 to arrive at 40 seats as an estimate. Some students struggle with the place value for their estimate. They question whether the answer is 40 or 400. Students need to check the reasonableness of their estimate in this case. Teachers can encourage students to check by multiplying 400 by 70. Working effectively with powers of 10 can improve students' estimation skills.

Rounding as an Estimation Strategy

Rounding to make estimates is a widely used technique, and for middle school students, rounding provides ample opportunities to make decisions based on the numbers and the situation.

> Here are the prices of various items in your basket at the grocery store: $12.59, $0.89, $2.36, $1.98, $22.87, and $4.39. Estimate the total cost.

Students can decide that they want to round to the nearest whole dollar. They would use 12 + 1 + 2 + 2 + 23 + 4 to arrive at their estimate of $44. Students can discuss whether or not to drop the $0.89. Some may argue that they want to be certain to have enough money rather than be embarrassed when they are asked to pay. These students will round all values up. Other students might suggest that the $0.89 does not change the total significantly and, therefore, it can be dropped. Some students might round to the nearest ten dollars in this case, 10 + 20. This would produce a significantly lower estimate.

For estimates involving subtraction, students can consider just rounding the number to be subtracted. Given 8526 − 2478, students can round 2478 to 2000 and then subtract to obtain an estimate of 6526. Knowing that they took less away than required by approximately 500, students may adjust the estimate to get 6000.

RESEARCH

J. Sowder and M. Wheeler (1989) reported in the *Journal for Research in Mathematics Education* that many students feared making an error when making estimates. Rather than estimating, students tended to solve the problem and then use an actual answer to create the estimate. This tendency increased in the middle grades. Consequently, it is important that teachers demonstrate that they clearly value different strategies for estimation as well as a range of acceptable estimates.

The rounding strategy can be used for multiplication as well. If numbers can be rounded to 10, 100, or 1000, the estimates can be quickly made. Students need to remember that if they raise both the factors, then the resulting estimate will be greater than the actual product. Students can discover that increasing one factor and decreasing the second factor yields a close estimate. Teachers can provide students with opportunities to make estimates and then compare their estimates to the actual products. Because the emphasis for such an experience is on developing estimation techniques, using a calculator to check the estimates can be helpful to build students' confidence in their estimates. Given specific contexts such as ordering off a menu, teachers can ask students whether or not their estimates would serve the intended purpose.

For division, students can work with compatible numbers or values that are easy to work with. In multiplication and division, compatible numbers are factors or multiples of each other. In addition, compatible numbers combine to make 10 or 100, for example. Working with 3104 ÷ 4, students can raise 3104 to 3200 to arrive at an estimate of 800. Considering 3104 ÷ 14, students might work with 2800 ÷ 14 or 3000 ÷ 15.

When helping students to become effective estimators, teachers need to give them many opportunities to use estimates. By understanding that they have choices in how they manipulate the numbers presented in the problem, students view mathematics as their tool rather than a series of steps to be memorized.

Estimation continues to play an important role as students work with rational numbers. Benchmark values prove effective in this context. Students can determine whether or not a particular value is closer to 0 or $\frac{1}{2}$. Locating values on a number line in a game format promotes students' estimation skills. For example, student teams can work with a set of ten cards each displaying a rational number to be placed on a number line. Students

Point Well Taken

"Estimation serves as an important companion to computation."
—*NCTM, 2000, p. 155*

REACT | **REFLECT**

Make a list of those tasks that require an exact answer. Make a second list of tasks in which an estimate will suffice. For example, balancing a checkbook might appear in the exact answer column, but calculating the number of miles traveled on a full tank of gas might be listed in the estimate column. Which column has more entries? What implications might the size of these two columns have on instruction?

are given directions to find the rational number that is closest to 1 or find the value that is greater than $\frac{3}{4}$ *but less than* $\frac{11}{12}$. The goal is for each team to be able to place all of the cards. Students can work collaboratively or competitively to place the cards on the number line. Clearly, there are many ways to position the cards. Spending time justifying their decisions helps students communicate clearly and solidify their understanding. Just as students use estimation with whole numbers, they need to use estimation when working with rational numbers. Given $3\frac{3}{4} \times 4\frac{1}{5}$, students should become comfortable providing an anticipated range of values, such as $12 <$ answer < 20. As students become more effective estimators, the range of values decreases. Students may round $3\frac{3}{4}$ *to* 4 and $4\frac{1}{5}$ *to* 4 to obtain 16 as an estimate. It is important to note that estimations involving rational numbers are dependent on a student's skills in working with whole numbers. Spending time to develop effective estimation and mental math strategies contributes significantly to students' mathematical success.

Typically, we tend to use estimates far more often than we calculate exact answers in our daily lives. Just the opposite is true for students in today's classrooms. If as adults we use estimates most of the time, we need to spend much more time promoting the use of estimates with students.

Implementation Strategies

Spending a few minutes either at the beginning or at the end of class doing mental math problems and estimates increases students' abilities to think flexibly, reinforces the importance of basic facts, and offers another opportunity for students to share strategies. Given a series of multiplication problems in a traditional textbook, teachers can ask students to find the largest or smallest product by estimating. Teachers can also prepare a transparency with two columns with one problem in each column. Using estimation skills, students then compare their estimates to find the lesser value. Teachers can also present a target number. Students are then asked to find the value closest to the target value. Students can bring in advertisement inserts from the newspaper. Students can then select items to total but not exceed $150. Placing a time limit on the work pushes students to use estimation. Another activity involves rapid calculations. Students can be shown a problem quickly on the overhead. Given a short period of time to view the problem, students are asked to find an estimate. Students then share their solution strategies. Even those students who may not feel comfortable under the pressure of timed activities will benefit from hearing the estimation strategies used by other students. Mental math problems can also present opportunities to apply the order of operations.

Point Well Taken

Mental-computation strategies "are flexible and can be adapted to suit the numbers concerned; they involve a definite, if not conscious, choice of strategy based on considering the numbers involved; and, almost always, they require understanding."

—*McIntosh in Morrow & Kenney, 1998, pp. 44–45*

Number Facts

Acquisition of the basic number facts can present challenges for some students. Teachers wonder whether or not they can continue with the curriculum if many of their students do not know the basic facts. "How can students estimate effectively?" or "How can my students work with factors if they do not know the multiplication tables?" are critical questions to be addressed.

Students who know their facts automatically have a great advantage over students who must construct each fact using prior knowledge. In middle school, students who need to work on the facts can take advantage of many websites that offer flash cards, number fact games, and other activities that encourage learning the basic facts. For those students who continually truly struggle with their facts, finger multiplication can make a significant difference.

Given that students know their multiplication facts through the five times tables, they can then represent all of the other facts for 6 through 10. A closed fist represents "five" and any finger lifted on that hand adds one more to that value of 5. Therefore, a hand with three fingers raised represents the value 8. To find the product of 8×6, represent the two numbers, one on each hand. (See Figure 6.6.)

The raised fingers count as tens. As shown in Figure 6.6, the three raised fingers on the left hand added together with the one raised finger on the right hand total 40. The fingers on the left hand that are *not* raised, 2, are multiplied with the fingers that are *not* raised on the right hand, 4 in this case. The product of 2 times 4 is added to the total number of tens: $6 \times 8 = 40 + 8$. Using this technique provides confidence to those students who have struggled trying to retain the multiplication tables. A word of caution is necessary here. Students need many opportunities to work with concrete experiences such as area models and skip counting in order to develop the basic multiplication facts. Finger multiplication is certainly not the first approach that should be used with students. It does provide students with an accessible strategy. Students who have had experience working with variables and the distributive property can verify how finger multiplication works. Refer to Chapter 7, Algebra: The Gateway, for this proof.

figure **6.6**

Finger Multiplication

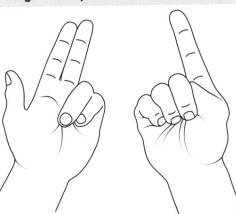

MISCONCEPTION

As middle school students work with the order of operations, many teachers rely on the acronym PEMDAS to help students remember the proper order. These letters stand for the order in which the operations should be calculated: P (parentheses), E (exponents), M (multiplication), D (division), A (addition), and S (subtraction). Frequently, teachers refer to PEMDAS as "Please excuse my dear Aunt Sally" as a method to help students remember the appropriate order. However, this acronym can contribute to a misconception as students tend to follow the order exactly. For multiplication and division, the calculation performed also depends on the order in which these two operations appear in the problem. This is also true for addition and subtraction.

AUTHOR'S **Recall**

One of my students had trouble learning the facts. His mother constantly drilled him before dinner, but her son resisted and tension between them increased. I suggested that she let the computer drill her son. Within two weeks, her son had mastered the multiplication facts; peace was restored in the house.

TRY THIS

Calculate $8 - 6/3 \times 2 + 4$. Did you get 8 or did you get 11?

Students tend to think that multiplication must always be calculated before division and all addition is to be done before subtraction. The order of operations requires that the operations be performed in order from left to right beginning with division and multiplication and then addition and subtraction. Consequently, we recommend that teachers present the acronym PEMDAS as shown in Figure 6.7. Writing the letters in vertical groupings helps students remember the hierarchy of the relationships. The arrows emphasize the fact that the operations at each level are calculated in the order that they occur in each case. When working with fractions, the numerators and denominators must be simplified according to the order of operations before working to simplify the entire fraction.

TRY THIS

Calculate the following:

$$\frac{14 \div 2(5) - 3}{8 + 2^2}$$

Did you get $\frac{8}{3}$ *or its equivalent* $2\frac{2}{3}$?

figure **6.7**

Visual Representation of the Order of Operations

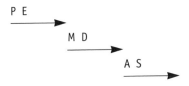

Here are two different approaches for introducing the order of operations. The first involves using different calculators. Many of the simple four-function calculators are not programmed to work with the order of operations. These calculators

REACT | REFLECT

In Chapter 3, The Practice of Effective Instruction, we discussed the importance of status issues. If you recognized that two students had low status in your class, which calculator would you want to give these students when you introduced the order of operations?

Did You **Know**?

The order of operations was formerly referred to as the order of precedence.

Point Well Taken

"Given the wide range of ways to represent rational numbers and the variety of meanings, it is not surprising that children are confused when dealing with rational numbers in any form."

—*Sheffield & Cruikshank, 2000, p. 232*

Did You **Know**?

The word *fraction* was first used by Geoffrey Chaucer (1342–1400) of *Canterbury Tales* fame.

simply follow the order in which the numbers are entered. Give some students the four-function calculators while other students use a more advanced calculator. Ask the students to find the answer to a problem involving the order of operations. An interesting discussion follows as the calculators present varying answers highlighting the need for the order of operations.

A second approach to introducing the order of operations involves football scores. Ask students to calculate the football team's final score if the team scored 2 touchdowns, 3 field goals, and 2 extra points. The problem $6 \times 2 + 3 \times 3 + 1 \times 2$ yields a very different result if we didn't follow the order of operations.

Rational Numbers

Rational numbers are defined as values that can be stated as a ratio $\frac{a}{b}$ in which a and b are integers and b does not equal zero. In elementary school, students experience fractions as parts of wholes. Students shade shapes, circle values in sets, and locate values on number lines. This part/whole relationship is fundamental. There are four other meanings of rational numbers that students need to understand in order to become mathematically proficient in working with rational numbers. Beyond the part/whole relationship, students must also work with the quotient meaning, ratio meaning, and operator meaning (Curcio, 1994, pp. 2–3). Students also need to work with the measure interpretation of rational numbers.

Part/Whole Interpretation

The part/whole relationship can be extended for middle school students to include investigations involving equal areas but not necessarily congruent parts. Given a geoboard or graph paper with a 4 × 4 square, students may be asked to show equal areas.

TRY THIS

Explore finding half of a 4 × 4 square cm grid. See if you can find ways that create equal areas but not necessarily congruent parts.

Students usually begin by making placing a line vertically or horizontally to divide the square in half. Creating a diagonal line provides another way to make equal halves. Students should also explore ways to create halves that are equal in area but not necessarily congruent. (See Figure 6.8.)

Students should also work with varying-sized pieces representing the whole. For example, students can explore the meaning of $\frac{1}{2}$ when given a picture of *half* of a circle. They can then compare the size of $\frac{1}{2}$ as it compares to $\frac{1}{2}$ of a *whole* circle. Changing the size of the original whole focuses students' attention on the fact that the same fractional value can represent different-sized pieces.

figure **6.8**

Representing Halves

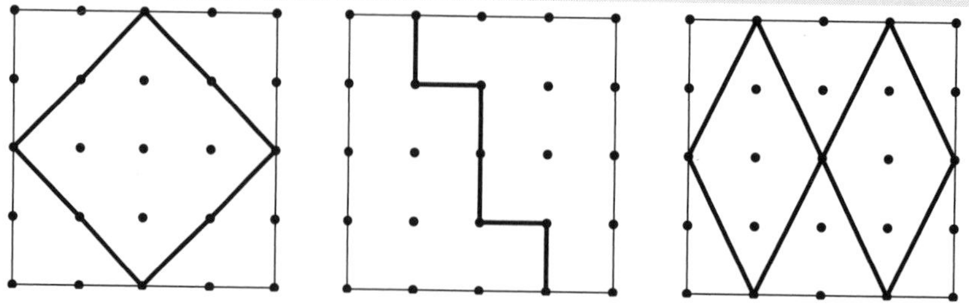

MISCONCEPTION

Students may struggle when working with multiplication and division of rational numbers. They have built an understanding that multiplication creates larger numbers and division yields smaller ones. Students need opportunities to confront their beliefs in terms of rational numbers.

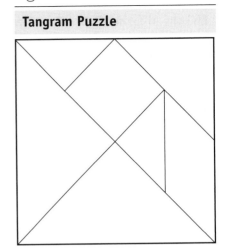

figure **6.9**

Tangram Puzzle

Tangram pieces also facilitate an understanding of parts of the whole. (See Figure 6.9.)

Students begin exploring this puzzle by separating the pieces, mixing them up, and then working to reform the original square. Students can also construct their own puzzle pieces. The directions for making tangrams can be found on several websites:

http://mathforum.org/trscavo/tangrams/construct.html
http://mathforum.org/trscavo/tangrams.html
www.ex.ac.uk/cimt/puzzles/tangrams/tangint.htm

In order to explore the concept of part/whole, students find the size of each individual piece given that the large square is one unit. In fact, any piece of the tangram can be called the whole and students can determine the size of the other pieces in terms of that whole.

Did You **Know**?

The fraction bar is call a *virgule*. The first European mathematician to use it was Fibonacci (c. 1175–1250). He may have derived the idea from the Persian mathematician al-Hassar.

TRY THIS

a. Using tangram pieces, if the area of the small square equals 1, then the size of the smallest triangle = _____.

b. If the area of the total puzzle equals 1, then what is the area of each piece?

c. If [diagram] equals the whole, then [diagram] = _____.

Finding the area relationships among the various tangram pieces helps students develop an understanding of the part/whole relationship.

Another useful strategy when thinking about part/whole relationships is called *unitizing*. Susan Lamon defines unitizing as the "process of mentally constructing different-sized chunks in terms of which to think about a given commodity" (Lamon in Litwiller, 2002, p. 80). Consider a case of tennis balls. There are 36 cans in each case. We can think about those 36 cans in a variety of ways. There are 36 individual cans, 2 (18 sets), 3 (12 sets), 4 (9 sets), and 6 (6 sets). Depending on the task, we can select the easiest grouping.

TRY THIS

The Athletic Outlet sells large quantities of tennis balls to school programs. The athletic director wants to be certain to get the best possible deal. The outlet offers 48 cans for $218.40 or 36 cans for $167.40. Which quantity of balls should the director purchase?

Most textbooks encourage students to find the unit price, the price per can in this case. Students can also consider changing the unit quantity, thereby making the division easier. The 48 cans can be thought of as 4 sets of 12 just as the 36 cans can be considered as 3 sets of 12. As the cans are now grouped into like sets or chunks of 12, students can compare the price using this chunk. When students divide $218.40 by 4, they find one 12-chunk costs $54.60. For the second option, students divide $167.40 by 3 to find the cost of the 12-chunk is $55.80. In this case, students work with a single-digit divisor as compared to

figure **6.10**

Chunks of Coins

a two-digit divisor that is needed if they find a unit price. Unitizing can also be used to determine how much of the whole a quantity represents. For example,

> Francine has 12 loaves of pumpkin bread. If she gives 3 loaves to her brother, what part of her original number of loaves does she give to her brother?

Students can approach this problem by unitizing:

$$\frac{3 \text{ loaves}}{12 \text{ loaves}} = \frac{1 \text{ (3 pack)}}{4 \text{ (3 pack)}}$$

Students can also use unitizing to find the whole given the part. For example,

> Elijah enjoys collecting state quarters and he now has 12 in his collection. These 12 quarters represent $\frac{2}{3}$ of his total collection. How many quarters does Elijah have in his collection?

Students can create chunks representing $\frac{2}{3}$ of Elijah's collection of coins. (See Figure 6.10.)

These 2 chunks of 6 quarters represent $\frac{2}{3}$ of the total collection. Students reason that one more third or chunk of six quarters will give the total amount of quarters. Note that students use unitizing without being given a lot of rules. Unitizing takes advantage of many of the number concepts that students already understand. Other advantages of unitizing include the following:

- Reasoning up or down while coordinating the size and number of pieces lays the groundwork for proportional reasoning.
- Recording the size of the chunks explains how one arrived at the fraction; that is, the notation captures students' thinking so that the teacher can better assess their progress.
- Unitizing aids self-assessment. Without the use of rules, students can check to see whether they have produced equivalent fractions because the number of chunks multiplied by the number in each chunk never changes. (Lamon in Litwiller, 2002, p. 82)

We continue to discuss this process of unitizing to help students develop proportional reasoning later in this chapter (see pages 154–155).

   PROCESS STANDARDS

Representation

Another representation that is helpful to students when working with part/whole relationships uses a diagram. Consider the following problem:

$\frac{3}{5}$ *of a number is 30. What is the number?*

Students can create a rectangle divided into five equal parts.

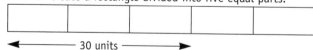

← —————— 30 units —————— →

Students reason that 3 units equal 30. So 1 unit equals 10. As there are 5 units, the original number must be 50. This way of modeling the problem helps students see the relationships within the problem and presents the problem in a visual context.

Quotient Interpretation

The quotient interpretation of rational numbers is often illustrated in practical contexts. Students are certainly interested in making fair shares and this view of rational numbers taps that interest.

TRY THIS

Ms. May Teech shares 5 loaves of pumpkin bread with 6 children. How much bread will each child receive?

Students may approach this relatively straightforward problem very differently than adults. Adults quickly compute that each student will get $\frac{5}{6}$ of a loaf ($5 \div 6 = \frac{5}{6}$). A student's difficulty with such a task is that the consideration of the whole changes as shares are distributed. (See Figure 6.11.)

In Figure 6.11, this student divides each loaf in half and then numbers each half according to the number of children. She then takes the fourth loaf and makes four equal pieces and uses one-half of the last loaf for two equal pieces so that there are six pieces, each the size of one-quarter of the loaf to share. Therefore, there is one-half of the last loaf to share among the six children. At this point, the student confronts the fact that she is not working with one whole. She wants to create six equal pieces out of the remaining half loaf. The size of each piece is one-sixth of the half loaf or one-twelfth of the whole loaf. Catherine Fosnot and Maarten Dolk identify this inherent difficulty when working with fractions as being caused by the fact that there are "relations on relations." Keeping track of the whole and the current working unit challenges students as well as adults (Fosnot & Dolk, 2002, p. 59).

TRY THIS

I have $\frac{2}{3}$ pint of ice cream. My serving scoop holds $\frac{1}{4}$ pint. How many servings can I make from the $\frac{2}{3}$ pint of ice cream using this scoop?

So far, we have looked at part/whole and quotient interpretations of rational numbers. The third interpretation involves ratios and rates.

Ratio Interpretation

Students use rational numbers in a ratio relationship as they compare quantities involving different categories. The ratio of boys to girls in a particular classroom and the number of buttons on a coat compared to the number of pockets are two examples. These relationships might both be expressed by the ratio 3:2 or $\frac{3}{2}$ or 3 to 2. Given the total number of students in the class, 25, students can then use the ratio to determine the number of girls in the class. Middle school students can explore ratios in their environment. An

figure **6.11**

Creating Equal Shares

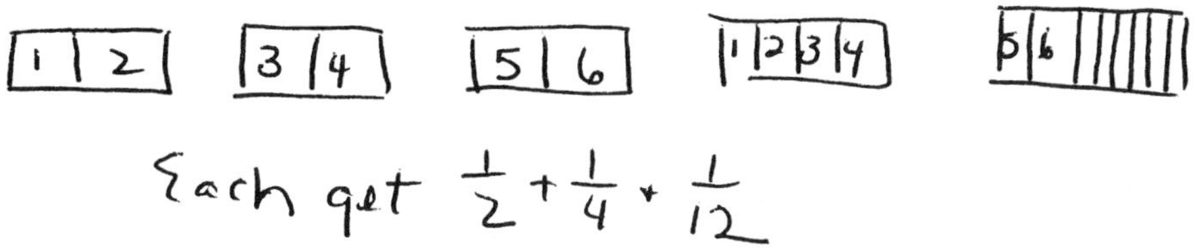

open-ended task to find ratios in the newspaper or simply make a list of where the students might expect to find ratios can generate interest. Because middle school students tend to enjoy activities about themselves, finding ratios as seen on their body creates interest and is an intriguing model for reference. Students can measure height, arm span, distance their navel is from the floor, length of their foot, and the length of their forearm. Students are surprised to find that the ratio of their arm span to their height is approximately 1:1 and that the ratio of their wrist circumference to the circumference of their neck is 1:2. A cautionary note: Middle school students may be experiencing growth spurts. This means that the ratios may be different from those indicated for adults. Consider taking the average height compared to the average arm span to avoid a lot of variation. As girls tend to reach their mature height before boys do, comparisons of the arm span to height ratios in terms of gender may generate interesting class discussions.

The concept of ratio extends to include the notion of rates. Miles per hour, gallons per day, and words read per minute are examples of common rates. Percents can be considered rates because any percent is a part compared to 100. For further discussion of the ratio interpretation of rational numbers, see Proportional Reasoning later in this chapter.

Operator Interpretation

The fourth meaning of rational numbers is called the operator meaning. Scale factors used in enlarging and reducing objects or pictures are rational numbers functioning as operators. Students can explore scale factors by taking a cartoon or a coloring book picture and tracing the outline onto quarter-inch graph paper. Students make an enlargement by drawing each element of the cartoon onto a large sheet of 1-inch graph paper. Students should predict how much greater the resulting design will be and determine the scale factor.

Measure Interpretation

The fifth meaning of ratio involves measurement. Students regularly work with units of measure that are less than one whole.

TRY THIS

Find the number of units each measuring $\frac{3}{4}$ of an inch in 1 foot.

Students can approach this problem in a variety of ways. They can use a ruler and actually count the number of $\frac{3}{4}$-units. Students can also directly calculate by dividing 12 inches by $\frac{3}{4}$. The method students use to solve the problem offers insights into their current level of understanding. Tracking their approaches over time provides important information as to students' progress in mathematics.

PROCESS STANDARDS

Connections

Rational numbers are seen in a variety of contexts and various fields of study inside and outside of mathematics. Ratios used in probability take on the parts of a whole interpretation, yet, when used in context of odds, the ratio is comparing quantities. The operator meaning of rational numbers is seen in geometry in terms of scale factors. Making such connections explicit for students provides greater understanding and increased retention.

These five meanings of rational numbers, part/whole relationship, the quotient, ratio, operator meaning, and measure interpretation all need to be experienced and explored by middle school students. Students without any formal training or exposure to the traditional algorithms can explore all of the examples explained in this section. Students need to develop their conceptual understanding of ratio before investigating formal procedures that employ ratios such as proportional reasoning. Before discussing proportional reasoning, we will look at the relationship between the various representations of rational numbers—fractions, decimals, and percents.

Fractions, Decimals, and Percents

Typically, students begin with fractions, proceed to decimals, and eventually work with percents. Students tend to see these three representations for rational numbers as uniquely different. When asked to change a decimal to a fraction or a fraction to a percent, many students struggle. Rather than treating them separately, we suggest that fractions, decimals, and percents be presented together so that students can explore the relationships among these representations.

PROCESS STANDARDS

Connections

Making connections among topics promotes retention. When students have opportunities to evaluate and analyze the varying features amid fractions, decimals and percents, they develop a deeper understanding. By seeing and understanding the similarities and differences in the uses of rational numbers, students realize that they have choices as to how they proceed in solving problems. Students gain a sense of control and, therefore, ownership of their mathematical thinking.

Linking Fractions, Decimals, and Percents

Number Line Equivalences, Blackline Master 6.1, presents a paper-folding exercise that highlights the relationship between the three representations of rational numbers. Students are given three number lines with each line having one of the following labels: fraction, decimal, or percent. Students fold the number lines by placing the endpoint on the left directly on top of the other endpoint. Students can hold the paper up to the light to be certain that the points match. They can then make a crease. Opening the fold, students then label the three numbers lines appropriately, $\frac{1}{2}$, 0.5, 50%. Next, students fold the number lines in half as before, and then they take the fold and place the fold directly on the endpoints. When they are certain as to the alignment, students then make a crease. Opening the paper reveals the number lines are now in fourths, and the students should label the three lines appropriately. Students repeat the folding process one more time to create eighths. For those students who might struggle with the process of folding the paper appropriately, it is helpful to prepare several number-line activity sheets prior to the start of class. The teacher can supply the folded sheets as needed. Consequently, the student can focus on the mathematics involved by labeling the lines and seeing the relationships, and the teacher has alleviated a student's possible frustration. As the students work to label the number lines, they begin to recognize significant patterns. Students recognize that $\frac{1}{4}$ = 0.25 and $\frac{1}{8}$ is half of $\frac{1}{4}$ and, therefore, the decimal equivalent of $\frac{1}{8}$ must be half of 0.25 or 0.125. They also see that if they know the decimal equivalent of $\frac{1}{8}$ they can find the decimal value of $\frac{3}{8}$ by multiplying by 3. Students should summarize their findings in writing and keep the chart in their notebooks as an available reference. Teachers can also ask students to compare quantities using these number lines. Teachers can also give students a list and ask them to order them using the three number lines as needed. The list might include $\frac{2}{3}$, 0.125, $\frac{5}{8}$, 75%, and $\frac{1}{4}$. As students solve problems, having the ability to choose which representation best fits the situation gives students options and provides students with opportunities to see mathematics as their tool.

Students also need to work with a variety of models as they develop their conceptual understanding of rational numbers. Area models, such as circles and rectangles, set models including counters, cubes or actual objects and linear models, as seen in the equivalence activity, Blackline Master 6.1, offer opportunities to build students' understanding of the five interpretations of rational numbers. We now look at the four arithmetic operations with rational numbers.

Operational Sense

One often hears the term *number sense* as a critical component of understanding mathematics. Along with number sense, students need to develop an operational sense. In the 2002 NCTM Yearbook, DeAnn Huinker defines operation sense in terms of the following seven abilities that students must have:

- Understand the meaning of each operation
- Develop the ability to describe and use each operation in appropriate contexts
- Understand the symbolic language
- Think flexibly between multiple representations such as concrete, pictorial, and symbolic
- Comprehend the relationships among and between the operations
- Compose and decompose numbers
- Anticipate the effect of using each operation (NCTM, 2002)

In terms of rational numbers, students need to explore the impact of each of the operations. Students should examine their understanding of the operations on whole numbers to realize that in some cases rational numbers do not work in the same manner. Students need to explore relationships such as division and multiplication with fractions. For example, students can discover that dividing by 3 is the same as multiplying by $\frac{1}{3}$ and dividing by $\frac{1}{2}$ is the same as multiplying by 2. Carefully constructed series of questions can help bring these understandings to light. (See Blackline Master 6.2, Operational Relationships.)

Addition and Subtraction

In the beginning of the chapter, we discussed how important it is for students to develop their conceptual understandings. Rather than lecturing and demonstrating how to add fractions, students need to work with concrete models. Fraction strips provide a hands-on tool to help students understand the importance of working with the same size pieces, common denominators. This also helps students develop an intuitive understanding of multiplication and division.

Using Fraction Strips

Student can make their own set of fraction strips, like those shown in Figure 6.12. Use five different colors of construction paper and make five strips each measuring 3 inches by 18 inches. Consider laminating these fraction strips for classroom sets.

The suggested colors are simply for ease of reference. Every student's set of fraction strips should use the same colors for the same-sized pieces. Students follow directions to make each strip based on folding and cutting halves. The $\frac{1}{2}$-size blue strip is folded in half and then cut to make two equal halves or fourths. The next strip completes the same folds as the previous strip and those pieces are folded in half again and cut to create eighths. Students should predict the number of creases that they will see when they unfold the strip as well as the number of pieces that will be created when those creases are cut. Some teachers prefer to make the strips for their students in order to save class time. After making their fraction strips, students should organize them as seen in Figure 6.12. Students should record the relationships between the number of pieces in each strip as compared to other

figure **6.12**

Fraction Strips

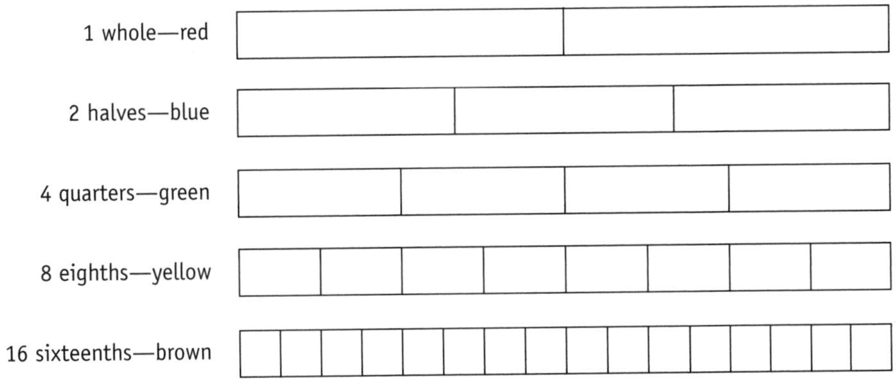

| 1 whole—red | | |

| 2 halves—blue | | |

| 4 quarters—green | | |

| 8 eighths—yellow | | |

| 16 sixteenths—brown | | |

strips. How many $\frac{1}{2}$-size strips make one whole strip? What do we call one blue strip? How many yellows (eighths) make one green piece? How many browns are needed to cover one yellow? Students should name the unit fraction for each strip and then find relationships among the various pieces. Students can also explore how many ways they can make 1 whole or $\frac{1}{2}$. Students can share and discuss their findings about equivalent fractions. Students can also record their findings on newsprint or posterboard that can be displayed around the classroom. Doing so validates students' contributions and students can refer to their posters as they continue their work with fractions.

Making One, Blackline Master 6.3, is a game that helps students focus on addition with unit fractions. Students can play cooperatively or competitively. Each team needs a fraction strip set and a cube labeled with $\frac{1}{2}, \frac{1}{4}, \frac{1}{8}, \frac{1}{16}, \frac{1}{8}, \frac{1}{16}$. Students roll the cube and then place the value rolled onto the red strip. The object of the game is to make one whole. The winner is the student who first covers the red strip, the whole, completely and exactly. Making more than one whole does not count. Students can also adapt this game to create a rule that they have to try to cover the red strip using one color in the easiest way. For this version, students roll the dice three times, taking the appropriate fraction strip piece as they roll. After the three rolls, they look to make the sum of those three pieces with one color and in the fewest number of pieces. For example, a student rolls $\frac{1}{4}, \frac{1}{8}, \frac{1}{4}$. This could be made by using 10 one-sixteenth pieces or 5 one-eighth pieces. As, $\frac{10}{16} = \frac{5}{8}$, the two fractions are equivalent. Using the smaller number of pieces is the winning solution.

Point Well Taken

"Mathematical games can foster mathematical communication as students explain and justify their moves to one another. In addition, games can motivate students and engage them in thinking about and applying concepts and skills."

—*www.nctm.org E-example 5.1*

MISCONCEPTION

Students are easily confused by the term *reducing* in regard to fractions. They tend to think that the fractions are getting smaller if they "reduce" them. Other more literal students view reducing fractions this way: $\frac{1}{2}, \frac{1}{2}, \frac{1}{2}$. In reality, the value of the fraction remains the same; it is the number of pieces relative to the size of the whole that changes. We suggest that students refer to equivalent fractions or simplifying fractions rather than reducing fractions.

Students can also use the fraction strips to explore subtraction of fractions. In a game called In the Red, students remove pieces from the red strip. Students use the same cube as in Making One and begin with the red strip covered by two half strips, or two blue pieces. After each roll, the student removes that quantity. For example, on the first roll, Jose rolls $\frac{1}{4}$. Jose must trade one blue piece (one-half) for two one-fourth pieces. He can then take away the appropriate amount ($\frac{1}{4}$). The winner is the first student to remove all of the pieces off the red strip. Students can use these fraction strips to gain a solid understanding of addition and subtraction of fractions. When they can describe steps in the process, it is time to work with other fractions that are not represented in the fraction strip set. Problems involving mixed numbers with like and unlike denominators can now be explored.

Internet Lesson Plan

Students often struggle comparing fractions. Going beyond using a model to work more symbolically presents difficulties. Students frequently do not understand why a common denominator is needed. All too often teachers demonstrate a cross-multiplication method that can confuse students, particularly if they have not developed any conceptual understanding. The website www.jasonproject.org/digital_labs/mathemagica/addition_fractions presents students with interactive scenarios so that they can see and evaluate what is happening as they compare fractions. In this lesson and others that appear in later chapters, we have not specified the length of time that each part of the lesson should take. Teachers' knowledge of their students, length of class time, and other variables contribute to the decision-making factors about allocating time.

Objectives
- Analyze patterns seen in applet
- Make conjectures about the meaning of the demonstrated steps
- Share their conjectures with their groups
- Relate action in the applet to steps used in comparing fractions

Materials
- Internet access
- Recording sheet

Prior Knowledge   Meaning of numerator and denominator

Lesson   Observe what approaches the students take as they decide which fraction is greater. Encourage students to write down an explanation supporting their reasoning. Tell the students that they will be working in pairs in the computer room using Mathemagica. Show them the blank screen as seen in Figure 6.13.

Tell the students that they will enter a fraction on the rectangle on the far left part the screen, $\frac{2}{3}$, in this case. They then enter the second fraction to be compared in the lower left rectangle. On the menu screen, they select "Go" and then pay close attention to what occurs. Instruct the students to repeat the process using different fractions. Their task is to determine the process that the screen is demonstrating.

Students work in pairs at the computers and then together in their group of four to exchange their ideas. Each member of the group should write a summary of their conjectures.

Close the lesson by having the students do an exit card on which they compare $\frac{1}{3}$ *and* $\frac{3}{8}$.

In your journal, explain how to compare two fractions to someone who doesn't understand yet.

Explanation of the Activity   After the students enter the fractions and click on "Go," the screen then displays the process of partitioning the top long rectangle on the right into the appropriate number of units. This is done in a staged process. The screen then shows the partitioning of the second fraction, $\frac{3}{5}$. The screen shows both of the long rectangles sectioned into fifteen units. The arrows then move to show the size of each original fraction in terms of the new denominator. The equivalent fractions are displayed, and the appropriate inequality sign is presented accordingly. Encourage the students to enter several pairs of fractions and watch carefully as the screen finds which fraction is greater. As students watch the screen, they need to focus on why different steps are being taken. With their partner, they need to write down what the steps are and why they occurred. Teachers can structure the students' exploration by supplying them with specific fractions to compare and they can supply them with specific questions to address. Teachers can also leave the exploration more open-ended as an alternative approach. In this case, the students are simply asked to explore to see if they can determine what is happening in each step and why it is happening. After investigating this applet, students should explain their discoveries.

figure **6.13**

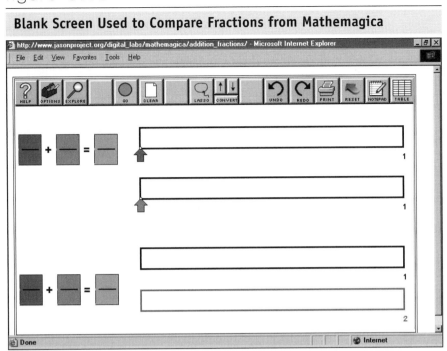

Blank Screen Used to Compare Fractions from Mathemagica

Used by permission of the Jason Foundation for Education.

Multiplication and Division

Using Fraction Strips

The fraction strips can also be used to explore both multiplication and division. Using specific language helps students understand the action taking place. For multiplication, the word *of* becomes meaningful. When taking $\frac{1}{2}$ *of* $\frac{1}{4}$, for example, students show the one-fourth piece and then look to find the size of the piece that is one-half of that one-fourth. Similarly, finding $\frac{1}{4}$ *of* $\frac{1}{2}$, students find the one-half piece and then look to see what piece is one-fourth of that one-half. As seen in these two examples, students can also explore the commutative property of multiplication. Considering division with fraction strips, language again plays an important role. For the problem $\frac{1}{2} \div \frac{1}{4}$, students think "$\frac{1}{2}$ has how many $\frac{1}{4}$s in it?" By placing the appropriate pieces on top of the one-half piece, students build a kinesthetic and visual understanding that two pieces the size of $\frac{1}{4}$ fit into the $\frac{1}{2}$. Labeling the strips on the reverse side with either the decimal or percent equivalences helps students relate the different representations. There are many manipulatives available to help develop a conceptual understanding of operations with fractions such as Cuisenaire Rods and Fraction Bars. Another model, an array, can help students see multiplication of rational numbers in action.

PROCESS STANDARDS

Representation

Frequently using common equivalences among all three representations of rational numbers helps keep these relationships in the forefront of students' minds. Using multiple models broadens and strengthens students' understanding.

Using Area Models

In elementary school, students used arrays to represent multiplication with whole numbers. They can extend this understanding to working with rational numbers as well. In

figure **6.14**

Using a 2 × 4 Area Model

figure **6.15**

Using an Area Model for Multiplication of Fractions

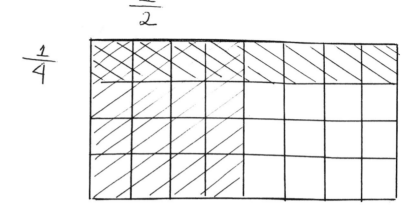

Figure 6.14, Judson used a 2 × 4 grid. After drawing the rectangle, Judson shaded one-half of it. He then put slash marks slanted in the opposite direction on one-fourth of the columns. The unit with both slash marks and the shading indicates the result of the product, $\frac{1}{8}$.

In Figure 6.15, Carolyn used a 4 by 8 unit array to find the product of $\frac{1}{2} \times \frac{1}{4}$.

She began shading by shading one-half of the sections appearing as columns with slash marks going up from left to right (///). She then shaded one-fourth of the units appearing as rows using \\\\ marks. She counted the units that had double shading and stated her answer as $\frac{4}{32}$. Comparing Judson and Carolyn's work leads to productive and insightful conversations. Students can determine whether or not the two solutions are equal. The process of verifying that the fractions are equivalent affords teachers the opportunity to discuss the identity property. Fractions, such as $\frac{1}{8}$, can be multiplied by $\frac{4}{4}$ to obtain the equivalent value $\frac{8}{32}$. Realizing that $\frac{4}{4}$ is indeed equivalent to 1 and that 1 multiplied by any number results in the same number are foundational understandings.

There are several websites that provide useful activities that engage students in the exploration of equivalent fractions.

> http://nlvm.usu.edu/en/nav/vlibrary.html
> www.aaamath.com/fra42a-idequivfract.html
> http://kidshub.org/kids/fractions.cfm

Using Question Strings

Providing students with carefully selected questions and asking them to look for patterns can help students as they work to develop conceptual understandings of multiplication and division of fractions (refer to Blackline Master 6.5, Can You See It?).

In Can You See It?, students solve the set of problems and then look for the pattern within the set. Students readily notice that the series of questions in each set yields the same answers. Teachers can pose such questions as "What is the pattern of change that happens to factors from one problem to the next?" "Does this same pattern hold when working with division?" Students should realize that when working with multiplication, one can double the first factor and take half of the second factor, and the product remains unchanged. This knowledge empowers students to make simpler problems! For example, given $14 \times 1\frac{1}{2}$, a student might think about doubling $1\frac{1}{2}$ and then taking half of 14. The student is then simply solving 7×3. When considering division problems, students discover that they can choose to make a simpler problem by multiplying the dividend and divisor by the same quantity. For example, $14 \div \frac{2}{3}$ can be approached by multiplying the dividend and divisor by 3. The simpler problem becomes $42 \div 2$. Using question strings is a powerful tool in a teacher's repertoire of skills that helps guide students' thinking.

REACT | REFLECT

Making a simpler problem is one strategy students can use. How does this approach compare to the algorithm involving inverting the divisor and then multiplying the fractions?

PROCESS STANDARDS

Reasoning and Proof

Placing the decision in the students' hands about what steps to take in order to reach a solution enables students to think about the context of the problem. Students are no longer memorizing steps nor are they trying to remember when to apply the rules. Teachers pose the problems and students use their current understanding to solve the problems. Sharing strategies strengthens their understanding, clarifies their reasoning, and offers opportunities to verify their solutions. Sharing solutions also allows fellow students to consider a new approach. Students can articulate the underlying rationale for taking each step in their chosen process. They should justify that the original problem and the simpler one are equivalent because the students have used a factor of 1. Students use strategies that they understand and strategies that they connected to in the process of development. Communicating their discoveries also promotes students' understanding and increases retention.

MISCONCEPTION

Students who are taught to change the mixed numbers to improper fractions and then multiply frequently forget that important first step. Given $2\frac{2}{3} \times 4\frac{1}{5}$, students state their solution as $8\frac{2}{15}$. Using their estimation skills, students can reason that the product is too small. In this case students have not multiplied by all of the factors: $(2 \times 4) + (2 \times \frac{1}{5}) + (\frac{2}{3} \times 4) + (\frac{2}{3} \times \frac{1}{5})$. Algorithms are indeed more efficient. This example points out the critical importance of conceptual understanding as a foundation.

Proportional Reasoning

Proportional reasoning is one of the most important topics in middle school mathematics. Proportional reasoning requires students to understand how quantities vary in relation to one another. It is a critical aspect of all mathematics topics to follow, for example, algebra (slope, direct and inverse variation), geometry (similar figures), probability (chance), and calculus (related rates). In middle school, students use proportional reasoning with similar figures, rate problems, percents, fractions, and scaling. Proportional reasoning is also a critical mathematics skill outside of the classroom. It is involved with grocery purchases, consumer topics, personal finances, and taxes. NCTM identifies proportional reasoning as one of the critical concepts in middle school that is "of such great importance that it merits whatever time and effort must be expended to assure its careful development" (NCTM, 1989, p. 82).

Proportional reasoning has proven to be a difficult topic for students in middle school and high school, and even for adults. Recent data from the Third International Mathematics and Science Study showed that problems requiring proportional reasoning are among the most challenging problems for students (Beaton et al., 1996). One study found that about half of a group of preservice teachers had difficulty reasoning proportionally (Cramer et al., 1989). Adults who cannot reason proportionally will have difficulty with applications of percents, rates, and scaling in real-world contexts. Consequently, it is important to spend sufficient time with proportional reasoning in the middle grades to ensure students have a strong foundational understanding to bring with them to high school and beyond.

TRY THIS

1. If you travel to a foreign country, you can exchange dollars for the currency used in the country. In England, you can exchange 3 dollars for 2 pounds. How many pounds could you exchange for 21 dollars?

2. Susie and Heather were running equally as fast around a track. Susie started first. When she had run nine laps, Heather had run three laps. When Heather had completed fifteen laps, how many laps had Susie run?

Did you use the same process for both problems? The first problem uses proportional reasoning. The second problem involves an additive relationship and proportional reasoning is not involved.

The study of proportionality typically begins in elementary school with various ratios such as three boys for every five girls or three telephones for every family. Ratios such as these are generally written as fractions but have a vastly different meaning than the part/whole fractions that we discussed earlier in this chapter. In a fraction such as $\frac{3}{4}$, the numerator indicates 3 items out of a group of 4 items, such as three students out of a study group of four students. In the ratio $\frac{3}{4}$, the 3 may represent one item, such as boys, and the denominator represents a completely different group or item, such as CDs. The groups are separate and distinct and may have no relationship except for that described by the ratio. It is important to determine how middle school students distinguish between their understanding of a part/whole fraction and a ratio. They look the same, but their meaning is quite different.

A further aspect of ratios and proportions that is different from what middle school students have previously studied is that all proportions involve multiplicative reasoning. The relationship between the two ratios of a proportion is not additive, but multiplicative. The following problem can help a teacher to gauge her students' understanding of proportional relationships.

Raven runs 6 laps for every 4 laps that Lydia runs. If Lydia runs 8 laps, how many laps does Raven run?

A student who reasons that this is an additive relationship will conclude that since Raven runs 4 additional laps $(4 + 4 = 8)$, then Lydia will run an additional 4 laps or 10 $(6 + 4)$ laps). The correct reasoning for this problem is multiplicative. Lydia runs double the number of laps stated at the start of the problem $(4 \times 2 = 8)$, so Raven will run double the number of laps stated in the beginning of the problem $(2 \times 6 = 12)$.

Students who cannot solve this problem correctly need to review the differences between ratios and fractions and how to form rates. The activities that follow may be used to introduce proportional reasoning to students as well as support students who are still having difficulty with proportional problems.

REACT | REFLECT

Compare Raven and Lydia's run around the track to Susie and Heather's race. What causes the two problems to be solved differently?

Using Rates

Students may be helped to reason proportionally by considering a variety of settings that demand proportional reasoning. Typically, problems involving rates are common settings that require proportional reasoning. For example, students could use a table to display data from a real-world context. Suppose Jan earns $3 per hour for baby-sitting. The rate table displayed here shows how much she earns for each hour of baby-sitting.

Hours Worked	1	2	3	4	5
Money Earned	3	6	9	12	15

For every subsequent hour spent baby-sitting Jan earns an additional $3.00. The rate table essentially shows skip counting by 3. Students should be able to determine what Jan would earn if she had 10 hours of baby-sitting by counting up from 5 hours. The next step would be to apply the multiplicative pattern from the table to determine how much Jan would earn for 20 hours of baby-sitting, 30 hours, 50 hours, and so forth by using the expression $3n$, where n represents the number of baby-sitting hours. Students can construct similar rate tables for other rate problems involving rates of pay, mileage, grocery prices, and so forth.

ASSESSMENT TIP

Teachers can provide students with a self-assessment scale before a new unit. Students can reflect on how confident they feel about a particular topic and then give themselves a rating. After completing the unit, students should rate themselves again. Identifying their individual growth can help students build confidence.

Once students are able to work with single rate applications, they can then move to working with proportions. A proportion is formed by two equal ratios. The concept of a rate table can be expanded to accommodate the two ratios of a proportion. A multiples table is helpful for students who are beginning to work with proportions to solve problems.

The following problem is a missing-term proportion problem. It is displayed in the multiples table in Figure 6.16.

Two packages of printer paper cost $5.00. What is the price of 8 packages of paper?

In Figure 6.16, the number of packages (2) and the related price (5) are circled. Next, the remaining number of packages of paper (8) is circled. Students can count down from 2 to 8 (three steps). They can then find the price of 8 packages by counting down three steps from 5 to 20.

Students can also write out the two rate columns separately as shown here.

2	5
4	10
6	15
8	20

figure **6.16**

Using Multiplication for Proportion Problems

1	(2)	3	4	(5)	6	7	8	9	10
2	4	6	8	10	12	14	16	18	20
3	6	9	12	15	18	21	24	27	30
4	(8)	12	16	20	24	28	32	36	40
5	10	15	20	25	30	35	40	45	50
6	12	18	24	30	36	42	48	54	60
7	14	21	28	35	42	49	56	63	70
8	16	24	32	40	48	56	64	72	80
9	18	27	36	45	54	63	72	81	90
10	20	30	40	50	60	70	80	90	100

Students should have many opportunities to display real-world rate problems on the multiples table. As they isolate the two columns from the table that apply to the problem, they will continue to focus on the multiplicative aspect of proportional reasoning in real-world applications.

Missing-Term Proportional Problems

Once students are comfortable using rate tables and multiplication charts to solve problems involving proportional reasoning, they are ready to move to two intermediate methods to solve missing-term proportion problems. The first method has been termed *unitizing*. In our discussion of the five meanings of rational numbers, we mentioned unitizing as a way to conceptually group objects. Consider the following problem:

Apples cost $2 for 3 pounds. What is the price of 12 pounds of apples?

This proportion may be written as

$$\frac{\$2}{3\ lb.} = \frac{x}{12\ lb.}$$

This proportion may be solved using the *unitizing* method as follows:

The description of 3 pounds of apples for $2 is a "chunk" or unit of related information. This chunk may be compared to the question in the problem in this way. How many chunks of 3 pounds are there in 12 pounds? There are 4 chunks (of 3 pounds) in 12 pounds; therefore there are 4 chunks of $2 in the price of the 12 pounds of apples or a total of $8 ($2 \times 4 = 8$). This idea of chunking, or unitizing, is very similar to simply forming equivalent fractions and finding the missing term. Consider the following interpretation of the same problem:

$$\frac{2}{3} \times \frac{4}{4} = \frac{?}{12}$$

The first representation for working with the price of apples and this one are not identical. The difference lies in the process of conceptualizing the problem. By immediately forming equivalent fractions and solving for the missing term, students may miss the rationale behind forming equivalent fractions and may also miss the multiplicative nature of the problem. They may simply be reducing it to a recipe-driven solution. Once students are able to internalize the chunking aspect of these proportions, they can beneficially think of the ratios in each proportion as equivalent fractions.

As stated previously, chunking is effective and efficient with proportions that are equivalent fractions. When working with proportions that are not equivalent, chunking can be used but the calculations become cumbersome. In such instances, students might decide to find the unit price. Consider this problem:

Apples sell at $2 for 5 pounds. How much will 8 pounds cost?

Did You **Know**?

By law grocery stores must post the unit prices for their items.

In this case the two ratios are not equivalent fractions and are not easily unitized. In this situation, the task is first to determine the unit price for the apples, that is, the price per pound. The price per pound for the apples is $\frac{2}{5}$ or 40 cents per pound. This result is then used to determine the price for 8 pounds ($8 \times 40 = \$3.20$).

Students can find the unit price to solve problems with solutions that are not integers, as well as with problems they can solve by chunking. Both procedures allow students to understand the relationships portrayed in the problem and then use their proportional reasoning to solve it.

An interesting finding about proportional reasoning is that any proportion can be interpreted in two distinct ways yet produce the same solution. Consider this problem:

A baker needs 12 cups of flour to bake 4 cakes. How many cups of flour will the baker need to bake 16 cakes?

The proportion may be understood in two different ways, as a Within proportion or as a Between proportion (Vergnaud, 1983).

Within

$$\frac{12\ cups}{4\ cakes} = \frac{x\ cups}{16\ cakes}$$

Between

$$\frac{4\ cakes}{16\ cakes} = \frac{12\ cups}{x\ cups}$$

In the Within representation, 12 cups of flour produce 4 cakes, so the relationship of cups of flour and cakes is a *within* relationship in the problem. The same is true with 16 cakes and a unknown number of cups of flour. In the Between representation, there is no direct relationship between 4 cakes and 16 cakes, nor between 12 cups of flour and the unknown cups of flour. Although the two proportions result in the same answer and are essentially equivalent, conceptually some students can make more sense of one proportion than the other. It is important to allow students to display both proportion forms in class so that students see two different ways to reason proportionally, either Within or Between. Studies show that students will select the proportion that makes more sense to them in terms of the problem. When students understand both the Within and Between ways to conceptualize a proportion, they have another problem-solving tool that they can use.

Using Cross-Products

The final aspect that students study about proportional reasoning in middle school is sometimes termed *cross-multiplication*. Cross-multiplication is used to solve missing-term proportion problems.

$$\frac{3}{5} = \frac{4}{x}$$
$$3x = 20$$
$$x = \frac{20}{3}$$

There are several advantages to using cross-multiplication: It is efficient; it quickly produces the correct answer, and it may be used with any missing-term proportion problem.

MISCONCEPTION

There are a number of cautions necessary with the cross-multiplication procedure. First, the name *cross-multiplication* can be confusing for students. They confuse this algorithm with the procedure for multiplying fractions.

$$\frac{2}{3} \times \frac{4}{5} = \qquad \frac{2}{3} = \frac{4}{x}$$

We suggest using the term *cross-product* to help students distinguish this algorithm from the one they use to multiply common fractions.

A second consideration is that students should not be rushed into using the cross-product algorithm before they have a foundational understanding of proportionality. The algorithm is easy to use, but successful use of it can mask poor proportional reasoning skills. Students who can employ the cross-product algorithm may only be positioning three numbers in a proportion and then solving for the missing term without any concept of proportional reasoning or application of proportionality to the problem. We suggest that the cross-product algorithm be the last concept that middle school students learn about proportions rather than one of the first.

When introducing the cross-product algorithm, it is important for students to understand the mathematics that support it. In the following example the solution can be determined by using equivalent fractions.

$$\frac{2}{5} = \frac{120}{x} \qquad \frac{2 \times 60}{5 \times 60} = \frac{120}{300} \qquad 300 = x$$

The resulting proportion $\frac{2}{5} = \frac{120}{300}$ may be used to demonstrate the cross-product algorithm. Students might explore the results of using the cross-product algorithm, namely,

$$\frac{2}{5} = \frac{120}{300}$$
$$2 \times 300 = 5 \times 120$$

In this case the resulting products are equal; that is, $5 \times 120 = 600$ and $2 \times 300 = 600$. Helping students understand why this is always so will help mitigate the rote memorization that students might employ when they use the algorithm. In this example, the scale factor between the original ratio ($\frac{2}{5}$) and the resulting ratio ($\frac{120}{300}$) is 60, as shown previously. When students employ the cross-product algorithm with this proportion, they are essentially using the scale factor.

$$\frac{2}{5} = \frac{120}{300}$$
$$\frac{2}{5} = \frac{2 \times 60}{5 \times 60}$$

By the cross-product algorithm

$$2 \times (5 \times 60) = 5 \times (2 \times 60)$$

Thus, the cross-product algorithm uses the scale factor that is imbedded in one of the ratios in any proportion. When the cross-product algorithm is used to solve for the missing term in a proportion, the same concept of the scale factor is still used to justify the algorithm. Once the two cross-products are found, then the missing term may be computed by solving the resulting equation.

$$\frac{2}{5} = \frac{120}{x}$$
$$2x = 600$$
$$x = 300$$

Point Well Taken

"An important conclusion of our research is that paying too much attention to specific methods of solution for proportional problems without also focusing on the underlying concepts and relationships of a problem situation may well turn out to be counterproductive."

—*Van Dooren et al., 2003, p. 208*

We can verify that the cross-product procedure works in more abstract terms.

Given $\frac{a}{b} = \frac{c}{d}$, we can multiply both sides of the equation by bd, which is the common denominator between the two fractions.

$$(bd)\frac{a}{b} = \frac{c}{d}(bd)$$

By simplifying $\frac{b}{b}$ to 1, and $\frac{d}{d}$ to 1, we obtain $ad = cb$, the cross-product. Rather than this abstract presentation, it is far more important for students to understand the conceptual development of the cross-product procedure so that they can be effective in its use.

The cross-product algorithm is a powerful tool that students will be able to use in a variety of mathematical areas for a wide range of practical applications. It is important to prepare students to understand and use the algorithm. Foundational work that precedes using the algorithm includes using intermediate methods suggested in this chapter and then moving to the cross-product algorithm as the final stage in learning how to solve problems that require proportional reasoning. Students who have had sufficient experiences solving proportions before they learn the cross-product algorithm will be able to successfully apply proportional reasoning to the middle school topics of percent, rates, and similar figures.

TRY THIS

What is Stan's error here? $\frac{3}{4} \times \frac{2}{3} = \frac{9}{8}$

REACT | REFLECT

How did you learn the cross-product algorithm? How well did you understand the mathematics behind the algorithm?

With this background on proportional reasoning, we will look at proportional reasoning in terms of working with percents.

Working with Percents

Working with percents challenges students because the tasks vary and the vocabulary itself is confusing. Consider a typical middle school problem:

> Angelo purchases a baseball glove during a 20% off sale. The cost of the glove was originally $90. How much does Angelo save by buying the glove on sale?

Each percent problem involves three values: base, rate, and percentage. The base in Angelo's problem is $90. The rate is 20% and the percentage is the amount he will save by buying the glove on sale. The vocabulary alone can be confusing for students and adults. The term *percentage* is often confused with the percent itself. In this case, the percent, 20%, is the rate in the problem. The percentage is the money saved. All problems involve finding one of the three values: base, rate, or percentage.

Traditionally, percent problems were presented as three different cases. The student had to determine which case the problem represented and then apply the appropriate rote procedure. We suggest that rote memorization is not beneficial as an operational procedure. As with fractions, students need to develop their conceptual understanding of percents. Working with percents in context helps students build that understanding and prepare for future work.

Students can approach Angelo's task by drawing a model as shown in Figure 6.17. Each of the sections represents 10% of the cost of the glove, or 10% of 90 or $9. Therefore, two sections, or 20%, of the cost equals $18. In the following problem, the rate and the percentage are known, and the base is the missing value.

> Francois paid $30 for a picture of the famous basketball player Michael Jordan. This price was 40% of the original price. What was the original price for this picture?

Students can show 40% of the original price as four 10% units. The first four units equal the 40% and $30; the second four units represent another $30. The remaining two units are half of the original and, therefore, represent 20% and $15. The sum gives the original price of the picture, $75. (See Figure 6.18.)

AUTHOR'S Recall

I recall learning to work with percents by distinguishing between three cases. Case 1 referred to finding a percent of a number. Finding the rate given the base and the percentage was called Case 2. Finding the base given the rate and the percentage was called Case 3. I first had to figure out which case the problem represented and then I applied the algorithm.

figure **6.17**

Model for 20% of $90

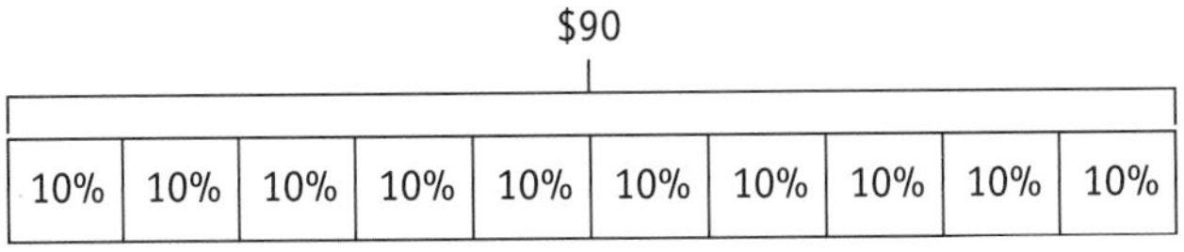

figure **6.18**

40% of What Value Is 30?

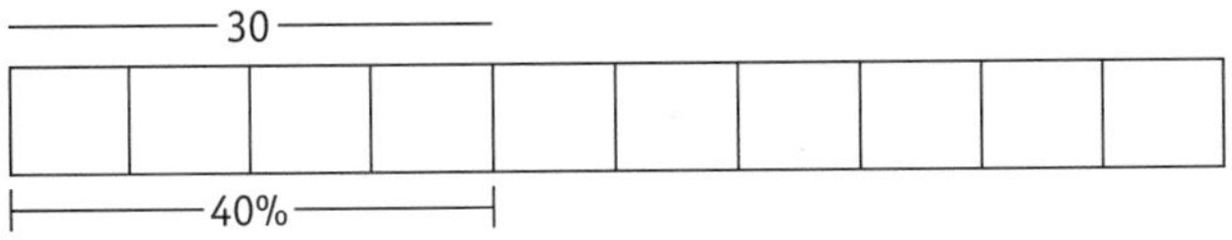

MISCONCEPTION

Traditionally, students have been taught to directly translate to find out the original price of the picture of Michael Jordan. Students might begin with 40% of what number is $30. Then they would represent the problem as $0.40x = 30$ where x represents the original price. Students would then solve the equation by dividing both sides by 0.40 to get $75. This method does not connect very well with what is happening in the problem. Students memorize the procedure with little understanding. We contend that students who work with models first will develop the necessary conceptual understanding. For these students, the related algorithm will be more transparent, and they will be able to use it effectively.

Because percents are always based on 100, these models work easily. Once students demonstrate mastery, they can use these rectangular models to work with similar problems involving fractions. For example,

> Shawna sold $\frac{2}{5}$ of her stamp collection. These 8 stamps were all different types. How many stamps did Shawna have in her collection before she sold those stamps?

In this case, students need to decide that the whole can be represented in fifths. Consequently, if $\frac{2}{5} = 8$ stamps, $\frac{4}{5} = 16$. The remaining unit, $\frac{1}{5}$, must equal 4 stamps. So the total number in the original collection is 20 stamps. (See Figure 6.19.)

RESEARCH

In *Teaching Children Mathematics*, Joan Moss shares her study on the teaching and learning of rational numbers in a measurement context beginning with percents. She cites several advantages of changing the order in which rational numbers are presented to students. Students can develop an intuitive understanding of comparison without having to follow a complicated procedure. A second advantage Moss notes is that every percent has an easily seen fractional equivalent. This is not true of every fraction, $\frac{1}{11}$, for example.

> By beginning with percents, we allow children to make their first conversions among the different representations of rational numbers in a direct and intuitive fashion and develop a better general understanding of how the three systems are related. (Moss, 2003, p. 336)

REACT | REFLECT

What is your reaction to Ms. Moss's research findings?

Finding the percent given the base and the rate can also be illustrated using this rectangular model.

TRY THIS

If 15 students out of the 75 students in the seventh grade class own more than one pet, what percent of the class owns more than one pet?

When looking for the percent, it is not always clear to students what the size of the rectangular model should be. Sometimes they look for a common value between the rate and percentage. Some students realize that 5 groups of 15 equal 75 and, therefore, the model can use fifths.

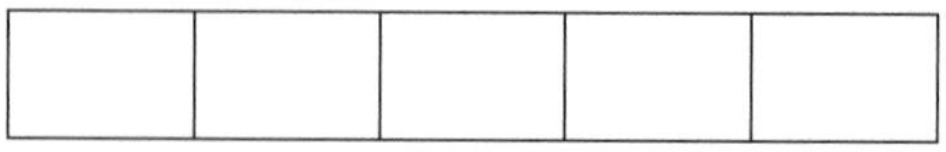

figure **6.19**

Using the Rectangle Model with Fractions

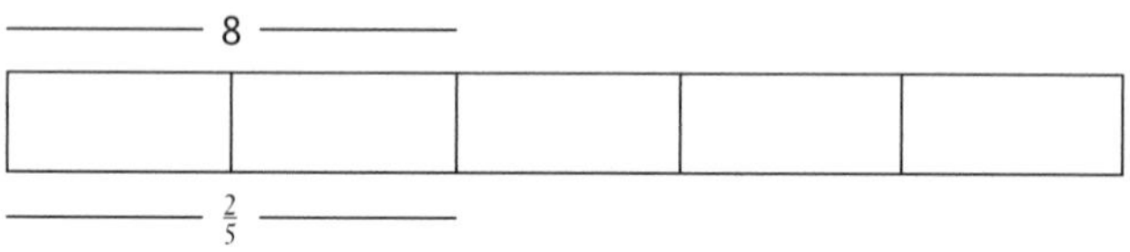

Students shade one box to represent the 15 students owning more than one pet. That unit represents one-fifth of the total. Because all percents are based on 100, students realize that each box represents 20%. Students who have developed proportional reasoning skills will appreciate the efficiency of the cross-product algorithm when working with percent problems.

These models work well to help students develop a conceptual understanding of each of the problems. These models can also be cumbersome particularly as the numbers become less compatible. In that case, students can set up the proportion and use the cross-product algorithm. This algorithm is efficient and reliable once students have developed the prerequisite skills in proportional reasoning. The rate is placed over 100 and the percentage is placed over the base. One of these values will be missing in the context of the problem.

TRY THIS

Mr. Cassava correctly predicted that 90% of his students will earn a B+ or better on the test. How many students are in his class if 27 earned a B+ or better?

Students can set up a proportion to solve this problem: $\frac{90}{100} = \frac{27}{x}$. The missing value in this case is the total number of students in Mr. Cassava's class. Students can find this base by applying the cross-product algorithm: $90x = 2700$. The total number of students, 30, is found as students divide both sides of the equation by 90.

MISCONCEPTION

In setting up the proportions, some teachers refer to the "is over of" method. The percent is always over 100 and then the value associated with the "is" is placed over the value associated with the "of" or total in the context of the problem. This is a formulaic approach and students seem to like it. However, as seen in the Try This involving Mr. Cassava's class, the problem is not stated so directly. In order to apply the "is over of" method, students need to think about the problem in the following way: 90% of his students earning B+ or better is 27.

Before leaving this chapter, we want to address one additional concept for middle school students. Developing a meaningful conceptual understanding of integers remains a critical component of the curriculum.

Integers

Integers are a subset of rational numbers. Positive and negative whole numbers and zero represent the set of integers. Middle school students have encountered these values previously at the intuitive level of understanding. They have considered debts and assets, temperature changes, and levels above and below sea level, for example. Over the years, teachers and researchers alike have struggled to develop the perfect manipulative or context that conveys the rules governing these values. As students relate to varying strategies differently, multiple representations and contexts prove beneficial for students' understanding.

Reminding students of where they have seen or used positive and negative numbers presents a solid beginning. Then looking for patterns on a number line places the integers in a familiar framework. Students can find patterns in terms of the size of the numbers on the number line. They can also see that for every positive value there is an opposite value. If the number line is folded in half around zero, students can easily see these pairings. Students also easily understand that every value and its opposite combine together to make zero. Such pairings are referred to as additive inverses. For example, the sum of 3 and its opposite, –3, equals 0 and similarly, the sum of –8 and +8 equals zero. Some of the more popular story situations used to help students understand addition and subtraction with integers are the postman and the cubes in the broth.

Did You **Know**?

Red is traditionally used to show accounts with a negative balance. The practice originated in Renaissance Italy. As the principles of modern accounting developed, one of the practices was to highlight any account in arrears in red.

Did You **Know**?

As recently as the sixteenth century, a leading mathematician termed the concept of negative numbers as absurd.

Using a Story Context

The postman story involves mail being delivered to the student's door. Sometimes the mail includes gifts of money and at other times bills to be paid. For each delivery, students need to determine the net amount received or the amount of money owed. For example, the postman delivered a bill for $5, a gift for $8, a second gift of $12, and then another bill for $13. Students record the transactions for the day's deliveries: –5, +8, +12, –13. This story becomes a little more complicated when the postman takes back a bill that was delivered yesterday. Taking away the bill amounts to a positive result!

The second popular story context involves hot cubes and cold cubes. When these cubes are placed in the broth, they affect the temperature of the broth. Five hot cubes will raise the temperature 5 degrees and six cold cubes will lower the temperature of the broth by 6 degrees (Fendel & Resek, 1997). Just as the postman delivers and takes away, the cubes are put into and also withdrawn from the kettle. Both of these stories place working with addition and subtraction in contexts that enable students to think about the outcomes. Another approach using two-colored chips provides students with a manipulative to represent integers.

Using Physical Models

Two-colored chips reinforce the concept of additive inverses, an integer and its opposite adding to zero. For example, the red side of the chip represents a negative 1 and the white side represents a positive 1. Students easily recognize that one white chip combined with one red chip equals zero. To model –3 + 4, students display three red chips and then four white ones. Students can match one white with one red chip until the one positive white chip remains. In some cases involving subtraction, students need to place pairs of chips on their desks in order to perform the operation required. Consider, for example, –3 – (+5). Students begin by placing three red chips. (See Figure 6.20.) Students realize that they do not have five white chips to remove; therefore, they place five pairs of white and red chips on their desks (Figure 6.20a and b). It is important that students recognize that these pairs have not changed the value shown by the chips because each pair equals zero. Students can now remove the five white chips to see the resulting eight red chips or –8 (Figure 6.20c).

Another approach to help students understand addition and subtraction of integers uses a number line. In order to provide a kinesthetic understanding, place paper recording tape from a calculator on the floor of the classroom. This large number line indicates the units from –10 to 10 about 1 foot apart. Students can walk this number line according to these directions:

- The first integer represents the starting position.
- The next sign indicates the operation and, therefore, the direction you face, left for the negative sign and right for the positive sign.
- Walk the number of spaces indicated by the second number and in the direction indicated (i.e., forward for positive value, backward for negative value).

Consider the following two problems:

$$-3 + 5$$

$$-1 - (-2)$$

In the first example, the student begins by standing on –3. He then faces the positive direction as the problem indicates addition. As the 5 is understood to be positive (we don't bother to write + (+5)), the student moves forward 5 spaces to end up on +2. In the second example, the student begins on –1 and turns to face the negative direction as indicated by the operational sign, subtraction. Now the student steps backward 2 spaces. Conse-

figure **6.20**

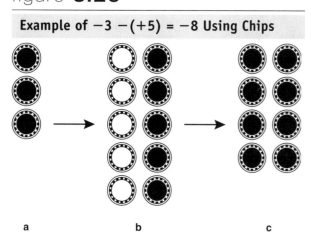

Example of –3 –(+5) = –8 Using Chips

a   b   c

On the Lighter Side

Clem gets it!

Rose Is Rose reprinted by permission of United Feature Syndicate, Inc.

quently, the student ends up at +1. Students observing the problem, record the problem as -1 − (-2) = 1.

There are distinct advantages to working with these two physical models. One advantage of working with the chips is that the students perform the action stated in the problem. They combine chips for addition and they take them away for subtraction. The advantage of using the number line reinforces the movement when combining integers and provides a kinesthetic opportunity to focus on addition and subtraction. When working with multiplication, students can use the chips in a repeated addition context. They can see that 4 groups of –3 equals –12, and considering the commutative property, students realize that –3 times 4 also equals –12. Students can also represent multiplication on a number line. (See Figure 6.21.) Multiplication with two negative factors represents a stumbling block for many students.

One approach to begin thinking about multiplication of integers uses statements such as the following: Raul states, "I am not **not** going to have lunch today." Although such a statement is not grammatically correct, it does illustrate the effect of two negatives working together. Raul is certainly going to eat lunch today. Students enjoy creating their own statements using double negatives, and they tend to go beyond double negatives to include many repeated "nots" and other double negative words such as "irregardless." Looking for patterns with these sentences provides a solid motivational approach to working with two negative factors.

Using Question Strings

Using a series of carefully designed examples presents students with the challenge of identifying the pattern and then predicting the next example in the series. Students should find the answer to each of the problems in Figure 6.22 and then look for patterns. In the

figure **6.21**

Number Line Modeling 3 × (−2)

```
◄———┼———┼———┼———┼———┼———┼———┼———┼———►
    -7  -6  -5  -4  -3  -2  -1   0   1
```

figure **6.22**

Identifying Patterns in Multiplication of Integers

SET A

$(2) \times (4) = \underline{\hspace{1cm}}$

$(2) \times (3) = \underline{\hspace{1cm}}$

$(2) \times (2) = \underline{\hspace{1cm}}$

$(2) \times (1) = \underline{\hspace{1cm}}$

$(2) \times (0) = \underline{\hspace{1cm}}$

$(2) \times (-1) = \underline{\hspace{1cm}}$

SET B

$(-2) \times (2) = \underline{\hspace{1cm}}$

$(-2) \times (1) = \underline{\hspace{1cm}}$

$(-2) \times (0) = \underline{\hspace{1cm}}$

$(-2) \times (-1) = \underline{\hspace{1cm}}$

$(-2) \times (-2) = \underline{\hspace{1cm}}$

$(-2) \times (-3) = \underline{\hspace{1cm}}$

table **6.1**   **Summary Chart for Multiplication of Integers**

FIRST FACTOR	SECOND FACTOR	PRODUCT
Positive (+)	Positive (+)	Positive (+)
Negative (–)	Positive (+)	Negative (–)
Positive (+)	Negative (–)	Negative (–)
Negative (–)	Negative (–)	Positive (+)

first set, students notice that the first factor remains the same and the second factor *decreases* by 1. The resulting product, however, *decreases* by 2. The last product entry is –2. The pattern could be continued to obtain further negative products. Several similar questions strings will help students understand that the product of a positive and negative number is negative. Similarly, as students work with the problems in set B, they soon confront multiplication with two negative factors. In order to keep the pattern consistent in terms of the product, students recognize that two negative factors create a positive result. After students have worked with the models and the set of problems, they are then ready to think about rules governing operations with integers. We suggest limiting the statement of rules to just multiplication and division. Students can make charts like the one in Table 6.1.

Students can build a similar chart regarding division after having discovered the same patterns through problem strings. We suggest that "rules" governing addition and subtraction with integers be avoided at first. The time spent articulating and memorizing these rules can be very confusing and, therefore, counterproductive. Students work more confidently by relying on their conceptual understanding and the models they used to build that understanding. To adequately develop the rules for adding and subtracting integers, students need to understand absolute value. Textbooks introduce the concept of absolute value and present the rules for all four operations with integers. We contend that students need to experience work with integers using concrete materials as well as place the use of integers into realistic contexts before working with rules governing the operations.

TRY THIS

Do these rules apply to addition or subtraction?

- If the signs are the same, add the digits.
- If the signs vary, subtract the digits and assign the sign of the digit with the largest absolute value.

Apply these rules to solve $4 + -6$.

SUMMARY

Middle school students thrive on active exploration and opportunities to articulate their findings. In order for students to develop *mathematical proficiency* as defined in Chapter 3, The Practice of Effective Instruction, they need opportunities to discover, form conjectures, justify their reasoning, and make connections. In short, students need to become young mathematicians! Teachers put problem solving up front by posing questions, and presenting problems and tasks to students. Students build their understanding as they use strategies to answer the problems presented to them. The following points are highlighted in this chapter:

- Students need time to experience mathematics in appropriate contexts.
- Algorithms are efficient and predictable in the hands of an accomplished student.
- Direct teaching of algorithms should be postponed until students have developed a conceptual understanding.
- Students need to develop number sense and operational sense; estimation and mental math activities can help students develop those important mathematical senses.
- The five interpretations of rational numbers present challenges for students.
- Linking the three representations of rational numbers, fractions, decimals and percents helps students make connections and develop an understanding of the appropriate uses for each.
- Proportional reasoning is a foundational mathematical skill. Time devoted to the careful development of this skill represents a major task for middle school students.
- Work with integers begins at the intuitive level and proceeds to concrete representations and then to the symbolic expressions.

Making sense of number and operations prepares students for all of their future work in mathematics. The act of building their understandings is the role to be embraced by students; providing experiences and challenging tasks, asking questions, and learning from students' work is the teacher's domain.

Student Performance on International and National Assessments

TIMSS

Divide: $\frac{6}{55} \div \frac{3}{25}$ (37% correct)

NAEP

Fifteen boxes each containing 8 radios can be repacked in 10 larger boxes each containing how many radios? (47% correct)

EXERCISES

From the Reading

1. Calculate. (Remember to use the order of operations.)
   a. $5 + 2^3 \times 3 - 6$
   b. $\frac{3^2 - 1}{2 + 3(2)}$

2. Place parentheses to make the statement true:
   $$4 + 3 + 6 + 4 - 1 = 25$$

3. Given 4 even numbers of consecutive integers, write an expression to find their sum.

4. Are all rational numbers integers? Are all integers rational numbers? Substantiate your responses.

5. You have been given a strip of paper that has been folded in half ten times. Theoretically, how many creases would be in that strip of paper?

6. Suppose you are teaching sixth graders and they are having trouble aligning decimal points. Develop one or two question strings for addition and subtraction of decimals.

7. Two competing store chains, BVS and Cooks, are offering the same product. Which deal is the better buy? Be certain to explain your thinking:

   BVS
   25% off on merchandise priced at $240

   Cooks
   40% off merchandise priced at $300

8. Shahid had 32 baseball cards: 25% of these cards were Chicago Cubs and 50% of the cards were players who had been playing in the big league for more than seven years. What percent of Shahid's cards were both Cubs and players in the league for more than seven years if 12 cards do not belong to either category?
   a. After solving this problem, reflect back on your process. Did you work with percents or did you use another representation of rational numbers?
   b. What problem-solving strategy did you use? Compare your strategy with classmates.

9. Given $\frac{3 + 4(3)}{3}$, a student responded that the "3s cancel so the answer is 4." How would you respond to this student?

On Your Own

1. Observe a mathematics class. Keep a chart noting the type of questions asked by the teacher. Categories might include questions that require factual knowledge, those that require rote learning, questions that ask for conclusions, and those that ask for analysis. A tape recorder might be helpful if available and if the teacher agrees to be recorded.

2. Here is a rather unique method for multiplication, commonly referred to as the Russian Peasant Method:

   Example: 18×52

   $$
   \begin{array}{rr}
   \cancel{18} & \cancel{52} \\
   9 & 104 \\
   \cancel{4} & \cancel{208} \\
   \cancel{2} & \cancel{416} \\
   1 & 832 \\
   \hline
    & 936
   \end{array}
   $$

   The numbers in the left column are found by dividing the factor above by 2 and ignoring any remainders. Then the second factor is doubled in the second column. Cross out any factors in the left column that are even. Add the right-hand column of the remaining factors.

   Try a few other problems: 33×41
   82×36

   What patterns do you notice? Why does this method work?

3. Create a game for students emphasizing estimation skills. Write out the rules for your game along with a clear definition of the "winner." Be certain to play your game to ensure that your directions are clear and your objectives are met.

4. If one finds the ratio of consecutive Fibonacci numbers (1, 1, 2, 3, 5, 8, 13 . . . see Chapter 3 for reference), the ratio approaches 1.618 as the values progress in the series. Create your own series of numbers using the guidelines of the Fibonacci series. Pick any two numbers. Add these together to form the third number in the series. Add the third and second number to form the fourth. Create ten terms in the series. Now find the ratio of the tenth term to the ninth term. Surprise!

5. Use an Internet search engine to find mathematical dictionaries. Find several different ways that rational numbers are explained. Quote the reference and then offer a critique in terms of your understanding of the definition.

 Portfolio Question

Research has demonstrated that many students do not equate success with effort. Many students think that success is linked with luck, ability, or other people (Marzano, Pickering, Pollock, 2001, p. 50). Write about a time during which you worked hard to achieve. Be as specific as possible. This might be a story for you to share with your students to help them realize the vital importance of effort.

Scenes from a Classroom

Ms. Siegal enjoys her seventh-grade class. They are currently working on all operations with fractions, and as we look in on her classroom, the students are sharing what they understood from the unit thus far. Ms. Siegal tries to ensure that she calls on everyone in the class, but she also knows that she has some very aggressive students who do a lot of speaking in these discussions.

Ms. Siegal has just called on Sergio. "I don't know," Sergio replied. Ms. Siegal asked if he would like more time to think about it. "I guess so" was the response, but he also mumbled something else under his breath that Ms. Siegal decided to ignore. After a few more discussion points were addressed, Ms. Siegal returned her attention to Sergio. "Do you have anything to add now, Sergio?" "No. Why do you keep calling on me? I didn't raise my hand." How would you respond to Sergio?

By remembering to check back in with Sergio, Ms. Siegal sends him a clear message that she would like him to participate. This scene does not give us any information about Sergio as a student. He may be someone who participates regularly when he is confident of the answer, or he may be the type of student who prefers to sit back and let others participate. Ms. Siegal values participation; she may not always call on every student in her class. Perhaps Sergio has avoided participating in the past. One way that Ms. Siegal can ensure that she calls on everyone is to use a system. Many teachers place popsicle sticks with each student's name on one stick in a jar. As she looks for someone to respond, she draws a stick out and calls on that student. Students quickly catch on to the fact that once their stick has been drawn, they do not have to focus for the remainder of the class. To avoid this situation, we suggest that teachers section the container in quarters. The unused sticks go in two of the sections and those that have been selected go into the other half. Students who are at their desks will not distinguish between the sections, and they will think that their stick has been replaced. Teachers can also require students to confirm their answer with a partner before offering a solution. By verifying the answer, two students have participated and the student who volunteers does not become as embarrassed if the solution is not correct. The importance of participating in the discussions cannot be overemphasized. One of the advantages of cooperative group work is that more students can participate orally for longer periods of time.

Preparing for Praxis

The average number of passengers who use a certain airport each year is 350 thousand. A newspaper reported the number as 350 million. The number reported in the newspaper was how many times the actual number?

A. 10
B. 100
C. 1,000
D. 10,000

RESOURCES

Math–Literature Connections

Enzensberger, H. (1997). *The number devil—A mathematical adventure.* New York: Henry Holt and Company.

Juster, N. (1961). *The phantom tollbooth.* New York: Random House.

LoPresti, A. (2003). *A place for zero (a math adventure).* Watertown, MA: Charlesbridge Publishing.

Nolting, A. C. (2003). *Pythagoras eagle and the music of spheres.* Mahomet, IL: Mayhaven Publishing.

Swartz, D. (1999). *If you hopped like a frog.* New York: Scholastic Press.

Tahan, M. (1993). *The man who counted: A collection of mathematical adventures.* Translated by L. Clark & A. Reid. New York: Norton.

Teacher's Bookcase

Enzensberger, H. M. (1997). *The number devil—A mathematical adventure.* New York: Henry Holt and Company.

In his dreams a boy encounters a devil who reveals the magic and wonder of numbers. This book can be used as a "read-aloud" as the chapters are short and discuss one concept at a time.

Humez, A., Humez, N., & Maguire, J. (1993). *Zero to lazy eight—The romance of numbers.* New York: Simon and Schuster.

The authors examine number words, their origins and their impact on our lives today. Delightful, entertaining, and fun resource linking numbers in a variety of unexpected ways!

Livio, M. (2002). *The golden ratio—The story of phi, the world's most astonishing number.* New York: Broadway Books.

An intriguing history of the golden ratio revealing not only its applications to nature but also its connections to the great pyramids, masterpieces such as Leonardo Da Vinci's Mona Lisa *and the stock market!*

Nahin, P. J. (1998). *An imaginary tale—The story of $\sqrt{-1}$.* **Princeton, NJ: Princeton University Press.**

The author explores the derivation of i. *An engaging history of the battles pursued by mathematicians arguing whether or not complex numbers even existed as well as discussion of the practical implications of such numbers today. Readers will find this informative and engaging.*

For Further Reading

Barnett, C., Goldstein, D., & Jackson, B. (Eds.). (1994). *Fractions, decimals, ratios, and percents: Hard to teach and hard to learn?* Portsmouth, NH: Heinemann Press.

The authors offer practical suggestions to help students develop conceptual understandings of rational numbers.

Links

This site reviews, practices, and offers explanations of topics.
www.math.com

This site offers instruction, practice, and answers to specific questions.
www.webmath.com

Students can ask Dr. Math questions.
www.mathforum.org/students

These websites offer practice on the basic facts.
www.aplusmath.com/Flashcards
www.edu4kids.com/math

This site places all of the multiplication facts in the context of exploring space.
www.gdbdp.com/multiflyer

This site offers Black Line Masters for a wide variety of topics including number facts and manipulatives such as fraction strips, pattern blocks, geoboards, and attribute blocks.
www.aldershot.ednet.ns.ca/BLM

REFERENCES

Beaton, A., Mills, I., Gonzalez, D., Kelly, D., & Smith, T. (1996). Mathematics achievement in the middle school: IEA's third international mathematics and science study. Boston: Center for the Study of Testing, Evaluation, and Educational Policy.

Bransford, J. D., Brown, A. L., & Cocking, R. R. (eds.). (1999). *How People learn: Brain, mind, experience and school.* Washington, DC: National Academy Press.

Cramer, K., Bezuk, N., & Behr, M. (1989). Proportional relationships and unit rates. *The Mathematics Teacher, 537–544.*

Curcio, F., & Bezuk, N. (1994). *Curriculum and evaluation standards for school mathematics addenda series, grades 5–8: Understanding rational numbers and proportions.* Reston, VA: NCTM.

Dahaene, S. (1997). *The number sense—How the mind creates mathematics.* New York: Oxford University Press.

Fendel, D., & Resek, D. (1997). *Interactive mathematics program, year 1.* Emeryville, CA: Key Curriculum Press.

Fosnot, C., & Dolk, M. (2002). *Young mathematicians at work—Constructing fractions, decimals and percents.* Portsmouth, NH: Heinemann.

Kilpatrick, J., Martin, W., & Schifter, D. (2003). *A research companion to principles and standards for school mathematics.* Reston, VA: National Council of Teachers of Mathematics.

Kilpatrick, J., Swafford, J., & Findell, B. (2001). *Adding it up—Helping children learn mathematics.* Washington, DC: National Academy Press,

Lamon, S. (2002). Part-whole comparisons with unitizing. In B. Litwillwer & B. Bright (Eds.), *Making sense of fractions, ratios, and proportions: 2002 yearbook.* Reston, VA: NCTM.

Lamon, S. (1994). Ratio and proportion. In G. Harel & J. Confrey (Eds.), *The development of multiplicative reasoning in the learning of mathematics.* Albany: State University of New York Press.

Lee, R. (2003, September). The triangle technique for solving direct variation problems. *Mathematics Teacher, 96,* 450–451.

Marzano, R., Pickering, D., Pollock, J. (2001). *Classroom instruction that works.* Alexandria, VA: Association for Supervision and Curriculum Development.

McClain, K., Cobb, P., & Bowers, J. (1998) A contextual investigation of three-digit addition and subtraction. In L. J. Morrow and M. J. Kenney (Eds.), *The teaching and learning of algorithms in school mathematics.* Reston, VA: NCTM.

Morrow, L., & Kenney, M. (1998). *The teaching and learning of algorithms in school mathematics.* Reston, VA: NCTM.

Moss, Joan. (2003, February). Introducing percents in linear measurement to foster an understanding of rational-number operatons. *Teaching Children Mathematics, 9,* 355–340.

National Council of Teachers of Mathematics. (1989). *Curriculum and evaluation standards for school mathematics.* Reston, VA: NCTM.

National Council of Teachers of Mathematics. (1998). *The teaching and learning of algorithms in school mathematics.* Reston, VA: NCTM.

National Council of Teachers of Mathematics. (2000). *Principles and standards for school mathematics.* Reston, VA: NCTM.

National Council of Teachers of Mathematics. (2002). *Making sense of fractions, ratios and proportions.* Reston, VA: NCTM.

Owens, D. (Ed.). (1993). *Research ideas for the classroom—Middle school mathematics. National Council of Teachers of Mathematics Research Interpretation Project.* New York: Macmillan.

Sheffield, L., & Cruikshank, D. (2000). *Teaching and learning elementary and middle school mathematics.* New York: John Wiley and Sons.

Sowder, J. T. & Wheeler, M. M. (1989). The development of concepts and procedures used in computational estimation. *Journal for Research in Mathematics Education, 20,* 130–146.

Tucker, B., Singleton, A. & Weaver. T. (2002). *Teaching mathematics to children: Designing and adapting instruction to meet the needs of diverse learners.* Upper Saddle River, NJ: Merrill Prentice Hall.

Van Dooren, W. et al. (2003, December). Improper applications of proportional reasoning. *Mathematics Teaching in the Middle School,* 208.

Vernaud, G. (1983). Multiplicative structures. In R. Lesh & M. Landau (Eds.), *Acquisition of mathematics concepts and processes.* New York: Academic Press.

Weinstein, E. (2005, February 26). 42nd Mersenne prime found. *MathWorld Headline News.* http://mathworld.wolfram.com/news/2005-02-26/mersenne

Number Line Equivalences

Fraction

Decimal

Percent

From Johnson & Norris, Teaching Today's Mathematics in the Middle Grades. Copyright © 2006 Allyn and Bacon, Pearson Education, Inc.

Operational Relationships

SET A	**SET B**
$\frac{1}{2}$ of 14 = _____	14 ÷ 2 = _____
$\frac{1}{2}$ of 12 = _____	12 ÷ 2 = _____
$\frac{1}{2}$ of 10 = _____	10 ÷ 2 = _____

What do you notice about Set A and Set B?

What conclusions can you make as a result?

Test your conclusions by making problem sets similar to Set A and Set B.

Explain why your conclusions are true.

 From Johnson & Norris, Teaching Today's Mathematics in the Middle Grades. Copyright © 2006 Allyn and Bacon, Pearson Education, Inc.

Making One!

Use the fraction strips seen in Figure 6.12. Record what you get on EACH roll. When you have covered up the red strip, write down all of the values and show that those fractions equal 1. You may not have to use all of the rolls.

ROUND 1

Turn

1 _____

2 _____

3 _____

4 _____

5 _____

6 _____

7 _____

8 _____

9 _____

10 _____

Write down the fractions you rolled to make 1.

ROUND 2

Turn

1 _____

2 _____

3 _____

4 _____

5 _____

6 _____

7 _____

8 _____

9 _____

10 _____

Write down the fractions you rolled to make 1.

Fraction Strips at Work!

Answer each of the following questions using your fraction strips. Be prepared to defend your answer.

SET A

1. What size piece do you get if you take $\frac{1}{2}$ of $\frac{1}{4}$?

2. What size piece do you get if you take $\frac{1}{4}$ of $\frac{1}{4}$?

3. What size piece do you get if you take $\frac{1}{2}$ of $\frac{1}{2}$?

4. What size piece do you get if you take $\frac{1}{2}$ of $\frac{1}{8}$?

5. What size piece do you get if you take $\frac{1}{8}$ of $\frac{1}{2}$?

6. Write down any patterns that you notice in the preceding problems.

SET B   Remember to use your fraction strips!

7. How many $\frac{1}{2}$-size strips are in 1 whole?

8. How many $\frac{1}{4}$-size strips are in 1 whole?

9. How many $\frac{1}{16}$-size strips are in $\frac{1}{4}$?

10. How many $\frac{1}{8}$-size strips are in $\frac{1}{2}$?

11. What do you notice about the problems in Set B?

12. Create one more problem like those in Set A.

13. Create one more problem like those in Set B.

14. What operation is at work in Set A? Is the same operation working in Set B? Explain your answer.

From Johnson & Norris, Teaching Today's Mathematics in the Middle Grades. Copyright © 2006 Allyn and Bacon, Pearson Education, Inc.

Can You See It?

In each problem series, solve the problems and then answer the questions.

SET A

$4 \times 8 =$ _____

$2 \times 16 =$ _____

$1 \times 32 =$ _____

$\frac{1}{2} \times 64 =$ _____

$\frac{1}{2} \times 128 =$ _____

SET B

$4 \times 6 =$ _____

$8 \times 3 =$ _____

$16 \times 1\frac{1}{2} =$ _____

$32 \times \frac{3}{4} =$ _____

$64 \times \frac{3}{8} =$ _____

QUESTIONS FOR SET A AND SET B:

1. What did you notice about the answers to Set A?

2. What caused this to happen?

3. Did this same pattern occur in Set B? Give reasons for your answer.

SET C

$4 \div 2 =$ _____

$8 \div 4 =$ _____

$16 \div 8 =$ _____

$32 \div 16 =$ _____

SET D

$8 \div \frac{1}{2} =$ _____

$4 \div \frac{1}{4} =$ _____

$2 \div \frac{1}{8} =$ _____

$1 \div \frac{1}{16} =$ _____

SET E

$4 \div \frac{1}{4} =$ _____

$8 \div \frac{1}{2} =$ _____

$16 \div 1 =$ _____

$32 \div 2 =$ _____

continued

From Johnson & Norris, Teaching Today's Mathematics in the Middle Grades. Copyright © 2006 Allyn and Bacon, Pearson Education, Inc.

Can You See It? (continued)

QUESTIONS FOR SET C AND SET D:

1. What operation occurred in Set C and Set D?

2. In Set C, what is the pattern that you see in terms of the numbers in each problem as you move from one problem to the next?

3. In Set D, is that same pattern continuing? Justify your answer.

QUESTIONS FOR SET E:

1. What is the pattern in Set E?

2. What is happening to cause the pattern to occur?

SUMMARY:

The answers to the problems within each set are the same.

1. For problems involving multiplication, what must happen to each factor to ensure the resulting answer will be the same?

2. Demonstrate this pattern by creating two problems.

3. Explain why this pattern works for multiplication.

4. For the problems involving division, what occurs to the divisor and dividend to ensure that the answer remains the same?

5. Demonstrate this pattern with division by creating two problems.

6. Explain why this pattern works for division.

 From Johnson & Norris, *Teaching Today's Mathematics in the Middle Grades.* Copyright © 2006 Allyn and Bacon, Pearson Education, Inc.

chapter seven

Algebra: The Gateway

Algebra. Some adults refer to this subject with pride. Others state that they just "didn't get it." Those in the latter category may have found ways to avoid mathematics as soon as possible in their educational careers. People who found algebra easily accessible might have also been told that they had the "mathematical genes" necessary for success. Fundamentally, algebra gained the reputation for being the gatekeeper for future success in the field. Those who found algebra easy were encouraged to pursue mathematics; those who struggled to master algebra were guided toward other disciplines. On the one hand, algebra was the gateway to higher mathematics; on the other, algebra served as the gatekeeper denying access to other branches of mathematics.

NCTM's *Principles and Standards for School Mathematics* addresses the concern of algebra as a gatekeeper by featuring algebra as a major standard in grades pre-K–12. Students now experience algebraic thinking early in their school experience. Young children look for patterns and for rules that govern those patterns. They balance scales and trade objects using proportional reasoning. They explore relationships through a variety of representations. Students begin to describe relationships and events mathematically. By explicitly highlighting their algebraic thinking, students gain experience and confidence in this mode of thought before ever reaching a formal Algebra 1 course.

In the middle school curriculum, students work with events and situations and describe them using a variety of representations. Students explore how one variable causes a change in a second variable. Students look for patterns and learn to express relationships symbolically. Students learn to identify functions as linear and nonlinear and explore their properties in tables, graphs, and equations. Building on experiences from elementary school, middle school students continue to develop and enrich their algebraic thinking.

What Is Algebra?

Some refer to algebra as generalized arithmetic. That is certainly a role that algebra performs. Both arithmetic and algebra provide ways to describe relationships. However, "although arithmetic is effective in describing static pictures of the world, algebra is dynamic and a necessary vehicle for describing a changing world" (Friel, Rachlin, & Doyle, 2001, p. 1). This descriptive and predictive nature of algebra provides students with a powerful tool to explore changing relationships, to use models to represent quantitative relationships, and to understand patterns, relations, and functions. Essentially, there are three types of algebraic activities to be included in school mathematics: representational activities, transformational activities, and generalizing and justifying activities (Kilpatrick, 2001). These activities are being incorporated into current middle school curricula and are providing meaningful foundations that enhance students' problem-solving skills. Incorporating the three types of algebraic activities in middle grades mathematics helps students

Did You **Know**?

The term *algebra* first appeared in the title of a book written in 825 by Persian mathematician al-Khwarizmi. The full title of the book was Hisab **al-jabr** w'al-muqabalah.

AUTHOR'S **Recall**

I recently asked several friends what they remember about their algebra course. Many responded by referring to those word problems that they were required to solve. "I remember trains heading toward each other at different rates and canoes being paddled up and down streams. Frankly, I simply did not care what time those trains met or how fast the current in the stream was moving."

access the important ideas. As stated in the National Council of Teachers of Mathematics Algebra Standard, instructional programs from prekindergarten through grade 12 should enable all students to

- Understand patterns, relations, and functions
- Represent and analyze mathematical situations and structures using algebraic symbols
- Use mathematical models to represent and understand quantitative relationships
- Analyze change in various contexts

These statements frame the standard. At each grade level grouping, the standard is further defined. For middle school students, the Algebra Standard states that all students should

- Understand patterns, relations, and functions
- Represent, analyze, and generalize a variety of patterns with tables, graphs, words and, when possible, symbolic rules
- Relate and compare different forms of representation for a relationship
- Identify functions as linear or nonlinear and contrast their properties from tables, graphs, or equations
- Represent and analyze mathematical situations and structures using algebraic symbols
- Develop an initial conceptual understanding of different uses of variables
- Explore relationships between symbolic expressions and graphs of lines, paying particular attention to the meaning of intercept and slope
- Use symbolic algebra to represent situations and to solve problems, especially those that involve linear relationships
- Recognize and generate equivalent forms for simple algebraic expressions and solve linear equations
- Use mathematical models to represent and understand quantitative relationships
- Model and solve contextualized problems using various representations, such as graphs, tables, and equations
- Analyze change in various contexts
- Use graphs to analyze the nature of changes in quantities in linear relationships (NCTM, 2000, p. 222)

Currently, there is a national discussion focusing on algebra. Some educators advocate that all eighth graders take a formal Algebra 1 course. The proponents of this view frequently site international testing, TIMSS, that showed the eighth-grade students in the United States scoring far below students from other countries. Opponents of an eighth-grade algebra course state that not all eighth graders are ready for the abstract thinking it requires. As this book is going to press, it is not clear how this debate will end. However, it is critically important that algebra as a strand maintain a prominent presence in the middle school curriculum.

TRY THIS

On page 30 in *Principles and Standards for School Mathematics*, NCTM shows a graph depicting the varying emphases that each standard ought to receive in each grade band. Describe what the graph indicates about the algebra standard.

In this chapter, we focus on algebra as a strand and we offer teachers specific problems to use with students. These problems illustrate the type of meaningful experiences appropriate for middle school students. We encourage readers to keep in mind the importance of students solving problems. Providing students with the opportunity to grapple with a task and see where their strategies lead them is a critical part of the learning process. As suggested in Chapter 3, The Practice of Effective Instruction, there are many options in terms of class structure; engaging middle school students in meaningful mathematics is the key!

Foundational Concepts

Before working with the three types of algebraic activities, there are several critically important foundational concepts. The meaning of the equal sign, the definition and role of a variable, and the creation of coordinate graphs are pivotal concepts that can be confusing to students.

Understanding the Equal Sign

In elementary classrooms, children see number sentences such as $3 + 5 = \square$. Many children interpret these sentences differently than we might anticipate. In *Children's Arithmetic*, Herbert Ginsburg offers the following children's interpretations:

> Kenneth interpreted + and = in terms of actions to be performed. So do other children. Presented with the same problem, Evelyn, also a first grader, maintained that $2 + 4 = \square$ means to "put number 6 in the box." She said that 2 and 4 are numbers, but $2 + 4$ is not a number. A second grader, Donna, referring to $3 + 4 = \square$, said that 'the equals sign means what it adds up to.' Another first grader, Tammy, said that the = sign means that "you're coming to the end" (Ginsburg, 1989 p. 112).

Students view such problems as actions. That interpretation may be appropriate for small numbers but it also needs to be extended to include the concept of balance: $2 + 4 = \square$ is another name for 6. We can also say that $2 + 4 + 1 = \square + 1$. Students also need to see the number sentence written this way: $\square = 2 + 4$. In this case, the "do something" or "the end is coming" interpretations do not fit the number sentence with the unknown quantity being stated first. Stressing the idea that there are many ways to express quantities in the early grades helps prepare students for future work with equations.

Varying Roles of Variables

A second critical concept involves variables and their different roles. Younger students work with the boxes as in the preceding number sentences. The boxes function as a placeholder for a value to be determined. Middle school students tend to think about one of the following strategies as they find what value goes in the box:

Consider $2 \square + 3 = 15$ or $2x + 3 = 15$. A student might read the line from left to right asking the question, "what times 2 when added with 3 equals 15?" Students guess a value and then check by substituting the value in the equation. Some educators refer to this as a guess and check approach. The second method, commonly referred to as "undoing," reverses the order of operations. Students subtract 3 and then divide by 2 to arrive at the answer of 6. A similar strategy involves covering up different components of the equation. In the preceding example, a student covers up the 2 and considers $\square + 3 = 15$. This leads to the result of 12 and then the student works with $2 \square = 12$ to reach the solution. These intuitive strategies for solving equations play an important role as children develop their ability to reason more abstractly. Students need many experiences working intuitively with such problems to facilitate the transition between arithmetic and algebra.

Two activities, Magic Tricks, Blackline Master 7.1, and Calendar Connection, demonstrate the power of variables and place variables into a useful context.

Did You **Know**?

The first mathematician to use alphabet letters for variables was French mathematician Francois Viete (1540–1603). He used vowels for unknown quantities and consonants for known values.

REACT | **REFLECT**

What does this cartoon suggest about this student's understanding of a variable?

"Just a darn minute — yesterday you said that X equals **two**!"

There's a reason they're called *variables*.

Used by permission of Rex F. May.

By working with Magic Tricks, students solve the first series of statements by selecting a value and proceeding through the steps. Students are genuinely surprised when they realize that everyone who calculated correctly arrives at the same result. Students may have tried integers, fractions, or decimals, all yielding the result of 4. As their curiosity rises, students begin to determine why the result is constant in spite of the fact that they chose different values to begin the series of steps. Some students perceive that each operation in the series of steps is later reversed by the opposite operation.

As students work to offer a proof that the trick will work using any value, they simply tend to substitute more values. These efforts do not *prove* that the trick will *always* work for any number. Teachers can encourage students to use a variable to represent any number. Because a variable represents the general case or any number, a variable can be used to prove that the series of steps will always yield 4.

Select any number:	x
Add 3:	$x + 3$
Multiply by 3:	$3(x + 3)$ or $3x + 9$
Add 3:	$3x + 12$
Divide by 3:	$x + 4$
Subtract original number:	4

After completing the second exercise, students write an explanation for both tricks. They can also make up their own Magic Tricks.

TRY THIS

Create your own Magic Trick. As you work, take note of your own strategies. How did you approach the task?

The role of a proof can be extended for more advanced middle school students. In Chapter 6, Making Sense of Number and Operations, we presented finger multiplication. Teachers can demonstrate the following proof of why finger multiplication works for those factors between 5 and 10 inclusively. Students need to understand the distributive property and multiplication of two binomials to appreciate this proof.

Let $a =$ the number of fingers raised on the left hand, and let $b =$ the fingers on the right hand. We are looking for the product of the numbers represented on the two hands: $(5 + a)(5 + b)$.

According to the finger multiplication process, the product of the two numbers is found by

1. Finding the sum of the raised fingers and then multiplying by 10 to obtain the tens digit $10(a + b)$
2. Finding the product of the remaining fingers (folded down) $(5 - a)(5 - b)$

Thus, the expression that describes the entire process is $10(a + b) + (5 - a)(5 - b)$. By simplifying the expression, we get the statement for the product, $(5 + a)(5 + b)$, which matches the original expression. Thus, the procedure will result in the correct numerical value (Tanton, 2004, p. 1).

A similar activity to Magic Tricks, Calendar Connection, allows the knowledgeable student to guess another's starting numbers without a lot of information. This activity uses variables and linear equations.

Many patterns can be seen in a monthly calendar. (See Figure 7.1.) Calendar Connection uses the relationship between dates that form a square on the calendar.

Students select dates that form a square such as 8, 9, 15, and 16. When performing the trick, one student tells another to pick a square and tell her the sum of the numbers forming the square. Knowing the sum and a little algebra, the student can "predict" the values that the second student selected. The values forming the square can be represented by $x, x + 1, x + 7,$ and $x + 8$ or $4x + 16$; $4x + 16$ equals the total sum of the numbers in the

figure **7.1**

Patterns in Monthly Calendars

June 2006

Sunday	Monday	Tuesday	Wednesday	Thursday	Friday	Saturday
				1	2	3
4	5	6	7	8	9	10
11	12	13	14	15	16	17
18	19	20	21	22	23	24
25	26	27	28	29	30	

square selected by the student. To predict which square was selected, the first student subtracts 16 from the total and divides by 4. Magic Tricks and Calendar Connection help students see the usefulness of variables. When presented with the more formal approach to solving linear equations, students are more likely to understand the rationale for the steps if they have had these experiences.

Another critical role of variables includes representing a range of values (Owens, 1993, p. 180). Rather than holding a place for one value, variables seen in this context represent many values. Given an expression, such as $2x + 3$, students determine the outcome based on several numerical values of x. Students can create a table of values as well as plot points on a coordinate graph. Given a completed table, students can also determine the rule or function.

As presented in NCTM's *Principles and Standards in School Mathematics*, variables extend beyond the placeholder function (NCTM, 2000, p. 225). Consider $x + y = y + x$. These variables represent a generalized statement illustrating the commutative property. Variables also take on the role of expressing formulas such as in "rate times time equals distance" or $R \times T = D$. Variables also express their relationship in terms of one another. Students can work with variables in different contexts and explore how one variable can cause a change in another. For example, consider the following: there are twice as many girls in the class as boys. Students can create a chart. If there are eight boys, students can determine the number of girls. They can also find the number of boys given the number of girls. Working in a variety of contexts, students begin to generalize that a change in one variable affects the values in a second variable. Students need a wide range of experiences to fully understand and appreciate the different roles of variables.

Creating generalized statements frequently challenges students.

TRY THIS

There are 16 students for every teacher in Small Town High School. Write an equation representing the relationship between the number of students and the number of teachers.

Did You **Know**?

We use x for an unknown because a printer ran out of letters. When French mathematician René Descartes sent his masterwork, *La Geometrie*, to Dutch printer Jan Maire, Maire found that he was running short of some of the letters. He asked Descartes if the choice of letters really mattered. Descartes replied that the letter choice was not critical, but he wanted unknowns represented by letters at the end of the alphabet. Consequently, Maire used x for all unknown values in the text. We have solved for x ever since.

Point Well Taken

"Logo, a programming language developed to help young students explore mathematical concepts, promotes many opportunities for algebraic thinking including the use of variables."
—Sarama, 1998

Many students respond by stating that $16s = 1t$, where s represents the number of students and t represents the number of teachers. In effect, such students have translated the statement from left to right. Such literal translations do not consider the meaning and context of the situation. By substituting values into the equation, students can realize their error. If we replace s with 10, and then solve the equation, we find that we have 160 teachers! Giving students such experiences as deriving the generalized statement from concrete representations, numeric charts, and graphs helps them establish a foundation on which they can build their abstract reasoning.

Graphing

Did You **Know**?

The term *graph* was coined by British mathematician James Joseph Sylvester in 1877.

Graphing represents the third foundational concept. Children work with many types of graphs early on in their schooling. Bar graphs and pictographs allow students to analyze the data to draw conclusions and see connections between the raw data and their graphical representation. Kindergarteners and first graders use tallies to gather data, display the results in a graphical representation, and then draw conclusions based on the information.

In elementary school, students investigate the various characteristics of the data such as the mean, median, mode, and range. In middle school, students use these measures of central tendency to help analyze situations and work to include the interpretation of events over time. For example, Figure 7.2 shows the graph of the number of people waiting outside a theater on opening night. Students can be asked to explain the graph in terms of the number of people as a function of time. What time do the doors open? What does the little bump between 8:00 and 8:10 indicate? Students should also be asked to create a graph based on a particular event.

1. *Encourage students to move beyond the bar graph.* Middle school students tend to focus on bar graphs. They have worked with them throughout their schooling, and they use this representation repeatedly. They use them even when they are working with two-variable data and they are investigating a possible relationship. Making students more receptive to using other graphs such as stem-and-leaf graphs, box plots, or scatterplots remains challenging for teachers. Each of these graphical representations provides varying pictures and insights. (See Chapter 10, Data Analysis: The Process.)

2. *Analyze where to place the variables on the coordinate graph.* Students often need assistance determining the independent and dependent variables. Some do not see that it can make a difference where the variables are placed. The variable that determines the value

figure **7.2**

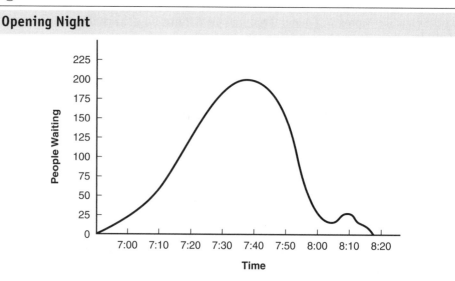

Opening Night

of the other is called the independent variable. For example, in Figure 7.2, the number of people is the dependent variable. The number of people entering the theater depends on the time, and therefore, time represents the independent variable. The independent variable is placed on the *x*-axis while the dependent variable goes on the *y*-axis. Students may also have trouble actually locating coordinate points. Some place the point in the middle of the square formed by the graph paper lines rather than placing the point at the intersection of the grid lines. Teachers can emphasize the purpose of the gridlines as tools to locate the point on the paper to help students move beyond shading in the square.

3. *Look at the type of data to determine if points on the graph should be connected.* Students see coordinate points forming a line and they automatically want to connect them. In many cases, the points function as solitary units, often referred to as discrete. The line should only be drawn if, within the context of the problem, the points represent a continuous relationship. In the upcoming discussion involving an activity entitled Messy Math, we offer an example and rationale for keeping the coordinate points as separate entities.

PROCESS STANDARDS

Representation and Connection

The process standards are rarely seen in isolation because they are continually intertwined.

> Most students will need extensive experience in interpreting relationships among quantities in a variety of problem contexts before they can work meaningfully with variables and symbolic expressions. An understanding of the meanings and uses of variables develops gradually as students create and use symbolic expressions and relate them to verbal, tabular, and graphical representations. (NCTM, 2000, p. 225)

Making the connection with verbal, tabular, and graphical representations helps students understand the various uses and meanings of variables.

MATH IN THE MEDIA

Recently, news reports have contained information about the connection between obesity and health risks. A formula has been created to determine the ratio between height and weight. This ratio, referred to as the Body Mass Index or BMI, can be calculated according to the following steps. Calculate your BMI.

1. Your weight in pounds   _____
2. Your height in inches   _____
3. Square your height   _____
4. Divide the result of step 1 by the result in step 3   _____
5. Multiply the result in step 4 by 703   _____ (BMI)

If the index is below 18.5, an individual is considered underweight; 18.5–24.9 is considered normal; 25.0–29.9 is overweight and any index above 30.0 may be cause for concern.

Take a moment to rewrite those steps into an algebraic equation to calculate the Body Mass Index. Do you prefer to see the steps or the algebraic equation in order to understand the connection between height and weight in terms of this index? Explain your reasoning.

Three Types of Algebraic Activities

As we mentioned earlier, there are fundamentally three types of algebraic activities: transformational, representational, and generalizing activities (Kilpatrick, 2001, p. 256).

Transformational activities or rule-based tasks involve simplifying expressions, solving equations, and basically following the rules to manipulate abstract symbols. Representational activities require students to use multiple representations of a given event. Making connections between the actual event and the multiple representations of the event helps students realize the power of algebra as a tool.

Representational and Generalizing Activities—The Rule of 5 at Work

The Rule of 5 provides a framework for students' thinking. As students approach many open-ended problems, they can rely on the Rule of 5 to guide their work. The five representations are as follows:

1. Concrete representation (use of manipulatives or pictures)
2. Numeric representation (chart or diagram)
3. Graphic representation
4. Symbolic representation
5. Verbal representation

The rule follows what many researchers, educational theorists, and teachers have known to be true—students need to begin with concrete experiences. By building, constructing, drawing, and representing the situation in concrete terms, students tap into several forms of their intelligences. As stated in Howard Gardner's theory of Multiple Intelligences, children access their kinesthetic, visual, and spatial intelligences as they use concrete manipulatives. (See Chapter 2, The Challenge of Middle School Learners, for more on learning styles.) As they work, students record their findings in a chart. This numeric expression provides an opportunity to evaluate patterns and changes. One of the habits of mind that teachers can encourage is getting students to determine from the chart what is changing and what is remaining the same. The corresponding graph is the third representation in the Rule of 5 and the graph offers opportunities to extend the pattern and relationship beyond the concrete models. By evaluating change as seen in both the numeric and graphical representations, students can begin to approach the generalized statement or symbolic representation, the fourth element in the Rule of 5, and an example of an algebraic generalizing activity. The last stage in the Rule of 5, verbal representation, provides opportunities for students to reflect back on the process and make connections with the previous representations. Students formalize and clarify their thinking as they present the solution orally or in writing.

PROCESS STANDARDS

Reasoning and Proof

Verbal representation, the final stage of the Rule of 5, emphasizes this process standard. As students provide explanations for their thinking, they are solidifying their understanding of the concept. Having opportunities to reflect and extend their thinking and then having to justify their thinking increases the likelihood that the students will retain and be able to use the knowledge acquired.

TRY THIS

With this overview of the Rule of 5, take a moment to complete the Black Line Master 7.2 entitled Messy Mathematics. Be certain to complete all five representations.

Seeing Change in Context

In Messy Mathematics, Blackline Master 7.2, students take a sheet of paper and rip that sheet into 5 pieces. They then take one of those pieces and rip it into 5 even smaller pieces. They are then asked to find the number of pieces after repeating the process 5 times, 10 times, *n* times.

As students begin the task of ripping the sheet of paper into 5 pieces, it is important that they see that stage 0 refers to the fact that they begin with one whole sheet of paper. The stage is referred to as 0 because they have not torn away any pieces. Students count the pieces of paper at each stage and record their results. As the paper pieces become smaller and smaller, students naturally turn to the chart to look for a pattern. The numeric representation is the second step in the Rule of 5. (See Table 7.1.)

As students look to describe what is happening in the chart, they see that as the stage number grows by 1, the total number of pieces increases by 4. Some students want to use 5 in the description because they created 5 pieces at each stage. Students realize that the actual change is 4 because one of the pieces used from the previous stage is ripped into 5 pieces. Students also graph these data as the next representation in the Rule of 5.

table **7.1**   Messy Mathematics

STAGE NUMBER	TOTAL NUMBER OF PIECES
0	1
1	5
2	9
3	13
4	17
5	21
6	25
7	29
8	33
9	37
10	41

MISCONCEPTION

As stated earlier, some students mistakenly think that placement of either variable on the axis does not matter. Students neglect to consider whether or not one variable governs another variable. For example, in Messy Mathematics, does the stage number determine the number of pieces or does the number of pieces determine the stage number? The independent and dependent variables in this case are clear. The number of pieces depends on the stage number and, therefore, number of pieces is the *dependent* variable. Teachers can help students establish the independent variable by asking them to define the word *independent* in their own words. Students can then interpret the meaning of an independent variable. Teachers can also ask students to create pairs of words. In each pair, the first word influences the second, age and height, for example. Students can then determine the independent variable and supply reasons for their choice. Justifying their responses with specific reasons helps clarify their thinking and enrich their understanding.

After the students have created the graph, they can describe what they notice about the graph. Responses should include that the points on the graph form a straight line. Students might also see the rate of change. As the *x*-value increases by 1, the *y*-value increases by 4. This can be seen on the calculator by creating a right angle between two points on the graph. (See Figure 7.3.)

As students come together to discuss their findings, they may consider whether or not the points should be connected. If they connect the points, they are indicating that the stages are not distinct. Consider, for example, a point between stage 2 and stage 3, say $2\frac{1}{2}$. How many pieces of paper would be created at stage $2\frac{1}{2}$? What would stage $2\frac{3}{4}$ look like in terms of pieces? None of these fractional stages are possible. As each stage requires the same number of pieces to be made, and each stage holds a finite number of pieces, there are no in-between steps such as stage $2\frac{1}{3}$. Each stage is a whole number. Consequently, the points on the graph are discrete and should not be connected.

figure **7.3**

Graph of Messy Mathematics

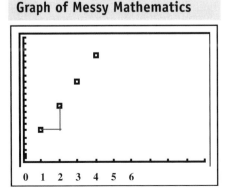

TRY THIS

Compare the graph of Opening Night in Figure 7.2 to the graph of the activity described in Messy Mathematics (p. 181). Explain why Opening Night's graph uses a line while the data points in Messy Mathematics are not connected.

Students might also see the connection between the point (0, 1), the y-intercept, and the original whole piece of paper at stage 0. Noting that the task began with the whole sheet of paper and making the connection to the y-intercept as the beginning of the graph helps students understand the y-intercept's role in this case. At this point, students should try to create the generalized statement to determine the number of pieces for any stage number. This is the next step in the Rule of 5, symbolic representation. Using the fact that the rate of change is 4, students might make several attempts at writing the equation until they conclude that $p = 4n + 1$, where $p =$ number of pieces and $n =$ the stage number. They should check to be certain that the coordinates of each point fit the equation. This trial-and-error process becomes easier with experience. Students may also develop another way of expressing the relationship between the stage number and the total number of pieces. A student might suggest that $p = 5n - (n - 1)$, for example. These varying and seemingly different equations provide the basis for a rich discussion.

It is important that students relate their equation back to the concrete event and explain the significance of their work. Using the equations stated previously, $p = 4n + 1$ or $p = 5n - (n - 1)$, encourage students to explore whether or not these two equations are equivalent. Students might also try substituting values for n and see if the same result occurs using both equations. Students also might graph the two equations on the calculator. If the equations are equivalent, one line will lie on top of the second. Students can also see the equivalence of these two equations by simplifying after distributing the negative sign to the values in parentheses. For example:

$$p = 5n - (n - 1)$$
$$p = 5n - n + 1$$

By then combining like terms, we get $p = 4n + 1$. Understanding the equivalence of the two equations is an example of a transformational activity, one of three types of algebraic activities mentioned in the beginning of this chapter. As an extension of this problem, students can explore the pattern if they rip the paper three times or if they tear the original paper into six pieces. Students may be able to predict the resulting pattern in each case.

TRY THIS

Use the Rule of 5 to work through the Building Blocks problem (Blackline Master 7.3). Compare the numeric, graphical, and symbolic representations.

Compare the multiple representations in this problem with those developed in the Messy Math problem. What do the numbers and variables represent in each context?

PROCESS STANDARDS

Communication

As the final step in the Rule of 5, students should write a statement summarizing the task and the process they used in arriving at the solution and provide an explanation for any conclusions that they make. Reflecting back on the experience helps students solidify their understanding and increases the likelihood of retention. Teachers should encourage students to go beyond simply telling the steps in the process of solution. Students should also explain why they took those steps. As they write, students often think of a connection that they had not previously understood. They may have understood an isolated component or a piece of information, but as they take time to analyze and synthesize what they saw and understood, they are more likely to construct their understanding in a manner that is useful to them. Highlighting these connections helps students' retention and furthers their understanding. Thus, students are more likely to extend and broaden their understanding. This writing component also raises questions for students that they may not have previously considered. Students can further their investigations and discussions based on their own questions.

Point Well Taken

"Each student should be expected not only to present and explain the strategy he or she used to solve the problem but also to analyze, compare, and contrast the meaningfulness, efficiency, and elegance of a variety of strategies. Explanations should include arguments and rationales, not just procedural descriptions and summaries."

—*NCTM, 2000, p. 268*

The Rule of 5 offers students an approach or guide as they are challenged by an open-ended task. By considering a concrete model, students become engaged with the problem. This seemingly simple act of involvement helps students get started on the path of a solution. All too often, teachers hear students state in frustration, "I can't do this." By using the concrete representation first, students have a starting point. The Rule of 5 supports students' thinking and helps them get started on what may appear to be a challenging task. Not all students will be able to generate the symbolic representation of each task, but the more opportunities they have to see what others have done, the more adept they become. The Rule of 5 places the emphasis on the solution process rather than highlighting the "right answer."

TRY THIS

NCTM pictorially displays the Rule of 5 using a pentagon in the *Navigations through Algebra* in grades 6–8. Make a sketch of a pentagon and draw in the diagonals. Label each vertex of the pentagon with one element of the Rule of 5. What conclusions can you make about the Rule of 5 based on this diagram?

The Rule of 5 is hierarchical yet interrelated. The rule is hierarchical in the sense that students approach a new task by first representing it in a concrete form using drawings, manipulatives, or in some cases, acting it out. The Rule of 5 is interrelated as each representation offers different information. Teachers can use the Rule of 5 to encourage students to make connections so that students think flexibly between these representations. As we have discussed in Chapter 5, Problem Solving: An Approach to Teaching and Learning Mathematics, the act of making connections deepens students' understanding and increases retention.

The Messy Mathematics problem provided an opportunity to explore a linear relationship. Students used the Rule of 5 to represent the relationship between stage numbers and the total number of pieces of paper. Students should make a connection between the rate of change as seen in the table and the graphical representation. In this case, students can relate the slope of the line that passes through the data points on the graph to the increase in the values in the table. As each stage increases by one, the total number of pieces of paper increases by four. Students again see the rate of change as it appears in the symbolic representation, $y = 4x + 1$. Students also connect the y-intercept with the table and the whole piece of paper. Both representational and generalizing activities are involved in Messy Mathematics. Specifically, Messy Mathematics provides middle school students with a concrete experience as an introduction to the more abstract equation, $y = mx + b$. Students need experiences with similar problems in order to solidify such important algebraic ideas as rate of change, or slope, and the use of multiple representations.

REACT | REFLECT

Look back on this chapter. What NCTM process standards have been addressed so far? Make a list and be ready to share your findings with your class or group.

TRY THIS

Take a moment to apply the Rule of 5 as you solve "Up and Down Staircases," Blackline Master 7.4.

Did You **Know**?

Raised numbers for exponents were first used by French mathematician René Descartes in 1637 in his book *La Geometrie*. Interestingly, Descartes still used *xx* for x^2 because it did not require a different typeset line.

Nonlinear Relationships

Up and Down Staircases, Blackline Master 7.4, presents a nonlinear relationship for students to explore. The number of blocks for each new staircase should be a familiar number to middle school students. Students should have had many experiences with perfect squares. Students have worked with perfect squares in number sequences, built patterns with blocks, and worked on square roots as an inverse operation: 1, 4, 9, 16, 25, 36, 49, 64, 81, 100, 121, and 144 are values that students should recognize as perfect squares. In Up and Down Staircases, perfect squares result with each new design.

As students recognize this pattern, they might predict what the graph will look like. The symbolic representation $b = s^2$ might be easily generated at this point. Students can determine which representation is easier to use in order to find the number of blocks in the hundredth staircase. Students should supply the reasons for their responses. Extending the graph may be the least preferred method as the graph curves, and using the chart might be tedious. Most students will recognize the ease of squaring 100 to find the total number of blocks. Students might inquire as to why the number of blocks in each staircase is a perfect square. Each side of the stairs can be rearranged to make a square and, therefore, a square number. (See Figure 7.4.)

Again, the final step in the Rule of 5 is the verbal statement. Students can provide the rationale for why the staircases result in perfect squares and how the graph of the relationship differs from the linear model as seen in Messy Mathematics.

One of the classic problems in middle school mathematics is the Handshake Problem. Students at a variety of ability levels can explore this problem. The problem can be presented to the same students in subsequent years as the mathematics that students apply to the problem can become increasingly sophisticated. The problem begins by posing the following question: If 10 people met for the first time and they greeted each other by shaking hands, how many handshakes would occur?

TRY THIS

Solve the Handshake Problem for 10, 20, 100, and *x* number of people. Take notes of the strategies you used.

In this case, students can actually shake hands as the concrete step. Working in small groups of three or four students, they can begin by observing the number of resulting handshakes as two, three, and four students meet. As some of the students are actually shaking hands, others can be recording the results in a chart as seen in Table 7.2.

As students recognize the increasing pattern in terms of the number of handshakes, students can easily complete the chart to find that when 10 people meet there are 45 handshakes. Students might also make a graph and then extend it to predict the number of handshakes that occur when 10 people meet. (See Figure 7.5.)

figure **7.4**

Stairs Arranged into a Square

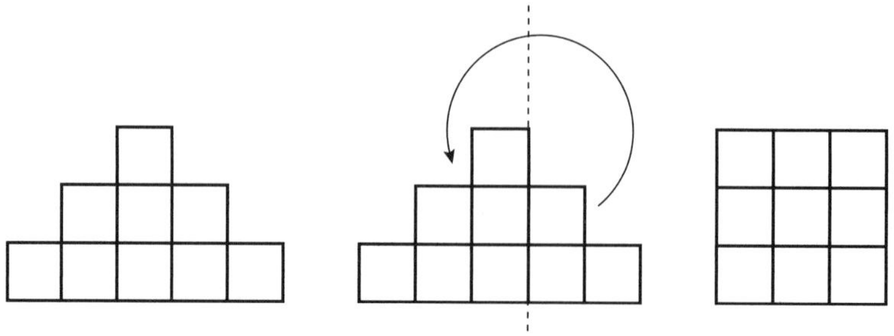

table **7.2**   **Handshake Problem**

STUDENTS	HANDSHAKES
1	0
2	1
3	3
4	6
5	10
6	15
7	21

figure **7.5**

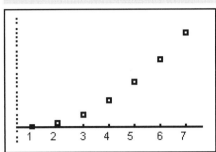

Graph of the Handshake Problem

By looking at the graph, students can sketch the continuation of the points. Students might consider the type of graph Figure 7.5 represents. Is the relationship between the number of students and the handshakes linear? Does this remind them of other graphs with which they have worked? Students should see that because the rate of change is not constant, the relationship between the number of people meeting and the resulting handshakes is not linear.

By asking students to determine the number of handshakes that would occur if 50 people or 100 people met, students begin to see that a generalized statement or symbolic representation is an easier method of solution as compared to a chart or graph.

As they begin to look for the equation, students might return to the modeling process. As students greet one another by shaking hands, the other students observe what happens and record what occurs in a diagram. (See Figure 7.6.)

This diagram indicates that once one person has met everyone, that person has finished. The next round begins with one less person. The lines in the diagrams in Figure 7.6 represent the number of handshakes that occur during the round. The equation that represents the number of handshakes in which $H =$ number of handshakes and $p =$ people is

$$H = \frac{p(p-1)}{2}$$

By referring to the diagrams, students can explain why 1 is subtracted from the number of people and why the result is divided by 2: for each round, the number of people has decreased by 1 and it takes 2 people to create 1 handshake. A meeting B is the same handshake as B meeting A. Dividing by 2 ensures that the greeting is not counted twice. Creating these generalized statements is a powerful tool that must be grounded in an event or context for middle school students.

figure **7.6**

Diagram of the Handshake Problem

A meets everyone. A ⟨ B C D E F

A is finished.

B meets everyone. B ⟨ C D E F

B is finished.

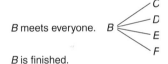

C meets everyone. C ⟨ D E F

C is finished.

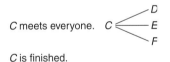

D meets everyone. D ⟨ E F

D is finished.

E and F meet. E —— F

REACHING DIVERSE LEARNERS

As students begin to study algebra, it is beneficial for diverse learners from different backgrounds to hear about mathematicians from different cultures. Persian mathematicians such as Al-Hazen, Al-Khwarizimi, and Abu'l-Wafa developed powerful mathematics and led interesting lives. Hindu mathematicians such as Bhaskara (see Bhaskara in Chapter 8) and Brahmagupta also extended our knowledge of algebra. There are many other mathematicians from non-Western backgrounds whose contributions to mathematics may be introduced into the curriculum. For biographies of mathematicians go to www.groups.dcs.st-andrews.ac.uk/~history/BiogIndex.html.

Students can also examine problems such as the Handshake Problem by analyzing the differences between the data at various stages in the problem. Recall the Messy Mathematics problem from earlier in this chapter. The data table for that problem follows:

STAGE	PIECES	DIFFERENCE
1	5	—
2	9	4
3	13	4
4	17	4

The difference between the number of pieces of paper in each of the stages is constant, each stage is 4 larger than the previous stage. A graph of these data will form a line, showing the relationship between the stages and pieces of paper is linear. A constant difference between the data in each of the stages also indicates a linear relationship. The resulting equation that describes the number of pieces (p) given stage (n) is $p = 4n + 1$. Contrast this result to the data from the Handshake Problem.

STUDENTS	HANDSHAKES	FIRST DIFFERENCE	SECOND DIFFERENCE
2	1	+1	
3	3	+2	+1
4	6	+3	+1
5	10	+4	+1

In this problem the number of handshakes at each stage increases as a new student is added to the problem. The difference in the number of handshakes at each stage is not constant, and each additional student adds an increasing number of handshakes to the total number of handshakes. However, when the differences themselves are compared, a *second difference* shows a constant, in this case a difference of 1. When the second difference in a series of data is constant, that indicates a quadratic relationship, not a linear one. The preceding discussion develops the formula

$$H = \frac{p(p-1)}{2} \text{ or } H = \frac{(p^2 - p)}{2}$$

Again, a graph of the data will verify the relationship between the number of students and the number of handshakes. In this case the data do not form a straight line but a quadratic curve. Thus, students can use the differences between the data at stages in a problem to determine if the relationship in the problem is linear or quadratic. In a linear relationship, the *first* difference is constant. In a quadratic relationship the *second* difference is constant.

TRY THIS

What is the relationship between data if the *third* difference between data in stages shows a constant?

For further discussion on finite differences go to www.math.ilstu.edu/day/courses/old/305/contentfinitedifferences.html.

PROCESS STANDARDS

Connections

One of the features that contribute to the classic nature of the Handshake Problem is its application to geometry, specifically, finding the number of diagonals in a polygon. Students can visualize a polygon with each vertex representing one person in the context of the Handshake Problem. By connecting each vertex to every other vertex, the sides of the polygon and the diagonals are drawn. Students can then work with a quadrilateral. When the vertices are connected, four line segments form the perimeter with two diagonals appearing in the interior of the polygon. (See Figure 7.7a.)

In the context of the Handshake Problem, when 4 people meet, 6 handshakes occur. Four of those handshakes are represented by the perimeter of the quadrilateral. After subtracting those handshakes represented by the perimeter, the remaining 2 handshakes are represented by the diagonals. Using a pentagon and counting all of the segments connecting the vertices, we can find the handshakes among 5 people. (See Figure 7.7b.) In this case, the result is 10. To find the number of diagonals of this pentagon, we can subtract the number of handshakes represented by the sides of the pentagon. The result is 5 diagonals, 10 − 5. The symbolic representation for the number of diagonals in a polygon is the same as the Handshake Problem, except that we subtract the number of sides of the polygon.

$$D = \text{number of diagonals}$$
$$n = \text{number of sides}$$
$$D = \frac{n(n-1)}{2} - n$$

The Handshake Problem highlights the cyclical nature of problem solving and how the steps in the Rule of 5 connect to each other. All of the representations in the Rule of 5 interconnect offering new information and varying perspectives. Students need to analyze and critique these five representations so that they can move flexibly between them. As students respond to open-ended tasks, the Rule of 5 serves as a framework and template for their work.

figure **7.7**

Geometric Interpretation of the Handshake Problem

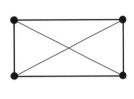
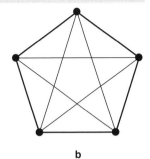

a   b

Did You **Know**?

German mathematician Michael Stifel (1486–1567) wrote an algebra text with some problems that had negative integers for solutions. He termed negative numbers as *numeri absurdi* or absurd numbers.

In the beginning of this chapter, we described algebra as a descriptive and predictive tool. In the previous activities, students worked with the descriptive nature of algebra as they wrote generalized statements. They then used these statements to then find larger values in a series of data. Students' thinking focused on making representations and generalizing an event. Students can also use the Rule of 5 as they explore situations requiring them to select the better option.

Making Predictions

In Pick a Deal, Blackline Master 7.5, students are asked to determine the better cable plan from two different perspectives. By using algebra, students describe the preferred options. Students can approach this problem using a chart or proceed directly to the graph. As they become more conversant with the rate of change and the *y*-intercept, they are more likely to proceed directly to the graph. They can observe when the slope of the line of one plan is steeper than the slope of the other line that plan becomes more expensive after the point of intersection. Graphing calculators can be used effectively; the trace function enables the students to investigate points on either line. (See Figure 7.8.)

The graphs of these equations, $y = 20x + 25$ for Stu Dent and $y = 10x + 80$ for Dr. Fay Mous, describe the situation. At 5.5 months the first plan becomes more expensive, but for Stu who is only planning to stay for just the five months, this first plan represents his better option. Students appreciate algebra as a tool after experiencing tasks that require the use of algebra in order to make decisions.

Another example of the predictive nature of algebra can be seen in the problem entitled Do the Wave, Blackline Master 7.6. Students use a stopwatch to time a small group completing the wave. The group is enlarged by two or three

figure **7.8**

Pick a Deal

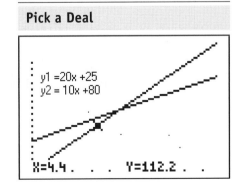

students and they are timed as they complete the wave. This process is repeated several more times. The data points are then graphed. Teachers can now ask students to predict how long it would take the entire class or school assembly to complete the wave. By extending the line on the graph, students can predict how long it will take the larger group to complete the wave. Students are generally surprised to discover that this relationship between the number of students and the time it takes to complete the wave is linear.

figure **7.9**

The Choice Is Yours!

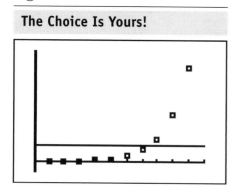

Another relationship to explore with middle school students involves exponential growth.

In Blackline Master 7.7, The Choice Is Yours!, students consider two varying options in terms of the number of minutes they will spend on homework for 30 consecutive school days. One choice remains constant and the other option starts at a very small number and doubles each day. By creating a chart for the two options, students quickly see the rapid growth pattern of the second option. They will also discern the point at which the first option becomes more desirable. Comparing the graphs of each option illustrates the exponential growth of the second option as compared to the consistent, horizontal line of the first option. (See Figure 7.9.)

PROCESS STANDARDS

Connections

Algebraic thinking and the Rule of 5 extend to other branches of mathematics: ". . . the topical strands of the mathematics curriculum, such as algebra, geometry, and data analysis, are highly interconnected, and many of the concepts presented under one strand will further develop and deepen when encountered again in another context" (Friel et al., 2001, p. 5).

Consider the following application in geometry:

> What happens to the perimeter and area of a square when you double the side length of the square?

Students tend to say that both the perimeter and area are doubled. Encourage them to draw a square and label the dimensions. Next, they should draw a second square with the side two times as long as the side of the first square. Creating a table with several pairs of squares followed by the calculations for the perimeter and area for each pair focuses students' attention on the resulting patterns. Students might develop a table similar to Table 7.3.

When students compare the perimeters of each of the squares they will realize that the perimeter doubles in each case as the side length doubles, as expected. What happens to the area? The area is four times larger. The symbolic representation provides the rationale as to why the area of the square is four times larger when the side is simply doubled. The area of the original square is $A = s^2$. The area of the second square with its side

table **7.3**   **Change in Perimeter and Area as Length of Side of Square Increases**

SIDE SQUARE A	PERIMETER	AREA	SIDE SQUARE B	PERIMETER	AREA
3 cm	12 cm	9 cm^2	6 cm	24 cm	36 cm^2
4 cm	16 cm	16 cm^2	8 cm	32 cm	64 cm^2
5 cm	20 cm	25 cm^2	10 cm	40 cm	100 cm^2
6 cm	24 cm	36 cm^2	12 cm	48 cm	144 cm^2

doubled is $A = (2s)^2$ or $4s^2$. Teachers might extend the students' thinking by asking what happens when the side of the square is tripled or is four times larger. The resulting area is the square of the scale factor, 3^2, 4^2. What happens to the volume of a cube if the edge is doubled? Observing whether or not students use the equation to determine the impact on the cube's volume or whether they approach the task by creating a table and investigating the results reveals how much they have acquired in terms of the pattern. Students who recreate the chart need that pattern to guide their thinking. Students who proceed directly to the equation realize that the volume will be the cube of the scale factor of the length of the edge of the original cube. This conclusion demonstrates a deeper level of understanding of the relationships.

ASSESSMENT TIP

The preceding relationships can also be seen on a graph. Teachers can present several opportunities to explore these changes in context. Possible scenarios might include enlarging a playground or swimming pool, creating a pasture for a farm animal, or enlarging a room in a house. Students can also use a spreadsheet to investigate these relationships.

Correlations and the Line of Best Fit

Algebra also connects with data analysis. As students gather data and then display the data in a table and on the graph sometimes called a scatter plot, they can investigate trends in the data. Students can then look for a possible relationship between the two variables. What does a positive relationship or correlation look like? How does a negative correlation compare to the positive correlation? (See Figure 7.10.)

Students can explore positive and negative correlations using examples from their own experiences. Teachers can place the following relationships in a problem for students to determine whether or not they think the variables are correlated:

- Height and age
- Walking rate and distance traveled
- Number of cell phones in use after the year 1990

Teachers can put restricting characteristics on these relationships to change the correlation. For example, a teacher can ask students to consider height and age for infants and then ask students to compare height and age for individuals older than 60. Students can also explore how a line can be used to describe the relationship between the two variables as seen in The Crickets' Chorus, Blackline Master 7.8.

In The Crickets' Chorus, students graph the relationship between the temperature and the number of cricket chirps per minute. After graphing the data on a scatter plot,

figure **7.10**

Correlations

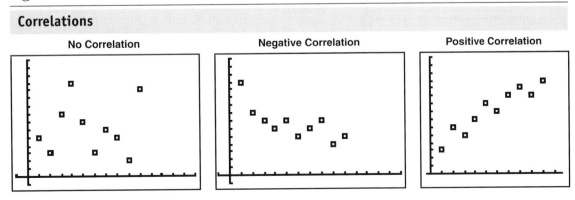

No Correlation   Negative Correlation   Positive Correlation

figure **7.11**

Line of Best Fit

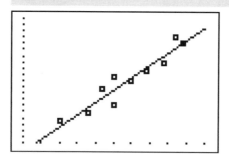 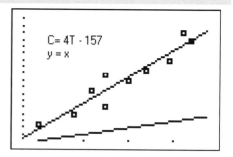

students explore a line that might fit or describe the data. Using string or a piece of un-cooked spaghetti, students place the line in the middle of the data on their graphs. The line, called the line of best fit, that best describes the relationship between the tempera-ture and the number of chirps is one that has half the points above the line and half the points below the line. This intuitive understanding of line of best fit prepares the students for the later work in statistics. (See Figure 7.11.)

With a graphing calculator, students can readily determine where the line crosses the y-axis. To gain an intuitive understanding of slope, students can enter a second equation such as $y = x$ to compare with the line representing the data. Students tend to describe the data line as more steep when moving up from left to right. The graph of $y = x$ ap-pears less steep and slowly increases from left to right. The slope of the lines for both graphs is positive. The use of a graphing calculator enhances this exploration. Students can focus on the relationship between the equation of the line, the graph, and the data points. (See Technology, page 193, in this chapter for more on this topic.)

Throughout most of this chapter, we have addressed the classification of algebraic activities involving representation and generalization. The third classification, transfor-mation, involves symbolic manipulation as in simplification of expressions and solving equations.

Transformational Activities

Typically, middle school students are presented with one-step equations such as $x + 5 = 8$. They have worked with such statements before, but students may now be required to fol-low the rules of algebra. Rather than using one of the strategies that they used success-fully in earlier grades, such as guess and check, students may be required to "balance the equation by doing the opposite operation." Some students can feel frustrated because they view the problem as trivial; others are easily confused by the various rules they are trying to remember. For students who are easily confused by the rules, algebra tiles provide a concrete and visual approach.

Algebra Tiles

Algebra tiles are based on an area model. The smallest square in Figure 7.12 measures 1 cm on each side and represents the unit. The long rectangle measures 1 cm wide and x cm long. Therefore, its area is x. The largest square measures x cm on each side so its area is x^2. To solve linear equations with alge-bra tiles, students work on a mat with a line down the center. The center line represents the equal sign in an equation. When working with $x + 5 = 8$, a student represents the left side of the equation by placing an x, a long rectangle, with 5 units on the

figure **7.12**

Algebra Tiles

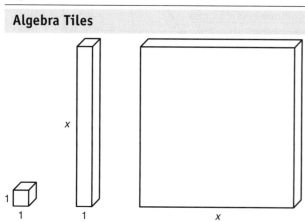

figure **7.13**

Using Algebra Tiles to Solve Linear Equations

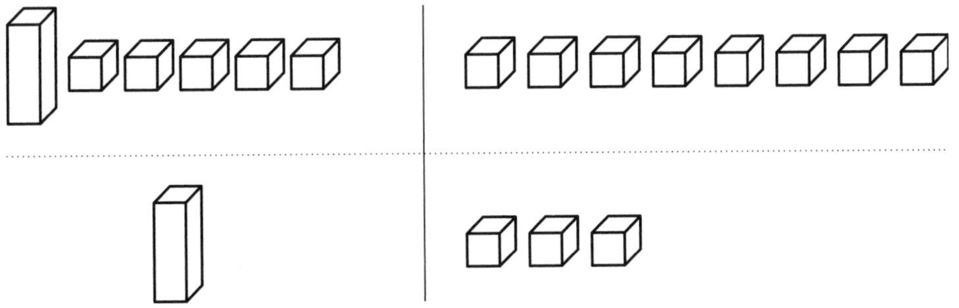

left of the center line. On the right of the center line, a student would place 8 units. (See Figure 7.13.)

To find out what the variable represents, students can remove five tiles from both sides. Students might also solve this equation by placing five negative units on both sides of the line. This maintains the balance of the equation. The five zero pairs on the left leave only the long rectangle or *x*. On the right, the five negative units create five zero pairs with five positive units, leaving only three units. Both methods are appropriate ways to think about solving the equation. (See Chapter 6, Making Sense of Number and Operations, for more about using manipulatives to work with integers.)

MISCONCEPTION

As students work with variables, they often confuse $2x$ and x^2. Using algebra tiles helps students visualize the differences between the aforementioned expressions. The large square represents x^2 and $2x$ is 2 long rectangles. Students can use the tiles to understand the meaning of combining like terms such as $x^2 + 3x + 2 + 2x^2 + 4x + 3$. Students readily see that they have 3 squares, 7 long rectangles, and 5 units as they combine the manipulatives that are the same shape.

One can argue that students need to "walk before they can run" and, therefore, they need to demonstrate mastery of the four operations seen in one-step equations. However, if students only follow the progression from one-step to two-step equations and then work with simplification requirements on both sides of the equation, students focus solely on the manipulation of symbols. Students tend to memorize the rules and lose sight of important understandings such as maintaining the balance and creating equivalent equations in simpler forms. Students do not see or appreciate algebra as a tool for representing the general case.

TRY THIS

Find the value of each of the following:

1. $\frac{5}{18} + \frac{13}{21} + \frac{13}{18} - \frac{13}{21}$

2. $[18.6 + 26.3 \div 1.3][3.2 \times 0.5 \times 0] + 6$

Look at your work. Did you show all of the steps?

Students tend to memorize the rules and rely on those rules in all situations. "Do the opposite" and "do the same operation to both sides of the equation" dictate students' thinking. They become so preoccupied with "showing all of the steps" that they tend to lose sight of the purpose for solving the equation in the first place! High school teachers report that many students remain stuck in the tedious process of showing every last detail of every last step.

Even though teachers encourage students not to waste time demonstrating that the solution is found by dividing both sides by 2, some students hang on to that final step and all of the details in previous steps. For these students, algebra has been reduced to the dance of the symbols. In the March 2003 issue of *Mathematics Teaching in the Middle School*, Andy and Rosemarie Reeves present a strong case for encouraging middle school students to view problems from different perspectives. Rather than habitually following a specified procedure, students need to take a step back and consider if there might be a more efficient approach. Repeatedly using the same procedure just because it worked in the past can be detrimental when the procedure is inappropriately applied in a new context. Hanging on to the "old way" can interfere with learning (Reeves & Reeves, 2003, pp. 374–377). Although we do want middle school students to solve algebraic equations, we also want them to see patterns and understand how those equations can help find answers to problems. Solving equations in context, as in Calendar Connection, demonstrates the usefulness of algebra.

The middle school curriculum that employs the Rule of 5 provides students with a meaningful framework. Students view the generalized statement as efficiently expressing the relationships within the event or context presented. Earlier in this chapter, we worked with the Messy Mathematics problem. After tearing up pieces of paper, making a table, and creating the graph, students worked toward writing the generalized statement. Students are motivated to find the solution employing the rule because extending the chart or graph becomes too laborious. As a result, students come to realize the efficiency of the equation and the power of algebra. Rich discussions occur as students compare their equations. Students arrive at the conclusion that $y = 4x + 1$ and $y = 5x - (x - 1)$ are equivalent equations by using the distributive property and combining like terms. Placing such transformational activities in context of a real problem helps students understand the value of the work. It also provides students with a sense of direction as they work with transformations. Rather than memorizing steps, students develop a sense of direction by knowing what the process does and where the process might take them as they work toward the answer. Another strategy that helps students solve any equation type is called backtracking.

Backtracking

Backtracking involves undoing the operations indicated in the equation in reverse order. It is as if students received a present. In order to discover what the gift is students need to unwrap it. They take off the ribbon, take off the paper, open the box, fold back the tissue paper, and there is the gift! Solving equations is a similar process. The gift is the solution or the value of the variable, and our task is to unwrap the variable. Consider this equation:

$$\frac{-3x + 5}{2} = 7$$

The steps taken to wrap the variable are

1. multiply by –3
2. add 5
3. divide by 2

In order to backtrack and solve this equation, we simply perform the opposite operation in reverse order:

1. multiply by 2
2. subtract 5
3. divide by –3

figure **7.14**

Backtracking

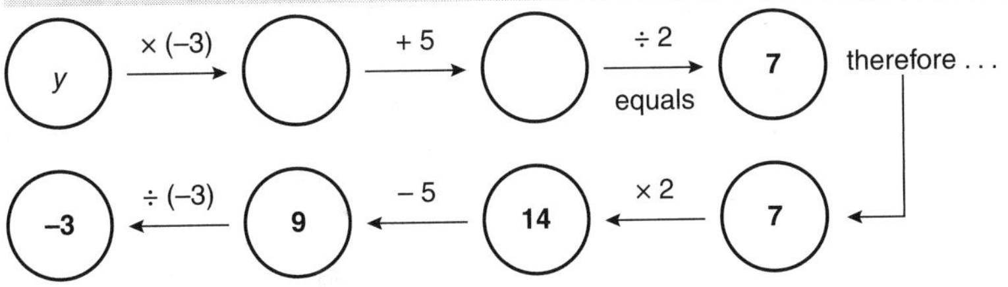

figure **7.15**

Backtracking—Activity to Prepare for Solving Equations

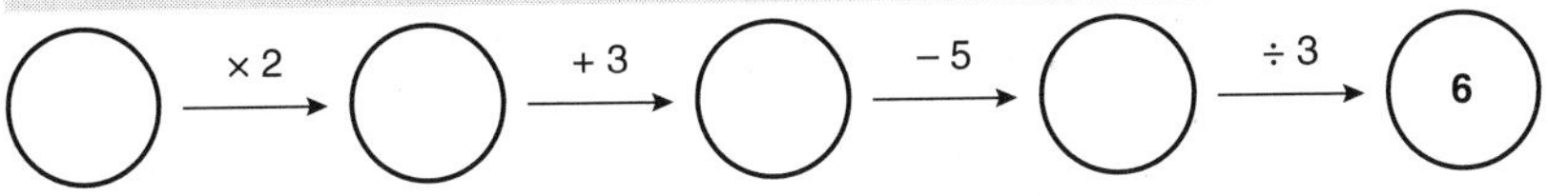

Some resources suggest making a diagram that works from left to right to indicate the order in which the variable was wrapped. The student can then draw the arrows in the reverse direction and perform the opposite operations. (See Figure 7.14.)

$$\frac{-3x + 5}{2} = 7$$

Students' understanding of the order of operations in the problem plays a critical role in the successful use of backtracking. Establishing the order in which the variable was wrapped up, to use the gift analogy, enables the students to determine the correct reverse order. Students can begin to use backtracking in preparation for solving equations. By giving them the series of steps and the answer, students can find the initial value. (See Figure 7.15.)

Technology

Technology plays a critical role as students explore and investigate relationships.

TRY THIS

Solve $2(x - 3) + 4 = 3x - 2(x - 1) - 3$ on a graphing calculator. Using "$y =$" set $y_1 = 2(x - 3)$ and $y_2 = 3x - 2(x - 1) - 3$. Graph these equations. What do you notice? Go to the table. Find the value of x when $y = 0$ for both equations.

"Technology is essential in teaching and learning mathematics; it influences the mathematics taught and enhances student learning" (NCTM, 2000 p. 11). This statement is one of the six principles and overarching themes of the *Principles and Standards for School Mathematics*. Specifically, technologies "furnish visual images of mathematical ideas, they facilitate organizing and analyzing data, and they compute efficiently and accurately. They can support student investigation by students in every area of mathematics, including geometry, statistics, algebra, measurement, and number. When technological tools are available, students can focus on decision making, reflection, reasoning and problem solving" (NCTM, 2000, p. 24).

Graphing Calculator

In an earlier discussion, we suggested that students' reliance on memorizing rules could be counterproductive to conceptual development. Consider the following equation:

$$3(x - 2) - 5x = 2x - [4 - (x + 3)]$$

figure **7.16**

Using a Calculator to Solve Linear Equations

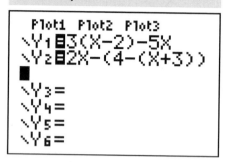

figure **7.17**

Point of Intersection Reveals the Solution

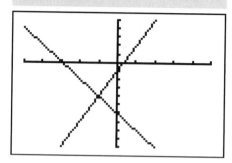

This equation may appear overwhelming to most students. However, some students are motivated by such a challenge and offering such a complex equation presents all students with an understanding of where this unit of study will take them and what they will be able to accomplish. With the aid of graphing calculators, students can explore the equation.

Students can set both the left and right sides of the equation equal to a unique y value, and then students can graph each side of the original equation separately. (See Figure 7.16.)

Students can then find the point of intersection $(-1, 4)$ of the two equations. The coordinate point indicates the value that satisfies both equations and, therefore, satisfies the original equation: $3(x - 2) - 5x = 2x - [4 - (x + 3)]$. To verify the solution, students can substitute -1 for x to determine that both sides are equal in the original equation. (See Figure 7.17.)

Using the table menu on the calculator, students can see a second representation of the solution. By searching for the value of x when the y values are the same (-4), students realize that -1 satisfies both sides of the equation.

After several experiences solving such complex equations using calculators, students will begin to understand the concept of balancing both sides of the equation. When students continue their understanding of the distributive, associative, and commutative properties as part of balancing the equation, then they are ready to work symbolically to solve linear equations.

Technology facilitates students' understanding of the algebraic big ideas, specifically, patterns, functions and relations, and change.

RESEARCH

Experimental studies involving spreadsheets have also shown enhanced student learning relative to traditional instruction. Studies of the use of spreadsheets have found that it is relatively easy for students to pass from a mixture of spreadsheet and algebraic notation to traditional algebraic symbolism (Kilpatrick et al., 2001, p. 265).

Did You Know?

Fibonacci's real name was Leonardo da Pisa because he was from Pisa, Italy. When he began writing about mathematics in 1202, he did so under the pen name of Fibonacci.

Spreadsheets

By using spreadsheets, students can explore patterns and relationships. The Fibonacci series intrigues middle school students as it can be seen in a wide variety of contexts including music, science, architecture, and nature. The series also offers interesting patterns to investigate. The series, 1, 1, 2, 3, 5, 8, 13, 21, 34 . . . , is based on a problem posed by Fibonacci about breeding rabbits.

Students can explore the numerical relationships in this series by using a spreadsheet. One approach to generating the series is to place the value 1 in the first cell and another 1 in the next cell below the first. Next, students can create a formula to add these two cells in the third cell. This third cell can then be copied for as many values in the series as desired. Here are some questions for students to explore:

1. Find the sum of the first *five* terms of the series. How does this sum relate to the seventh term in the series?
2. Find the sum of the first *eight* terms of the series. How does this sum relate to the tenth term in the series?
3. Predict the sum of the first *thirteen* terms in the series.
4. Create a new column in the spreadsheet for the squares of the terms. Add each pair of consecutive squares to make a new sequence. What pattern do you see?

Investigating the Fibonacci series provides extensive opportunities for discovering connections between mathematics and other disciplines.

Middle school students can use spreadsheets to investigate savings. How much money will they have at the end of their senior year in high school if they begin saving $1 per day now? Assume that the money is deposited in a bank that offers a 4% interest rate compounded semiannually. Suppose the students deposited $100 initially, and they add $50 dollars at the end of the second quarter and then again at the end of the fourth quarter. Students can create a spreadsheet such as the one in Table 7.4.

By using spreadsheets, students can explore various changes in the original conditions of the problem. What happens if the beginning deposit is larger? What happens if the bank compounds the interest annually? Is there another form of investment, such as bonds or certificates of deposit, that might yield a higher interest rate? Such investigations place the mathematics in an attractive context for middle school students, and students use mathematics as a tool to explore the given situation.

Technology also supports students' investigative approach when working with functions. After students have had experiences plotting and locating points on a coordinate grid and using a table to make graphs by hand, they are ready to explore relationships using technology. Technology provides the mechanics so that students concentrate on evaluating the patterns and relationships rather than the calculations.

After students have explored linear relationships in practical situations as in Building Blocks, Blackline Master 7.3 and Messy Mathematics, Blackline Master 7.2, they are ready to look at the characteristics of linear equations in general. In this chapter, our Internet lesson focuses on the slope and *y*-intercept using the website http://nlvm.usu.edu/en/nav/vlibrary.html that offers virtual manipulatives. In this case, students will use the graphing program.

Point Well Taken

"Research has shown that instruction that makes productive use of computer and calculator technology has beneficial effects on understanding and learning algebraic representation."
—*Kilpatrick, 2001, p. 420*

Did You **Know**?

The term *function* was first used by German mathematician Gottfried Leibniz (1646–1716) in 1673. Leibniz is also credited with introducing the term *coordinate* in 1682.

table **7.4**   **Using Spreadsheets**

GRADE LEVEL	INITIAL DEPOSIT	SECOND QUARTER	FOURTH QUARTER	TOTAL SAVINGS
6	$100	100(1.02) + = 152	152(1.02) + = 205	$205
7	$205	205(1.02) + = 259.10	259.10(1.02) + 50 = 314.30	$314.30
8				
9				
10				
11				
12				

Internet Lesson

Goals   Students discover patterns regarding the *y*-intercept and the slope of linear equations

Objectives   Students will

- Explain how the *y*-intercept affects the graph of the linear equation
- Explain how the slope affects the graph of the linear equation
- Predict the location of the graph given the equation
- Write about their discoveries in their journals

Lesson   Preview lesson by connecting with a previous problem, Messy Mathematics.

$$p = 4n + 1$$

What do those variables represent in terms of the problem?

Why did the 4 appear in the equation? What did the 1 represent?

Today, we are going to explore linear equations in general. You will work with your technology partners to discover relationships. You will be using the virtual manipulatives website. Here is a transparency of the page that you will be working on.

Explain features and vocabulary. (See Figure 7.18.) Remind students of cooperative skills that the class is working currently working on:

- Listening carefully
- Offering help when asked
- Asking for help when needed

figure **7.18**

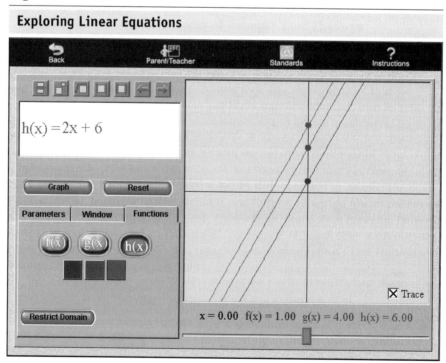

Used by permission of the National Library of Virtual Manipulatives, © 2003, Utah State University.

$$y = x$$
$$y = x + 3$$
$$y = x - 1$$

What is the same in each equation?

What is different?

What happens to the graph as a result of this difference?

Predict what the graph of this equation will look like: $f(x) = x - 3$.
Make a sketch below.

Clear the screen. Now graph these three equations on your calculator:
$y = x$, $y = 3x$, $y = -2x$
What is the same in each equation?

What is different?

What happens to the graph as a result of this difference?

Compare $y = 2x$ and $y = -2x$. What is the same in each equation?

What is different?

What happens to the graph as a result of this difference?

Predict what each graph will look like given each equation. Make a sketch.

$f(x) = 2x + 1$ $g(x) = -3x + 1$ $h(x) = 4x - 5$

Journal: Write about what you discovered today about graphs of the equations. Be specific and provide examples.

Which of the cooperative skills did you and your partner do well today?

Explain the function notation $f(x)$, $g(x)$, and $h(x)$ as ways of distinguishing the graphs of the three different equations. Students can work with three equations at a time. The graphs will appear in the three colors: blue, red, and green. Provide students with a worksheet detailing the equations you want them to focus on in the beginning of their work (see page 196).

As students work with their partners, listen to their conversations. Note the appropriate skills and behaviors that have been previously discussed with students so that those can be highlighted to the class.

Closure   Before students leave the computer room, ask students to turn their chairs away from the screens and focus their attention on you. This is a quick check-in. Ask students to close their eyes. You give this directive to students, "Thumbs up if you think that you and your partner worked well today." Write these two equations on the board or a transparency. Instruct students to open their eyes and indicate "Thumbs up if you can predict what this graph will look like for each of these equations: $y = 2x + 1$ and $y = -3x + 2$. As an exit card today, sketch the graph of $y = -x + 2$." Highlight those positive behaviors by sharing them with the class. Be certain to mention those students who did an exemplary job.

The lesson can be extended using graphing calculators. After frequent experiences in examining the effects of changes in the slope and y-intercepts, challenge students to write the equation of the line appearing on the overhead projector. Be certain to cover the projector with a piece of paper as you enter the equation in the calculator so that it is not visible to students. Graph this equation and then remove the paper so the students see the resulting graph. They work with their calculators to match the target equation. As their confidence builds, a variety of linear equations can be presented including those with negative and fractional slopes. Students can explore parabolas as well. Again, students need to have many experiences in problem-solving activities, such as the Handshake Problem, prior to exploring the symbolic representation and the placement of its resulting graph on the coordinate grid. There are many sources for algebraic activities and lessons on the Web.

> National Library of Virtual Mathematics Manipulatives:
>   http://nlvm.usu.edu/en/nav/vlibrary.html
> Mathemagica Applets site: www.mathemagica.org/home.nfs?a=mathemagica
> Function Machine Algebraic Reasoning in Number Patterns:
>   www.learner.org/teacherslab/math/patterns/mystery/index.phtml
> Opportunities to explore functions and correlations:
>   www.explorelearning.com.math.
> A variety of problems and interactive activities: www.mathforum.org/mathtools

Technology continues to influence mathematics curricula. "This technology demands new visions of school algebra that shift the emphasis away from symbolic manipulation toward conceptual understanding, symbol sense, and mathematical modeling" (Heid et al., 1995, p. 1). With increased use of technology, students explore mathematical domains as teachers facilitate problem-solving opportunities. Students will ask "what if?" and teachers may find themselves participating as learners in the investigation. "Research has shown that instruction that makes productive use of computer and calculator technology has beneficial effects on understanding and learning algebraic representation" (Kilpatrick et al., 2001, p. 420). As students explore the varying algebraic representations and begin to ask probing questions, they embrace more of the ownership of their learning.

Point Well Taken

"The study of patterns and relationships in the middle grades should focus on patterns that relate to linear functions, which arise when there is a constant rate of change. Students should solve problems in which they use tables, graphs, words, and symbolic expressions to represent and examine functions and patterns of change."

—NCTM, 2000, p. 223

SUMMARY

Middle school students begin rich, problem solving tasks with a concrete representation. When students use blocks, drawings, handshakes, or manipulatives, the problem becomes accessible to them. Investigating the relationships and recording the findings in a chart provides the numerical representation that can then be graphed. These steps can support students as they look to represent the event symbolically. Writing or telling a summary of the task as a form of reflection and clarification of their thinking promotes students' communication skills. The Rule of 5 provides a framework for students as they respond to open-ended questions as seen on most state tests. By experiencing the connections between the different representations, students can articulate their understanding about their reasons for selecting the table or graph to solve the problem. Students come to realize that not every problem requires them to demonstrate all five steps. Students can decide the most effective tools for each situation. It is helpful that students move through all the steps as they are first introduced to these multiple forms of representation. The Rule of 5 supports students' thinking as they build a firm foundation for their high school mathematics experience.

NCTM promotes the increased emphasis of algebraic reasoning in elementary and middle school curriculum. Such experiences play a critical role in making algebra accessible to all students. Students will come to understand the predictive and descriptive nature of algebra and be able to use algebra as a tool in their lives. Algebra will be seen as the gateway to higher mathematics.

The following are highlights from this chapter:

- The Rule of 5 guides students' thinking as they solve problems.
- All three types of algebraic activities, representational, transformational, and generalizing activities, are appropriate for middle school students.
- Technology plays a critical role in the exploration of many algebraic concepts.
- Manipulatives can help students access algebraic concepts.
- Reliance on the memorization of rules can be counterproductive to conceptual development.

Student Performance on
International and National Assessments

TIMSS

A book publisher sent 140 copies of a certain book to a bookstore. The publisher packed the books in two types of boxes. One type of box held 8 copies of the book, and the other held 12 copies of the book. The boxes are all full, and there were equal numbers of both types of boxes.

How many boxes holding 12 books were sent to the bookstore? (26% correct)

What fraction of the books was in the smaller boxes? (12% correct)

NAEP

If $\frac{2}{25} = \frac{n}{500}$, then $n =$ (48% correct)

A. 10
B. 20
C. 30
D. 40
E. 50

EXERCISES

From the Reading

1. A student has just submitted his work on the Messy Mathematics problem. He wrote the equation $p = 5n - (n - 1)$. If $p =$ the total number of pieces and $n =$ the stage number, what explanation might you anticipate the student use to support his equation?

2. Explain how to find the slope and y-intercept from a graph, table, and equation.

3. Reflect back on your learning experiences in algebra. How do your experiences compare to the approach used in the chapter?

4. A student is riding her bike from school to her home. Graph her progress in terms of distance traveled as a

function of time. Include a written explanation of the graph.

5. Use a graphing calculator to explore the relationship between the following two equations: $y = (x - 2)^2 + 3$ and $y = x^2 - 4x + 7$. Describe the relationship. Provide an explanation as to why the relationship exists.

6. Complete the problems in "Try This" on page 191. After finding the solution, look back at your work. Did you show every step? Is there a shortcut that made the task easier?

7. Try this "magic trick" that uses phone numbers. (Use a calculator.) Explain why it works.

   Put the first three digits after your area code of your phone number on the display.

   Multiply by 80.

   Add 1.

   Multiply by 250.

   Add the last four digits of your phone number.

   Add the last four digits again.

   Subtract 250.

   Divide by 2.

8. How would you respond to students who write down just the answers on their homework papers?

9. Find the sum of any five consecutive integers. Demontrate that the sum of any five consecutive integers is equal to five times the middle number. Does this pattern hold for any number of values in the series?

10. Write a lesson plan involving technology that includes the objective of having students discover the *y*-intercept.

On Your Own

1. Go to the NCTM website www.nctm.org. Explore the many e-examples found in Middle School Algebra.

2. Go to www.mathforum.org and look for the activity Traffic Jam. Use the interactive applet to work on the problem. Use the Rule of 5 to extend your algebraic thinking.

3. Go online to the Math Forum website www.math forum.org/algpow. Find the Problems of the Week focusing on algebra. Select one of the problems. Write a critique of the problem. Be certain to include a description of the task and the mathematics involved in the solution process. Do you think that the problem will engage middle school students? Do you consider it to be a "good" problem?

4. Do local districts require algebra in the eighth grade? Find out.

5. Conduct an Internet search for commercial, algebraic manipulatives.

 Portfolio

Discuss the Rule of 5 and its impact on lesson planning.

Scenes from a Classroom

Ms. Noether handed back the quizzes to her eighth-grade class and asked the students to work with their partner to go over any questions they might have. She emphasized the importance that both students needed to be able to explain the correct solution. Ms. Noether told the class that she would ask various students to explain some of the problems before the end of class. The class began working and Ms. Noether seemed pleased that the students were taking their roles seriously. As the students continued to work, one group called her to their desk.

Amy caught Ms. Noether's attention first and said, "We don't understand why I got so many points taken off here. I did just about the same thing as Brian. We both made one mistake. He lost one point but I lost three." Ms. Noether seemed a little concerned that she may have made an error on Amy's test. As class was coming to a close, she told Brian and Amy that she would take their quizzes and reconsider the grading of that particular problem. Brian was concerned that he might have more points taken away if he resubmitted his paper. Ms. Noether replied, "Don't worry. I'm looking at Amy's paper to see if she deserves more points. Remember our understanding that if I make a mistake correcting your paper I will not penalize you for telling me. It's more important that you learn from your mistake." With that remark, Brian was reassured and class was dismissed.

Here is the problem in question:

$$-3x - 5(2x + 1) = 2x - 6. \text{ (See Figure 7.19.)}$$

Before reading further, respond to the following:

Compare the two solutions. If this problem was worth 5 points on the quiz, how many points would you give each student? Be ready to explain your thinking.

Some teachers feel strongly that a student's work should be completely correct in order to earn any points on a particular problem. These teachers demand accuracy in mathematics and support their policy by saying, "Errors are not valued. After all, I don't want them building bridges that don't quite reach from one shoreline to the other." Because both Amy and Brian made an error, neither one would earn points for their work. Other teachers state that students should earn points for the correct mathematics demonstrated in their work. If a student makes an error in the beginning of the problem and then works correctly through the remainder of the problem,

figure **7.19**

Comparison of Student Work

Amy's Work

$$3x - 5(2x + 1) = 2x - 6$$
$$3x - 10x + 5 = 2x - 6$$
$$-7x + 5 = 2x - 6$$
$$-9x = -11$$
$$x = \frac{11}{9}$$

Brian's Work

$$3x - 5x - 5 = 2x - 6$$
$$-2x - 5 = 2x - 6$$
$$-4x = -6 - 5$$
$$-4x = -11$$
$$x = \frac{11}{4}$$

the student should earn partial credit. Amy made a common error in using the distributive property in the second line of her solution ($-5(2x + 1) = -10x - 5$, not $-10x + 5$). Brian's error occurred in the third line of his solution as he combines -6 and -5 rather than using $+5$. Some teachers might award both students 4 out of 5 possible points. Other teachers might argue that Amy only deserves 3 out of 5 points because she made the mistake in the very first line of her solution. Giving partial credit must be done consistently. In order to determine the number of points to be allocated, teachers should take the test themselves. They can then experience the complexities of the problems and assign points accordingly. Inevitably, students present situations in their work that teachers did not foresee. As the teacher determines the appropriate number of points for the new situation, these points should be awarded consistently. A teacher needs to be fair and consistent in dealing with the issues of assigning partial credit.

Another issue is raised in this scene. Brian is worried that if he gives back his quiz he might end up losing more points. Ms. Noether assures him that she will not take any additional points off his grade. This is a policy that allows students to look at their mistakes. If a teacher has made a mistake in the student's favor, she will not take off additional points. A teacher can always give more points to a deserving student's work. Being open to reevaluate a student's work helps maintain the lines of communication between teacher and students.

Preparing for PRAXIS

If $a^3 \cdot b^2 \cdot a^4 \cdot b^3$ can be written as $a^7 b^5$, then $2^3 \cdot 3^4 \cdot 2^2 \cdot 3^3$ can be written as

A. $2^5 \cdot 3^7$
B. $4^5 \cdot 9^7$
C. 6^{12}
D. 36^{12}

RESOURCES

Math–Literature Connections

Anno, M. (1995) *Anno's magic seeds.* New York: Philomel Books.
Glass, J. (2000). *Counting sheep.* New York: Random House.
Pittman, H. C. (1986). *A grain of rice.* New York: Scholastic Press.

Pinczes, E. (1993). *One hundred hungry ants.* Boston: Houghton Mifflin.

Teacher's Bookcase

Billstein, R. (1998). Language and representation in algebra: A view from the middle. In *The nature and role of*

algebra in K–14 curriculum. Reston, VA: National Council of Teachers of Mathematics and National Science Education Board.

> *This resource summarizes of the proceedings from a national symposium on May 27 and 28, 1997. Nationally recognized educators share their thinking on a vision for algebra in K–14 classrooms.*

Burns, M. (2000). *About teaching mathematics.* Sausalito, CA: Math Solutions Publications.

> *This work offers research on how children learn mathematics and rich problems to use with students. The book also includes classroom management strategies and problem-solving approaches.*

Friel, S. (Ed.). (2001). *Navigating through algebra in grades 6–8.* Reston, VA: NCTM.

> *This valuable resource explains the Algebra Standard and offers classroom activities to use with middle school students.*

Kilpatrick, J., et al., (2001). *Adding it up—Helping children learn mathematics.* Washington, DC: National Academy Press.

> *A significant work summarizing the latest research on children's understanding of mathematics.*

Ma, L. (1999). *Knowing and teaching elementary mathematics.* Mahwah, NJ: Lawrence Erlbaum Associates.

> *A fascinating comparison of teachers' knowledge of mathematical content between China and the United States.*

Saphier, J., & Gower, J. (1997). *The skillful teacher.* Carlisle, MA: Research for Better Teaching.

> *A comprehensive resource that acknowledges the complexity of teaching and provides common vocabulary on which to build a vast repertoire of skills.*

For Further Reading

Billings, E., & Lakatos, T. (2003, May). Lisa's lemonade stand: Exploring algebraic ideas. In *Mathematics Teaching in the Middle School,* 456–460.

> *The authors discuss a series of engaging activities requiring students to connect events with their graphical representations. The authors stress the importance of providing students with opportunities to interpret and analyze change as seen on the graphs.*

Lannin, J. (2003, March). **Developing algebraic reasoning through generalization.** In *Mathematics Teaching in the Middle School.*

> *The author presents six strategies that students use when developing generalizations: counting, recursion, whole object, contextual, guess and check, rate adjustment.*

Links

This site is a listing of online activities relating to algebra.
www.illuminations.nctm.org/swr/list

The Algebra Game card series includes four topic packages: Linear, Quadratic, Conic, and Trig Equations. Each deck provides students with opportunities to match the tabular, symbolic, and graphical representations of the functions. A teacher's guide offers suggestions for further activities and explorations. The Algebra Game is manufactured by Math Studio.
www.mathstudio.com

See this website for a review of teasers by Tobbs, a software manufactured by Sunburst Communications. Using this software, students solve puzzles involving linear relationships and other problem-solving strategies.
www.atarimagazines.com/v3n6/educational.html

REFERENCES

Billstein, R. (1998). Language and representation in algebra: A view from the middle. In *The Nature and Role of Algebra in K–14 Curriculum.* Reston, VA: National Council of Teachers of Mathematics and National Science Education Board.

Bochner, S. (1996). *The role of mathematics in the rise of science.* Princeton, NJ: Princeton University Press.

Burns, M. (2000). *About teaching mathematics.* Sausalito, CA: Math Solutions Publications.

Driscoll, M. (1999) *Fostering algebraic thinking.* Portsmouth, NH: Heinemann.

Friel, S., Rachlin, S., & Doyle, D. (2001). *Navigating through algebra in grades 6–8.* Reston, VA: NCTM.

Garland, T. H. (1987). *Fascinating fibonaccis—Mystery and magic in numbers.* Palo Alto, CA: Dale Seymour Publications.

Ginsburg, H. (1989). *Children's arithmetic.* Austin, TX: Pro-ed.

Heid, K., Choate, J., Sheets, C., & Zbiek, R. (1995). *Curriculum and evaluation standards for school mathematics: Algebra in a technological world.* Addenda Series. Reston, VA: NCTM.

Hiebert, J., et al. (1997). *Making sense—Teaching and learning mathematics with understanding.* Portsmouth, NH: Heinemann.

Kelley, J. (1992). Comparing options. Teaching Mathematics with Calculators: A National Workshop, Mathematical Association of America.

Kilpatrick, J., et al. (2001). *Adding it up—Helping children learn mathematics.* Washington, DC: National Academy Press.

National Council of Teachers of Mathematics. (2000). *Principles and Standards for School Mathematics.* Reston, VA: NCTM.

Owens, D. (Ed.). (1993). *Research ideas for the classroom—Middle grades mathematics.* Reston, VA: NCTM.

Pederson, K. (1987). *Trivia math: Algebra and geometry.* Palo Alto, CA: Creative Publications.

Reeves, A., & Reeves, R. (2003, March). Encouraging students to think about how they think. In *Mathematics teaching in the middle school* (pp. 374–377). Reston, VA: NCTM.

Sarama, J., & Clements, D. (1998). Using computers for algebraic thinking. In *Teaching Children Mathematics.* Reston, VA: NCTM.

Tanton, J. (2004, November). *The St. Mark's Institute of Mathematics newsletter.* Southborough, MA: St. Mark's School.

Verschaffel, L., De Corte, E., & Vierstraete, H. (1999). Upper elementary school pupils' difficulty in modeling and solving nonstandard additive word problems involving ordinal numbers. *Journal for Research in Mathematics Education, 30*(3), 265–286.

Magic Tricks

1. Select any number:

    Add 3

    Multiply by 3

    Add 3

    Divide by 3

    Subtract your selected number

        The result is . . .

2. Select any number:

    Multiply by 2

    Add 2

    Divide by 2

    Subtract 1

        The result is . . .

Explain WHY these magic tricks work.

Prove that each trick will work for any problem.

 From Johnson & Norris, Teaching Today's Mathematics in the Middle Grades. Copyright © 2006 Allyn and Bacon, Pearson Education, Inc.

Messy Mathematics

Take a sheet of paper. Cut this sheet into 5 pieces. (This represents stage 1.) Take any one of those pieces and cut that piece into 5 pieces. (This represents stage 2.) Repeat this process and record the total number of pieces after each stage in the table below. How many pieces of paper will there be after the fifth round . . . seventh round . . . nth round?

Stage 0	1 piece
Stage 1	5 pieces
Stage 2	___ pieces
Stage 3	___ pieces
Stage 4	___ pieces
Stage 5	___ pieces
Stage 6	___ pieces
Stage 7	___ pieces
Stage n	___ pieces

After completing the chart, graph your results. Then respond to the following questions in writing:

1. How did you set up your graph? (What values were indicated on each axis? What scale did you select?) Explain your thinking.

2. What do you notice about your graph?

3. What is the connection between your general statement for the nth stage and the graph?

4. Did you connect the points on the graph? Why or why not?

Source: Adapted from Pederson, K. (1987). *Trivia math: Algebra and geometry.* Palo Alto, CA: Creative Publications.

Building Blocks

Suppose you make a building using 100 cubes. Now you want to paint the building on all sides and the top. (Don't worry about the base of the tower.) How many squares would you have to paint?

Use the strategy of beginning with a simpler problem. Begin with one cube. As shown in the table, five sides need to be painted. Make the second building by stacking 2 cubes. In this case, nine sides need to be painted. Continue making the buildings with 3, 4, and 5 cubes.

Fill in the chart and then look for a pattern.

BLOCKS	SQUARE FACES TO PAINT
1	5
2	9
3	
4	
5	
6	
n	

Do you see a pattern? Describe the pattern.

Use graph paper to create a graph of the chart.
What do you notice about the graph?

Write an equation that describes the pattern.

How many sides will need to be painted for a building using 100 cubes?

Source: Adapted from Burns, M. (2000). About teaching mathematics: A K–8 resource. Sausalito, CA: Math Solutions Publications, p. 115.

 From Johnson & Norris, Teaching Today's Mathematics in the Middle Grades. Copyright © 2006 Allyn and Bacon, Pearson Education, Inc.

Up and Down Staircases

1. Look at the pattern below. Use tiles, blocks, or graph paper to create the next two patterns.

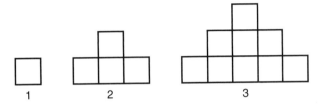

2. Fill in the chart:

STAIR NUMBER	NUMBER OF BLOCKS
1	1
2	4
3	———
4	———
5	———

3. How many blocks will be in the tenth staircase?

4. How many blocks will be in the fiftieth staircase?

5. Make a graph of the chart above. Include stair numbers 1–10 on your graph.

6. What do you notice about this graph?

7. Write the generalized statement for this pattern. What equation will represent the number of blocks in the *n* staircase?

Source: Adapted from Isaacs, A., et al. (1998). Patterns and Functions. *Bridges to classroom mathematics—Staff developers' guide: Mathematics for elementary teachers.* Lexington, MA: COMAP, p. 17.

Pick a Deal!

The cable company in your area offers two pricing options hoping to interest more customers.

  Plan 1: $25 installation fee plus $20 per month.

  Plan 2: $80 installation fee plus $10 per month.

Find the better deal from the point of view of each of the following two people. Select the better deal for each person. Describe in detail why you made your selections. Include a graph to help justify your response.

1. Stu Dent has just moved onto the university campus. He is an exchange student and is planning to stay five months.

2. Dr. Fay Mous comes to the university with her family for a three-year appointment.

Source: Adapted from Kelley, J. (1992). Comparing options. In *Teaching mathematics with calculators: A national workshop*. Washington, DC: Mathematical Association of America.

Do the Wave

1. Begin by asking students if they have ever been at a sporting event during which all of the spectators "did the wave."

2. Continue questioning:

What happened?

How long did the wave take?

Does it depend on the number of people participating?

Can we predict how long a wave might take?

3. Establish a common definition of a wave.

Stand

Raise hands over head

Sit down

After one person has reached the chair, the next one stands.

Each person must wait until the previous one has sat down.

4. Conduct the experiment:

First trial: Time 3 students

Second trial: Time 8 students

Third trial: Time 15 students

Graph the results: Time as a function of number of students

Predict the result of the entire class "doing the wave" based on the graph obtained.

Fourth trial: Time the entire class

5. Discuss results.

6. You can extend this activity and involve the entire school or grade team. Predict how long it will take everyone to do the wave. Have the graph prepared to show on transparency.

The Choice Is Yours!

Miss Take decides to offer her class choices in terms of the amount of time they will spend on homework. She announces to her class that they can decided between two options:

OPTION A: For the next 30 school days you will spend a total of 180 minutes on your homework each night.

OPTION B: Starting today, you will have 1 minute of homework. On the next day, you will have 2 minutes of homework and then 4 minutes on the following day. Every day the amount of time doubles. This continues for 30 days.

Help Miss Take's class decide which is the better option. Be certain to prepare your reasons in a convincing written statement.

 From Johnson & Norris, Teaching Today's Mathematics in the Middle Grades. Copyright © 2006 Allyn and Bacon, Pearson Education, Inc.

The Crickets' Chorus

Scientists have gathered the following data of the number of chirps per minute and the corresponding temperature in Fahrenheit.

NUMBER OF CHIRPS	TEMPERATURE (°F)
136	72
165	84
98	68
110	75
150	80
210	94
84	60
158	75
221	92
178	89

1. Do you think that there is a relationship between the number of chirps the cricket makes and the temperature? Explain your reasoning.

2. Create a scatter plot of the data. Which is the independent variable? Provide a reason for your answer.

3. By looking at the graph of the data, do you think that your response was correct in question 1?

4. Find the line that describes the relationship. You may sketch the line on a graph or use the graphing calculator.

5. Describe the equation of the line. How does the equation relate the crickets' chirping and the temperature?

chapter **eight**

Geometry: Moving beyond Formulas

Did You **Know**?

Euclidean geometry is named for Greek mathematician Euclid (c. 300 B.C.E.). Euclid catalogued all the geometry known at the time into a collection of postulates and logically developed theorems.

Point Well Taken

"Geometry enables us to describe, analyze, and understand our physical world, so there is little wonder that it holds a central place in mathematics."

—*Pugalee et al., 2001, p. 1*

Our word *geometry* is derived from Greek words meaning "to measure the earth." The earliest civilizations used geometry to plant fields, build shelters, and find their way.

As early societies became more sophisticated, the study of geometry became increasingly logical and abstract, culminating in the Euclidean geometry of postulate, theorem, and proof. Geometry, more than any other topic in mathematics, is most easily found in and applied to the real world from even a child's perspective.

Primary school children use geometry to navigate their world and make sense of two- and three-dimensional representations of it. They need to be able to locate toys, their bed, their clothes, and they need to know their location in relation to the neighborhood, their classroom, and their home. They play with miniature cars, dolls, and action figures and build houses, castles, and model planes. The geometry they study in elementary school supports their practical needs. It is visual, tactile, and literal. As students progress in their schooling, they study increasingly abstract aspects of geometry such as angle and area measure, special shapes, and relationships such as the Pythagorean Theorem and the Golden Rectangle. For most students their study of geometry culminates with deduction in Euclidean geometry in high school.

Despite this innate development of geometry in the early grades and an appreciation for its practical value, many middle school and secondary school students find geometry to be a challenging undertaking. There are a number of reasons that middle school students in particular find geometry difficult. Some of the reasons will be considered in the course of this chapter. First, it is important to review the NCTM Geometry Standard.

NCTM Standards

There are four strands to the Geometry Standard for all grade levels. The specific recommendations for grades 6–8 follow:

1. *Analyze characteristics* and properties of two- and three-dimensional geometric shapes and develop mathematical arguments about geometric relationships.
   - Precisely describe, classify, and understand relationships among types of two- and three-dimensional objects using their defining properties.
   - Understand relationships among the angles, side lengths, perimeters, areas, and volumes of similar objects.
   - Create and critique inductive and deductive arguments concerning geometric ideas and relationships, such as congruence, similarity, and the Pythagorean relationship.

2. *Specify locations* and describe spatial relationships using coordinate geometry and other representational systems.

- Use coordinate geometry to represent and examine the properties of geometric shapes.
- Use coordinate geometry to examine special geometric shapes, such as regular polygons or those with pairs of parallel or perpendicular sides.

3. *Apply transformations* and use symmetry to analyze mathematical situations.

- Describe sizes, positions, and orientations of shapes under informal transformations such as flips, turns, slides, and scaling.
- Examine the congruence, similarity, and line or rotational symmetry of objects using transformations.

4. *Use visualization,* spatial reasoning, and geometric modeling to solve problems.

- Draw geometric objects with specified properties, such as side lengths or angle measures.
- Use two-dimensional representations of three-dimensional objects to visualize and solve problems such as those involving surface area and volume.
- Use visual tools such as networks to represent and solve problems.
- Use geometric models to represent and explain numerical and algebraic relationships.
- Recognize and apply geometric ideas and relationships in areas outside the mathematics classroom, such as art, science, and everyday life (NCTM, 2000, p. 232).

The four strands offer a comprehensive vision of geometry at the middle school level. Notice that one of the strands focuses on visualization and spatial reasoning. We likewise focus on spatial reasoning as one of the topics in this chapter. Other topics are the Pythagorean Theorem, categorization of figures, specifically quadrilaterals, and similarity. Before beginning to consider these topics, it is critical to examine geometry thinking in and of itself, so that teachers can understand and use it in their teaching.

Van Hiele Levels of Geometry Thinking

In the 1950s Piet van Hiele and Dina van Hiele-Geldoff, a Dutch couple, were middle school teachers in the Netherlands. In the course of their teaching middle school students, they began to collect impressions, data, and anecdotal evidence about the geometry understanding of their students. They refined their findings and developed what they called levels of geometric thinking. The van Hieles suggested that there were five distinct levels of geometry thinking, and every student had to pass through each preceding level in order to reason at a higher level. Students who attempted to work with concepts and problems that were at a higher level of geometry thinking than they had achieved were likely to fail in the attempt.

The five van Hiele levels of geometry thinking are

- Level 0: Visualization
- Level 1: Analysis
- Level 2: Abstraction
- Level 3: Deduction
- Level 4: Rigor

A cursory examination of the titles of each level suggests that higher van Hiele levels demand more complex geometry thinking. This is, in fact, what the van Hiele model of geometry thinking postulates and has been supported by a number of research studies. Each van Hiele level consists of distinct properties that contribute to an understanding of geometry appropriate for that level. The van Hieles envisioned levels of geometry

Point Well Taken

"Geometry provides a rich context for the development of mathematical reasoning, including inductive and deductive reasoning, making and validating conjectures, and classifying and defining geometric objects."

—*NCTM, 2000, p. 233*

figure **8.1**

Triangles

Recognized as Triangles   Not Recognized as Triangles

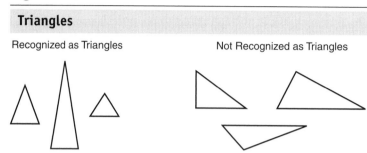

Did You **Know**?

The van Hieles numbered their levels of geometry thinking to match the European scheme for numbering the floors of a build-ing. In Europe the ground floor is Floor 0, the next floor is Floor 1, and so forth.

thinking that began with the foundation or ground level at Level 0, to be followed by sub-sequent levels that build on one another in succession. A student who wishes to reach Level 2 must enter geometry thinking at Level 0 and then progress through Level 1 to Level 2. Descriptions of the thinking for each level will help to clarify the van Hiele levels of geom-etry thinking.

Level 0: Visualization

A student who is thinking at Level 0 will recognize various shapes by visual inspection alone. The student at this level will identify a triangle because "it looks like a triangle." There is no explicit understanding that triangles have three sides or three angles and may be identified by the number of sides and/or angles. For many students at this level trian-gles must be equilateral or isosceles with their bases parallel to the bottom of the page. As shown in Figure 8.1, triangles that deviate too far from the expected shape may not be recognized as triangles.

Young children operate at this initial van Hiele level. However, it is not uncommon to find middle and even high school students who are still thinking at this early level.

Level 1: Analysis

At this level a student is beginning to analyze a figure to determine all of its characteris-tics or properties. A student at this level will examine a square and determine that a square has four sides with the same lengths and four right angles. In addition the student may also observe that opposite sides are parallel and the diagonals are not only congruent but also perpendicular bisectors of each other. Similar data might also be gathered about other quadrilaterals, angles on parallel lines, and regular polygons. Students at this level might even compose lists of properties and compare them for different figures, but the com-parison is simply done by matching properties from one list to another list rather than using the properties as a means to distinguish between figures. (See page 233 for a table of properties of quadrilaterals.) A student at this level can tell the difference between a rectangle and a square and can give as a reason that a square has congruent sides whereas a rectangle does not. However, at this level a student would not fully grasp that a square is a special case of a rectangle. Such reasoning takes place at Level 2.

Level 2: Abstraction

Did You **Know**?

Venn diagrams are named for En-glish mathematician John Venn (1834–1923). He used them to represent relationships in a new algebra that used sets instead of numbers. His idea to use circles to help categorize items was not new. The same concept had been used over 100 years earlier but never caught the attention of most mathematicians.

At this level of geometry thinking a student is able to compare figures and their proper-ties. The comparison is more than the matching of a checklist of properties as described for Level 1. At this level a student can compare and contrast properties as a means for distinguishing between figures and defining them. A student at this level will understand that a square is a "special" rectangle, one with congruent sides and perpendicular diago-nals, for example. The Venn diagram in Figure 8.2 is one means students at this level can use for comparing quadrilaterals.

A student thinking at the abstraction level would be able to reason that a square is also a special case of a rhombus. It has all the properties of a rhombus and in addition has right angles and congruent diagonals.

TRY THIS

Consider the diagonals of a rhombus, a rectangle, and a square. Use the characteristics of each figure to help you to write alternate definitions of all three figures.

figure **8.2**

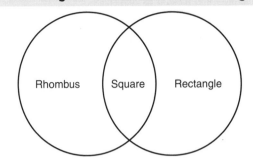

Venn Diagram of Rhombus and Rectangle

Level 3: Deduction

A student thinking at this level can reason deductively about various geometric concepts and problems and make valid conclusions that apply to all cases and not simply to the specific problem at hand. A student reasoning at this level can provide a logical argument or proof for a conclusion. For example, to show that the sum of the measures of interior angles of a hexagon is 720°, a student at this level might draw a hexagon with an interior point, as shown in Figure 8.3.

The student can then draw segments from random interior point Q to each vertex, forming six triangles. The sum of the measures of the angles in the six triangles is $6 \times 180° = 1080$. This sum includes the angles about point Q that are not interior angles of the hexagon. The sum of the angles about point Q is 360°; thus, the sum of the angles of the hexagon is $1080 - 360 = 720°$. The deductive thinking shown here may be applied to any hexagon and by extension to any polygon.

figure **8.3**

Finding the Interior Angle Sum of a Hexagon

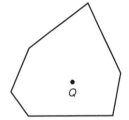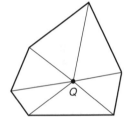

TRY THIS

Using similar reasoning as before, develop a formula to determine the interior measures of any n-gon.

Given a related task, students thinking at Level 0 may recognize a regular hexagon with a traditional orientation, so that one side is "at the bottom," that is, parallel to the bottom of the page of a text. They might not recognize a random hexagon with a non-traditional orientation. A student at Level 1 could identify any hexagon by counting the number of sides but would likely be confused by a hexagon with segments drawn from interior point Q to each vertex. In such a case a Level 1 student may see only a series of triangles and not a hexagon with interior segments. A student at Level 2 might measure the angles of various polygons and discern the pattern to the sum of interior angles. The reasonable conjecture from the pattern is that each additional side increases the angle sum by 180°, so the angle sum of a hexagon is 720°. The interior angle sum of additional polygons may be determined using the pattern to extend the table shown here.

SIDES	ANGLE SUM
3	180
4	360
5	540
6	(720)

The conjecture is based on a pattern of results from measuring angles and is not a proof of the angle sum for a hexagon. In order to verify the conjecture, it is necessary to provide

figure **8.4**

Geometry on a Sphere

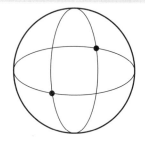

a logical argument or proof such as the preceding one. This level of thinking in geometry is typical for a high school geometry class. By the end of a typical high school geometry class the goal is for all students to be reasoning at Level 3.

Level 4: Rigor

Students reasoning at this level are thinking about geometry in different systems and developing the consequences of the limits and idiosyncrasies of those systems. For example, in the familiar Euclidean geometry, two lines meet at only one point. In spherical geometry (geometry on the surface of a sphere) this is not true. By definition all lines in spherical geometry must be great circles, circles on the surface of the sphere with the same diameter as the sphere itself (see Figure 8.4). Two circles or lines, such as a line through the North and South Poles and a line around the equator, will meet at two points!

Other systems of geometry such as hyperbolic, affine, and projective have their own sets of postulates and theorems that distinguish them from each other. This van Hiele level is generally found in graduate-level mathematics courses.

TRY THIS

Draw a triangle in spherical geometry whose angles total more than 180°.

The van Hieles found that all students had to begin thinking about geometry at Level 0 and progress through each subsequent level until they reached Level 3 in secondary school. Students can neither skip levels nor the related experiences required to build up geometric thinking appropriate for those levels. They also found that the levels were only remotely related to chronological age. A child who begins to reason at Level 0 will remain at that level without appropriate activities and experiences, both in and out of school, to move on to subsequent levels. Unlike some mathematical thinking such as conservation of area, moving from one level to the next is not automatic with physical age or maturity. Thus, a middle school mathematics class may have students who are thinking at several different van Hiele levels.

When there are students in a class who are at a lower than expected van Hiele level, it is necessary to help these students move to the appropriate level. This may mean providing different activities at the appropriate van Hiele level for them. Middle school students require a fewer number of experiences to move from one van Hiele level to the next than do elementary school students. For example, middle school students at van Hiele Level 0 require neither the number nor the duration of activities and explorations that a student at grade 3 would require to move to thinking at van Hiele Level 1. However, it is critical not to make the mistake of assuming that students can quickly move to the appropriate van Hiele level by means of a few activities. The van Hieles found that all students had to move through each successive level by means of sufficient experiences, regardless of age, although older students could do so somewhat more rapidly.

Because there are likely to be some students at several van Hiele levels in a typical middle school class, it is necessary to provide activities that will help students at lower levels move up to the appropriate level for their class. However, teachers can plan some activities that are based on upper van Hiele levels to stretch the geometry thinking of all students and strengthen the geometry understanding of students who are thinking at these higher van Hiele levels. At the middle school, students who are still thinking at lower van Hiele levels can, nevertheless, engage in activities that lead into and may be partly grounded in van Hiele Level 2.

An example of an activity that can challenge several levels of geometry thinking is an exploration of the properties of various quadrilaterals. Students could be directed to use rulers and protractors to determine the properties of side lengths, diagonal lengths, and angle measures of several parallelograms and rectangles. A student working at Level 0

Point Well Taken

"For middle grade students, attention must be focused on levels 0, 1, and 2 of the van Hiele model. If students are having trouble learning geometry, one might hypothesize according to this model that they are being taught at a higher level than they have attained. Moreover, two individuals (perhaps teacher and student, or student and textbook author) who reason at different levels cannot understand each other."

—Kloosterman & Gainey, 1993, p. 9

Point Well Taken

"The expanding logical capabilities of students in grades 5–8 allow them to draw inferences and make logical deductions from geometric problem situations."

—NCTM, 1989, p. 112

might create a chart of all the properties. Students at Level 1 could be expected to compare and contrast the properties of the two figures, using the properties to build descriptions of the two figures that might be used to identify and distinguish between them. Students at Level 2 might use those descriptions to build definitions of these figures. These students might also be expected to define one figure in terms of another, as for example, a rectangle in reference to a parallelogram and then explain why the definition suggests that a rectangle is a special parallelogram.

As middle school teachers strive to assist their students to move through the van Hiele levels to Level 2, it is important to keep in mind that students cannot fully function at a higher van Hiele level than their own thinking level. For example, for students thinking at Level 1, most class activities and tasks should be designed for Level 1 thinking. However, included with these Level 1 activities should be extensions that stretch students' thinking by requiring Level 2 thinking. In addition, interspersed in the Level 1 activities should be a few Level 2 activities. These Level 2 tasks make explicit what was implicit at Level 1. As students become comfortable and more accomplished with the Level 1 activities, they can engage more frequently with Level 2 tasks, until the focus of the class is more on Level 2 activities, with Level 1 activities and tasks interspersed among them.

By the end of middle school all students should be reasoning at van Hiele Level 2. Thus, they will be prepared for activities, problems, and explorations in high school geometry that will move them into van Hiele Level 3, Deduction. This does not mean that students working at lower van Hiele levels cannot engage in activities that promote Level 3 thinking. Young children learn how to play games like Clue and Battleship quite successfully. These games require deductive reasoning and younger children can manifest deduction in a variety of geometric settings. The difficulty occurs, for example, when a student is thinking at van Hiele Level 1 and *all* the class activities and explorations are geared for van Hiele Level 3. In such a situation the Level 1 thinker may become frustrated and resort to rote memorization. This student will be unable to accomplish the Level 3 tasks except through rote, algorithmic methods. The result is that there is a reduction of the Level 3 tasks to a Level 1 task, even if the task is successfully completed.

As students move through the various van Hiele levels, class activities and experiences should employ a wide array of manipulatives. The van Hieles found that a student who studies geometry without the benefit of manipulatives is working under a severe disadvantage. This is especially true for students who are thinking at the lower van Hiele levels. These students benefit from explorations with manipulatives to set a firm foundation on which they will build their geometry understandings. When students use manipulatives such as geoboards, polyhedron models, and framework shapes to represent various geometry relationships, these relationships are more easily understood and better remembered than by simply committing the given relationships to memory.

As described in Chapter 3, The Practice of Effective Instruction, these manipulatives help students identify various concepts and relationships and provide them a point of reference for understanding and recalling them. When students can represent geometric relationships with more than one manipulative, they are ready to move from the concrete stage of understanding to the ikonic stage. After representing a relationship with more than one manipulative, students could then be expected to describe or explain the relationship with diagrams, a verbal report, or a written summation. This stage can then be followed up with the symbolic stage, where students express the relationship with brevity of a symbolic statement, such as a formula or a concise statement of the relationship as in a postulate or theorem.

Research subsequent to the van Hieles' findings has helped to clarify some aspects of the van Hiele levels of geometry thinking. It is possible to be at different van Hiele levels for different concepts. A student may be at van Hiele Level 2 regarding polygons and at van Hiele Level 0 regarding symmetry due to an uneven background of beneficial and effective geometry experiences. Thus, students are continually developing their levels of geometry thinking according to the specific geometry topic they are studying.

AUTHOR'S **Recall**

I recall teaching grade 7 mathematics during my first teaching year with no geometry manipulatives in the entire school. The consensus was that all a mathematics teacher needed was chalk and a blackboard.

figure **8.5**

A Square Rotated 45°

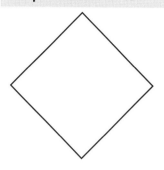

AUTHOR'S **Recall**

I remember working with grade 4 teachers at a large elementary school complex. Each wing of the school housed a separate school, and all of them fed into a common cafeteria, library, and gymnasium. To help students find their way back to their school from the common areas, each wing had its own color (red, green, blue, yellow) and a shape that was prominently displayed on doors, corridors, and floors. One of the shapes was a square and another was a diamond. The "diamond" was a square rotated 45°, demonstrating that even architects who command salaries of thousands of dollars may not recognize a square in a different orientation!

REACT | **REFLECT**

Recall some of your experiences with geometry activities in middle school and high school. Assign van Hiele levels to them.

MISCONCEPTION

Many middle school students (and adults) at Level 2 of geometry thinking can easily recognize a square, provide a reasonable definition of a square and list its properties, and compare it to a rectangle or rhombus. Yet they will identify the shape in Figure 8.5 as a diamond, not a square. Why?

What has happened is that the "diamond" is actually a square that has been rotated 45° so that, in the words of one middle school student, it is "standing on one of its angles." Many middle school students who have only seen squares oriented with sides horizontal and vertical will not recognize a square in a different orientation.

A similar difficulty exists for middle grades students who are examining right triangles. Middle grades students can usually identify the hypotenuse of a right triangle and can usually parrot the facts that the hypotenuse is opposite the right angle and is the longest side. However, many students will simply look for the "slanted side" and call that the hypotenuse. In Figure 8.6, triangles a–d all have a slanted hypotenuse, that is, a hypotenuse that is neither vertical nor horizontal. However, in triangle e the hypotenuse is not slanted. Students have difficulty with this figure because the orientation is unusual—it does not have the legs in horizontal and vertical orientation.

Both misconceptions may be remedied by displaying geometric figures in a variety of orientations and not in the common orientations as shown here. By showing quadrilaterals, triangles, and other figures in unusual orientations, students will recognize them when they see them in unexpected displays. Note that the failure to recognize figures in different orientations in this case is not a matter of being at a low van Hiele level but is rather a lack of experience with seeing them in uncommon orientations.

There are several tests used to indicate van Hiele thinking. You might administer one of these tests to your students at the start of the year to gauge the geometry thinking level of the class as a whole and also for individual students. Knowing the specific van Hiele level of students can help you to plan appropriate activities for them.

For more information about a test to determine van Hiele levels in students, go to ERIC Resume for ED372924 at www.eric.ed.gov.

TRY THIS

Predict your van Hiele level of geometry thinking. Then take the van Hiele test and compare your test result with your prediction. Are they the same? If not, why do you think your test result was different?

Classroom teachers can employ the van Hiele levels of geometry thinking to provide a framework for selecting appropriate tasks for middle school students. The tasks we describe in this chapter all relate to five major topics in geometry: spatial sense, symmetry, triangle relationships (Pythagorean Theorem), categorizing shapes (hierarchy of quadrilaterals), and similarity. Additional topics of angle measure, perimeter, area, and volume measures are considered in Chapter 9, Measurement: Behind the Units.

figure **8.6**

Right Triangles in Different Orientations

a   b   c   d   e

Spatial Sense

One of the most critical aspects of geometry thinking at any level is spatial sense. Without the ability to recognize figures, envision shapes in different positions, and form composite figures, a student would be unable to advance in geometry thinking. Spatial sense transcends all geometry topics and is an integral part of all of them.

Spatial sense is one of the major concepts that is included in the NCTM *Standards* for geometry:

- Specify locations and describe spatial relationships using coordinate geometry and other representational systems.
- Use visualization, spatial reasoning, and geometric modeling to solve problems.

Spatial sense has two distinct aspects: spatial visualization and spatial orientation. In spatial visualization the viewer remains in a fixed position and the figure changes positions or orientation with regard to the viewer, much like rotating a cube in your hand as you observe it. In spatial orientation the figure remains in one position and the viewer changes his or her viewing point and so sees the figure from different aspects, much like placing a cube on a desk and then walking around the desk while looking at the cube from different positions. Both aspects of spatial sense are critical to an understanding of many mathematics topics and to succeed in everyday tasks. It is a rare day when a child or an adult does not have to plan a walk from one place to another, whether from the bedroom to the kitchen, the classroom to the cafeteria, or the car to the office. Being able to visualize the walk before taking it is a distinct advantage.

Spatial sense is prized by all mathematics teachers, yet it is infrequently taught in school classrooms. There are several reasons for this: Spatial sense is difficult to quantify. The tasks that require spatial sense do not lend themselves to simple right or wrong responses, but rather to drawings, descriptions, and explanations. In a crowded curriculum spatial sense is frequently eliminated in favor of more concrete studies such as rational numbers or area relationships. Some teachers may have the erroneous view that spatial sense is an innate ability that develops long before school age and cannot be greatly enhanced by school activities. Finally, many may believe that spatial sense is developed by engaging in tasks that, while focusing on a different concept, require some spatial sense to complete, such as studying the properties of polyhedrons and other solids.

In point of fact, spatial sense is developed during preschool years by children who build with Legos, complete jigsaw puzzles, climb on or around a jungle gym, and play with miniature action figures along with many other play activities. Some children, however, do not engage in any spatial sense building activities and so enter school with a poorly defined spatial sense. For many children their spatial sense is never developed via classroom experiences for reasons suggested earlier. It is our stand that spatial sense requires explicit activities throughout the mathematics curriculum in order to be fully developed by every student. To that end we suggest some possible activities to help students develop their spatial sense.

In Two Dimensions

Students might be given a brief glimpse of a figure and then asked to sketch it. Students who can reproduce the figure shown in Figure 8.7 when they have only 1–2 seconds to view it have developed one aspect of their spatial sense. One or two seconds is not enough to memorize or duplicate every angle and segment length of this figure. Thus, students must gain a holistic view of the figure in order to reproduce it. To one middle school student this figure resembled a rectangle with a cutoff corner and a single diagonal. Another saw a building with a crooked roof

Point Well Taken

"Students' skills in visualizing and reasoning about spatial relationships are fundamental in geometry."

—NCTM, 2000, p. 237

Point Well Taken

"Spatial thinking develops unequally at school age even in students under identical teaching conditions."

—Yakimanskya, 1991, p. 25

figure **8.7**

Reflecting a Figure across Coordinate Axes

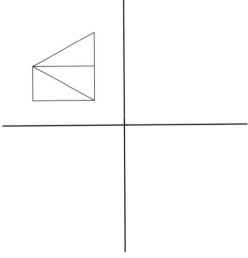

and a crossbeam. In both cases these students were able to visualize the figure as a whole and relate it to more familiar shapes.

Some students with a poorly developed spatial sense may need some remediation in the form of longer time to view the figure before drawing it. Some students may even need to draw the figure while they observe it. In both cases, these students will benefit from hearing how their peers were able to visualize the diagram in a holistic sense. As these students become more adept at drawing figures, their observation time may be gradually decreased.

The same images may be used with coordinate axes and transformations to develop another aspect of spatial sense. In this activity students draw the image of the figure after it is reflected across the *y*-axis. After students discuss their results, they might draw the image of the figure after it is reflected across the *x*-axis. (Teachers can prepare two transparencies of an image and coordinate axes as shown previously, then the top transparency may be physically flipped to clearly show the reflection across either of the axes.) For students to fully benefit from this activity, it must be repeated with different figures throughout the school year and not for a few days during a special "Spatial Sense" Week.

TRY THIS

Reflect the shape in Figure 8.7 across the *x*-axis and then across the *y*-axis. Is the result the same as reflecting the figure first across the *y*-axis and then across the *x*-axis? In other words, is reflection of figures across coordinate axes commutative?

An aspect of spatial sense that is particularly useful in a high school geometry class is the ability to see individual and composite figures in a single diagram. In Figure 8.8 there are a number of different triangles. How many can you see? (See Blackline Master 8.1, How Many Triangles?)

Many middle school students will see only the distinct triangles that are individually lettered *a, b, c, d, e, f, g, h*. Some will see other triangles, composite triangles that are formed by combining individual triangles, such as triangle *ab*. Other students will notice the symmetry in the figure and reason that the top half contains as many triangles as the bottom half and so will diminish the amount of searching they need to do to find all the triangles. The triangles in this figure are *a, b, c, d, e, f, g, h, i, j, ab, bc, cd, de, fg, gh hi, ij, bi, ch, abc, bcd, cde, fgh, ghi, hij, abcd, bcde, fhgi, ghij, abji, cdhg, cdefgh, abcde,* and *fghij*. There are 35 triangles in all.

For students with developing spatial sense this task can be a daunting challenge. They will require some experiences with simple images, such as one the ones shown in Figure 8.9.

The following Internet sites can help students develop their spatial sense in two dimensions:

Activity 6.4.1 at http://standards.nctm.org
www.learner.org/teacherslab/math/geometry/shape/quilts/index.html
www.bbc.co.uk/education/mathsfile/shockwave/games/bathroom.html
Geometry 6–8 at http://nlvm.usu.edu/en/nav/vlibrary.html

figure **8.8**

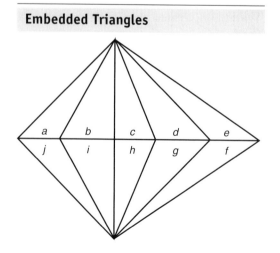

Embedded Triangles

figure **8.9**

Embedded Figures

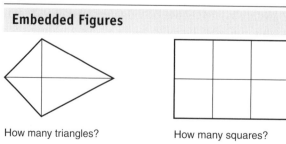

How many triangles?   How many squares?

TRY THIS

Go to one of the sites listed and try one of the activities. How might this activity help students improve their spatial sense?

Did You **Know**?

The term *net* was first used in a mathematical sense by German artist Albrecht Dürer (1465–1532). Dürer was interested in the mathematics of the newly emerging aspect of perspective in art. Dürer thought the geometry nets resembled fishing nets.

In Three Dimensions

Spatial sense also involves three-dimensional figures. An activity involving nets can help students in several areas of spatial sense. The sketch in Figure 8.10 shows the net of a cube. A net is a two-dimensional figure that can be folded up to form a three-dimensional figure.

For any net, each polygon must share at least one full side with another shape. No partial sharing of sides is permitted (see Figure 8.11).

Students might work with a manipulative such as Geofix shapes or 1-inch grid paper to find all the nets of a cube. Students verify their nets by folding up the Geofix squares or drawing their nets onto grid paper, cutting out the nets, and then folding them up to make a cube. When students find a net, they record it on graph or grid paper. As students work to find the different possibilities it is beneficial to encourage them to make an organized search.

The student who simply combines squares with no plan for searching for all of the nets will likely not find all of them. Middle school students will be encouraged to make an organized search if they are not told the number of possible nets. Instead, they might be required to explain how they are convinced they have found all possibilities, beyond simply claiming "There aren't any more." One way middle school students can make an

figure **8.10**

Net of a Cube

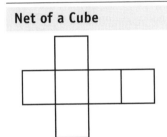

figure **8.11**

Correct and Incorrect Nets

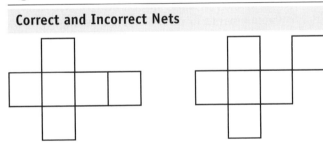

Geofix shapes
Used by permission of Didax, Inc.

<figure>figure **8.12**

Possible Net of a Cube

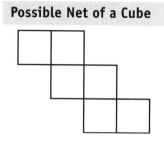</figure>

organized search is to form all the possible nets with six squares in a row (0), five squares in a row (0), four squares in a row (6), and so forth. After students have found all the nets, they might be challenged to try to fold up each net to form a cube in their mind, using their Geofix shapes to help visualize folding up each two-dimensional net to form a three-dimensional cube. This is especially important for those students who have not developed their spatial sense as well as their classmates have.

TRY THIS

Examine Figure 8.12. Is this the net of a cube?

Another spatial sense aspect of this activity is found in the possible solutions students draw. The examples in Figure 8.13 show several versions of the same net in different orientations. It is important for students to rotate and/or reflect potential nets to determine if they are duplicates. The second net is a reflection of the first net. The third net is a reflection and subsequent rotation of the first net. All three are different orientations of the same net.

What can be done to help students who form the same net in different orientations as shown here and think the nets are different? These students can be encouraged to build one of the nets and then perform the appropriate transformation, either a reflection or a rotation, to produce the other orientations. Thus, they will be able to clearly discern how the nets they thought were different are actually identical.

The website www.peda.com/poly allows students to fold and unfold nets for many different polyhedrons.

<figure>figure **8.13**

Nets with Geofix Shapes

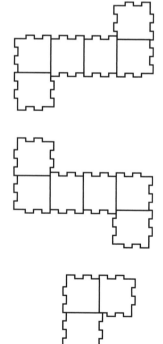</figure>

MISCONCEPTION

Many middle school students consider the preceding examples of a single net to be three separate and distinct nets. One reason for this common misconception may be found in their use of arrays to develop whole number multiplication.

The two arrays in Figure 8.14 represent two different multiplication facts: 3×2 and 2×3. Although the two multiplication facts are essentially equivalent (by the commutative property), they are considered distinct facts by younger children. In addition, the two arrays are also considered distinct arrays. In a geometric context, of course, the two arrays are congruent. One array is a rotation of the other. Similarly, when students have the experience of physically rotating or reflecting the same figure into different orientations, they establish that different orientations do not result in different geometric figures.

In the nets activity students need to visualize turning a two-dimensional net into a three-dimensional cube. This ability to move from two to three dimensions is a hallmark of spatial sense. The following activity asks students to picture and then sketch a three-dimensional shape as a two-dimensional figure.

<figure>figure **8.14**

Rectangular Arrays

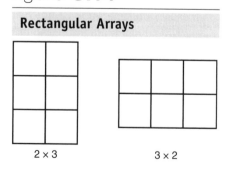

2 × 3   3 × 2</figure>

For this activity students need a cube such as one pictured in Figure 8.15. Students might fill the cube to about $\frac{1}{3}$ its volume with water and then set the cube on a horizontal surface such as a table or desk. The surface of the water will be in the shape of a square, the same shape as the cross section of the cube when cut by a plane parallel to the bases of the cube.

Students can then tilt the cube to various orientations to find other cross sections represented by the surface of the water. Stu-

View Thru' Shapes

Used by Permission of
Classroom Products, Inc.,
www.classroomprdcts.com.

figure **8.15**

Cross Section of a Cube

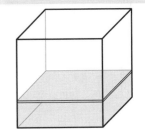

dents might be asked to make a list of cross sections, along with accompanying sketches on templates of cubes, or draw the complete sketches for each of the cross sections, including the cube. (See Blackline Master 8.2, Cross Sections of a Cube.)

Two sites that contain interactive activities with cross sections are

www.learner.org/teacherslab/math/geometry/space/shadows/index.html
Geometry 6-8 at http://nlvm.usu.edu/en/nav/vlibrary.html

TRY THIS

Can you see how to make a hexagonal-shaped cross section of a cube? Make a drawing to show the hexagonal cross section.

One final spatial sense activity involves interpreting a two-dimensional drawing as a three-dimensional figure. In this case the spatial sense being developed is the ability to visualize the three-dimensional object that is represented by a drawing. Teachers expect students to interpret two-dimensional images as three-dimensional objects, frequently using photographs, sketches, and diagrams to represent real-life objects. Many times middle school students have not had the appropriate experiences to be able to readily make such interpretations. Activities such as these will help all students develop this aspect of spatial sense.

In Figure 8.16 three views of a block figure are offered. The task for students is to build the block figure based on the three views.

In this case there is a single block figure that matches the given views. In the student activity sheet with several of these problems (see Blackline Master 8.3), the last problem is ambiguous. There is more than one distinct possibility given the three views. Such an outcome will help students expand their spatial sense even further to accommodate more than their initial solutions to the views.

figure **8.16**

Views of a Block Figure

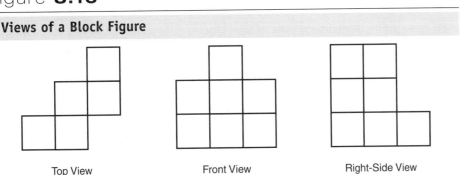

Top View   Front View   Right-Side View

REACT | **REFLECT**

Give your response to a parent who claims that "you're either born with spatial sense, or you're not."

Texas Instruments
TI-73 Calculator

Courtesy of Texas
Instruments.

TRY THIS

What is the minimum number of cubes required to build the block structure in Figure 8.16?

There are several websites that ask students to build structures, count blocks in existing structures, and recognize different orientations for the same structure.

www.learner.org/teacherslab/math/geometry/space/plotplan/index.html
www.fi.uu.nl/rekenweb/en

Technology

New and emerging technologies have a multitude of uses in the middle school mathematics classroom. Two outstanding dynamic geometry software programs are Cabri Geometry and The Geometer's Sketchpad. Both software programs allow for interactive explorations of relationships that would be difficult to explore by other means. Some calculators are designed to display geometry relationships. The calculator pictured here enables students to draw and analyze characteristics of two- and three-dimensional shapes.

Consider the problem shown here:

What is true about the three altitudes of a triangle?

Students can use dynamic software to construct the altitudes to the sides of a triangle. The altitudes will share a single point (i.e., they are concurrent). Students can now distort the triangle to examine how the location of the point changes as different triangles are represented. The concurrent point is inside all acute triangles and outside all obtuse triangles. Other concurrent points of triangles may be explored with dynamic software, including medians, perpendicular bisectors of the sides, and angle bisectors.

The alternative to exploring this problem with software is for students in small groups to construct or paper fold all three altitudes in different triangles, and then look for some patterns to their group results beside the fact that the altitudes meet at a single point. The dynamic software enables students to observe the point's location in a much shorter time.

After students have performed explorations such as those discussed here, another problem students might explore using dynamic geometry software is the following:

A telephone company is setting up telephone poles so it can run telephone lines to each house in a new housing development. The location of the telephone pole should

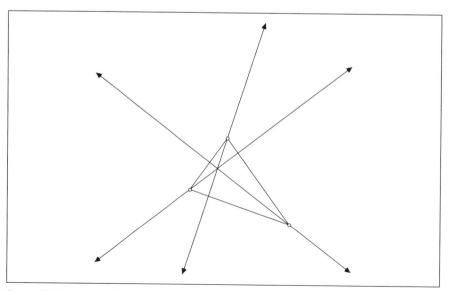

Source: The Geometer's Sketchpad. Used by permission of Key Curriculum Press, 1150 65th Street, Emeryville, CA 94608, 1-800-995-MATH, www.keypress.com/sketchpad.

be at the point (*C*) that the total length of line to the two houses from the telephone pole (*AC* + *BC*) is a minimum. Where on the edge of the road should the company locate the telephone pole?

Students can create a diagram similar to Figure 8.17 with the software, and then they can slide point *C* along line *t* to find the minimum sum of the two segment lengths (*AC* + *BC*). Many students are surprised that point *C* is not "in the middle" of line *t*. Once students locate the point of minimum distance in one diagram, they are ready to find point *C* in additional diagrams with point *A* and point *B* in different locations. After locating point *C* in several diagrams, they are ready to explore how the location of point *C* is related to the locations of point *A* and point *B*.

TRY THIS

Trace the preceding diagram. Find point *Q*, the reflection point of point *A*. Explain why the minimum distance point (point *C*) is where $\overline{QB}$ intersects line *t*.

PROCESS STANDARDS

Communication

Communication is a critical part of the study of mathematics. The most brilliant mathematicians must be able to communicate their findings. If they are unable to do so, their discoveries benefit no one and are not remembered. Middle school students must have ample opportunities to communicate, explain, conjecture, and discuss their geometry. As they do so, they clarify their own thinking processes and illuminate geometry for others. Selecting problems and tasks that enable students to talk about mathematics is a key part of the communication process for students.

Students might examine another of the concurrent points of a triangle by first examining several triangles and then relating their findings. For example, students could cut out various types of triangles they have drawn on wax paper, patty paper (delicatessen sandwich paper), or origami paper. They can then fold the perpendicular bisectors of all three sides of the triangles (see Figure 8.18). Students can communicate their findings to their group and then from the group to the entire class.

One finding will be obvious to all students—the crease lines all meet at a single point, so they are concurrent. Further investigation about this concurrent point will reveal that the point is inside the triangle if the triangle is acute and outside the triangle when the triangle is obtuse. Students might conjecture about the location of the concurrent point (called the circumcenter) for a right triangle. Some additional paper folding will reveal that the point lies on the edge of the triangle, on the midpoint of the hypotenuse. As an alternative, students could engage in the same exploration using dynamic geometry software.

Asking students to explore and then relate their findings to their class can empower students to discover and build their own understanding of mathematics. Such discovery tasks are engaging and provide students the freedom and responsibility to develop mathematical thinking for themselves.

TRY THIS

Paper-fold the three angle bisectors of several different triangles. What is your conjecture?

One aspect of spatial sense that many students begin to develop even before they study it in middle school is line symmetry. In middle school, students study

figure **8.17**

Telephone Pole Problem

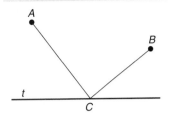

Did You **Know**?

Greek mathematician Heron (c. 65–c. 125) was the first to propose this minimum-distance problem. He is also known for using steam engines to drive carriages, animate water fountains, and power machines that dispensed food and drink.

REACT REFLECT

Students can explore the concurrent point of the three altitudes of a triangle using a straightedge and compass, by paper folding, and with technology. If you could use only one of these methods to explore the altitudes of a triangle, which would you prefer? Why?

figure **8.18**

Perpendicular Bisectors of a Triangle

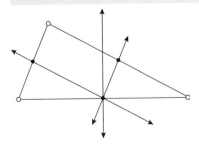

line, reflection, and rotation symmetry. We now discuss some aspects of symmetry in the middle school curriculum.

Symmetry

Line Symmetry

figure **8.19**

Line Symmetry in an Isosceles Trapezoid

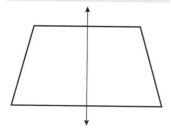

Most students have a sense of symmetry from a young age. Buildings, furniture, commercial logos, and their own faces exemplify symmetry for students, and they build a sense of symmetry as they develop their spatial sense. In earlier grades students usually learn the "paper-fold" test for determining whether a figure displays symmetry. The paper-fold test stipulates that if a figure can be folded onto itself along a line, then that figure has line symmetry. The isosceles trapezoid in Figure 8.19 can be folded onto itself along line t, so line t is the line of symmetry and the isosceles trapezoid is a figure with line symmetry. In terms of a transformation, the figure on one side of the symmetry line can be reflected onto the figure on the other side of the symmetry line. The symmetry line also divides the isosceles trapezoid into two congruent figures.

MISCONCEPTION

Many students enter middle school with the mistaken idea that if a line divides a figure into two congruent parts, then the line must be a line of symmetry. It is true that a necessary condition of a line of symmetry is that it divides a figure into two congruent parts. However, that condition alone is not sufficient to identify a line of symmetry. Consider the parallelogram in Figure 8.20.

The diagonal clearly divides the parallelogram into two identical triangles, but the diagonal is not a line of symmetry. The paper-fold test is not true for the diagonal. In fact, there are no lines of symmetry in this parallelogram.

To help students avoid this misconception, it is beneficial to include in their study of symmetry many examples of figures with lines that divide figures into congruent parts, yet are not lines of symmetry such as diagonals of parallelograms and rectangles.

TRY THIS

How many lines of symmetry does a regular octagon have?

The parallelogram does have rotational symmetry about the point of intersection of its two diagonals. If the parallelogram is rotated 180° it will rotate unto itself. During a

The MIRA reveals line symmetry
by showing reflections.

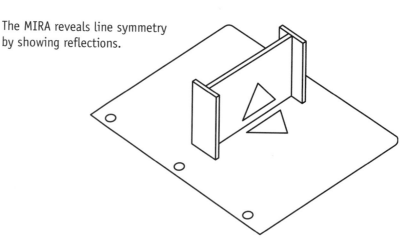

figure **8.20**

Examining a Parallelogram for Line Symmetry

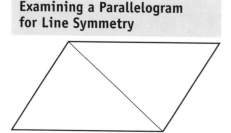

full turn of 360° the parallelogram will rotate unto itself twice. This is called two-fold rotational symmetry.

TRY THIS

What is the rotational symmetry of an equilateral triangle? A regular hexagon?

Although the paper-fold test is an effective means for determining line symmetry, it is not practical. In most instances, it is not possible to cut out a figure and fold it onto itself to check for line symmetry. Some middle school students have a well-developed spatial sense and can imagine the results of folding along a line to check for symmetry, but many students need another way to determine symmetry.

After having appropriate experiences with lines of symmetry in elementary school, middle school students are ready to fully understand line symmetry and to use its definition to verify lines of symmetry in figures. When a figure has line symmetry, every point in the figure on one side of the symmetry line has a matching or corresponding point on the opposite side of the symmetry line. Figure 8.21 shows several pairs of corresponding points. By the definition of a symmetry line, each point (A) and its matching point (A') are the same distance from the symmetry line l. As shown here, $\overline{AX} = \overline{XA}'$

figure **8.21**

Line Symmetry in the Plane

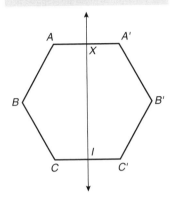

TRY THIS

Trace Figure 8.21 and draw in $\overline{BB}'$ and $\overline{CC}'$. How is symmetry line l related to each of these two segments?

The relationship of corresponding points in a figure with line symmetry can be represented on a coordinate grid. In Figure 8.22, the y-axis is a line of symmetry for rectangle $ABCD$. Points A and B are corresponding points for the line of symmetry. Students can use the coordinates to verify that both points are the same distance from the symmetry line.

Students can use the relationship of corresponding points to locate a line of symmetry in a figure. Where is the horizontal line of symmetry for rectangle $ABDC$ in Figure 8.23? The symmetry line has to be located so it is equidistant from points A and C and also points B and D. The line equidistant between the points must pass through coordinates that are midway between the points. In this figure the line of symmetry is the line $x = 6$.

Students might first find the symmetry line by locating it with the help of grid lines on coordinate axes, essentially "eyeballing" where it is located. Once students can locate a symmetry line this way, they can be encouraged to look for patterns in the coordinates of two points on each side of the line and the equation of the symmetry line itself. Students will discover that the symmetry line passes through the "average" of the coordinates of the two points.

figure **8.22**

Line Symmetry in the Coordinate Plane

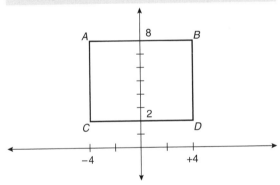

figure **8.23**

Rectangle in the Coordinate Plane

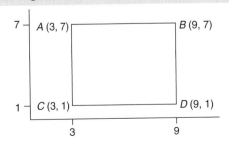

TRY THIS

Find the missing coordinates for point R in rectangle $PQRS$ if the symmetry line is the line $y = 4$. $P(-4,8)$, $Q(4,8)$.

As students progress through middle school, they develop the relationships of points and lines of symmetry on a grid to help them to determine line and rotational symmetry and to apply symmetry to various situations.

MATH IN THE MEDIA

Beauty is in the eye of the beholder, or is it? Do we have a natural sense of beauty or is it learned? Researchers explored this question with infants younger than six months. In a series of experiments infants were shown photographs of human faces with varying degrees of symmetry. The infants stared longer at those faces they found appealing and averted their sight from those they did not. Invariably the infants found the faces that showed the greatest degree of symmetry to be the most appealing. They quickly changed their sight when shown faces with low degrees of symmetry. The conclusion? A sense of symmetry seems to be hardwired into the human brain. Infants too young to appreciate symmetry because of social convention were fixated on symmetric faces. And whose face was the most beautiful of them all? Actress Sharon Stone, the epitome of symmetry.

Three-Dimensional Symmetry

figure **8.24**

Symmetry Plane in a Cube

Another aspect of symmetry students may consider in middle school is plane symmetry with three-dimensional figures. A plane of symmetry divides a three-dimensional figure into two identical parts so that each point on one-half of the figure has a corresponding point on the other half of the figure. Similar to line symmetry, the two corresponding points are equidistant from the plane of symmetry and the symmetry plane is the perpendicular bisector of the segment joining the two points. Unlike line symmetry, there is no paper-fold test that verifies plane symmetry. In the cube in Figure 8.24 the horizontal plane is a symmetry plane. Point A and point C are corresponding points that are equidistant from the plane. The plane of symmetry is perpendicular to and bisects $\overline{AC}$.

When middle school students examine the planes of symmetry in three-dimensional figures, they benefit from using models of the figures. Styrofoam or clay models can be sliced with taut string to represent a symmetry plane. Students are then able to see a physical representation of the effects of a symmetry plane. Eventually students do not need models to envision symmetry lines and planes and can draw and work with lines and planes.

TRY THIS

Make sketches to show all nine symmetry planes in a cube.

REACT | REFLECT

What is your personal preference for advertising logos? Do you prefer a logo with line and/or rotational symmetry, such as the Mercedes Benz logo, or do you find a logo with no symmetry more appealing? Why?

Symmetry is strongly related to spatial sense. Some middle school students will be able to picture lines and planes of symmetry immediately. Many other students, especially those needing remediation, will require sufficient experiences with sketches of two-dimensional figures and models of three-dimensional figures before they are able to work easily with symmetry relationships. With ample opportunities to explore relationships, as described here, middle school students can fully understand symmetry in geometric figures and can recognize line and rotational symmetry in advertising logo images.

These sites are representative of interactive Internet sites that focus on symmetry.

www.uu.fi.nl/rekenweb/en (See Mirror)
www.learner.org/teacherslab/math/geometry/shape/index.html

NCTM

PROCESS STANDARDS

Representation

Middle school students will benefit from seeing and employing multiple representations of concepts and solutions to problems. When students are able to envision different representations for a single concept, they are able to select the representation that resonates with them and employ it effectively. They are also able to understand different representations that others use to depict a relationship or problem solution.

The solution to the following problem is an example of using multiple representations.

The sides of a rectangle are in a 2:3 ratio. The area of the rectangle is 600 square feet. What are the side lengths of the rectangle?

The solution to the problem may be represented several ways. One student may use a table of values to determine the answer.

BASE LENGTH	HEIGHT	AREA
2	3	6
4	6	24
10	15	150
20	30	600

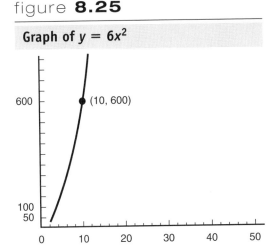

figure **8.25**

Graph of $y = 6x^2$

Another student might employ equations to solve the problem.

side length $= 2x$, height $= 3x$
$$(2x)(3x) = 600$$
$$6x^2 = 600$$
$$x^2 = 100$$
$$x = 10$$
$$2x = 20 \qquad 3x = 30$$

Another student might represent the problem graphically. (See Figure 8.25.)

Although these representations are quite varied, each one effectively solves the problem and shows understanding at the ikonic or symbolic level (see Bruner's understanding scheme in Chapter 3, The Practice of Effective Instruction). Middle school students benefit from having the opportunity to work with different representations such as these and will select the appropriate representation for concepts and problem solutions according to the specific task at hand. Research suggests that their selection will be made on the basis of what makes the most sense to them at that time and for that problem. Consequently, opportunities to share and discuss the characteristics of the different approaches are advantageous for all students. It is during these discussions that students can observe other solution strategies and can be encouraged to move from ikonic representations and solutions to symbolic ones.

The Pythagorean Theorem

The Pythagorean Theorem is the most famous theorem in mathematics. Even people who don't know anything about the Pythagorean Theorem have at least heard of it. Middle school is the time to introduce the Pythagorean Theorem to students. Early explorations with the Pythagorean Theorem will prepare students for understanding the theorem and all of its implications in later grades, including formal proofs of the theorem.

Generally middle school students will accept the relationships presented by the theorem and can use it in appropriate problems without needing a formal proof to justify its use. We suggest that some supporting explorations accompany the use of the theorem. The activities that follow, Black Line Masters, and Internet sites cited later will all enable students who are thinking at van Hiele levels below Level 3 to gather supporting evidence for the theorem.

The Pythagorean Theorem describes the relationships between the side lengths of any right triangle. In any right triangle the sum of the squares of the two side lengths is equal to the square of the length of the hypotenuse. Thus, in the right triangle shown in Figure 8.26 the lengths of the sides are always in the following relationship: The sum of

Did You **Know**?

There are literally hundreds of proofs of the Pythagorean Theorem, including proofs by Leonardo da Vinci, Isaac Newton, Galileo, and U.S. President James Garfield.

Did You **Know**?

Pythagoras (c. 570 B.C.E.–c. 500 B.C.E.) is a legendary figure among ancient Greek mathematicians. Pythagoras and his followers worshipped number instead of the panoply of gods as was the norm. Pythagoras is also credited with inventing our musical scale of eight notes. Some historians claim he won a gold medal in Olympic boxing.

figure **8.26**

Right Triangle

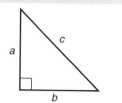

Point Well Taken

"At this level (grades 5–8) geometry should focus on investigating and using geometric ideas and relationships rather than on memorizing definitions and formulas."
—*NCTM, 1989, p. 112*

figure **8.27**

The Pythagorean Theorem

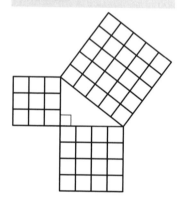

figure **8.28**

Proof of the Pythagorean Theorem by Dissection

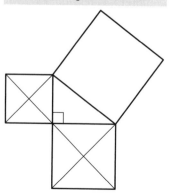

the squares of the lengths of the legs is equal to the square of the length of the hypotenuse. In terms of Figure 8.26, the Pythagorean Theorem may be expressed symbolically in the familiar form of $a^2 + b^2 = c^2$.

For example, if the length of side a is 5 and the length of side b is 12, then the length of side c is determined by the Pythagorean Theorem, as shown here.

$$a^2 + b^2 = c^2$$
$$5^2 + 12^2 = c^2$$
$$25 + 144 = c^2$$
$$169 = c^2$$
$$\sqrt{169} = c^2$$
$$13 = c$$

Not all side lengths of right triangles are whole numbers as, for example, a right triangle with legs 5 and 7. In this case

$$a^2 + b^2 = c^2$$
$$25 + 49 = c^2$$
$$74 = c^2$$
$$\sqrt{74} = c$$

TRY THIS

In the movie *The Wizard of Oz* the scarecrow recites the following to demonstrate how brilliant his new brain has made him: "The sum of the square roots of any two sides in an isosceles triangle is equal to the square root of the remaining side." What is the scarecrow's mistake?

It is quite possible for students to simply memorize the Pythagorean Theorem and then apply it to any number of skill and word problems. We suggest providing students with exploratory experiences for them to build a basic understanding of the Pythagorean Theorem, such as Blackline Masters 8.4–8.8, before expecting students to solve either skill or application problems.

In the diagram in Figure 8.27, a square has been drawn on each side of the right triangle. The sum of the areas of the two smaller squares is equal to the area of the largest square. In Figure 8.27 students can count or compute the areas of the squares to verify the Pythagorean Theorem. This activity may be repeated with other right triangles with whole numbers for their side lengths.

Triangles with whole numbers for side lengths may also be used to help students understand the Pythagorean Theorem. In addition to computing the areas of squares on each side of a right triangle, the diagrams in Figure 8.28 offer students the opportunity to cut up the two smaller squares and verify they are equal in area to the largest square. In these diagrams students can cut and paste the composite pieces of the smaller squares of side lengths a and b (i.e., they represent an a-square and a b-square, with area of $a \times a$ and $b \times b$ or a^2 and b^2) into the large c-square. Students can show by several cases of dissections and rearranging that $a^2 + b^2 = c^2$. (See Blackline Masters 8.5–8.9, Pythagorean Puzzle 1–5.)

There are also several Internet sites where students can manipulate various geometric figures to support or prove the Pythagorean Theorem.

www.albertaonline.ab.ca/resources/Mathapplets.htm
www.ies.co.jp/math/products/geo2/menu.html
www.mathsnet.net

TRY THIS

The shortest proof of the Pythagorean Theorem is in Figure 8.29. Can you see how to support the Pythagorean Theorem using the diagram? The Indian mathematician Bhaskara (c. 1100) had the areas of the composite shapes in mind when he developed this "obvious" proof. Compute the areas of the smaller square and the four right triangles. Show how the area sum of the small square and the four right triangles is equal to the area of the large square ($c \times c = c^2$).

When students first compute side lengths using the Pythagorean Theorem, it can be beneficial to use Pythagorean Triples. Pythagorean Triples are side lengths of a right triangle that are whole numbers. There are an infinite number of Pythagorean Triples, including 3-4-5 ($3^2 + 4^2 = 5^2$) and 5-12-13 ($5^2 + 12^2 = 13^2$) and their multiples. (See Figure 8.30.)

Students enjoy generating Pythagorean Triples and then challenging classmates to solve for one of the side lengths of their Pythagorean Triple triangle. In addition, students strengthen the connections between geometry and algebra when they are able to verify Plato's formula or generate Pythagorean Triples.

Right triangle problems involving irrational numbers create the perfect opportunity for students to use a calculator. (See Chapter 6, Making Sense of Number and Operations, for a discussion of irrational numbers.)

ASSESSMENT TIP

The following is an attempt to find the value of c in Figure 8.31. What is the common error shown?

$$a^2 + b^2 = c^2, \quad 6^2 + 10^2 = c^2, \quad 36 + 100 = c^2, \quad 136 = c^2, \quad c = \sqrt{136}$$

TRY THIS

The diagonal length of a square or rectangle can be determined with the Pythagorean Theorem. The diagonal length in a rectangular solid can be found using an extension of the Pythagorean Theorem. If the dimensions of a rectangular solid are width = 6, length = 8, and height = 4, find the diagonal length.

As with any mathematics topic, students should have many experiences solving Pythagorean Theorem problems in context. Here are two examples of problems in context that students can solve using the Pythagorean Theorem.

Kit is tying to get from one corner of a garden to the opposite corner. She decides to take a path on the diagonal instead of walking along the perimeter. The dimensions of the garden are 60 feet × 80 feet. How much shorter is Kit's diagonal path compared to her perimeter path?

Robin has a 10-foot-long ladder. He leans it against a wall so that the bottom of the ladder is 2 feet from the base of the wall. How far up the wall will the top of the ladder reach?

figure **8.29**

Bhaskara's Proof of the Pythagorean Theorem

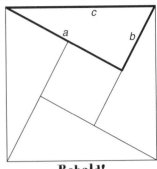

Behold!

Did You **Know**?

One formula for generating Pythagorean Triples was discovered by Greek philosopher Plato. For any integers $m < n$, the integer side lengths of a right triangle are: $n^2 - m^2$, $2mn$, and $n^2 + m^2$.

figure **8.30**

Pythagorean Triples

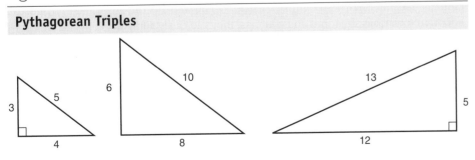

figure **8.31**

Right Triangle

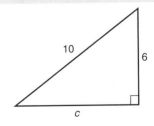

REACT | REFLECT

Explore one of the Internet sites listed, and then write a problem using the Pythagorean Theorem that would engage a typical seventh-grade student.

There are many resources that contain such context problems. Among the Internet sites that contain context problems for the Pythagorean Theorem are

www.stfx.ca/special/mathproblems/welcome.html
www.wits.ac.za/ssproule/pow.htm
http://mathforum.org/geopow/solutions

PROCESS STANDARDS

Connections

The Pythagorean Theorem is useful for forging powerful connections between geometry and algebra. For example, the distance formula in coordinate geometry is an application of the Pythagorean Theorem. Students who understand the Pythagorean Theorem will have a firm foundation for learning the distance formula in coordinate geometry.

In Figure 8.32 the length of $\overline{AB}$ may be found by drawing in $\triangle ABC$ so that $\overline{AB}$ is the hypotenuse. According to the Pythagorean Theorem, $BC^2 + AC^2 = AB^2$, $BC = x_2 - x_1$, $AC = y_2 - y_1$. Thus, $(x_1 - x_2)^2 + (y_1 - y_2)^2 = AB^2$, or

$$AB = \sqrt{(x_1 - x_2)^2 + (y_1 - y_2)^2}$$

The Pythagorean Theorem can also be employed to help students explore how to simplify radical expressions. Students familiar with the Pythagorean Theorem can use Figure 8.33 to compute the length of $\overline{AB}$ in triangle ABC to equal to $\sqrt{2}$. Students can easily see that since $\overline{AF}$ is composed of four segments each the length of $\overline{AB}$, then $AF = 4\sqrt{2}$. However, by using right triangle AFQ, $AF = \sqrt{32}$. Thus, $4\sqrt{2} = \sqrt{32}$. Students can initially verify these two expressions are equivalent by entering both into a calculator.

Similarly, $AC = 2\sqrt{2} = \sqrt{8}$, and $AD = 3\sqrt{2} = \sqrt{16}$. In small groups students can examine how $\sqrt{32} = 4\sqrt{2}$, $\sqrt{18} = 3\sqrt{2}$, and $\sqrt{8} = 2\sqrt{2}$. Students can then test their simplification method by simplifying expressions such as $\sqrt{75}$, $\sqrt{48}$, and $\sqrt{120}$. Students can explore this same relationship using the geoboard screen on a TI-73 calculator.

An interesting extension of the Pythagorean Theorem for middle school students is the converse of the Theorem. That is, if the three side lengths of a triangle do fit the Pythagorean Theorem, then the triangle is a right triangle. For example, a 3-4-5 triangle has to be a right triangle because the three side lengths fit the equation for a right triangle that the Pythagorean Theorem stipulates. Conversely, a triangle with side lengths 3-4-6 is not a right triangle because its side lengths do not fit the equation.

figure **8.32**

The Distance Formula in a Right Triangle

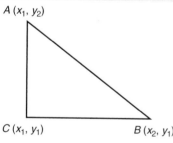

figure **8.33**

Irrational Segment Lengths on a Geoboard

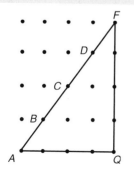

$a^2 + b^2 = c^2$	$a^2 + b^2 = c^2$
$3^2 + 4^2 = 5^2$	$3^2 + 4^2 = 6^2$
$9 + 16 = 25$	$9 + 16 < 36$

Converse of the Pythagorean Theorem

This relationship is fairly straightforward, and once students can apply the Pythagorean Theorem to various situations and contexts, they can easily apply the converse. It can be beneficial for students to explore the converse by examining different triangles, such as the three triangles shown in Figure 8.34. After a few explorations, students will be able to use the converse to determine if a triangle is acute, right, or obtuse.

In triangle a the square of the length of the hypotenuse is less than the sum of the squares of the lengths of the two legs ($6^2 + 9^2 > 9^2$). In brief, the hypotenuse is not long enough to form a right triangle with the two legs. As the diagram shows, the two legs must form an acute angle to meet the two ends of the hypotenuse. Triangle b shows a right

figure **8.34**

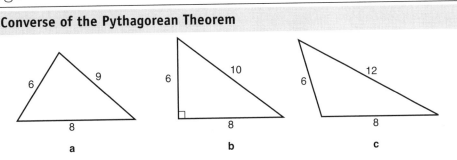

Converse of the Pythagorean Theorem

triangle ($6^2 + 8^2 = 10^2$). In triangle c the square of the length of the hypotenuse is larger than the sum of the squares of the lengths of the two legs ($6^2 + 8^2 < 12^2$). Thus, the two legs must form an obtuse angle in order to meet the ends of the hypotenuse. Students might try to form various triangles using lengths of straws or coffee stirrers cut to whole numbers of inches. They will be able to represent the three possible situations shown here and clarify how to determine if a triangle is acute, right, or obtuse by using the converse of the Pythagorean Theorem.

Hierarchy of Quadrilaterals

By the middle grades students should have a working knowledge of the properties of geometric figures, especially quadrilaterals. Middle grades students are now ready to compare properties among and between quadrilaterals (and other figures) in a way the van Hieles described for van Hiele Level 2: Abstraction. Students can now consider whether a rectangle is always a square or whether a square is always a rectangle.

To begin this level of study of quadrilaterals, it can help to have students gather data from a number of quadrilaterals. Students might use rulers and protractors to gather the data displayed in Table 8.1 from several cardboard shapes of these quadrilaterals.

Students will notice from Table 8.1 that a square has all the properties listed, whereas all the other quadrilaterals have only some or none of the listed properties. Students may be encouraged to use these properties to define figures, as for example, a parallelogram is a quadrilateral with two pairs of opposite sides parallel or a parallelogram is a quadrilateral with two pairs of opposite sides congruent. Either of these will suffice as a definition for a parallelogram, although the generally accepted definition is related to its name,

table **8.1** **Properties of Quadrilaterals**

QUADRILATERAL	OPPOSITE SIDES EQUAL IN LENGTH	4 EQUAL SIDES	RIGHT ANGLES (2 PAIRS)	PARALLEL SIDES (2 PAIRS)	CONGRUENT DIAGONALS	PERPENDICULAR DIAGONALS
Parallelogram	y	n	n	y	n	n
Rectangle	y	n	y	y	y	n
Rhombus	y	y	n	y	n	y
Square	y	y	y	y	y	y
Kite	n	n	n	n	n	y
Trapezoid	n	n	n	n	n	n
Isosceles trapezoid	n	n	n	n	y	n

Did You **Know**?

In 1817 Charles O'Hara built the Trapezium House in Petersburg, Virginia. Legend has it that the house has neither parallel walls nor right angles because O'Hara was told by his West Indian slave that such a house could not harbor ghosts and spirits.

and so opposite pairs of parallel sides is the universally accepted definition. If the property of parallel sides is the determining (and only) property used to identify a parallelogram, students might be challenged to determine what other shapes are properly termed *parallelograms* according to their data table. In the table rectangles, rhombuses, and squares all have two pairs of parallel sides, and so all of them should be considered parallelograms.

MISCONCEPTION

Many students understand squares and rectangles to be separate and distinct shapes with some common properties. They do not perceive the square as a special rectangle, nor do they see either shape as a parallelogram. Furthermore, some students wonder how different shapes (such as rhombus and rectangle) can belong to the same category (parallelograms).

One way students begin to clarify the relationships between quadrilaterals is to first consider all of them to be parallelograms, because they all have two pairs of parallel sides. Students can then refine the relationships between these quadrilaterals by considering rectangles, rhombuses, and squares to be special parallelograms, parallelograms with special or additional properties. For example, a rhombus is a parallelogram with all sides congruent.

TRY THIS

Complete the sentence: A rectangle is a parallelogram with . . .

The Venn diagram in Figure 8.35 can also assist students to internalize the relationships between these quadrilaterals.

Students might be given the Venn diagram shown in Figure 8.35 with one or two circles labeled and asked to label the rest of the diagram. Or students might be challenged to explain what it means to be in two circles at once, in the overlap, as are squares pictured here.

Another visual aid for students can be a quadrilateral family tree. In the family tree in Figure 8.36, all shapes descend from the general category of quadrilaterals.

Notice that the family tree for a square can be traced back through either a rectangle or a rhombus, thus supporting the fact that a square is a special rhombus and a special rectangle. Students could make the case that a square has to be considered a type of rectangle and rhombus based on this "lineage." Observe that in this tree neither the kite nor the trapezoid are related to the parallelogram. Students can be challenged to build a complete quadrilateral tree and explain the genealogy of each quadrilateral to the class.

Point Well Taken

"The informal knowledge and intuitive notions developed in the elementary grades receive more-careful examination and more-precise description in the middle grades."

—*Pugalee et al., 2001, p. 10*

figure **8.35**

Quadrilateral Relationships

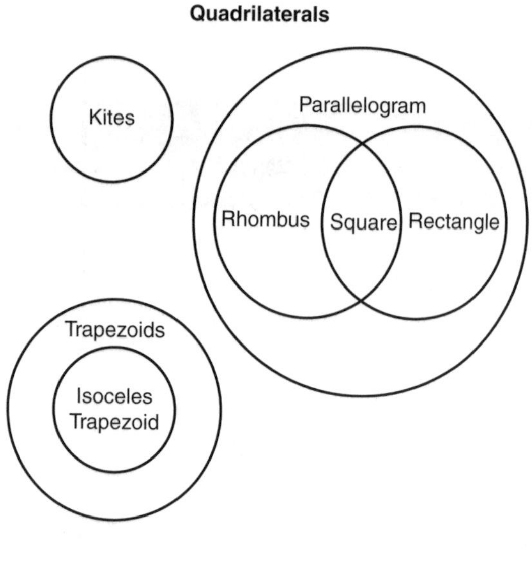

Quadrilaterals

Kites

Parallelogram

Rhombus | Square | Rectangle

Trapezoids

Isoceles Trapezoid

figure **8.36**

Quadrilateral Family Tree

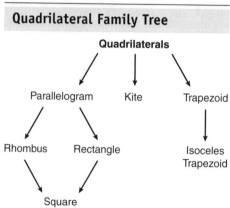

Quadrilaterals

Parallelogram — Kite — Trapezoid

Rhombus — Rectangle

Square

Isoceles Trapezoid

An interesting extension of this quadrilateral hierarchy is that in Canada and Europe the definition of trapezoid differs from the generally accepted definition in the United States. The customary definition of a trapezoid in the United States is a quadrilateral with *only* or *exactly two* parallel sides. Thus, trapezoids and parallelograms are entirely separate categories of quadrilaterals. The alternate definition of a trapezoid used in Canada and Europe (and in some American textbooks) is a quadrilateral with *at least two* parallel sides. As a consequence, trapezoids can have one or two pairs of parallel sides. Students might be challenged to change the Venn diagram (or the quadrilateral tree) to accommodate this alternate definition, as shown in Figure 8.37.

The alternate definition for trapezoid means that a parallelogram is a type of trapezoid, one with two pairs of parallel sides and not just a single pair. The rest of the diagram then falls into place and looks similar to the first arrangement with the common trapezoid definition.

TRY THIS

Draw a new quadrilateral family tree using the alternate trapezoid definition.

figure **8.37**

Alternative Quadrilateral Relationships

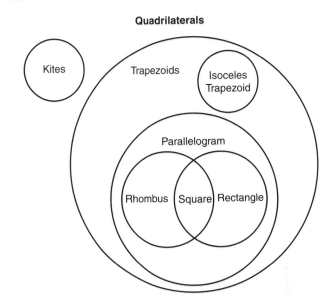

An alternative way to classify quadrilaterals is not by segment length, parallel sides, or angle measure but by lines of symmetry. Notice how the lines of symmetry for the quadrilaterals support the relationships shown in the Venn diagram and the quadrilateral tree.

Quadrilateral	Number of Symmetry Lines
Parallelogram	0
Trapezoid	0
Isosceles trapezoid	1 (bisector of the bases)
Kite	1 (bisector of one pair of opposite angles)
Rhombus	2 (bisector of both pairs of opposite angles)
Rectangle	2 (bisector of both pairs of opposite sides)
Square	4 (bisector of both pairs of opposite angles, bisectors of both pairs of opposite sides)

Did You **Know**?

The Greek word for *trapezoid* means "table." Perhaps your school has trapezoid-shaped tables or tables whose legs form the legs of an isosceles trapezoid with the table top and the floor. The Greek word for *rhombus* relates to an amulet suspended on a string. Early Greeks looked into the future by spinning a rhombus-shaped amulet.

On the Lighter Side

Dilbert empathizes with the rectangle.

Dilbert © by Scott Adams. Reprinted by permission of United Feature Syndicate, Inc.

When students understand how the various quadrilaterals are related to each other, they will find there is little need to memorize a table of properties. Instead they can reason, for example, that a rectangle has all the properties of a parallelogram and also several that are particular to the rectangle. Similarly, a square has all the properties of a rectangle and a rhombus. Students who never reach this level of understanding are relegated to memorizing a set of unrelated facts by rote, facts that can be confusing and quickly forgotten.

TRY THIS

Use a Venn diagram to categorize equilateral, isosceles, and scalene triangles.

MATH IN THE MEDIA

On the German version of the popular television show *Who Wants to Be a Millionaire?* the 8,000-euro question for one contestant was:

Every rectangle is:
a. a rhombus
b. a square
c. a trapezoid
d. a parallelogram

The contestant was confused by the question and what she thought were two perfectly good answers (c and d), so she skipped the question and kept her winnings to that point (4,000 euros). In the following days the broadcast station received tons of letters and phone calls pointing out that the question was unfair because it had two answers. The response of the show's producers was that they checked three encyclopedias and all three agreed that only parallelogram was the correct response. Rather than try to settle the question of whether a rectangle is always a trapezoid (which it is if the definition of a trapezoid is a quadrilateral with *at least two* parallel sides), the producers invited the contestant back the following week to continue the contest with a new 8,000-euro question.

Tessellations

Tessellations are an interesting geometry topic for middle grades students. A tessellation is a covering of the plane using geometric figures with no gaps or overlaps. Tessellations are familiar to the general population via the art of Dutch artist M. C. Escher (1898–1972), whose tessellations include birds, reptiles, and other animals. A search for Escher with an Internet search engine will produce many sites that display his works. One type of tessellation is a *tiling*, a tessellation that is closely aligned to angle measure.

Tilings

This type of tessellation involves only regular polygons. There are three *regular* tessellations, each composed of a single regular polygon. Students might experiment with several regular polygons to determine that only the equilateral triangle, square, and regular hexagon will tile a plane. (See Figure 8.38.)

Once students determine these three regular tilings, they might examine the angles about each vertex point in the tilings. In each case, the angles about each point total 360° (6 × 60° for the equilateral triangle, 4 × 90° for the square, and 3 × 120° for the regular hexagon). Students could then be asked to use the angle relationships about a point to explain why regular pentagons or other regular polygons cannot tile a plane. In the diagram in Figure 8.39, the three pentagons meet at point *Q*. Each angle of a regular pentagon is

figure **8.38**

Regular Tilings

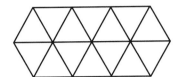 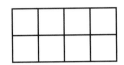 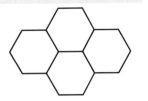

figure **8.39**

Regular Pentagons Cannot Tile a Plane

figure **8.40**

One of Eight Semiregular Tilings

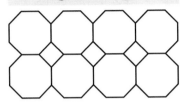

108°, so the total of the three angles meeting at point Q is 324° (3 × 108°). Three pentagons cannot tessellate a plane because their angles total less than 360°. There is a gap between the three pentagons at point Q.

There are eight *semiregular* tiling patterns. Semiregular tilings consist of two or more regular polygons, each with equal side lengths. In addition, each point in the tiling has the same arrangement of polygons meeting at that point. One of the semiregular tilings is shown in Figure 8.40. It is composed of squares and regular octagons.

The notation for this semiregular tiling is 4.8.8. This notation uses the number of sides of each polygon to indicate the arrangement of the polygons at each vertex. In this tiling the polygon arrangement is square-octagon-octagon. The angles at each vertex of this tiling are 90° + 135° + 135° = 360°. The other seven semiregular tilings are 3.12.12, 4.6.12, 3.6.3.6, 3.4.6.4, 3.3.3.3.6, 3.3.3.4.4, and 3.3.4.3.4. Note that the notation begins with the polygon(s) with the smallest number of sides. It then lists the other polygons in order around the vertex point. The notation 8.4.8 names the same tiling that is usually represented as 4.8.8.

Students might be challenged to find these semiregular tilings by either fitting regular polygons together or by examining combinations of interior angle measures of regular polygons to find those combinations that total 360°. (For templates of regular polygons to use for tiling explorations see www.nzmaths.co.nz/Geometry/Symmetry/Fitness.htm.)

Students could also use Internet sites to explore tilings. We have chosen tilings as our topic for this chapter's Internet Lesson Plan.

Internet Lesson Plan

Tiling the Plane

Objectives

Process	Directed teaching to a large group, then small group work. Students work cooperatively using their assigned roles (facilitator, team captain, reporter, and recorder).
Mathematics	Find and analyze tilings with regular polygons. Write a conjecture about the relationship of interior angle measures of polygons that tile a plane.
Materials	1 Internet-connected class computer and image projector; individual computers for each group (http://nlvm.usu.edu/en/nav/vlibrary.html)
Previous Knowledge	Method to compute single interior angle measures of regular polygons

Lesson

1. As they enter the room, students write the number of the problems that they would like the class to discuss on the homework board.
2. Warm-up problem reviewing yesterday's lesson

   One interior angle of a regular polygon is 135. Name the polygon.

3. Review agenda for the day
   Warm-up
   Tiling a plane with regular polygons
   Homework demos by students
   Wrap-up
4. Students sit in groups of four. Attention focused on the computer projection.
   Looking for patterns
   Making conjectures
   Drawing conclusions
   Summarizing findings
5. Demonstrate to students how the applet works. Clicking on a figure moves it into the active screen. Then the polygon may be dragged by the cursor and/or rotated as needed.
6. Have students conjecture in their groups about which individual polygons will tile the plane. (The applet uses equilateral triangles, squares, regular hexagons, regular octagons, and regular dodecagons.) Ask each group to use the applet to try to tile with each polygon and record their results.
7. Have individual students use the applet to show that equilateral triangles, squares, and regular hexagons will tile the plane.
8. Students in each group examine the interior angles of these polygons and make a conjecture about why they tile the plane.
9. Using their conjectures, students explain why a pentagon cannot tile a plane.
10. Students present group conjectures to the class.
11. Discuss with the class the need for the angles at each vertex to total 360°. In a pentagon they total only 324° (3 × 108°).
12. Define a semiregular tiling as composed of two or more polygons. Ask students to find all the semiregular tilings using the applet and their conjecture about angles of polygons that tile a plane.

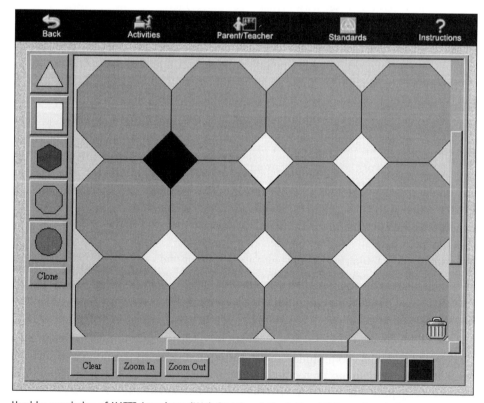

Used by permission of MATTI Associates (Utah State) and the National Science Foundation.

13. Students fill in the following table as they work.

TILING POLYGONS	INDIVIDUAL ANGLE MEASURES	ANGLE TOTAL AT EACH POINT

14. The groups report their findings to the class.

15. Teacher summarizes those cooperative processes in which groups excelled.

16. Students volunteer to post requested homework problems on the board and explain their thinking.

17. Wrap-up to the lesson: Students write an exit card and give it to the teacher as they leave the classroom.

    Describe how your group reached its conjecture(s).

    What did you contribute to your group today?

Creating Tessellations

Students can create original tessellations by deforming a square or a regular hexagon. One method for designing a shape that will tessellate might be called the "chomp and paste" method. As shown in Figure 8.41, a square is chomped from one side and this chomped shape is then pasted to the opposite side. This process may be repeated on the other pair

Did You **Know**?

The word *tessellation* is derived from the Latin word *tesserea,* a word that described the small tiles used to form Roman mosaics, such as those found in Ravenna, Italy.

figure **8.41**

Tessellation Using the Chomp and Paste Method

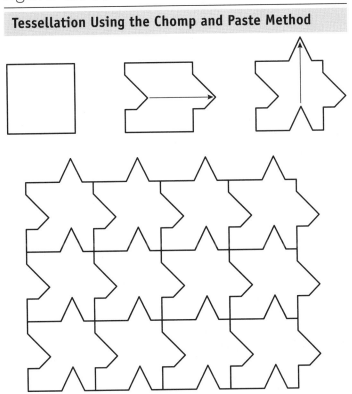

of sides. The resulting figure will always tessellate. The tessellating figure in the diagram is an abstract shape, but if it is colored and appropriately decorated, it might resemble an animal, character, or some other real-life figure.

Students might also create tessellations by performing rotations and reflections with quadrilaterals and equilateral triangles. For more about tessellations or to create your own tessellations, see http://mathforum.org/sum95/suzanne/tess.intro.html or www.shodor.org/interactivate/activities/tessellate/index.html.

TRY THIS

Create your own original tessellation using the "chomp and paste" method with a square or regular hexagon.

Similarity

The study of similar figures in geometry is challenging for many students. They must extend their spatial sense to easily recognize and visualize similar figures. In addition, students must expand their proportional thinking that is needed to fully apply similar figures to real-world situations. (For a full discussion of proportionality, see Chapter 6, Making Sense of Number and Operations.) At the end of elementary school and the start of middle school, students begin to analyze similar figures and use the properties of similar figures to identify them. The two pairs of figures shown in Figure 8.42 are similar.

The corresponding or matching angles are congruent, and the corresponding side lengths have the same ratio, or are in a proportion. $\triangle ABC \sim \triangle QRS$ so $<A \cong <Q, <B \cong <R$, and $<C \cong <S$. In addition, $\frac{AB}{QR} = \frac{BC}{RS} = \frac{CA}{SQ}$. In the same way mathing angles are congruent and matching sides are in the same ratio for the two similar quadrilaterals.

TRY THIS

Write out the pairs of congruent angles and the ratios for corresponding sides of two similar pentagons. Pentagon *STACK* ~ Pentagon *FLING*.

To either introduce or review similar figures, students might be given several pairs of similar cardboard triangles. Students can manipulate similar pairs to show that corresponding angles are congruent by placing the smaller figure on top of the larger figure and nestling one angle on top of its corresponding angle. When students do so, the resulting figure will appear as shown in Figure 8.43.

Students might be asked to consider how the two nonoverlapping sides of the two triangles are related. (They are parallel.) Students might repeat the process with the other two angles of the triangles and with several more triangles to clarify that all corresponding angle are congruent.

To begin to consider the side lengths students might arrange their triangle pairs as shown in Figure 8.44.

When students arrange similar figures in this manner, the relationship of side lengths begins to emerge. Clearly, each corresponding side in the larger triangle is longer. The smaller figure grows so that each side increases proportionally and it will be congruent to the larger figure. In addition, students' spatial sense will suggest that each larger side is larger in the same proportion.

After having students experiment with several pairs of similar triangles as suggested previously, teachers should

figure **8.42**

Similar Figures

$\triangle ABC \sim \triangle QRS$

Quadrilateral *BATH* ~ Quadrilateral *ROCK*

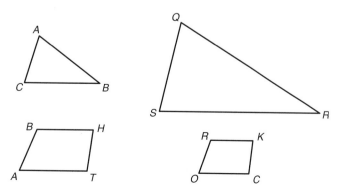

figure **8.43**

Similar Triangles with Manipulatives

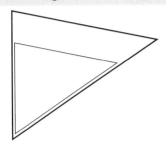

figure **8.44**

Embedded Similar Triangles

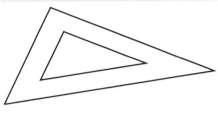

provide opportunities to collect measurement data from their figures. Students can use rulers and protractors to measure side lengths and angles and record them in a table. After gathering data from several pairs of similar figures, students should recognize that the corresponding angles are congruent. In the case of triangles, if the corresponding angles are congruent, then the triangles must be similar. For all other figures the corresponding angles must be congruent and corresponding sides must be in the same ratio. (If only congruent angles were necessary to identify all corresponding figures, then squares and rectangles could be considered similar because their corresponding angles are congruent.)

REACT | REFLECT

Did you study similar figures with the help of transformations? If so, how did using a transformation approach help? If not, how might using a transformation approach help?

RESEARCH

Proportional reasoning is one of the key concepts developed in the middle grades. Proportionality has applications throughout mathematics from slope and similar figures to related rates and calculus applications. An interesting finding by two different research studies was that of all proportional reasoning problems within reach of high school students, it was the problems in a geometric context that were most difficult (Kaput & West, 1994; Lamon, 1994). Students had the lowest success levels with proportion problems involving a missing segment or a missing length.

The implications for the classroom are clear. Students may be able to solve proportions with apparent fluency by employing the cross-product method but their success masks their superficial understanding of proportional relationships in geometric contexts. More time needs to be spent helping students understand the applications of proportional reasoning to geometric settings, whether discovering the relationships of similar figures, solving for missing segments, or applying proportionality to real-world problems. (See Chapter 6, Making Sense of Number and Operations, for more on proportional reasoning.)

TRY THIS

$\triangle ABC \sim \triangle QRS$. $AB = 12$, $BC = 20$, $QR = 18$, $RS = ?$

Dilations

Another way to consider similar figures is by means of transformations, specifically dilations. Middle school students will have had some previous experience with translations (slides), reflections (flips), and rotations (turns). Dilations are properly introduced in middle school.

In Figure 8.45 $\triangle ABC$ is a dilation of $\triangle FOX$. Since $\triangle ABC$ is larger, it is called an enlargement of $\triangle FOX$. If $\triangle ABC$ were smaller, it would be considered a

figure **8.45**

Similar Triangles

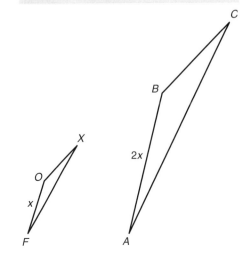

Did You **Know**?

The symbol for similar (~) is called a tilde and was first used to represent similarity by German mathematician Gottfried Wilhelm Leibniz (1616–1703).

reduction of ΔFOX. A comparison of $\overline{AB}$ and $\overline{FO}$ shows that $\overline{AB}$ is twice as long as $\overline{FO}$. Since all corresponding sides of similar figures are in the same ratio, each side of ΔABC is twice the length of the matching side of ΔFOX. This may be expressed as a scale factor. The scale factor to expand ΔFOX to the size of ΔABC is 2. Conversely, the scale factor needed to shrink ΔABC to the size of ΔFOX is $\frac{1}{2}$.

As with the other transformations that middle school students study, dilations may be beneficially represented on coordinate axes. (See Figure 8.46.)

A matrix of the coordinate points of the two triangles may be used to show enlargements and reductions. In this case the scale factor describes the enlargement of ΔFOX to ΔABC.

ΔFOX			ΔABC	
2	2		4	4
3	6	Scale factor 2	6	12
5	8		10	16

A scale factor of $\frac{1}{2}$ applied to the matrix of vertex coordinates describes the shrinking of ΔABC to ΔFOX.

ΔABC			ΔFOX	
4	4		2	2
6	12	Scale factor $\frac{1}{2}$	3	6
10	16		5	8

figure **8.46**

Similar Triangles on Coordinate Axes

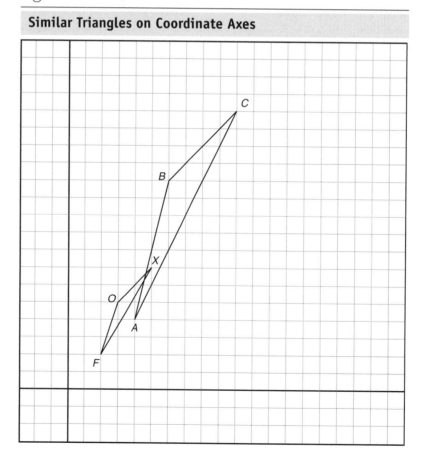

In a similar fashion, the knowledge and skills that students began to develop in the elementary grades may be used in the middle grades to represent and clarify all the transformations, not simply dilations. Representing all transformations in a coordinate grid, as with dilations here, is helpful to all students.

A site that provides students with the opportunity to apply transformations to similar figures is http://standards.nctm.org/document/eexamples/chap6/6.4/index.htm.

REACHING DIVERSE LEARNERS

Geometry is a visual study accompanied by many vocabulary words, some of which originated in ancient Greece. Words such as *scalene, isosceles, rhombus,* and *perpendicular* can be challenging for English-language learners to understand. To help English-language learners to better understand classroom conversations, it is beneficial for teachers to write new vocabulary words along with their definitions on the board as they are introduced. Teachers can also use graphic organizers as an aid to introduce vocabulary. Various geometric objects around the classroom could be labeled in several languages to further assist English-language learners to understand new vocabulary.

Area and Volume Relationships

There is one aspect of similar figures that can be the source of difficulty for all geometry students. It is the relationship between areas and volumes of similar figures. Many middle school students will find the study of similar figures challenging, especially when area and volume are considered. We have discussed this relationship from an algebraic standpoint (see Chapter 7, Algebra: The Gateway), but here we consider it geometrically.

TRY THIS

Sketch a square with twice the area of the square in Figure 8.47.

Most students will attempt to solve this problem by doubling the length of the sides of the square, reasoning that if the side lengths are doubled, then the perimeter is doubled, and so the area is also doubled. Such mistaken thinking has been the study of mathematicians from the time of Plato. In *Meno*, Plato describes how Socrates corrected the erroneous thinking of a slave named Meno with this same problem.

Figure 8.48 shows the original square and a square with side lengths that have been doubled.

The larger square is clearly more than twice the area of the original square. What is the area of the larger square compared to the smaller square? When grid lines are drawn in the larger square (see Figure 8.49), the area of the larger square is apparent. The area of the larger square is four times as large as the area of the original square.

Although such a result is strongly visual as shown here, students find the area and volume relationships between similar figures to be counterintuitive. One reason is that students have consistently compared figures by using linear measures. They compared themselves to others when they were younger by observing heights. For young children, large objects are large, in part, because of their height. The taller the object, the larger it is. In this instance, students tend to compare the original square and its double by observing only the side lengths. Since the side lengths in the larger square are twice as long, it seems reasonable to conclude that the area will be twice as large. The side lengths and perimeters are in the same linear relationship, and so students conclude that the areas will show an identical linear relationship.

What if the side lengths of a square or another plane figure are increased by another factor such as 3 or 4? How does the area of the enlarged figure compare to the area of

figure **8.47**

Square

figure **8.48**

Enlarging a Square

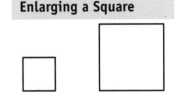

figure **8.49**

Enlarging a Square

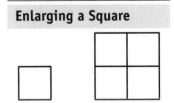

Point Well Taken

"The study of geometry in grades 5–8 links the informal explorations begun in grades K–4 to the more formal processes studied in grades 9–12."

—*NCTM, 1989, p. 112*

figure **8.50**

Enlarging Squares

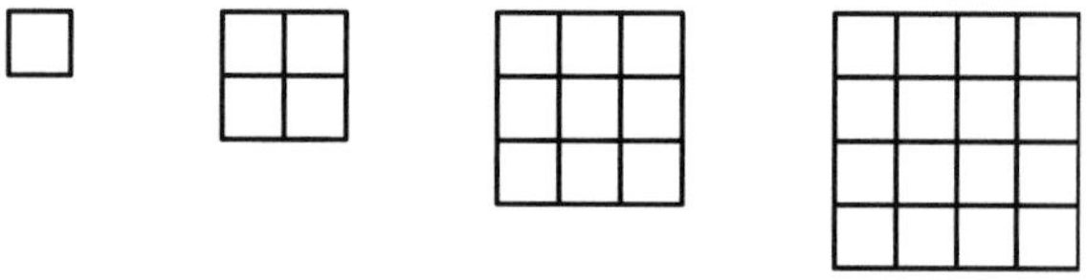

the original figure? This relationship can be represented by a series of enlargements as shown in Figure 8.50.

This table shows the data from these figures.

SIDE LENGTH	AREA
1	1 or $(?)^2$
2	4 or $(?)^2$
3	9 or $(?)^2$
4	16 or $(?^2)$

Notice that the area of each succeeding square is found by squaring the factor by which the side length was increased. Based on this pattern, we would predict that when the side length of a square is increased by a factor of 5, then the area of the enlarged square will have an area that has been increased by a factor of 25 (5^2).

This relationship may also be examined algebraically. A square of side length q has an area of q^2. If the side length is doubled to $2q$, then the area of the new square is found by using the area formula for the enlarged square, $A = s^2 = (2q)^2 = 4q^2$. The enlargement has an area that is four times as large as the original square. Similarly, other enlargements will show the same quadratic area relationships.

$$(3q)^2 = 9q^2$$
$$(4q)^2 = 16q^2$$

TRY THIS

You'll find in Chapter 7, Algebra: The Gateway, that we use this same problem but with a different emphasis. How do the varying developments of this same problem compare in these two chapters?

When middle school students have many opportunities to examine similar figures and compare sides lengths and areas, they will be able to understand the nonlinear relationship between the areas of similar figures and express in their own words that the ratio of the areas of similar figures is the square of the ratio of the side lengths. One activity to help students understand the area relationship between the areas of similar figures is to have students employ a series of squares with unit lengths. Students might construct a table of data from pairs of squares and note how the area ratios differ from the linear ratios.

SIDE LENGTH SQUARE *A*/ SIDE LENGTH SQUARE *B*	PERIMETER SQUARE *A*/ PERIMETER SQUARE *B*	AREA SQUARE *A*/ AREA SQUARE *B*
$\frac{1}{2}$	$\frac{1}{2}$	$\frac{1}{4}$
$\frac{2}{3}$	$\frac{2}{3}$	$\frac{4}{9}$

Another activity might employ an applet from the Internet. Students could explore the relationship between area and perimeters of figures with the applet at http://standards.nctm.org/document/eexamples/chap7/7.3/index.htm.

This relationship of linear and area ratios of similar figures can be extended to three dimensions. The relationship of surface areas for similar solids is the same as for plane figures. The ratio of the surface areas is the square of the ratio of any linear measure. The volumes of similar solids present a new relationship. Students might begin to examine the relationship between similar solids by building block figures, as shown in Figure 8.51, and collecting the data.

EDGE LENGTH	VOLUME
1	1
2	8
3	27
4	64

figure **8.51**

Enlarging Cubes

1 × 1 × 1 cube   2 × 2 × 2 cube   3 × 3 × 3 cube   4 × 4 × 4 cube

The volume relationships are clearly not linear. That is, when the edge length is increased by a factor of 2, for example, the volume does not increase by a factor of 2. As the table shows, the increase is not similar to the area relationship. In the case of volume, the relationship is cubic, in contrast to the area relationship, which is quadratic (or based on the square of the linear factor). The ratio of the volume of similar solids is found by cubing the ratio of the edge lengths. When the edge length of a cube is doubled, then the resulting volume shows a 2^3 or eightfold increase.

TRY THIS

The problem of doubling the volume of a cube dates from ancient Greece. It is called the Delian Problem. Research the context of the Delian Problem using the search engine at www.dogpile.com.

TRY THIS

Granny Jones Cookie Company plans to enlarge its boxes by doubling all the linear dimensions. How much more ribbon, cardboard, and cookies will the larger box need compared to the original box?

PROCESS STANDARDS

Reasoning and Proof

Reasoning and proof would seem to be very closely connected to geometry. Although proof is a part of all mathematics, it is in geometry that most students confront proofs. The process of proof first begins with collecting data to construct a conjecture. Conjecture lies at the heart of all geometric theorems. Conjecture, in turn, is based on patterns from collected data. The use of patterning to solve problems both in geometry and in other fields of mathematics is a powerful one. In geometry, students can make conjectures leading to proofs based on patterns from gathered data, whether it is discovering that all vertical angles have the same measure or that rectangles have two lines of symmetry.

The problem here exemplifies how patterning may be used to solve a problem in a geometric context.

How many rectangles can be formed by a series of ten dominoes laid end to end?

As shown in Figure 8.52, the first two dominoes form three rectangles: *a*, *b*, and *ab*. The first three dominoes form six rectangles: *a*, *b*, *c*, *ab*, *bc*, and *abc*.

The table reveals the pattern to the total number of rectangles formed by any specific number of dominoes.

NUMBER OF DOMINOES	NUMBER OF RECTANGLES
1	1
2	3
3	6
4	10
5	15

figure **8.52**

Row of Dominoes

a	b	c

figure **8.53**

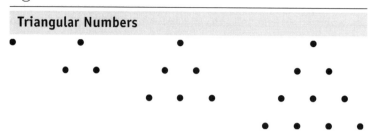

Triangular Numbers

The pattern for the number of rectangles resembles the solution to the Handshake Problem in Chapter 7, Algebra: The Gateway. The pattern of numbers is also known as triangular numbers because each number may be represented as a triangular array of points. (See Figure 8.53.)

SUMMARY

Students bring more knowledge about geometry to middle school than any other mathematics topic. As NCTM states: "Students come to the study of geometry in the middle grades with informal knowledge about points, lines, planes, and a variety of two- and three-dimensional shapes; with experiences in visualizing lines, angles, and other polygons; and with intuitive notions about shapes built from years of interacting with objects in their daily lives" (NCTM, 2000, p. 233). It is critical to build on these informally gathered conceptualizations. In middle school, students move from intuitive, visual understandings of geometry to induction, categorization, and deduction. Students are helped to do so with many activities and experiences that employ manipulatives, models, and real-world applications.

The following are highlights of this chapter:

- The van Hiele levels of geometry thinking indicate that students must pass through increasingly complex stages of geometry thinking: visualization, analysis, abstraction, deduction, and rigor. Teachers must ensure that the majority of class activities and student thinking are at the same van Hiele level.
- Spatial sense is a building block of geometry. In middle school, students focus on visualizing and drawing three-dimensional figures. Although students can develop their spatial sense outside of school by solving jigsaw puzzles and the like, they also require activities and experiences in school that specifically build spatial sense.
- When students study the Pythagorean Theorem, they must do more than memorize it by rote and apply it to word problems. Middle school students need to build a fundamental understanding of the relationship between side lengths of a right triangle and have the opportunity to apply the Theorem in real-life situations.
- Middle school students can usually recognize special quadrilaterals and list some of their properties. As they advance in their geometry thinking, middle school students use the quadrilateral properties to categorize them and define them. Rather than memorize a chart with all the properties, students should be able to recognize the relationships between the quadrilaterals and reason, for example, that a square has all the properties of a rectangle and it is, therefore, a special rectangle.
- Middle school students consider similar figures from several aspects. They need to fully develop their proportional or multiplicative thinking to understand the relationship between side lengths of similar figures. They also can benefit from considering similar figures from a transformational view by considering similar figures as dilations of one another.

Student Performance on
International and National Assessments

TIMSS

Which of these angles has a measure closest to 30°? (64% correct)

A. a
B. b
C. c
D. d

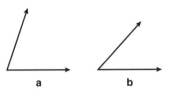

NAEP

When the rectangle in the accompanying figure is folded along the dotted line, Point *P* will touch which of the lettered points? (39% correct)

A. *A*
B. *B*
C. *C*
D. *D*
E. *E*

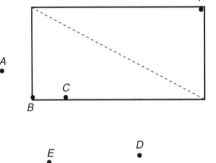

EXERCISES

From the Reading

1. How will you use what you know about the van Hiele levels of geometry thinking in your classroom?

2. Draw the symmetry lines for a rectangle, rhombus, and square.

3. How many lines of symmetry does a regular dodecagon have?

4. Draw all the nets of a cube.

5. Solve for *x* in the triangle in the accompanying figure.

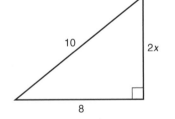

6. How are manipulatives helpful to students in geometry? What type of student might have difficulty using manipulatives?

7. Define a square in terms of a special rhombus.

8. Draw two different quadrilaterals that are neither similar nor congruent but with congruent corresponding angles.

9. The coordinates of a quadrilateral *QXYZ* are *Q*(3, 2) *X* (5, 4) *Y*(8, –2) *Z*(–3, –6). What are the coordinates of the image of *QXYZ* under a dilation with a scale factor of 3? Of $\frac{1}{2}$?

10. What may happen if a student who is at Level 1 of geometry thinking is in a class whose activities are predominantly Level 2 activities?

11. Why should spatial activities be spaced across the year rather than restricted to geometry units?

12. Make a Venn diagram to categorize these quadrilaterals but use lines of symmetry as the descriptor for the sets: parallelogram, rhombus, kite, trapezoid, rectangle, and square.

On Your Own

1. Interview a middle school teacher to determine what role manipulatives and/or the computer play in the classroom.

2. Research the meaning of the Greek words from which we derive *isosceles* and *scalene*.

3. All crossword puzzles show symmetry. Examine a crossword puzzle from a local newspaper or a national magazine. What type of symmetry does the crossword puzzle display?

4. Examine a middle grades mathematics textbook. Does the textbook contain recommended classroom activities that require manipulatives?

 Portfolio Question

What new understandings about teaching geometry have you acquired as a result of working through this chapter?

Scenes from a Classroom

We look in on Mr. Euclid's class as he begins a unit on quadrilaterals with his sixth graders.

Mr. Euclid: Today we are going to begin to study the properties of quadrilaterals. Let's make a list of the names of the quadrilaterals we will study. Who can name a quadrilateral?

Carole: A square.

Latoya: A parallelogram.

Sharon: A trapezoval.

Jacko: You mean a trapezoid.

Shawna: Yeah, that's what I meant.

Mr. Euclid: There are two others we will study. Anyone?

Trumaine: I know, a rectangle.

Mr. Euclid: Very good, now there is one more. What is it?

Frieda: I got it. It's a rhombus.

Mr. Euclid: Yes, we have five of them. Now we are going to study all their properties in this chapter. There are a lot of properties, and so I have prepared a chart of them to help you learn them.

Mr. Euclid passes out a chart similar to Table 8.1.

Mr. Euclid: Don't wait until the test to learn these properties. Start tonight with some of the parallelogram properties and keep learning some new ones every night. That way when we finish the chapter, you will be ready for the text.

Before reading our comments, respond to these questions.

1. How is Mr. Euclid trying to help his students?
2. How effective do you think his method will be?
3. What alternative approach might he take to help his students learn the properties?

Mr. Euclid is depending on his students' rote memory to help them to learn these properties. Few students can learn all these properties by using brute force memorization. Those who do will find that their resulting knowledge is fleeting and they will need to memorize the properties again next year and the year after that. Mr. Euclid's students will benefit from explorations that enable them to explore the properties of each quadrilateral and to discover the relationships among them. For example, students might measure segment lengths and angle measures

of various quadrilaterals. As they record these properties, students will notice that the square, rectangle, and rhombus all have the properties of a parallelogram. Rather than learn a series of properties for a rectangle, they can focus on those properties that distinguish a rectangle from a parallelogram. In addition they will note that the square has all the properties of a rectangle and rhombus, as well as the parallelogram. Again, instead of learning a series of properties for a square, they can recall the properties of a parallelogram, rectangle, and rhombus.

When students can explore the properties of a specific quadrilateral and compare them to others, they develop knowledge about the properties that will not be forgotten as easily as memorized facts. In addition, they will be able to reconstruct those properties that they may forget by recalling how the particular quadrilateral is related to other quadrilaterals.

Preparing for Praxis

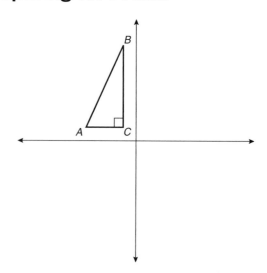

Which figure on the facing page results if right triangle *ABC* is flipped (reflected) across the *y*-axis and then turned (rotated) clockwise about point *C* by 90 degrees?

RESOURCES

Math–Literature Connections

Abbott, E. (1992). *Flatland.* New York: Dover Publications, Inc.

Ellis, J. (2004). *What's your angle, Pythagoras?* Watertown, MA: Charlesbridge Publishing.

Juster, N. (2000). *The dot and the line: A romance in lower mathematics.* San Francisco: Chronicle Books.

Juster, N. (1988). *The phantom tollbooth.* New York: Bullseye Books.

Neuschwander, N. (1999). *Sir Cumference and the dragon of pi: A math adventure.* Watertown, MA: Charlesbridge Publishing.

Neuschwander, N. (2003). *Sir Cumference and the sword in the cone: A math adventure.* Watertown, MA: Charlesbridge Publishing.

Sleator, W. (1998). *The boy who reversed himself.* New York: Puffin Books.

Stewart, I. (2001). *Flatterland.* Cambridge, MA: Perseus Publishing.

Teacher's Bookcase

Abbott, E. A. (1937). *Flatland: A romance of many dimensions.* Boston: Little & Brown.

This book is a classic that uses a land of two-dimensional characters to introduce students to geometries of different dimensions.

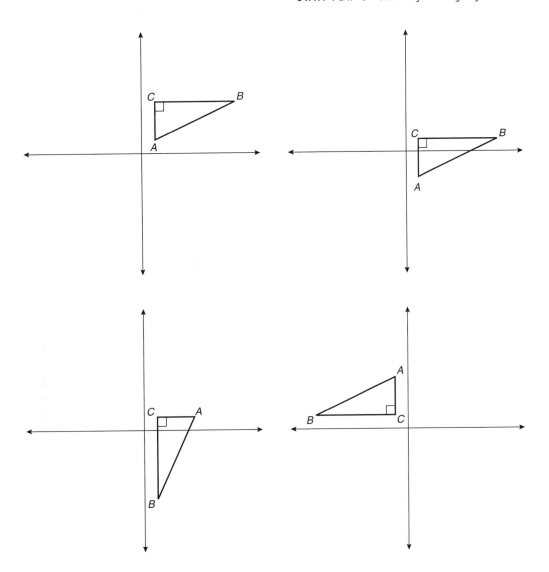

Enderson, M. C., & Manouchehri, A. (1998). **Technology-based geometric explorations for the middle grades.** In L. Leutzinger (Ed.), *Mathematics in the middle* (pp. 193–200). Reston, VA: NCTM & National Middle School Association.

This text is a collection of activities appropriate for use with dynamic geometry.

Garland, T. (1987). **Fascinating Fibonaccis: Mystery and magic in numbers.** Palo Alto, CA: Dale Seymour Publications.

This book contains whimsical drawings to help middle schoolers grasp the significance of the golden ratio in math, music, nature, and more.

Golomb, S. (1996). **Polyominoes: Puzzles, patterns, problems, and packings.** Princeton, NJ: Princeton University Press.

This is an updated version of a classic text. Golomb describes polyominoes, including pentominos, and develops important mathematics extensions from activities with various polyominoes.

Johnson, A. (1997). **Building geometry: Activities for polydron frameworks.** Palo Alto, CA: Dale Seymour Publications.

The text offers many activities for exploring polyhedrons, from Platonic solids to dihedral prisms, using any number of commercial or hand-made manipulatives.

Pohl, V. (1986). **How to enrich geometry using string designs.** Reston, VA: NCTM.

This resource shows how to draw straight-line curves and then use string to produce three-dimensional artwork using mathematics principles.

Pugale, D., et al. (2001). **Navigating through geometry: 6–8.** Reston, VA: NCTM.

This book contains a discussion of middle school geometry and is accompanied by many activities with Black Line Masters. The text also includes a CD with interactive applets designed for middle school students.

Seymour, D., & Britton, J. (1989). **Introduction to tessellations.** Palo Alto, CA: Dale Seymour Publications.

This is an excellent introduction to tessellations with many student examples included.

Silverstein, S. (1981). **Missing piece meets the big O.** New York: Harper Collins.

A delightful tale relating area to perimeter by a master storyteller.

For Further Reading

Chapin, S., & Canavan, N. (2003). Crossing the bridge to formal proportional reasoning. *Mathematics Teaching in the Middle School, 8*(8), 420–425.

The authors describe a program they used to help middle school students successfully develop strategies to apply proportions to real-world problems.

Ferrer, B. et al. (2001). By the unit or the square unit. *Mathematics Teaching in the Middle School, 7*(3), 132–137.

In this article the author team describes difficulties middle school students have distinguishing between area and perimeter. They include effective activities they have used to help students understand both concepts.

Peterson, B. (2000). From tessellations to polyhedra: Big polyhedra. *Mathematics Teaching in the Middle School, 5*(6), 348–357.

This article bridges the gap between tessellations and three dimensions, culminating with semiregular polyhedrons. Activities and Black Line Master sheets are included for classroom use.

Stein, M., & Bovalino, J. (2001). Manipulatives: One piece of the puzzle. *Mathematics Teaching in the Middle School, 6*(5), 142–145.

This article presents the advantages of using manipulatives but cautions that there are some concerns for teachers when they use them.

Strutchens, M. et al. (2001). Assessing geometric and measurement understanding using manipulatives. *Mathematics Teaching in the Middle School, 6*(7), 402–405.

The authors discuss specific ways to employ manipulatives as an assessment tool.

Weinber, S. et al. (2003). The giants project. *Mathematics Teaching in the Middle School, 8*(8), 406–413.

The authors describe a project they used with middle schoolers to help them expand and apply their proportional reasoning skills.

Links

Cabri dynamic geometry software
www.ti.com

Geometer's sketchpad dynamic geometry software
www.keypress.com

Varied geometry topics and activities
www.cut-the-knot.org/content.shtml

Geometry through Art
mathforum.com/~sarah/shapiro

The Geometry Junkyard
www.ics.uci.edu/~eppstein/junkyard

Sacred Geometry
www.intent.com/sg/

Fibonacci Numbers
www.mcs.surrey.ac.uk/Personal/R.Knott/Fibonacci

Fold and unfold polyhedra
www.peda.com/poly

Interactive geometry software programs
http://forum.swarthmore.edu/dynamic.html

REFERENCES

Fuys, D., Geddes, D. & Tischler, R. (1988). The van Hiele model of thinking in geometry among adolescents. *Journal for Research in Mathematics Education,* Monograph Number 3.

Kaput, J., & West, M. (1994). Missing values proportional reasoning problems: Factors affecting informal reasoning patterns. In G. Harrel & J. Confrey (Eds.), *Development of multiplicative reasoning in the learning of mathematics* (pp. 237–291). Albany: State University Press.

Kloosterman, P., & Gainey, P. (1993). Students' thinking: Middle grades mathematics. In D. Owens (Ed.), *Research ideas for the classroom: Middle grades mathematics.* Reston, VA: NCTM.

Lamon, S. (1994). Ratio and proportion. In T. Carpenter, E. Fennema, & T. Romberg (Eds.), *Rational numbers: An integration of research* (pp. 131–155). Hillsdale, NJ: Lawrence Erlbaum.

National Council of Teachers of Mathematics. (1994). *Principles and Standards of School Mathematics.* Reston, VA: NCTM.

National Council of Teachers of Mathematics. (1989). *Curriculum and Evaluation Standards for School Mathematics.* Reston, VA: NCTM.

Pugalee, D., Frykholm, J., Johnson, A., Sloven, H., Malloy, C., & Preston, R. (2002). *Navigating through geometry in grades 6–8.* Reston, VA: NCTM.

Yakimanskya, I. S. (1991). The development of spatial thinking in school children. In P. Wilson & J. Davis (Eds.) and R. Silverman (Trans.), *Soviet studies in mathematics education,* Vol. 3. Reston, VA: NCTM.

How Many Triangles?

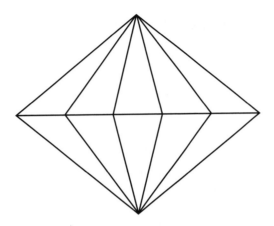

How many triangles do you think there are here? Find out. Count all the triangles and compare your answer to a partner's answer.

Explain your process. How do you know you found all the triangles?

Cross Sections of a Cube

The accompanying cube shows a square-shaped cross section. What other cross sections are possible when a cube is intersected by a plane?

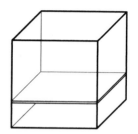

Draw the cross sections in the cubes provided here and describe the cross section below each cube.

 From Johnson & Norris, Teaching Today's Mathematics in the Middle Grades. Copyright © 2006 Allyn and Bacon, Pearson Education, Inc.

Block Structures

For each of these structures, give the minimum number of blocks needed to build it.

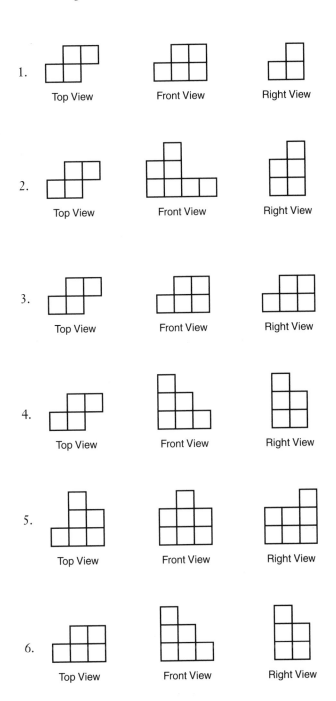

1. Top View   Front View   Right View

2. Top View   Front View   Right View

3. Top View   Front View   Right View

4. Top View   Front View   Right View

5. Top View   Front View   Right View

6. Top View   Front View   Right View

Pythagorean Puzzle 1

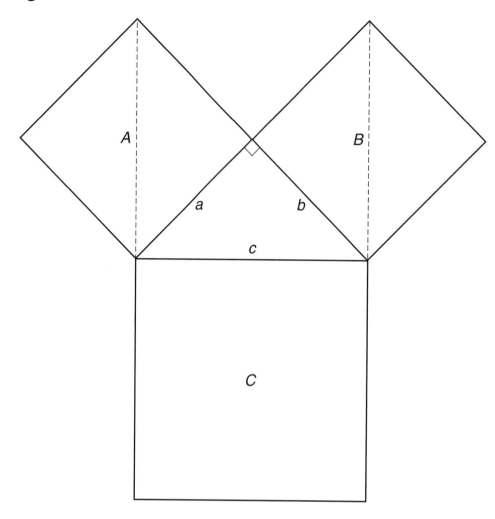

Notice the right triangle with leg *a*, leg *b*, and hypotenuse *c*.
Notice too that c^2 is the algebraic way to write a square with side length *c*.

1. Cut out square *A* and square *B*.
2. Cut square *A* and square *B* along the dashed lines.
3. Tape or paste these four pieces to cover square *C*.
4. What is the relationship between $a^2 + b^2$ and c^2?
   (*Note:* The term a^2 is read aloud as "*a*-squared.")

Pythagorean Puzzle 2

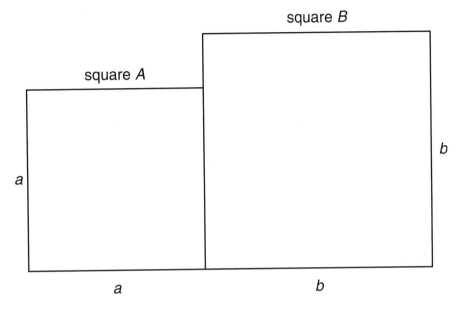

square A

square B

a

a

b

b

square C

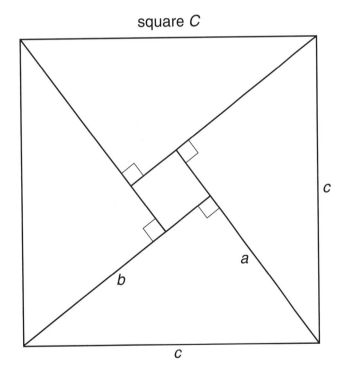

c

a

b

c

Notice the right triangle with leg *a*, leg *b*, and hypotenuse *c*.
Notice too that c^2 is the algebraic way to write a square with side length *c*.

1. Cut out the five pieces from square *C*.
2. Tape or paste these pieces to cover square *A* and square *B*.
3. What is the relationship between $a^2 + b^2$ and c^2?
   (*Note:* The term a^2 is read aloud as "*a*-squared.")

Pythagorean Puzzle 3

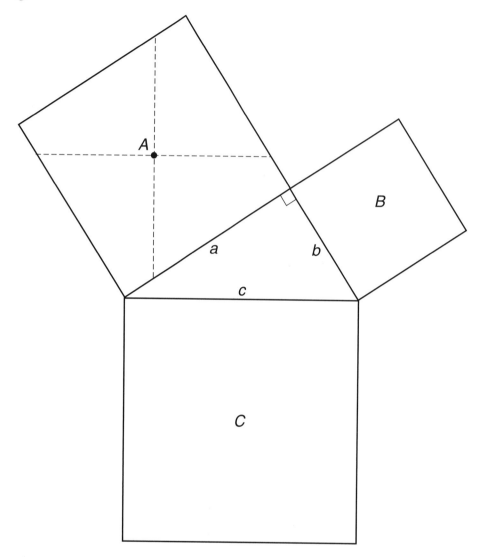

Notice the right triangle with leg *a*, leg *b*, and hypotenuse *c*.
Notice too that c^2 is the algebraic way to write a square with side length *c*.

1. Cut out square *A* and square *B*.
2. Cut square *A* along dashed lines.
3. Tape or paste these four pieces to cover square *C*.
4. What is the relationship between $a^2 + b^2$ and c^2?
   (*Note:* The term a^2 is read aloud as "*a*-squared.")

Pythagorean Puzzle 4

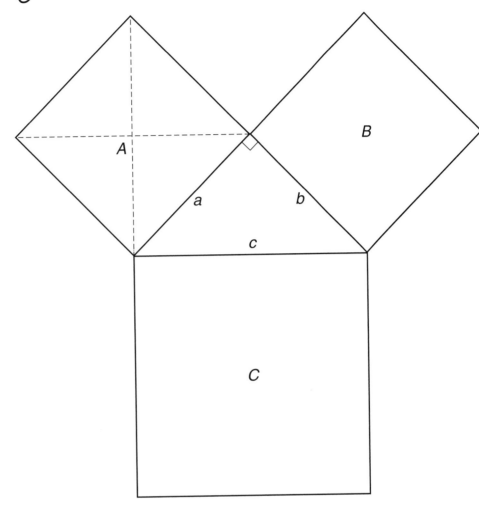

Notice the right triangle with leg *a*, leg *b*, and hypotenuse *c*.
Notice too that c^2 is the algebraic way to write a square with side length *c*.

1. Cut out square *A* and square *B*.
2. Cut square *A* along the dashed lines.
3. Tape or paste these four pieces to cover square *C*.
4. What is the relationship between $a^2 + b^2$ and c^2?
   (*Note:* The term a^2 is read aloud as "*a*-squared.")

Pythagorean Puzzle 5

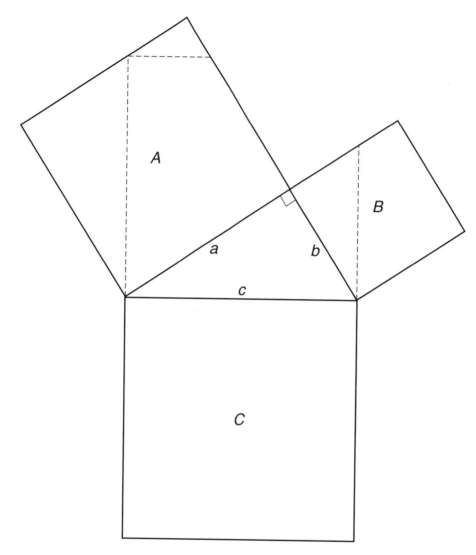

Notice the right triangle with leg *a*, leg *b*, and hypotenuse *c*.
Notice too that c^2 is the algebraic way to write a square with side length *c*.

1. Cut out square *A* and square *B*.
2. Cut square *A* and square *B* along the dashed lines.
3. Tape or paste these four pieces to cover square *C*.
4. What is the relationship between $a^2 + b^2$ and c^2?
    (*Note:* the term a^2 is read aloud as "*a*-squared.")

Measurement: Behind the Units

Measurement is more closely aligned to the real world and to concrete applications than nearly any other branch of mathematics. The earliest societies had a need to quantify linear, weight, area, and other physical attributes. As a result they established primitive measurement systems. As civilizations advanced, they developed measurement systems that became increasingly more complex and were applied to more physical attributes. Today we can measure nanoseconds, the number of light-years across the universe, and the diameters of atoms.

In primary school, children use an intuitive measuring system when they compare their size to other children, their height to the height of a table or a countertop, and their stuffed animal to the real thing. As children progress through elementary school, they continue to make comparisons between concrete objects by direct comparison and with invented and customary measuring scales and units.

In middle school the study of measurement builds on the foundations laid in earlier grades and expands students' understanding of measurement to perimeter and area relationships, to surface area and volume relationships, and to algebraic expressions for these relationships. They also develop facility with both the customary and metric measurement systems.

At first glance, it may appear that measurement should be a less challenging mathematics topic than algebra or probability, but this is not the case. On the 1999 TIMSS, grade 8 students from the United States scored below average on measurement questions. On Measurement achievement the United States ranked twenty-fifth out of 38 countries, with a Measurement test score of 39%. The U.S. grade 8 students were *above* average on questions from Fractions and Number Sense, Algebra, and Data Representation, Analysis, and Probability. Clearly, there is much to do to improve our middle school students' achievement in measurement (International Association for the Evaluation of Educational Achievement, 2005).

Point Well Taken

"From earlier instruction in school and life experience outside school, middle-grades students know that measurement is a process that assigns numerical values to spatial and physical attributes such as length."
—NCTM, 2000, p. 241

NCTM Standards

The general NCTM Measurement Standard and specific recommendations for grades 6–8 are as follows:

1. *Understand measurable attributes* of objects and the units, systems, and processes of measurement.
   - Understand both metric and customary systems of measurement.
   - Understand relationships among units and convert from one unit to another within the same system.
   - Understand, select, and use units of appropriate size and type to measure angles, perimeter, area, surface area, and volume.

2. *Apply appropriate techniques, tools, and formulas* to determine measurements.

- Use common benchmarks to select appropriate methods for estimating measurements.
- Select and apply techniques and tools to accurately find length, area, volume, and angle measures to appropriate levels of precision.
- Develop and use formulas to determine the circumference of circles and the area of triangles, parallelograms, trapezoids, and circles and develop strategies to find the area of more complex shapes.
- Develop strategies to determine the surface area and volume of selected prisms, pyramids, and cylinders.
- Solve problems involving scale factors, using ratio and proportion.
- Solve simple problems involving rates and derived measurements for such attributes as velocity and density (NCTM, 2000, p. 241).

The two measurement strands for grades 6–8 offer a comprehensive goal for measurement instruction in the middle grades. Notice that the first strand is devoted to helping middle school students gain a foundational understanding of the metric and customary measurement systems, the relationships between various units within each system, and appropriate selection and uses of measurement units. The focus of the second strand involves quantitative topics with applications of measurement concepts.

At its simplest level a measurement is a number and a unit, such as 3 feet, 3 quarts, 5 square meters, and 12 cubic inches. Although many word problems include measurement data in their context, some students tend to ignore the measurement unit until the final answer, when they affix the same unit given in the problem onto their answer. Thus, providing problems with a measurement context may not be sufficient to ensure students will acquire a full understanding of measurement concepts.

Point Well Taken

"In the middle grades, students should build on their formal and informal experiences with measurable attributes like length, area and volume; with units of measurement; and with systems of measurement."

—NCTM, 2000, p. 241

Benchmarks

One of the goals for middle school measurement is for students to build their understanding of measurement systems by constructing benchmarks. Students should add to the benchmarks they may have already created in earlier grades, expanding their benchmarks to include weight and capacity in both customary and metric systems. In earlier grades students may have found that their finger or part of their finger was about 1 inch long. Similarly, they may have discovered a part of their arm or their leg that was about 1 foot long. These personal benchmarks need to be reviewed to account for their physical growth, and other benchmarks need to be added to them. Some potential benchmarks are the following:

- A typical textbook weighs about 2 pounds or 1 kilogram.
- A doorway in a house is about 2 meters or 7 feet tall.
- A quart or a liter contains a bit more than two cans of soda.
- A doorknob is about 1 meter above the floor.
- A comfortable temperature range is 70°F–80°F or 25°C–30°C.

Students might also use a computer-based ranger (CBR) to record the distance to an object as students approach it and then walk away. As students record and plot the data, they will improve their ability to gauge distances and develop helpful benchmarks.

Along with developing personal benchmarks, students should also have ample opportunities to select appropriate measurement units for specific tasks. For example, in the middle grades students should be able to determine the appropriate measurement unit for finding the width of the classroom (feet or miles), the weight of a single potato (milligrams or grams), and the distance from Boston to Vancouver (meters or kilometers). Some of the students' facility with appropriate units can come from outside of school experiences, but it is critical to provide appropriate classroom experiences for students to ensure they can select the appropriate measurement unit for a specific measuring task. Otherwise, they may never develop a confidence with measures in real-life contexts and will have difficulty making the many decisions an adult makes that deal with measurements, from carpeting a room to seeding a lawn. Accordingly, all students should have many opportunities to determine the appropriate unit in problems set in real-world settings, such as:

- Is the appropriate unit for the length of a picture frame inches or yards?
- Is the appropriate unit of weight for an adult kilograms or grams?
- Is the appropriate unit of length for the distance from school to a student's house meters or kilometers?

Ample opportunities to discuss the proper unit in such problems strengthen students' understanding of measurement concepts.

In addition to selecting the proper measurement unit, students could then expand the data in a problem to each possible unit as, for example, the weight of an adult could reasonably be 70 kilograms or 70,000 grams. Students might then discuss why 70 kilograms is a better choice than 70,000 grams to represent the adult's weight. Students might also consider problems such as the following:

Is the area of a new carpet that Jamie's parents bought for her house 120 ft^2, 12 ft^2, or 1200 ft^2? (Note that ft^2 represents square feet; in.^{2} represents square inches; and yd^3 represents cubic yards.)

Again, students should explain their answers to their group and the class. By examining their answers to such problems in real-world contexts, students solidify their conceptualization of measurement beyond computation and memorization.

Another basic aspect of measurement that middle school students should understand is that every measurement is an approximation, no matter how carefully measured. An example of this is a football field. The field must measure exactly 100 yards from goal line to goal line, but an actual measurement will probably show the distance is a fraction of an inch off. Such a small difference between the declared length and the actual length is of no consequence for a football field. Similarly, a person who claims his height is 6 feet 2 inches is not exactly that height, and a segment that is drawn to be exactly 6 inches long may be off by the width of the marks on the ruler. Nevertheless, students strive to obtain what they consider to be exact measurements. Because of their prior experience with exact answers in counting and number operations, middle grades students find it difficult to develop a sense of approximation with measurement.

Teachers can help students to understand the approximation aspect of measurements by drawing several circles with the following diameters: 2.5 cm, 3 cm, and 3.4 cm, and then cutting them out. Each of the circles in Figure 9.1 measures 3 cm in diameter, to the nearest centimeter, but they are clearly different sizes. Another set of circles might include diameters of $2\frac{3}{4}$ inches, 3 inches, and $3\frac{3}{8}$ inches. To the nearest $\frac{1}{2}$ inch, each of these circles has a 3-inch diameter, but they are clearly different sizes. Thus, the range of possible circle sizes depends on the degree of precision. There is always some variance in the range due to the limitations of the measurement. As a result, every measurement must be

> ## Point Well Taken
>
> "Students' experiences with measurement on the (middle) school level shape their facility with measurement as an adult."
> —Meeks & Wheeler, 2003, p. 193

> ## Point Well Taken
>
> "Measurement activities can and should require a dynamic interaction between students and their environment. . . . Measurement should be an active exploration of the real world."
> —NCTM, 1989, p. 116

figure **9.1**

Circles to Show Approximation

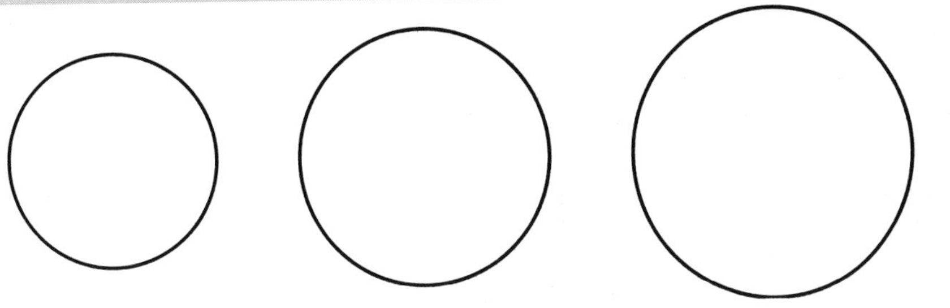

approximate to some degree of precision no matter how expressed. (See Blackline Master 9.1, How Close Is Close?)

TRY THIS

A garden fence measures 58 feet to the nearest foot. What is the range for the length of the fence?

Measurement Systems

Did You **Know**?

The metric system was developed shortly after the French Revolution (1789) by a committee established by the revolutionary government. The committee was one of many created to eliminate all vestiges of the former monarchy, including the traditional measurement systems.

Middle school students should have had numerous experiences with the metric and U.S. or customary measurement systems in elementary school. It is in the middle grades that students should become fully competent when working within each measurement system, making conversions within each system, solving real-world applications with them, and applying benchmarks for various measurement units in each system. We recommend that students continue to use both measurement systems throughout the middle school years. Although students will have studied the metric system for several years in the lower grades, there is usually a need to revisit this topic with some students. We do not intend to review every aspect of the metric system here but will highlight those aspects that are critical for a competent understanding of the system.

REACHING DIVERSE LEARNERS

One main topic in measurement is the metric system. Students who are new to the United States learned the metric system in their previous school. These students could give personal experiences of how they learned the metric system and describe how they used it in their country. They could also peer tutor students to help them understand and apply the metric system.

The Metric System

The metric system is based on successive powers of 10. The chart shown here shows the relationship between the various units. Notice that the basic unit measures for length (meter), mass (gram), and capacity (liter) all use the same prefixes to indicate other measurement units within the metric system.

1000	100	10		.1	.01	.001
kilo	hecto	deca	GRAM	deci	centi	milli
kilo	hecto	deca	METER	deci	centi	milli
kilo	hecto	deca	LITER	deci	centi	milli

Did You **Know**?

The original kilogram, a bar of platinum dating from the time of the French Revolution, still exists. It is stored in an airtight vault in Sevres, France.

The Greek prefixes (*kilo-*, *hecto-*, *deca-*) designate units larger than the unit measure (gram, meter, liter), and the Latin prefixes (*deci-*, *centi-*, *milli-*) designate those measures smaller than the unit measure. The symbols for each prefix are as follows: kilo, hecto, deka, deci, centi, and milli. Note that these are *symbols*, not abbreviations, so they do not require a trailing period. Converting from one unit, such as kilograms, to another unit, such as grams, is accomplished by using a conversion factor that is a multiple of 10, in this case 1000. When students contrast this simple relationship between metric measures to the morass of conversion factors in the customary system (2 cups = 1 quart, 16 ounces = 1 pound, 36 inches = 1 yard, 5,280 feet = 1 mile), they will appreciate why all other industrialized nations around the world have adopted the metric system. Although the metric system is not fully incorporated into our society, we see liters of soda and metric equivalents on most packaging. Running events in track and field are no longer in yards but in meters, and any company doing business with the federal government must supply metric measures for any product.

Another important aspect of the metric system is that the three basic measurement units (meter, liter, and gram) are related. A cube that is 1 centimeter on each edge contains a milliliter of water. The weight of a milliliter of water is a gram. This connection between length, capacity, and weight in the metric system is in stark contrast to the customary system where feet, pounds, and gallons have nothing in common.

In addition to establishing useful benchmarks for various measurement units, students should also formulate benchmarks between the customary and metric systems. Although NCTM discourages skill computations to convert between the two measurement systems, benchmarks of various measures between the two systems can be useful. Students might remember that a meter is only slightly longer than a yard or that a kilometer is a bit longer than half a mile. Similarly, a kilogram is a bit more than 2 pounds and a quart is just barely smaller than a liter. A poster or visual model showing these comparisons can help students to remember the relationships.

The Customary System

By the time students reach middle school they should have had sufficient experiences with converting measures within both the customary and the metric systems so that the focus in middle grades can be on other aspects of measurement, such as area and volume relationships. However, some students may still have difficulty converting measurements, despite knowing the appropriate conversion factors. A student who is trying to convert 156 inches into feet likely will know that 1 foot = 12 inches. The difficulty that some students can have with such a problem arises when they try to decide whether to multiply or divide by 12.

There are two ways students might reflect about this seemingly simple problem of having to convert 156 inches into feet. In one method, students should think about the fact that a foot is longer than an inch. That means that fewer feet are needed to equal the same length as a specific number of inches. As the size of a unit increases, the number of units needed for a specific length (or any attribute) decreases. The answer to the problem is the number of feet that are equivalent to 156 inches. Because a foot is longer than an inch, the number of feet that is equal in length to 156 inches is smaller than 156. This conversion may be solved by dividing by 12, resulting in a smaller number of feet than inches.

A second approach is to write the problem in a proportion, as follows.

$$\frac{12 \text{ inches}}{1 \text{ foot}} = \frac{156 \text{ inches}}{x \text{ feet}}$$

In this case students can solve for the missing term by means of equivalent fractions, because 12 is a factor of 156. For conversions that do not lend themselves to such a solution, such as 150 inches = ? feet, students can write the problem as a proportion and use cross products. It is critical that students fully understand proportional reasoning before they employ the cross-product algorithm (see Chapter 6, Making Sense of Number and Operations, for more on the cross-product algorithm in proportions).

There are many other equivalent measures that students should know ranging from 32 fluid ounces in a quart to 16 ounces in a pound. Students may benefit from a graphic organizer in addition to a table of equivalent measures as they try to remember these various equivalents. One student designed the organizer in Figure 9.2 to help her recall liquid measures.

The large G represents gallons. The four large Qs on the G shows there are 4 quarts to a gallon. She then placed 2 P's representing pints on each quart, and then 2 C's for cups on each pint. Finally, she put an 8 in each cup for 8 ounces in a cup. Graphic organizers such as this can be quite helpful for some students because they can visualize the relative size and relationships between various measures.

REACT | REFLECT

How confident are you with the metric system? Why do you think this is so?

Point Well Taken

"Work in the metric system ties nicely to students' emerging understanding of, and proficiency in, decimal computation and the use of scientific notation to express large numbers."
—NCTM, 2000, p. 241

Did You **Know**?

Since 1983 a meter is defined as the distance light travels in a vacuum in $\frac{1}{299,792,458}$ second.

AUTHOR'S **Recall**

I remember during my first year of teaching a school board member saying that "the metric system is a Communist-backed plot to undermine our American traditions."

Point Well Taken

"In the middle grades [students] should become proficient in converting measurements to different units within a system, recognizing new equivalences, such as 1 square yard equals 9 square feet and 1 cubic meter equals 1,000,000 cubic centimeters."
—NCTM, 2000, p. 241

Did You **Know**?

Our word *mile* comes from the Latin phrase *mille passus*, meaning one thousand paces. A pace is about 5 feet, so 1,000 paces is approximately a mile.

figure **9.2**

Graphic Organizer

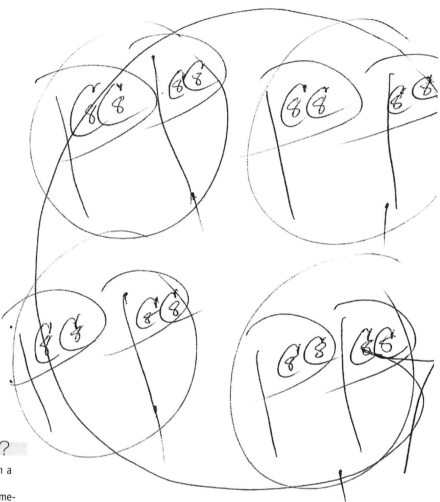

Did You **Know**?

The word *yard* is derived from a Middle English term meaning "wrap around the waist." In medieval times a sash around the waist doubled as a handy yardstick. The length of a yard was formally established by King Henry I of England (1069–1135) as the distance from the end of his outstretched hand to the tip of the royal nose. It took another 400 years for the official length to be inscribed on a bronze bar.

At www.bbc.co.uk/education/mathsfile/shockwave/games/animal.html, students must determine what conversion weight (metric or customary) will balance a specific weight of animal on the other side of the scale (e.g., 2.34 kg = 234 g, 2,340 g, or 23.4 g).

Did You **Know**?

A *jiffy* is a length of time. It is $\frac{1}{100}$ of a second.

Did You **Know**?

A picosecond is one-trillionth of a second.

MATH IN THE MEDIA

In this day and age of technology standardization, there is a movement afoot in Cambridge, Massachusetts, to introduce a new measurement length—the smoot. The smoot was first used by Lambda Chi Alpha, a fraternity at the Massachusetts Institute of Technology. The smoot is based on the height of Oliver R. Smoot, Jr., who was rolled, end to end, across the Charles River on Harvard Bridge in October 1958 as a fraternity prank. The fraternity determined that the length of the bridge was 364.4 smoots plus one ear. As his fraternity brothers rolled Smoot across the bridge, they dutifully marked 10-smoot lengths along the bridge sidewalk. The markings have been re-marked semiannually by the later members of the fraternity to preserve them.

Although it is doubtful that the smoot will ever become as mainstream as the yard or the inch, Smoot himself remains hopeful. He recently mused, "I understand that the yard got its start as the length of the king's arm." So even if the smoot hasn't caught the public's attention yet, Smoot is still optimistic that "maybe there's a future for the microsmoot or the kilosmoot."

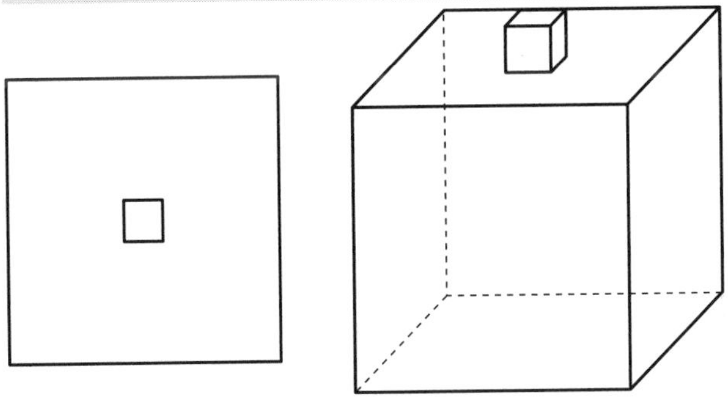

Did You **Know**?

The Fibonacci sequence (1, 1, 2, 3, 5, 8, 13, 21, 34, . . .) may be used by tourists in a foreign country to convert between miles and kilometers. For example, 8 miles is equal to 13 kilometers, and 34 kilometers is equal to 21 miles.

MISCONCEPTION

An aspect of measurement conversion that can be troublesome for middle grades students involves square and cubic units. Even after students understand the concepts of area and volume and can use the appropriate formulas to compute both of them, they can still have difficulty with conversions in square and cubic measures. The reason is that the conversion factors are not the same as with linear measures. The first measurement units students learn involve some application of linear units—their height, the length of a ski pole, the height of a bicycle, or the height of a door. The subsequent development of measurement skills and related applications still focuses on linear dimensions. Most adults can estimate a distance of 6 feet but would have more difficulty estimating an area of 6 square feet or a volume of 6 cubic feet. The tendency is for students to see all measurement conversions through the lens of linear conversion factors. In linear measure 1 foot equals 12 inches, but 1 *square* foot equals 144 square inches and 1 *cubic* foot equals 1,728 cubic inches.

There are several ways that teachers can help students put aside this misconception. Students might consider square and cubic conversions as follows:

$$1 \text{ foot} = 12 \text{ inches}$$
$$1 \text{ square foot} = 12^2 \text{ square inches}$$
$$1 \text{ cubic foot} = 12^3 \text{ cubic inches}$$

Note that if square units are involved, then the linear conversion factor, in this case 12 inches to a foot, is *squared,* resulting in 12^2 or 144 square inches per square foot. In like manner, when cubic units are involved, the linear conversion factor of 12 is now *cubed,* resulting in 12^3 or 1,728 cubic inches per cubic foot. All other area and volume conversions may be represented the same way, by either squaring or cubing the appropriate linear conversion factor. When students pay close attention to the measurement units (square or cubic), they then have an indication of the conversion factor they must use. When students think about area and volume conversion factors as extensions of the linear factors as shown here, they need not memorize a new set of conversion factors but instead can derive the needed factor from the linear conversion factors.

Another effective aid to help students remember that linear conversion units are not used with square and cubic measures might be a visual display such as Figure 9.3. Groups of students can build cubic inches and cubic feet and square inches and square feet out of cardboard to get a sense of the difference between these conversion factors and linear conversion factors. A casual glance at a square inch centered in a square foot quickly shows that it will take more than 12 square inches to cover 1 square foot. Similarly, a cubic inch set on top of a cubic foot clearly shows that many more than 12 cubic inches fill a cubic foot.

Many students need only a quick reminder that square and cubic conversion units are different from linear units, and they are able to work correctly with area and volume units. A model students themselves have built provides the visual reminder to them about the different conversion factors. Students could also build metric models, but generally a single visual display that shows how different area and volume conversions units is sufficient to create a mnemonic reminder for students.

REACT | **REFLECT**

What misconception does Lanier display here?
$$3 \text{ ft}^2 = 36 \text{ in.}^2$$

figure **9.3**

Square and Cubic Inches and Square and Cubic Feet

TRY THIS

How many cubic feet in 2 cubic yards?

Angle Measure

One measurement attribute that students first consider in middle grades is angle measure. Students in upper elementary school begin to study individual angles. They can usually recognize right angles and straight angles and memorize their respective measures. However, the ability to recognize specific angles such as these can mask students' confusion about what is actually measured when an angle is declared to measure 60°. The confusion is understandable because most early measurement concepts involve attributes that students measure by employing a ruler for length, unit containers for capacity, scales for weight, and clocks for time. An angle does not have an easily measured dimension for determining its size. Students tend to view an angle through the filter of linear measure. Students can mistakenly think the lengths of the rays, or the distance between the rays, indicate the measure of the angle.

Point Well Taken

"It remains a major challenge to help students develop understanding of angle and its measure."
—*Lehrer, 2003, p. 187*

ASSESSMENT TIP

It is important to help students who confuse linear measure with angle measure. Showing students the three angles in Figure 9.4 (which are all congruent) and asking them to rank them in order of magnitude can help a teacher to determine which students require some remediation or foundational understanding about angle measure.

Degree measure is a proportional measure and so is not studied extensively in lower grades because younger students cannot reason about proportions to the degree of sophistication needed for angle measure.

Most students know that a circle has 360 degrees from watching basketball players spin a full 360° when making a slam dunk or from watching snowboarders spin two full revolutions or 720°. This forms a good foundation to understanding angle measure, but it still does not explain how an angle is measured in degrees. The fact that all circles, *regardless of size*, contain 360 degrees is counterintuitive to all that students have learned previously about measurement; a longer stick has more inches, a larger poster has more square inches, and a bigger rock weighs more. Nevertheless, by middle grades, students can understand the proportional relationships of degree measure. Consider ∠*ABC* shown in Figure 9.5.

figure **9.4**

Congruent Angles

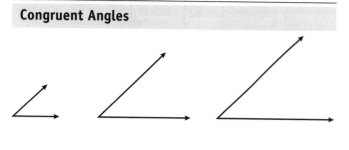

figure **9.5**

Angle Measurement

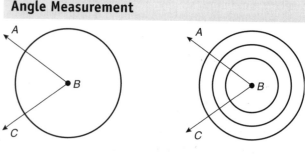

a   b

In Figure 9.5, ∠*ABC* takes up $\frac{1}{6}$ of circle *B*. Because a circle is defined as consisting of 360°, then ∠*ABC* is $\frac{1}{6}$ × 360° = 60°. The lengths of ray *BA* and ray *BC* are irrelevant regarding the degree measure of ∠*ABC*. A smaller circle or a larger circle as shown in part *b* results in ∠*ABC* taking up $\frac{1}{6}$ of these other circles. ∠*ABC* will take up $\frac{1}{6}$ of any circle that is added to the diagram. (In each case, the circles must have point *B* as their center.)

In all three cases, $\frac{1}{6}$ of each circle represents 60°. Similarly, $\frac{1}{4}$ of a circle is 90° and $\frac{1}{2}$ of any circle is 180°. Just as the lengths of the rays are unimportant for degree measure, so is the distance between the rays. The linear relationship that seems to be an intuitive method for comparing angles proves to be misleading. Angle measures can be determined only by employing degree measures with an appropriate circle.

Once students understand what a degree measure is actually quantifying, they can readily understand how to use a protractor to measure angles (See Figure 9.6). However, many students are confused when trying to read the degree measure from a typical protractor.

The angle shown here has been properly aligned with the protractor, and the degree measure may be read by determining the reading for where ray *BA* passes through the protractor. However, the reading for ray *BA* may be given as 60° or 120°. Some students try to memorize a jingle about which scale to employ by thinking about which end of the protractor is aligned with the angle. We suggest a different approach—benchmarks.

As previously mentioned, students have a strong visual connection to a straight angle and a right angle. These visual connections may be used with an angle wheel (see Blackline Master 9.2) to help students develop their ability to estimate angle size. The angle wheel is designed to display a shaded angle to the class (and an angle reading toward the teacher). A teacher can quickly display an angle wheel reading to students and ask for the measure. It is best if the degree measure of each displayed angle is a multiple of 10. If a student gives an incorrect estimation of a displayed angle, the teacher can offer hints, "higher" or " lower," before asking another student for a new estimate. Several students will be able to read angles on the angle wheel in a matter of only a minute or two. A few class sessions consisting of two or three minutes with the angle wheel can suffice for students to develop a reasonable skill at angle estimation and, more importantly, using a right angle as a benchmark. (See Figure 9.7.)

In a short time students will easily recognize acute angles and obtuse angles by comparing them to the visual image they have for a right angle. This right angle benchmark can be used when reading the angle in the protractor displayed in Figure 9.6. If students

figure **9.6**

Using a Protractor to Measure ∠ABC

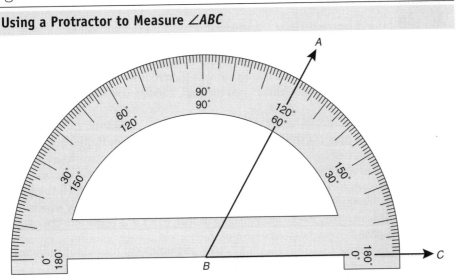

figure **9.7**

The Angle Wheel

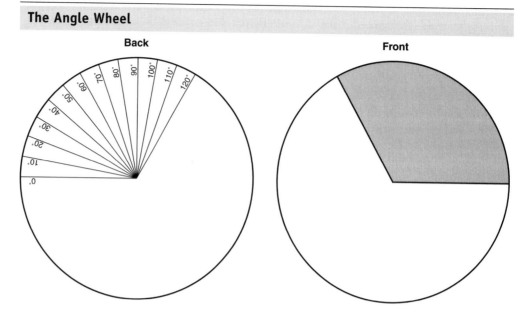

Back   Front

consider how this angle compares to their benchmark of a right angle, then they can eas-ily tell it is a 60° angle and not a 120° angle.

Once students are able to estimate angle size using benchmarks and can properly use a protractor to measure angles, they will generally have no further difficulties with an-gles per se. The future study of angles in parallel lines, in polygons, and in degrees of ro-tation in transformations becomes more a case of distinguishing features of angle relationships rather than a study of angle measure.

Students can use a circular geoboard with several concentric circles to create angles with specific measures. The applet with such a geoboard is at http://nlvm.usu.edu/en/nav/category_g_3_t_3.html. At the site http://descartes.cnice.mecd.es/ingles/1st&2nd_secondary_educ/measuring_angles/angulos1.htm, students can change the size of an an-gle as the measure is displayed. They can also measure angles on a protractor.

REACT | REFLECT

How would you explain to a sixth grader that the lengths of an angle's sides are not re-lated to its angle measure?

RESEARCH

Swiss researcher Jean Piaget found in his research that younger children tend to view height rather than width as the predominant linear measure, even when examining volume (Piaget et al., 1960). Young children will think a tall, thin cylinder will hold more than a large bowl, because the bowl is so much shorter. Even when the cylinder is filled with water, and then the water is poured into the bowl, children still think the cylinder con-tains more water.

Surprisingly, adults retain some sense of height-to-width dominance. In a recent study adults were asked to pour the same amount of liquid into a short, squat glass and into a tall thin glass. In most cases adults poured substantially less into the tall glass. When the exper-iment was repeated with bartenders, they also poured far less into the tall glass. One conclu-sion of the study is that even for professionals such as bartenders, the tendency is still to think of "tall as more" compared to short and wide. Most of the subjects in the study were aware of their tendency, and so they overcompensated by pouring much less liquid into the tall glass (*Science News*, 2003).

figure **9.8**

Using the Geometer's Sketchpad to Explore Angle Measure

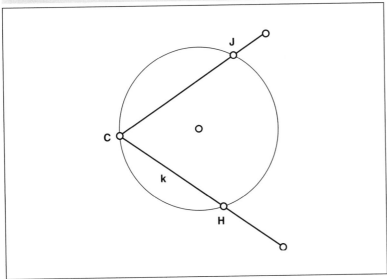

Source: The Geometer's Sketchpad. Used by permission of Key Curriculum Press, 1150 65th Street, Emeryville, CA 94608, 1-800-995-MATH, www.keypress.com/sketchpad.

Technology

We have shown in previous discussions how technology can be used in its various media to help students understand measurement concepts by employing Computer Based Laboratories, the Internet, Cabri geoboards, and dynamic geometry software. Dynamic geometry software can be especially helpful when students are exploring angle measures on a circle. In Figure 9.8, ∠1 has rays that pass through the endpoints of $\overline{JH}$. The measure of $\overwidehat{JH}$ is 80°. As the vertex point of the angle is dragged to different places on the circle, the measure of ∠1 remains the same (40°), as does the intercepted arc ($\overwidehat{JH}$). The conjecture is quickly determined: the measure of an inscribed angle is equal to one-half the measure of the inscribed arc. Other angle and arc relationships may be explored in the same fashion.

Area and Perimeter

Polygons

By the middle grades, students will have had many experiences with the concepts of perimeter and area, using string for forming a boundary to determine perimeter and small squares and other shapes for covering a surface to determine area. By the middle grades they will also have worked with some perimeter and area formulas. However, students in the middle grades and beyond still continue to confuse the two terms and their respective formulas. Although practice using the various formulas in context can be helpful, it can be especially beneficial to continually stress the basic difference between perimeter and area while considering these measurement topics. Perimeter is a linear distance, for example, the length of fencing around a lawn or the frame around a painting. Area is a covering measurement, for example, the amount of grass seed needed for a lawn or the amount of carpet needed for a dining room.

Generally students can easily determine the perimeter of a polygon, once they have the proper concept in mind, by computing the sum of the side lengths. Area presents a

Point Well Taken

"About one-third of eighth grade students in the United States could not draw a rectangle with an area of 12 square units on a grid."

—*Strutchens, 2003, p. 189*

figure **9.9**

Area of a Rectangle

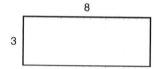

Point Well Taken

Whenever possible, students should develop formulas and procedures meaningfully through investigation rather than memorize them.

—*NCTM, 2000, p. 244*

figure **9.10**

Width and Length in a Rectangle

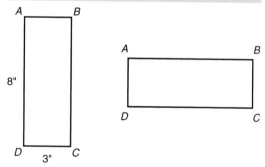

greater challenge to middle school students because the polygons that are studied in middle grades each have their own distinct formula, and for some students the task becomes one of memorizing the respective formulas without any foundational understanding. Students who do so are unlikely to recall these memorized formulas, will confuse which formula matches which polygon, or will forget specific formulas.

We recommend that students have ample exploration activities to develop a foundational understanding for the various area formulas and repeat these activities even if students had engaged in them in earlier grades. In the middle grades the goal is to develop working formulas for computing areas from activities such as those that follow.

In elementary school, students use rectangular arrays to generate the basic ideas of multiplication. It is a short step from using arrays for multiplication facts to developing the formula for the area of a rectangle.

An 8×3 array would represent the number sentence $8 \times 3 = 24$. The rectangle in Figure 9.9 has an area that is determined in the same way as the array number sentence 8 in. $\times$ 3 in. $= 24$ in.^{2} Most students have learned in elementary school that the area of a rectangle is the product of the length and width of the rectangle, or $l \times w = A$. While this is an effective formula, we recommend that students think of the area as the product of the base and height, or $b \times h = A$. Using base and height in place of length and width will allow middle grades students to relate subsequent area formulas to each other as discussed later. Another reason for using $b \times h = A$ is that the terms *base* and *height* do not have the same connotation as *length* and *width*. Given the first rectangle in Figure 9.10, many upper elementary school students would have difficulty identifying side *AD* as a width.

However, they could easily do so in the second rectangle. The reason is that length and width carry with them the idea of comparative size. That is, the width is considered shorter than the length, and so the first rectangle presents a problem to students who have this misconception. Using base length $\times$ height = area will help students leave behind the misconception of the width as the shorter of the two sides in a rectangle. Base and height do not carry with them any sense of qualitative lengths. Students will understand that one rectangle is the rotation of the other and that which side is the "base" and which is the "height" is unimportant insofar as computing the area.

Before considering the area formulas of various polygons, it is important to discuss the concept of square measure because students will compute it for the rectangle shown in Figure 9.10. Once students understand that area is a covering and perimeter is a length, it is important to clarify that any area measure must be expressed in *square* units. Again, reference to rectangles as arrays will call this to mind for most students. At first, students can draw in the lines of the rectangle arrays to reveal the squares, thus helping to define the unit of measure for a square unit. As students perform computations to determine area measures, it is important that they use the measurement unit in their calculations. For the rectangles in Figure 9.10 a student might compute the area as follows:

$$b \times h = A$$
$$3 \text{ in.} \times 8 \text{ in.} = A$$
$$24 \text{ in.}^2 = A$$

As suggested earlier, some students might complete their computations and then simply assign a unit to their answer. The inclination to tack on the unit after the computation can tend to remove a problem from its context and turn it into a simple computation with a final step of units labeling. We suggest that units are an integral part of any problem involving area (or another measure) and the units should appear throughout the problem. This way students have the measures in mind as they are solving the problem, and rather than affixing an appropriate unit to their answer, they will have determined the unit measure as a result of their computation.

There is another advantage to having students use appropriate units in their computation. From the preceding problem, 3 in. × 8 in. = A. The solution might be expressed this way:

$$A = (3 \text{ in.})(8 \text{ in.}) = 24 \text{ in.}^2$$

Note that the label of the computed answer, in.^{2}, is an algebraic way of representing square inches. When students study area formulas in this format, they can see the results of multiplying exponents in a geometric setting.

The common polygons that middle school students will study include parallelograms, triangles, rhombuses, and trapezoids. Students who simply memorize individual area formulas for each of these will likely need to relearn most of them in subsequent years of school and eventually will forget them soon after they leave their formal geometry class in high school. In order for students to recall these respective formulas, it is necessary for them to understand their relationship to each other by engaging in activities such as the ones that follow.

Students can cut any parallelogram into two parts and then rearrange the two parts to form a rectangle. The resulting rectangle in Figure 9.11 has the same base length and height as the original parallelogram, and so these lengths may be used in the parallelogram to find its area using the same area formula as for the rectangle; i.e., $A = b \times h$.

MISCONCEPTION

When students compute the area of a rectangle, they use the base and height, which are also the side lengths. In a parallelogram the side lengths are not the base and height, but some students will still use side lengths to determine the area of a parallelogram. For the parallelogram in Figure 9.12, some students will compute an area of 54 ft^2 (9 ft × 6 ft), instead of using the height to compute the correct area of 36 ft^2 (9 ft × 4 ft).

Even students who have learned their area formulas and can compute areas of various shapes may not have a deep conceptual understanding of area. For many students computing the area (or volume) of a figure is simply a matter of plugging numbers into a formula and then computing the answer. Such a cursory method leads to students using the wrong data from a figure to compute its area. Certainly teachers can point out such erroneous methods to students as they study various shapes, either by calling students' attention to the incorrect approach or by presenting to students the incorrect process in a problem and asking them to determine what is wrong.

We suggest that at times students gather the data they need for an area or volume formula. Students might be given a cardboard shape, such as a parallelogram or a trapezoid, and then measure with a ruler to determine the data for the respective formula. This will help students develop a sense of what segment lengths are critical for determining the area of a figure and engenders in students a sense of how the data are used in the formula.

figure **9.11**

Area of a Parallelogram

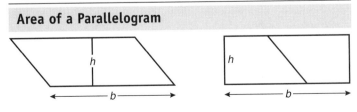

figure **9.12**

Base and Height of a Parallelogram

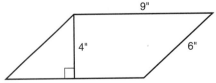

figure **9.13**

Area of a Triangle

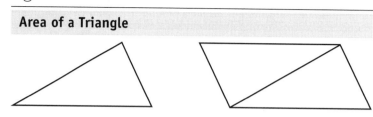

When students study triangle area, they should explore the following idea.

As Figure 9.13 shows, any triangle can be duplicated and then the two triangles combined to form a single parallelogram. How does the base of the original triangle compare to the base of the resulting parallelogram? How do their altitudes compare? In both cases they are the same length. Because students already know how to compute the area of a parallelogram, they can use that formula to compute the area of a triangle, which is one-half the area of the parallelogram or $A = \frac{1}{2}(bh)$.

Sometimes students will try to apply the $\frac{1}{2}$ in the triangle formula to both the base and the height. Students who try to do so are likely recalling the distributive law and are misapplying the law to this situation.

There are several ways teachers can address this mistaken process. A review of the distributive law can be helpful, along with several examples and nonexamples of the correct procedure for students to examine, such as

$$3 \times 4 \times 5 \overset{?}{=} 12 \times 5 \qquad 3 \times 4 \times 5 \overset{?}{=} 12 \times 15 \qquad 3 \times 4 \times 5 \overset{?}{=} 3 \times 15$$

An examination of the diagram in Figure 9.14 can also benefit students. In Figure 9.14, the area of the parallelogram is determined by $A = bh = 6\ \text{cm} \times 10\ \text{cm} = 60\ \text{cm}^2$. The area of one of the triangles must be 30 because the area of one triangle is one-half the area of the parallelogram. If the computed area of the triangle is not 30, then students can focus on their computation methods to determine why the computed area is not the same as one-half the area of the parallelogram.

figure **9.14**

Area of a Triangle Related to the Area of a Parallelogram

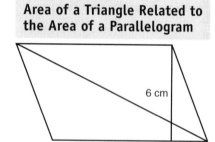

6 cm

10 cm

MISCONCEPTION

Many students who can correctly compute the area of a triangle using the area formula believe there is only one base and height from which the area is determined. Few students understand that any side of a triangle can be considered the base and each side has a respective altitude or height.

To help students expand their thinking about altitudes and bases in triangles, it is advantageous for them to use a straightedge to draw all three altitudes in various triangles. Figure 9.15 shows the three altitudes in an acute triangle. It is best to begin with acute triangles, then build to right triangles (whose legs are altitudes), and then to obtuse triangle (whose sides need to be extended in order to draw altitudes).

figure **9.15**

The Three Altitudes of a Triangle

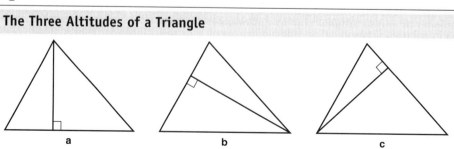

a   b   c

In Figure 9.15, the three altitudes are displayed in each of the three congruent triangles. Triangle a shows the common orientation for triangles, the base-is-the-bottom orientation. The altitudes in triangle b and triangle c are quite difficult for students to draw at first, especially in this orientation. Students could rotate their papers to orient the triangles into the familiar base-is-the-bottom orientation at first to help them draw additional altitudes of the triangle. After a few experiences drawing all the altitudes of a triangle, students need no longer rotate the triangle into the base-on-the-bottom position.

Students' inability to see or draw more than one altitude in a triangle is more a function of not having seen triangles in different orientations than it is a characteristic of a van Hiele level (see Chapter 8, Geometry: Moving Beyond Formulas). Once students can confidently draw all the altitudes of a triangle, they might be asked to determine the area of cardboard triangles. In this case a group could be given three copies of the same triangle and students asked to determine the area by measuring and computing with a different altitude on each triangle. Students can draw the respective altitudes on each triangle and also the height and base length they used to compute the area. Naturally the areas of all three triangles should be very close, allowing for measurement rounding. When students compute the same area using each of the altitudes, they further solidify their understanding that every triangle has three altitudes, each of which may be used to compute the area. This concept may then be extended to other figures as, for example, finding the two altitudes on a parallelogram.

figure **9.16**

Parallelogram

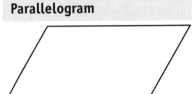

TRY THIS

Draw the two altitudes in the parallelogram in Figure 9.16.

PROCESS STANDARDS

Communication

The ability to communicate one's findings during exploration activities is an integral part of individual and group advancement in mathematics. In this activity students examine the areas of triangles on a geoboard. The task is to find all seven noncongruent triangles on a geoboard with an area of 1 square unit. Most students easily find the two shown here in Figure 9.17 (figure x) and then are perplexed when attempting to find any additional triangles.

Once students begin to discuss the formula for triangle area and focus on the base and height of the given triangles, they can then search for additional noncongruent triangles on the geoboard with a base and height of 1 and 2 units.

Another of the seven triangles is shown in Figure 9.17 (figure y). It is difficult for most students to visually determine that the area of this triangle is the same as triangle a and triangle b shown in figure x, 1 square unit. By keying on the base length and height of the tri-

figure **9.17**

Triangles on a Geoboard

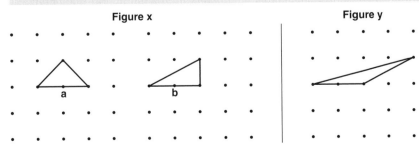

angle in figure y, students can explain to group members that it must have an area of 1 square unit. Then students are on their way to discovering the other 1-square unit triangles on their own rather than having a classmate show all the possible triangles.

TRY THIS

Draw all seven triangles with a one-square unit area that are possible on a geoboard.

Elementary school students can recognize a trapezoid but it is not until middle school that they learn to compute areas. The formula is confusing to students because it includes a fraction ($\frac{1}{2}$) and an addition operation in the formula. Students who try to memorize the formula without any understanding tend to confuse the addition operation with multiplication because all the other area formulas involve multiplication exclusively. Because the formula resembles the triangle area formula, students may get confused. If students have the opportunity to explore the area of a trapezoid, they can construct an understanding of the formula that will eliminate the need for rote memorization.

Any trapezoid can be duplicated and then the two identical trapezoids can be combined to form a parallelogram, much like any triangle can be duplicated and then the two combined to form a single parallelogram.

As shown in Figure 9.18, the new parallelogram has the same height as the original trapezoid. The base of the new parallelogram is the sum of the two bases of the original trapezoid. We find the area of the parallelogram by $A = bh$ or $A = (b_1 + b_2)h$. Because the original trapezoid area is one-half the area of the composite parallelogram, we can write the formula for the area of any trapezoid as $A = \frac{1}{2}(b_1 + b_2)h$. Developing the formula this way helps students understand the addition operation as part of the formula and, like the triangle activity, clarifies the role of the fraction $\frac{1}{2}$ in the formula.

figure **9.18**

Area of a Trapezoid

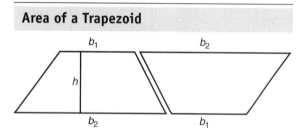

TRY THIS

In Figure 9.19 parts of a trapezoid (figure a) have been cut up and rearranged to form a rectangle (figure b). Explain how the trapezoid formula is developed by this method. The middle segment in figure b may be formed by folding one base of the original trapezoid onto the other base.

MISCONCEPTION

In lower grades students begin their study of area by examining squares. The area for any square may be determined by the perimeter and vice versa. For example, a square with area 25 m² has a side length of 5 meters and a perimeter of 4 × 5, or 20 meters. Conversely, a square with a perimeter of 48 feet has a side length of 12 feet ($\frac{48}{4}$) and an area of 144 square feet. Many middle school students believe that the

figure **9.19**

Alternate Method for the Area of a Trapezoid

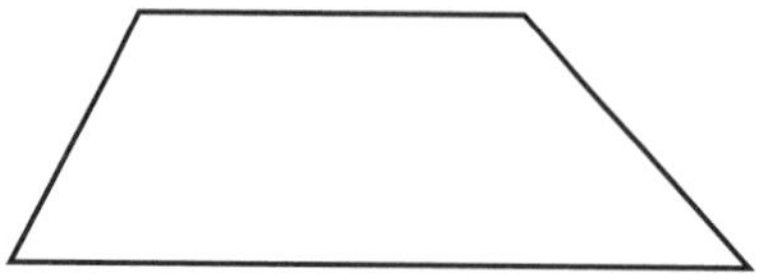

Figure a 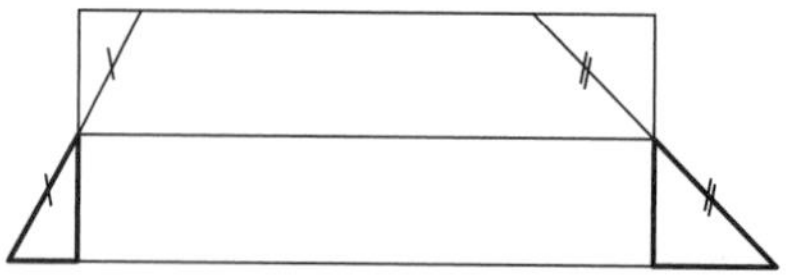   Figure b table **9.1**   **Integer Side Lengths for a Rectangle with a 20-ft. Perimeter**

BASE	HEIGHT	PERIMETER	AREA
9 ft	1 ft	20 ft	9 ft^2
8 ft	2 ft	20 ft	16 ft^2
7 ft	3 ft	20 ft	21 ft^2
6 ft	4 ft	20 ft	24 ft^2
5 ft	5 ft	20 ft	25 ft^2

same relationship exists for rectangles. That is, given the perimeter (or area) of a rectangle, one can determine its area (or perimeter).

To help students overcome this misconception, they might consider a rectangle with a fixed perimeter of 20 feet and build a data table as shown in Table 9.1.

The data show that a rectangle with a fixed perimeter of 20 feet can have many different dimensions and resulting areas. Students might repeat this process with other rectangles to solidify their understanding of area–perimeter relationships. Sufficient attention to such data can help students understand the ambiguity of trying to determine the area of a rectangle with perimeter 100 feet. Are the dimensions (in feet) of the rectangle 49×1, 48×2, 47×3? It is impossible to be sure.

Another activity that can help students remove this misconception that area and perimeter are directly related is to have them cut enough string to form a 2×2 square on a geoboard. Students can then try to use the same length of string to form the perimeter of another rectangle (such as a 1×3). Students will discover that the 1×3 rectangle has the same perimeter but a different area (3 units compared to 4 units for the square). Students might also form rectangles with square tiles. For example 12 tiles can be used to form three different rectangles (3×4, 2×6, 1×12), all with the same area (12 tiles) but with different perimeters. The 3×4 rectangle has the shortest perimeter of the three possible rectangles. If students repeat this activity with 16 tiles, they will get similar results; several different rectangles, all with different perimeters, can have an area of 16 square units. In this case, the rectangle with the shortest perimeter is the square of side 4.

The results of the tiles activity and the data in Table 9.1 point to an interesting relationship that does exist between area and perimeter. Students will enjoy exploring the minimum perimeter rectangle for any given area. The data in Table 9.1 and the results of the tiles activity suggest that a rectangle in the shape of a square has the shortest perimeter for a given area. In the table the rectangle with the largest area is in the shape of a square. Notice how the graph in Figure 9.20 displays the data for the minimum perimeter of various rectangles with an area of 36 square units. It shows that the rectangle with the minimum perimeter has a width of 6, and so it also has a base of 6. The minimum perimeter rectangle is a 6×6 square. By using Table 9.1, the results of the tiles activity, and the graph, students can make the conjecture that for a given area the rectangle with the shortest perimeter is a square. (See Blackline Master 9.5, Minimum Perimeter.)

At www.mste.uiuc.edu/carvell/rectperim/RectPerim2.html students can explore the relationship between the area and the perimeter of rectangles.

Did You **Know**?

It was Greek mathematician Zenodorus (c. 200 B.C.E.–140 B.C.E.) who first wrote about polygons with minimum perimeter and maximum area.

TRY THIS

Given 100 feet of fence, what shape would enclose the largest area? (No, it's not a square.)

figure **9.20**

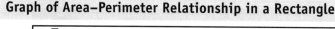

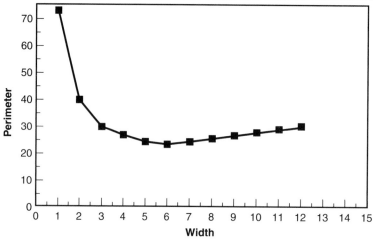

Graph of Area–Perimeter Relationship in a Rectangle

ASSESSMENT TIP

When students apply area formulas to problems, they tend to make common errors. As mentioned earlier, one common error is when students use the two sides of a parallelogram to find the area. Another common error is for students to multiply the base lengths of the trapezoid instead of finding their sum. A teacher who is aware of these and other common errors can help students to avoid them by posting such a solution on the board and asking students to correct the error. Teachers should also have students provide a rationale about why it is in error. As with other misconceptions, a teacher should be alert to this and help students correct them as soon as they arise. When students repeat the same misconception a number of times, it becomes ingrained in their understanding and very resistant to correction.

Did You **Know**?

The first mathematician to use π for the circumference/diameter ratio was William Jones in 1707. He selected π for the symbol because it is the first letter of the Greek word for *perimeter*.

Did You **Know**?

The French mathematician Compte de Buffon derived the value of π by flipping a loaf of French bread on a tile floor. (See Blackline Master 9.3, Flipping for π.)

Circles

The formulas for the circumference and area of a circle use the most famous symbol in mathematics, π. The Greek letter π has been used as the title of a science fiction movie, a snowboard model, and even a men's cologne. The symbol π is used to represent the ratio of the circumference of a circle to the length of the diameter ($\pi = C/d$).

Middle school students first use π when computing the circumferences and areas of circles. For many students the use of π is simply a matter of memorizing formulas and employing an appropriate value for π to substitute into the formulas. Middle school students can easily memorize the value of pi to be 3.14 or $\frac{22}{7}$, but if all they understand about π is a memorized value, then the real use of π is lost to them. Such rote memorization leads to confusion about the formulas and hides a real understanding of the value of π from students.

TRY THIS

Replicate Buffon's experiment at www.mste.uiuc.edu/reese/buffon/buffon.html.

To help middle grades students develop a fundamental understanding of π, students in grade 6 might gather a few disks such as the tops of margarine tubs, the tops of potato chip cylinders, the tops of peanut canisters, and so forth. They can then compare the length of string fitted across the diameter to the length of a string that is tightly fitted around the circumference of their disks. Their results will be that the ratio of *C/d* is always a bit more than 3. This result is sufficient for students to begin to understand the relationship of π to circles. Once students understand the value of π to be approximately 3, they are ready to examine the relationship of π to the circumference of a circle. Since π = *C/d* or about 3, students might then be asked how to determine the circumference if only the diameter of a circle is known. (Because π is about 3, then the circumference is about three times as long as the diameter.) Thus, the circumference of a 10-inch diameter dinner plate is about 30 inches. Sufficient experiences of gathering data in such a manner will help students gain a foundational understanding of the approximate value of π and its relationship to the circumference of a circle. When students determine approximate circumference lengths using 3 for the value of π, they are able to focus on the relationship between π, the diameter, and the circumference (*C* = π*d*) rather than focus on computing with either 3.14 or $\frac{22}{7}$. (See Blackline Master 9.4, Curve and Straight.)

TRY THIS

Approximately how long is the circumference of a hula hoop?

After sufficient developmental activities in grade 6 employing 3 for the value of π, students in grade 7 and 8 are ready to use the approximations of π (3.14 or $\frac{22}{7}$) in problems and applications involving both circumference and area.

TRY THIS

Compare the circumference of a three-ball tennis can to its height. Predict which one is longer and then measure and compute to find out.

Students can also explore the value of π by using the Internet. We have chosen a π exploration for the Internet Lesson Plan for this chapter.

Internet Lesson Plan

This lesson plan uses a simple applet to help students conjecture that the value of *C/d* is the same for all circles. In addition, students will discover that the value of π is slightly more than 3.

This lesson plan actually extends across several days. The reason is to allow students the opportunity to access a computer for the assignment. As we mentioned earlier (Chapter 2, The Challenge of Middle School Learners), equity is an issue when students must use computers outside of the classroom. This plan allows two days' time for students to complete the assignment, so that students without a computer in their home can have ample time to access one. It may be that even more time is needed by some students, and the plan could be revised to reflect that.

Objectives

Process	Gather data using a computer program.
	Work independently to explore the relationship between the circumference of a circle and its diameter.
	Make conjectures in small groups about results of exploration.
Mathematics	Create and analyze data.
	Conjecture about the value of $\frac{C}{d}$.
Materials	Internet connection
Previous knowledge	Circumference, diameter, radius

Did You **Know**?

The first 10 decimal places for π are 3.1415926536. See www.joyofpi.com for a link to a site that displays 1 million places of π.

Did You **Know**?

In 2001 a team of mathematicians at the University of Tokyo led by Dr. Yasumasa Kanada announced a new world record for decimal places of π. The team used a supercomputer for 400 hours to calculate π to over 1.24 trillion places.

Lesson

Day 1   Distribute Internet Exploration Sheet to students near the end of class. Tell students that they will discuss their results in a small group in two days time. After their discussion, each student will turn in a summary of their group's conjecture(s).

Day 2

1. Warm-up problem from high-stakes test:

   $$5 + \tfrac{3}{2} \times 6 - 3 + 4 \div 2 = ?$$

2. Review agenda for the day:
   a. Warm-up
   b. Describe/define circumference, radius, diameter
   c. Homework demos by students
   d. Wrap-up

3. After students have had a chance to work on the computer to gather data, they will then work in small groups to analyze their findings. Each group writes up their conjectures and turns them in.

4. One group reports its findings to the entire class. A class discussion follows of the group's findings, focusing on the validity and reasonableness of the conjecture(s). Students ask questions about the group's findings. Other groups compare their results. In the discussion, clarify for students that the ratio of C/d is known as π.

5. Students volunteer to post homework on the board and explain their thinking.

6. Wrap-up to lesson. Students write an exit card and give it to the teacher as they leave.

   What data did we collect today? What did we discover?
   How did you help your group reach its conjecture(s)?

As an extension, students could be asked to find the mean of the C/d ratio for all data collected by the class. The mean will approximate the commonly used approximation of 3.14. Further discussion about the value of π can focus on its irrational nature. In the applet students can observe that either the diameter or the circumference must be rounded to a unit value, indicating that the value of π cannot be represented as the ratio of two integer values.

Student Sheet

For this assignment you will use the Internet to explore the value of π.

1. Go to www.arcytech.org/java.

2. Select Discovering the Value of π.

3. Start by selecting the size of the circle. Move the vertical scale and watch the size of the circle increase. Read the scale and record the diameter of the circle.

4. Next roll the circle by dragging on the horizontal bar.

5. Roll the circle until the tick mark is again on the bottom of the circle. Record the circumference.

6. Record the data for eight circles in a table like this one:

Circumference	Diameter	$\frac{c}{d}$ (Decimal form)

7. Summarize your findings.

8. Write out a conjecture based on your findings to share with your group.

MISCONCEPTION

One misconception that arises from the study of circumference and areas of circles is that π is exactly $\frac{22}{7}$ or 3.14. However, π is an irrational number, and students may have agreed that it has an infinite number of digits in its representation, but for purposes of skill and application problems, students will use one of the two approximations (3.14 or $\frac{22}{7}$) or leave the answer to a problem in the common form, such as 15π. In either case, though, the value for π becomes either the decimal or common fraction approximation through repeated employment of these accepted approximations.

It is important to stress for students that any approximation for π that students use is just that, and any computation involving an approximation of π must itself be an approximation. When students give an answer involving an approximation for π, they might be challenged to explain how accurate (or inaccurate) their answer is.

Did You **Know**?

Hiroyuki Goto holds the world record for memorizing π. It took him just over nine hours to recite 42,000 digits.

Students can explore the formula for the area of a circle by dissecting and then rearranging the parts of a circle. Students can take a circle and fold it in half successively three times so that there are eight sectors to the circle when it is unfolded. Students can then cut out the eight sectors and rearrange them as shown in Figure 9.21 to form a figure that resembles a parallelogram.

The height of the resulting parallelogram is equal to the radius of the original circle. The base of the resulting parallelogram is equal to one-half the circumference of the circle. Students can then substitute these values into the area formula for a parallelogram as follows:

$$A = bh \qquad\qquad C = 2\pi r$$
$$A = \pi r \times r \qquad\quad C/2 = \pi r$$
$$A = \pi r^2$$

Students can repeat the activity with a circle folded in half four times to form 16 sectors. The resulting parallelogram will more closely resemble an actual parallelogram.

figure **9.21**

Area of a Circle

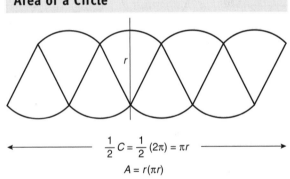

$$\frac{1}{2}C = \frac{1}{2}(2\pi) = \pi r$$
$$A = r(\pi r)$$

On the Lighter Side

Frank closes in on the area formula for a circle.

Frank & Ernest © by Bob Thaves. Reprinted by permission of Newspaper Enterprise Association, Inc.

Did You **Know**?

The record for computing the value of π by hand is 707 places in 1873 by William Shanks. In 1945 a calculator was used to check his figures. Shanks had made an error in the 527th place!

PROCESS STANDARDS

Connections

This activity can be used to introduce students to ideas from calculus. Students can easily conjecture that the more sectors that are formed in the original circle, the more closely the resulting figure will be to a parallelogram. They might then conjecture that with an infinite number of sectors, the resulting figure will appear to be a parallelogram to even the most discerning student. This aspect of infinite numbers of pieces that are infinitely small is one hallmark of integral calculus. Ultimately, as the number of sectors in the circle approaches infinity, the shape of the resulting figure will approach a real parallelogram.

MISCONCEPTION

Some middle school students are confused when the area of a circle is designated as a number of *square* units. There are several reasons for this. When they study area concepts in the lower grades, children usually work with square and rectangular arrays that are subdivided into square units. When the concept of area is extended to triangles and parallelograms, students can still envision square units as a unit of area because triangles and parallelograms can be dissected and the resulting pieces rearranged into a rectangle. These same students can have great difficulty picturing a circle subdivided into square units. Appropriate time and supporting activities are required for such students to fully accept and understand that the square unit is a basic area unit for any shape, even those with curved lines.

One approach is to have students use small unit circles (1-inch diameter) to determine the area of a rectangle (3 inches × 4 inches) and a larger circle (4-inch diameter) by covering each figure with the circles. In both cases, there will be gaps or overlaps. Students can repeat the same process using a unit square (1-inch side length). This time there are no gaps or overlaps when the squares are used to cover each figure. The unit square covers the rectangle perfectly. To be sure, the unit square does not cover the circle perfectly, but neither did the unit circle. In fact, the unit square gives a better approximation of the circle area than does the unit circle. In any event, students can see for themselves that a unit circle will not cover a circle and so is not an effective unit for area measure.

Did You **Know**?

The method for finding the area of a circle described in Try This was first proposed by Chinese mathematician Liu Hui.

TRY THIS

Cut out a circle and fold it to form 16 sectors. How closely does the resulting figure resemble a parallelogram?

MISCONCEPTION

It is not uncommon for students to understand the difference between perimeter and area, yet confuse the two formulas for circumference and area of a circle. The key here is not several worksheets of area and circumference problems. Such problems only strengthen numerical computation, not any understanding of the two concepts. Rather, students should be asked to explain why they chose the formula they did to solve a problem.

One suggestion for helping students is to have them use $C = \pi d$ rather than $C = 2\pi r$. The formula $C = 2\pi r$ resembles the formula for area, $A = \pi r^2$, and can prove to be a source of confusion, especially for less-able students. It may also help students to reflect on which formula results in the proper unit for area measure, square units. Only $A = \pi r^2$, with the length of the radius squared, results in square units.

There are many different sites on the Internet that discuss some aspect of π. A search engine such as www.dogpile.com lists over 100 sites related to π. One of the best is www.joyofpi.com, which contains may facts about π and has links to many other sites. For a million digits of π go to www.cecm.sfu.ca/organics/papers/borwein/paper/html/local/billdigits.html. At arcytech.org/java/pi/measuring.html students can record the diameter and circumferences of ten different circles and use their data to make conclusions about the value of π.

TRY THIS

Many mathematics classes hold a special celebration at exactly 1:59 on March 14. Why?

In Chapter 7, Algebra: The Gateway, and Chapter 8, Geometry: Moving Beyond Formulas, we discussed the relationship of perimeter and area ratios. Many students have difficulty understanding how the two respective ratios can be different yet related. One website that allows students to experiment with similar figures and relate perimeter and area (and also volume) ratios is http://standards.nctm.org/document/eexamples/chap6/6.3/index.html.

Volume

Point Well Taken

"Students need to have deeper experiences with surface area and volume, instead of just computing with formulas."

—*Strutchens, 2003, p. 204*

Just as manipulative activities helped students understand area relationships with two-dimensional figures, so will similar activities help students understand surface area and volume relationships of three-dimensional figures. In order for students to fully understand area and volume of solids, it is essential that they are able to visualize three-dimensional figures from the two-dimensional figures shown in their textbooks. (See Chapter 8, Geometry: Moving Beyond Formulas, for more on visual sense in geometry.)

The surface area of solids is best introduced by having students build nets for specific figures and then unfold them. A net is a two-dimensional figure that folds up to form a three-dimensional shape. Students can break up the nets into their composite shapes and compute the areas of each of the composite polygons. Consider the two nets in Figure 9.22. The net for a rectangular prism is composed of six rectangles. Every rectangular box has six faces, and the net for any box, or rectangular prism, will show the six faces. Students might verify this by decomposing cereal boxes and other packaging boxes to form their nets.

The second net is for a cylinder. Most students can readily identify the shape of the two bases of a cylinder, but fewer will be able to visualize that the remaining surface area of a cylinder is in the shape of a rectangle. Students can verify this by peeling labels off cans and flattening them. The dimensions of the resulting rectangle can then be related to the height of the can and the circumference of the base.

Rather than develop formal steps for computing surface area, including any formulas, it is best to allow students sufficient time to explore figures, measure various lengths, and use the resulting data to compute areas of the various faces. This allows students time and opportunity to fully develop their visual sense about the surface area of solids. Students can then use this foundation to build the formal surface area formulas they will study in a formal geometry course at the secondary school level.

Beneficial activities involving the volume of three-dimensional figures can come from building block figures, examining them, and sketching them. Block figures can be employed to help students gain a sense of volume and the basic volume formula for solid figures.

Students might be asked to build a 2 × 3 array with cubes. Students can easily determine by visual inspection that the resulting rectangular

figure **9.22**

Nets of a Prism and a Cylinder

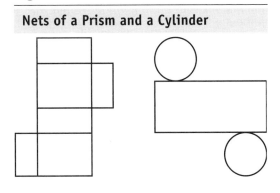

table **9.2**	Volume for a Rectangular Prism	
BASE AREA	**HEIGHT**	**VOLUME**
6	1	6
6	2	12
6	3	18
6	4	24
6	5	30

prism has a volume of 6 cubes. When students add another layer to the array of blocks, the volume of the resulting prism is 12 cubes. Subsequent layers increase the volume by 6. Students might display their findings in a chart as shown here in Table 9.2.

Clearly, every layer increases the volume by the same amount, by the number of cubes per layer, the area of the base. This leads students to the basic volume formula:

$$\text{Volume} = \text{Base area} \times \text{height}$$
$$V = Bh$$

This basic relationship can also be explored with cylinders. For every layer or unit of height that is added to a cylinder, the volume will increase. A graduated cylinder or simply an empty can with markings will easily demonstrate that as more layers of water are poured into the cylinder, the volume increases according to the height of the water, just as the volume of the rectangular prisms increased according to the number of layers of blocks. Thus, the formula for the volume of a cylinder may also be represented as $V = Bh$, since a cylinder may be thought of as a special kind of prism. It has a base that resembles a many-sided polygon; in this case the base is a circle, which can be considered a polygon with an infinite number of sides.

MISCONCEPTION

Earlier in this chapter we described the tendency of some students to conclude that the length of a rectangle is always longer than its width. In a similar sense, some students think the height of a rectangular prism must be longer than either the base length or base width.

To help students discard such a misconception, it can be instructive to have them examine a cardboard box like a cereal box. They might orient it in the three different ways shown in Figure 9.23 so that each orientation has a different face for its base. Students can then make the needed measurements and compute the volume for each orientation. Naturally, they are the

figure **9.23**

Three Orientations of the Same Rectangular Prism

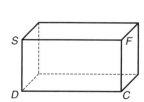
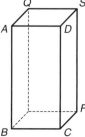
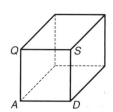

same, even though each orientation has a different base. Students could repeat this process with another box or two to help them understand that the base length, width, and height are interchangeable among the three segments according to the orientation of the box. It is important to help students perceive that the rectangular prism remains unchanged in edge length and volume regardless of its orientation.

TRY THIS

Why is the volume of a rectangular prism unaffected by its orientation?

Similar Solids

Many geometry relationships are predicated on segment lengths or angle measures. Similar figures, for example, are recognized by their angle measures and their side lengths. Any two figures are similar if their corresponding angles are congruent and their corresponding segment lengths have the same ratio. In addition, the areas of any two similar figures are in a ratio that is the square of the ratio between linear dimensions. These relationships for similar polygons are also true for any similar solids. All corresponding angles are congruent, corresponding linear dimensions have the same ratio, and any corresponding areas have the square of the linear ratio. The volumes of similar solids are also in a proportion, one that is the cube of the ratio between the linear dimensions. Thus, measurement is integrally intertwined with the study of similarity, both as an essential part of basic definitions and as a real-world application of its principles.

Students can explore the surface areas and volumes of similar solids by gathering data for a table. The data table should display linear dimensions and ratios of corresponding lengths as shown in Table 9.3. The ratio between the corresponding lengths can be compared to the ratio between surface areas and between volumes. By analyzing the data students will be able to develop the square and cubic ratios of the areas and volumes of similar solids.

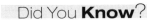

Did You **Know**?

A giant like Paul Bunyan or King Kong cannot exist with the same structure as a normal-sized man or ape. For example, if Paul Bunyan is ten times the height of a normal human (60 feet versus 6 feet), then his surface area is 100 times as large and his volume or mass is 1,000 times as large. Even though Paul Bunyan's leg bones increase in size, they cannot support such a large increase in total weight.

PROCESS STANDARDS

Reasoning

An interesting activity is to have students use two pieces of paper (same size) to make two different cylinders, one with the short side as the height, and the other with the long side as the height. Clearly, they both have the same surface area. What about the volumes? Just as students mistakenly relate perimeter to area with two-dimensional figures, so many students (and adults) will relate surface area and volume, reasoning that if the surface areas are equal, then so must the volumes be equal. Students might stand the taller cylinder inside the shorter cylinder and fill the taller cylinder with packing nuggets to examine a potential relationship (see Figure 9.24).

figure **9.24**

Comparing Cylinders

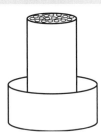

table **9.3**   **Volumes and Areas for Similar Cubes**

CUBE EDGES	RATIO OF EDGE LENGTHS	RATIO OF AREAS	RATIO OF VOLUMES
1 in., 2 in.	$\frac{1}{2}$	$\frac{1}{4}$	$\frac{1}{8}$
1 in., 3 in.	$\frac{1}{3}$	$\frac{1}{9}$	$\frac{1}{27}$
2 in., 3 in.	$\frac{2}{3}$	$\frac{4}{9}$	$\frac{8}{27}$

When the taller cylinder is lifted, the nuggets remain and fill the shorter cylinder, but not completely. Students can work in groups to explore and then offer the reasons why such a counterintuitive result happens.

Point Well Taken

"By the end of middle school students should understand perimeter, area, surface area, and volume and should have developed strategies and general formulas to measure these attributes in selected figures."

—*NCTM, 2003, p. 208*

TRY THIS

Explain why the volumes of the two cylinders in Figure 9.23 are not the same. Assume that the paper used is standard $8\frac{1}{2}" \times 11"$ paper.

The volumes of pyramids and cones can be explored using commercially produced solids such as View-Thru' Blocks or by means of solids constructed using a heavy grade of paper or oak tag to trace the nets of the solids. (See Blackline Master 9.6, Cube and Pyramid Templates, for a cube and pyramid with congruent bases and heights.)

As students examine the cube and pyramid, they should verify that the bases are congruent and their heights are the same. The task is for students to determine how the volume of the pyramid compares to the volume of the cube. Students can fill the pyramids with rice, popping corn, or inert packing material and then pour the pyramids' contents into the cube. The volumes of three pyramids will fill the cone. Thus, students can easily conclude that for any pyramid $V = \frac{1}{3}Bh$. A similar experiment with a cone will demonstrate an identical relationship between the cone and a cylinder with congruent bases and equal heights.

There are a number of Internet sites that are very effective in representing volume relationships. At www.explorelearning.com students can collect data about rectangular prisms and cylinders in a table and then use the data to develop the formulas for volume. At www.shodor.org/interactivate/activities/index.html students can change any dimension of a rectangular or triangular prism and view the effects of the change on both the surface area on volume of the resulting solid. At http://nlvm.usu.edu/en/nav/category_g_4_t_4.html students can make qualitative comparisons between the volumes of various solids (and so improve their visual sense for volume) by pouring the contents of one solid into another.

PROCESS STANDARDS

Representation

Students benefit when geometric relationships are represented in a variety of ways. The relationship among solids with common linear dimensions is an example of a relationship that students can represent in several ways. Consider how the volume of a hemisphere compares to the volume of a cone. When both have congruent radii, and the height of the cone is congruent to its radius, the relationship between the volumes can be examined in several ways. Plastic models such as Power Solids might be used, and students can fill the cone and pour the contents into the hemisphere to determine that the hemisphere has twice the volume of the cone. Both might be compared to the volume of a sphere with the same radius. Obviously two of the hemispheres will fill the sphere. Four cones will also fill the sphere; thus, two hemisphere volumes are the same as four cone volumes. Finally, the relationship might be compared algebraically.

$$\text{Cone volume: } \tfrac{1}{3}\pi r^2 h \qquad \text{Hemisphere volume: } \tfrac{2}{3}\pi r^3$$

By representing the same relationship in a variety of ways, students will understand that the relationship transcends any specific manipulative and yet can benefit from using concrete models to duplicate abstract relationships that they can examine algebraically.

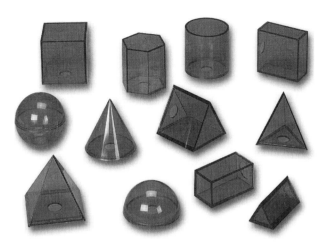

Power Solids
Courtesy of Nasco, Inc.

TRY THIS

Complete the algebraic exploration to demonstrate the relationship between the volumes of a cone and hemisphere.

SUMMARY

Measurement systems were developed in response to the need to compare and quantify various physical attributes. As a result, measurement is inherently related to geometry and real-world contexts. In middle school, students continue to work in both the customary and metric systems as they develop benchmarks and the ability to select the appropriate measurement units for various tasks. They also explore perimeter and area measures with polygons and area and volume relationships with polyhedrons.

The following are highlights of this chapter:

- A measure is a number with a unit.
- NCTM suggests that computational measurement conversions are made within the metric and customary systems and not between them.
- Students should be aware of measurement units during the problem solution and not only when the solution is written.
- Students should have a repertoire of benchmarks to help them estimate various measurements in real-world settings.
- Students should build their understanding of area and volume relationships by exploring these relationships with polygons and polyhedrons.
- Rote memorization of formulas can lead to misconceptions.

Student Performance on International and National Assessments

TIMSS

The ratio of each side of a square to its perimeter is (56% correct)

- A. $\frac{1}{1}$
- B. $\frac{1}{2}$
- C. $\frac{1}{3}$
- D. $\frac{1}{4}$

NAEP

The cruise ship *Titanic* was 882 feet long. Which of the following is about that length? (46% correct)

- A. Two moving van lengths
- B. Fifty car lengths
- C. One hundred skateboard lengths
- D. Five hundred school bus lengths
- E. One thousand bicycle lengths

EXERCISES

From the Reading

1. Use the areas of the two triangles in Figure 9.25 to develop the standard area formula of a trapezoid.

figure **9.25**

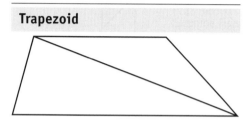

Trapezoid

2. Why do you think the United States has not adopted the metric system as the national measurement system?

3. Develop personal benchmarks for a meter, liter, and kilogram.

4. How would you explain to a middle school student that 3 cubic yards are not equal to 9 cubic feet?

5. Explain to a middle school student why square units are used for the area of a circle.

6. Find the area of a circle with a circumference of 12π feet.

7. What is the area of the largest rectangle that can be enclosed with a fence that is 400 feet long?

8. If the side lengths of a hexagon are doubled, by what factor is the area of the original hexagon increased?

9. How many square inches are there in a square yard?

10. Why does a protractor show two readings for every measured angle?

On Your Own

1. Research the metric system to determine the role of the French Revolution in its origin.

2. Interview ten adults to find out how many remember that 1 mile = 5,280 feet.

3. Interview five adults about their support for a complete change to metric measures in the United States.

4. Ms. Educator has designed a project for her seventh-grade class. Students will build a scale model of the solar system. She plans to use a tennis ball–sized sphere for Earth and let the students build spheres for the other planets and the sun. What critical fact has she forgotten to consider?

Portfolio Question

What will you need to do to feel comfortable and confident about teaching the metric system?

Scenes from a Classroom

Ms. Agnesi is in the middle of a chapter on measurement with her fifth-grade class. Among the topics in the chapter are the metric and customary measurement systems. Ms. Agnesi wants her students to develop a sense of how each system is used in the real world and how they compare to each other. So, she has prepared a series of worksheets for her students to complete as they move through the chapter. The problems shown here are typical of the problems on her worksheets.

$$2.3 \text{ m} = ? \text{ ft.}$$
$$4.5 \text{ mi.} = ? \text{ km}$$
$$1.51 = ? \text{ qt.}$$
$$235 \text{ cm} = ? \text{ ft.}$$

Along with the worksheets, Ms. Agnesi gives her students a measurements conversion sheet. It is full of conversion factors in the following form:

$$1 \text{ in.} = 2.54 \text{ cm}$$
$$1 \text{ mi.} = 6.25 \text{ km}$$
$$1 \text{ kg} = 2.2 \text{ lb.}$$
$$1 \text{ lb.} = 454 \text{ g}$$

Before reading our comments, respond to these questions.

1. How successfully do you think these worksheets will meet her expectations?
2. How else might Ms. Agnesi help her students develop an understanding of the two measurement systems?

The worksheets that Ms. Agnesi gives her students are essentially rote computation sheets using the conversion factors from the conversion sheet. All students need to do to solve these problems is to select the conversion factor from the sheet and then multiply or divide. A student who solves these problems will have very little sense of either measurement system in the real world and even less about how the two systems are related.

Students will be better served by having the opportunity to develop benchmarks for each of the measurement systems. For example, a liter is half a large bottle of soda, a gram is the weight of three small paper clips, and a foot is a bit longer than the length of a student's foot. What about conversions between the two systems? NCTM discourages converting between the two systems and suggests the time is better spent establishing a few benchmarks to gain a rough sense of how the systems compare, as for example, a liter is a bit larger than a quart or a meter is a bit longer than a yard. Other beneficial activities include determining the appropriate unit of measure for a context, such as deciding whether to use a meter or a centimeter to find the length of a pencil, or a pound or ton to find the weight of an automobile.

Preparing for Praxis

The large rectangular block in the accompanying figure was made by stacking smaller blocks, all of which are the same size. What are the dimensions in centimeters of each of the smaller blocks?

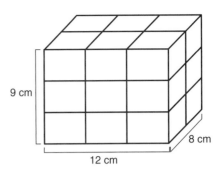

A. $3 \times 2 \times 3$
B. $3 \times 3 \times 3$
C. $3 \times 4 \times 3$
D. $4 \times 4 \times 3$

RESOURCES

Math–Literature Connections

Ackerman, K. (1998). *Araminta's paint box.* New York: Simon & Schuster Children's Books.

Lasky, K. (2003). *The man who made time travel.* New York: Farrar, Strauss and Giroux.

Lasky, K., & Hawkes, K. (1994). *The librarian who measured the Earth.* Boston: Little, Brown.

Major, J. (1995). *The silk route: 7,000 miles of history.* New York: HarperCollins Publishers.

Neuschwander, N. (2001.) *Sir Cumference and the great knight of Angleland: A math adventure.* Watertown, MA: Charlesbridge.

Swift, J. (1991). *Gulliver's travels.* New York: Dover.

Teacher's Bookcase

Clements, D., & Bright, G. (Eds.). (2003). *Learning and teaching measurement: 2003 yearbook.* Reston, VA: NCTM.

This NCTM text is a collection of articles on measurement from mathematics educators around the world. Some articles focus on lower grades, but many are appropriate for middle school classrooms.

Diagram Group. (1994). *Measurements and conversions: A complete guide.* New York: Diagram Group.

Everything you want to know about measurement conversions, complete with formulas, charts, diagrams, and so forth.

Dilke, O. (1987). *Reading the past: Mathematics and measurement.* London: British Museum Press.

This book explores measurement in the ancient Mediterranean cultures of Egypt and Babylon.

Huong, N. (1999). *Math logic: Perimeter, area, and volume.* Bellevue, WA: Logical Connections.

This text presents a discussion of the aspects of dimension. Earlier discussions about perimeter and area may be helpful for review or remediation for middle school students. The discussions and activities dealing with surface area and volume can be beneficial for all middle schoolers.

Johnson, A. (1994). *Classic math: History topics for the classroom.* Palo Alto, CA: Dale Seymour Publications.

This book contains the history of various aspects of measurement and the word origins of many measurement words.

Strauss, S. (1995). *The sizesaurus: From hectares to decibels to calories, a witty compendium of measurements.* New York: Kodansha International.

This book contains clever applications of various measurements and a brief history of some such as the metric system. It is written at an upper middle school level.

For Further Reading

Berry III, R., & Wiggins, J. (2001). Measurement in the middle grades. *Mathematics Teaching in the Middle School,* 7(3), 154–156.

The authors use the NCTM Measurement Standard to organize angle measurement using manipulatives and dynamic geometry software. The authors describe several class activities they used to teach angle measure.

Buhl, D., Oursland, M., & Finco, K. (2003). The legend of Paul Bunyan: An exploration in measurement. *Mathematics Teaching in the Middle School,* 8(8), 441–448.

The author employs the legend of giant Paul Bunyan to exemplify the relationships between linear, area, and volume measures of similar solids. In the article the author describes a class project involving building models of Paul, his ox Babe, and some of their personal effects with clay to explore the measurement relationships.

Ferrer, B., Hunter, B., Irwin, K., Sheldon, M., Irwin, K., Thompson, C., & Vistro-yu, C. (2001). By the unit or the square unit? *Mathematics Teaching in the Middle School,* 7(3), 132–137.

The article reviews difficulties students have distinguishing between perimeter and area and provides some reasons for their misconceptions. The author team includes several activities they used with middle school students to improve their understanding of area and perimeter.

Hartletzer, S. (2003). Ratios of linear, area, and volume measures of similar solids. *Mathematics Teaching in the Middle School,* 8(5), 228–236.

The author delineates a classroom exploration involving paper cubes and balloons that students use to gather data for relating linear, area, and volume measures of similar solids.

Kaplan, G. (2003). Eureka! or don't throw out the crown with the bath water. *Mathematics Teaching in the Middle School,* 8(9), 484–488.

This article applies Archimedes' method of inscribed and circumscribed polygons to help students derive a value for π.

Moore, S., & Bintz, W. (2002). Teaching geometry and measurement through literature. *Mathematics Teaching in the Middle School, 8*(2), 78–84.

> *The authors reference a number of literature texts as sources of explorations, discussions, and activities that develop measurement concepts in middle school students. The article includes a very helpful list of references.*

Preston, R., & Thompson, T. (2004). Integrating measurement across the curriculum. *Mathematics Teaching in the Middle School, 9*(8), 438–441.

> *In this article the authors stress the whys and hows for including measurement across the mathematics curriculum from algebra to data analysis.*

Thompson, T., & Preston, R. (2004). Measurement in the middle grades: Insights from NAEP and TIMMS. *Mathematics Teaching in the Middle School, 9*(9), 514–519.

> *The authors use the results of U.S. students on NAEP and TIMSS to formulate a program that integrates measurement across the mathematics curriculum.*

Links

Comprehensive measurement dictionary
www.unc.edu/~rowlett/units

Compute measurement conversions
www.convert-me.com/en

Solve and create measurement conversion problems
http://nlvm.usu.edu/en/nav/category_g_4_t_4.html

REFERENCES

Boston, M., & Smith, M. (2003). Providing opportunities for students and teachers to "measure up." In *Learning and teaching measurement: 2003 NCTM yearbook* (p. 208). Reston, VA: NCTM.

International Association for the Evaluation of Educational Achievement. (2005). Trends in international mathematics and science study. http://timss.bc.edu/timss2003.html

Lehrer, R. (2003). Developing understanding of measurement. In J. Kilpatrick, W. Martin, & D. Schifter (Eds.), *A research companion to Principles and Standards for School Mathematics.* Reston, VA: NCTM.

Lehrer, R., Jenkins, M., & Osana, H. (1998). Longitudinal study of children's reasoning about space and geometry. In R. Lehrer & D. Chazen (Eds.), *Developing learning environments for understanding of geometry and space* (pp. 137–167). Mahwah, NJ: Erlbaum.

Meeks, V., & Wheeler, R. (2003). Introduction: Part 2. In *Learning and teaching measurement: 2003 NCTM yearbook* (p. 193). Reston, VA: NCTM.

National Council of Teachers of Mathematics. (1989). *Curriculum and evaluation standards for school mathematics.* Reston, VA: NCTM.

National Council of Teachers of Mathematics. (2000). *Principles and standards of school mathematics.* Reston, VA: NCTM.

Piaget, J., B. Inhelder, & Z. Sinclair. *The child's conception of geometry.* New York: Basic Books, 1960.

Shape of beverage glass influences how much people pour and drink. (2003, October 3). *Science News.*

Strutchens, M., Martin, W., & Kenney, P. (2003). What students should know about measurement: Perspectives from the National Assessment of Educational Progress. In *Learning and teaching measurement: 2003 NCTM yearbook* (p. 204). Reston, VA: NCTM.

TIMSS. http://timss.bc.edu/timss2003.html

How Close Is Close?

How hard can it be to find the area of your school desk? If it's a rectangle, you measure the base length and the height and then use the formula $A = bh$. But there is more to it than that. What you use for measuring units can make a difference.

For this exploration you are going to use inches, centimeters, and millimeters for the lengths of the sides. Measure the side lengths to the nearest unit. Fill in the data table with your measurements.

	BASE LENGTH	HEIGHT	AREA
Nearest inch			
Nearest centimeter			
Nearest millimeter			

Why is there a difference in the areas?

Which area is closest to the actual area? Why?

How far apart are the two extreme areas?

The Angle Wheel

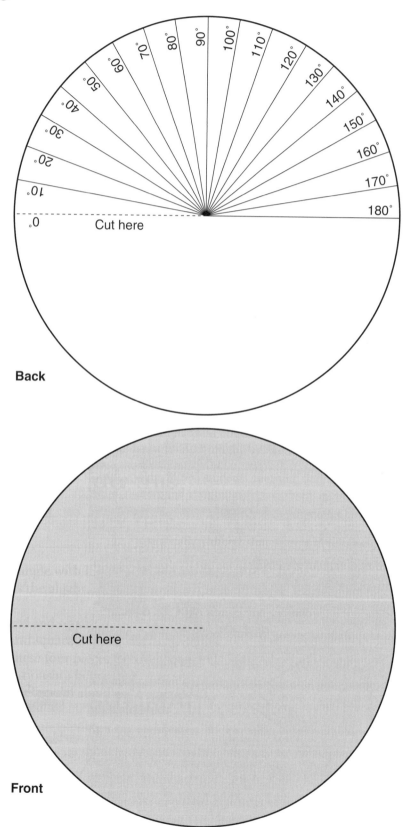

Back

Front

 From Johnson & Norris, Teaching Today's Mathematics in the Middle Grades. Copyright © 2006 Allyn and Bacon, Pearson Education, Inc.

Flipping for π

Did you know you can generate the value of π by flipping a piece of spaghetti? The Count of Buffoon discovered this simulation over 200 years ago. Here are the instructions.

1. Break off a 1-inch piece of uncooked spaghetti.

2. Drop the spaghetti segment onto the parallel lines at the bottom of this page.

3. Record whether the spaghetti segment comes to rest on one of the parallel lines. If the spaghetti didn't come to rest between two parallel lines, drop the spaghetti again.

4. Repeat the process for a total of 25 times.

5. Use your data to evaluate the following equation:

$$\pi = 2\left(\frac{\text{tries}}{\text{hits}}\right)$$

6. Be sure to record your data. We will combine the class data for a class result.

Curve and Straight

For this activity you will measure the distance across, or diameter, and the circumference, or distance around, several circular-shaped objects. Measuring the diameter of a circle is fairly simple. Measuring the circumference is a little tricky. To measure the circumference of the circle, use a piece of string. Fit the string all the way around and mark where it fits the circle. Unwrap the string and measure it. Record your data in the table provided.

OBJECT	CIRCUMFERENCE	DIAMETER	$\frac{C}{d}$ (TO NEAREST WHOLE NUMBER)
1			
2			
3			
4			
5			
6			

 From Johnson & Norris, Teaching Today's Mathematics in the Middle Grades. Copyright © 2006 Allyn and Bacon, Pearson Education, Inc.

Minimum Perimeter

For this activity you will use the tiles to form different rectangles. In the example provided, six tiles were used to form a rectangle.

AREA	SKETCH	PERIMETER
6	⬚⬚⬚ 2 / 3	10

PART A

Use 24 tiles to form as many different rectangles as possible. Fill in the following data table.

AREA	SKETCH	PERIMETER
24		
24		
24		
24		
24		

continued

Minimum Perimeter *(continued)*

PART B

Sketch all possible rectangles for 36 tiles. Fill in the following data table.

AREA	SKETCH	PERIMETER
36		

Use your findings to describe the dimensions of the rectangular garden with the largest area that can be enclosed by a 100-foot fence.

 From Johnson & Norris, *Teaching Today's Mathematics in the Middle Grades.* Copyright © 2006 Allyn and Bacon, Pearson Education, Inc.

Cube and Pyramid Templates

From Johnson & Norris, Teaching Today's Mathematics in the Middle Grades. Copyright © 2006 Allyn and Bacon, Pearson Education, Inc. 295

chapter ten

Data Analysis: The Process

In the middle grades, students gather data, represent data in a variety of ways, look for trends within the data, question the data, and summarize the data. It is through this interaction with the data that students learn the appropriate tools and strategies to help them make sense of the information—a necessary lifetime skill. Data analysis is a process. It involves a series of predictable steps as well as cycling back to reconnect with individual data points and the original question being addressed. As seen in Figure 10.1, data analysis begins with a problem to be resolved. Directing students' attention to an actual problem or question that they would like to answer motivates them and places their learning in a real context. Formulating the question and determining how information is to be gathered that addresses the question are critical steps in the process. After the data have been collected, analysis begins by organizing the data and then working to represent the data appropriately. The arrows in Figure 10.1 illustrate that as students work to represent the data, questions may arise that cause them to go back to the original question or the data.

figure **10.1**

Cyclical Nature of the Data Analysis Process

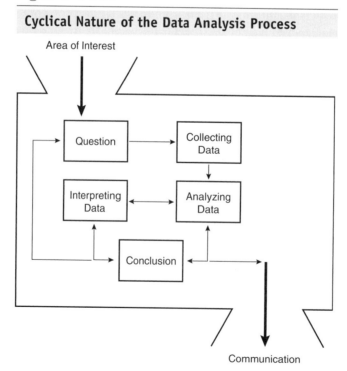

Area of Interest

Question → Collecting Data

Interpreting Data ↔ Analyzing Data

Conclusion

Communication

Interpreting the representations and then drawing conclusions based on those representations may also lead back to the original problem and question being addressed. It is important that students remain connected to the purpose of the process.

PROCESS STANDARDS

Connections

Data analysis can also be viewed in light of the writing process. (See Figure 10.2.)

Data analysis and the writing process begin with a problem, question, or topic to be explored. By generating their own questions and formulating ways to address their concerns, students become engaged in the data analysis process, which stimulates significant motivation. As in the writing process where students establish a thesis to be explained, in data analysis students define the techniques to be used in the process of collecting the information. Surveys and polls are common strategies selected by middle school students. Defining the questions, carefully considering the type of anticipated responses, and conducting small trials to ensure the validity of the questions constitute steps leading to the collection of the data. These steps correspond to brainstorming and establishing the thesis statement in the writing process. In data analysis, students gather the data and then begin the work of analyzing the data. Looking for trends, clusters, and numerical summaries and developing several representations for the data help provide information about the data. Students also need to go back to individual data points and ask questions about the implications of specific items. This is the recursive nature in the process of data analysis. Students can verify whether or not a data point is an outlier and then determine whether or not to include that item in the graphical representations. Their conclusion incorporates reasons for their decisions about outliers. As students work through the process of data analysis, it is important that they stay connected to the original purpose and the question that they are addressing. Making the connection between data analysis and the writing process enhances students' understanding of the cyclical nature of both processes.

Point Well Taken

". . . students need to develop ways to reason logically about data—not memorize rules and procedures. . . . Students' experiences with data, graphs and representative values need to reflect the expectation that they reason about situations rather than simply apply rules and algorithms."
—McClain, 1999, p. 380

figure **10.2**

Data Analysis and the Writing Process

DATA ANALYSIS	WRITING PROCESS
Identify Problem	Brainstorm
Establish Data Collection Techniques	Establish Thesis
Gather Data	Outline or Map
Analysis of Data	Draft
Representations	
Statistical summary	
Revisit Hypothesis	Revise and Edit
Revisit Data	
Conclusion	Conclusion

NCTM Standards

The NCTM's *Principles and Standards for School Mathematics* states that school mathematics programs should enable students to

- Formulate questions that can be addressed with data
- Collect, organize, and display relevant data to answer questions
- Select and use appropriate statistical methods to analyze data
- Develop and evaluate inferences and predictions that are based on data

Specifically, for students in grades 6–8, the standards state that students should

- Formulate questions, design studies, and collect data about a characteristic shared by two populations or different characteristics within one population
- Select, create, and use appropriate graphical representations of data, including histograms, box plots, and scatter plots
- Find, use, and interpret measures of center and spread, including mean and interquartile range
- Discuss and understand the correspondence between data sets and their graphical representations, especially histograms, stem-and-leaf plots, box plots, and scatter plots

Point Well Taken

"Understanding data representation and analysis involves many complex issues, from sorting through what different numbers on the graph mean, to choosing appropriate measures to summarize and compare groups, to identifying relationships between variables. Through multiple experiences with a variety of data sets, students begin to develop the tools and concepts they need to use data themselves and to interpret data that they will use throughout life."
—Konald & Higgins, 2003, p. 213

Did You **Know**?

John Graunt (1620–1674) was the first to make an organized analysis of data. He examined birth notices and burial records to estimate the population in London.

- Use observations about differences between two or more samples to make conjectures about populations from which the samples were taken
- Make conjectures about possible relationships between two characteristics of a sample on the basis of scatter plots of the data and approximate lines of best fit
- Use conjectures to formulate new questions and plan new studies to answer them (NCTM, 2000, p. 248)

In today's world, we are bombarded by data. Having the knowledge and skill to interpret the data and their implications is fundamental. In this chapter, we provide an overview of the various graphical representations and types of data. We discuss the measures of central tendency and measures of dispersion and the importance of summarizing data with these measures. We look specifically at the process of data analysis within the context of activities that we suggest for middle school students and, finally, we consider ways data and the presentation of data can be misleading.

Overview of Graphical Representations

Did You **Know**?

The earliest published graph was barometric pressure against time by Dr. Plot in 1668.

Graphical representations vary depending on the specific data and the question being addressed. Line plots, stem-and-leaf plots, bar graphs (case-value bar graphs, frequency bar graphs, double bar graphs, and stacked bar graphs), histograms, box plots, line graphs, scatter plots, and circle graphs offer different views with advantages and disadvantages. Matching the appropriate views for the particular data set and question being explored remains a critical component of the data analysis process. Comparing these representations helps clarify their strengths and weaknesses in certain situations.

Line Plot

Line plots are often used to quickly organize data and get an understanding of the distribution of the data points. They are frequently used as a first step toward organizing the data. (See Figure 10.3.)

This line plot quickly displays the smallest and largest number of M&M's in a package. This graph also shows the clusters or groups of data points at 24 and 25 and then again between 28 and 31 inclusively. Students can also observe that there are three modes in this data set: 24, 28, and 31. Mode, the data point most frequently seen in the set, will be discussed later in the chapter with the other averages, mean and median. (See Measures of Central Tendency.) Line plots are typically used when the number of data points is relatively small, 25 or fewer, and the range of the data is reasonably tight. Line plots also point out any gaps that exist in the data set. It is also important to note that the scale used in line plots must be uniform and is typically a conveniently rounded value such as multiples of 5 or 10 (Landwehr & Watkins, 1986, p. 5). In Figure 10.3, we simply chose to use units and only displayed those units that were between the maximum and minimum values.

figure **10.3**

Line Plot

Number of M&M's in a Small Package

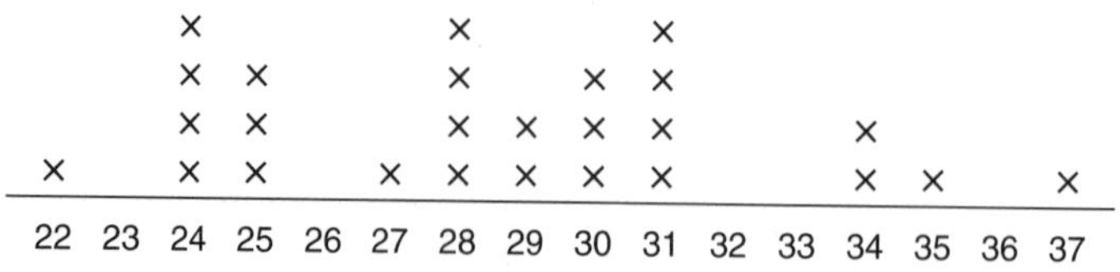

Stem-and-Leaf Plot

Another way to display these M&M data is in a stem-and-leaf plot, or simply a stem plot. This plot separates the tens and units digits. The tens digit represents the *stem* and the units digits are the *leaves*. In Figure 10.4, we have spread out the tens digits using a bullet. This allows the graph to appear less dense. Values from 30 through 34 are presented next to the 3 stem and the values from 35 to 39 are placed next to the bullet below the 3 stem. In this presentation, the individual data points are seen along with the minimum and maximum values. The data appear to be tightly grouped. Figure 10.4 is referred to as an ordered stem plot as the data have been organized so that the smallest values are closest to the stem.

TRY THIS

Create a new stem plot using the data in Figure 10.4 but do not separate the stem values using bullets. Compare your graph with the one presented.

It is important to note that stem plots include a key such as the one in Figure 10.4. Stem plots can also be used to make comparisons. In Figure 10.5, two classes compared the number of hours that each member of the class watched television for a one-week period. Students then made a back-to-back stem plot to compare their results.

Students noticed that the data were not very spread out and, therefore, students elected to use the asterisk.

MISCONCEPTION

Students often confuse the key on the left-hand side of the plot. They need to remember that the stem represents the tens digit and the key on the left side of plot is displayed with the tens digit on the right of the vertical line as in the key in Figure 10.5. Teachers can remind students that the key is written in the way that the data are presented. On the left side of the back-to-back plot the leaf is first and then the stem. On the right side of the plot, the stem occurs first and then the leaf.

Because these data are ordered from least to greatest, students can find the median, or middle value in the data, for each class simply by counting. In both classes, the median number of hours spent watching television is 12. Students observe that Mr. Dolison's class has a wider range and the shapes of both data sets are similar. Students also noted that Mr. Dolison's class has two more students than Ms. Eddington's class. When using back-to-back stem-and-leaf plots, it is important that the two data sets have approximately the same number of values. If these two class sizes differed dramatically, the stem plot

figure 10.4

Stem-and-Leaf Plot

1	
•	
2	2, 4, 4, 4, 4
•	5, 5, 5, 7, 8, 8, 8, 8, 9
3	0, 0, 0, 1, 1, 1, 1, 4
•	5, 7
4	

2 | 4 = 24

figure 10.5

Back-to-Back Stem-and-Leaf Plot Comparing Hours of TV Watched between Two Different Classes

Mr. Dolison's Class		Ms. Eddington's Class
2, 1	0	4, 4
9, 8, 8, 7, 6, 5	*	5, 8, 8, 8, 8
3, 3, 2, 2, 1, 0, 0	1	0, 2, 2, 2, 2, 4
8, 8, 8, 7, 7, 5, 5	*	6, 7, 8, 9, 9
2, 0, 0	2	0, 0
	*	5, 5
1	3	

2 | 1 = 12 hours   1 | 2 = 12 hours

could be misleading. Bar graphs also display individual data as well as group comparisons, and there are several different types of bar graphs: case value, frequency, double, and stacked bar graphs.

Bar Graph

Looking at the case-value bar graph (see Figure 10.6), each individual case is represented by name. Students can quickly tell the height of each student. Compare the case-value representation to the bar graph representing the same data in Figure 10.7.

Figures 10.6 and 10.7 use the same data set yet present varying displays.

figure **10.6**

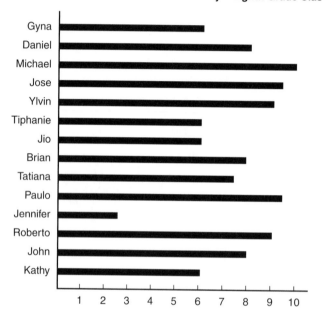

figure **10.7**

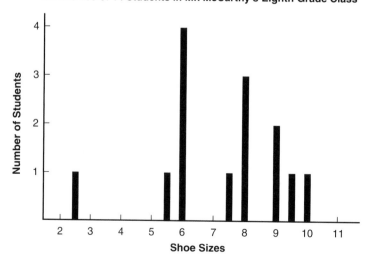

TRY THIS

Compare Figures 10.6 and 10.7. What are the similarities? What are the differences?

The case-value graph displays the individual with his or her shoe size. Students see, for example, that Gyna, Tiphanie, and Jio all wear size 6 shoes. In the frequency bar graph, students know that three students wear size 6, but they do not know their identity. Case-value bar graphs are typically used in elementary grades to display categorical data. Double bar graphs and stacked bar graphs present a comparison of two groups. For example, the double bar graph in Figure 10.8 shows the comparison of boys' and girls' favorite fruits.

Students quickly observe the number of students selecting each fruit and that apples are preferred by both girls and boys.

Stacked bar graphs also compare two groups, but the bars for each category place one group on top of one another as in Figure 10.9.

Histogram

A type of graph often confused with a bar graph is a histogram.

Histograms are used to display continuous data such as age in years, measurements involving height and weight, and ratings based on a continuous scale (Lappan et al., 1998, p. 1b). Histograms group the data within consistent intervals and the height of the bar shows the number of data points within that interval. Figure 10.10 displays a histogram for the scores on a recent algebra test.

This representation of the data has grouped the scores in intervals of 5 and a perfect score is 75. Each interval includes the lower boundary but not the upper boundary. For example, only one student scored between 45 and 49 inclusively.

The shape of the distribution in Figure 10.10 is weighted toward the higher scores. The height of each bar indicates the number of students who achieved within that range of scores. Two-thirds of the students scored 60 points ($\frac{60}{75} = 0.80$) or more, resulting in grades of 80% or better. Because the scores are grouped in intervals, individual results cannot be seen on the histogram. If the situation requires seeing the individual data

figure **10.8**

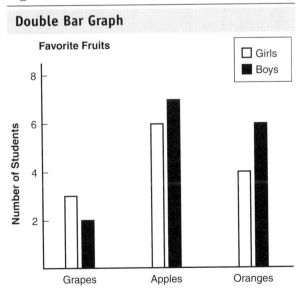

figure **10.9**

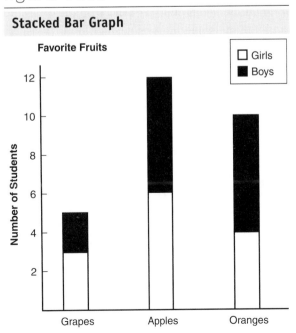

figure **10.10**

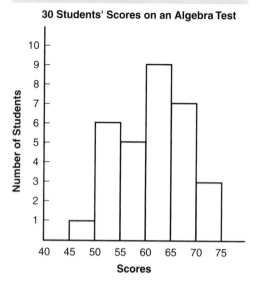

Histogram of Scores

30 Students' Scores on an Algebra Test

REACT | **REFLECT**

As the teacher of this class, what does this histogram tell you about the overall performance of the class?

points, a stem-and-leaf plot can be used. In both graphs, students can see the shape of the data and the trend in the data toward the higher scores. (See Figure 10.11.) Because the stem-and-leaf plot uses the same scale as the histogram, the shape of the two graphs is the same. By rotating the histogram so that the bars become horizontal, students readily see that the shapes of the histogram and the stem-and-leaf plot are the same.

The choice as to the size of the intervals depends on the data set and the desired message. Consider the two histograms in Figure 10.12.

TRY THIS

Compare the two graphs in Figure 10.12. What effect does the histogram have with the greater range in the intervals on the scale?

As students compare the two graphs in Figure 10.12 that use the same data, they observe that the heights of the bars vary because there are more scores included in the larger intervals. They also notice that graph B loses some of the details, as there are not as many bars. The impact of the message that the students did very well on this algebra test is also not as powerful in graph A as compared to graph B. In the first graph, $\frac{20}{30}$ students or 66.6% of the class scored 80% or better, $\frac{60}{75} = 0.8 = 80\%$, but this is not as easily seen. In the second graph, the larger bars attract attention. Those bars representing the higher test scores create a greater visual impact even though only 19 out of 30 students scored higher than 60 points, or $0.633 \approx 63\%$, as compared to 66.6% in Figure 10.11 A. The first graph indicates that the distribution of scores is skewed. There are several intervals containing just two students. The tail of the distribution extends in the direction of the lower scores and, therefore, it is said to be negatively skewed. For the students, such a negatively skewed distribution represents the fact that many of the students performed well on the test. In the second graph, no skewed distribution is apparent. As seen in these two histograms, the scale choice can affect the message delivered by the graph.

It is also important to note that the bars in the histograms are placed next to one another and, within each graph, the intervals are the same size. By comparison, the bars used in bar graphs show separate items as seen in Figure 10.8, Favorite Fruits. Teachers can provide students with different data sets and have the students select to construct either

figure **10.11**

Comparing a Histogram with a Stem-and-Leaf Plot

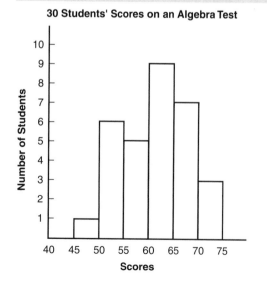

30 Students' Scores on an Algebra Test

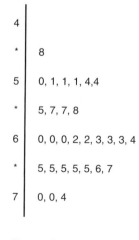

30 Students' Scores on an Algebra Test

4	
*	8
5	0, 1, 1, 1, 4, 4
*	5, 7, 7, 8
6	0, 0, 0, 2, 2, 3, 3, 3, 4
*	5, 5, 5, 5, 5, 6, 7
7	0, 0, 4

Key: 5 | 1 = 51

figure **10.12**

Comparison of Scales

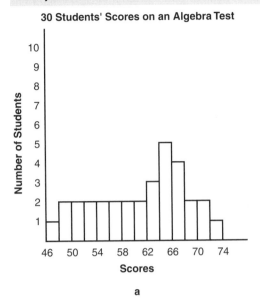

a

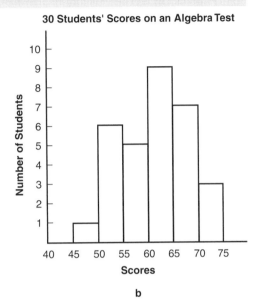

b

a bar graph or histogram. Students can then compare the features of each graph. (See Blackline Master 10.1.)

Histograms can also be created using the percent frequencies. Rather than the number of individual students indicated by the height of the bar, the percent of the number of students out of the total class scoring in that interval is indicated by the height of each bar. Histograms and box-and-whisker plots, or box plots, help to reveal trends within the data.

Box-and-Whisker Plot

A box-and-whisker plot illustrates trends in the data as it displays a five-point summary of the data. This summary includes the median, the first and third quartiles, and the least and greatest value in the data set. The first quartile, Q1, represents the median of the lower half of the data. Similarly, the third quartile, Q3, is the median of the upper half of the data. Figure 10.13 shows a box plot for the number of TV hours watched by Mr. Dolison's class.

This box plot shows the trends within the data set. It provides a sense of the distribution of the data. The middle segment in the box represents the median, 12. The first quartile, Q1, and the third quartile, Q3, are the two ends of the box. The plot, therefore, displays 25% of the data within each section, each whisker equally 25%, and the box represents 50% of the data. The distance between Q1 and Q3 is referred to as the interquartile range (IQR). We can compare the number of hours watched for the two classes by placing both graphs on the same axes. (See Figure 10.14.)

TRY THIS

Compare the box-and-whisker plots in Figure 10.14 to the back-to-back stem-and-leaf plots in Figure 10.5.

Students can compare these two data sets by looking at the graphic display. The top box plot for Mr. Dolison's class has a wider range;

figure **10.13**

Box-and-Whisker Plot

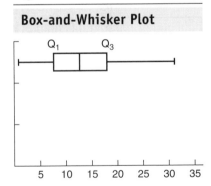

figure **10.14**

Comparison of the Two Classes

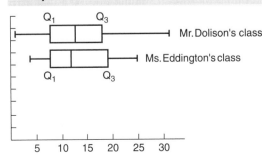

specifically, the whiskers are both longer than the other class. Ms. Eddington's plot reveals that the third quartile is more spread out as compared to the third quartile in Dolison's graph. Students quickly see that the first quartiles are the same, yet Mr. Dolison's class data covers a greater range in this quartile. The box in each case represents 50% of the data. Students may question whether or not the maximum point, 31 hours in Mr. Dolison's class, is vastly different than other values in the set. Such different points in a set are referred to as outliers and the process of considering outliers can affect the interpretation of the data. The formal definition of an outlier involves finding the interquartile range and multiplying it by 1.5. A data point is said to be an outlier if it lies above or below the third or first quartile beyond the distance of $1.5 \times$ IQR. For example, the interquartile range for Mr. Dolison's class data is 10, and $1.5 \times 10 = 15$. Consequently, the point that lies a distance greater than 15 from either the first or third quartiles would be an outlier. In this case, 31 does not lie 15 units beyond the third quartile so it would not be considered an outlier. Box plots are especially helpful when there are many values in the data sets and the number of values in each set are drastically different. Because the box plot indicates trends in the data, the number of values in each set may differ.

Line Graph

Another graph used to represent data is called a line graph. This graph is typically used when working with continuous data like a histogram. However, the line plot is used to show changes over time. Changes in temperature, plant growth, and the length of one's shadow might all be graphed using a line plot. In all of these examples, the change occurs over the continuous variable, time. (See Figure 10.15.)

This line graph shows the change in the length of the shadow over a period of time. The line is drawn between each data point because the time continues to advance even though an actual data point was not taken.

TRY THIS

Compare the line graph in Figure 10.15 with the graphs shown in Chapter 7, Algebra: The Gateway, specifically the graph of the Handshake Problem and Messy Mathematics. How are these three graphs similar? How are they different?

figure **10.15**

Line Graph

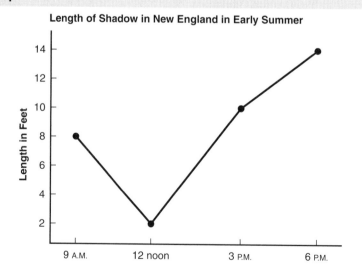

Every point between the plotted values represents the length of the shadow at that moment. Every possible length of the shadow is indicated by the connected line. The graph of the Handshake Problem in Figure 7.6 shows points that are not connected. The number of handshakes that occur for each group of individuals is discrete. It is not possible to have 3.5 handshakes. The graph for Messy Mathematics, Figure 7.3, also uses discrete data because there are no half stages involved in the process of ripping the paper.

Scatter Plot

Scatter plots are used when two measurements are taken on the same element in the set. For example, data indicating length of one's arm span and one's height or data finding the amount of one's salary and the time spent at the company would be graphed using a scatter plot. Figure 10.16 shows a scatter plot of 16 adults' elbow to wrist length as compared to their foot length.

PROCESS STANDARDS

Connections

Middle school students can connect their understanding of linear equations as they use a line to describe the data. Teachers can display the scatter plot in Figure 10.16 on an overhead projector and then lead a discussion about using a line, called the line of best fit, to describe the data. Teachers can place a thin piece of spaghetti or a toothpick on the data so that half the points are above the line and half the data points are below the line. Teachers should encourage students to describe the relationship seen in this scatter plot. As the length of the foot increases, the distance between the elbow and the wrist increases. This graph demonstrates a positive correlation between the two variables. (See Chapter 7, Algebra: The Gateway, for further discussion of correlation.) Middle school students can use a graphing calculator to determine the actual line of best fit and the resulting equation of that line. Graphing data in a scatter plot helps to quickly demonstrate whether or not two characteristics are related.

AUTHOR'S **Recall**

I was watching a colleague making a presentation during a workshop. He was working with data and displaying the group's data on the overhead projector. As he was talking, a particular point caught his eye. As he discussed the relevance of that point, he heard someone in the audience whisper that the point was not in their data set. My colleague looked down at the projector and suddenly realized that the point in question was actually a speck of dirt. He looked at the participants, looked down at the data, and then blew the speck away.

figure **10.16**

Scatter Plot

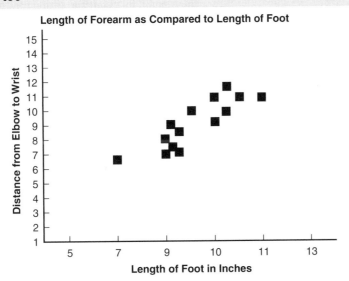

figure **10.17**

Circle Graph

Students' Favorite Fruits

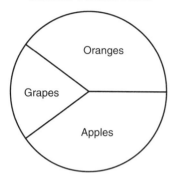

Did You **Know**?

Florence Nightingale (1820–1910), famous for founding the modern profession of nursing, was the first to use a pie chart. She employed pie charts to support her campaign to use modern sanitary practices in military hospitals.

Did You **Know**?

British mathematician James Sylvester (1814–1897) first used the term *graph* in 1878. He was a tutor of Florence Nightingale.

Did You **Know**?

The word *average* is taken form a Persian word meaning "damaged goods." During the Renaissance, the average was used to determine profits and losses of investors in goods of merchants' ships.

Circle Graph

Finally, a circle graph presents categories as a percent of the whole. Many curricula feature circle graphs as a context for students to practice working with percents and degree measure. Circle graphs offer a quick visual representation of all the parts. The sum of all of these parts should be 100%, but rounding to the nearest whole percent or nearest tenth of 1% can cause the sum to vary slightly from 100%. When this is the case, students need to look for the cause and be able to justify it. A circle graph is often referred to as a pie chart. (See Figure 10.17.)

All of these graphs, bar graphs, histograms, line plots, stem-and-leaf plots, box plots, line graphs, scatter plots, and circle graphs, offer different advantages. Part of the task involved in data analysis is matching the data to the appropriate representation. In some cases, several views are needed to get the full understanding of the data. Essentially, there are two types of data: categorical and numerical. Categorical data represent specific groups such as fruit, gender, or transportation. Categorical data are displayed in the circle graph. Data that refer to measures or counts are numerical. The number of hours spent watching TV illustrates numerical data. As students consider the problem to be addressed, they also need to consider the type of information that will help them address the problem. Before delving into data analysis as a process, we will look at the measures of central tendency and measures of dispersion.

MATH IN THE MEDIA

News articles often convey the role that data analysis plays in decision making. Headlines such as "Data show court disparities: Caseload dispensation, budgets, and staffing differ widely in analysis" (*Boston Globe*, January 8, 2004) discuss changes that might occur as a result of data analysis. Data analysis appears in many news articles. Students can create a bulletin board display of those articles that they find over the course of a term.

Measures of Central Tendency

Characterizing a data set by finding the typical data point helps students understand the data. Where do the data points tend to fall or cluster? Where is the center of the distribution? For middle school students, there are three methods to describe the average: median, mode, and mean.

The median is the point in the middle of the data set. By ordering the points from smallest to largest, students can locate the median by counting. If there is an even number of values, the median is found by adding the two values in the middle and dividing by two.

TRY THIS

Find the median for the following set: 10, 12, 15, 18.

Thus, the median of an even number of values in the set is the arithmetic average of the two middle values. The median does not always exist within the set. For example, for a set containing 10, 12, 15, 18, the median is 13.5. It is halfway between the two middle values in the set.

The mode is simply the most frequently appearing data point in the set. In some cases, the data do not contain a recurring value and, consequently, the mode does not exist. On the other hand, some sets have more than one mode.

The mean is the measure of central tendency most people refer to when considering an average. Students in the elementary grades are taught to find the average of a series of

figure **10.18**

Characteristics of the Mean

1. The mean is located between the extreme values.

2. The sum of the deviations from the mean is zero.

3. The mean is influenced by values other than the mean.

4. The mean does not necessarily equal one of the values that was summed.

5. The mean can be a fraction that has no counterpart in physical reality.

6. When one calculates the mean, a value of zero, if it appears, must be taken into account.

7. The mean value is representative of the values that were averaged.

Source: Strauss & Bichler, 1988.

figure **10.19**

Data to Help Explore the Characteristics of the Mean

You be the judge!

Students have recently completed a fund-raising drive to help a neighborhood shelter. The 24 students were divided into groups and their efforts are listed below in terms of the amount of money each student raised in the group:

Group 1	Group 2	Group 3	Group 4	Group 5
65	55	50	60	80
40	45	50	55	50
30	35	35	40	20
25	30	25	25	0
20	15	20		30

Which group did the best job fund-raising?

Source: Bremigan, 2003, p. 23

numbers as a way to practice addition and division skills. At this level, students rarely understand the descriptive nature of the mean. Middle school students need to experience the mean beyond a set of calculations. Strauss and Bichler defined seven characteristics of the mean. These features provide a framework to expand students' experiences so that they develop a rich understanding of the mean. (See Figure 10.18.)

In the *Principles and Standards of School Mathematics*, the National Council of Teachers of Mathematics emphasizes the importance of working with mathematics in a realistic setting. Middle school students can explore the mean in a context, such as the data in Figure 10.19.

Making the decision about which group did the best job provides ample opportunity for students to explore the various characteristics of the mean. Students usually begin by finding the total amount of money earned by each group. The fact that all five groups have the same total pushes students to look beyond that strategy. They quickly see that group 4 has one less member in the group and that one member in group 5 did not raise any money. Students need to consider these two issues as they look to determine which group did the best in terms of fund-raising. Students realize that they need to look for the average contribution of each member within the group as well as compare the range of contributions within each group. Teachers can also direct students' attention to the difference between a group's mean and a member's contribution. Students are very surprised to realize that the sum of these differences is always 0. (See Figure 10.20.)

Students can experience the power of the mean and develop an appreciation for this measure of central tendency in the class activity Meaning of the Mean. (See Blackline Master 10.2, Meaning of the Mean: Data Recording Sheet.) In this activity, the teacher posts two parallel lines approximately 2 feet long somewhere in the classroom. The distance between these two lines should be about 30 to 35 cm and be a fractional value. Students are given a recording sheet. Before class, the teacher prepares a meter stick by covering all of the indicated measurements with masking tape. Then with dark ink the teacher marks off 10 centimeters and 80 centimeters on the meter stick. During class, the teacher places the ruler perpendicularly across the two parallel lines. The students in turn estimate where the ruler hits the first line and then where the ruler hits the second line. These

figure **10.20**

Finding the Sum of the Deviations from the Mean

GROUP 1	DIFFERENCE FROM MEAN
65	$65 - 36 = 29$
40	$40 - 36 = 4$
30	$30 - 36 = -6$
25	$25 - 36 = -11$
20	$20 - 36 = -16$

Sum of deviations from the mean = 0

estimates are recorded. The teacher repositions the ruler so that the next student can estimate where the ruler hits the first and second lines. The students calculate the estimated distance between the two parallel lines by subtracting the first estimate from the second. The students then calculate the mean for those estimated distances. The greater number of students' estimates, the closer the mean and the actual measurement will be. Before removing the masking tape from the ruler, students can discuss how close they think the mean will be to the actual distance. Students are frequently surprised at how close the estimated mean is to the actual distance. Students should go back to the actual data to see if there were any patterns in their estimates.

PROCESS STANDARDS

Connections

Students' learning can be enhanced through reflection. In Blackline Master 10.3, Meaning of the Mean: Reflection, students are asked to review the steps taken during the class activity and then draw conclusions about the meaning of the mean. Opportunities to clarify and extend their thinking occur as they write. "Writing can be a way to find out what they know and what they do not know about a particular subject. Informal writing encourages students to struggle with new material, to let themselves wonder, speculate, and experiment with ideas" (Countryman, 1992, p. 88).

Students can also explore characteristics of the mean by building data sets that have the same mean but different elements in the set. For example, students can work with five elements in the set with both sets having a mean of 3: 3, 3, 3, 3, 3 and 1, 1, 1, 1, 11. Students can also look at a given data set and make changes to the data in order to meet certain specific requirements. For example, given a set 8, 9, 10, 11, 12, add two more elements so that the mean stays the same. Is the median affected by this change? If you add a large number, 50, to this set what happens to the mean? Is this new mean descriptive of the set? Students should also consider which measure of central tendency best fits the data set's purpose. For example, when a store clerk places an order for a particular shoe style, she considers buying greater quantities in the average size. In this case, the clerk uses the mode as the average because the mode indicates the most popular shoe size. The mean shoe size is likely to be a number such as 6.38 and not a real shoe size. The median shoe size may be a size that is not as popular. In real estate, the average price of a home in a community appears in newspapers. In this case, the average is the median because a few very expensive homes (outliers) will raise the mean value. The median is not as sensitive to outliers as it represents the middle value in the set. There may not be any mode values in the prices of homes.

TRY THIS

If you wanted to know if you could afford a hotel room in Paris, France, would you ask about the mean, median, or mode room rate? Explain your reasoning.

The Blackline Master 10.4, Can This Be True?, asks students to determine how three teachers could report to the principal that their class had the highest average in the entire seventh grade on a test. Students are given three line plots to compare. Each plot represents a different class's test results. Students soon realize that each teacher is reporting a different average, and they can describe the visual impact of the mean, median and mode as seen on these line plots.

TRY THIS

Describe three different situations that require using different measures of central tendency.

Along with the measures of central tendency, the measures of dispersion add to the description of a data set.

Measures of Dispersion

Measures of dispersion characterize the spread of the data. Maximum and minimum points and the range covered between these points are measures of dispersion. The range is a numerical value found by taking the difference between the maximum and minimum values. In everyday language, we often hear that the range covers a specific interval. In Figure 10.19, group 1 contributed $65 as the maximum and $20 as the minimum. The range for this group is $45. Some students have a tendency to say that the range goes from 20 to 65. Mathematically, the range is a single value. Other measures of dispersion include the interquartile range and standard deviation.

As stated earlier, the interquartile range is found by subtracting the first quartile from the third. This measure reveals the spread of 50% of the data and is easily seen as the box in the box-and-whisker plots. Middle school students can develop an intuitive understanding of the standard deviation by investigating different data sets and using a calculator. Standard deviation is "an average of individual deviations from the mean" (Philips, 1992, p. 35). It measures the spread of the data and can be seen on the intuitive level by comparing data sets.

TRY THIS

Using the five groups in Figure 10.18, create a table to compare the mean, interquartile range (Q3–Q1), and standard deviation for each group. Use a calculator to determine these values. Compare the groups. What patterns emerge?

Using the data in Figure 10.19, students can begin to see patterns even in this small data sample. With the statistical features on a calculator, students can determine the values as shown in Figure 10.21. Students can work in small groups to look for patterns in the chart and make conjectures as to what they think the standard deviation represents.

Students see that group 5 has the largest standard deviation and the largest interquartile range. Even though this group's mean is the same as most of the other groups, the measures of dispersion are greater. Students also note that group 4 has the highest mean and median, yet the standard deviation and the interquartile range are closely aligned with groups 1, 2, and 3. The comparison of group 2 with group 3 stimulates interesting discussion points. The only value that differs between these two groups is the standard deviation. Referring back to the original data reveals the cause for this discrepancy. Group 2 has the greater range, 40. Group 3's range is 30 and, therefore, has the smaller standard

figure **10.21**

Comparison of the Group Results in the Fund-Raising Drive

	Group 1	Group 2	Group 3	Group 4	Group 5
$\bar{X}$ (mean)	36	36	36	45	36
Q_1 (1st Quartile)	22.5	22.5	22.5	32.5	10
Median	30	35	35	47.5	30
Q_3 (3rd Quartile)	52.5	50	50	57.5	65
SD (standard deviation)	17.8	15.1	13.8	15.8	30.4
IQR (Interquartile Range)	30	27.5	27.5	25	55

figure **10.22**

Visual Comparison of Group 2, Group 3, and Group 5

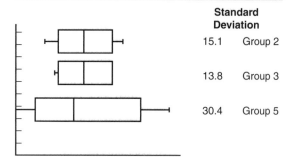

	Standard Deviation	
	15.1	Group 2
	13.8	Group 3
	30.4	Group 5

Point Well Taken

"There is a connection between the standard deviation and the box plot. Two-thirds of the data fall between 1 standard deviation above and 1 standard deviation below the mean. The box in the box-and-whiskers plot includes 50% of the data."

—*Zawojewski, 1991, p. 31*

deviation. Because of the tedious process involved in calculating standard deviations, middle school students do not need to do so for any data set. Their time is better spent evaluating the standard deviations with a calculator. Building an understanding that the standard deviation describes the spread of the data and making the connection with the visual representations for the data provide a solid foundation for later work in data analysis in high school. In Figure 10.22, box plots for groups 2, 3, and 5 are shown.

Middle school students can easily recognize the connection between the length of the box and the standard deviation. Making the connection between the visual representation and the statistical measures used to describe characteristics within and between data sets provides an important framework on which to work with the process of data analysis.

PROCESS STANDARDS

NCTM

Reasoning and Proof

By working with data in a context, students discover the meaning of the standard deviation. In this way, students are using inductive reasoning as they look for patterns and relationships within the data set and between sets. Students can build data sets according to given specifications. For example, students can create a set of 30 elements that has a mean of 20 and a standard deviation around 5. Using a graphing calculator, students might begin by creating a list containing 30 elements that all have a value of 20 and realize that the set has a mean of 20 but a standard deviation of 0. They can then change some of values in the data set to keep the mean constant while finding a standard deviation of 5. They can then change the parameters to build a data set with the same mean but a standard deviation around 10. Students should also suggest a practical context for each set by defining the group to which each set might belong.

REACHING DIVERSE LEARNERS

It is always interesting to students when they use real-life data for analysis or representation. These data will interest diverse learners if, at times, the data reflect the students' background and culture. For example, students might gather population statistics or other demographic information from their own country or a neighboring country for class analysis. They could examine data from sports or crafts that are popular in their culture.

Engaging Middle School Students in the Data Analysis Process

The data analysis process begins with a problem, an area of concern, that relates to students' experiences and knowledge base. Which music store offers the best deal on CDs? How much food is wasted in the cafeteria? What are the characteristics of the average seventh grader in our school? Typically, the problem is stated in general terms. The task then becomes clarifying the problem into specific, quantifiable questions.

Defining the Question

Changing the problem statement into questions to be explored is the first step in the data analysis process. Suppose that a class has decided to explore the characteristics of seventh graders. Students need to define areas that they think would help classify seventh graders. Students tend to list areas in terms of their "favorites" such as music, school subjects, sports, movies, video games, and so on. Students also list characteristics such as number of siblings in their family, distance they live from school, and time they spend doing activities outside of school. As students work to clarify the area of study into specific questions to be addressed, they need to consider the method they anticipate using and the type of data they expect to collect.

For example, students decide to determine whether boys tend to be better students than girls. This general area needs to be defined further. What factors need to be considered when determining "better student"? Grades and time spent studying represent two possibilities. As students consider the factors, they may redefine the problem to be addressed. They may want to know whether or not there is a correlation between time spent studying and the resulting test score. Students then need to clarify how the data will be collected.

Collecting the Data

Care needs to be taken when many students participate in the data collection. Students need to clarify the steps in the process of data collection so that all of those participating follow the same procedures. Students need to decide whether or not to conduct a survey or develop a recording sheet for every seventh grader to complete over a specified time period. If students decide to conduct a poll, they need to write very specific questions. Conducting short, trial surveys helps students clarify the questions. For example, asking "How many brothers and sisters do you have?" can be interpreted in a variety of ways to include step-siblings or any children living in the house. Students can hear the varying interpretations of their questions and then edit the survey appropriately. As students write survey questions, they also need to consider the type of data, categorical or numerical, they expect to collect. Considering whether or not to limit the choices when working with categorical data is also important. For example, the question "What is your favorite TV show?" might elicit a very wide range of responses. Students might anticipate this by offering a list of five shows and an "other" category. In doing so, they need to be careful as they design the question so that the "other" category does not overwhelm the remaining options in terms of the number of responses. Suppose students decided to have every class member maintain a recording sheet in order to collect data on his or her question: Is there a correlation between time spent studying and the resulting test score? Students need to determine the format and categories for this recording sheet. They also might enlist several volunteers to use the sheet for a few days as a trial run to determine whether or not the categories sufficiently address their stated question. Students also need to determine the length of time that the data collection will occur. (See Blackline Master 10.5 and Blackline Master 10.6 for examples of recording sheets.) When conducting surveys, the sampling process is another factor to consider.

MATH IN THE MEDIA

The poll taken in the 1936 presidential election dramatically states the case for using an appropriate sample. *Literary Digest* predicted a major victory for Alfred Langdon over Franklin Roosevelt using a sample size of over 2 million people. The sample size was clearly large enough, but the sample was not representative. The *Literary Digest* sent questionnaires to those households having a telephone and/or a car. Consequently, individuals who did not have those assets were not included in the survey. This is a dramatic example of the importance of conducting a random sample that is representative of the population involved in the question being addressed.

Students need to carefully consider the population participating in the statistical study. There are times when the entire population can be involved as in a class survey.

On the Lighter Side

That's one way to keep the election outcome suspenseful.

Used by permission of Tribune Media Services.

For other questions, a much larger population could be involved as in a national election. Because it is not feasible to poll every registered voter, a representative sample of those voters is needed. Students need to determine how a representative sample can be obtained. For example, students might randomly select people from a phone book in randomly selected states. Students may decide that they really need to select all of the states in order to have an appropriate representation for a national survey and only contact 25 people who have been randomly selected in each state. Determining an appropriate sample for their particular school helps students understand the value of a representative sample. Another issue to consider is how the sample is obtained. Students may decide to stand in the corridor and ask questions of individuals who pass by. If this hallway is located near the main school entrance, the students will probably get a representative sample. If the hallway is on the sixth-grade corridor, the sample might easily contain only sixth-grade students.

RESEARCH

The concept of a random sample is often difficult for students to embrace. According to research conducted by Victoria Jacobs (1999), some students think that the only way to be certain is to ask everyone. They find extending information from a sample to a bigger population troublesome. "When faced with conflicting results from samples collected in different ways, nearly a third of the students did not differentiate between results produced by biased versus unbiased sampling methods. Rather, they based conclusions on personal experience or said that they would ask a trusted authority, such as a teacher or principal, to estimate outcomes" (Konold, 2003, p. 196). Students can discuss different sampling techniques and focus on whether or not they think the sample is biased. Random sampling, restricted sampling, and self-selected sampling strategies can be compared and discussed (Jacobs, 1999, p. 240).

Point Well Taken

"Data are usually somewhat helpless in the form we first collect them. A stack of completed questionnaires is like a messy room in a need of a good cleaning."

—*Konold & Higgins, 2003, p. 199*

Analyzing the Data

Once the data sheets are gathered, the task of organizing the information begins. Students may decide to make a line plot of the total number of minutes studied as a way to begin organizing the data, or they may decide to create a bar graph for total number of minutes studied per subject area for the entire class. They can calculate the measures of central tendency for each subject area. Students may also begin asking more questions of the data such as "Is one subject easier than another?" This interrogation of the data (McClain, 1999) helps students make sense of the data within the given context. Students may discover that individuals who recorded time for studying for a language test may be referring to several different languages. Students need to go back to the data to determine which languages were being referenced in each case. In order to answer the question, students may make a scatter plot of grades as a function of time spent studying. They might also consider creating a histogram with intervals of time and frequency of honors grades. These representations may lead the students back to the data in order to ask more questions or back to the data for further clarification. This process of interpreting the data continues to cycle back to the question and the data until acceptable conclusions are reached. Checking to ensure that they have answered their intended question and that they communicate their results is the last step in the process of data analysis.

Point Well Taken

"The notion of interrogating the data, then, involves the entire process of a statistical investigation."
—*Bright et al., 2003, p. 12*

RESEARCH

Students have difficulty moving beyond looking for individual characteristics seen in the data to seeing the data as an aggregate. Students' early experiences in data collection often focus on "favorite" categories such as ice cream, movies, or sports. Students tend to look at their own responses in terms of all the others. Research (Hancock et al., 1992) reveals that students will continue to explore individual characteristics until they are involved in a question requiring group summaries. The question of whether or not studying for longer time periods results in better grades is a question that helps focus students' attention on group characteristics.

PROCESS STANDARDS

NCTM

Representation

Data analysis includes multiple representations of the data. Students can use a line plot to organize the data and to indicate where clusters might fall. These same data can be represented in a histogram to reveal the spread and shape of the data. Students might also calculate measures of central tendency in order to describe the data set in terms of a number summary. These multiple representations add information about the data so that appropriate interpretations and conclusions can be made.

Internet Lesson Plan

Students can take advantage of the graphing tools that appear on many websites. The following lesson uses http://nces.ed.gov/nceskids/graphing.

Objectives
- To gather and organize data
- To analyze different representations for the same data
- To use graphing tools to create different graphs

Materials
- Internet connection
- Meter sticks or yard sticks
- Post-it notes

Prior Knowledge   Familiarity with bar graphs, scatter plots, line graphs, and circle graphs.

Lesson   To introduce this lesson, ask students to all stand up and raise their arms to shoulder height. Say, "You are as tall as the distance from the tip of your middle finger on one hand to the tip of your middle finger on the other hand. Do you think that this is true?"

Students work in their collaborative groups to find their height and arm span. In order to measure their arm span effectively, they should face a wall and outstretch their arms. A partner places a Post-it Note on the wall where the tip of the middle finger reaches and then places a second Post-it Note where the other middle finger reaches on the other side. Students then measure the distance between the two notes.

After students have found their own measurements, they need to gather the data for the entire class. Ask the students to predict what the data might look like if their arm span and their height are the same. What graph might be best to display the data? After students have gathered the data, they then go to the graphing tool on the website http://nces.ed.gov/nceskids/graphing.

Working with a partner, students represent their data on several graphs. They enter the data and then explore the various graphs. After exploring several different representations, students select one that they feel best represents the data.

To close the lesson, provide opportunities for students to discuss their findings and share their graphs. (Responses may be completed for homework.) Ask students to respond in their journals to the following questions:

What graph best represented the data? Explain.
What conclusions can you draw based on the data and the graph?

PROCESS STANDARDS

Communication

The data analysis process concludes as students communicate their conclusions. Making presentations to the other classes, explaining their graphs and conclusions, and writing a formal report of their findings put closure on their work. These activities provide opportunities for reflection and help students clarify their thinking. Students solidify their understandings in the process of summarizing their steps in the data analysis process. They can critique their approach and offer suggestions for further study. The importance of this final stage must not be overlooked.

As students work with all of the various data representations, they need to be aware that some representations can be misleading. Consequently, it is important for students to realize some of the factors that contribute to deceptive or ambiguous representations.

Misleading Graphs and Statistics

Misleading graphs and statistics can pique students' interest. By being aware of techniques used, students become savvy in terms of the messages being conveyed. Points to consider when looking at graphs include the source, illustrative graphics, scale used, date, sample size, and questions asked. When looking at data, middle school students can investigate how these data are grouped and consider the sizes of the groups being compared.

The source of the information can add to the reliability of the data or the source can raise some suspicion about the information's credibility. Suppose, for example, a bar graph depicts favorite vacation spots. The data source is Travel Industry Association. Such a graph may raise some suspicion as to the motive for presenting the data. Students should inquire as to the sample size and how many choices each participant could select in the survey. In our example, suppose that people could have selected more than one destina-

Point Well Taken

"Scaling decisions represent ideas about how to frame the data. Thus, they should be tailored to the questions one wants to answer."

—*Konold & Higgins, 2003, p. 201*

tion. Students should also check to see if the data given in percents total 100. Students can make conjectures as to why they think the data do not equal 100%.

Another interesting technique frequently used to mislead the reader involves the use of graphics. Suppose data were gathered about whether or not stock market analysts were anticipating a downward trend in the stock market in the coming quarter. A circle graph could indicate that most analysts did not think the market would lose ground financially. Graphics added to this circle graph might include people running away with worried faces and lines of individuals waiting in front of a bank. Such graphics distract the reader and suggest a different interpretation of the data. Teachers can encourage students to look beyond the graphics in order to interpret the data appropriately.

The scale choice can make a significant difference on the impact of a graph's message. Truncating a graph can increase the impact of the difference between two quantities. For example, cereal boxes frequently include a graph of the amount of sugar contained in the product. By cutting the scale, the difference between the amount of sugar contained in each product looks greater. (See Figure 10.23.)

Teachers can make copies of the side of the cereal boxes and students can then extend the bars to compare the impact if a full scale were shown. (See Figure 10.24 and Figure 10.25.)

Students readily see the impact of elongating the bars. The difference of 1 gram of sugar appears minimal.

Additional aspects to consider when reading graphs are the date of the information, how the information was obtained, the sample size used, and how current the data are. Sometimes the information is no longer relevant. Asking how the information was obtained as well as the sample size used are other important factors.

TRY THIS

Using the data that follow, create two different bar graphs. The first graph should indicate that there is much less sugar in Fit n' Trim as compared to Chunks of Chocolate and Honey Wheat cereals. The second graph should send the message that there is not a significant difference.

BRAND	GRAMS OF SUGAR
Fit n' Trim	8
Chunks of Chocolate	10
Honey Wheat	11

figure **10.23**

Truncating the Scale to Change the Message

Kellogg's® and Rice Krispies Treats® Cereal are registered trademarks of Kellogg Company. All rights reserved. Used with permission.

figure **10.25**

Extending the Bars Changes the Impact of the Graph

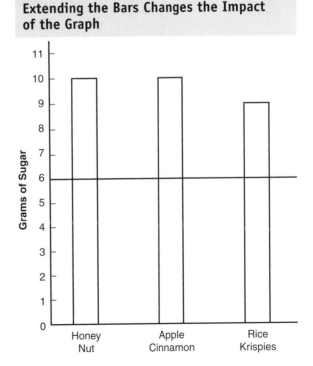

figure **10.24**

Grams of Sugar in Cereals

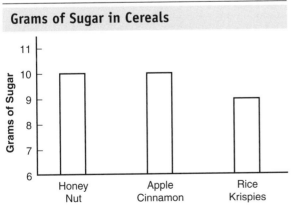

ASSESSMENT TIP

After looking at the impact of scale choice, source, illustrative graphics, date, sample size, and questions asked in gathering the data, students can apply their understandings. Students can create two different graphs using the same information: one graph to highlight a particular message and the other graph to negate that same message.

Sometimes data and groups of data can give surprising results. Middle school students can explore Simpson's Paradox to increase their awareness of ways that data can be presented.

TRY THIS

Select which candy you think is the most popular choice of the middle school students at Candace Sweet Middle School. Be certain to justify your answer.

Suppose that the students in Candace Sweet Middle School conducted a survey as to their favorite candy given three choices. Students' choices along with their grade appear in Figure 10.26.

Students can discuss which candy they think is the favorite of those students surveyed. Typically students suggest that Caramel Kiss is the most popular because two out of three classes selected it as their favorite. Students can also view the data in terms of the whole group. Finding the total number of students and the total number of votes for each candy presents a different picture: 287 students participated in the survey and 96 voted for Chocolate Chunk as compared to 90 votes for Caramel Kiss and 91 for Peanut Butter Bar. It is interesting to note that the favorite candy of two classes turns out to be the least favorite of the entire group. This is an example of Simpson's Paradox as the direction of comparison reverses when groups are combined to form a single group. For more information on Simpson's Paradox, go to http://exploringdata.cqu.edu.au/sim_par.htm.

PROCESS STANDARDS

Connections

Data analysis is strongly linked to probability. As the next chapter on probability demonstrates, students gather data as an integral part of their work comparing experimental probability to theoretical probability. Active student participation remains a key factor as students build their understanding.

figure **10.26**

Data Exhibiting Simpson's Paradox

CANDY SURVEY

Grade	Chocolate Chunk	Caramel Kiss	Peanut Butter Bar
Grade 6	28	37	24
Grade 7	26	39	31
Grade 8	42	24	36

Technology

Technology plays a critical role in data analysis. Calculators, spreadsheets with graphing capabilities, facilitate the data analysis process so that students can focus their attention on interpreting and summarizing the results of the data collection. There are also several websites that offer interactive applets to help students understand many statistical concepts.

www.ups.edu/community/tofu
http://illuminations.nctm.org

These sites offer data to explore with middle school students.

www.census.gov
http://nces.ed.gov/nceskids
www.usatoday.com/educate/home.htm?Loc=vanity

A useful software tool to use with middle school students is Tabletop. This tool allows students to work with prepared databases or their own data and begin the process of analysis by creating line plots, bar graphs, and scatter plots. A particularly useful feature to help students focus on group characteristics is Tabletop's capability to make Venn diagrams.

SUMMARY

Data analysis is a complex, nonlinear process. As seen in Figure 10.1 at the beginning of the chapter, the process frequently cycles back to the original question and the actual data. Providing students opportunities to work through the process of data analysis engages them and supports them as they challenge themselves to address real problem situations.

Making sense of information, understanding descriptive measures such as mean, median, and range, and being alert as to misleading representations are critical skills. Students explore these concepts as they work with data asking questions and searching for explanations. Working within the context of an actual problem makes the data analysis experience come alive. Students can gain meaningful understandings as they explore varying data sets presented to them, but applying their knowledge in a real situation has more long-lasting benefits.

The following are highlights of this chapter:

- Writing process and data analysis have parallel features.
- As students begin the process, they need to carefully articulate the question to be addressed.
- Students should anticipate the type of data that will be helpful in answering their question.
- Careful consideration must be given to how the data are to be collected, including the sample size and sampling techniques.
- Summary statistics such as measures of central tendency and measures of dispersion are descriptive. Students can select those measures that aptly characterize the data set.
- Experience with misleading graphs heightens students' awareness and adds to their knowledge base.
- Data analysis is a process that cycles back to the original questions asked and the actual data.
- Multiple representations of the data lead to more robust understandings.

Point Well Taken

"Simplistic views can lead to the use of recipe approaches to reasoning with data and to the treatment of data as numbers only, stripped of context and practical importance. Conversely, staying grounded in the data and attentive to what they have to say keeps tools of data analysis— the collecting, graphing, and averaging—in their appropriate, supportive role."
—*Russell et al., 2002, p. 166*

Student Performance on
International and National Assessments

TIMSS

Chris plans to order 24 issues of a magazine. He reads the following advertisements for two magazines. *Ceds* are units of currency in his country.

Ad #1

Teen Life Magazine

24 issues
First four issues FREE
The rest cost
3 *ceds* each.

Ad #2

Teen News Magazine

24 issues
First 6 issues FREE
The rest cost 3.5 *ceds* each.

Which magazine is the least expensive for 24 issues? How much less expensive? Show your work.

NAEP

SCORE	NUMBER OF STUDENTS
90	1
80	3
70	4
60	0
50	3

The accompanying table shows the scores of a group of 11 students on a history test. What is the average (mean) score of the group to the nearest whole number? (19% correct)

EXERCISES

From the Reading

1. Romona gathered the heights of everyone in her seventh-grade class. She decided to make a scatter plot indicating the boys' heights on one axis and the girls' heights on the other axis. As Romona's teacher, how would you respond to her?

2. Go through the beginning steps involved in data analysis as described in this chapter. With a partner, decide on an area to explore and then articulate the question. Describe how you would gather the data on this question. If you are taking a survey, develop the questions, conduct a trial, and then edit the questions as necessary.

3. This chapter presented a comparison of the writing process to the data analysis process. Reflect on this analogy.

4. The data set that follows shows the foot length in inches for 18 individuals. Summarize this set and create an appropriate graph.

   4.5, 8.5, 9.5, 10, 10.5, 11, 11, 11.5,
   12.5, 13, 13.5, 14, 14, 15, 15, 16, 19

5. Create a data set with 10 items that has a mean of 12 and a standard deviation approximating 6.

6. Compare a stem-and-leaf plot with a box-and-whisker plot. What are the advantages and disadvantages of each?

7. Design a way to test whether or not a paper clip on the nose of a paper airplane increases the distance that the plane flies.

8. Describe the circular nature of data analysis.

9. Suppose you saw six stacks of pennies with the following number of pennies in the stacks: 6, 2, 8, 5, 8, and 1. Make all of the stacks equal. Make a chart to record the change that occurred in each stack. Find the sum of those changes.

10. Write a paragraph to explain the difference between discrete and continuous data.

On Your Own

1. Look through magazines and newspapers to find misleading graphs for a bulletin board display. How might you make this display interactive for students?

2. Devise a lesson plan that engages students in comparing two different graphs of the same data. Define the objectives of the lesson and include the data to be used.

3. Write two survey questions that might help define the food to be served at a Math Night for parents. Be certain to conduct several trial runs of your questions to be certain that they ask the question that you intended. Show your original questions and your edited versions.

Portfolio Question

What has been your experience with data analysis? What specific ideas and suggestions do you want to incorporate in your teaching from this chapter?

Scenes from a Classroom

This is Ms. May Take's second year of teaching and she is using a problem-solving approach in her sixth-grade mathematics class. She has a traditional textbook that she uses for practice problems or an occasional homework set. During the first four weeks of the year, the class studied probability and they are currently working on gathering and analyzing data. For last night's assignment, the students looked for articles in newspapers and magazines that refer to the word *average*. Today, the class will explore whether or not they can determine which average was actually being used. On this particular morning, Ms. Take was waiting for the arrival of one of her student's parents.

"I'm not one to criticize, but I can't follow what is happening in this math class," Ms. Raphael offered as her opening remark. "My son is reading the paper for math class! What happened to the way that I was taught math—we practiced calculations. How can I help my son if he doesn't bring home a textbook?" Take a moment to respond to each of the following:

How would you respond to this parent?
How might the school community address this parent's need?

It is always helpful to begin a discussion with a parent by paraphrasing what the parent has said. By doing so, the parent feels heard and the teacher can be assured that she understands the issue. The parent also has an opportunity to clarify her concern if necessary. Ms. Take can also feel pleased that this parent is taking an active interest in her son's mathematics class. Ms. Take can begin her response to the parent with such a compliment. The teacher can also validate the parent's feelings of frustration about not having a specific resource available. Ms. Take can explain that the emphasis for middle school mathematics is placed on the active engagement of the students. Through exploration, discovery, and opportunities to discuss their thinking, students are building their understanding. Ms. Take might provide a short, written summary of the units that the class will cover during the year and a paragraph explaining some of her beliefs as to how children learn mathematics. Ms. Take can also offer this parent a specific set of questions that she can use to help her son as he works on math assignments. The problem solving heuristic mentioned in Chapter 5, Problem Solving: An Approach to Teaching and Learning Mathematics, can be explained to the parent. Ms. Take can also suggest to the parent that she use some leading questions that allow her son to continue to think about the task such as "I don't understand what you mean when you said . . ." or "Tell me more about. . . ."

It is also important for the school as a community to support parents in the request to understand the curricula. School leadership needs to take the responsibility to inform parents on all aspects of the school program. It is also critical that school leaders support Ms. Take's efforts as she implements a problem-solving approach. Principals need to understand the impact of educational research and provide opportunities for teachers to enhance their professional practice. Attending workshops, taking courses, or participating in a lesson study group with colleagues are some opportunities that schools can offer.

Preparing for Praxis

Robin's test scores are as follows:

88, 86, 98, 92, 90, 86

In an ordered set of numbers, the median is the middle number if there is a middle number; otherwise, the median is the average of the two middle numbers. If Robin had the test scores given previously, what was her median score?

A. 89
B. 90
C. 92
D. 95

RESOURCES

Math–Literature Connections

Guinness Book of World Records. (2004). www.guinnessworld records.com.
Singh, S. (2002). *The code book: How to make it, break it, hack it, crack it*. New York: Delacorte Press.

Teacher's Bookcase

Bernstein, P. (1996). *Against the odds—The remarkable story of risk*. New York: John Wiley and Sons.
  Bernstein explores the nature of risk in our society and our apparent need to minimize it. In the process, he clarifies the concepts of sampling, probability, and deviation.
Paulos, J. A. (1998). *Innumeracy*. New York: Hill and Wang.

  This book provides a thought-provoking and stimulating account of the various misapplications and inappropriate interpretations of mathematics. Paulos discusses the stock market, diet and medical claims, sports, elections, drug testing, and much more.
Paulos, J. A. (1998). *Once upon a number*. New York: Basic Books.
  Paulos links number with stories and extends this concept to demonstrate how real-world situations can be dealt with through mathematical means.
Steen, L. A. (Ed.). (1990). *On the shoulders of giants*. Washington, DC: National Academy Press.
  Five essays explore mathematics as a language and science of patterns. They offer imaginative ways that can be developed to engage students.

For Further Reading

Harper, S. (2004, February). Students' interpretation of misleading graphs. *Mathematics Teaching in the Middle School, 9*(6), 340.

> *Author provides examples of students' analysis of several misleading graphs and offers practical suggestions for the classroom.*

Hitch, C., & Armstrong, G. (2004, January). **Daily activities for data analysis.** *Arithmetic Teacher, 41*(5), 242–245.

> *Authors provide insights into how to develop sampling strategies and issues surrounding quality control with upper elementary students.*

McClain, K., & Schmitt, P. (2004, January). **Teachers grow mathematically together: A case study from data analysis.** *Mathematics Teaching in the Middle School, 9*(5), 274.

> *An interesting account of how teachers worked collaboratively to develop their understanding of the process of data analysis.*

Link

Sunburst is the manufacturer of Tabletop, a data analysis tool enabling middle school students to work with large data sets. **http://store.sunburst.com**

REFERENCES

Bremigan, E. (2003). Developing a meaningful mean. *Mathematics Teaching in the Middle School, 9*(1), 23.

Bright, G., Brewer, W., McClain, K., & Mooney, E. (2003). *Navigating through data analysis in grades 6–8.* Reston, VA: NCTM.

Countryman, J. (1992). *Writing to learn mathematics.* Portsmouth, NH: Heinemann.

Friel, S., Curcio, F., & Bright, G. (2001). Making sense of graphs: Critical factors influencing comprehension and instructional implications. *Journal for Research in Mathematics Education, 32,* 124–158.

Hancock, C., Kaput, J. J., & Goldsmith, L. T. (1992). Authentic inquiry with data: Critical barriers to classroom implementation. *Educational Psychologist, 27,* 337–364.

Jacobs, V. (2003, December). How do students think about statistical data before instruction? *Mathematics Teaching in the Middle School, 5*(4), 240–246, 263.

Konold, C., & Higgins, T. (2003). Reasoning about data. In Kilpatrick, Martin, & Schifter. *A research companion to principles and standards for school mathematics.* Reston, VA: NCTM.

Landwehr, J. M., & Watkins A. E. (1986). *Exploring data.* Palo Alto, CA: Dale Seymour Publications.

Lappan, G., Fey, J., Fitzgerald, W., Friel, S., & Phillips, E. (1998). Samples and populations. In *Connected Mathematics.* White Plains, NY: Dale Seymour Publications.

McClain, K. (1999). Reflecting on students' understanding of data. *Mathematics Teaching in Middle School, 4,* 374–380.

Philips, J. (1992). *How to think about statistics.* New York: W. H. Freeman,

Russell, S. J., Schifter, D., & Bastable, V. (2002). *Developing mathematical ideas—Working with data.* Parsippany, NJ: Dale Seymour Publications.

Strauss, S., & Bichler, E. (1988). The development of children's concepts of the arithmetic average. *Journal for Research in Mathematics Education, 19,* 64–80.

Zawojewski, J. (1991). *Dealing with data and chance.* Addenda Series Grades 5–8. Reston, VA: NCTM.

Histogram or Bar Graph: The Choice Is Yours

For each data set, create either a bar graph or histogram. Be ready to explain the reason for your selection.

1. The small community theater kept track of ticket sales for its showings of old movie classics during the year.

Month	Jan	Feb	March	April	May	June	July	Aug	Sept	Oct	Nov	Dec
Tickets	41	38	26	31	14	22	35	32	18	21	38	46

Based on your graph, what conclusions can you draw about ticket sales?

2. Freddy Ford kept track of his used car sales. Here are his data:

PRICE RANGE IN DOLLARS	NUMBER OF CARS SOLD
0–999	4
1000–1999	3
2000–2999	8
3000–3999	21
4000–4999	36
5000–5999	48
6000–6999	31
7000–7999	27
8000–8999	16
9000–9999	11

What advice do you have for Freddy in terms of pricing his cars?
What graph might best advertise Freddy's car sales?

Meaning of the Mean: Data

LINE 1	LINE 2	DISTANCE
_____	_____	_____
_____	_____	_____
_____	_____	_____
_____	_____	_____
_____	_____	_____
_____	_____	_____
_____	_____	_____
_____	_____	_____
_____	_____	_____
_____	_____	_____
_____	_____	_____
_____	_____	_____
_____	_____	_____
_____	_____	_____
_____	_____	_____
_____	_____	_____
_____	_____	_____
_____	_____	_____
_____	_____	_____
_____	_____	_____

 From Johnson & Norris, Teaching Today's Mathematics in the Middle Grades. Copyright © 2006 Allyn and Bacon, Pearson Education, Inc.

Meaning of the Mean: Reflection

Consider the activity we just did to answer the following questions:

1. What did we do first?

2. What did the group calculate?

3. How close was the mean to the actual distance between the two lines?

4. Are you surprised?

5. Why does the mean work?

Can This Be True?

Three different seventh-grade math teachers raced into the principal's office. Each teacher excitedly said, "My class had the highest average in the entire seventh grade!" The principal was pleased when Mr. LaPlante told her his news, but then she became a little confused when Ms. Tissiere arrived to report her news that her class had the highest average. By the time Mr. Alkala arrived with his news, the principal was concerned! How can these three teachers be saying exactly the same thing?

Using the accompanying graphs, help the principal by deciding what these teachers are reporting is indeed true.

Mr. LaPlante's Class

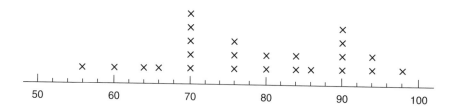

Ms. Tissiere's Class

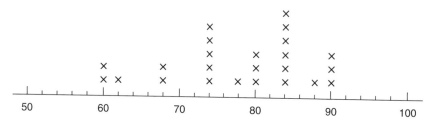

Mr. Alkala's Class

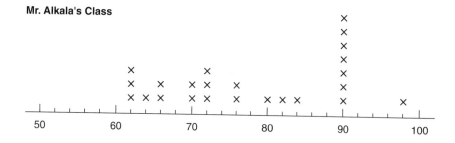

 From Johnson & Norris, Teaching Today's Mathematics in the Middle Grades. Copyright © 2006 Allyn and Bacon, Pearson Education, Inc.

Minutes Spent Studying

Name: _____ Beginning Date: _____

Ending Date: _____

RECORDING SHEET

Date	Subject	Time (Begin)	Time (End)	Total Minutes

Grades Earned

RECORDING SHEET (PART 2)

TEST RESULTS

Date	Subject	Grade

 From Johnson & Norris, Teaching Today's Mathematics in the Middle Grades. Copyright © 2006 Allyn and Bacon, Pearson Education, Inc.

chapter eleven

Probability: Measures of Uncertainty

The principles of probability affect our everyday lives in many ways. Some areas where probability is important are the weather ("There is a 60% chance of rain today"), insurance rates (males between the ages of 18–24 have the highest probability of having an automobile accident), and entertainment (the odds in favor of the Red Sox winning the World Series are 6 to 8). Middle school students find probability to be interesting and full of real-world applications. Probability is engaging to students because they have had many experiences with spinners, dice, and similar random generators in the games they have played from earliest school days like Chutes and Ladders and Monopoly. In the minds of middle schoolers, probability can help them to predict their next spin or next roll of the dice. Students easily perceive the real world applications of probability.

More importantly, probability is challenging to middle school students because it brings misconceptions, superstitions, prejudices, and personal experiences into the mix of their study. These factors combine to render probability counterintuitive to many students and adults, resulting in what might be termed *subjective probability*. The student who thinks he will roll 8 "because it's my lucky number" is laboring under the weight of his superstitions as he tries to determine the probability of rolling 8. An adult who plays the lottery using a "lucky date" is under the same misconception, that is, that her own personal beliefs or experiences will affect the outcome of a random event. A student who believes she is going to roll doubles in Monopoly because she "always gets doubles when I need it" is thinking like the adult who reasons that the chances of getting into an accident on Highway 128 are very high because he has seen several accidents in the past few weeks. In these cases, personal experiences have overtaken rational consideration of the facts and clouded their understanding of the probability principles of the situation. A 1993 experiment offered adults the chance to select a red jellybean from a bowl with 1 red jellybean out of 10 in the bowl or from a bowl with 7 red jellybeans out of 100. Many adults preferred the bowl with 7 red jellybeans. Even though they knew the chance of selecting a red jellybean was worse ($\frac{7}{100}$ versus $\frac{1}{10}$), they *felt* as if their chances were better (Achenbach, 2003). Because subjective probability intuitions are deeply held, it is important that students have many opportunities to explore probability settings, generate and gather data, and evaluate their results. When students have ample opportunities to explore probability situations, gather and analyze data from experiments and simulations, and create and perform their own experiments, they will be better able to set aside those incorrect intuitions arising from subjective probability and reason logically about probability situations. We will suggest students regularly explore probability situations with simulations to clarify their thinking about probability.

Point Well Taken

"Solutions to probability problems often seem counterintuitive even for teachers. Students (and adults) can simultaneously follow the logical reasoning needed to justify a solution and yet be intuitively unwilling to believe or accept that reasoning."

—*Bright & Hoffer, 1993, p. 84*

Point Well Taken

"Unlike many other mathematical topics, probability instruction must compete with possibly strongly held intuitive beliefs and strategies that may be inconsistent with the instruction."

—*Bright & Hoffer, 1993, p. 87*

Point Well Taken

"Part of the difficulty in internalizing ideas of probability is that people are inclined to look for order in the world. . . . The notion that random events are a fundamental part of some mathematical situations is often difficult for students to understand."

—*Bright et al., 2003, p. 51*

REACT | REFLECT

What are some factors that increase insurance premiums for a life insurance policy? Why does each of these factors elevate the premiums?

Did You **Know**?

According to the Institute of Life Insurance, the probability that death will occur for an American within one year is $\frac{1.35}{1000}$ at age 5, $\frac{1.79}{1000}$ at age 20, $\frac{3.53}{1000}$ at age 40, $\frac{20.34}{1000}$ at age 60, and $\frac{109.98}{1000}$ at age 80.

PROCESS STANDARDS

Connections

The study of probability is intimately related to gathering and interpreting data, whether data from simulations, experiments, or past events. Such data are used to expose probability relationships, support probability computations, and inform probability theory. Especially in the case of empirical data is data collection critical. For example, insurance rates for automobiles are established on the basis of thousands of pieces of data collected over many years and across many different categories. Among the factors that affect insurance premiums are type of automobile, residence, age, gender, driving record, scholastic record, and so forth. The probability that a driver in one or more categories will be involved in an accident is based on an analysis of the data. The insurance premiums are directly related to the likelihood that a person will be involved in an accident. Although it is impossible to determine with absolute certainty the probability that a specific individual will be involved in an accident, based on extensive records, the individual's risk of an accident is related to those factors that apply to that individual.

An Overview

Probability is an integral part of any middle school mathematics curriculum. The middle school experiences build on preliminary explorations in the elementary grades. These early explorations focus on determining the randomness of events, classifying events as likely and unlikely at first, and then qualifying these descriptions to include additional categories such as very likely, very unlikely, and others. Students can respond to statements such as "My neighbors all have televisions" in terms of being very likely or unlikely. Students stating that this statement is "certain" must support their response in terms of having personal knowledge that all of the neighbors do indeed have televisions. Students can then connect such verbal phrases to corresponding fractions and percents. "Equally likely as unlikely" can be stated as $\frac{1}{2}$ and 50%. Linking their understanding of such categories to equivalent ratios and percents provides a strong foundation. Students also gain an understanding that all probabilities range from 0 (an impossible event) to 1 (a certain event).

Point Well Taken

"Chance has its reason."
—*Petronius, c. 50*

NCTM Standards

In middle school students begin to display probabilities as ratios and explore various facets of probability. The NCTM standards for probability in grades 6–8 are as follows:

- Understand and apply basic concepts of probability
- Understand and use appropriate terminology to describe complementary and mutually exclusive events
- Use proportionality and a basic understanding of probability to make and test conjectures about the results of experiments and simulations
- Compute probabilities for simple compound events, using such methods as organized lists, tree diagrams, and area models (NCTM, 2000, p. 249)

Did You **Know**?

French mathematicians Pierre de Fermat (1601–1665) and Blaise Pascal (1623–1662) were co-founders of probability theory. Fermat and Pascal developed their ideas about probability during a long correspondence.

Probability in Middle School

Probability is essentially the ratio between two numbers: the desired or specified outcome (rolling a 7) and all possible outcomes, sometimes called the sample space (all 36 possible resulting throws of a pair dice). The probability or chance of picking a green marble out of a bag with 3 green, 4 red, and 5 blue marbles is $\frac{3}{12}$. (Note that the probability $\frac{3}{12}$ may also be expressed as 3:12.) That is, there are 3 ways to select a green marble (the specified outcome) and there are 12 ways to select any single marble from the bag (the sample space). Note that although ratio is a critical part of the probability study, the probability ratio can be thought of as a fraction that displays a part/whole relationship. Students who are not yet able to reason proportionally can still begin their study of probability by thinking of the probability ratio as a part/whole relationship. In terms of the bag of marbles, the part/whole relationship that describes the chance of selecting a blue marble is $\frac{5}{12}$, where 5 represents the part of the whole that describes how many different ways or events the blue marble can be picked, compared to all 12 marbles, the total number of outcomes for selecting a marble from the bag.

In this problem, the ratio $\frac{3}{12}$ can be simplified to $\frac{1}{4}$. Although doing so can be advantageous in some cases, we suggest that for a setting such as this the ratio remain $\frac{3}{12}$. When $\frac{3}{12}$ is maintained, students can readily make the connection to the original problem. Three marbles out of 12 are clearly represented in the fraction $\frac{3}{12}$. Students can also compare $\frac{3}{12}$ to any other probability fractions in the problem. Because all the probability fractions are based on 12 marbles in the bag, they will all have the same denominator of 12.

In the marble example, the assumption is that the marble selection is totally random. In other words, the chance of picking any one marble is no different from picking any other marble. If some circumstance about this bag of marbles were to affect the random selections, then the probability would change. Consider a bag of marbles with blue marbles on the top of a pile of marbles in the bag and green marbles on the bottom of the bag. In this case, the chance of selecting a green marble would not be $\frac{3}{12}$ because the arrangement of the marbles is not random, a necessary condition for probability relationships. Because green marbles are on the bottom of the pile and blue marbles are on the top of the pile, the chances of selecting a blue marble are better than they would be for selecting a blue marble from a bag of marbles where the marbles are randomly mixed together. When the probability of an event is totally random, the event may be termed *fair*. A fair coin is one that when flipped results in heads or tails as being equally likely. A fair deck of 52 playing cards is one in which a club can be drawn 25% of the time.

Interspersed throughout this chapter are activities and problems that produce results that seem counterintuitive. We present these problems to exemplify the difficulty students and adults have with probability situations. These problems are designed to be used with students. The goal is not to confuse or frustrate students but to expand their thinking about probability situations and to encourage them to confront their erroneous intuition so they are prepared to adjust it to meet the realities of probability. Students need many opportunities to explore the probability situations such as the ones we present in this chapter. They need to conduct experiments and then gather and interpret the resulting data. They need to perform simulations and use the data to make conjectures about the probabilities involved. Students need to draw diagrams, create charts, and in other ways represent probability situations. When students have many opportunities to examine probability situations in the ways we will highlight and demonstrate in this chapter, they will be better able to understand the theoretical probability principles involved and correctly apply them. For more of these types of problems and a lively discussion about them go to www.cut-the-knot.org/probability.shtml.

For middle school students one of the most appealing aspects of probability is the prospect of foretelling the future, that is, predicting the outcome of the next spin, coin flip, or roll of the dice. Probability can reveal tendencies in events over the long run but not the specific outcome of a single event. There are three methods that middle school students can use to determine probability: experiments, simulations, and theoretical computations. Each of these is a valuable means of determining probability for a given situation and middle school students should have experiences employing all three of them as they study probability. Connecting the results from an experiment or simulation to the theoretical probability helps students build their understanding of probability that extends beyond their intuition.

Did You **Know**?

The first book written about probability was by Italian mathematician Girolamo Cardano in 1520. *The Book of Chance* gave gambling tips on backgammon, dice, and cards drawn from the writer's extensive experiences.

Point Well Taken

"Although probability computations can appear to be simple work with fractions, students must grapple with many conceptual challenges in order to understand probability. Misconceptions about probability have been held not only by many students but also by many adults."
—Konold, 1989, p. 254

REACT | REFLECT

The chances of winning a lottery like Powerball are so small as to be essentially impossible, yet many people play Powerball faithfully every week. Why do you think this is so?

Point Well Taken

"The ideas of probability deal more with predictions over the long run than with predictions of individualized outcomes."
—Bright, 2001, p. 51

Did You **Know**?

There is a higher probability of landing on Illinois Avenue than on any other space on a Monopoly board.

Point Well Taken

"Students' lack of experience with physical situations that embody probability concepts seems to be an important part of the explanation of poor performance."

—*Bright & Hoffer, 1993, p. 83*

Point Well Taken

"Students need to develop their probabilistic thinking by frequent experience with actual experiments."

—*PSSM, 2000, p. 254*

Experimental Probability

Experimental or empirical probability involves gathering data from probability settings and using the data to make conclusions about the probabilities involved. Students require many experiences with physical settings that represent probability situations. They must have ample opportunities to gather, collate, and evaluate experimental data from individual and class experiments. Students can reason that they will select a red card from a regular deck of playing cards 50% of the time. They also need opportunities to actually make random selections from the deck of cards to see if their data from the experiment coincide with what they have reasoned. The probability statement based on the data from actually selecting the cards is referred to as experimental probability and the probability based on reasoning is called the theoretical probability. Students begin to realize that the greater number of selections from the deck of cards that they make, the greater the likelihood that the experimental and theoretical probabilities will be close.

In the bag of marbles situation, students might be given a bag with an indeterminate number of red, blue, and green marbles. The task could be to determine the probability of picking a green marble from the bag. If students knew the contents of the bag, they could quickly establish the theoretical probability of drawing each marble color. In this instance, students cannot look inside the bag; they can only make repeated drawings from the bag. Suppose 500 drawings from the bag produced the following results: 401 green, 47 blue, and 52 red. It might be reasonable to conclude that the ratio of green:blue:red marbles is about 8:1:1. Additional drawings could support this conjecture.

Law of Large Numbers

What if a student made only 10 drawings from the bag and had the following results: 3 green, 4 blue, 3 red? These results might lead the student to conjecture that there is an equal number of each color. Such a result does not match the previous drawing with 500 marbles, yet it is perfectly possible. This result illustrates the Law of Large Numbers. When any probability conjecture is based on experimental data, there must be a large number of trials to support the conjecture. This is especially so if students are trying to gather experimental data to support or to develop theoretical probability. Experimental probability is based on the results of all the trials. Theoretical probability is defined by ratio of the number of successful outcomes over the total number of possible outcomes. The Law of Large Numbers suggests that the greater number of trials used in the experiment, the greater likelihood that the experimental probability and the theoretical probability will match or be close in value. The tendency for students is to perform a few trials and make a conjecture based on too few events. A student who draws three black marbles from a bag will usually conjecture that the bag is full of black marbles. In the student's mind the fourth black marble "confirms" the conjecture, regardless of how many marbles are in the bag.

When teachers assign experimental probability tasks to students, it is important to ensure that there will be a sufficient number of trials to satisfy the Law of Large Numbers. Consider the following activity: Students might be asked to determine the probability of flipping a thumbtack and having the tack land on its head, with the point sticking up. In a class of 25 students the Law of large Numbers could be satisfied by having each student flip 10 tacks a total of 10 times, for 100 trials. As a class, the total number of trials (2,500) will be sufficient to allow students to make a reasonable conjecture about the likelihood of a tack landing on its head. A student who ignores the Law of Large Numbers might have each classmate flip a single tack and make a conjecture based on only these data. Such a small number of events is insufficient to support a well-grounded conjecture.

REACHING DIVERSE STUDENTS

It is critical that teachers make allowances for students with physical disabilities. For example, when studying probability, a student with physical disabilities may not be able to roll dice or flip coins to generate class data. This student could still participate fully and gather data by visiting any of several Internet sites that contain virtual data generators. These sites replicate flipping a coin, spinning a spinner, and other events, all electronically.

Throughout this chapter we will cite interactive Internet sites that can help students understand probability concepts. The site we have chosen for the Internet Lesson Plan in this chapter examines the Law of Large Numbers.

Internet Lesson Plan

Objectives

- Record experimental data
- In pairs analyze results and make conjectures

Mathematics

- Explain the relationship between theoretical and experimental probability
- Discover the Law of Large Numbers
- Conjecture about the probabilities of rolling dice

Materials   Internet connection

Previous knowledge   Probability ratios

Class Organization   Students work in pairs at computer terminals

Lesson

1. Warm up with a problem from a recent class. What is the probability of picking a red card from a deck of 52 playing cards?
2. Review the agenda for the day.
   a. Warm-up
   b. Homework demos by students
   c. Law of Large Numbers exploration in computer lab
   d. Wrap-up
3. Students volunteer to post homework on the board and explain their thinking.
4. Students pair off with a partner from their group and go to the computer lab.
5. Students are directed to go to the activity at http://nces.ed.gov/nceskids/probability. Once there, they record results for 10, 100, 500, 1,000, 5,000, and 9,999 trials.
6. Using their data, pairs of students answer these questions:
   Are the results about the same for different number of tosses?
   If you did the same experiment again, which results would you predict would be about the same?
   Predict how 50,000 tosses would come out.
7. Wrap up the lesson by having the students write an exit card and give it to the teacher as they leave.
   How many rolls of pyramid dice would be enough for you to predict how the dice roll?
   How did you share computer time with your partner?

This plan uses a computer lab so that students can work on computer explorations during class. When students run the simulation, they will likely find that the results for 10 tosses differ from the results for 100, and perhaps the results for 100 differ from 1,000. As students perform more dice rolls, they will find the cumulative results begin to resemble each other. That is the point of the Law of Large Numbers. The results for 5,000 tosses will hardly differ from the results of 50,000 or 500,000 tosses but may differ dramatically from 10 or 50 rolls. Notice that this applet also records how many times each of the 36 possible rolls of the dice is generated.

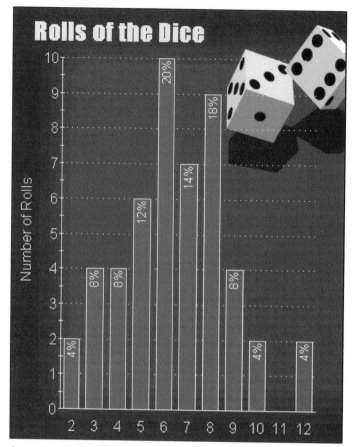

Source: Retrieved from http://nces.ed.gov/nceskids/probability.

Die1	Die2	Rolls	Die1	Die2	Rolls	Die1	Die2	Rolls
•	•	2	•	•	1	•	•	2
•	•	2	•	•	4	•	•	0
•	•	2	•	•	3	•	•	1
•	•	0	•	•	1	•	•	1
•	•	1	•	•	2	•	•	0
•	•	1	•	•	0	•	•	0
•	•	2	•	•	2	•	•	0
•	•	1	•	•	1	•	•	2
•	•	0	•	•	3	•	•	3
•	•	3	•	•	1	•	•	0
•	•	2	•	•	0	•	•	0
•	•	3	•	•	2	•	•	2

Source: Retrieved from http://nces.ed.gov/nceskids/probability.

MISCONCEPTION

In this chapter the misconceptions that we will detail have more to do with students' beliefs about probability than with their erroneous thinking with probability computations. Probability is where students "use different, sometimes competing, intuitive theories when reasoning about probability tasks" (Shaughnessy, 2003, p. 219). A teacher who knows about some of the commonly held misconceptions can help her students dismiss them and replace these mistaken ideas with accurate beliefs. Students have many experiences employing patterns to solve problems, to determine the next or an nth term, and to make conjectures in geometry. When students try to use the same level of patterning in probability, they are likely to be led astray. The reason is that they do not consider the Law of Large Numbers. Given a series of numbers, the next term is usually found after examining a few members of the series. Likewise, with inductive conclusions in geometric settings, the conjecture may be reasonably made after a few examples (see Chapter 8, Geometry: Moving Beyond Formulas). When students apply the same level of patterns to probability, they make incorrect conjectures based on only a few examples. "It is important that students be allowed to confront their often faulty intuitions in settings that are non-threatening" (Bright, Frierson, Tarr, & Thomas, 2003, p. 87).

Students may be helped in several ways to see the need for a large number of trials before making a conjecture about the probabilities involved. When every student in the class performs a number of trials in an experiment, the individual students' results can be compared with the class result. Individual students' results are most always different from the combined class results. Individual students might keep track of the results of flipping a thumbtack and determine the experimental probability based on 10, 25, 50, and 100 flips. The conjectured probability will differ according to the number of tosses. By examining data they themselves generate and then comparing it to the class data, students can build essential probability understandings.

Experimental probability tasks may also be used to develop theoretical probability to support previously determined probabilities. For example, most students know that the results of flipping a coin are $\frac{50}{50}$ for heads or tails. Students might gather experimental data to validate their belief in $\frac{50}{50}$ probability of a "fair coin" or collect data about the toss of a pair of dice to develop the related probabilities.

Did You **Know**?

English mathematician Karl Pearson (1857–1936) flipped a coin 24,000 times to experimentally verify the theoretical $\frac{50}{50}$ predictions for the flip of a coin. He recorded 12,012 heads (50.05% of his flips were heads).

TRY THIS

Replicate the tacks activity with three classmates. How many times will each of you flip the tacks to satisfy the Law of Large Numbers?

Other experimental activities could involve students flipping paper cups or toothpaste caps, dropping playing cards (face up or face down?), or rolling a pencil on the desk (print up, down, or to the side?) among others. Students strengthen their understanding of probability as they compare their experimental probability results to the theoretical probability of a situation. Students who have little experience developing experimental conjectures, who have not had the opportunity to gather data they have generated, and who are computing probabilities by juggling numbers will have a brittle understanding of probability. Their probability understanding will many times fall victim to their inconsistent intuitions, superstitions, and mistaken conclusions. By providing a wide range of probability experiments and explorations as described in this chapter, a teacher can keep such erroneous thinking to a minimum. It is during these experiments that students compare experimental results with the theoretical probability and enhance their understanding.

Point Well Taken

"Teachers should give middle-grades students numerous opportunities to engage in probabilistic thinking about simple situations from which students can develop notions of chance."

—NCTM, 2000, p. 253

PROCESS STANDARDS

Communication

The study of probability demands more communication between students and between student and teacher than any other middle school mathematics topic because it is fraught with many counterintuitive concepts. Middle school students bring their superstitions, likes and dislikes, and flawed intuitions to every probability situation. As a result, they are frequently adjusting their conclusions and beliefs about probabilistic settings. Because many probability problems can lead students to incorrect conclusions, many middle school students are reluctant to divulge their thinking or conclusions to an entire class for fear of being wrong (again!). In order to foster real communication in probability settings it is important to provide students with many opportunities to work in pairs and small groups as they explore probability relationships. "This approach [pairs and small groups] is often very effective with students in middle grades because they can try out their ideas in the relative privacy of a small group before opening themselves up to the entire class" (NCTM, 2000, p. 272).

Consider an exploration involving a bag of 25 marbles. The tally of marbles picked out of the bag *without replacing* is 5 green, 1 red, and 2 blue. What conjectures might students make? It is hard to make any declarations with so little data, but some students would claim there are more green marbles than any other color and perhaps that there is the same number of red and blue marbles. Few would venture more than this but it is not unreasonable to suggest there may be another marble color in the bag. Also, green may not be the dominant color, and blue and red marbles are not equal in number. Then, again, they might be. More data would result in more valid conjectures, but these early conjectures help to frame data collection and its interpretation. As more data are collected, students can adjust their conjectures. We believe most students would likely hold some of the conjectures supplied here, but few would voice them to a whole class for fear of being wrong. They will be more willing to do so with a partner, and then both of them can report them to their group. Once the group agrees on conjectures, reporting them to the entire class is not nearly as threatening as doing so alone. As middle school students develop their probability understanding it is important for them to collect data, make conjectures based on the data, and then examine their conjectures by considering their reasonableness, comparing the data to additional data collections, and drawing possible conclusions. Such experiments point to the nature of uncertainty inherent in probability. In the context of the bag of marbles, students decide what the most likely color combination of marbles might be contained in the bag. Students are only certain about the contents of the bag as they look inside and count the marbles.

AUTHOR'S **Recall**

I remember first learning the principles of probability in high school. There was no probability at all in the middle grades mathematics curriculum.

Simulations

Simulations are used to represent a probability setting. Data are gathered from the simulation and then used to develop the probabilities for the real-world situation. There are several reasons why mathematicians use simulations to develop probabilities. In some cases the mathematics involved is too difficult or unavailable for computing the probability. In other cases it is impossible or inconvenient to empirically replicate the setting so that the generated data can then be used to develop the probabilities involved. Finally, there may be no data from previous settings that may be used to generate probability relationships. In such cases, mathematicians model a simulation to generate data that they can examine to develop the probability of the situation. In the case of middle school students, simulations help them to build proper intuitions about probability. Simulations engage students in a discovery process that empowers them as they use the data to develop previously unknown relationships. Students build a better understanding of theoretical probability as they connect it with experimental probability of the event. They are also employing a technique that is used by mathematicians and students alike. Finally, simulations introduce students to the effectiveness of mathematical modeling. We will employ simulations as a means to clarify some probability settings. Consider this problem:

> Your Uncle Lenny presents you with six identical envelopes. Two of these envelopes contain some money. You can select any two of these envelopes at random. What is the probability that you will get some money?

In this case, students are likely to say that the probability of getting some money is $\frac{2}{6}$. By conducting the simulation, students can determine the experimental probability. Students can then create the entire sample space of outcomes to determine the theoretical probability.

Students first must ensure that they understand the situation. From the six envelopes, they are to select two envelopes. After selecting the pair of envelopes, students then look inside to see if either one or both of the envelopes contain some money. They then replace the envelopes and shuffle them before making the next selection. Students also need to decide on a variety of tools to use in this simulation. They can use actual envelopes with slips of paper indicating the money. Students can also roll one die two times to select the envelopes randomly. If the same number appears on the second roll, the students roll again. Students can select any two numbers to represent the envelopes with the money in them. Depending on the number of students in the class that are working in teams, the number of trials can be determined. Suppose that the class has 28 students and they are working in teams of two. Each team can conduct 20 trials resulting in 280 total trials for the class. For each of the 20 trials, students indicate whether or not they found money in an envelope. Students determine their experimental probability by stating the number of trials that they obtained some money over their total number of trials, in this case, 20. After gathering the class data, students can determine the experimental probability for the class. Suppose that the students selected an envelope with money 167 times. The probability for this event is stated: *P*(selecting envelope with money) $= \frac{167}{280}$ or 0.596 or 59.6% of the time. Students might ask why the individual team's experimental probability varies from the class's result. Hopefully, members of the class will realize the influence of the Law of Large Numbers at work.

Students are now ready to investigate the theoretical probability for this event by creating the sample space for all of the possibilities. The problem-solving strategy of making an organized list helps in this situation. (See Chapter 5, Problem Solving: An Approach to Teaching and Learning Mathematics, for more on this strategy and others.) Here is one way to represent the sample space for selecting envelopes that have been numbered from 1 to 6:

```
1,2
1,3   2,3
1,4   2,4   3,4
1,5   2,5   3,5   4,5
1,6   2,6   3,6   4,6   5,6
```

As each envelope is selected and not returned to the group until after both envelopes have been selected, no envelope can be selected twice. Duplicate pairings have been eliminated from the sample space as 1, 2 is the same as 2, 1. Students can arbitrarily select two numbers that indicate the envelopes containing the money. They can now determine the theoretical probability as $\frac{9}{15} = 60\%$. Conducting the simulation and comparing the experimental and theoretical probabilities lead students toward a more meaningful understanding of probability.

Consider the following problem:

> Sugar Crunchies, the breakfast of cool kids, has begun a new promotion. Each box will contain one of six action figures from the new hit movie *Bored of the Rings*. How many boxes of Sugar Crunchies would a family have to buy to be likely to collect them all? (See Blackline Master 11.1, Collect Them All.)

Did You Know?

The probability simulation known as the Monte Carlo Method was first used during World War II by American scientists seeking to determine the level of lead shielding needed for radioactive materials. The scientists used a simulation of short segments falling on parallel lines to help them to predict what level of shielding would be sufficient.

Did You Know?

The term *Monte Carlo Method* was coined by mathematicians Stanislaw Ulam (1909–1984) and John Von Neumann (1903–1957). They named this type of simulation Monte Carlo after the famous gambling casino in Monaco because their computer simulations resembled games of chance.

The mathematics needed to solve this problem using theoretical approaches is beyond most middle school students. It is also beyond reason to gather experimental data by purchasing hundreds of boxes of cereal at random locations across the United States. A simulation of the problem will enable students to generate a meaningful solution.

The problem setting involves several assumptions. The distribution of the action figures and the placement of the cereal boxes on the grocery store shelves must be totally random. The cereal company has to produce the same number of each action figure. These assumptions also mandate that the action figures be randomly collected by any cereal purchase. A simulation of this situation requires a tool that randomly generates any one of six possibilities. Rolling a single number cube will simulate this setting, where students keep track of the number of rolls they need before each number comes up. Other tools to be considered for this simulation are cards or random number generators on some calculators. Students can select one card from a set of six cards or students can use a calculator programmed to select one number randomly from 1 to 6. Other simulations can involve different random event generators such as a coins or spinners. In all simulations, the Law of Large Numbers must be considered. A class of 25 students who perform several complete trials each will produce a reasonable amount of data to fulfill the Law of Large Numbers for the Sugar Crunchies problem.

A virtual representation of this simulation is at www.mste.uiuc.edu/users/reese/cereal/default.html.

TRY THIS

Work with a classmate to simulate the Sugar Crunchies problem. You should have a least 20 different complete trials to have a reasonable amount of data.

Another simulation for students to explore involves the gender of children in a family. For example, what are the chances of a couple having three boys out of a family of five children? For all intents and purposes, the gender of a child at birth is $\frac{50}{50}$ for girl or boy. A random data generator with a $\frac{50}{50}$ probability is a fair coin. In this case, five flipped coins can represent the five children in the family. Students could determine the sample space for the problem by listing all the possibilities for a family of five children (5 girls; 4 girls 1 boy; 3 girls 2 boys; 2 girls 3 boys; 1 girl 4 boys; 5 boys) and then flip the five coins and categorize each flip of the five coins. After a reasonable number of tosses, (perhaps 25 tosses of five coins per student), the data gathered by the entire class should approach the theoretical probability. (See Blackline Master 11.2, A Happy Family.) Having students generate their own data via probability experiments helps them gain a firsthand understanding of the Law of Large Numbers in a way that they could not by simply "crunching" numbers in a probability ratio.

Technology

Computers and some calculators offer students the opportunity to execute simulations of many different probability experiments. The Internet has many sites devoted to probability simulations such as flipping a coin or rolling dice. Calculators such as the TI-73 can simulate flipping a coin or rolling a pair of dice. Such simulations should be used in conjunction with the physical models and not in place of them. Of course, electronic simulations allow students to perform hundreds of trials in a matter of seconds. These interactive programs will also collate and display the resulting data for students, so they can then concentrate on interpreting their results. At Internet sites students can roll virtual dice, spin virtual spinners, and flip virtual coins hundreds of times in a matter of moments and then interpret the resulting data. They can also design their own spinners and dice and observe the effect on their data. For some students the experience of electronic simulations is sufficient for them to develop their probabilistic thinking. However, some students might simply view a screen and then click on a button or two without really thinking about the generated data. Such students require more experience with the physical

Did You **Know**?

George Louis Leclerc, le Compte de Buffon (1707–1788), was a wealthy French nobleman who dabbled in mathematics as a hobby. He used a probability simulation to generate the value of π.

Point Well Taken

"Prior to using computer simulations students should generate trials with hands-on materials, so that they can experience how an experiment really happens."

—*Bright, 2001, p. 88*

models that actually generate data. They need to perform the experiments, gather and collate the data, and then make conjectures based on the data they themselves have generated in order to fully develop their probability sense.

Nevertheless, computer simulations can be effective, especially when the virtual experiment and simulation are preceded by experiencing the actual event. Students can then most beneficially compare experimental data from computer simulations to their predictions or theoretical computations. In addition, they can observe as the data are collated during the simulation of 100, 1,000, or more trials, and see for themselves the application of the Law of Large Numbers.

The following sites are coin-flipping simulations:

www.shodor.org/interactivate/activities/chances/index.html
www2.whidbey.net/ohmsmath/webwork/javascript/cointoss.htm

The following sites offer adjustable spinners and dice simulations:

www.shodor.org/interactivate/activities/spinner/index.html
www2.whidbey.net/ohmsmath/webwork/javascript/spinner.htm

Theoretical Probability

Theoretical probability involves using the principles of probability theory to compute the probability of a specific event. Some theoretical probability is within reach of all middle school students and can be initially explored with fairly straightforward situations such as marbles in a bag or the flip of a coin. In both cases the situations present well-defined outcomes and clear sample spaces. However, seemingly simple events, such as rolling a pair of dice, can present unexpected difficulties for students. In the case of rolling a pair of dice, students will be able to determine the sample space in part. The results of rolling a pair of dice are the numbers 2–12 inclusive. However, not all numbers have an equal probability of coming up, something students probably know from experiments in elementary grades or their experience with any one of the many board games that use dice. Students need a strategy to determine the sample space and the desired outcomes for this and other probability events. (See Blackline Master 11.3, Let It Roll.)

One means for determining the full sample space and desired outcomes is to use a chart. The following chart shows the sample space for the sum of two dice. For example, the sum of rolling a 2 and a 3 is determined by finding the intersection of the 2 row and the 3 column (and also the 3 row and the 2 column).

Notice that the sum of 7 occurs most often (six times), followed by 6 and 8 (five times each), down to 2 and 12 (one time each). The table also shows that there are 36 different possibilities in the sample space. According to the table, the chance of rolling a 7 is $\frac{6}{36}$, the highest probability for any sum. It may appear a fairly simple task to design and fill in this table, but it can prove to be quite challenging for middle school students. As suggested earlier, students may assume that every number 2–12 has the same chance of coming up and so will think the sample space contains 11 possibilities, 2–12.

Point Well Taken

"Computer simulations may help students avoid or overcome erroneous probabilistic thinking."
—*NCTM, 2000, p. 254*

Point Well Taken

"Students in the middle grades must actively participate in experiments with probability so that they develop an understanding of the relationship between the numerical expression of a probability and the events that give rise to these numbers."
—*NCTM, 1989, p. 109*

Blue Die

	1	2	3	4	5	6
1	2	3	4	5	6	7
2	3	4	5	6	7	8
3	4	5	6	7	8	9
4	5	6	7	8	9	10
5	6	7	8	9	10	11
6	7	8	9	10	11	12

Red Die

MISCONCEPTION

A common misconception is when students try to determine a specific outcome with the dice, for example, rolling a 7. It is not unusual for students to predict only three ways to roll a 7: 6–1, 5–2, 4–3. What causes such a misconception? One cause is that by middle school students have seen the commutative property of addition and multiplication in many different settings. This setting seems to be another one where 6 and 1 and 1 and 6 are the same situation, where they are equivalent by the commutative property. Although they have identical sums and addends, they are not the same physical situation. This

Did You **Know**?

The earliest known dice were excavated at the ruins of the Sumerian city of Ur and date from 2000 B.C.E. They are tetrahedrons with two faces colored and two faces plain.

can be difficult for students to understand. In many cases they still believe them to be identical, even after they grudgingly accept the teacher's explanation that they are different.

One way to help students overcome this misconception is to use two different colored dice in all dice experiments, for example, red and green. This makes it easier for students to understand that 6(red) and 1(green) is not the same as 1(red) and 6(green). Once students understand that the commutative property of addition has no role to play in determining desired outcomes, they will be able to generate and understand tables such as the one shown previously.

TRY THIS

Who has a better chance to win at a game of dice, a person betting on 6 or 7, or a person betting on either 3, 4, 8, 9, or 10? Explain your answer.

An interesting way to display this sample space is shown here. Notice that when the tops of the columns are connected by a continuous curve, the result approximates a "normal" curve, which is used to develop standard deviations. The standard deviation is used for statistical analysis of large amounts of data such as population trends or nationwide test scores.

2	(1,1)
3	(1,2), (2,1)
4	(1,3), (3,1), (2,2)
5	(1,4), (4,1), (3,2), (2,3)
6	(1,5), (5,1), (2,4), (4,2), (3,3)
7	(1,6), (6,1), (1,5), (5,1), (3,4), (4,3)
8	(6,2), (2,6), (5,3), (3,5), (4,4)
9	(6,3), (3,6), (5,4), (4,5)
10	(6,4), (4,6), (5,5)
11	(6,5), (5,6)
12	(6,6)

Did You **Know**?

Pascal invented the game of roulette to help him explore probability relationships.

Another method for generating sample spaces and desired outcomes is a probability tree diagram. Students can use a probability tree to explore the following problem.

TRY THIS

Suppose that there are four socks in a drawer. Two socks are blue and two socks are red. What is the probability that if you reach into the drawer without looking and select two socks that you will select a matching pair of socks?

figure **11.1**

Sock in Drawer Probability Tree

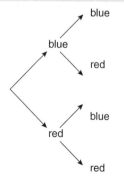

Many students and adults will argue that there are three distinct possibilities: a pair of blue socks, a pair of red socks, or a pair of one of each. They would then mistakenly conclude that the probability of selecting a pair of matching socks is $\frac{2}{3}$. The probability tree in Figure 11.1 can help students to identify all the possibilities in the sample space and the desired outcome.

In the tree, each vertex shows the two possibilities for a sock, blue or red. The sample space is found by following the tree from the starting vertex to each final limb. In the diagram the sample space is blue-blue, blue-red, red-blue and red-red. The sample space has four possibilities, and the desired outcome of a pair of red socks or a pair of blue socks occurs two times. Thus, the probability of selecting a matching pair is $\frac{2}{4}$ or 50%. What is the probability of selecting two red socks? In this case, only one branch of the tree results in red-red, so the probability of a person selecting two red socks is $\frac{1}{4}$. Students could also explore this problem with a simulation using four coins.

Although the following problem seems fairly straightforward, the results of this problem can be counterintuitive for some students.

There are three cards in this experiment. One card is red on the front and back. One card is green on the front and back, and one card is red on the front and green on the back. One card is dealt out on a table. It is green. What is the probability of finding green on the other side when you turn it over?

Many students and adults answer $\frac{1}{2}$ because it could be the green-green card or the green-red card. (Because the card shows green, the red-red card is eliminated.) A closer examination reveals the correct answer of $\frac{2}{3}$. It can help to designate the cards as g1-g2, g3-r1, and r2-r3. When green is showing on the card that is dealt, it can be one of three card faces. The green face could be g1, g2, or g3. In the case of g1 or g2, the opposite side is also green. In the case of g3, the opposite side is red. Thus, the probability of turning the card over to reveal another green face is $\frac{2}{3}$. Students can duplicate this experiment and gather data that will support the $\frac{2}{3}$ ratio. Giving students the opportunity to conduct experiments and determine the experimental probability helps them make connections and understand the theoretical probability. Probability in the classroom should include experiments, conjectures, and discussions.

A related probability setting involves multiple descriptions or conditions for the desired outcome. For example, the chance of selecting a club from a deck of cards is $\frac{13}{52}$. The desired probability is a single outcome: clubs. The desired outcome could be a combination such as the probability of selecting a club *or* a diamond. In this case the probability is the sum of the individual outcomes $P(\text{club}) + P(\text{diamond}) = \frac{13}{52} + \frac{13}{52} = \frac{26}{52} = \frac{1}{2}$. What is the probability that a stranger you meet lives in a state that begins with M or with O? (Assume the stranger's residence in any of the fifty states is equally likely.) There are eight states that begin with M and two that begin with O. The probability is $\frac{8}{50} + \frac{2}{50}$, or $\frac{10}{50} = \frac{1}{5}$. The outcomes in these two problems involve distinct conditions. They have nothing in common. Such outcomes are termed *mutually exclusive*.

TRY THIS

What is the probability that a number from 1–100 will be a prime number or a perfect square?

A more challenging setting involves outcomes that are not mutually exclusive, outcomes that have one or more items in common. For example, what is the probability of selecting a club or a queen from a deck of cards? There are 13 clubs and 4 queens, but one of the queens is also a club, so the probability must take into consideration the card that these two outcomes have in common, the queen of clubs. So the probability is $\frac{13}{52} + \frac{4}{52} - \frac{1}{52}$ or $\frac{16}{52}$.

TRY THIS

What is the probability of rolling a prime number or an odd number with a pair of dice?

ASSESSMENT TIP

Many times students will determine a non–mutually exclusive probability without thinking of any common events in the two probability outcomes. For example, students may determine that the probability of picking a king or a club from a deck of cards is $\frac{17}{52}$: $P(\text{king}) + P(\text{club}) = \frac{4}{52} + \frac{13}{52}$). Their error is in forgetting that one of the 13 clubs is also a king. The correct probability is $\frac{16}{52}$.

Some students will quickly understand how to solve non–mutually exclusive probability problems. They will compute the probability for each outcome, find the sum, and

figure **11.2**

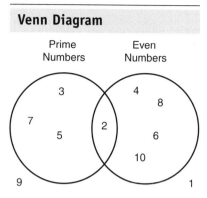

Venn Diagram

Did You **Know**?

English mathematician John Venn (1834–1923) invented Venn diagrams to help solve problems in a new algebra, Boolean algebra.

then subtract from the outcome the term(s) in common. This method is efficient but is also fragile. Students who memorize this process can easily forget it and revert to the erroneous thinking described earlier. It is beneficial for students to represent the situation in a diagram for a time. A Venn diagram can help students represent outcomes that are not mutually exclusive. Consider a spinner with 1–10 equally represented on the face of the spinner. What is the probability of spinning an even number or a prime number? The Venn diagram in Figure 11.2 shows the sets of both outcomes.

Both outcomes have the number 2 in common, as shown by its location in the diagram. The Venn diagram helps students determine that the probability of spinning an even number or a prime number is $\frac{8}{10}$. (Note: 1 and 9 do not appear in either circle, as they are neither prime nor even.)

As with other probability situations, students need to have ample opportunities to explore these types of problems and represent them employing Venn diagrams, so that they are confident using Venn diagrams to solve probability situations.

TRY THIS

Use a Venn diagram to represent the probability of selecting a queen or a club from a deck of cards.

This problem can expose faulty intuitions about probability.

Students are given two identical bags along with 2 red blocks and 2 blue blocks. The task is to put the blocks into the bags in such a way that a person selecting a single bag and then selecting a single block from the bag will maximize the chances of picking a blue block.

Students usually put one of each color into the two bags (blue-red and blue-red). The probability of selecting one bag is $\frac{1}{2}$. The probability of then selecting a blue block from either bag is $(\frac{1}{2})(\frac{1}{2}) = \frac{1}{4}$. Consequently, there is a 50% probability of picking a blue block from either of the two bags $(\frac{1}{4} + \frac{1}{4})$. A better arrangement is to put a single blue block in one bag and the remaining three blocks into the second bag. Now the chance of selecting a blue block is $\frac{2}{3}$ $(\frac{1}{2} + \frac{1}{6})$. Students can conduct experiments and collect the data to verify this arrangement results in selecting a blue block more often than the blue-red split of blocks. Students can also make an organized list of the possible arrangements of blocks and then calculate the theoretical probability. See Figure 11.3.

As students actually conduct the experiment, they soon realize that they are not guaranteed to select the blue block even though they have used the arrangement with the highest probability. Through such experiments, students begin to understand the meaning of probability as a measure of uncertainty.

figure **11.3**

Possible Arrangements of Blocks

BAG A	BAG B	Theoretical Probability	
2 Blue	2 Red	$\left[\frac{1}{2}\right]\left[\frac{1}{2}\right]$	$\frac{1}{4}$
1 Blue 1 Red	1 Blue 1 Red	$\left[\frac{1}{2}\right]\left[\frac{1}{2}\right] + \left[\frac{1}{2}\right]\left[\frac{1}{2}\right]$	$\frac{1}{2}$
1 Blue 2 Red	1 Blue	$\left[\frac{1}{2}\right]\left[\frac{1}{3}\right] + \left[\frac{1}{2}\right]\left[1\right]$	$\frac{2}{3}$

Expected Value

An interesting application of probability that appeals to middle school students is expected value. Expected value settings require students to apply probability principles to determine the expected outcome, usually in terms of some financial payment. Consider the following problem:

Our class plans to run this spinner during Parent's Night to raise money for computers. What is a reasonable price to charge people to play the spinner game?

The expected payout for the spinner in Figure 11.4 is a function of the probability of the spinner landing in each of the numbered sectors. The probability of the spinner arm landing on any sector is related to the fractional part of the spinner each sector represents. The probability for each sector is 1: $\frac{1}{8}$, 2: $\frac{1}{8}$, 3: $\frac{1}{4}$, and 4: $\frac{1}{2}$. The winnings for each sector are shown on the spinner and they may be combined with the probabilities to determine the expected value for this spinner.

$$\frac{1}{8} \times \$6 + \frac{1}{8} \times \$6 + \frac{1}{4} \times \$4 + \frac{1}{2} \times \$1$$

$$\$.75 \quad + \quad \$.75 \quad + \$1.00 \quad + \$.50 = \$3.00$$

For this spinner the expected value or expected payout is $3.00. If the class charges $3.00 to play, in the long run they will break even. If the class charges anything less, they will lose money, and if the class charges more, they will make money. (See Blackline Master 11.4, Wheel of Money.)

To solve a problem such as this students must apply the principles of probability and the Law of Large Numbers and then decide in the context of the problem what an appropriate playing fee might be, in contrast to a fee that makes money. Students might conduct experiments with spinners, keeping in mind the Law of Large Numbers. They could also determine the expected value by computing it according to theoretical probability. The two results should be reasonably close, verifying their computations and giving the students the data they need to decide how much to charge for playing the game. A playing fee of $10 will make money but solicit very few participants. A fee of $4.00 or $3.50 will also make money and would likely solicit many more players.

Gambling casinos determine the expected value for all their games of chance and determine the playing fee accordingly. Naturally, casinos adjust the fee so that they turn a profit. Any expected value is subject to the Law of Large Numbers, and the expected value describes the results after many events or trials.

Compound Probability

To this point most of the problems have involved a single-stage event with a single condition or a combination of conditions. As seen in the blocks in a bag problem, a more complex type of probability setting involves multiple events, events whose outcomes that are related to preceding outcomes, for example, trying to determine the probability of flipping a coin to get four heads in a row. This type of probability is called *compound probability*. In this problem, in order for a heads on the third flip to count toward four heads in a row, the two flips before it had to produce heads. A probability tree can help students understand this problem.

Students can use the tree in Figure 11.5 to compute the probability of flipping four heads in a row. Each single flip of the coin has a $\frac{1}{2}$ chance of coming up heads. In this case, there are four coin flips, each of which has a $\frac{1}{2}$ probability of coming up heads. After flipping a head ($\frac{1}{2}$ chance), the probability of

figure **11.4**

Expected Value Spinner

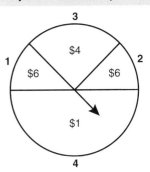

figure **11.5**

Four Coin Flip Probability Tree

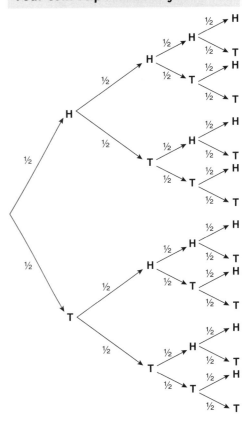

flipping a head on the next flip is also $\frac{1}{2}$. Combining these two probabilities results in a $\frac{1}{4}$ chance of getting two heads in a row. An examination of the tree shows that out of the four possible outcomes for two flips, only one of them is HH. For four flips there are 16 distinct branches on the tree, so there are 16 possible outcomes in the sample space. Only one branch on the entire tree results in HHHH, so the probability is $\frac{1}{16}$ for flipping four heads in a row.

After students have had many opportunities to explore a number of multiple events probability settings such as the ones described in this chapter, they will understand that the relationship between the individual outcomes is multiplicative and not additive. In this problem the probability of flipping four heads in a row is the product of each outcome $\left(\frac{1}{2} \times \frac{1}{2} \times \frac{1}{2} \times \frac{1}{2} = \frac{1}{16}\right)$.

ASSESSMENT TIP

At times students can confuse compound probability with multiple outcomes and are not sure whether to sum or multiply the individual probabilities. Teachers can help students by having them work to solve many problems of each type and then calling students' attention to the reason they sum or multiply to determine the probability.

figure **11.6**

Five-Child Probability Tree

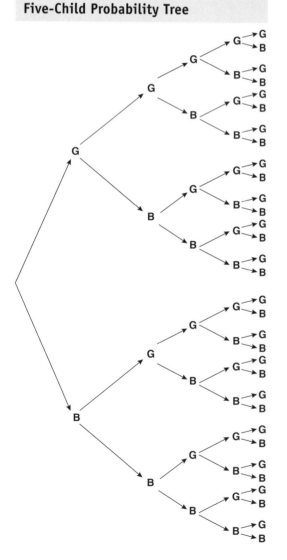

Once students can solve simple multiple event problems, they are ready to solve the following type of problem:

A bag of marbles has 2 green, 3 blue, and 3 red marbles. What is the probability of selecting 2 green marbles in a row if the first green marble is not placed back into the bag after it is picked?

This problem resembles a simple multiple event problem with the added dimension that the first marble selected is not returned to the bag. The solution strategy is the same as shown for the preceding multiple event problem. In this case the probability of selecting the first green marble is $\frac{2}{8}$. When the first green marble is selected, there is only one green marble left in the bag. The total number of marbles in the bag also decreases by 1, so that there are now only 7 marbles left in the bag. The probability for the second outcome, selecting a green marble from a total of 7 marbles, is $\frac{1}{7}$. When the two probabilities are combined, the probability of selecting two green marbles in a row from the bag is $\frac{2}{8} \times \frac{1}{7} = \frac{2}{56}$ or $\frac{1}{28}$. The difficulty for students comes when they must determine the probability of the second outcome, that is, selecting a second green marble. Students who have memorized and now mimic the teacher's demonstration or the book's procedure can have difficulty determining this second probability outcome. Many times a student who finds this type of problem challenging will remember to deduct the green marble for the second probability ratio but will neglect to deduct a marble from the total or sample space. Thus, the student will compute the following probability for selecting two green marbles in a row as follows: $\frac{2}{8} \times \frac{1}{8} = \frac{2}{64} = \frac{1}{32}$. A student who can visualize the situation will be able to produce both outcome ratios correctly.

An Internet site that simulates drawing marbles from a bag with and without replacement is at www.shodor.org/interactivate/activities/marbles/index.html.

Recall the problem about gender combinations of children in a family (p. 336). After generating data for the problem by flipping coins, students could also design a probability tree and use theoretical probability principles to solve the problem. The tree in Figure 11.6 reveals that there are 10 possibilities for three boys in a family of five children out of a total of 32 possibilities.

The paths of the probability limbs that result in three boys are the following: GGBBB, GBGBB, GBBGB, GBBBG, BGGBB, BGBBG, BGBGB, BBGGB, BBGBG, and BBBGG. Both simulation and theoretical approaches are reasonable solution strategies for this problem, and the experimental results from the simulation and the computation using the probability tree verify each other. With many opportunities to solve these types of problems, students should feel comfortable using both of these strategies to solve problems that are difficult to compute using principles of probability theory.

Another approach to this problem uses Pascal's Triangle. Figure 11.7 shows Pascal's Triangle. It is named for one of its discoverers, French mathematician Blaise Pascal (1623–1662).

Each cell in the triangle is the sum of the two cells above it, to the left and to the right. The rows of the triangle are numbered beginning with row 0. In row 5, the cell with 10 is the sum of the cells above (4 + 6). In row 6, the cell with 20 is the sum of the two cells above (10 + 10). The first and last term of every row is always 1.

Pascal's Triangle has many mathematical applications. Younger children may have explored the triangle by looking for patterns in rows and diagonals. The sum of the terms in each of the rows forms a pattern, as do the sum of various diagonals. In elementary school many children had the opportunity to divide up Pascal's Triangle into equilateral triangular cells. They then colored cells of various numbers, such as even numbers or prime numbers, and observed the resulting geometric patterns.

figure **11.7**

Pascal's Triangle

```
             1
           1   1
         1   2   1
       1   3   3   1
     1   4   6   4   1
   1   5  10  10   5   1
 1   6  15  20  15   6   1
1  7  21  35  35  21  7  1
```

TRY THIS

Locate the Fibonacci series in Pascal's Triangle. Do you think that the appearance of the series in the triangle is a coincidence or by design? Explain your reasoning.

In this problem Pascal's Triangle can be used to explore gender combinations of the children in a family. Think of each number as the vertex of a path. The number at each vertex indicates the number of different paths from the apex of the triangle to the vertex (all paths must move forward or down, no moving backward). At each vertex there is a choice to move in two directions, left or right. Just as with a coin flip there are two distinct possibilities. For example, there are three separate and distinct paths from the apex to each 3 cell.

TRY THIS

What is the sum of the terms in the tenth row of Pascal's Triangle?

Row 5 has six cells, each of which represents one of the six possibilities in the family problem. When the possibilities are arranged in decreasing magnitude for either one of the two genders, the cell numbers match the categories. The gender categories are (G for girl, B for boy), GGGGG, GGGGB, GGGBB, GGBBB, GBBBB, and BBBBB. These six categories now align with the six numbers in row 5 of Pascal's Triangle, so that out of 32 possibilities the gender combinations are GGGGG-1, GBBBB-5, GGBBB-10, GGGBB-10, GBBBB-5, and BBBBB-1. Notice that $2^5 = 32$; thus, the row number (5) helps to determine the total number of possible combinations. The probability of having three boys in a family of five children is $\frac{10}{32}$ (the same probability as having three girls out of five children). In a problem involving six children (and seven gender combinations), row 6 of Pascal's Triangle contains the data needed to determine the probability. Because we use row 6 there are 2^6 or 64 possible gender combinations in this problem. A similar problem could involve setting light switches in a theatrical light board with seven switches. Each switch has an on and off position. How many different settings are possible? Because row 6 has seven cells to match the seven switches, there are 2^6 or 64 possible on/off settings for the light board.

Did You **Know**?

Indian mathematician Halayudha and Chinese mathematician Chu Shih-Cheih both wrote about Pascal's Triangle centuries before Pascal.

TRY THIS

Write out the next two rows of Pascal's Triangle.

PROCESS STANDARDS

Connections

There is an interesting application of Pascal's Triangle to algebra. The cells in Pascal's Triangle provide the coefficients needed for expanding a binomial. Consider this problem: $(a + b)^4$. This binomial can be expanded by multiplying $(a + b)(a + b)$, then multiplying that partial product by $(a + b)$, and then multiplying the resulting partial product by $(a + b)$ one final time. For larger coefficients the number of multiplications increases. The process soon becomes tedious, and a problem such as expand $(a + b)^7$ is boring and time-consuming.

The expansion $(a + b)^7$ can be rapidly found using Pascal's Triangle. The first task is to list all the terms in order of exponents for one of the variables. In decreasing order of a the terms are $a^7, a^6b^1, a^5b^2, a^4b^3, a^3b^4, a^2b^5, a^1b^6, b^7$. What about the coefficients? There are eight terms in the binomial expansion. Row 7 in Pascal's Triangle has eight cells that will provide the coefficients for the eight terms in the expansion (notice that the row number 7 corresponds to the exponent of the binomial). Thus, $(a + b)^7 = 1a^7 + 7a^6b^1 + 21a^5b^2 + 35a^4b^3 + 35a^3b^4 + 21a^2b^5 + 7a^1b^6 + 1b^7$. The reason Pascal's Triangle generates the coefficients for a binomial is because the binomial is composed of only two terms and every partial product is the product of some power of the two terms. Similarly, each path through Pascal's Triangle moves left or right and each path is a combination of left and right paths from each vertex.

Did You **Know**?

Sir Isaac Newton discovered what he named binomial expansion (which you have done before) using Pascal's Triangle.

TRY THIS

$(x + q)^8 = ?$

MATH IN THE MEDIA

Many advertising campaigns are based on winning a grand prize by collecting a specially numbered bottle cap or token inside the package. In the Philippines the Pepsi-Cola company developed such a promotion. Consumers who found the winning bottle caps would receive $40,000.

Gina Cruz drank several bottles of Pepsi every day for several months and saved every bottle cap in hopes of winning the grand prize. When the magic number was announced, Gina was overjoyed. Not only did she have a winning bottle cap, she had two of them! Her joy turned to disappointment and then anger. She was not the only winner. There were thousands of winners, all with bottle cap 349. A computer error had generated 800,000 winning numbers instead of the 18 the promotion planned.

The company paid out $20 "goodwill" prizes to the holders of the sham bottle caps. Gina was disappointed. Will she continue to drink Pepsi? Bet on it. She intends to use the $40 to buy more bottles. The elusive caps are still out there.

In some settings compound probability can be difficult to understand. A counter-intuitive problem that involves compound probability is the birthday problem.

How many people must be in a room so that there is a better than even chance that two people share the same birthday?

The answer is surprising. When there are 23 people in the room there is a better than even chance that two of them share the same birthday. We can solve this problem the same way we solved the gender combination problem, but we will approach it from the aspect of *not* matching birth dates. What are the chances the first person will not match someone else's birth date? The first person selected has a $\frac{365}{365}$ chance of not matching anyone else's birthday. What about the second person selected? He or she has a $\frac{364}{365}$ chance of not matching anyone's birth date, because one potential birthday match is taken up by the first person. The third person selected has a $\frac{363}{365}$ chance of not matching anyone's birth date, and so forth. The product of these individual outcomes is the probability of *not* matching a birth date in the room. (See Chapter 5 for another perspective on this problem.)

$$\left(\frac{365}{365} \times \frac{364}{365} \times \frac{363}{365} \times \frac{362}{365} \cdots\right)$$

When this expression is evaluated for 23 terms, the result is 0.4927 that there is no match of a birthday. That means that for 23 people there is a 0.5073 chance of *matching* a birth date. This is a better than even chance (0.50) of matching a birthday. Naturally, the more people in the room, the higher the probability of a birthday match. A teacher with 25 students in the class has a much better than even chance of finding a matching birthday (60%). Each additional student in the class increases the likelihood of a birthday match. The probability of not matching birthdays and the probability of matching a birth date are referred to as complementary probabilities. One way to find the probability of an event, as demonstrated in this birthday problem, is to find the complement of the event and then subtract from 1 to find the probability of the event itself.

This problem is another example of a probability setting that can be counterintuitive to students. There are only 25 students and 1 teacher in a room, yet it is likely there is a birthday match. This is hard to understand when students compare the 26 birth dates to an entire calendar and think the probability is $\frac{26}{365}$. The error comes in thinking of a single event matching the 26 birth dates. Instead, each birth date of people in the class is matched against every one else's birth date, and the chances are far higher when that is part of the consideration. A website that offers a simulation of the birthday problem is at www.mste.uiuc.edu/java/java/birthday/birthday.html.

As an extension of the birthday problem, note the table here. It represents the number of people in the room (*n*) and the smallest number of persons (*s*) for which the probability of a match is better than 50%. For example, when there are 25 people in the room, the probability exceeds 50% that a match will be found by the time the 15th person announces their birth date. These results may be obtained by expanding the computation strategy used for the original birthday problem (Nymann, 1975).

n	23	24	25	26	27	28	29	31	33	36	40	46
s	20	17	15	14	13	12	11	10	9	8	7	6

One last problem whose results run against intuition is a problem that received national publicity thanks to columnist Marilyn Vos Savant. The problem involved the strategy for winning a television game show. In the show contestants were shown three doors and could pick one of the three doors to win a grand prize. The contestant picks one door but does not open it. At this point the host opens another door (a losing door). The contestant is given the choice of keeping the original door selection or switching to the remaining door. What is the better strategy, stay or switch?

Surprisingly, switching is the best strategy. When Ms. Vos Savant gave that answer in her column, she touched off a firestorm in the mathematics community. Even university-level professors were divided on the better strategy. To paraphrase Ms. Savant, consider the situation this way. At the start of the game, there is a $\frac{1}{3}$ chance the prize is behind the door the contestant selected (door 1), and a $\frac{2}{3}$ chance it is behind the other two doors (door 2, door 3). When the host reveals that door 2 has a joke prize, the option is now to stay with door 1 or switch to door 3. Door 1 still has the original $\frac{1}{3}$ chance of winning because nothing has happened to change the prize or selection of door 1. Door 3 is the only other choice, and so it has $\frac{2}{3}$ chance of being the winning door. Switching is better! As with the

REACT | **REFLECT**

Did you think the results of this problem are counterintuitive? Why?

other problems that we have described that run against intuition, students should simulate the game show and collect data to explore the probabilities.

See www.mste.uiuc.edu/pavel/java/dilemma for an interactive simulation of this problem, called Monty's Dilemma in honor of game show host Monty Hall. (See Blackline Master 11.5, Stay or Switch.)

PROCESS STANDARD

NCTM

Reasoning and Proof

For each of the nonintuitive problems, we have suggested that students should replicate the experiment and gather data to verify the theoretical solution. Collecting, collating, and evaluating data is a critical part of reasoning for middle school students. The data that students gather can then be evaluated from several different viewpoints. "Tasks that require the generation and organization of data to make, validate, or refute a conjecture are often appropriate for developing mathematical reasoning" (NCTM, 2000, p. 265). Students develop their mathematical reasoning when they collate data in a meaningful way, when they conjecture about the probability of a specific situation based on the experimental data they have gathered, when they validate or refute probabilities developed by theoretical principles, and when they make predictions of future events based on the probabilities they have found.

Did You **Know**?

The chances of getting a straight flush (five consecutive cards, all the same suit) in poker are 1 in 72,192. The chances of getting a 13-card suit in bridge are 1 in 158,753,389,899.

A misunderstanding that plagues students and adults alike is the Gambler's Fallacy. A student with a shallow understanding of probability will believe that the various probabilities of an event are equally distributed across the sample space. For example, when rolling a single number cube, they might expect to obtain all six possible numbers (1, 2, 3, 4, 5, 6) with only six rolls. A more difficult misunderstanding to correct involves the confusion between the probability of a single event and the compound probability involving a sequence of events. Every student and adult know the probability of flipping a heads with a fair coin is $\frac{1}{2}$. The difficulty comes when a person has flipped a coin and gotten heads five times in a row. At this point students and adults alike will reason that "tails is due" and expect tails to be flipped next, or conversely, view this as a lucky coin and think it flips mostly heads. In both cases, the misunderstanding involves not the probability of the individual flip of a coin but rather in viewing the entire series of flips as somehow linked to each other. The coin has no memory and any single flip has a $\frac{1}{2}$ chance of coming up heads, regardless of that happened with the previous flip. Similarly, a basketball player who misses several shots in a row is "cold" while one who makes several shots in a row is "hot." In both cases the streaks are simply part of the player's normal shooting performance and in the long run the streaks will counterbalance each other and the player's shooting percentage remains stable. A baseball player who has not had a hit in several appearances at the plate is termed "due for a hit," when in fact the string of hitless attempts is simply part of the player's entire hitting record. Such examples are interesting and helpful in evaluating a player's chances of success in a game.

A more insidious case of the Gambler's Fallacy involves gambling with slot machines. One stereotype of a gambler is a person who sits at the same slot machine, loading coin after coin into the slot. The Gambler's Fallacy here mandates that the machine has to pay off sooner or later, and so the longer the gambler can play the same slot machine, the better the chances of winning. In point of fact, the chance of winning is the same on every pull of the slot machine handle. A gambler has the same chance of winning whether staying with a single slot machine or changing machines after every pull. It makes no difference. Similarly, the person whose lucky number has not yet come up on the lottery might reason that his or her chances improve with every disappointment and so is encouraged to "stay with it" because the number is eventually going to come up.

As with other misconceptions described in this chapter, students require ample occasions with these situations. When students gather and interpret data they have gener-

Point Well Taken

"One of the faulty intuitions that students bring to the study of probability is that if an expected outcome has not occurred for several trials of an experiment, then that outcome is likely to occur on the next trial."

—*Bright et al., 2003, p. 51*

ated, they are able to develop the groundwork for the probability principles involved. For example, students could record each result of each of 25 coin flips in order. They then might examine the flip that follows two tails or three tails. They will find that the results conform to the $\frac{50}{50}$ probability of a single coin flip, and no streak of heads or tails, no matter how long, will affect the next flip of the coin.

REACT | **REFLECT**

Explain the following statement: The lottery is a tax on people who can't do mathematics.

MISCONCEPTION

Many times students are ready to predict the outcome of a single event based on the probabilities of a given situation. Given a bag of marbles with 10 green and 20 blue, blue has twice the chance of green to be picked ($\frac{20}{30}$ versus $\frac{10}{30}$). After picking a green marble, some students will predict the next marble picked has to be blue. Students who hurry to make this prediction do not understand that the probability of a situation does not describe an individual event, such as the next event. Rather, probability data describe the proportions of different outcomes over a long range of outcomes. A person selecting a marble out of the bag will select a blue marble twice as often as a green marble, but not on the next selection, or even the next ten selections. The probability of selecting a blue marble is twice as likely as selecting a green marble over a large number of selections. Probability will not predict an individual outcome, but rather the results of many events or outcomes.

Students who want to predict a specific event with certainty need to be helped to understand that probability results will describe tendencies over many events, not for specific events. When students have the opportunity to perform many experiments and then collect and analyze the data, they can remedy their misconceptions. Given the bag of marbles described here, students could record each selection they make from the bag and then examine sets of three drawings to determine if each group of three shows the $\frac{2}{3}$ probability of drawing a blue marble. When students determine that not every group shows the $\frac{2}{3}$ probability of the situation, they can better understand that the $\frac{2}{3}$ probability refers to the results of many trials and not the results of each individual trial.

TRY THIS

Adapt the probability tree in Figure 11.6 to show the probability of flipping five heads in a row.

We have discussed various methods to help determine theoretical probability from data tables, probability trees, and applying the principles of probability theory. Another method that students will find effective is to use geometry principles to solve probability problems.

On the Lighter Side

General Halftrack falls victim to the Gambler's Fallacy.
Reprinted with permission of King Features Syndicate.

figure **11.8**

Spinner

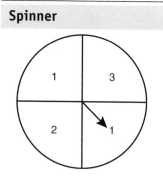

figure **11.9**

Compound Probability Tree

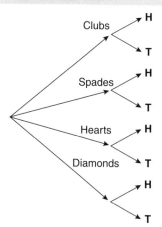

Geometric Probability

Some students may benefit from representing probability problems using geometry. In elementary school, students used spinners to explore probability. In the spinner in Figure 11.8, even young students can tell that 1 will come up twice as often as either 2 or 3.

In this case they are comparing the areas of the different outcomes on the entire spinner face (sample space) and making a conjecture based on how the areas compare. A typical target with a bull's-eye also represents principles of geometric probability. Although not a random probability setting, a target with a bull's-eye also helps students develop their geometric sense of probability. Students understand that the smaller the area of a target, the less likely they are to hit it. Consequently, most targets they have seen assign more points to the smaller areas. In addition to those probability settings that are related to areas, geometry can solve probability problems with no geometry context. Consider the following problem:

> What is the probability of drawing a club from a deck of cards and flipping a coin and getting heads?

This is a compound probability problem that can be solved by finding the product of the individual probabilities ($\frac{1}{4} \times \frac{1}{2} = \frac{1}{8}$) or by making a probability tree as in Figure 11.9.

Another solution strategy is to represent the problem geometrically. In the first rectangle in Figure 11.10, the possibility of selecting a club from a deck of cards ($\frac{1}{4}$) is represented. The second rectangle shows how the probability of flipping a coin can be added to the rectangle to find the probability of drawing a club and flipping heads. In the second rectangle 1 cell out of 8 lies in both clubs and heads. The second rectangle illustrates that there is $\frac{1}{8}$ probability of picking a club and flipping a head.

Another example of geometric probability is this problem.

> Mandy Torpedoes is trying to find the Warrior Queen of Neverland. Her journey is a confusing series of roads, paths, and trails. Some of them lead to Neverland and some lead to Knoware, the home of the dreaded Worksheet Monster. Here is a simple map of the trip Mandy must take. She doesn't have a map and so she has to guess which route to take every time she comes to a place the path branches out. What is the probability Mandy will get to Neverland?

The path in Figure 11.11 first divides into two branches. This can be represented by the rectangle in Figure 11.12. Now, each part of the rectangle can be divided to show the three paths for the upper branch and the two paths for the lower branch (Figure 11.13). The resulting rectangle can be further subdivided so that the resulting areas have a common subdivision unit. As shown in the second rectangle of Figure 11.13, the chance of reaching Neverland is $\frac{7}{12}$ and of reaching Knoware is $\frac{5}{12}$.

figure **11.10**

Area Representation of Probability

			Heads $\frac{1}{2}$	Tails $\frac{1}{2}$
$\frac{1}{4}$ clubs		$\frac{1}{4}$ clubs		
$\frac{1}{4}$ spades		$\frac{1}{4}$ spades		
$\frac{1}{4}$ hearts		$\frac{1}{4}$ hearts		
$\frac{1}{4}$ diamonds		$\frac{1}{4}$ diamonds		

figure **11.11**

Pathways to Neverland

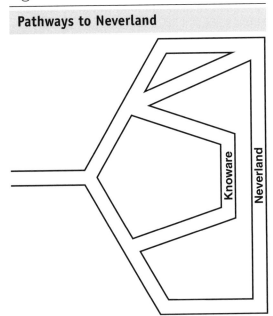

figure **11.12**

Partial Area Representation of Neverland's Problem

figure **11.13**

Final Area Representation of Neverland's Problem

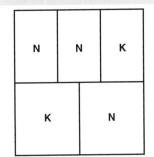

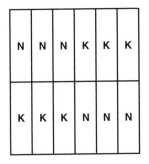

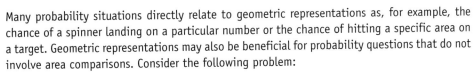

PROCESS STANDARDS

Representation

Many probability situations directly relate to geometric representations as, for example, the chance of a spinner landing on a particular number or the chance of hitting a specific area on a target. Geometric representations may also be beneficial for probability questions that do not involve area comparisons. Consider the following problem:

Lois Terms is driving in a line of cars through a Falling Rock Zone. There is about 150 feet between each car, and the cars are each about 15 feet long. If a rock strikes a car or falls within 30 feet in front of a car, it will cause an accident. What is the probability that a falling rock will cause an accident?

This problem can be represented on a segment. In Figure 11.14, $\overline{AB}$ represents the distance between a car (150 feet) plus the length of the car itself (15 feet), for a total of 165 feet. In the diagram $\overline{QS}$ represents the danger zone of a falling rock, the length of the car (15 feet) plus the 30 feet in front of the car, for a total of 45 feet.

The two segments represent the probability of a falling rock causing an accident. Any location of $\overline{QS}$ along $\overline{AB}$ represents an accident. The probability of a falling rock causing an accident is $\frac{45}{165}$. Although some students may solve this problem more quickly by simply using the data to form the probability ratio, others will benefit from an additional means to represent probability situations. Students who add another problem-solving strategy to their repertoire gain additional means to solve problems in the future. This representation allows students to develop a visual representation of the problem and the resulting probability. Such visualizations are critical for students who do not reason abstractly. If students have sufficient experiences to be confident and comfortable with all these methods, they will have an effective repertoire of strategies to use to solve probability problems.

figure **11.14**

Linear Representation of Probability

Q —— 45 ft —— S

A ———————— 165 ft ———————— B

Three Internet sites that enable students to use geometry contexts to solve probability problems are

www.explorelearning.com/index.cfm?method=cResource.dspResourcesForCourse
&CourseID=233
www.mste.uiuc.edu/activity/estpi
www.mste.uiuc.edu/activity/rocket

RESEARCH

Students' responses to probability tasks are widely varied, reflecting both their own personal intuitions and experiences, as well as their partial understanding of probability relationships. Konold introduced the terminology *outcome approach* to describe a group of students' responses to probability tasks (Konold et al., 1993). Students who form an outcome approach to probability thinking do not understand that the result of a single experiment is significant only when it is included with many other experiments so as to lead to a conclusion about the likelihood of the event. These students perceive each single experiment as a separate, distinct happening and "believe their task is to correctly predict the outcome of an independent probability experiment rather than to recognize what is likely to occur or what would occur more often if the experiment were repeated" (Shaughnessy, 2003).

For example, students shown a jar with an equal number of red and green marbles predicted an abnormally wide range for the next selection of ten marbles. Their predictions ranged from 1 to 10 reds with explanations such as "It could be any number of reds," or "Anything could happen." These students focus on a *single event* and conceive of probability as predictive of a *single* event rather than predicting the *likelihood* of a specific event in a sample space. In other words, many students focus on the next event in a situation rather than on the likelihood of an event over many trials. When students in class exhibit such beliefs, it is necessary to help them understand, through experiences such as those described in preceding paragraphs, that probability can determine the likelihood of an event based on many previous events, and even then they cannot predict the next event with 100% accuracy.

Odds

It is customary to express probability ratios in a part/whole form, where the part represents the desired outcome and the whole represents the sample space or all possible outcomes. Sometimes probability is represented as odds, generally with sporting events. When a probability is represented by odds, it is a part/part ratio. It is a ratio of the desired outcome/undesired outcome. For example, the chance of selecting a green marble from a bag of 2 green, 2 blue, and 5 red marbles is $\frac{2}{9}$. The odds in favor of selecting a green marble are $\frac{2}{7}$ (usually represented as 2:7), where 7 represents the number of unfavorable events (2 blue and 5 red marbles). Notice that when odds are represented in fraction form the sum of the numerator and denominator of an odds ratio is equal to the number of elements in the sample space.

For some it is easier to tell the likelihood of a team winning a competition or a horse winning a race when the odds are given instead of the probability ratio. A horse whose odds of winning are 3:8 has a less than even chance (1:1) of winning, whereas a horse with odds of winning posted at 5:4 has a greater than even chance of winning. The same conclusions could be made from the probability ratios of 3:11 and 5:9, respectively, but for some the odds are easier to interpret and so have remained a staple of athletic contests around the world.

TRY THIS

The probability of the Red Sox winning the World Series is $\frac{6}{8}$. What are the odds of the Red Sox winning the World Series?

One last consideration when developing probability relationships with middle school students is the topic of gambling. We have already touched on gambling in a few parts of this chapter. It is important to help students understand that gambling may be a form of entertainment or recreation, but it is an expensive one. The principles of probability clearly reveal that it is impossible to win at any game of chance in the long run. There are ample studies that describe the addiction that the urge to gamble has on people, including teenagers. A recent study of nearly 7,000 eighth-grade students in the United States found that over one-third of them had gambled in the past year. According to the International Youth Centre at McGill University, more than half of Canadian students ages 12–17 are considered recreational gamblers, and 4%–6% are already pathological gamblers. The concern of experts is that high-stakes gamblers who start young are the most likely to develop addiction problems. The proliferation of lotteries and casinos across the United States and Canada makes gambling so much easier for everyone. Gambling has become a respected pastime, even in social organizations. In addition, the Internet is now the site of hundreds of virtual casinos, providing young people anonymity, immediate access, and, with a credit card, the ability to gamble with money they do not have. These all pressure the average student to "play the lottery," "try your luck" or "place a bet." It is the teacher's obligation to clarify the mathematics involved in games of chance so that students do not fall prey to the insidious nature of gambling and become another statistic for gambling addiction.

These two Internet sites present real-life settings for probability problems. In the first site a forest fire spreads or dies out according to an adjustable probability ratio. In the second site students adjust the numbers of fish in a tank to match probability ratios.

> www.shodor.org/interactivate/activities/fire1/index.html
> www.bbc.co.uk/education/mathsfile/shockwave/games/fish.html

REACT | REFLECT

What may contribute to the addictive nature of gambling for some persons?

SUMMARY

Middle school students will find probability to be intriguing and challenging. It is, however, the most counterintuitive topic in mathematics. Students bring past experiences, superstitions, beliefs, hunches, and hopes to the study of probability, and these cloud their ability to think probabilistically. A student who chants a lucky phrase might think that will influence the roll of a pair of dice. A student who has rarely rolled doubles in the past few board games she has played is likely to believe she is incapable of rolling doubles in the future. Adults are not immune to faulty probability reasoning as the booming gambling industry and proliferation of lotteries demonstrate.

The laws of probability follow well-defined boundaries. If an event is random, then the outcome over a large number of trials can be predicted. Probability will not predict the outcome of a single or the next event but only the tendency of events over many repetitions. Students who study probability should generate, gather, collate, and interpret data to reason effectively. Finding experimental probabilities by conducting experiments and simulations helps students develop a meaningful connection and greater appreciation for theoretical probability. Students can appreciate probability as a measure of uncertainty.

The following are highlights of this chapter:

- Probability is a part/whole ratio of a desired event compared to all possible outcomes (sample space).
- Probability principles apply to random or fair events.

- Probability cannot predict the outcome of a single event but only the tendencies of events over many trials.
- There are three ways the probability of a situation can be determined: compute the theoretical probability, collect experimental data, and perform simulations.
- The Law of Large Numbers stipulates that a large number of events is needed for the principles of probability to be revealed.
- The Gambler's Fallacy describes the mistaken belief that a previous event affects the results of a new and independent event.
- Pascal's Triangle is useful for students to determine the theoretical probability of some events.
- Odds are an alternative method for representing probability.

Student Performance on International and National Assessments

TIMSS

Each of the six faces of a certain cube is painted either red or blue. When the cube is tossed the probability of the cube landing with the red face up is $\frac{2}{3}$. How many faces are red? (47% correct)

A. One
B. Two
C. Three
D. Four
E. Five

NAEP

Nine chips numbered 1–9 are placed in a sack and then mixed up. Madeline picks one chip from the sack. What is the probability Madeline draws a chip with an even number? (53% correct)

A. $\frac{1}{9}$
B. $\frac{2}{9}$
C. $\frac{4}{9}$
D. $\frac{1}{2}$
E. $\frac{4}{5}$

EXERCISES

From the Reading

1. Use Pascal's Triangle to determine the probability of having four boys out of eight children in a family.

2. Write about a situation that has a probability of 0. Be ready to support your reasoning.

3. What would you do to help a seventh-grade student understand the Gambler's Fallacy?

4. What are the chances of flipping a coin to get six heads in a row?

5. Why are simulations used to study probability?

6. What are the chances of selecting a red card or a king from a deck of cards?

7. What are the odds against rolling a 6 with a number cube?

8. A sack has 3 blue, 4 red, and 2 green marbles. What are the chances of picking 2 red marbles in a row if you replace the first marble you pick? If you do not replace the first marble picked?

9. Why is the Law of Large Numbers important for classroom experiments?

On Your Own

1. Interview an adult who plays the lottery. Ask how he or she determines the numbers to play. Does this person have a lucky number or play hunches? Does he or she use a method based on the Gambler's Fallacy?

2. Go to www.mste.uiuc.edu/reese/buffon/buffon.html and replicate Buffon's experiment that produced the value of π.

3. Visit a middle school classroom and ask a few students about any lucky numbers that they can roll with number cubes.

4. Examine the lottery in your state. What is the profile of a typical participant?

Portfolio Question

What role do hunches play in your thinking about probability situations? Why?

Scenes from a Classroom

Ms. Somerville is reviewing probability ratios with her grade 5 students by using a paper bag with different combinations of marbles in it. She has just put 4 blue, 5 green, and 3 red marbles into the bag.

Ms. Somerville: OK, you all know how many of each color I put in the bag. So, what is the probability of picking a green marble from the bag? Yes, Latrell?

Latrell: That would be 5 out of 12 or $\frac{5}{12}$.

Ms. Somerville: That's right. Now, Danielle, what is the chance of my picking a blue marble out of the bag?

Danielle: It's 4 out of 12 or $\frac{4}{12}$.

Hector: You could make that $\frac{1}{3}$, right?

Ms. Somerville: Yes. Either answer is correct. Now, what are the odds of picking a red marble? Fila?

Fila: That is 3 out of 12 or $\frac{3}{12}$ or $\frac{1}{4}$.

Ms. Somerville: That's right. Very good. Let's try a different bag of marbles so we can . . .

Before reading our comments, respond to these questions.

1. Examine Ms. Somerville's questions carefully. What question needs adjustment?
2. How would you improve her questions?

Ms. Somerville has been a bit casual with her vocabulary, a tendency most teachers have to carefully monitor. In corridor talk, the distinction between odds and probability is blurred to insignificance. However, in mathematics, the two terms have different meanings, as discussed earlier in this chapter. By using *odds* and *probability* interchangeably, Ms. Somerville has made it difficult, if not impossible, for her students to recall and understand the difference between odds and probability. Carelessness about mathematics vocabulary can extend to *congruent* and *equal*, *combination* and *permutation*, and *line* and *segment*. Although there is no need to become pedantic about the vocabulary to use before students, it is critical that mathematics terms are used according to their definitions.

Preparing for Praxis

In order to estimate the population of snails in a certain woodland, a biologist captured and marked 84 snails that were then released into the woodland. Fifteen days later the biologist captured 90 snails from the woodland, 12 of which bore the markings of the previously captured snails. If all of the marked snails were still active in the woodland when the second group of snails was captured, what should the biologist estimate the snail population to be based on the probabilities suggested by this experiment?

A. 630
B. 1,010
C. 1,040
D. 1,080

RESOURCES

Math–Literature Connections

Bruce, C. (2001). *Conned again Watson: Cautionary tales of logic, math and probability.* Cambridge, MA: Perseus Publishing.

Cushman, J. (1991). *Do you wanna bet?* London: Clarion.

Holtzman, C. (1977). *No fair!* New York: Scholastic.

L'Engle, M. (1973). *A wrinkle in time.* New York: Bantam Doubleday Dell Books for Young Readers.

Rowland, M. (1997). *In the next three seconds.* London: Egmont Children's Books.

Van Allsberg, C. (1981). *Jumanji.* Boston: Houghton Mifflin.

Teacher's Bookcase

Bright, G., Frierson, D., Tarr, J., & Thomas, C. (2003). *Navigating through probability in grades 6–8.* Reston, VA: NCTM.

This book from NCTM is an excellent source of activities and interactive applets on the included CD.

Peterson, I. (1998). *The jungles of randomness: A mathematical safari.* New York: John Wiley & Sons, Inc.

Peterson is a well-known mathematics writer whose book contains several chapters dealing with nonroutine applications of probability in real-life situations.

Shulte A., & Smart, J. (Eds.). (1981). *Teaching statistics and probability: 1981 yearbook of the National Council of Teachers of Mathematics.* Reston, VA: NCTM.

This book is a collection of chapters dealing with probability topics in the classroom at all levels.

Weaver, J. (2001). *What are the odds?: The chances of extraordinary events in everyday life.* Amherst, NY: Prometheus Books.

This book is written for mainstream audiences. It presents the odds of various social events such as accident rates and mortality rates. The statistical information can prove to be quite interesting to middle schoolers.

Further Reading

Abaugh, F., Scholten, C., & Essex, K. (2001). Data in the middle grades: A probability web quest. *Mathematics Teaching in the Middle School, 7*(2), 90–95.

In this article the authors describe how to use Internet-based materials and applets to introduce principles of probability.

Aspinwall, L., & Shaw, K. (2000). Enriching students' mathematical intuitions with probability games and tree diagrams. *Mathematics Teaching in the Middle School, 6*(4), 214–220.

This article presents several games for students to explore using tree diagrams in order to build their intuitions in probability.

Bright, G., & Hoffer, K. (1993). Measurement, probability, statistics, and graphing. In D. T. Owens (Ed.), *Research ideas for the classroom: Middle grades mathematics.* **Reston, VA: NCTM.**

This chapter covers a wide range of topics but includes some interesting observations about how probability is best presented to middle school students.

Ewbank, W., & Ginter, J. (2002). Probability on a budget. *Mathematics Teaching in the Middle School, 7(7), 280–283.*

This article presents several exploration lesson plans designed to help students understand probability. The experiments involve cheaply made manipulatives and so are easily incorporated into a middle school classroom.

Freda, A. (1998). Roll the dice: An introduction to probability. *Mathematics Teaching in Middle School, 4(2), 85–89.*

The author describes a class project involving different numbers of dice and a difference game. Students gather data about the game, develop a simulation on a graphing calculator, and devise winning strategies based on probability principles.

Kader, G., & Perry, M. (1998). Push-penny: What is your expected score? *Mathematics Teaching in the Middle School, 3(5), 370–377.*

The author describes an activity with pennies touching parallel lines. Students examine experimental, theoretical, and simulated data to form conclusions about the probability of the events described in the article.

Noron, R. (2001). Determining probabilities by examining underlying structures. *Mathematics Teaching in the Middle School, 7(2), 79–86.*

In this article a class lesson with middle schoolers is described in detail. The lesson leads students from collecting and collating data from games of dice to formulating theoretical probabilities.

Weist, L., & Quinn, R. (1999). Exploring probability through an even-odds dice game. *Mathematics Teaching in the Middle School, 4(6), 358–362.*

In this article the authors describe probability explorations using several types of dice. Students develop game strategies based on probability principles and the data they generate.

Links

Probability applets
www.shodor.org/interactivate/activities/index.html#pro
http://nlvm.usu.edu/en/nav/topic_t_5.html

REFERENCES

Achenbach, J. (2003, September). Time to hit the panic button. *National Geographic.*

Bright, G., Frierson, D., Tarr, J., & Thomas, C. (2003). *Navigating through probability in grades 6–8.* Reston, VA: NCTM.

Bright, G., & Hoffer, K. (1993). Measurement, probability, statistics, and graphing. In D. T. Owens (Ed.), *Research ideas for the classroom: Middle grades mathematics.* Reston, VA: NCTM.

Konold, C. (1989). Informal conceptions of probability. *Cognition and Instruction, 6, 59–98.*

Konold, C., Pollatsek, A., Well, A., Lohemier, J., & Lipson, A. (1993). Inconsistencies in students' reasoning about probability. *Journal for Research in Mathematics Education, 24, 392–414.*

National Council of Teachers of Mathematics. (1989). *Curriculum and evaluation standards for school mathematics.* Reston, VA: NCTM.

National Council of Teachers of Mathematics. (2000). *Professional standards for school mathematics.* Reston, VA: NCTM.

Nymann, K. (1975). Another generalization of the birthday problem. *Mathematics Magazine, 48, 46–47.*

Shaughnessy, M. (2003). Research on students' understanding of probability. In J. Kilpatrick, W. Martin, & D. Schifter (Eds.), *A research companion to principles and standards for school mathematics.* Reston, VA: NCTM.

Collect Them All

Sugar Crunchies, the favorite breakfast cereal of star basketball player Mandy Torpedoes, has started a new set of collectible action figures. The action figures are from the new movie *Bored of the Rings*. There is one action figure in each box. The Sugar Crunchies company makes the same number of each figure and distributes them randomly around the country. How many boxes will your family have to buy so you can collect all six action figures?

To find out you will have to carry out a simulation. Use a single number cube. Each number of the cube will represent one of the action figures. Record how many rolls you need before all six numbers come up. Try this four times. Be sure to record all your data. We will combine all the class data to get an answer.

Trial 1   _____ rolls

Trial 2   _____ rolls

Trial 3   _____ rolls

Trial 4   _____ rolls

From Johnson & Norris, *Teaching Today's Mathematics in the Middle Grades.* Copyright © 2006 Allyn and Bacon, Pearson Education, Inc.

A Happy Family

You just heard that a new family is moving into your neighborhood. There are five children in the family. You wonder if there are more girls or more boys in the family. You can use what you know about probability simulations to get some idea. Find out the probability of the family having three girls and two boys.

First, write out all six possibilities in a family of five children.

1. 5 girls

2.

3.

4.

5.

6. 5 boys

A child can be a boy or a girl. So, you can use the flip of a coin to represent a child's gender. For five children, you will need to flip five coins.

Work with your group. Each one of you should flip five coins at least 25 times. Keep track of what each result shows in a table. Be sure your table has all six possible girl-boy combinations.

After you gather all your group data, tell the probability of the family having three girls. Also tell the probability of the family having three boys.

Three girls: _____   Three boys: _____

 From Johnson & Norris, *Teaching Today's Mathematics in the Middle Grades.* Copyright © 2006 Allyn and Bacon, Pearson Education, Inc.

Let It Roll

You have probably used dice or number cubes to play games like Monopoly or Clue. What numbers can you get by rolling two dice? That's right—any number from 2 to 12 can come up. Do some numbers come up more than others? How much harder is it to roll some numbers than it is to roll others? Find out.

First, make a chart to figure out all the possible number combinations that you can roll with two dice. Use your chart to make probability ratios for each number.

Put your chart here.

Next, roll a pair of dice 100 times and keep track of what numbers come up. Combine your results with three other people in class. Give the percent that each number was rolled. Write your probability ratios from your chart and your data from the rolls on the accompanying chart.

NUMBER	PROBABILITY RATIO	ACTUAL ROLLS	PERCENT OF ROLLS
2			
3			
4			
5			
6			
7			
8			
9			
10			
11			
12			

Wheel of Money

The local school Fundraisers Club plans to use the spinner you see here at the next Activity Day to help raise money for school clubs and athletic teams. The dollar amounts are the payoff for each pat of the spinner. The club is not sure how much to charge people to play the spinner game. What do you think?

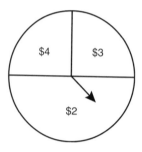

1. What is the expected value for this spinner?

2. What should the club charge to make a reasonable amount of money on each spin?

Design your own spinner with four different regions on it. Make the expected value $5.00. Draw your spinner here.

 From Johnson & Norris, Teaching Today's Mathematics in the Middle Grades. Copyright © 2006 Allyn and Bacon, Pearson Education, Inc.

Stay or Switch?

Will you stay or switch? That's the choice you have on a popular television game show. On the show you try to find the grand prize that is behind one of three doors. Sounds simple, right? But there is more to it.

Suppose you pick door 1. The game show host then opens one of the other doors, say, door 2. Door 2 has a consolation prize. You then have the choice of staying with door 1 or switching to door 3. The grand prize is behind one of those doors. So, will you switch or not? Does it really make any difference?

To find out, play the game 25 times with a partner. Place three playing cards face down. Decide ahead of time which of the cards is the grand prize winner. One of you will act as the game show host. As the host places the cards face down, it is important to keep track of which card is the grand prize winner. With your partner, you will keep track of the number of times that you win according to one of the following strategies:

Half of the class will always switch after the host reveals the door with the joke prize. The other half of the class will never switch after the host reveals the door with the joke prize.

Determine the experimental probability for winning the grand prize for your 25 trials.

12

Teaching as a Career: The Journey Begins

Teaching is an incredibly complex craft. It seems that the more we begin to understand about teaching, the more we realize that there is so much more to know and assimilate. Throughout this book, we have highlighted several themes: the active engagement of students as they build their understandings, the importance of problem solving, and the varied and balanced role of assessment. We have also intertwined pedagogy with content. Meaningful mathematics presented through effective pedagogical approaches explained in this book will make a difference for all students. In this chapter we look at the professionalism of teaching and offer some closing thoughts for teachers as they begin their professional journey.

Professionalism of Teaching

In 1989, the National Council of Teachers of Mathematics (NCTM) published the *Curriculum and Evaluation Standards for School Mathematics*. The volume identified changes to be made in the curricula and placed an increased emphasis on student involvement. NCTM had set the stage for all disciplines to raise the bar for students and teachers. These standards led the way for increased accountability for teachers. In 1991, NCTM published *Professional Standards for Teaching Mathematics*. This work clearly defined the factors necessary to implement NCTM's standards and called for the "professionalism of teachers" (NCTM, 1991, p. 4). This professionalism entailed a high degree of responsibility, decision making, and preparation. *Professional Standards for Teaching Mathematics* includes standards for teaching and for the evaluation of teaching. These standards also provide guidelines for the professional development of teachers of mathematics and detail the needed support of mathematics teachers from within the community, including the responsibilities of government and businesses. All at once, teachers of mathematics were seen as "objects and agents of change" (Merseth, 2003, p. xiv). Teachers were viewed as objects of change because they needed to be supported as they incorporated new strategies. Concurrently, teachers were seen as agents of change because they could significantly impact student learning in their classrooms. A greater emphasis was then placed on high-quality professional development for teachers.

The American Council on Education (ACE) stated, "The success of the student depends most of all on the quality of the teacher" (1999, p. 5). As professionals, it is incumbent upon us all to actively engage in our own development. Teaching is a journey; the journey encourages us to continue to grow and learn while we are engaging in our craft. If we as teachers are learning and growing, so will our students. As you enter the profession and begin your journey, we offer the following thoughts.

Point Well Taken

"Effective teachers are those who can stimulate students to *learn* mathematics. Educational research offers compelling evidence that students learn mathematics well only when they *construct* their own mathematical understanding. To understand what they learn, they must enact for themselves verbs that permeate the mathematics curriculum 'examine,' 'represent,' 'transform,' 'solve,' 'apply,' 'prove,' 'communicate.' This happens most readily when students work in groups, engage in discussion, make presentations, and in other ways take charge of their learning."

—*National Research Council, 1989, pp. 58–59*

Beginning the Professional Journey

Finding the Right Match

As you begin to interview, finding the right match between you and the school is fundamental to your success. This process can seem similar to finding the right college; some individuals get an intuitive feeling and they can see themselves in the building. Others analyze the opportunities between districts. Some factors to consider as you pursue options:

- What is the school's vision for education? Can you align yourself with that vision?
- Is the opportunity tapping into your talents?
- Do you see others within the building with whom you can relate?
- What opportunities are available for your continued professional growth?
- What is the school structure in terms of grade-level groups or teams? Is the school departmentalized? Is the school organized by teams of teachers working with the same students?
- What are the additional duties required of every teacher?
- Is there a published salary scale?
- How is the administration viewed by teachers?
- Is there a formal mentor program for new teachers?
- How committed is the community to supporting education?

Before you go to a school for an interview, you can find many of the answers to the preceding questions on a website. Be certain to prepare for each interview. Also consider possible questions that might be asked of you. Here are some examples of questions commonly used in the interview process:

- Describe how you plan a lesson.
- How do you know that a lesson has been successful?
- What are the important concepts in mathematics at this grade level?
- How might you handle a difficult parent conference?
- What impact has the NCTM *Standards* and state guidelines had on your thinking about mathematics education?
- Describe your ideal classroom.
- Where does technology fit into the teaching and learning of mathematics?

Those First Few Weeks

Ideally, you will have time to get to know some of your colleagues, especially those whose classrooms are near yours. These neighbors can provide those quick and necessary answers. Other people in the building to be sure to get to know are the office and custodial staff. These individuals can help enormously with many difficulties that may arise. Some new teachers feel that if they ask a lot of questions that they will be perceived as inadequate. This is simply not the case: Understanding the rules, procedures, and policies is fundamental to your success.

Establish class routines early. Students will push against whatever the rules may be. By clearly stating expectations and making certain that the class understands the rational for these guidelines, you help students settle in to begin the real work—learning. Collaborate with colleagues as to what classroom procedures they have found effective. Discuss options about consequences of student behavior. What are the support systems available to you? Do not wait for a discipline situation to occur to find out what your options might be. Be firm, be fair, and occasionally be flexible. There are always extenuating circumstances.

There will certainly be highs and lows during that first year. Remember those positive moments; record them in a journal. Throw away those negative thoughts and reminders

Point Well Taken

"Those who can, do, those who can think, teach."

—*George Bernard Shaw*

of failed lessons, missed opportunities, and misunderstandings. Build from the positive and walk confidently into the next year knowing that you will not repeat the same mistakes; you will simply find new ones! We all do!

Professional Development Opportunities

"Probably nothing within a school has more impact on students in terms of skills development, self-confidence, and classroom behavior than the personal and professional growth of teachers" (Barth, 1990, p. 49). Teachers need to be actively engaged in their own professional development if growth is to occur. "When teachers observe, examine, question, and reflect on their ideas and develop new practices that lead toward their ideals, students come alive. When teachers stop growing, so do their students" (Barth, 1990, p. 50).

Join the National Council of Teachers of Mathematics
TRY THIS

Go to www.nctm.org. You can register online and receive the professional journal, *Mathematics Teaching in the Middle School.*

Membership in this national organization provides you with informative articles about the learning and teaching of mathematics as well as information about local and national conferences. Attending a conference provides opportunities to learn and to connect with colleagues. Attending a conference with a colleague pays additional benefits as you begin to incorporate some of the ideas from the conference. You can support each other in the implementation process. Conferences also provide opportunities to connect with other teachers with common interests. Casual conversations about common struggles and possible solutions can be one of the several beneficial outcomes of attending a conference. Many publishers display the latest curricula, technology innovations, and manipulatives at conferences. Conferences also provide an opportunity to evaluate some of these programs and explore further those items of interest. When you join NCTM, also join your state organization. These local organizations also provide conferences and great networking potential.

Take a Course

Being on the student side of the desk can bring a fresh perspective. Understanding what students experience from a personal perspective can be very informative. Taking classes can also be supportive and stimulating especially if these classes deal with aspects of the craft of teaching. Occasionally, schools have agreements with area colleges and universities so that tuition is reduced. School districts have also been known to offer tuition reimbursements.

Volunteer for Work with a Coach

Many schools have embraced a coaching model. Experienced teachers are hired to come to work with other teachers. This work is usually focused on content, but many pedagogical approaches naturally weave throughout the discussions. Coaches can help you create professional goals, strategize as to how these goals can be reached and support you as you proceed toward those goals. Relationships formed through the coaching experience are valuable assets and frequently develop into friendships that extend beyond any anticipated timetable.

Solicit Student Feedback

Teachers can gain valuable insights by asking students their opinions about aspects of the course. Questions pertaining to student understanding as a unit progresses or the amount of time spent on homework open the lines of communication between students and teachers. After the first grading period, consider asking students about one aspect of the course that they would change and one aspect that they do not want to change. Asking students to respond to questions in writing anonymously ensures that students will offer their own thoughts and opinions. Students tend to appreciate being asked such questions and frequently will offer concrete suggestions that teachers can incorporate into the class routines.

Participate in a Lesson Study Group

Participating in a lesson study group offers opportunities to connect with colleagues from various disciplines and work together for common understanding. Frequently, lesson study groups are facilitated by an external consultant. Teachers volunteer to focus on a particular topic—proportional reasoning, for example. The teachers meet on a regular basis to explore the research on a topic and begin to define the desired student outcomes for a unit. As the planning proceeds, teachers volunteer to teach an initial lesson. Other teachers observe the lesson and then meet to discuss the strengths and weaknesses of the lesson. That revised lesson is then taught by another member of the team and critiqued by the group. This process continues until the unit is finalized. Many schools then share these units with other teachers within the district.

Volunteer for Committees

Participating on a district committee can also lead to professional growth. Connecting with teachers across the district can help you extend your network and provide you with insights about the issues in other buildings.

Grants and Awards

Money is available to support initiatives. Working with colleagues to write a proposal, the thrill of receiving the funds, and the implementation process all contribute to a teacher's professional growth. Here are just a few sites to explore:

> www.nctm.org/about/met
> www.nctm.org/about/toyota
> www.nsf.gov

There are also search engines to help find available funding such as www.freeus governmentgrants.com.

One of the most prestigious awards for math and science teachers is the Presidential Award for Excellence in Teaching Mathematics. Currently, this award includes a $10,000 grant and a celebration week in Washington, D.C., with other awardees. Individual teachers are nominated by administrators, colleagues, or parents and then complete a lengthy application that includes a videotaped lesson. The application is sent to a state committee and finalists are then forwarded to the national committee for selection. This award is indeed an honor and continues to enrich the lives of the awardees throughout their careers.

We hope this book has helped you understand many of the issues facing middle school mathematics teachers and given you insights and strategies on how to create an effective learning environment. We also hope this book will serve as a resource for you by providing problems to use with students in your classroom. Throughout this book, we have intertwined pedagogy with content. Content driven by skills is not retained; neither will sound pedagogical practices improve poor content. Rather, engaging content and effective pedagogy go hand in hand. Mathematics teaching is a complex craft; it is a profession carrying many intrinsic rewards: lifelong friendships, the returning student who tells you that you are the reason that he or she has chosen to be a teacher, the look of joy as a concept is understood, and a simple "thanks" at the end of the day. Welcome to our profession.

EXERCISES

Portfolio: A Summative Assessment

This is an opportunity to reflect on the content of this book by creating a portfolio. Begin by reviewing the summaries and exercises from each chapter. Read your responses to the portfolio questions.

Build the portfolio by selecting two responses to the portfolio questions. Also select two problems from different chapter exercises to include in your portfolio. Write a short statement supporting your reasons for selecting each piece as an entry in your portfolio.

Respond to the following questions. Each question is a separate entry in the portfolio:

- What specific information in this text do you want to be certain to incorporate into your teaching?
- Do you have any lingering questions?

Write three specific goals for yourself. Be as clear and precise as possible and include a timeline for delivery.

REFERENCES

American Council on Education. (1999). *To touch the future: Transforming the way teachers are taught. An action agenda for college and university presidents.* Washington, DC: ACE.

Barth, R. (1990). *Improving schools from within.* San Francisco: Jossey-Bass.

Merseth, K. (2003). *Windows on teaching math.* New York: Teachers College Press.

National Council of Teachers of Mathematics. (1991). *Professional standards for teaching mathematics.* Reston, VA: NCTM.

National Research Council. (1989). *Everybody counts: A report on the future of mathematics education.* Washington, DC: National Academy Press.

Index